Policy-Making in the European Union

SIXTH EDITION

Edited by

Helen Wallace, Mark A. Pollack, and Alasdair R. Young

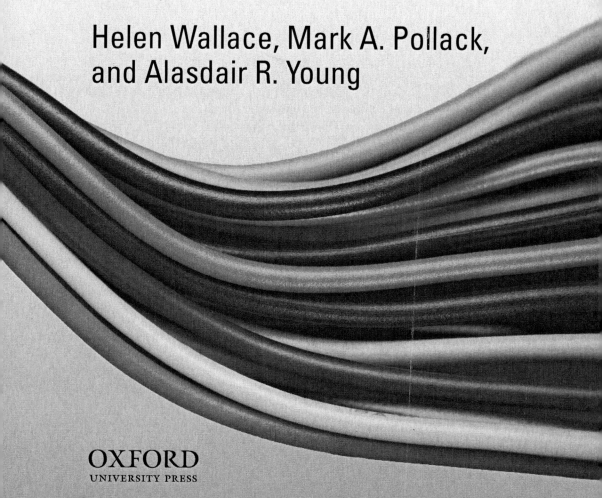

OXFORD

UNIVERSITY PRESS

OXFORD
UNIVERSITY PRESS

Great Clarendon Street, Oxford OX2 6DP

Oxford University Press is a department of the University of Oxford.
It furthers the University's objective of excellence in research, scholarship,
and education by publishing worldwide in

Oxford New York

Auckland Cape Town Dar es Salaam Hong Kong Karachi
Kuala Lumpur Madrid Melbourne Mexico City Nairobi
New Delhi Shanghai Taipei Toronto

With offices in

Argentina Austria Brazil Chile Czech Republic France Greece
Guatemala Hungary Italy Japan Poland Portugal Singapore
South Korea Switzerland Thailand Turkey Ukraine Vietnam

Oxford is a registered trade mark of Oxford University Press
in the UK and in certain other countries

Published in the United States
by Oxford University Press Inc., New York

© Oxford University Press 2010

British Library Cataloguing in Publication Data
Data available

Library of Congress Cataloging in Publication Data
Data available

Typeset by MPS Limited, A Macmillan Company
Printed in Great Britain on acid-free paper by
Ashford Colour Press Ltd,
Gosport, Hampshire

ISBN 978–0–19–954482–0

3 5 7 9 10 8 6 4 2

▌ OUTLINE CONTENTS

PART I   Institutions, Process, and Analytical Approaches

PART II   Policies

PART III   Conclusions

▌ DETAILED CONTENTS

▐ PART I   Institutions, Process, and Analytical Approaches

▌ PREFACE

This is a new book which builds on five previous editions. It follows the pattern established in *Policy-Making in the European Communities* (1977), extended and developed in the second, third, fourth, and fifth editions of 1983, 1996, 2000, and 2005. All of the chapters have been rewritten, many extensively, with references to the earlier versions as appropriate. Readers who wish to understand the historical development of EU policies and policy-making in more detail are encouraged to refer back to earlier editions, to gain a broader sense of how patterns of policy-making and institutional interaction have changed over the past three decades.

In the years since the last edition went to press the European Union (EU) has enlarged from twenty-five to twenty-seven members, with yet more would-be members waiting in the wings. This most recent enlargement notwithstanding, the EU policy process continues to operate and to evolve, despite the persistent difficulties of winning support for institutional reforms. Our previous edition went to press as the Constitutional Treaty awaited ratification, and indeed it failed to win consent in France and The Netherlands. Its more modest successor, the Treaty of Lisbon, was ratified in November 2009. Nonetheless, economic and monetary union (EMU) has been consolidated and additional member states have joined the eurozone. However, the pursuit of the 'Lisbon strategy', agreed in March 2000 with the goal of making of the EU the 'most dynamic knowledge-based economy in the world' by 2010, has produced more meagre results. The financial crisis which has hit the global economy recently poses European policy-makers with daunting challenges, on which several of our case studies and our concluding chapter comment.

Europeans have witnessed other profound changes in the global environment and have found themselves struggling to define collective responses. Security concerns are well to the fore, as the military interventions in Afghanistan and Iraq continue to elude resolution and instabilities persist around Europe's neighbourhood. Nonetheless, European foreign and security policy cooperation has proceeded pragmatically to gain momentum and to acquire responsibilities. In parallel and in response to the international turbulence, European policy collaboration on internal security, on migration, and on justice and home affairs has continued to develop. Latterly policies to deal with energy security and climate change have also risen in salience.

This volume is a study of policy-making, not of European integration as such. We do not therefore plunge into discussions of the broader political processes of the EU. Other dimensions of the EU are well covered in the companion volumes in *The New European Union Series*. Our aim here is to provide a detailed picture of the diversity of EU policy-making across a range of policy domains, to identify predominant patterns, and characteristic styles and trends over time.

The first edition was produced to fill a gap in what was then a thin academic literature on west European integration. Since then European academic research has mushroomed, contributing to a broadening flow of empirical and theoretical publications. We have included in this edition a new chapter by Alasdair Young setting out how to situate EU policy-making in the broader literature of policy analysis. This complements the chapter by Mark Pollack on EU-related theories.

The fifteen case studies have been chosen both to cover the most important fields of EU activity and to illustrate the range of policy domains in which EU institutions now operate. Familiar issues of distribution and redistribution, the single market, agriculture, competition, external trade, monetary integration, and foreign policy have been covered in each of the five editions. The expansion of the EU's policy agenda since the early 1980s is reflected in the inclusion of case studies of environmental regulation, the social dimension, employment policy, biotechnology, and justice and home affairs. We have added to this edition a case study of energy policy, given its increased importance for policy-makers.

Fifteen of the nineteen authors of this volume contributed to the fifth edition, and the other four are welcome new conscripts. The editorial team has been reshaped. William Wallace has ceded his role as co-editor, but remains as co-author of Chapter 18, as well as a staunch supporter of the volume. Alasdair Young has become a co-editor, as well as author of Chapters 3 and 5. The authors come from a range of nationalities and intellectual traditions. This volume continues to benefit from informal ties and friendships among contributors since the first edition, sustained through exchanges of visits and children as well as through conferences and shared research. Special thanks go to those authors who have succeeded in producing both chapters and babies at the same time.

We would like to thank Ruth Anderson and her colleagues Claire Brewer, Catherine Page, and Joanna Hardern for their patience, hard work, and encouragement as the book has taken shape at Oxford University Press, as well as John Peterson, series co-editor, for his constant vigilance and commitment. Lauren Albright has done a splendid job in editing and compiling the manuscript, while Malcolm Todd did a scrupulous copy-edit of the manuscript, and Scott Brown helped make possible our ever-growing index. The European University Institute, the London School of Economics and Political Science, Temple University, and the University of Glasgow all provided financial support at various stages of the project. A special debt is owed to Josef Falke and Stephan Leibfried for compiling the remarkable statistics on the caseloads of the European courts, which appear in the Appendix.

Box 4.1 in Chapter 4 also appeared in Chapter 10 of the volume *The Council of Ministers* by Fiona Hayes-Renshaw and Helen Wallace, and is reproduced here with the kind permission of the authors and of Palgrave Macmillan. Thanks are due to Renaud Dehousse and Florence Deloche-Gaudez for access to the database of the Institut des Études Politiques in Paris in order to update Figure 4.2.

Table 5.1 is reproduced by kind permission of the Royal Institute of International Affairs. Chapter 14 includes material taken from Chapter 6 of *When Cooperation Fails: The International Law and Politics of Genetically Modified Foods* by Mark Pollack and Greg Shaffer (2009), by permission of Oxford University Press. Figure 15.1 (map of gas pipelines) is reproduced with permission from *Natural Gas Market Review* (OECD/IEA), 2008, for which the International Energy Agency holds the copyright.

MAP, HW, ARY
Philadelphia, London, and Glasgow
November 2009

▌ LIST OF FIGURES

▍ LIST OF BOXES

▊ LIST OF TABLES

ABBREVIATIONS AND ACRONYMS

ACER	Agency for the Cooperation of Energy Regulators
ACP	African, Caribbean, and Pacific countries
AFSJ	area of freedom, security and justice
AP	accession partnership
APEC	Asia Pacific Economic Cooperation
ASEAN	Association of South East Asian Nations
Benelux	Belgium, The Netherlands, and Luxembourg
BEPGs	Broad Economic Policy Guidelines
BKA	*Bundeskartellamt*
BRIC	Biotechnology Regulation Inter-Service Committee
BSC	Biotechnology Steering Committee
BSE	bovine spongiform encephalopathy
CAP	common agricultural policy
CARDS	Community Assistance for Reconstruction, Development and Stabilization
CATS	Coordinating Committee for Police and Judicial Cooperation in Criminal Matters
CCP	common commercial policy
CEAS	common European asylum system
CEECs	countries of central and eastern Europe
CEEP	European Centre of Enterprises with Public Participation and of Enterprises of General Economic Interest
CEER	Council of European Energy Regulators
CEFIC	European Chemical Industry Council
CEN	Committee for European Norms (Standards)
CENELEC	Committee for European Electrical Norms (Standards)
CEPOL	European Police College
CET	common external tariff
CF	Cohesion Fund
CFI	Court of First Instance
CFP	common fisheries policy
CFSP	common foreign and security policy
CHODs	Chiefs of Defence Staffs of the member states

CIS	Commonwealth of Independent States (ex-USSR)
CITES	Convention on International Trade in Endangered Species
CIVCOM	Committee for Civilian Aspects of Crisis Management
CMOs	common market organizations
CNE	Climate Network Europe
COA	Court of Auditors
COGs	chiefs of government
COMAGRI	Agriculture and Rural Development Committee (of the EP)
COPA	Committee of Professional Agricultural Organizations
COPS	*Comité politique et de sécurité*; French acronym for PSC
CoR	Committee of the Regions
Coreper	Committee of Permanent Representatives
COSAC	*Conférence des organes spécialisées aux affaires européennes*
CPCC	Civilian Planning and Conduct Capability
CPCMU	Conflict Prevention and Crisis Management Unit
CSCE	Conference on Security and Cooperation in Europe
CT	Constitutional Treaty
CTEU	Consolidated Treaty of the European Union
DAC	Development Assistance Committee
DDA	Doha Development Agenda
DG	Directorate-General (for European Commission, see Table 4.1)
DG AGRI	Directorate-General for Agriculture
DG BUDG	Directorate-General for Budget
DG COMP	Directorate-General for Competition
DG ELARG	Directorate-General for Enlargement
DG EMPL	Directorate-General for Employment
DG ENV	Directorate-Generate for Environment
DG JAI	Directorate-General for Justice and Home Affairs
DG JLS	Directorate-General for Justice, Liberty and Security
DG MARKT	Directorate-General for Internal Market and Services
DG RELEX	Directorate-General for External Relations
DG SANCO	Directorate-General for Health and Consumer Protection
DG TRADE	Directorate-General for Trade
DG TREN	Directorate-General for Energy and Transport
DM	Deutschmark
DNA	deoxyribonucleic acid
DoJ	Department of Justice (US)

DRC	Democratic Republic of Congo
DSU	Dispute Settlement Understanding
EA	Europe agreement
EAFRD	European Agricultural Fund for Rural Development
EAGGF	European Agricultural Guidance and Guarantee Fund
EaP	Eastern Partnership
EAP	Environmental Action Programme
EAW	European arrest warrant
EBA	Everything But Arms
EBRD	European Bank for Reconstruction and Development
EC	European Community
EC6	Belgium, France, Federal Republic of Germany, Italy Luxembourg, and The Netherlands
EC9	EC6 plus Denmark, Ireland, UK
EC10	EC9 plus Greece
EC12	EC10 plus Portugal, Spain
EC/EU15	EC12 plus Austria, Finland, Sweden
ECB	European Central Bank
ECHA	European Chemicals Agency
ECHO	European Humanitarian Aid Department
ECJ	European Court of Justice
ECN	European Competition Network
ECO	European Cartel Office
Ecofin	Council of Ministers for Economic and Financial Affairs
ECOWAS	Economic Community of Western African States
ECR	European Court of Justice Reports
ECSC	European Coal and Steel Community
ECT	Energy Charter Treaty
ecu	European currency unit
EDA	European Defence Agency
EdF	*Electricité de France*
EDF	European Development Fund
EEA	European Economic Area
EEC	European Economic Community
EEG	European Employment Guidelines
EES	European Employment Strategy
EET	European Employment Taskforce

EFSA	European Food Safety Authority
EFTA	European Free Trade Association
EGTC	European Grouping for Territorial Cooperation
EIB	European Investment Bank
ELOs	European Liaison Officers
EMBO	European Molecular Biology Organization
EMCDDA	European Monitoring Centre on Drugs and Drug Addiction
EMCO	Employment Committee
EMEA	European Agency for the Evaluation of Medicinal Products
EMI	European Monetary Institute
EMS	European Monetary System
EMU	economic and monetary union
ENP	European neighbourhood policy
ENVI	Environment, Public Health, and Food Safety Committee (of the EP)
EP	European Parliament
EPA	economic partnership agreement
EPC	European political cooperation
EPN	European Patrol Network
EPP	European People's Party
EPSCO	Employment, Social Policy, Health and Consumer Affairs Council
ERDF	European Regional Development Fund
ERGEG	European Regulators Group for Electricity and Gas
ERM	exchange-rate mechanism
ERT	European Round Table of Industrialists
ESA	European Space Agency
ESC	Economic and Social Committee
ESCB	European System of Central Banks
ESDC	European Security and Defence College
ESDI	European security and defence identity
ESDP	European security and defence policy
ESF	European Services Forum
ESF	European Social Fund
ESRC	European Systemic Risk Council
ESS	European Security Strategy
ETS	emissions trading system
ETSO	European Transmission System Operators' Association
ETUC	European Trade Union Confederation

EU	European Union
EU/EC15	EC12 plus Austria, Finland, Sweden
EU25	EU15 plus Cyprus, Czech Republic, Estonia, Hungary, Latvia, Lithuania, Malta, Poland, Slovakia, Slovenia
EU27	EU25 plus Bulgaria and Romania
EUHR	EU High Representative
EUMC	European Monitoring Centre on Racism and Xenophobia
EUMC	European Union Military Committee
Euratom	European Atomic Energy Community
euro (€)	name of the single currency for EMU
Eurodac	European system for collecting fingerprints from asylum-seekers (from French abbrev.)
Eurogroup	European group within Nato from 1970
Eurojust	EU body to coordinate investigation and prosecution of serious cross-border and organized crime
Europol	European Police Office
EUSRs	European Union Special Representatives
FBI	Federal Bureau of Investigation (US)
FCO	Foreign and Commonwealth Office
FIFG	Financial Instrument for Fisheries Guidance
FRA	Fundamental Rights Agency
Frontex	Agency for the Management of Operational Cooperation at the External Borders
FSC	Foreign Sales Corporation Tax (US)
FTA	Free Trade Agreement
FTAA	Free Trade Area of the Americas
FTC	Federal Trade Commission
FYROM	former Yugoslav Republic of Macedonia
G5	Group of 5 EU countries for JHA: France, Germany, Italy, Spain, and the UK
G6	G5 plus Poland
G7	Group of 7 (western economic powers): Canada, France, Germany, Italy, Japan, UK, US
G8	G7 plus Russia
G20	A coalition of developing countries active in the Doha Round of multilateral trade talks
GAC	General Affairs Council
GAERC	General Affairs and External Relations Council
GATT	General Agreement on Tariffs and Trade

GDP	gross domestic product
GDR	German Democratic Republic
GMO	genetically modified organism
GNI	gross national income
GNP	gross national product
GPA	Government Procurement Agreement
GSP	Generalized System of Preferences
GTE	Gas Transmission for Europe
HR/SG	High Representative/Secretary General
ICTY	International Criminal Tribunal for the former Yugoslavia
IEA	International Energy Agency
IEEP	Institute for European Environmental Policy
IGC	Intergovernmental Conference
IIA	inter-institutional agreement
IMCO	Internal Market and Consumer Protection Committee (of the EP)
IMF	International Monetary Fund
IMPs	Integrated Mediterranean Programmes
IMPEL	European Network for the Implementation and Enforcement of Environmental Law
INTA	International Trade Committee (of the EP)
IPA	Instrument for Pre-Accession Assistance
IPPC	integrated pollution prevention and control (EU)
IPR	intellectual property rights
IR	international relations
ISPA	Instrument for Structural Policies for Pre-Accession Aid
IT	information technology
ITRE	Industry, Research, and Energy Committee (of the EP)
JHA	justice and home affairs
K4	committee of senior officials for JHA (now Article 36 Committee)
LDC	less developed country
LNG	liquefied natural gas
MEP	member of the European Parliament
Mercosur	Common Market of the Southern Cone
MFN	most-favoured nation (in GATT)
MLG	multi-level governance
Monuc	United Nations Mission in the Democratic Republic of the Congo
MTR	Mid-Term Review of Uruguay Round

NAMA	non-agricultural market access
NAP	national action plan
Nato	North Atlantic Treaty Organization
NCA	national competition authority
NCBs	national central banks
NGO	non-governmental organization
NIC	newly industrializing country
NPAAs	national programmes for the adoption of the *acquis*
NSRF	National Strategic Reference Framework
NTB	non-tariff barrier
NUTS	nomenclature of territorial units for statistics (from the French)
OECD	Organization for Economic Cooperation and Development
OFT	Office of Fair Trading (UK)
OLAF	European Anti-Fraud Office, *Office de la Lutte Anti-Fraude*, formerly UCLAF
OMC	open method of coordination
OSCE	Organization for Security and Cooperation in Europe
OU	ownership unbundling
PCA	partnership and cooperation agreement
PCTF	European Police Chiefs' Task Force
PESC	*politique étrangère et de sécurité commune*
Phare	*Pologne, Hongrie: assistance à la restructuration des économies* (extended to other CEECs)
PJCCM	police and judicial cooperation in criminal matters
PSC	Political and Security Committee
QMV	qualified majority voting
QR	quantitative restriction
R&D	research and development
RABITs	Rapid Border Intervention Teams
rDNA	recombinant DNA
SAAs	stabilization and association agreements
SACU	Southern Africa Customs Union
SAD	Statement of Assurance
SAP	stabilization and association process
SAPS	single area payment scheme
SAPARD	Special Accession Programme for Agriculture and Rural Development
SCA	Special Committee on Agriculture
SCD	subsidies and countervailing duties

SCIFA	Strategic Committee on Immigration, Frontiers and Asylum
SCIFA+	SCIFA plus heads of national border control authorities
SEA	Single European Act
SEM	single European market
SFP(S)	single farm payment (scheme)
SGP	Stability and Growth Pact
SIC	Schengen Implementing Convention
SIS	Schengen Information System
SME	small and medium-sized enterprises
SPS	sanitary and phytosanitary
T&C	textiles and clothing
TACIS	Technical Assistance for the CIS countries
TAIEX	Technical Assistance Information Exchange Office
TBR	Trade Barriers Regulation
TBT	technical barriers to trade
TCA	trade and cooperation agreement
TEC	Consolidated Treaty establishing the European Community, Revised Treaty of Rome
T&E	European Federation for Transport and Environment
TEN	Trans-European Network
TEU	Treaty on European Union
ToA	Treaty of Amsterdam
ToL	Treaty of Lisbon
ToN	Treaty of Nice
TPA	Trade Promotion Authority
Trevi	Terrorism, Radicalism, Extremism, Violence, Information (agreement on internal security cooperation)
TRIPs	Trade-Related Intellectual Property Rights
troika	grouping of three successive Council presidencies
UCLAF	*Unité de coordination de la lutte anti-fraude*, now OLAF
UEAPME	European Association of Craft, Small and Medium-sized Enterprises (*union européenne de l'artisan et des petites et moyennes enterprises*)
UK	United Kingdom
UN	United Nations
UNFCCC	United Nations Framework Convention on Climate Change
UNICE	Union of Industrial and Employers' Confederations of Europe (since 2007 Business Europe)
Unifil	United Nations Interim Force in Lebanon

Unprofor	United Nations Protection Force in Bosnia
UR	Uruguay Round
US	United States
USTR	United States Trade Representative
VAT	value-added tax
VERs	'voluntary' export restraint agreements
VIS	Visa Information System
WEU	Western European Union
WG	working group
WTO	World Trade Organization
WWF	World-Wide Fund for Nature

■ LIST OF CONTRIBUTORS

DAVID ALLEN	Loughborough University
DAVID BUCHAN	Oxford Institute for Energy Studies
BASTIAN GIEGERICH	International Institute for Strategic Studies
DERMOT HODSON	Birkbeck College
BRIGID LAFFAN	University College Dublin
SANDRA LAVENEX	University of Lucerne
STEPHAN LEIBFRIED	University of Bremen
ANDREA LENSCHOW	University of Osnabrück
JOHANNES LINDNER	European Central Bank
MARK A. POLLACK	Temple University
MARTIN RHODES	University of Denver
CHRISTILLA ROEDERER-RYNNING	University of Southern Denmark
ULRICH SEDELMEIER	University of Minnesota
GREGORY C. SHAFFER	London School of Economics and Political Science
HELEN WALLACE	London School of Economics and Political Science
WILLIAM WALLACE	London School of Economics and Political Science
STEPHEN WILKS	University of Exeter
STEPHEN WOOLCOCK	London School of Economics and Political Science
ALASDAIR R. YOUNG	University of Glasgow

▌ TABLE OF CASES

European Court of Justice (ECJ) and Court of First Instance (CFI)

European Court of Justice Reports (ECR), are available on-line at *http://www.curia.eu.int/*
en/content/juris/index.htm

■ TABLE OF LEGISLATION

Regulations

Directives

Decisions

Sources:

- The Official Journal of the European Communities:

  http://europa.eu.int/eur-lex/en/oj/

- European Commission, DG Competition: *http://europa.eu.int/comm/competition/index_en.html*

- EUR-Lex database: *http://eur-lex.europa.eu/*

▌ EDITORS' NOTE

A number of problems of dating, numbering, and nomenclature should be noted.

Generally in this volume for convenience we use the term European Union (EU) to embrace the family of arrangements under different treaties, even though it was not formally introduced until 1992. Where specifically relevant we refer to individual Communities or the European Community (EC).

Table 1.1 sets out the main treaties, including treaty revisions and enlargements. Treaty reforms are dated to their year of signature by member governments, rather than to the completion of negotiations (often the year before), or ratification (often the year after). The well-intentioned renumbering of treaty articles, agreed as an afterthought to the Treaty of Amsterdam (ToA), has created immense difficulties for all students of European Union. This Consolidated Treaty on European Union (CTEU), agreed in 1997, confusingly contains the Consolidated Treaty establishing the European Community (TEC). We generally quote treaty articles under this new numbering, but special care is needed to follow the two parallel sets of numbering that cover the common foreign and security policy and justice and home affairs. For the Treaty of Lisbon (ToL), ratified as we went to press, we identify potentially relevant amendments.

The Treaty of Lisbon, in turn, should not be confused with the so-called 'Lisbon Agenda' or 'Lisbon Strategy' for economic reform, adopted at the March 2000 Lisbon European Council with the aim of making the EU 'the most competitive and dynamic knowledge-based economy in the world', and whose impact, and variable successes, are discussed in a number of the chapters of the volume.

As regards terminology, readers will notice that we frequently refer to 'member government' rather than 'member state'. Although, strictly speaking, it is 'states' that sign and are parties to treaties and conventions, it is the member 'governments' which negotiate policies and legislation, or implement them at home, acting not only as representatives of states, but as the domestically accountable executive authorities.

There is also an issue about how to refer to the twelve member states that joined the EU in 2004 and 2007. While we appreciate that these states are very different, a central issue for this volume is how policy-making in the EU has been affected by the accessions of these states. It is therefore useful to have a shorthand for referring to them collectively. We are not aware of a more succinct way of referring to these states collectively than as the 'new' member states, even though at the time of writing (June 2009) those states that joined in 2004 have been members for five years.

Gross domestic product (GDP) is the most commonly used measure of the value of production in the area concerned (a country or a region). Gross national product (GNP) is GDP plus net transfers of factor incomes, i.e. the repatriated profits of member-state multinationals overseas, and less the profits of non-national multinationals operating in the member state. In most countries the difference between the two may be insignificant, but in countries such as Ireland the difference between the two may be as high as 25 per cent. Recently, gross national income (GNI) has become the more commonly used name for GNP.

Until September 1999 Directorates-General (DGs) of the European Commission were generally known by their numbers, e.g. DGVI for Agriculture. Numbers have latterly been replaced by functional names. The two nomenclatures are set out in Table 4.1, since for earlier material the numbers remain relevant.

The ecu, or European currency unit, referred to in some chapters was the unit of account adopted for certain EU transactions or statistical comparisons. It has been replaced by the euro with the advent of economic and monetary union.

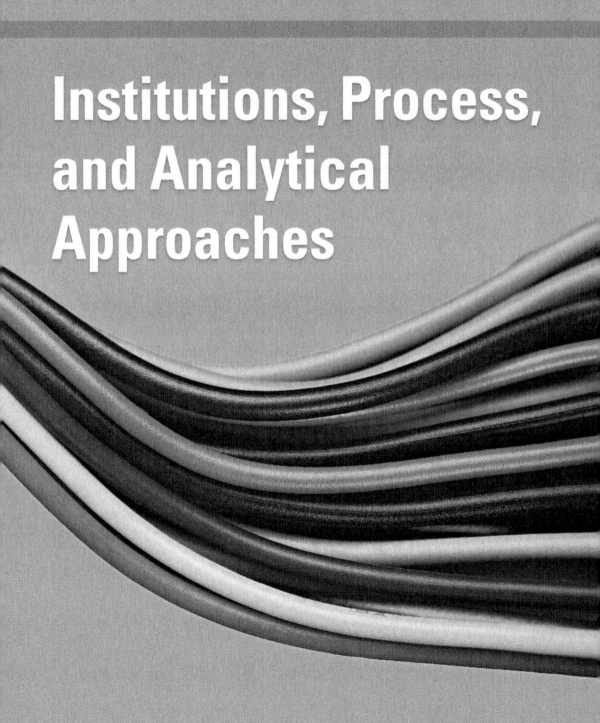

PART I

Institutions, Process, and Analytical Approaches

CHAPTER 1

An Overview

Helen Wallace, Mark A. Pollack, and Alasdair R. Young

Introduction

The European Union (EU) is perhaps the most important agent of change in contemporary government and policy-making in Europe. EU decisions pervade the policy-making activities of individual European countries, both the member states and their neighbours. Moreover, given the importance of the EU's market, its activities can affect profoundly the lives of people around the world. Given the importance and pervasiveness of EU policies, it is vital to understand how such policies are made, which is the key aim of this volume.

More specifically, this book, like its five predecessors, seeks to understand the processes that produce EU policies: that is, the decisions (or non-decisions) by EU public authorities facing choices between alternative courses of public action (Peterson and Bomberg 1999: 4). We do not advance any single theory of EU policy-making, although we do draw extensively on theories of European integration, international cooperation, comparative politics, and contemporary governance in our search for vocabulary to understand and explain our subject. Similarly, we make no effort to identify a single EU policy style, but instead classify and explore empirically the extraordinary and ever-increasing diversity of 'policy modes' whereby the preferences of national governments, sub-national actors, and supranational organizations are changed into common policies.

The volume is organized in three parts. In Part I we sketch the broad contours of the EU policy process and relevant analytical approaches for understanding that process. Chapter 2 surveys the many theories that have been put forward to explain both European integration as a process, and the European Union as a political system. Chapter 3 situates policy-making in the EU in the wider literature on policy-making, drawing on theories developed in comparative politics and international relations. Chapter 4 explains the various EU institutions through which policies are articulated and presents a classification of five 'policy modes', drawn from the scholarly literature and empirical practice, which serve as an analytic backdrop for the analysis of policy-making in specific sectors.

Part II consists of fifteen case studies, which cover the main policy domains in which the EU dimension is significant. We have included: policies that have been core European business from the outset, such as competition policy, the common agricultural policy (CAP), and trade policy; policies that have become central to the EU as it has developed—such as the budget, the structural funds, the single European market (SEM), economic and monetary union (EMU), and the environment, as well as enlargement; policies that illustrate more recent areas of European engagement, such as common foreign and security policy (CFSP), justice and home affairs (JHA), employment, and biotechnology; and policies in which recent developments have given new content to old policy ambitions, such as energy and social policy. The policies are also selected to illustrate the variety of policy-making patterns, from extensive delegation to supranational institutions—as in competition policy, monetary policy, and trade policy—to relatively loose coordination among member states, as in defence, employment, and aspects of justice and home affairs, and everything in between. Energy policy reappears in this edition in recognition of both its growing importance for the EU and its multi-faceted character. The policy cases carried over from previous editions have been extensively revised and updated.

Part III, the concluding chapter, summarizes the broad findings of the volume, identifying contemporary trends in EU policy-making and offering some observations about EU policy-making under the multiple stresses of enlargement, institutional stalemate, and financial crisis. In addition, the Appendix contains valuable tables of the cases adjudicated by the European Court of Justice (ECJ) and the Court of First Instance (CFI), which indicate the pattern of cases over time and across sectors.

The EU and its predecessors

For convenience, we have generally used the term European Union (EU) in this volume. The EU is built out of three originally separate Communities, each with different powers, characteristics, and policy domains, complemented by other 'pillars' of organized cooperation. Treaty amendments over the years have revised the original treaties and made provision for the accession of new member states. These various treaties are summarized in Table 1.1. As this volume goes to press the Treaty of Lisbon (ToL) has just been ratified by all member states and awaits implementation. The chapters in this volume indicate the new provisions relevant to each topic.

Membership of the EU had expanded from six countries in 1951 to fifteen by 1995, and to twenty-seven in 2007, with further enlargement in prospect. Croatia and Turkey were involved in accession negotiations as of June 2009, with other countries from the Western Balkans and Iceland acknowledged as potential candidates (see Chapter 17).

Some preliminary observations

Four broad points need to be made clear at the outset. First, the EU policy process is based on west European experience. Until 2004 the member countries of the EU, and its various precursors, were west European countries with market economies and liberal democratic polities, even though some, notably Greece, Portugal, and Spain, had moved quite swiftly from authoritarian regimes to EU membership in the 1980s, and from 1991 Germany included as new *Länder* what had been the German Democratic Republic under a communist regime. It is not our contention that these countries all neatly fitted into a single political and economic mould, but nonetheless they have some strong shared characteristics which permeate the EU policy process.

TABLE 1.1   The main treaties including treaty revisions and enlargements

Year*	Treaty	Outcome
1951	Treaty of Paris	European Coal and Steel Community (ECSC) (signed by Belgium, the Federal Republic of Germany, France, Italy, Luxembourg, and The Netherlands)
1957	Treaty of Rome	European Economic Community (EEC)
1957	Treaty of Rome	European Atomic Energy Community (Euratom)
1965–6	Luxembourg crisis and compromise	Interrupts extension of qualified majority voting (QMV)
1965	Merger Treaty	Combines institutions into single set
1970	Budgetary Treaty	'Own resources' (i.e. revenue) created; some budgetary powers for European Parliament (EP)
1972	Act of Accession	Admits Denmark, Ireland, and UK from 1973
1975	Budgetary Treaty	More powers to EP; new Court of Auditors
1978	Treaty revision	For direct elections to EP
1980	Act of Accession	Admits Greece from 1981
1985	Act of Accession	Admits Portugal and Spain from 1986
1986	Single European Act (SEA)	More QMV in Council; some legislative power for EP; new Court of First Instance; introduces cohesion; expands policy scope, especially single European market (SEM)
1992	Treaty on European Union (Maastricht) (TEU)	Three-pillar structure of European Union; common foreign and security policy (CFSP) and justice and home affairs (JHA); more QMV in Council; formalizes European Council; some co-decision for EP; new Committee of the Regions; expands policy scope, especially for economic and monetary union (EMU); introduces subsidiarity and citizenship; Social Protocol (UK opt-out)
1994	Act of Accession	Admits Austria, Finland, and Sweden from 1995 (but negative vote on accession in Norway)
1997	Treaty of Amsterdam (ToA)	More legislative powers to EP, and stronger requirement for its 'assent' on (e.g.) enlargement and Commission appointments; introduces 'flexibility' (some member states cooperating without others); modest extra QMV in Council; incorporates Schengen and develops JHA; reverses UK social opt-out

1997	Consolidated Treaty on European Union (CTEU)	'Simplifies' the treaties by combining into a single set, and therefore renumbering, the provisions of earlier treaties
2001	Treaty of Nice (ToN)	Intended to streamline the EU institutions for further enlargement
2003	Act of Accession	Admits Cyprus, Czech Republic, Estonia, Hungary, Latvia, Lithuania, Malta, Poland, Slovakia, and Slovenia from May 2004
2004	Constitutional Treaty (CT)	Wide-ranging reorganization of treaties into three parts: I—main 'constitutional' provisions; II—The Charter of Fundamental Rights; III—The Policies and functioning of the Union, and some institutional changes; not ratified after negative referendums in France and The Netherlands
2005	Act of Accession	Admits Bulgaria and Romania, activated January 2007
2007	Treaty of Lisbon (ToL)	Modified version of CT— ratification completed in November 2009

*Note: dates of signature.

However, the EU has now enlarged eastwards to embrace already ten central and east European countries, with very different inheritances. One important question which follows is whether this fit between country characteristics and European process will be sustainable in a larger and more diverse Union.

A second preliminary point is that dense multilateralism is a strong feature of the west European experience in which the EU is embedded. The EU constitutes a particularly intense form of multilateralism, but western Europe constituted a region of countries with an apparent predisposition to engage in cross-border regime-building. In part this relates to specific features of history and geography, but it seems also to be connected to a political culture of investing in institutionalized cooperation with neighbours and partners, at least in the period since the second world war. This is part of the reason why transnational policy development has become more structured and more iterative in the EU than in most other regions of the world.

Thirdly, the EU has, since its inception, been active in a rather wide array of policy domains, and indeed has over the decades extended its policy scope. Most international or transnational regimes are more one-dimensional. Part of our contention in this volume is that this array of policy domains has generated not one, but several, modes of policy-making, as the case studies reveal. Moreover, the same EU institutions, and the same national policy-makers, have different characteristics, exhibit different patterns of behaviour, and produce different kinds of outcome, depending on the policy domain and depending on the period. Thus, as we shall see, there is no single and catch-all way of capturing the essence of EU policy-making. All generalizations need to be nuanced, although, as will be seen in Chapter 4, five main variants of the policy process can be identified.

Fourthly, this volume goes to press at a moment when the EU is facing important challenges. The implications of eastern enlargement are only just becoming clear, which the contributions to this volume explore. The questions hang in the air as how, the Treaty of Lisbon will be implemented. The contributions to this volume consider what impacts Lisbon would likely have on the policy-making process of the EU. In addition, the financial crisis in 2007–8 has precipitated the sharp contraction of the real economy; transformed public finances as revenues have shrunk and government expenditure has increased, in some cases dramatically; and potentially altered the balance between state and market. At the time of writing it was unclear how deep or how protracted the economic contraction will be, although a number of contributions to the volume reflect on the EU's preliminary response to the crisis.

There are also broad changes in the nature of EU policy-making. The proliferation of patterns of policy-making identified in the previous volume has continued and, if anything, accelerated. A striking feature of these patterns of policy-making is that they are constructed to a large extent outside the classical Community framework. Some EU institutions, so far at least, have been on the margins of the main developments. In particular the Commission, the European Court of Justice (ECJ), and the European Parliament (EP) have been less central actors, while the main dynamics have been found in the intensive interactions between national policy-makers, with both new agencies, such as the European Central Bank (ECB) (see Chapter 7) or Europol (see Chapter 19), and new consultative forums, notably to pursue the Lisbon Strategy on economic reform (see Chapter 12). The investments being made in new institutional arrangements have been designed to underpin this structured transgovernmentalism rather than to incorporate them within the traditional Community procedures (communitarization). The case study chapters suggest that this may be a sustained pattern, not a mere staging post in the transition from nationally rooted policy to 'communitarization'. Tempting though it is to interpret this as the triumph of 'intergovernmentalism' (a process in which traditional states predominate) over 'supranationalism' (a process in which new European institutions enjoy political autonomy and authority), we argue that the story is more nuanced, with the emergence of new, varied, and hybrid policy modes emerging across our fifteen issue areas.

Chapters 2 and 3 therefore take a broad and eclectic approach in identifying a deliberately wide range of theories and concepts with which to examine and to explain EU policy-making. We argue that care should be taken to avoid overly sharp dichotomies between supranationalism, on the one hand, and intergovernmentalism, on the other, or between theoretical templates from comparative politics, on the one hand, and international relations, on the other. Instead, we look to a variety of approaches, drawing on diverse theoretical traditions and from both comparative politics and international relations, in order explicitly to 'mainstream' the study of the EU by linking EU policy processes to comparable domestic and international processes, particularly in multi-layered polities. Our aim is not to prove or falsify any particular theory, but to use all available theoretical tools to understand EU policy-making in all its complexity.

The EU in context

Most studies of the EU concentrate on describing what happens in and through the special institutions of the EU, located in Brussels, Luxembourg, and Strasbourg: the European Commission; the Council of the EU; the European Council; the European Parliament (EP); and the European Court of Justice (ECJ).[1] Each of these institutions, and others, is introduced in detail in Chapter 4. However, we should be careful not to regard these EU institutions as existing in a vacuum. Most of the policy-makers who devise and operate EU rules and legislation are from the member states themselves. They are people who spend the greater part of their time as national policy-makers, for whom the European dimension is an extended policy arena, not a separate activity. Indeed, much of EU policy is prepared and carried out by national policy-makers and agents who do not spend much, if any, time in Brussels. Instead, what they do is consider how EU regimes might help or hinder their regular activities, and apply the results of EU agreements on the ground in their normal daily work. If we could calculate the proportions we might well find that in practice something like 80 per cent of that normal daily life was framed by domestic preoccupations and constraints. Much the same is true of the social and economic groups, or political representatives, who seek to influence the development and content of EU policy.

On the face of it, it might appear that it cannot simultaneously be the case that 80 per cent of the member states' socio-economic legislation is shaped by the EU, while 80 per cent of the policy context of national policy-makers is framed by domestic concerns. Yet precisely what distinguishes the EU as a policy arena is that it rests on a kind of amalgam of these two levels of governance. Country-defined policy demands and policy capabilities are set in a shared European framework to generate collective policies, most of which are then implemented back in the countries concerned. Moreover, as we shall see from several of the case studies in this volume, how those European policies operate varies a good deal between one EU member state and another. In other words, the EU policy process is one which has differentiated outcomes, with significant variations between countries. Hence it is just as important to understand the national institutional settings as to understand the EU-level institutions in order to get a grip on the EU policy process as a whole (H. Wallace 1973, 1999).

This two-level picture does not, however, describe the whole story. In all EU countries there are other levels of infranational government, that is local or regional authorities, the responsibilities of which are to varying extents shaped by EU regimes. Many of these authorities have occasional direct contacts with the EU institutions, and in some countries may be the key ones for implementing specific EU policies and legislation. In addition, and increasingly, national policy processes in Europe depend on other kinds of agencies and institutions, which lie between the public and the private spheres and also vary a good deal in character from one country to another. One striking feature of western Europe in the past decade or so, an experience now replicated in central and eastern Europe, has been the proliferation of bodies with public policy functions outside the central governments. This is especially so in the regulatory arena, perhaps the most extensive domain of EU policy activity. The shift towards more autonomous or semi-autonomous agencies, or to forms of 'self-regulation', represents a move away from the inherited heavy-state version of government towards a kind of partnership model. What the EU policy process does is to add another layer, making cross-agency coordination one of its key features, as we shall see in several of our case studies.

Even this multi-faceted picture does not encompass the whole story. The EU arena is only part of a wider pattern of making policy beyond the nation-state. In many areas of public policy, including those within which the EU is active, there are broader transnational consultations and regimes. These vary a great deal in their robustness and intensity, but they are part of a continuum of policy-making that spreads from the country level, through the European arena, to the global level. Many of the same policy-makers are active across these different levels, and policy development consists of choices between these levels or the assignment of different segments of a given policy domain to different levels. Several of our policy case studies illustrate this phenomenon, and mostly stress its increased salience. One important question to bear in mind here is whether or not the EU institutions provide the main junction box through which connections are made between the country level and the global level.

One further preliminary point needs to be made. Most accounts of the EU policy process work from the EU treaties outwards, starting from the policy powers explicitly assigned to the European level of governance, and then considering extensions of policy powers, or refusals to extend policy powers. Such accounts place the EU at the centre of the picture, and tend to make the EU appear the fulcrum of policy-making. Other European transnational policy regimes—and there are many—tend to be viewed as second-best solutions, or weaker forms of policy cooperation. This volume takes issue with this image. Instead we argue that the EU is only one, even if by far the most invasive, arena for building European policy regimes. Hence we need to compare and contrast the EU with these other policy regimes, both the highly structured (such as the North Atlantic Treaty Organization (Nato) for defence), and the relatively informal (such as in the past have enabled national police forces to develop cross-border cooperation). Then we can consider with more nuance why the EU process is especially important in some policy domains, but not in others, just as we can examine how experiences in other kinds of European policy regime might be changing the character of the EU policy process.

In short, the EU policy process needs to be viewed through several sets of spectacles. Different lenses may be needed depending on the division of powers and influences between these different levels and arenas of policy development. Certainly, we then need to focus squarely on what happens in and through the EU institutions. But we need peripheral vision to take in the country-level processes (both national and infranational), the global level, and the alternative European frameworks. And we need to be aware that policy-making shifts between these in a fluid and dynamic way.

The EU as a unique arena—or perhaps not

Most accounts of the EU policy process, as we have noted, concentrate on the EU's own institutions. Their main features and characteristics are set out in Chapter 4, and their roles in the policy process will be a recurrent theme in this volume. We shall observe general features that are present in most areas of EU policy, as well as features that are specific to particular sectors, issues, events, and periods.

But how far do the particular features of the EU's institutional system produce a distinctive kind of policy process? It has been commonplace for commentators on the EU to stress its distinctive features, and indeed often to argue that they result in a unique kind of politics. Whether such an assertion is warranted is a question to keep in mind in reading subsequent chapters. In forming an answer to the question it is important to reflect on what other political arrangements might be appropriately compared with those of the EU. Some would say loose-knit states, such as Canada or Switzerland, mostly confederal in character, or a federal state like the United States of America, Belgium, or Germany. Others would say some multilateral regimes, especially those which focus on the political economy, such as the Organization for Economic Cooperation and Development (OECD), or the various regional customs unions and free trade areas elsewhere in the world. Depending on which comparators are chosen, different 'benchmarks' will be useful for evaluating the EU institutions and their performance.

As we shall see in Chapter 2, this issue has been one of the longest-running sources of controversy among political analysts of the EU. On one side of the debate are ranged those who see the EU as one example, perhaps a particularly richly developed example, of a transnational or international organization. On the other side of the debate are those who view the EU as a kind of polity-in-the-making, and, in this sense, state-like. The analyses of the EU's institutions conducted in these two camps differ considerably. A third camp argues that contemporary politics in Europe are changing anyway, with traditional forms of politics and government being transformed in quite radical ways. The net result, it is argued, is that it is more appropriate to talk of 'governance' than of 'government'. The EU has, according to this view, emerged as part of a reconfigured pattern of European governance, with an evolution of institutional arrangements and associated processes that have interestingly novel characteristics.

This volume starts out closer to the third camp than to either of the first two. However, subsequent chapters will reveal some policy sectors in which the EU has powers as extensive as those normally associated with country-level governance, while other chapters will describe much lighter and more fragile European regimes. The institutional patterns vary between these two kinds of cases. Chapter 4 provides an anatomical overview of the institutions together with a broad characterization of five main policy modes that vary across issue areas and across time. Subsequent case studies identify many of the variations of institutional patterns that are observable in specific areas of policy, along with the organic features of the institutional processes. These variations make the EU policy process a challenging one to characterize and hence the subject of lively argument for both practitioners and analysts.

However distinctive and unusual the EU institutions might be argued to be, we should not forget that the people, groups, and organizations which are active within these institutions are for the most part going about their 'normal' business in seeking policy and political outcomes. There is no reason to suppose that their activities have different purposes simply because the institutional arena is different from the others in which they are involved. The politics of the EU are just that—normal politics, with whatever one thinks are the normal features of domestic politics, and by extension policy-making, in European countries. Nonetheless, we need to be alert to differences in behaviour, in opportunities, and in constraints that arise from being involved in a multi-level and multi-layered process. It is around this feature of the EU that much of the most interesting analytical debate takes place, to which we turn in Chapters 2 and 3.

Note

1 Those new to the subject should note the existence of an entirely separate organization—the Council of Europe, created in 1949, based in Strasbourg, originally with only west European members, but now with a continent-wide membership of forty-seven countries. It has a classical intergovernmental structure, except for the rather autonomous European Court of Human Rights.

FURTHER READING

A good understanding of the recent history of Europe is a valuable starting point. Dinan (2004) provides a straightforward overview of the development of the EU. Milward (2000) offers a robust critique of much of the orthodoxy surrounding interpretations of the EU. Moravcsik (1998) submits the history of the EU to fine-grained political analysis. For insights into the deeper history Mazower (1999) is an excellent and provoking volume, usefully complemented by the more social scientific insights of Stein Rokkan, whose collected writings are drawn together by Flora (1999). Scharpf (1999) draws together very succinctly many of the contemporary challenges to governance in western Europe, some of which are also interestingly surveyed by Kapteyn (1996) and Majone (2005). Kohler-Koch (2003) addresses the EU governance debate more broadly. For an attempt to situate European integration in both its global and its domestic contexts, see Laffan, O'Donnell and Smith (1999). For the link to 'pan-Europe', see also H. Wallace (2001*a*: Ch. 1), and Schimmelfennig and Sedelmeier (2005*a*).

Dinan, D. (2004), *Europe Recast: A History of European Union* (Basingstoke: Palgrave Macmillan).

Flora, P. (1999) (ed.), *State Formation, Nation-Building and Mass Politics in Europe: The Theory of Stein Rokkan* (Oxford: Oxford University Press).

Kapteyn, P. (1996), *The Stateless Market: The European Dilemma of Integration and Civilization* (London: Routledge).

Kohler-Koch, B. (2003) (ed.), *Linking EU and National Governance* (Oxford: Oxford University Press).

Laffan, B., O'Donnell, R., and Smith, M. (1999), *Europe's Experimental Union: Rethinking Integration* (London: Routledge).

Majone, G. (2005), *Dilemmas of European Integration: The Ambiguities and Pitfalls of Integration by Stealth* (Oxford: Oxford University Press).

Mazower, M. (1999), *Dark Continent: Europe's Twentieth Century* (London: Penguin).

Milward, A. S. (2000), *The European Rescue of the Nation-State*, 2nd edn. (London: Routledge).

Moravcsik, A. (1998), *The Choice for Europe: Social Purpose and State Power from Messina to Maastricht* (Ithaca, NY: Cornell University Press).

Scharpf, F. W. (1999), *Governing in Europe: Effective and Democratic?* (Oxford: Oxford University Press).

Schimmelfennig, F., and Sedelmeier, U. (2005*a*) (eds.), *The Europeanisation of Central and Eastern Europe* (Ithaca, NY: Cornell University Press).

Wallace, H. (2001*a*) (ed.), *Interlocking Dimensions of European Integration* (Basingstoke: Palgrave Macmillan).

CHAPTER 2

Theorizing EU Policy-Making

Mark A. Pollack

▌ Summary

Our understanding of European Union (EU) policy-making and policy processes is shaped largely by the language of theory, and an understanding of the main currents of EU-related theories is therefore a useful starting point for the case studies in this volume. Three primary currents or strands of theory are identified and explored. First, we examine the various theories of European integration, which sought to explain the process of EU development from the origins of the Union to the present day. This body of theory initially pitted neo-functionalist models of integration through spill-over against intergovernmentalist models emphasizing the continuing dominance of national governments; later, this debate was largely supplanted by a second debate pitting rational-choice theorists against constructivist analyses.

Secondly, we survey the increasing number of studies that approach the EU through the lenses of comparative politics and comparative public policy, focusing on the federal or quasi-federal aspects of the EU and its legislative, executive, and judicial politics. Thirdly and finally, we examine the 'governance approach' to the EU, which theorizes the Union as an experiment in non-hierarchical, public-private, and deliberative governance, and focuses in large part on the normative questions of the EU's democratic legitimacy. Taken together, these theories pose important questions and provide distinctive hypotheses about the key actors and the dominant processes in EU policy-making.

Introduction

This chapter sketches the theoretical background for the book, by surveying theories of European integration, comparative politics, and governance, laying out clearly the analytical concepts that will subsequently be employed by our contributors.[1] The chapter does not seek to come up with a single theory to explain European integration, or even the policy process within the EU, a project beyond the scope of this volume. Indeed, a consistent theme of this book from its first edition onwards has been the need to guard against overgeneralizing about 'the' EU policy process, but instead being open to the prospect that policy-making may differ considerably and systematically across issue areas. Nevertheless, theories of European integration and public policy-making are useful in providing us with the analytical tools with which to chart and explain variation in EU policy-making both across issue areas and over time, and these theories inform the language and the categories of analysis used in the subsequent chapters of the volume.

This chapter is organized in four parts. The first provides a brief overview of the most influential theories of European integration, namely neo-functionalism, intergovernmentalism, institutionalism, and constructivism, paying particular attention to the implications of each theory for our specific focus on EU policy-making. The second section looks beyond the integration literature, drawing on rationalist theories of comparative public policy for a set of analytical categories that can be used to analyse the participants, processes, and policies that we observe in the EU. In doing so, we pay special attention to the concept of the EU as a political system, characterized by a vertical and a horizontal separation of powers, which, we argue, has implications for the nature of policy-making and the key actors in the EU policy process. The third section examines the recent development of a 'governance approach' to the European Union. The governance approach emphasizes a series of interrelated concepts, including: the non-hierarchical or 'network' character of EU policy-making; the emergence of 'multi-level governance' implicating sub-national, national, and supranational actors; the challenge to the governance capacity of national governments and the limited governance capacity and legitimacy of the EU; and the prospect for 'deliberative supranationalism' as a partial response to the challenge of democratic legitimacy beyond the nation-state. The fourth section concludes with a brief restatement of the primary theoretical debates in EU studies today, and the questions that they raise for the study of policy-making in the European Union.

Theories of European integration

For many years, the academic study of the European Communities (EC), as they were then called, was virtually synonymous with the study of European *integration*. The initially modest and largely technocratic achievements of the EC seemed less significant than the potential that they represented for the gradual integration of the countries of western Europe into something else: a supranational polity. When the integration process was going well, as during the 1950s and early 1960s, neo-functionalists and other theorists sought to explain the process whereby European integration proceeded from modest sectoral beginnings to something broader and more ambitious. When things seemed to be going badly, as from the 1960s until the early 1980s, intergovernmentalists and others sought to explain why the integration process had not proceeded as smoothly as its founders had hoped. Regardless of the differences among these bodies of theory, we can say clearly that the early literature on the EC sought to explain the process of European *integration* (rather than, say, policy-making), and that in doing so it drew largely (but not exclusively) on theories of international relations.

In the first edition of this volume, Carole Webb (1977) surveyed the debate among the then-dominant schools of European integration, neo-functionalism, and intergovernmentalism, drawing from each approach a set of implications and hypotheses about the nature of the EC policy process. Similarly, here we review neo-functionalism and its views about the EU policy process, and then the intergovernmentalist response, as well as the updating of 'liberal intergovernmentalism' by Andrew Moravcsik in the 1990s. In addition, we examine more recent bodies of integration theory—institutionalism and constructivism—which offer very different views of the integration process and very different implications for EU policy-making.

Neo-functionalism

In 1958, on the eve of the establishment of the European Economic Community (EEC) and European Atomic Energy Community (Euratom), Ernst Haas published his seminal work, *The Uniting of Europe*, setting out a 'neo-functionalist' theory of regional integration. As elaborated in subsequent texts by Haas and other scholars (e.g. E. Haas 1961; Lindberg 1963; Lindberg and Scheingold 1970), neo-functionalism posited a process of 'functional spill-over', in which the initial decision by governments to place a certain sector, such as coal and steel, under the authority of central institutions creates pressures to extend the authority of the institutions into neighbouring areas of policy, such as currency exchange rates, taxation, and wages. Thus, neo-functionalists predicted, sectoral integration would produce the unintended and unforeseen consequence of promoting further integration in additional issue areas.

George (1991) identifies a second strand of the spill-over process, which he calls 'political' spill-over, in which both supranational actors (such as the Commission) and sub-national actors (interest groups or others within the member states) create additional pressures for further integration. At the sub-national level, Haas suggested that interest groups operating in an integrated sector would have to interact with the international organization charged with the management of their sector. Over time, these groups would come to appreciate the benefits from integration, and would thereby transfer their demands, expectations, and even their loyalties from national governments to a new centre, thus becoming an important force for further integration. At the supranational level, moreover, bodies such as the Commission would encourage such a transfer of loyalties, promoting European policies and brokering bargains among the member states so as to 'upgrade the common interest'. As a result of such sectoral and political spill-over, neo-functionalists predicted, sectoral integration would become self-sustaining, leading to the creation of a new political entity with its centre in Brussels.

For our purposes in this book, the most important contribution of neo-functionalists to the study of EU policy-making was their conceptualization of a 'Community method' of policy-making. As Webb pointed out, this ideal-type Community method was based largely on the observation of a few specific sectors (the common agricultural policy (CAP), see Chapter 8, and the customs union, see Chapter 5) during the formative years of the Community, and presented a distinct picture of EC policy-making as a process driven by an entrepreneurial Commission and featuring supranational deliberation among member-state representatives in the Council. The Community method in this view was not just a legal set of policy-making institutions but a 'procedural code' conditioning the expectations and the behaviour of the Commission and the member governments as participants in the process.

This Community method, Webb suggested, characterized EEC decision-making during the period from 1958 to 1963, as the original six member states met alongside the Commission to put in place the essential elements of the EEC customs union and the CAP. By 1965, however, Charles de Gaulle, the French President, had precipitated the so-called 'Luxembourg crisis', insisting on the importance of state sovereignty and arguably violating the implicit procedural code of the Community method. The EEC, which had been scheduled to move to extensive qualified majority voting (QMV) in 1966, continued to take most decisions de facto by unanimity, the Commission emerged weakened from its confrontation with de Gaulle, and the nation-state appeared to have reasserted itself. These tendencies were reinforced, moreover, by developments in the 1970s, when economic recession led to the rise of new non-tariff barriers to trade among EC member states and when the intergovernmental aspects of the Community were strengthened by the creation in 1974 of the European Council, a regular summit meeting of EU heads of state and government. In addition, the Committee of Permanent Representatives (Coreper), an intergovernmental body of member-state representatives, emerged as a crucial decision-making body preparing legislation for adoption by the Council of Ministers. Similarly, empirical studies showed the importance of national gatekeeping institutions (H. Wallace 1973). Even some of the major advances of this period, such as the creation of the European Monetary System (EMS) in 1978 (see Chapter 7), were taken outside the structure of the EEC Treaty, and with no formal role for the Commission or other supranational EC institutions.

Intergovernmentalism

Reflecting these developments, a new 'intergovernmentalist' school of integration theory emerged, beginning with Stanley Hoffmann's (1966) claim that the nation-state, far from being obsolete, had proven 'obstinate'. Most obviously with de Gaulle, but later with the accession of new member states such as the UK, Ireland, and Denmark in 1973, member governments made clear that they would resist the gradual transfer of sovereignty to the Community, and that EC decision-making would reflect the continuing primacy of the nation-state. Under these circumstances, Haas himself (1975) pronounced the 'obsolescence of regional integration theory', while other scholars such as Paul Taylor (1983), and William Wallace (1982) argued that neo-functionalists had underestimated the resilience of the nation-state. At the same time, historical scholarship by Alan Milward and others (Milward and Lynch 1993; Milward 2000) supported the view that EU member governments, rather than supranational organizations, played the central role in the historical development of the EU and were strengthened, rather than weakened, as a result of the integration process. And indeed, the early editions of *Policy-Making in the European Communities* found significant evidence of intergovernmental bargaining as the dominant mode of policy-making in many (but not all) issue areas.

Liberal intergovernmentalism

The period from the mid-1960s through the mid-1980s has been characterized as 'the doldrums era', both for the integration process and for scholarship on the EU (Keeler 2005; Jupille 2005). While a dedicated core of EU scholars continued to advance the empirical study of the EU during this period, much of this work either eschewed grand theoretical claims about the integration process or accepted with minor modifications the theoretical language of the neo-functionalist/intergovernmentalist debate. With the 'relaunching' of the integration process in the mid-1980s, however, scholarship on the EU exploded, and the theoretical debate was revived. While some of this scholarship viewed the relaunching of the integration process as a vindication of earlier neo-functionalist models (Sandholtz and Zysman 1989; Tranholm-Mikkelsen 1991), Andrew Moravcsik (1993a, 1998) argued influentially that even these steps forward could be accounted for by a revised intergovernmental model emphasizing the power and preferences of EU member states.

Moravcsik's 'liberal intergovernmentalism' is a three-step model, which combines: (1) a liberal theory of national preference formation with (2) an intergovernmental model of EU-level bargaining, and (3) a model of institutional choice emphasizing the role of international institutions in providing 'credible commitments' for member governments. In the first or liberal stage of the model, national chiefs of government (COGs) aggregate the interests of their domestic constituencies, as well as their own interests, and articulate their respective national preferences towards the EU. Thus, national preferences are complex, reflecting the distinctive economics, parties, and institutions of each member state, and they are determined *domestically*, not shaped by participation in the EU, as some neo-functionalists had proposed.

In the second or intergovernmental stage, national governments bring their preferences to the bargaining table in Brussels, where agreements reflect the relative power of each member state, and where supranational organizations such as the Commission exert little or no influence over policy outcomes. By contrast with neo-functionalists, who emphasized the entrepreneurial and brokering roles of the Commission and the upgrading of the common interest among member states in the Council, Moravcsik and other intergovernmentalists emphasized the hardball bargaining among member states and the importance of bargaining power, package deals, and 'side payments' as determinants of intergovernmental bargains on the most important EU decisions.

Third and finally, Moravcsik puts forward a rational-choice theory of institutional choice, arguing that EU member states adopt particular EU institutions—pooling sovereignty through QMV, or delegating sovereignty to supranational actors like the Commission and the Court—in order to increase the credibility of their mutual commitments. In this view, sovereign states seeking to cooperate among themselves invariably face a strong temptation to cheat or 'defect' from their agreements. Pooling and delegating sovereignty through international organizations, he argues, allows states to commit themselves credibly to their mutual promises, by monitoring state compliance with international agreements and filling in the blanks of broad international treaties, such as those that have constituted the EC/EU.

In empirical terms, Moravcsik argues that the EU's historic intergovernmental agreements, such as the 1957 Treaties of Rome and the 1992 Treaty on European Union (TEU), were not driven primarily by supranational entrepreneurs, unintended spillovers from earlier integration, or transnational coalitions of interest groups, but rather by a gradual process of preference convergence among the most powerful member states, which then struck central bargains among themselves, offered side-payments to smaller member states, and delegated strictly limited powers to supranational organizations that remained more or less obedient servants of the member states.

Overarching the three steps of this model is a 'rationalist framework' of international cooperation. The relevant actors are assumed to have fixed preferences (for wealth, power, etc.), and act systematically to achieve those preferences within the constraints posed by the institutions within which they act (Moravcsik 1998: 19–20; Moravcsik and Schimmelfennig 2009).

During the 1990s, liberal intergovernmentalism emerged as arguably the leading theory of European integration, yet its basic theoretical assumptions were questioned by international relations scholars coming from two different directions. A first group of scholars, collected under the rubrics of rational-choice institutionalism and historical institutionalism, accepted Moravcsik's rationalist assumptions, but rejected his spare, institution-free model of intergovernmental bargaining as an accurate description of the EU policy process. By contrast, a second school of thought, drawing from sociological institutionalism and constructivism, raised more fundamental objections to the methodological individualism of rational-choice theory in favour of an approach in which national preferences and identities were shaped, at least in part, by EU norms and rules.

The 'new institutionalisms'

The rise of institutionalist analysis of the EU did not develop in isolation, but reflected a gradual and widespread re-introduction of institutions into a large body of theories (such as pluralism, Marxism, and neo-realism), in which institutions had been either absent or considered epiphenomenal, reflections of deeper causal factors or processes such as the distribution of power in domestic societies or in the international system. By contrast with these institution-free accounts of politics, which dominated much of political science between the 1950s and the 1970s, three primary 'institutionalisms' developed during the course of the 1980s and early 1990s, each with a distinct definition of institutions and a distinct account of how they 'matter' in the study of politics (March and Olsen 1984, 1989; Hall and Taylor 1996).

Rational-choice institutionalism began with the effort by American political scientists to understand the origins and effects of US Congressional institutions on legislative behaviour and policy outcomes. By contrast with early rational-choice models of US legislative behaviour, which depicted legislative politics as a series of simple-majority votes among Congressional representatives, institutionalists such as Kenneth Shepsle (1979, 1986) argued that Congressional institutions, and in particular the committee system, could shape legislative outcomes and make those outcomes durable in the face of subsequent challenges. Congressional institutions, in this view, could produce 'structure-induced equilibrium', by ruling some alternatives as permissible or impermissible, and by structuring the voting power and the veto power of various actors in the decision-making process. Subsequently, Shepsle and others turned their attention to the problem of 'equilibrium institutions', namely, how actors choose or design institutions to secure mutual gains, and how those institutions change or persist over time.

The subsequent development of the rational-choice approach to institutions produced a number of theoretical offshoots with potential applications to both comparative and international politics. For example, rational-choice institutionalists have examined in some detail the 'agenda-setting' power of Congressional committees, which can send draft legislation to the floor that is often easier to adopt than it is to amend. In another offshoot, students of the US Congress have developed 'principal-agent' models of Congressional delegation to regulatory bureaucracies and to courts, and they have problematized the conditions under which legislative principals are able—or unable—to control their respective agents (Moe 1984; Kiewiet and McCubbins 1991). More recently, Epstein and O'Halloran (1999), and others (Huber and Shipan 2002) have pioneered a 'transaction-cost approach' to the design of political institutions, arguing that legislators deliberately and systematically design political institutions to minimize the transaction costs associated with the making of public policy.

Although originally formulated and applied in the context of American political institutions, rational-choice institutionalist insights 'travelled' to other domestic and international contexts, and were quickly taken up by students of the EU. Responding to the increasing importance of EU institutional rules, such as the cooperation and co-decision procedures, these authors argued that purely intergovernmental models of EU decision-making underestimated the causal importance of formal EU rules in shaping policy outcomes. In an early application of rational-choice theory to the EU, for example, Fritz Scharpf (1988) argued that the inefficiency and rigidity of the CAP and other EU policies was due not simply to the EU's intergovernmentalism, but also to specific institutional rules, such as unanimous decision-making and the 'default condition' in the event that the member states failed to agree on a common policy (see Chapter 8). By the mid-1990s, George Tsebelis, Geoffrey Garrett, and many others sought to model both the choice and the functioning of EU institutions in rational-choice terms. Many of these studies fall essentially into the comparative study of executive, legislative, and judicial politics, and are therefore reviewed in the second part of this chapter.

By contrast, sociological institutionalism and constructivist approaches in international relations defined institutions much more broadly to include informal norms and conventions as well as formal rules. They argued that such institutions could 'constitute' actors, shaping their identities and hence their preferences in ways that rational-choice approaches could not capture (see next section).

Historical institutionalists took up a position between these two camps, focusing on the effects of institutions *over time*, in particular on the ways in which a given set of institutions, once established, can influence or constrain the behaviour of the actors who established them (Hall 1986; Thelen and Steinmo 1992). In perhaps the most sophisticated presentation of this thinking, Paul Pierson (2000) has argued that political institutions are characterized by what economists call 'increasing returns', insofar as they create incentives for actors to stick with and not abandon existing institutions, adapting them only incrementally in response to changing circumstances. Thus, politics should be characterized by certain interrelated phenomena, including: *inertia*, or 'lock-ins', whereby existing institutions may remain in equilibrium for extended periods despite considerable political change; a critical role for *timing and sequencing*, in which relatively small and contingent events at critical junctures early in a sequence shape events that occur later; and *path-dependence*, in which early decisions provide incentives for actors to perpetuate institutional and policy choices inherited from the past, even when the resulting outcomes are manifestly inefficient. In recent years, these insights have been applied increasingly to the development of the EU, with various authors emphasizing the temporal dimension of European integration (Armstrong and Bulmer 1998).

Pierson's (1996*b*) study of path-dependence in the EU, for example, seeks to understand European integration as a process that unfolds over time, and the conditions under which path-dependent processes are most likely to occur. Working from essentially rationalist assumptions, Pierson argues that, despite the initial primacy of member governments in the design of EU institutions and policies, 'gaps' may occur in the ability of member governments to control the subsequent development of institutions and policies, for four reasons. First, member governments in democratic societies may, because of electoral concerns, apply a high 'discount rate' to the future, agreeing to EU policies that lead to a long-term loss of national control in return for short-term electoral returns. Secondly, even when governments do not heavily discount the future, unintended consequences of institutional choices can create additional gaps, which member governments may or may not be able to close through subsequent action. Thirdly, the preferences of member governments are likely to change over time, most obviously because of electoral turnover, leaving new governments with new preferences to inherit an *acquis communautaire* negotiated by, and according to the preferences of, a previous government. Finally, EU institutions and policies can become locked-in not only as a result of change-resistant institutions from above, but also through the incremental growth of entrenched support for existing institutions *from below*, as societal actors adapt to and develop a vested interest in the continuation of specific EU policies.

In sum, for both rational-choice and historical institutionalists, EU institutions 'matter', shaping both the policy process and policy outcomes in predictable ways, and indeed shaping the long-term process of European integration. In both cases, however, the effects of EU institutions are assumed to influence only the incentives confronting the various public and private actors—the actors themselves are assumed to remain unchanged in their fundamental preferences and identities. Indeed, despite their differences on substantive issues, liberal intergovernmentalism, rational-choice institutionalism, and most historical institutionalism arguably constitute a shared rationalist research agenda—a community of scholars operating from similar basic assumptions and seeking to test hypotheses about the most important determinants of European integration.

Constructivism, and reshaping European identities and preferences

Constructivist theory, like rational choice, did not begin as a theory of European integration, but rather as a broader 'metatheoretical' orientation with potential implications for the study of the EU. As Risse (2004: 161) explains in an excellent survey:

it is probably most useful to describe constructivism as based on a social ontology which insists that human agents do not exist independently from their social environment and its collectively shared systems of meanings ('culture' in a broad sense). This is in contrast to the methodological individualism of rational choice according to which '[t]he elementary unit of social life is the individual human action'. The fundamental insight of the agency-structure debate, which lies at the heart of many social constructivist works, is not only that structures and agents are mutually co-determined. The crucial point is that constructivists insist on the *constitutiveness* of (social) structures and agents. The social environment in which we find ourselves, 'constitutes' who we are, our identities as social beings.

For constructivists, institutions are understood broadly to include not only formal rules but also informal norms, and these rules and norms are expected to 'constitute' actors, i.e. to shape their identities and their preferences. Actor preferences, therefore, are not exogenously given and fixed, as in rationalist models, but *endogenous* to institutions, and individuals' identities shaped and re-shaped by their social environment. Taking this argument to its logical conclusion, constructivists generally reject the rationalist conception of actors as utility-maximizers operating according to a 'logic of consequentiality', in favour of March and Olsen's (1989: 160–2) conception of a 'logic of appropriateness'. In this view, actors confronting a given situation do not consult a fixed set of preferences and calculate their actions in order to maximize their expected utility, but look to socially constructed roles and institutional rules and ask what sort of behaviour is appropriate in that situation. Constructivism, therefore, offers a fundamentally different view of human agency from rational-choice approaches, and it suggests that institutions influence individual identities, preferences, and behaviour in more profound ways than those hypothesized by rational-choice theorists.

Consistent with these hypotheses, a growing number of scholars have suggested that EU institutions shape not only the behaviour, but also the preferences and identities of individuals and member governments. This argument has been put most forcefully by Thomas Christiansen, Knud Erik Jørgensen, and Antje Wiener (1999: 529):

A significant amount of evidence suggests that, as a process, European integration has a transformative impact on the European state system and its constituent units. European integration itself has changed over the years, and it is reasonable to assume that in the process agents' identity and subsequently their interests have equally changed. While this aspect of change can be theorized within constructivist perspectives, it will remain largely invisible in approaches that neglect processes of identity formation and/ or assume interests to be given exogenously.

Not surprisingly, such arguments were forcefully rebutted by rationalist theorists, resulting in a major 'metatheoretical debate' (Moravcsik 1999; Checkel and Moravcsik 2001).

In recent years constructivist scholars have produced a spate of empirical work, seeking rigorously to test hypotheses about socialization, norm-diffusion, and collective preference formation in the EU, using a range of qualitative and quantitative research methods. The results of these studies are somewhat mixed, with some scholars finding evidence of socialization among long-standing EU members (Lewis 2005) and/or new and candidate members (Gheciu 2005), but the predominant finding has been that EU socialization of both Commission (Hooghe 2005) and national officials has been less far-reaching than expected. In a series of rigorous studies, for example, students of EU enlargement examined the attitudes and policies of new and candidate members of the Union, finding only weak evidence of socialization, and arguing that EU 'conditionality' or 'external incentives', rather than socialization, provided the strongest explanation of these states' behaviour (Kelley 2004; Schimmelfennig and Sedelmeier 2005a). A collective research project on international socialization in Europe, led by Jeffrey Checkel (2005), produced similar findings, concluding that, 'while there are good conceptual reasons for expecting a predominance of international socialization in Europe, the empirical cases instead suggest that effects of socialization are often weak and secondary to dynamics at the national level' (Zürn and Checkel 2005: 1047).

Integration theory today

European integration theory is far more complex than it was in 1977 when the first edition of this volume was published. In place of the traditional neo-functionalist/ intergovernmentalist debate, the 1990s witnessed the emergence of a new dichotomy in EU studies, pitting rationalist scholars against constructivists. During the late 1990s, it appeared that this debate might well turn into a metatheoretical dialogue of the deaf, with rationalists dismissing constructivists as 'soft', and constructivists denouncing rationalists for their obsessive commitment to parsimony and formal models. The past several years, however, have witnessed the emergence of a more productive dialogue between the two approaches (Jupille, Caporaso, and Checkel 2003), and a steady stream of empirical studies allowing us to adjudicate between the competing claims of the two approaches. Furthermore, whereas the neo-functionalist/intergovernmentalist debate was limited almost exclusively to the study of European integration, the contemporary rationalist/constructivist debate in EU studies mirrors larger debates among those same schools in the broader field of international relations theory. Indeed, not only are EU studies *relevant* to the wider study of international relations, they are in many ways the *vanguard* of international relations theory, insofar as the EU serves as a laboratory for broader processes such as globalization, institutionalization, and socialization.

Despite these substantial measures of progress, the literature on European integration has not produced any consensus on the likely future direction of the integration process. At the risk of overgeneralizing, more optimistic theorists tend to be drawn from the ranks of neo-functionalists and constructivists, who point to the potential for further integration, the former through functional and political spill-overs, and the latter through gradual Europeanization of both élite and mass preferences and identities. Rationalist and intergovernmentalist critics, on the other hand, tend to be sceptical regarding claims of both spill-over and socialization, pointing to the strains of EU enlargement and the difficulties of ratifying both the Constitutional Treaty and the subsequent Treaty of Lisbon. For these scholars, the EU may well represent an 'equilibrium polity', one in which functional pressures for further integration are essentially spent, and in which the current level of institutional and policy integration is unlikely to change substantially for the foreseeable future (Moravcsik 2001: 163). Hence, while the literature on European integration has advanced substantially over the past decade, a consensus on the causes and the future of the integration process remains as elusive as ever.

The EU as a political system

Thus far we have examined the EU literature as one concerned overwhelmingly with the causes and the direction of European integration as a process, with its theoretical inspiration primarily from the study of international relations. However, many scholars have approached the EU very differently, as a polity or political system akin to other *domestic* political systems. This tendency was most pronounced in the work of federalist writers, who explicitly compared the EU to federal and confederal systems in Germany, Switzerland, and the US (Pinder 1968; C. J. Friedrich 1969; Capelletti, Seccombe, and Weiler 1986; Scharpf 1988; Burgess 1989; Sbragia 1992a, 1992b, 1993), as well as in the work of systems theorists like Lindberg and Scheingold (1970), who saw the EU as a political system characterized by political demands (inputs), governmental actors, and public policies (outputs). At the same time, an increasing number of EU scholars, not least the editors and authors of the first (1977) edition of *Policy-Making in the European Union*, deliberately sought to bracket the question of integration and the EU's final destination, focusing instead on a better understanding of the EU policy process in all its complexity and diversity.

By the mid-1990s, the dominance of international relations came under serious challenge, with a growing number of scholars seeking explicitly to understand the EU as a political system using the theoretical tools developed in the study of domestic polities. This perspective was championed most effectively by Simon Hix (1994, 1999, 2005), who issued a call to arms to comparativists. Previous studies of the EU, Hix argued, had neglected the *politics* of the Union, as well as its characteristics as a *political* system. The EU, he contended, was clearly less than a Weberian state, lacking in particular a monopoly on the legitimate use of force; yet he echoed Lindberg and Scheingold by suggesting that the EU could be theorized as a political system, with a dense web of legislative, executive, and judicial institutions that adopted binding public policies and hence influenced the 'authoritative allocation of values' in European society. Furthermore, Hix suggested that EU politics takes place in a two-dimensional space, with integration representing one dimension, alongside a second dimension spanning the traditional left-right divide over the extent and nature of government intervention in the economy. Hence the EU could, and should, be studied using 'the tools, methods and cross-systemic theories from the general study of government, politics, and policy-making. In this way, teaching and research on the EU can be part of the political science mainstream' (Hix 1999: 2).

Hix's call to arms among comparativists has not escaped criticism, with a number of authors arguing that the aim of EU scholars should not be to reject international relations in favour of comparative politics, but rather to understand the interactions between domestic and international politics (Hurrell and Menon 1996). Nevertheless, comparative political scientists *have* moved increasingly into EU studies, in part because the EU has intruded increasingly into what had previously been seen as exclusively 'domestic' arenas, and in part because an increasing number of scholars accepted Hix's claim that the EU could be theorized as a 'political system' (Jupille 2005).

Although such comparative work on the EU is extraordinarily diverse, much of it can fairly be characterized as comparative, rational-choice, and positivist in nature. First, much of the work on EU politics proceeds from the assumption that the EU is not a *sui generis* system of governance, but is a variant on existing political systems. It can therefore be studied and understood with the aid of 'off-the-shelf' models of policy-making in other (primarily national) contexts. In recent years, a growing number of these theories have drawn from American politics, since the EU arguably resembles the US in possessing both a vertical and a horizontal separation of powers.

Secondly, most of the work reviewed in this section is either implicitly or explicitly rationalist, taking the assumption that actors (be they states, individuals, or supranational organizations) have fixed, exogenously determined preferences, and act systematically to maximize those preferences within the constraints of the EU's institutional system. A growing subset draws not only on the language of rational choice (i.e. 'soft' rational choice), but also elaborates formal and game-theoretic models of EU decision-making.

Thirdly and finally, much of the work discussed here can be characterized as implicitly or explicitly 'positivist', adopting and adapting the standards of the natural sciences, seeking to test theory-driven hypotheses systematically, and often (though by no means always) using quantitative as well as qualitative methods (see e.g. Gabel, Hix, and Schneider 2002 on EU studies as 'normal science'). A complete survey of this literature would take us beyond the remit of this chapter, although many elements of it are addressed by

Alasdair Young in Chapter 3. In this section, I focus narrowly on two dimensions that are most relevant to the study of policy-making, namely the vertical or 'federal' division of powers between the EU and member-state levels, and the horizontal separation of powers among the legislative, executive, and judicial branches of the Union.

The vertical separation of powers: the EU as a federal system

The EU did not begin life as a federal union, nor, in the view of most analysts, does it constitute a fully developed federation today. In political terms, the very term 'federal' was contentious and referred to obliquely as 'the f-word'; and in analytical terms some scholars question whether the EU can or should be accurately described as a federal state:

> The contemporary EU is far narrower and weaker a federation than any extant national federation—so weak, indeed, that we might question whether it is a federation at all. . . . The EU was designed as, and remains primarily, a limited international institution to coordinate national regulation of trade in goods and services, and the resulting flows of economic factors. Its substantive scope and institutional prerogatives are limited accordingly. The EU constitutional order is not only barely a federal state; it is barely recognizable as a state at all.

(Moravcsik 2001: 163–4)

Nevertheless, federalism was a powerful *normative* ideal motivating many of the founders of the European movement and much of the early scholarship on the EU. Recognizing the strong resistance of national governments to directly federal proposals, Jean Monnet and his colleagues opted instead for a more sectoral and incremental approach, more accurately captured in neo-functionalist theory than in traditional federalist approaches. By the 1980s, however, the EC had developed features with analytical similarities to those of existing federations. Theories of federalism therefore took on greater importance, not just as a normative ideal motivating European integration, but as a positive theoretical framework, capable of explaining and predicting the workings of the EU as a political system.

The term federalism has been the subject of numerous overlapping definitions, but most rely on the three elements emphasized by R. Daniel Kelemen (2003: 185), who defines federalism as 'an institutional arrangement in which: (a) public authority is divided between state governments and a central government; (b) each level of government has some issues on which it makes final decisions; and (c) a federal high court adjudicates disputes concerning federalism'. In most federal systems, moreover, the structure of representation is twofold, with popular or functional interests represented directly through a directly elected lower house, while territorial units are typically represented in an upper house, whose members may be either directly elected (as in the US Senate) or appointed by state governments (as in the German *Bundesrat*). In both of these senses, the EU *already* constitutes a federal system, with a constitutionally guaranteed separation of powers between the EU and member-state levels, and a dual system of representation through the European Parliament (EP) and the Council of Ministers. Hence the literature on comparative federalism provides a useful toolkit for thinking about policy-making in the EU.

Perhaps the most difficult issue, as in other federal systems, is the question of the distribution of powers among the federal and state levels of government, which can vary both across issue areas and over time (H. Wallace 2000). While the division of powers between the two levels may be constitutionally guaranteed, these constitutional assignments of authority are often stated in vague terms, and in practice federal and state governments frequently enjoy concurrent rather than exclusive jurisdiction in most issue areas. Both the US Constitution and the EC/EU treaties, for example, feature broad and flexible clauses which authorize the federal legislature to regulate interstate commerce or indeed to adopt any legislation deemed to be 'necessary and proper' in achieving the fundamental aims of the federation. We often see cycles or rhythms of federalism in which federal governments centralize power and authority, followed periodically by backlashes in which states seek a rebalancing or devolution of power back to the states. In this view, the history of the EU can be viewed as a series of centralizing initiatives (e.g. the founding years of the 1950s, and the relaunching of the integration process in the 1980s), followed by periods of retrenchment or devolution (e.g. the Gaullist-led resistance of the 1960s and the post-Maastricht backlash of the 1990s) (Donahue and Pollack 2001: 98). The struggle over European integration, in this view, is not a *sui generis* process, but is a constitutionally structured process of oscillation between states and central governments familiar from other federal systems.

Students of comparative federalism have, however, pointed to an exceptional aspect of the EU, namely the absence or at least the weakness of 'fiscal federalism', and the dominance of 'regulatory federalism' (Börzel and Hosli 2003: 180–1). Most federal systems engage in substantial fiscal transfers across state boundaries, but the EU budget has been capped at a relatively small 1.27 per cent of EU GDP, predominantly devoted to agricultural and cohesion spending (see Chapters 8, 9, and 10). The EU is therefore unable to engage in substantial redistribution or macroeconomic stabilization through fiscal policy (see Chapter 7), and only indirectly influences the structure of European welfare states, which remain predominantly national (see Chapter 11). In contrast, the Union has engaged primarily in regulatory activity (see Chapters 5, 11–15), earning it the moniker of a 'regulatory state' (Majone 1996: Chs. 4, 5). The regulatory output of the Union, in Majone's view, has been driven by both demand and supply factors. On the demand side, the imperative of creating a single internal market has put pressure on EU member states to adopt common or harmonized EU-wide regulations, most notably on products, in order to ensure the free movement of goods, services, labour, and capital throughout the Union. On the supply side, an entrepreneurial European Commission has seen regulation as a viable way to enhance its own policy competence despite the financial limits imposed by the EU's strict budgetary ceiling.

In empirical terms, the Union has engaged in a vast EU-wide project of economic regulation, driven largely by the creation and maintenance of the internal market, and these EU regulations have been adopted according to a 'regulatory mode' of governance (see Chapter 4). As in other federal systems, the adoption of far-reaching central regulations has taken the Union into areas of regulation not originally envisaged by the framers of the treaties, generating significant controversy and increasing demands since the 1990s for adherence to the principle of 'subsidiarity', the notion that the EU should govern as close as possible to the citizen and therefore that it should engage in regulation only where necessary to ensure the completion of the internal market and/or other fundamental aims of the treaties. Even in the regulatory field, therefore, the vertical separation of powers is not fixed but fluid, and the result resembles not so much a layer cake as a marble cake, in which EU and member-state authorities are concurrent, intermixed, and constantly in flux.

The horizontal separation of powers

Unlike the parliamentary states of western Europe, but like the US, the EU has a horizontal separation of powers in which three distinct branches of government take the leading role in the legislative, executive, and judicial functions of government, respectively. This does not mean that any one institution enjoys sole control of any of these three functions; indeed, as Amie Kreppel (2002: 5) points out, the Madisonian conception of the separation of powers 'requires to a certain extent a co-mingling of powers in all three arenas (executive, legislative, and judicial)'. In the case of the EU, for example, the legislative function is today shared by the Council of Ministers and the EP, with an agenda-setting role for the Commission; the executive function is shared by the Commission, the member states, and (in some areas) independent regulatory agencies; and the judicial function is shared by the ECJ, the Court of First Instance (CFI), and a wide array of national courts bound directly to the ECJ through the preliminary reference procedure (see Chapter 4).

Reflecting this separation of powers, comparative-politics scholars have over the past decade devoted extraordinary attention to theorizing, predicting, and explaining legislative, executive, and judicial behaviour using off-the-shelf theories drawn from the study of American and comparative politics. Many of these theories are reviewed in Chapter 3, where Alasdair Young provides comparative analysis of the EU 'policy cycle', from agenda-setting through to implementation. We focus here on some of the applications of comparative analysis to the legislative, executive, and judicial policies of the EU, demonstrating briefly the promise and limits of such applications.

Legislative politics: towards bicameralism

A first strand within the rationalist/comparativist literature, most relevant to our concerns with EU policy-making, is the large and growing literature on the EU legislative process. Drawing heavily on theories of legislative behaviour (i.e. the ways in which legislators vote) and legislative organization (the ways in which legislatures organize their business), scholars have sought to understand the legislative process in the EU, focusing on three major questions: legislative politics within the European Parliament; voting power and voting patterns in the Council of Ministers; and the respective powers of these two bodies in the EU legislative process (McElroy 2007).

The European Parliament (EP) has been the subject of extensive theoretical modelling and empirical study over the past two decades, with a growing number of scholars studying the legislative organization of the EP and the voting behaviour of its members (MEPs). Early studies of the Parliament emphasized the striking fact that, in spite of the multinational nature of the Parliament, the best predictor of MEP voting behaviour is not nationality but an MEP's 'party group', with the various party groups demonstrating extraordinarily high measures of cohesion in roll-call votes. These MEPs, moreover, were shown to contest elections and cast their votes in a two-dimensional 'issue space', including not only the familiar nationalism/supranationalism dimension but also and especially the more traditional, 'domestic' dimension of left-right contestation. Perhaps most fundamentally, these scholars have shown, the EP can increasingly be studied as a 'normal parliament' whose members vote predictably and cohesively within a political space dominated by the familiar contestation between parties of the left and right (Tsebelis and Garrett 2000; Kreppel 2001; Hix, Noury, and Roland 2007).

By contrast with this rich EP literature, the rational-choice literature on the Council of Ministers until recently focused on the relatively narrow question of member-state voting power under different decision rules. In recent years, however, the study of the Council has undergone a renaissance, driven in part by the increasing public availability of Council voting records and data-sets such as the Decision-Making in the European Union (DEU) project (R. Thomson et al. 2006). This thriving literature has produced new theoretical conjectures, and new qualitative and quantitative empirical tests, on issues such as the relative power of EU member states in the Council; the coalition patterns among member states within the Council (which appear to break down largely on geographical or North-South lines); the Council's tradition of consensus decision-making, rather than minimum-winning coalitions; and the as-yet uneven evidence for the socialization of national officials in the Council and its subsidiary committees and working groups (see Mattila 2004; Hayes-Renshaw and Wallace 2006; and Naurin and Wallace 2008).

Third and finally, a large and ever-growing literature has attempted to model in rational-choice terms, and to study empirically, the inter-institutional relations among the Commission (as agenda-setter) and the Council and Parliament, under different legislative procedures. Over the course of the 1980s and the 1990s, the legislative powers of the EP have grown sequentially, from the relatively modest and non-binding 'consultation procedure' through the creation of the 'cooperation' and 'assent' procedures in the 1980s, and the creation and reform of a 'co-decision procedure' in the 1990s. This expansion of EP legislative power, and the complex nature of the new legislative procedures, has fostered the development of a burgeoning literature and led to several vigorous debates among rational-choice scholars about the nature and extent of the EP's and the Council's respective influence across the various procedures. Such studies have shown that the institutional power and impact of the EP on legislative outcomes has grown substantially over time with the move from consultation to cooperation to the two different versions of co-decision in the Maastricht and Amsterdam Treaties (see e.g. Tsebelis et al. 2001; Hix, Noury and Roland 2007; and the review in McElroy 2007). Today, the powers of Parliament vary by issue and by the treaty basis for any particular policy, ranging from the limited influence of the consultation procedure to the revised co-decision procedure in which 'the Council and the Parliament are now co-equal legislators and the EU's legislative regime is truly bicameral' (Tsebelis and Garrett 2000: 24). Several case studies in this volume illustrate the role of the EP in the legislative, as well as the budgetary, processes of the EU.

Executive politics: delegation and discretion

The study of EU executive politics, and especially the role of the European Commission, is a perennial issue in European integration theory, with neo-functionalists and intergovernmentalists debating the causal role of the executive Commission for decades. Nevertheless, rational-choice and principal-agent analysis have emerged over the past decade as the dominant approach to the study of the Commission and other executive actors such as the European Central Bank and the growing body of EU agencies (Tallberg 2007).

These studies generally address two specific sets of questions. First, they ask why and under what conditions a group of (member-state) *principals* might delegate powers to (supranational) *agents*, such as the Commission, the European Central Bank, or the Court of Justice. Simplifying considerably, such *transaction-cost* accounts of delegation argue that member-state principals, as rational actors, delegate powers to supranational organizations primarily to lower the transaction costs of policy-making, in particular by allowing member governments to commit themselves credibly to international agreements and to benefit from the policy-relevant expertise provided by supranational actors. Despite differences in emphasis, the empirical work of these scholars has collectively demonstrated that EU member governments do indeed delegate powers to the Commission, the European Central Bank and the Court of Justice largely to reduce the transaction costs of policy-making, in particular through the monitoring of member-state compliance, the filling-in of framework treaties ('incomplete contracts'), and the speedy and efficient adoption of implementing regulations that would otherwise have to be adopted in a time-consuming legislative process by the member governments themselves (Pollack 1997, 2003; Moravcsik 1998; Majone 2000a; Franchino 2004, 2007).

In addition to the question of delegation, rational-choice institutionalists have devoted greater attention to a second question posed by principal-agent models: what if an agent—such as the European Commission, the Court of Justice, or the European Central Bank—behaves in ways that diverge from the preferences of the principals?

The answer to this question lies primarily in the administrative procedures that the principals may establish to define *ex ante* the scope of agency activities, as well as the oversight procedures that allow for *ex post* oversight and sanctioning of errant agents. Applied to the European Union, principal-agent analysis therefore leads to the hypothesis that agency autonomy is likely to vary across issue areas and over time, as a function of the preferences of the member states, the distribution of information between principals and agents, and the decision rules governing the application of sanctions or the adoption of new legislation. By and large, empirical studies of executive politics in the EU have supported these hypotheses, pointing in particular to the significance of decision rules as a crucial determinant of executive autonomy (Pollack 1997, 2003; Tallberg 2000; Tsebelis and Garrett 2001; Franchino 2007).

Finally, students of executive politics in the EU have turned increasingly to the study of relatively new phenomena, notably the ECB and a diverse array of regulatory agencies at the EU level. The ECB, now the collective central bank of the Eurozone, is without doubt the most spectacular example of supranational delegation in the history of the EU. Indeed, both rational-choice scholars and EU practitioners have referred to the ECB as the most independent central bank in the world, due to the long and non-renewable terms of its members and the insulation of the Bank and its mandate, which can be altered only by a unanimous agreement of the member states (see Chapter 7). At the same time, the EU's member states have created a growing number of regulatory agencies, such as the European Medicines Agency (EMEA) and the European Food Safety Authority (EFSA), among more than a dozen others, each with their own rules and their own powers and responsibilities in the EU policy process (see e.g. Chapter 14 on the regulatory role of EFSA).

Judicial politics and the ECJ

Rational-choice institutionalists have also engaged in increasingly sophisticated research into the nature of EU judicial politics and the role of the ECJ in the integration process. Geoffrey Garrett (1992) first drew on principal-agent analysis to argue that the Court, as an agent of the EU's member governments, was bound to follow the wishes of the most powerful member states. These member states, Garrett claimed, had established the ECJ as a means to solve problems of incomplete contracting and monitoring compliance with EU obligations, and they rationally accepted ECJ jurisprudence, even when rulings went against them, because of their longer-term interest in the enforcement of EU law. In such a setting, Garrett and Weingast (1993: 189) argued, the ECJ might identify 'constructed focal points' among multiple equilibrium outcomes, but the Court was unlikely to rule against the preferences of powerful EU member states, as Burley and Mattli (1993) had suggested in a famous article drawing on neo-functionalist theory.

Other scholars have argued forcefully that Garrett's model overestimated the control mechanisms available to powerful member states and the ease of sanctioning an activist Court, which has been far more autonomous than Garrett suggests. Such accounts suggest that the Court has been able to pursue the process of legal integration far beyond the collective preferences of the member governments, in part due to the high costs to member states in overruling or failing to comply with ECJ decisions, and in part because the ECJ enjoys powerful allies in the form of individual litigants and national courts which refer hundreds of cases per year to the ECJ via the 'preliminary reference' procedure of Article 234 TEC (ex Art. 177 EEC) (Weiler 1994; Mattli and Slaughter 1995, 1998; Stone Sweet and Caporaso 1998; Stone Sweet and Brunell 1998a, 1998b; Alter 2001). According to Stone Sweet and Caporaso (1998: 129), 'the move to supremacy and direct effect must be understood as audacious acts of agency' by the Court.

More recently, as Lisa Conant (2007b) points out, the literature on the ECJ and legal integration has increasingly moved from the traditional question of the ECJ's relationship with national governments, towards the study of the ECJ's other interlocutors, including most notably the national courts that bring the majority of cases before the ECJ, and the individual litigants who use EU law to achieve their aims within national legal systems. Such studies have problematized and sought to explain the complex and ambivalent relationship between the ECJ and national courts, as well as the varying litigation strategies of 'one-shot' litigants and 'repeat players' before the courts (Mattli and Slaughter 1998; Alter 2001; Conant 2002). These and other studies have demonstrated the complexities of ECJ legal integration, the interrelationships among supranational, national, and sub-national political and legal actors, and the limits of EU law in national legal contexts.

Towards normal science?

Students of the EU have thus approached the study of policy-making employing the theoretical tools of comparative politics, formal and informal models drawn from rational choice, and a positivist commitment to systematic empirical testing. The resulting literature, although sometimes highly abstract and inaccessible to the general reader, has substantially advanced our understanding of EU policy-making, of the respective roles and influence of the Commission, Council, Parliament, and Court, and increasingly of the relationship between EU institutions and their national and sub-national interlocutors. Furthermore, with the creation and dissemination of a range of new databases, the scope for systematic testing and falsification of theories is certain to increase in the years to come, making the EU an increasingly promising arena for the practice of 'normal science'.

The governance approach: the EU as a polity

The reader might easily conclude from the chapter so far that the story of theorizing about the EU is a linear progression from international-relations theories to comparative-politics theories. Such a story, however, would be misleading. International-relations scholars continue to theorize about and carry out empirical research about the process of European integration, the workings of EU institutions, and the EU's role in the global order (see Chapter 18). Just as importantly, these approaches now co-exist with a third approach, typically labelled the 'governance approach', which draws on both IR and comparative politics and considers the EU as neither a traditional international organization *nor* as a domestic 'political system', but rather as a new and emerging system of 'governance without government'.

The governance approach is not a single theory of the EU or of European integration, but rather a cluster of related theories emphasizing common themes (Jachtenfuchs 2001, 2007; Jachtenfuchs and Kohler-Koch 2004). Hix (1998) has usefully contrasted the governance school to its rationalist/comparativist/positivist alternative, arguing that the governance approach constitutes a distinctive research agenda across four dimensions.

First, the governance approach theorizes EU governance as non-hierarchical, mobilizing networks of private as well as public actors, who engage in deliberation and problem-solving efforts guided as much by informal as by formal institutions. Secondly, the practitioners of the governance approach are suspicious of 'off-the-shelf' models, advocating the need for a new vocabulary to capture the distinctive features of EU governance (Schmitter 1996; Eriksen and Fossum 2000: 2; Bache and Flinders 2004: 2). Thirdly, students of EU governance often (although not always) emphasize the capacity of the EU to foster 'deliberation' and 'persuasion'—a model of policy-making in which actors are open to changing their beliefs and their preferences, and in which good arguments can matter as much as, or more than, bargaining power (Risse 2000). Fourthly, governance theorists frequently express a normative concern with the 'democratic deficit' in the EU, with many emphasizing the potential for the EU as a 'deliberative democracy' (Joerges 2001*a*).

The literature on 'governance' thus defined has exploded in recent years (Jachtenfuchs 1995; Scharpf 1999; Jachtenfuchs 2001; Hooghe and Marks 2001; Jachtenfuchs and Kohler-Koch 2004; Bache and Flinders 2004; Jachtenfuchs 2007). I focus here on five key issues: (1) the concept of 'governance'; (2) early applications to the EU, in the literatures on 'multi-level governance' and policy networks; (3) the growing literature on the 'Europeanization' of both existing member states and new and candidate members; (4) a substantial literature on the governance capacity of member states and of EU institutions, and the problems of legitimacy faced by the latter; and (5) a new and novel set of claims about the EU as a process of 'deliberative supranationalism' capable of resolving these normative dilemmas.

Governing without government

In Hix's (1998) critique, the governance approach is presented as a *sui generis* approach, treating the EU as fundamentally different from other polities and therefore requiring new—as opposed to 'off-the-shelf'—theoretical approaches. Nonetheless, the EU governance literature draws heavily on the concept(s) of governance worked out by students of both comparative politics *and* international relations.

Within the field of comparative politics, the term governance has appeared with increasing frequency, but with different definitions and different emphases—indeed, Rod Rhodes (1996) identifies at least six distinct uses of the term in the literature. At their most far-reaching, however, theorists of governance put forward the radical claim that contemporary governments lack the knowledge and information required to solve complex economic and social problems, and that governance should therefore be conceived more broadly as the negotiated interactions of public and private actors in a given policy arena. In this view, modern society is 'radically decentred', and government features as only one actor among many in the larger process of socio-economic governance (Kooiman 1993). Hence, in Rhodes' (1996: 660) terms, governance—as distinct from government—takes place through organized networks of public and private actors which 'steer' public policy towards common ends.

International-relations scholars have also increasingly embraced the notion of 'governance without government' with Rosenau (1992: 4) and others suggesting that international affairs may be 'governed' by various different types of networks, including 'transgovernmental' networks of lower-level government or judicial actors interacting across borders with their foreign counterparts (Slaughter 2004), and 'transnational' networks of private actors forming a sort of 'global civil society' (Wapner 1996). This approach to governance, emphasizing networks of public and private actors 'steering' EU public policy, has gained widespread acceptance in EU studies, most notably in the study of 'multi-level governance' and policy networks.

Multi-level governance and EU policy networks

By most accounts (Jachtenfuchs 2001; Bache and Flinders 2004: 3), the governance approach to the EU can be traced, at least in part, to Gary Marks' (1992, 1993) work on the making and implementation of the EU's structural funds. Writing in opposition to intergovernmentalists, Marks argued that the structural funds of the 1980s and 1990s provided evidence for a very different image of the EU, one in which central governments were losing control both to the Commission (which played a key part in designing and implementing the funds), and to local and regional governments inside each member state (which were granted a 'partnership' role in planning and implementation). In making this argument, Bache and Flinders (2004: 3) point out, Marks and his colleagues placed a dual emphasis, first on the 'multi-level' interdependence of territorial governments at the European, national, and sub-national level, and second on the development of new public-private policy networks transcending all three levels.

Later studies of the EU structural funds questioned Marks' far-reaching empirical claims, noting in particular that EU member governments played central roles in the successive reforms of the funds, and that these member states remained effective 'gatekeepers', containing the inroads of both the Commission and sub-national governments into the traditional preserve of state sovereignty (Pollack 1995; Bache 1998; see also Chapter 10). Following these challenges, proponents of the multi-level governance approach have conceded the more varied, nuanced influence of EU policies on territorial governance, documenting how national governments have maintained gatekeeping roles in some countries, such as the UK and Greece, while other countries have witnessed 'an immense shift of authority' from national governments to the European arena and to sub-national, regional governments in a substantial number of states such as France, Italy, Spain, and Belgium (Hooghe 1996; Hooghe and Marks 2001; Bache and Flinders 2004).

Other scholars have focused on the horizontal or network aspects of European integration, drawing on network theory to describe and explain the workings of transnational and transgovernmental networks that can vary from the relatively closed 'policy communities' of public and private actors in areas such as research and technological development to the more open and porous 'issue networks' prevailing in areas such as environmental regulation (Peterson and Bomberg 1999; Peterson 2009). This network form of governance, moreover, has been accentuated further over the past decade by the creation of formal and informal networks of national reg-ulators, in areas such as financial regulation and competition policy (see Chapter 6; for a general discussion of policy networks in the EU, see also Chapter 3).

Europeanization

An increasingly significant offshoot from the multi-level governance tradition exam-ines the phenomenon of 'Europeanization', the process whereby EU institutions and policies influence national institutions and policies within the various member states. In general terms, such studies date to the 1970s, when a small number of scholars examined how EU membership had influenced national political institutions and pub-lic policies (see e.g. H. Wallace 1973). During the 1990s, the study of Europeanization became a cottage industry, with a growing number of studies seeking to explain both the process of Europeanization and the significant variation in outcomes observed across both member states and issue areas. In one particularly influential formulation, Cowles, Caporaso, and Risse (2001) suggested that the extent of Europeanization should be the dual product of: (1) adaptational pressures resulting from the varying 'goodness of fit' between EU and national institutions and policies; and (2) domes-tic intervening variables, including the number of veto points and the organizational and political cultures embedded in existing national institutions. These theories, in turn, have informed a growing literature on the implementation of EU policies 'on the ground' in the various member states, which remains a disputed and understudied topic (see e.g. Falkner et al. 2005; Hartlapp and Falkner 2008; and Chapter 3).

Subsequently, scholars have sketched alternative rationalist and constructivist mechanisms whereby the EU might influence national politics—in the first instance by constraining national choices, in the second case by instilling new norms and reshaping national identities and preferences (Kelley 2004; Börzel and Risse 2007). More recently, Frank Schimmelfennig and Ulrich Sedelmeier (2002, 2005a) have led teams of researchers who tested alternative rationalist and constructivist hypotheses about the effect of EU membership on the new member states. They find some evidence of EU-led policy learning and socialization, as predicted by constructivist models, but the content and the timing of policy reforms in the new members suggest that the greatest impact of the EU has resulted from explicit EU conditionality, a classic rationalist mechanism.

A democratic deficit?

A third major branch of the governance approach to the EU emerged out of the European political economy literature of the 1980s and 1990s, associated with scholars such as Wolfgang Streeck (1998) and Fritz Scharpf (1999). Much of this work analyses and undertakes a normative critique of an EU that purportedly undermines the autonomy and domestic governance capacity of the member states through 'negative integration', while failing to establish governance capacity that is both substantial and democratically legitimate at the supranational EU level. This critique is typically made in two stages.

First, it is argued, EU internal market regulations and ECJ decisions have increasingly eroded, invalidated, or replaced national social regulations, thereby thwarting the social aims and the democratically expressed preferences of national electorates and their legislatures. Moreover, even where EU legislation and ECJ jurisprudence leave national laws, taxation systems, and welfare programmes untouched, it is often argued that the free movement provisions of the Union may set in train a process of regulatory competition in which national governments face pressures to adjust national regulations in an effort to make them more attractive to mobile capital. This may lead to a 'race to the bottom', in which national governments compete to lower the tax burden and the regulatory burdens on businesses threatening to move to other jurisdictions. The recent adoption of the euro, and the limitations on national budget deficits contained in the EU Stability and Growth Pact, have arguably constrained national autonomy still further, depriving states of fiscal policy tools that have proven effective in the past pursuit of economic and social goals (see Chapter 7). In the words of Claus Offe (2000), the *acquis communautaire* (the body of rules and legislation mandated by the EU) now threatens the *acquis nationale* of strong liberal democracy and well-developed welfare states. The extent and character of this purported race to the bottom remain a matter of dispute, with Scharpf (1999) and others acknowledging that the extent of competitive deregulation appears to vary systematically across issue areas. But either way, the prospect of the undermining of national regulations and welfare states poses important analytic as well as normative challenges.

This challenge to national governance raises a second question: whether the race to the bottom might be averted, and democracy regained, at the EU level. On this score, many contributors to the debate are pessimistic, pointing to: the distant and opaque nature of EU decision-making; the strong role of indirectly elected officials in the Council of Ministers and unelected officials in the European Commission;

the weakness of the EP and the second-order nature of its elections; and the bias in the treaties in favour of market liberalization over social regulation (Williams 1991; Scharpf 1999; Greven 2000). Furthermore, even if these institutional flaws in the EU treaties were to be addressed, Joseph Weiler (1995) has suggested that Europe lacks a *demos*, a group of people united by a sense of community or 'we-feeling' that could provide the constituent basis for an EU-level democracy. Other scholars, writing from the perspectives of critical theory (Manners 2007) and feminist theory (Prügl 2007), raise additional challenges to the EU's legitimacy, questioning the locus of public power in the Union, the inclusion of the concerns of peoples of various classes, genders, and ethnicities, and negative as well as the positive impacts of the EU's public policies. For all these reasons, governance theorists argue, the EU faces a 'democratic deficit' and a profound crisis of legitimacy.

Much of the governance literature is given over to proposals for increasing the democratic accountability and the governance capacity of the Union. Whereas in the past EU institutions had relied primarily on 'output legitimacy' (i.e. the efficiency or popularity of EU policy outputs), today there are increased calls for reforms that would increase the 'input legitimacy' (i.e. the democratic accountability of EU institutions to the electorate).

We can identify three distinct reform tracks in the literature: constitutionalization, parliamentarization, and deliberation. The first and most modest of these proposals is 'constitutionalization', the creation of overarching rules and procedural controls that would ensure minimum levels of transparency and public participation in EU policy-making. Andrew Moravcsik (2002), for example, has suggested that the EU's existing treaties (as opposed to the proposed Constitutional Treaty that was rejected in 2005) *already* contain sufficient checks and balances to address concerns about the EU's democratic legitimacy within the circumscribed limits of its powers.

Critics of the EU's democratic legitimacy, however, argue that such procedural safeguards are insufficient to produce an EU that is open and responsive to its citizens. In this context, the second proposed reform track, parliamentarization, would involve *inter alia* the strengthening of the EP's legislative and budgetary powers; a strengthening of EU party groups; the increased salience of EU (rather than national) issues in European elections; and the subordination of the Commission to the Parliament as in the national parliamentary systems of Europe (Hix 2008*b*). Others, however, have cast doubt on the parliamentary model, suggesting that such an approach could exacerbate, rather than ameliorate, the EU's crisis of legitimacy by subjecting national communities, or *demoi*, to a long-term minority position in an EU of twenty-seven or more members (Weiler 1995), and by threatening the independence and neutrality of the European Commission (Majone 2000*b*).

For these reasons, an increasing number of authors have suggested a third model for the EU, namely a 'deliberative democracy' in which citizens, or at least their representatives, would collectively deliberate in search of the best solution to common problems.

Argument, persuasion, and the 'deliberative turn'

This emphasis on deliberation as a characteristic feature of EU policy-making derives largely from the work of Jürgen Habermas (1985, 1998), whose theory of communicative action has been adapted to the study of international relations and to the study of EU governance. The core claim of the approach, as popularized by Risse (2000) in the field of international relations, is that there are not two but three 'logics of social action', namely: the logic of consequentiality (or utility maximization) emphasized by rational-choice theorists; the logic of appropriateness (or rule-following behaviour) associated with constructivist theory; and a 'logic of arguing' derived largely from Habermas's theory of communicative action.

In Risse's (2000: 7) logic of arguing, political actors do not simply bargain based on fixed preferences and relative power, they may also 'argue', questioning their own beliefs and interests and being open to persuasion and the power of a better argument. In the view of many democratic theorists, such argumentative processes lead to the promise of a normatively desirable 'deliberative democracy', in which societal actors engage in a sincere collective search for truth and for the best available public policy, and in which even the losers in such debates accept the outcome by virtue of their participation in the deliberative process and their understanding of the principled arguments put forward by their fellow citizens (Elster 1998; Bohman 1998).

Despite the purported benefits of such deliberative democracy, Risse (2000: 19–20) concedes that genuine argumentative rationality is likely only under a fairly restrictive set of preconditions, including notably:

- the existence of a common lifeworld provided by a high degree of international institutionalization in the respective issue area;
- uncertainty of interests and/or lack of knowledge about the situation among the actors; and
- international institutions based on non-hierarchical relations enabling dense interactions in informal, network-like settings.

These conditions are by no means satisfied everywhere in international politics. Where they are present, however, constructivist scholars predict that international actors will engage in arguing rather than bargaining.

The promise of deliberation has received extraordinary attention within the study of the EU in recent years, most notably among scholars looking for a new normative basis for a democratically legitimate EU (Joerges 2001a; Eriksen and Fossum 2000, 2003). Empirical studies of deliberation face significant methodological hurdles in distinguishing between arguing and bargaining, or between genuine communicative action and 'cheap talk' (Checkel 2001; Magnette 2004: 208). Despite these challenges, EU scholars have identified the promise of deliberation in three EU-related forums: comitology committees, the Constitutional Convention of 2003–4, and the 'new governance' mechanisms of the EU's 'Open Method of Coordination' (OMC). With regard to the first, Christian Joerges and Jürgen Neyer (1997*a*, 1997*b*) argue that EU comitology committees provide a forum in which national and supranational experts meet and *deliberate* in a search for the best or most efficient solutions to common policy problems, arguing on the basis of informal norms, good arguments, and a search for consensus. Critics, however, question both the empirical basis of this claim, noting that evidence of deliberation in such committees remains partial and sketchy (Pollack 2003: 114–45), as well as the normative value of committee deliberations that take place largely outside the public eye (Zürn 2000).

A second EU arena often identified as a promising venue for deliberation was the Convention on the Future of Europe, which met in 2003 to consider changes to the EU treaties and proposed a draft Constitution, although here again the evidence for genuine deliberation, as opposed to bargaining from fixed interests, remains unclear and controversial (Maurer 2003*a*; Closa 2004; Magnette 2004).

Thirdly, the promise of deliberation has also been emphasized by students of the OMC, codified and endorsed by the Lisbon European Council in March 2000. This is a non-binding form of policy coordination, based on the collective establishment of policy guidelines, targets, and benchmarks, coupled with a system of periodic 'peer review' in which member governments present their respective national programmes for consideration and comment by their EU counterparts (see Chapter 4). The OMC remains controversial both politically and in the academic community (see Chapter 12). For many commentators, the OMC offered a flexible means to address common policy issues without encroaching on sensitive areas of national sovereignty, representing a 'third way' between communitarization and purely national governance and a potential test case for Habermasian deliberation (Hodson and Maher 2001; Scott and Trubek 2002). Careful empirical work, however, has at least tempered the more far-reaching claims put forward by the supporters of the OMC. A number of scholars have argued that when it comes to politically sensitive questions, national representatives revert to a presentation of fixed national positions, engaging clearly in bargaining rather than arguing behaviour (see, e.g. Jacobsson and Vifell 2003; Jobelius 2003; Borrás and Jacobsson 2004; De la Porte and Nanz 2004; and Chapter 12).

Legitimate governance?

The governance approach to the EU draws on comparative politics as well as international relations and asks analytically and normatively important questions about the workings of EU policy networks, the variable transformation and Europeanization of national institutions and politics, the democratic legitimacy of the EU as a political system, and the prospects for deliberative policy-making at the EU level. Certainly, the governance approach is not without its flaws or critics, and even its proponents concede that it remains a constellation of interrelated claims rather than a single, coherent theory. In empirical terms, moreover, one can argue that the analytical and normative elaboration of the governance approach has outpaced the empirical work needed to assess the plausibility of its claims. Nevertheless, students of EU governance have made significant progress in formulating a research agenda and in producing more empirical evidence and more nuanced claims about territorial change, Europeanization, and deliberation in an enlarged EU.

Conclusions

In 1972, Donald Puchala likened theorists of EU integration to blind men touching an elephant, each one feeling a different part of the elephant and purporting to describe a very different animal. Today, theories of the EU are even more diverse, comprising three distinct approaches with lively debates both within and across all three. Puchala's metaphor suggested the relative immaturity and weakness of integration theory and the partiality of its insights. Yet there is a more optimistic reading of the dizzying array of theories purporting to provide insights into the workings of the EU and the *telos* of European integration.

The past decade of scholarship in EU studies witnessed at least a partial retreat from grand theorizing about the integration process in favour of a series of mid-range questions about a variety of topics including the workings of the EU's legislative, executive, and judicial processes; the prospects of socialization or deliberation in EU institutions; the effects of European integration on national institutions and policies; and a wide range of other questions. These more fine-grained questions, in turn, have prompted scholars to undertake increasingly sophisticated empirical testing of their various hypotheses, replacing sterile 'metatheoretical' debates with the careful and patient accumulation of empirical findings that allow us to adjudicate with increasing precision among contending theories from all three traditions. The implications of these theories for our understanding of the EU policy process are explored at length by Alasdair Young in Chapter 3.

Note

1 This chapter draws from the earlier and more extensive version in the 5th edition of this volume. The author is grateful to Helen Wallace and Alasdair Young for excellent comments on this version. Any remaining flaws or omissions are the responsibility of the author.

FURTHER READING

Excellent introductions to European integration theories can be found in Rosamond's (2000) clear and concise text, and in the essays in Jørgensen, Pollack and Rosamond (2007) and Wiener and Diez (2009). Keeler (2005) and Jupille (2005) provide illuminating and thorough analyses of trends in the literature, especially the US literature, over the past five decades. E. Haas (2004 [1958]) remains the *locus classicus* on neo-functionalism, and Hoffmann (1966) the founding text on intergovernmentalism. For more recent developments, see Moravcsik (1998) and Moravcsik and Schimmelfennig (2009) on liberal intergovernmentalism; Pollack (2009) on institutionalism; and Risse (2009) and Jupille, Caporaso, and Checkel (2003) on constructivism. Hix (2005) deftly reviews comparative-politics approaches to various aspects of EU policy-making. The governance literature remains extremely diverse, but useful overviews are provided by Scharpf (1999), Hooghe and Marks (2001), and Jachtenfuchs (2007).

Haas, E. B. (2004) [1958], *The Uniting of Europe* (Stanford, CA: Stanford University Press); reprinted in 2004 by Notre Dame University Press.

Hix, S. (2005), *The Political System of the European Union*, 2nd edn. (Basingstoke: Palgrave Macmillan).

Hoffmann, S. (1966), 'Obstinate or Obsolete? The Fate of the Nation-State and the Case of Western Europe', *Daedalus*, 95/3: 862–915.

Hooghe, L., and Marks, G. (2001), *Multi-Level Governance and European Integration* (Lanham, MD: Rowman & Littlefield).

Jachtenfuchs, M. (2007), 'The European Union as a Polity (II)', in K. E. Jørgensen, M. A. Pollack, and B. Rosamond (eds.) (2007), *The Handbook of European Union Politics* (London: Sage), 159–73.

Jørgensen, K. E., Pollack, M. A., and Rosamond, B. (eds.) (2007), *The Handbook of European Union Politics* (London: Sage).

Jupille, J. (2005), 'Knowing Europe: Metatheory and Methodology in EU Studies', in M. Cini and A. Bourne (eds.), *Palgrave Advances in European Union Studies* (Basingstoke: Palgrave Macmillan), 209–32.

Jupille, J., Caporaso, J. A., and Checkel, J. (2003), 'Integrating Institutions: Rationalism, Constructivism, and the Study of the European Union', *Comparative Political Studies*, 36/1–2: 7–40.

Keeler, J. T. S. (2005), 'Mapping EU Studies: The Evolution from Boutique to Boom Field 1960–2001', *Journal of Common Market Studies*, 43/3: 551-82.

Moravcsik, A. (1998), *The Choice for Europe: Social Purpose and State Power from Messina to Maastricht* (Ithaca, NY: Cornell University Press).

Moravcsik, A., and Schimmelfennig, F. (2009), 'Liberal Intergovernmentalism', in A. Wiener and T. Diez (eds.), *European Integration Theory*, 2nd edn. (Oxford: Oxford University Press), 67-87.

Pollack, M. A. (2009), 'The New Institutionalism and European Integration', in A. Wiener and T. Diez (eds.), *European Integration Theory*, 2nd edn. (Oxford: Oxford University Press), 125–43.

Risse, T. (2009), 'Social Constructivism and European Integration', in A. Wiener and T. Diez (eds.), *European Integration Theory*, 2nd edn. (Oxford: Oxford University Press), 144–61.

Rosamond, B. (2000), *Theories of European Integration* (Basingstoke: Palgrave).

Scharpf, F. W. (1999), *Governing in Europe: Democratic and Effective?* (Oxford: Oxford University Press).

Wiener, A., and Diez, T. (2009) (eds.), *European Integration Theory*, 2nd edn. (Oxford: Oxford University Press).

CHAPTER 3

The European Policy Process in Comparative Perspective

Alasdair R. Young

▌ Summary

Policy-making in the European Union (EU) is particularly complex and is distinctive. Nonetheless, it can be fruitfully studied by drawing upon insights from the analysis of policy-making within states and cooperation among states. This chapter sets out the stages of the policy-making process—agenda-setting, policy formation, decision-making, implementation, and feedback—introduces the prevailing approaches to analysing each of these stages, and discusses how these apply to studying policy-making in the EU. It argues that theories rooted in comparative politics and international relations can explain different phases of the EU's policy process. This chapter also helps to explain why policy-making varies across issue areas within the EU.

Introduction[1]

Policy-making is extremely complex even within traditional states (Hurrell and Menon 1996; Scharpf 1997: 29; John 1998; Sabatier 1999). It is even more so in the European Union where institutional structures are more in flux, the allocation of authority is more contested, and multiple levels of governance engage a multitude of actors (Hurrell and Menon 1996; McCormick 2006). Nonetheless, this chapter echoes the central theme of this volume by contending that EU policy-making can be fruitfully studied using general tools of political science (see also Sbragia 1992a; Peterson and Bomberg 1999; Hix 2005). This chapter does not aim to provide an introduction to the wealth of literature on policy-making in all of its myriad forms; rather it aims to introduce those analytical approaches and debates drawn from comparative politics and international relations that are most commonly deployed, implicitly or explicitly, to explain policy-making in the EU. This chapter therefore situates EU policy-making in a broad comparative perspective, drawing on both policy-making within states and cooperation among them.[2]

This chapter is intended to serve as a stepping stone between the grand theories of European integration and the different approaches to studying the EU discussed in Chapter 2 and the patterns of policy-making and roles of the key institutions developed in Chapter 4. It begins by introducing the policy cycle. It then makes the case that there has been convergence between comparative politics and international relations with regard to the analysis of at least certain aspects of the policy process. The chapter then introduces the literatures on the different phases of the policy cycle—agenda-setting, policy formation, decision-making, and implementation—and relates them to the study of the EU before examining policy feedback. It concludes by drawing out the implications for explaining policy-making in the EU.

Policy-making and the policy cycle

The policy-making process is commonly depicted heuristically as a 'policy cycle' (also known as the 'stages heuristic') (see Figure 3.1): a self-conscious simplification of a complex phenomenon in order to facilitate our understanding (John 1998: 23–7, 36; Sabatier 1999: 6–7; McCormick 2006: 13–14; Richardson 2006: 7; Hague and Harrop 2007: 378). The policy cycle is usually depicted as commencing with an issue being put on the political agenda; that is, it becomes an issue of concern (agenda-setting). Once a decision has been taken to address a particular issue, it is necessary to formulate specific proposals for action (policy formulation) and decide what course of action to pursue, or not (policy decision). If a policy decision is taken, then the policy must be put into effect (implementation). The policy cycle emphasizes that the story does not stop with policy implementation, but that the intended, inadequate, and unintended effects of policies often feed back into the policy process.

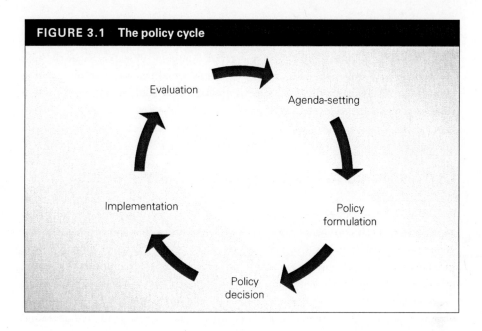

FIGURE 3.1   The policy cycle

The policy cycle has been criticized for being misleading (see Sabatier 1999: 7). First, the stages of the policy process are not as discrete as the heuristic implies. For instance, policy formulation may well occur as officials seek to implement vague legislation. Second, Kingdon (2003: 205–6) contends that problem identification (agenda-setting) and solution specification (policy formulation) do not necessarily occur in the sequence depicted in the policy cycle: policies are sometimes developed in advance of there being a specific problem to solve and these alternatives are advocated prior to an opportunity to push them on to the agenda. Third, the cycle does not explicitly capture the interaction between multiple policies being pursued in a particular policy domain. This often comes up as the issue of policy coherence, namely whether different policies support or impede each other's objectives (see, e.g. Streeck and Thelen 2005: 19–22; Carbone 2008: 325–7). Fourth, the heuristic can give the impression that there is a single policy cycle when in reality there are multiple, asynchronous policy cycles operating at different levels of governance. As a consequence, some have characterized the policy process as a 'garbage can', in which policies emerge in a manner much less predictable than that suggested by rational decision-making in response to an identified problem (Cohen et al. 1972; and, with specific reference to the EU, Richardson 2006: 24). While these criticisms do not necessarily condemn the policy cycle as a heuristic device, they should caution against being seduced by its simplicity.

A more fundamental critique of the policy cycle is that it does not provide the basis for a causal theory of policy-making that applies across the policy cycle (Sabatier 1999: 7). Rather, different analytical approaches have been applied to try to explain each individual stage (see, e.g. Peterson and Bomberg 1999; Richardson 2006: 7). There is, however, no agreement on a 'grand theory' of policy-making (Scharpf 1997: 19; John 1998: 195; Peterson and Bomberg 1999: 272; Sabatier 1999: 261; Richardson 2006: 7). This chapter does not seek to develop an overarching explanation of the policy process; rather it highlights the analytical approaches that have been developed to explain the different stages of the policy process.

Convergence in the analysis of policy-making

Hurrell and Menon (1996) and Risse-Kappen (1996) have argued for drawing on insights from both comparative politics and international relations in order to explain policy-making in the EU. Both contributions highlight developments in the international-relations literature—notably with regard to the implications of complex interdependence for state behaviour, attention to the roles of non-state actors, and the consequences of increasing institutionalization of international cooperation—that depict relations at the international level in ways increasingly analogous to those found at the domestic level (more generally see Milner 1998). The literature on international cooperation in particular is concerned with the central questions of policy-making: whether there should be cooperation (which conflates whether there should be action and by whom) and what form it should take, including in terms of substance (see, e.g. Rosenau and Czempiel 1992; O. R. Young 1999; Keohane and Nye 2001).

This chapter also points to changes in how policy-making within states is analysed, particularly the decreased emphasis on hierarchy, that increase the resonance with analyses of international cooperation. These analytical changes are in response to and in recognition of real-world changes. Beginning in the 1980s, privatization, administrative reforms inspired by the New Public Management, changes in territorial politics (such as devolution in the UK), increased economic interdependence, and the development of policy-making beyond the state (not least by the EU) contributed to governing within European states being understood as occurring less through hierarchical authority structures and more through negotiation and persuasion within more decentralized networks (R. Rhodes 1997; Peters 2001; Kahler 2002: 58; Goodin et al. 2006: 11–12; Goetz 2008). As a result of both of these shifts, approaches to analysing aspects of international cooperation and domestic policy-making have become more similar.

The players in the policy process

Before turning to ways of understanding the policy process, it is first necessary to identify the actors that engage in that process. Wherever policy-making occurs—within states, in the EU, or in the wider international arena—it involves the interaction of multiple actors that want different things and bring different resources and capabilities to the policy process.

The main actors in the policy processes of liberal democracies are politicians, bureaucrats, and interest groups. Politicians, either as legislators or as members of government, are the key decision-makers. Bureaucrats advise politicians in government, take some policy decisions, and implement policies. Interest groups seek to promote policies and to influence politicians' and bureaucrats' decisions and often play a role in implementing policy.

While politicians in government always matter in the policy process, how important legislators are depends on the distribution of power amongst political institutions (see under decision-making below). Within political science there are intense debates about how politicians do and should act. Some (e.g. Dahl 1961; Beer 1982; Baumgartner and Leech 1998; Grossman and Helpman 2001) depict them as being highly responsive to societal pressures, constituency demands, and/or interest-group lobbying. More typically, authors assume that politicians have their own preferences, informed by their own experiences and political beliefs, as well as being influenced by societal pressures (Derthick and Quirk 1986; Putnam 1988; Atkinson and Coleman 1989; Evans 1993).

Bureaucrats also tend to be depicted as having specific interests, which may be purposive (concerned with achieving policy goals, including greater European integration) or reflexive (concerned with enhancing the power and prestige of their particular branch of the bureaucracy) (Niskanen 1971; Peters 1992: 115–16; also Dunleavy 1997). The tendency for bureaucracies to have functionally determined preferences is captured by the aphorism popularized by Graham Allison (1969: 711) that 'where you stand depends on where you sit.'

Interest groups are non-profit, non-violent associations of individuals or other organizations that are independent of governments that aggregate interests and inject them into the policy process (Keck and Sikkink 1997; Clark et al. 1998; Halliday 2001; Price 2003; Hawkins 2004). All interest groups must contend with the 'logic of collective action' (Olson 1965). That is, they must overcome the free-rider problem: that individuals or firms are able to enjoy the benefits of collective action (a policy) without incurring the costs of realizing it. The free-rider problem is more acute the more actors are involved (it is harder to identify free riders with larger numbers) and the more diffuse the benefits of action (the lower the individual incentive to act). This implies that it is easier for producers to organize than for consumers or people concerned about the environment (for a critical discussion, see G. Jordan 1998). There are, however, ways for consumers and environmentalists to overcome the collective action problem, not least because members are motivated by non-material considerations (G. Jordan and Maloney 1996; A. R. Young 1998), but such groups tend to be fewer and more poorly resourced than producer interests. Moreover, many firms have the resources individually to participate in the policy process. Politicians and bureaucrats generally welcome the input of interest groups and firms into the policy process because they provide information, which helps to inform policy options and choices, and because many represent actors that are affected by the policies and compliance is likely to be better (and therefore policy effectiveness greater) if the affected actors have been part of the process (Lindblom 1977; Beer 1982). Producer interests tend to be particularly well equipped to provide these benefits to policy-makers, giving them a 'privileged position' in the policy process (Lindblom 1977).

These actors play roles in the EU process that are slightly different from those they perform at the national level. In the EU the bureaucrats in the Commission have a greater role in agenda-setting and policy formulation and a lesser one in policy implementation than their counterparts within states. Members of the European Parliament (MEPs) are directly elected, but their role tends to be more circumscribed than that of national parliamentarians (see Chapter 4). National ministers sit together in the Council of Ministers and play an important role in adopting legislation, albeit one in which they represent their own interests as well as those of their constituents (see Chapter 4). European interest groups tend to be associations of national associations, which can present problems for agreeing common positions, although there are a growing number of European groups that have direct memberships (Greenwood and Young 2005). Producer groups enjoy privileged access to EU policy-makers, particularly focusing on the Commission, which combined with their organizational and information resources have led many analysts to characterize the EU as an 'élite pluralist environment' (see Coen 2007: 335).

Moreover, informed by the debate in integration theory between neo-functionalism and (liberal) intergovernmentalism (see Chapter 2), there is also a vigorous strand of the EU policy-making literature that considers the extent to which the EU's supranational institutions—the Commission, European Court of Justice (ECJ), and European Parliament (EP)—influence the EU policy-making process. In this context they tend to be treated as distinctive, unitary actors, although each of these is a composite institution with complex internal politics (see Chapter 4).

Policy makes politics

Which interest groups, firms, and parts of the state engage in the policy process and how much autonomy the government has from societal actors vary with the type of policy at issue. In the EU the policy in question also influences at what level of governance authority lies and which decision rules apply at the EU level. Theodore Lowi (1964; 1972: 299) contended that 'policy determines politics', identifying three main types of policy—distributive, regulatory, and redistributive—each characterized by a different type of politics.[3] Distributive policies, for which there are no visible losers within the polity because the individual costs are very small and are spread widely, such as 'pork-barrel' spending from the public purse, are characterized by supportive relations between interest groups and policy-makers and mutual non-interference among interest groups. Regulatory policy, including rules governing who can provide which services, which produces concentrated winners and losers, by contrast, leads to interest-group competition. Redistributive policies, such as those associated with the welfare state, which involve the transfer of resources from one diffuse group to another, are characterized by politics divided along class lines. Despite its prominence and popularity, Lowi's scheme has been extensively criticized, particularly because the typology is difficult to apply to the messy reality of policy-making (Heidenheimer 1985: 455).

Wilson (1980) developed a more nuanced analysis grounded explicitly in the distribution of anticipated costs and benefits. Where the distribution of both costs and benefits is broad, majoritarian politics is likely to occur. Where benefits are diffuse and costs concentrated, such as in consumer and environmental protection (see Chapters 13 and 14), policy will be blocked by the vested interests that benefit from the status quo, unless a policy entrepreneur can mobilize latent public opinion in favour of policy change. Where anticipated costs and benefits are both concentrated, such as in economic regulation in which some firms gain at the expense of others, interest-group competition is expected (see Chapters 5 and 15). Policies that have narrow benefits and diffuse costs, such as economic regulations that shield producers from competition, are likely to be characterized by clientelistic politics (see Chapters 5 and 15). The crucial insight to take away from this discussion, however, is straightforward—different types of policy are characterized by different types of politics, even if the precise contours are difficult to pin down (John 1998: 7).

Foreign policy has tended to be treated as distinct from domestic policy-making. In particular, policies that concern the most basic concerns of the state (particularly security) are thought to be subject to 'high politics', in which heads of government are prominent and societal actors passive (see Chapter 18). Other policies, such as trade (see Chapter 16) and international environmental policies (see Chapter 13), however, have been depicted as subject to 'low politics', in which societal actors engage actively and which are addressed lower down the political hierarchy (Keohane and Nye 2001: 22–3; Hill 2003: 4), and thus look more similar to domestic politics. Governments are thus thought to have more autonomy from societal pressures when pursuing some types of foreign policy than others.

This high/low politics distinction is problematic, however. It assumes a hierarchy among issues that is not sustainable as non-military issues—including financial crises, pandemics, and environmental degradation (including climate change)—can have profound implications for states (Keohane and Nye 2001: 22–3; Hill 2003: 4). Moreover, foreign policy, even when its focus is security, often engages politicians, bureaucrats, and interest groups in ways similar to domestic politics (Allison 1971; Lowi 1972; Risse-Kappen 1991; Evans 1993; Hill 2003), and arguably is coming increasingly to resemble domestic politics (Hill 2003). Conversely, there are claims that issues, such as energy (see Chapter 15), traditionally thought of as domestic can be 'securitized'; that is, it can be 'presented as an existential threat, requiring emergency measures and justifying actions outside the normal bounds of political procedure' (Buzan et al. 1998: 24). It is, therefore, not easy and is probably unhelpful to designate certain issues as high or low politics a priori. This discussion, however, does draw attention to variation in how much autonomy the government has from societal actors when making policy choices.

Policy has particularly profound effects on politics in the EU (see Chapter 4). Whether competence (authority) resides with the member states or the EU or is shared between them varies across policy areas. Moreover, the roles of the institutions differ between policy areas at the EU level, as can the decision rule in the Council. Consequently, it is essential to understand the institutional context within which a policy decision is taken.

Agenda-setting: deciding what to decide

Deciding what to decide is a crucial part of the policy-making process and one that often takes place in a context where there is a great deal of uncertainty. Deciding what to decide actually involves two steps in the policy cycle: agenda-setting and policy formation. Whether an issue attracts political attention in part reflects the character of the issue—how serious the problem is; whether there has been a change in the severity of the problem; whether it stands for a more general problem, such as the threatened extinction of a specific animal as emblematic of diminishing biodiversity; and whether it has emotional appeal, as some issues, such as those involving children or bodily harm, are more likely to garner sympathy from publics and policy-makers (Keck and Sikkink 1998: 26; Page 2006: 216).

There is, however, a significant degree of agency in agenda-setting, with policy entrepreneurs, be they interest groups, politicians, or others, identifying and exploiting opportunities to push a policy and presenting ('framing') it in a way that resonates politically (Kingdon 2003: 204–5; Price 2003: 583; Page 2006: 215). Framing an issue is most likely to be successful if it can be linked with existing widely held norms or concerns (Price 2003: 597; Hawkins 2004: 780).

An 'epistemic community' is a distinctive type of political entrepreneur. It is 'a network of professionals with recognized expertise and competence in a particular domain and an authoritative claim to policy-relevant knowledge within that domain or issue-area' (P. Haas 1992: 3). The members of an epistemic community share a set of normative and principled beliefs, causal beliefs, notions for weighing and evaluating knowledge, and a common set of problems to which they direct their expertise. The impact of epistemic communities tends to be particularly acute in highly technical areas, such as with respect to the environment (P. Haas 1992; Zito 2001; this volume, Chapter 13) and economic and monetary union (Verdun 1999; McNamara 2005). Epistemic communities affect the policy agenda by articulating cause-and-effect relationships and in doing so help to specify problems and propose solutions (P. Haas 1992: 14).

Events can also be crucial for creating opportunities for policy entrepreneurs to promote policies (Downs 1972: 39; Kingdon 2003: 197; Page 2006: 216). Crises can contribute to converting conditions that can be ignored into problems that need to be addressed (Kingdon 2003). For example, a series of regulatory failures concerning food safety in Europe during the 1980s, most notably bovine spongiform encephalopathy (BSE), contributed to the adoption of a more precautionary approach to regulating food safety (Vogel 2003: 568; this volume, Chapter 14). The significance of events injects an important element of contingency into the policy-making process.

The agenda-setting literature, however, has been criticized for being too conditioned by the US political system in which it developed (Page 2006: 208–9). In particular, the US political system is relatively non-hierarchical: policy initiatives can come from many directions. In parliamentary democracies the fusing of legislative and executive branches of government through party control tends to produce executive dominance, which means that there is one key audience that must be convinced if an issue is to get on the agenda (Page 2006: 208–9).

The EU combines pluralism with executive dominance. Its vertical and horizontal divisions of power create a great many access points (Peters 1994; Richardson 2006: 5). In those policy areas in which the European Commission has the exclusive right of initiative, however, the Commission is the key audience that must be persuaded to put an issue forward (Majone 2005: 231; Daviter 2007: 655). As the Commission's structure is highly fragmented with overlapping internal responsibilities, however, alternatives are available for a policy advocate looking for bureaucratic allies to develop a policy proposal (Peters 1994: 14). In addition, the Commission can be asked by the European Council or the Parliament to advance a policy initiative, and it is common for EU legislation to have built-in deadlines for reforms. Nonetheless, the Commission is the pre-eminent policy entrepreneur in the EU and it actively frames policy proposals in order to construct political support (Garrett and Weingast 1993; Jabko 2006; Daviter 2007: 659). The Commission, however, is constrained in that it needs external support from other EU institutional actors—either from influential member states, the EP, or the ECJ—if the agenda it is promoting is to have a realistic chance of adoption (Tallberg 2007: 204–5).

Policy formulation: what are the alternatives?

Before policy decisions can be taken the range of alternatives must be narrowed. As discussed above, this process does not necessarily neatly follow agenda-setting. Whatever the sequencing, the formulation of policy is seen as involving a different set of actors from those who participate in agenda-setting and is most commonly depicted as the product of policy networks (Peterson 1995; Richardson 2006: 7).

Policy networks are 'sets of formal institutional and informal linkages between governmental and other actors structured around shared if endlessly negotiated beliefs and interests in public policy-making and implementation' (R. Rhodes

2006: 426).[4] While most of the policy network literature focuses on domestic policy, it has been applied to explaining foreign policy (Risse-Kappen 1991; Hocking 2004) and international relations (Keck and Sikkink 1998; Reinicke 1999–2000). Policy networks are seen as influencing policy choices by shaping which groups participate in the policy process (R. Rhodes 1997: 9; Peterson 2004). The term 'policy network' captures a variety of different types of relationship between public and private actors from tightly integrated 'policy communities' to loosely affiliated 'issue networks' (Peterson 2004: 120). Policy communities—which have stable memberships, exclude outsiders, and have members who depend heavily on each other for resources—are seen as having significant impacts on policy formulation and tend to promote policy continuity in the interests of the participating incumbents. Issue networks by contrast have open and unstable memberships, which tend to contain competing policy preferences (Peterson 2004: 120).

There are three particular actors within policy networks that warrant special attention: producers, epistemic communities, and advocacy coalitions. The resource dependencies at the heart of policy network analysis are usually seen as privileging producer interests because it is often their behaviour that has to be changed, which means that they have detailed information about the costs and likely success of policy alternatives and they can either drag their feet on implementation or can lend their support to the initiative (Olson 1965; Lindblom 1977; Beer 1982). Epistemic communities are not only important in agenda-setting, but also advance solutions to identified policy problems (Peterson 2004; R. Rhodes 2006: 425). Sabatier and Jenkins-Smith (1993; Sabatier 1998) contend that policy networks tend to contain between one and four 'advocacy coalitions', 'each composed of actors from various governmental and private organizations who both (a) share a set of normative and causal beliefs and (b) engage in a non-trivial degree of co-ordinated activity over time' (Sabatier 1998: 103). Advocacy coalitions are thus networks within networks, which compete to advance their preferred policy solutions.

Policy network analysis is, however, seen by many as providing nothing more than a description of what is happening, rather than an explanation of how policy is made (John 1998: 86; Peterson 2004: 126–7). Dowding (1995: 137) contends that the metaphor of the network has no explanatory value, as the nature of the network and its impact on policy outcomes are both determined by the power relations among the actors involved. Further, Kingdon's (2003) 'policy streams' approach implies that policy formulation does not necessarily follow an issue being put on the agenda, as is implied in the policy network approach.

There are also a number of criticisms of the policy network approach that are particular to the EU. One is that EU policy-making is too fluid—with different focuses of authority and different constellations of actors involved in individual policy decisions even within the same policy area—to be captured by the network concept (Kassim 1994: 20–2). Further, because implementation of most EU rules is carried out by the member states, the Commission has a limited direct role in policy delivery, reducing the intensity of its engagement with societal actors and its dependence on them. Moreover, because there are public and private participants from twenty-seven member states as well as the EU-level participants, actors involved in the policy process have very different value systems and often have very different views of problems and possible solutions, which makes it difficult for groups to agree common positions that can be injected coherently into the policy process. Thus it is relatively rare to find policy communities at the EU level, with the most notable exception being in agriculture, but even that policy community is eroding as agriculture is reframed as a trade and budgetary and environmental issue (see Chapter 8). Policy formulation, therefore, is a relatively open process in the EU (Richardson 2000: 1013), but, as with agenda setting, the Commission is the pivotal actor in policy formation in those policy areas where it has sole right of initiative (Kassim 1994: 23). Crucially, its central role in agenda-setting and policy formulation give the Commission a significant say in many EU policies even if its role in decision-making is limited (Hix 2005: 74).

Decision-making: choosing what (not) to do

Although there is convergence between comparative-politics and international-relations approaches regarding agenda-setting and policy formulation, there is much less common ground with regard to decision-making. This is due in large part to decision-making within domestic contexts taking place through highly institutionalized procedures, including voting, while decision-making in international relations—as in examples of international cooperation—usually takes place by consensus. Even in those international organizations in which binding decisions are taken by votes—such as the International Monetary Fund and the United Nations Security Council—decisions require super-majorities and powerful actors retain vetoes. Thus the two sub-disciplines generally seek to explain decision-making in very different contexts.

These differences, however, are a boon when it comes to explaining decision-making in the EU because the context of policy-making varies extensively across policy areas (see Chapter 4), from unanimous decision-making among the member states, for example in foreign and security policy (Chapter 18), to decisions taken on the basis of qualified majority voting (QMV) amongst the member states in conjunction with the EP on a proposal from the European Commission, for example with regard to the single market (Chapter 5) and the environment (Chapter 13), with many combinations in between. Thus some aspects of EU decision-making have features similar to the executive and legislative politics of domestic policy-making, while others are more similar to international negotiations.

The analysis of decision-making in the EU is rooted primarily in the 'new institutionalisms': historical institutionalism, rational-choice institutionalism, and sociological institutionalism (Hall and Taylor 1996; Aspinwall and Schneider

1999; Peters 1999; Pollack 2004; and see Chapter 2). The historical and rational choice variants have tended to be applied more frequently to studies of policy-making (Nugent 2006), particularly with regard to executive politics, primarily in the Commission, and legislative politics, focused on the EP. Both sociological and rational-choice institutionalist approaches, however, have been applied to analyses of decision-making in the Council of Ministers.

Executive politics: delegated decision-making

Executive politics is most often associated with providing political leadership, such as through agenda-setting and policy formation, and overseeing the implementation of legislation. Our focus here, however, is on the delegation of decision-making responsibility to executive bodies. Both comparative-politics and international-relations literatures consider the decision to delegate responsibilities, but it is the comparative politics literature, particularly that on delegation by the US Congress to independent regulatory agencies, that focuses on the delegation of decision-making, rather than of agenda-setting or monitoring compliance (for a review see Pollack 2003: 20–34; and see Chapter 2). This literature is rooted in rationalism, particularly principal-agent analysis. A key insight is that the principal(s) and agent have different preferences and that the act of delegation gives the agent scope to pursue its own preferences, rather than those of the principal(s).

The benefits of delegating decision-making are considered to be particularly pronounced under certain circumstances, such as a significant need for policy-relevant expertise due to the technical or scientific complexity of a policy area (see Chapter 2). In the EU the specialized agencies—such as the European Medicines Evaluation Agency and the European Food Safety Authority (see Chapter 14)—have been given the task of providing expert advice to the Commission, which formally takes decisions (at least under certain circumstances) (Krapohl 2004; Eberlein and Grande 2005). The delegation of decision-making is also more likely where doubts about politicians' commitment to a policy can undermine its effectiveness. The problem of commitments not being credible is likely to be pronounced when there is a conflict between short-run costs and long-run benefits (time inconsistency), such as in monetary policy (see Chapter 7), or a when policy delivers diffuse benefits, but imposes concentrated costs and therefore generates strong political pressure to abandon the policy, such as in competition policy (see Chapter 6). Decision-making may also be delegated in order to make it harder for successors to reverse the policy.

Alternatively, sociological institutionalists contend that delegation occurs not necessarily because it is efficient, but because it is perceived as a legitimate and appropriate institutional design. Thus, institutional designs are copied through processes of emulation and diffusion. In this view, the creation of a European Central Bank (ECB) was shaped by the acceptance of monetarist ideas and the view that independent central banks were appropriate (McNamara 2005).

Where decision-making is delegated, two different views of bureaucratic decision-making prevail. One view, rooted primarily in the analysis of independent regulatory agencies in the US, stresses the importance of technical expertise and legal mandates and sees value in insulating decision-makers from political pressures, so that decisions can be taken for the greater good rather than to benefit the powerful. Giandomenico Majone (1994: 94) has argued that the Commission, because it is pan-European and not democratically elected, is more insulated from political pressures and is therefore more likely to take difficult decisions and less likely to be captured than national regulators.

A much messier view of bureaucratic politics comes primarily from the analysis of US foreign policy, not least Graham Allison's study of the Cuban Missile Crisis (Allison 1969, 1971; Allison and Zelikow 1999), which depicts bureaucratic politics as bargaining among different sections of the executive with different preferences (for a rare application to the EU, see Rosenthal 1975). In this view decisions reflect compromise and consensus among the participants (Rosati 1981). While much of the European integration literature has treated the Commission as if it is a unitary actor and focused on its influence relative to the member states, the policy-making literature has pointed out vigorous differences within the Commission (see, e.g. Chapter 13).

An important implication of the principal-agent approach, however, is that the bureaucratic agent is not completely free to take decisions, but is constrained by the principals' preferences. How constraining the principals' preferences are depends how able they are to monitor the agent's behaviour and whether they are able to sanction behaviour they dislike, which in turn depends on whether some of the principals approve of what the agent is doing and are able to shield it (Pollack 2003). In this view, any analysis of Commission decision-making must consider what authority has been delegated to it and how its preferences relate to those of the member states on the issue in question.

Legislative politics or international negotiation?

Because of the separation of executive and legislative authority, the legislative politics of the EU, especially in the EP, is arguably more closely analogous to that of the US than to those of most EU member states (Hix 2005; McElroy 2007). Consequently, authors seeking to understand EU legislative politics have drawn extensively on theories developed to explain decision-making in the US Congress, particularly the House of Representatives. Care, however, is required when drawing such comparisons, not least because the connection between voters and representatives is much weaker in the EP than in the House of Representatives, because the powers of the Council and EP are not as equal as are those of the Senate and the House, and because the executive–legislative division of powers is much less strict in the EU than in the US (McElroy 2007: 176). Moreover, despite its legislative role, the Council appears to operate in many respects like an international negotiation.

'Pure' legislative politics in the European Parliament

The theory of 'minimum-winning coalitions' (Riker 1962) is particularly commonly applied to EU decision-making. A minimum-winning coalition, by involving the minimum number of votes needed to secure victory, means that there are fewer interests to accommodate and gives the members of the coalition, particularly those decisive in creating a winning majority, greater influence over the policy. It is more precise, however, to think in terms of 'minimum-connected-winning' coalitions among legislators or parties that have policy preferences that are relatively closely related (Axelrod 1970). In parliamentary systems such coalition-building is less likely on a policy-by-policy basis, but similar dynamics are evident in the creation of coalition governments (Swaan 1973; Felsenthal and Machover 2004). Contrary to these expectations, however, the EP has had a tendency to form oversized voting coalitions, ostensibly to increase the EP's influence relative to the Council. Recent studies, however, have pointed to a tentative retreat from oversized coalitions toward more 'normal' patterns of minimum-winning coalitions on the left or the right (Kreppel and Hix 2003; Hix and Noury 2009).

Given that the EP is a supranational legislature, in which electoral connections are notably weak, much attention has been paid to what motivates parliamentarians' voting behaviour (McElroy 2007: 177–8). Strikingly, the best predictor of MEP voting behaviour is not nationality, but an MEP's 'party group', with the centre-left Party of European Socialists, the centre-right European People's Party, and other smaller party groups demonstrating extraordinarily high measures of cohesion in empirical studies of roll-call votes (Kreppel 2001). MEPs, moreover, contest elections and cast their votes in a two-dimensional 'issue space,' including not only the familiar nationalism/supranationalism dimension, but also a more traditional, 'domestic' dimension of left–right contestation (Hix 2001; Hix et al. 2007; McElroy 2007).[5]

Legislating, bargaining, or arguing? Decision-making in the Council

There is greater debate about how the Council takes decisions. Theories of coalition formation have also been extensively applied to the Council of Ministers, at least when QMV applies.[6] A number of scholars have used increasingly elaborate formal models of Council voting to establish the relative bargaining power of various member states (Bueno de Mesquita and Stokman 1994; Hosli 1994; Felsenthal and Machover 1997). One implication of this analysis is that the relative preferences of member governments are relevant; governments with preferences close to the centre of the range of preferences on a given issue are more likely to be in a winning majority independent of their formal voting weight, while other governments may be 'preference outliers', and therefore more likely to be isolated in EU decision-making. There is also evidence that the member state holding the Council presidency has extra influence, through its capacity to shape the agenda (Tallberg 2006) and by exploiting its superior information about the positions of the other member states when the final decision is taken (Schalk et al. 2007; R. Thomson 2008) in order to shape outcomes to reflect more closely its own preferences.

It is worth noting, however, that only a minority of legislative decisions are taken by ministers in the Council, with most reached by consensus among officials (Häge 2008; and see Chapter 4). Moreover, even when QMV applies, the Council tends to seek consensus whenever possible (see Chapter 4), so that models of procedures, such as minimum-winning coalitions, appear to provide a poor guide to understanding day-to-day practice in the Council even in those policies in which voting occurs (Hayes-Renshaw and Wallace 2006; Schneider et al. 2006).

Bargaining models, which have been extensively developed and applied to international negotiations, appear to perform better at predicting decisions (Schneider et al. 2006). In bargaining, policy is agreed through a process of identifying an outcome that makes none worse off—producing 'lowest common denominator' outcomes—or through the use of issue linkage, inducements, or threats (Putnam 1988). Bargaining outcomes, whether among states, among coalition partners, or in industrial relations, are expected to reflect the relative power of the actors, which, in turn, is shaped, by their 'best alternatives to negotiated agreement' (BATNA) (Fisher and Ury 1982; Garrett and Tsebelis 1996). The best alternative can involve being content with the status quo or having the capacity to realize objectives unilaterally or through cooperation with an alternative set of actors (Moravcsik 1998; Keohane and Nye 2001). The implication is that the actor that has the best alternative to an agreement will have the greatest say in the outcome.

A particular variant of bargaining analysis is Fritz Scharpf's (1988: 239; 2006) 'joint-decision trap' in which there is no solution that all veto players prefer to the status quo. Scharpf (2006: 847) has stressed that the 'joint-decision trap' is not a general condition of EU policy-making, but applies when institutions create an 'extreme variant of a multiple-veto player system' and where transaction costs are high, notably where the Commission does not have the right of initiative. Scharpf (2006: 851) argues, however, that agenda-setting by the Commission does not imply much softening of the pessimistic implications of the joint-decision trap because the diversity of the member states' preferences may still mean there is no solution acceptable to all (or a qualified majority of) member states. The implication is that the 'logic of the joint decision trap' is 'strong' in an EU of twenty-seven member states (Scharpf 2006: 851).

Arguably, side-payments or package deals ('log rolling') are ways of overcoming the joint-decision trap (Peters 1997), although Scharpf (2006) is sceptical about the availability of such bargaining techniques within the EU's fragmented policy-making process. In international negotiations in highly institutionalized settings, of which the EU is a prime example, however, cooperation is facilitated because the participants are aware that they will be interacting repeatedly in the future and as their experience of successful cooperation accumulates (Axelrod 1984; Peters 1997). This can generate 'diffuse reciprocity', in which governments acquiesce in the short run in the expectation of favourable consideration of their concerns at some point in the future (Keohane 1986: 4). Being able to accommodate diffuse reciprocity may be one of the key reasons why bargaining models are better at predicting policy-making in the EU than procedural models, which are blind to iteration (Schneider et al. 2006: 304–5).

In contrast to rationalist bargaining, constructivists contend that deliberation, argument, and persuasion—the 'logic of arguing'—can produce a reasoned consensus that is superior to a lowest-common-denominator outcome even in international negotiations (Risse 2000; and see Chapter 2). The policy-making literature in general now recognizes that reason-giving is important at all stages of the policy process (Goodin et al. 2006: 7). A key question is whether actors are simply trying to persuade others to change their positions by appeals to principle ('rhetorical action') or if they are genuinely open to being persuaded to change their own positions ('argumentative rationality') (Risse 2000: 7). Argumentative rationality is thought to be most likely to occur under particular conditions (Risse 2000: 10–11; and see Chapter 2), which are particularly intense in the EU. The likelihood that argumentative rationality will apply also depends on the issue under consideration. It is most likely to occur—actors are most likely to be open to persuasion—under situations of uncertainty, where actors are not sure about their preferences and/or those of the other actors or are uncertain about the appropriate norm or how to resolve tensions among rules (Joerges and Neyer 1997b; Risse 2002: 601).

Rationalists also accept that persuasion, albeit of a more limited kind, can occur through exposure to new causal ideas (Goldstein and Keohane 1993; Sabatier and Jenkins-Smith 1993). New causal ideas can help to clarify the nature of problems confronted and/or introduce actors to new ways of realizing their objectives, including through presenting new policy alternatives ('policy learning').

Uncertainty is most likely to occur when issues are first identified, that is during agenda-setting and policy formulation. Once the parameters of the problem have been agreed and responses formulated, the distributional implications of the alternatives become clearer, and even advocates of constructivism concede that bargaining may replace arguing (Joerges and Neyer 1997b; Risse 2000: 20, 2002: 607). Theories of international negotiation, therefore, appear to capture decision-making in the Council better, even when QMV is permitted, than do theories developed to explain legislative behaviour.

Inter-institutional power dynamics

Although there are a few policy areas, such as foreign and security policy (Chapter 18) and aspects of justice and home affairs (Chapter 19), in which the Council is essentially the sole decision-maker, in most areas of EU policy the Commission and EP have roles in decision-making. Most of the existing literature on interaction of the EU's institutions in decision-making, which is rooted in rationalist modelling, finds that the EP's influence is much greater under the co-decision procedure than under the cooperation procedure, arguably to the extent that it is a co-legislator with the Council (Schneider et al. 2006: 303; McElroy 2007: 186). The Commission, by contrast, is widely considered to have lost influence as the EP's has increased (Thomson and Hosli 2006: 414; see Chapter 4).

The existing literature on inter-institutional politics, however, tends to treat the institutions as unitary actors, neglecting the competing preferences behind the common, institutional positions (McElroy 2007: 186). Analyses of specific decisions, however, illustrate how actors within particular institutions, notably the Council, have been able to use the positions of the other institutions to shift legislation towards their preferences (Tsebelis 1994; A. R. Young and Wallace 2000).

The formal powers of the EU's institutions and the decision rules in the Council matter because the more actors there are that can block a decision—'veto players'— the harder it is to reach an agreement (Tsebelis 1995). If there is to be an agreement it must be acceptable to all veto players, which means that it must accommodate the concerns of the actor that is least enthusiastic about change. In the EU there are a great many veto players: the Commission may choose not to advance a proposal; under co-decision either the EP or the Council can block legislation; under unanimity each member state is a veto player; and under QMV a minority of states can block decisions. The need to accommodate so many veto players in order to adopt a policy led Simon Hix (2008a: 589) to characterize the EU as 'a hyper-consensus system of government'.

In such a highly consensual policy process, securing agreement requires a potent coalition across the key decision-makers. This often requires a coalition across two levels of governance: among the EU's institutions and within the member states. Constructing such coalitions is difficult and demanding. Policy networks, which link officials and interest groups across the EU's member states and to the Commission, and epistemic communities, through persuading key actors in different institutions, can play vital roles in constructing such coalitions (Peters 1997; Zito 2001). Thus cooperation among policy actors without formal roles in the policy process can be decisive to the adoption of policy.

Implementation: national legislative and executive politics

Once a decision has been taken, further steps are usually required in order to put it into effect. The difficulty of reaching agreement in the EU makes implementation particularly important because decisions often contain messy compromises and/or vague language, which leave significant room for discretion in how the policies are put into practice (Treib 2008). In addition, many, but far from all, EU decisions—in the form of directives—must be incorporated ('transposed' in EU parlance) into national law before they are translated into practice by national bureaucracies (see Chapter 4). Thus there is a very significant component of decision-making in the implementation phase of EU policy-making.

The analysis of implementation in the EU context, as within states, is concerned primarily with the EU's internal policies, which occur within a legal hierarchy.[7] The literature on implementation includes discussions of how particular policies are carried out, most notably with regard to competition policy (see Chapter 6), cohesion and structural funds (see Chapter 10), and the novel modes of implementation adopted in employment policy (see Chapter 12), as well as with respect to the common fisheries policy (Lequesne 2005). The more systematic academic literature on implementation in the EU, however, has been narrow and partial, focusing overwhelmingly on the implementation of directives and in only a few policy areas, most notably the environment and social policy (Treib 2008).

Different internal policies, however, target the behaviour of different types of actor and in different ways. For some policies, whether national or EU—such as setting interest rates (Chapter 7), approving/blocking mergers or imposing fines for anti-competitive behaviour (Chapter 6)—taking the decision and implementing it are essentially the same thing: no steps beyond taking the EU-level decision are required. There are other EU policies—such as budgetary policy (Chapter 9), aspects of justice and home affairs (Chapter 19), and the fiscal disciplines of the Stability and Growth Pact (Chapter 7)—in which the targets of policy are governments. Most EU policies, however, seek to influence the behaviour of individuals and firms within the member states. Although some such policies are implemented via 'regulations', which apply directly within the member states, the implementation literature focuses primarily on directives.

Because directives, except under limited circumstances, must be transposed into national law in order to have effect they share some of the characteristics of international agreements. Consequently, there is a significant degree of overlap between explanations of 'implementation' in the EU and international-relations explanations of 'compliance'. In both the EU-implementation (Treib 2008) and IR-compliance (Young 2009) literatures there is increasing attention to the impact of domestic politics on whether and how international obligations are translated into policy change.

In these accounts, whether and how implementation (compliance) occurs depends on the preferences of key societal actors and the government regarding the new obligation relative to the status quo, and crucially whether any of those opposed to implementation are 'veto players' (for surveys see Treib 2008; A. R. Young 2009). Arguably, such a politicized approach to implementation is found only in some EU member states, with implementation being apolitical in some or accepted as appropriate, despite the costs, in yet others (Falkner et al. 2007). Moreover, whether implementation is politicized varies with the type of measure required—with legislation being more likely to produce contestation than administrative change (Steunenberg 2007)—and the political salience of the issue (Treib 2008; A. R. Young 2009). This broad level of agreement masks a degree of disagreement about the relative importance of rationalist or constructivist considerations (Börzel and Risse 2007; A. R. Young 2009). Moreover, these considerations address the will to implement EU rules, but there is also the issue of whether the member state has the administrative capacity to do so effectively.

Although most academic interest has focused on explaining transposition (Treib 2008), some scholars have begun to consider how national bureaucracies have changed in order to carry out EU policies and how variance among member states' administrative responses can be explained (Kassim et al. 2000; Knill 2001; Jordan 2003; Falkner et al.

2005; Toshkov 2007; Falkner and Treib 2008). A particular strand of this research examines the proliferation of (quasi-)independent agencies within the member states (Majone 2000*b*; Thatcher and Stone Sweet 2002; Kelemen 2002, 2004; Coen and Thatcher 2005) and how they are integrated into European networks (Eberlein and Grande 2005; Egeberg 2008). This literature, therefore, has been more concerned with the EU's impact on national institutions than with how national institutions actually implement and enforce EU policies (see Trondal 2007: 966–8 for a review).

The EU implementation literature, therefore, has largely neglected enforcement and implementation within the member states, how policy translates into action on the ground (Falkner et al. 2005: 17; Treib 2008: 14; an exception is Versluis 2007). In part this reflects the general neglect of implementation by political science (Goodin et al. 2006: 17; Hague and Harrop 2007: 382). A compounding cause is the difficulty of establishing systematically whether an EU law has been properly applied (see Falkner et al. 2005: 33–5 for a discussion), let alone what explains that outcome. There is, however, extensive variation among member states and across policy areas concerning which and how many branches of the bureaucracy are involved, whether central, regional, or even local government is responsible, and whether enforcement is carried out by the state or private actors (Falkner et al. 2005: 35–6).

Despite the disagreements and limited answers, three crucial implications emerge from the analysis of policy implementation in the EU. First, the impact of EU decisions, in terms of both costs and associated political and administrative challenges, varies among member states (Héritier et al. 2001: 9; Börzel and Risse 2007). Second, member states—due to differences in both legislative and executive politics, as well as local circumstances—adopt very different national policies in order to implement 'common' EU policies. Third, member states, whether intentionally or not, do not always comply with EU rules.

Judicial politics: adjudicating disputes

It is with respect to how the EU deals with non-compliance that the EU differs most sharply from member international organizations. In the EU the domestic political process of implementation is supervised by the Commission, aided and abetted by societal actors and member governments, and may be subject to adjudication before national or European courts (Tallberg 2003). Both rationalist and constructivist accounts recognize that the Commission by threatening legal action can create pressure for policy adaptation, although the outcomes may be less than intended (Börzel and Risse 2007: 492; for an analysis of how it performs this role, see Hartlapp 2007).

As much of the oversight of implementation occurs through (or with the threat of) legal action, how the EU's legal order functions is essential to understanding the implementation of many, but by no means all, EU policies. The European legal order is much more highly developed than those commonly found among states, and consequently has become the subject of debate between intergovernmentalists and neo-functionalists (see Chapter 2).

Beyond the integration-centric question of the independence of the ECJ (see Chapter 2), there are a number of aspects of judicial politics that are more common to comparative politics than international relations (Conant 2007a). One concerns which actors are most able to take advantage of the opportunities to challenge national (and European) policies under EU law. Although even relatively disenfranchised actors have made use of the European legal system, more politically powerful actors have tended to make more and better use of litigation to challenge (predominantly national) policies that they dislike (Conant 2007a).

The direct implications of court rulings tend to be quite narrow, requiring member state governments to accommodate only the specific requirements of the judgment (Conant 2007a), although governments may extend the implications to other similar circumstances. The implications of court judgments, however, may be developed and exploited by policy entrepreneurs, as the European Commission famously did in developing the concept of 'mutual recognition' on the basis of the ECJ's *Cassis de Dijon* ruling (Alter and Meunier-Aitsahalia 1994; and see Chapter 5). Even the narrow implications of the ECJ's rulings, however, can be significant, at least with respect to specific policies. On several occasions, such as on the EU's agreement with the US about providing the names of transatlantic airline passengers (see Chapter 19), the ECJ has ruled, usually at the request of the European Parliament, that an EU rule was adopted using an improper procedure and that a different decision-rule should apply. The ECJ's ruling against the Council for failing to adopt a common transport policy raised the spectre of court-imposed deregulation of road haulage, which raised the cost-of-no-agreement for those opposed to liberalization and strengthened the hands of those that wanted more far-reaching liberalization (A. R. Young 1995). ECJ rulings have also had significant implications for member states' social and employment policies (see Chapters 11 and 12). Conversely, the ECJ has had an important impact on EU regulatory politics as a result of upholding the legitimacy of national environmental and consumer regulations (Vogel 1995; Joerges and Neyer 1997b; A. R. Young and Wallace 2000; and see Chapter 5). Thus even though the EU's legal system formally only adjudicates on how the EU's treaties and rules are applied (implemented), its rulings can have significant implications for other phases of the policy cycle by pushing issues up the agenda, generating new concepts, or changing bargaining dynamics by foreclosing options, particularly that of not acting.

Policy feedback: completing and shaping the policy cycle

The process of implementing policies, therefore, generates outcomes that feed back into the policy process, 'completing' the policy cycle. There are three distinct, but not unrelated, ways through which policy implementation feeds back into the policy cycle: evaluations of effectiveness, political feedback loops, and spill-over.

The most basic feedback loop involves evaluation of a policy's effectiveness. If the implemented policy does not address the problem that it was intended to, there might well be pressure to take additional action. It is worth noting that a policy's effectiveness is not directly related to the quality of its implementation (Raustiala and Slaughter 2002): a perfectly implemented policy may be ineffective if it was insufficiently ambitious or if an inappropriate approach was chosen. Conversely, the aims of the policy may be realized in the absence of implementation as the result of other, unrelated changes.

Evaluation of policy effectiveness is arguably particularly problematic within the EU. Because the EU is a multi-level polity in which policy initiation resides primarily with the Commission and policy implementation resides primarily with the bureaucracies of the member states, there is significant 'distance' between those who put policy into practice and those responsible for initiating it, which stretches the feedback loop (Falkner et al. 2005: 33–5; Hartlapp 2007). A key aim of the Commission's initiatives to build transnational networks of regulators (discussed above under implementation) is to shrink this distance. Policy feedback within the EU, however, is also complicated by the weakness of the mechanisms, which are embedded in national polities, for linking society and government—political participation, political parties, and interest groups—which is commonly known as the EU's 'democratic deficit' (see Chapter 2). This means that the Commission does not have access to the same sources of feedback on what is wanted and what is working that democratic national governments do.

Beyond the effectiveness of a policy there are also more political feedback loops that can be either 'positive', reinforcing the policy, or 'negative', undermining it. 'Positive feedback' occurs because actors that have adjusted their expectations and behaviours to a policy or that benefit from it will mobilize to defend it (Pierson 1993: 596; 2000: 251). These actors enjoy a political advantage in that, unless the policy has a built-in expiration date, the policy represents the default position (Pierson 2000: 262). The significant number of veto players in the EU, therefore, reinforces the resilience of a policy. Such 'path-dependence' makes policies difficult to change.

Path-dependence, therefore, has several important implications for the analysis of policy-making (Pierson 2000: 263). First, it stresses the significance of the timing and sequencing of decisions. Decisions taken earlier will constrain those taken later. Second, even apparently small events, if they occur at a crucial moment ('critical junctures'), can have significant, enduring effects (Pierson 2000: 251). Third, over time policies may become sub-optimal: they may perform a function that is no longer valued or at a cost that is no longer acceptable (Pierson 2000: 264; Streeck and Thelen 2005: 28). Fourth, path-dependence may be sufficiently strong as to lead to there being non-decisions, in which previously viable alternatives are not considered (Pierson 1993: 609). Path-dependence suggests that policy change occurs as the product of 'punctuated equilibrium': long periods of policy stability disrupted by abrupt change when the mismatch between the policy and its objectives becomes unsustainable or when there is an external shock.

The 'stickiness' of policies should not, however, be overstated (Streeck and Thelen 2005; Hall and Thelen 2009).[8] As noted in the discussion of implementation, there is significant scope for policies to change during their translation into practice. Moreover, policies are continuously being contested by those that did not get their way when the policy was adopted, by new actors or by established actors whose interests the policy no longer serves (Streeck and Thelen 2005; Hall and Thelen 2009). As a consequence of these dynamics, policies may gradually atrophy, be re-directed to new purposes, or even collapse (Streeck and Thelen 2005). Thus, while there is positive feedback supporting policy stability, there is also negative feedback creating pressure for change. The result, as is arguably the case with respect to the common agricultural policy (see Chapter 8), is a *'politics* of institutional stability' (Hall and Thelen 2009: 6), in which the suitability of existing policies is continuously assessed against existing or plausible alternatives.

The third feedback process in the EU involves 'functional spill-over', which is central to the neo-functionalist account of integration (see Chapter 2). Spill-over does not involve feedback into the same policy process, but creates incentives for additional policy development. For example, a successful policy might cause a new set of problems, either unintended or unanticipated, such as the elimination of border controls within the EU creating incentives for enhanced cooperation with respect to immigration and policing (see Chapter 19). Alternatively, further policy development might be seen as enhancing the results of an existing policy, such as the development of a single currency augmenting the creation of the single European market (see Chapter 7). Crucially, actors must make the connection between these policy problems or opportunities and push them onto the policy agenda. Functional spill-over, therefore, is not automatic and requires agency.

Conclusions

This chapter has used the heuristic of the policy cycle to structure the discussion of how theories of policy-making drawn from both comparative politics and international relations can be fruitfully applied to the analysis of policy-making in the EU. The implication is that theories rooted in the different sub-disciplines explain different phases of the policy cycle better than others. The convergence in comparative-politics and international-relations approaches to explaining agenda-setting and policy formation means that there is a common set of debates, if not a single analytical approach. Comparative-politics approaches are better suited to explaining EU-level executive decision-making and the politics of the European Parliament, but insights from international relations, albeit accommodating the highly institutionalized nature of the EU, are more useful when trying to understand decision-making in the Council. The first stage of policy implementation within the EU (transposition) is illuminated better by international-relations approaches, although how the policies are actually translated into practice is the purview of comparative politics, even if the existing literature is rather underdeveloped, with the notable exception of judicial politics. Comparative politics also provides the most extensive discussion of the dynamics of policy feedback. Thus, which sub-discipline is more appropriate depends on what one is trying to explain. Crucially, moreover, there are lively debates within each sub-discipline—primarily between rationalism and constructivism—about how policies are made.

Despite the need to tailor analytical tools to subjects of enquiry, several general implications can be drawn from the preceding discussion. First, every aspect of policy-making is contestable, from whether a condition is a problem that needs to be addressed to how it might be addressed to how it will be addressed to how that decision will be carried out to whether that choice should be revisited. Second, therefore, attention to actors is essential: agency is central to policy-making. Third, ideas matter. What actors want is shaped by ideas, at the very least in the sense of ends–means understandings, and actors use ideas to pursue their objectives by trying to persuade others. Fourth, institutional settings at the very least have impli-cations for which actors are most likely to prevail and arguably shape what those actors want. Consequently, this chapter helps to explain why policy-making in the EU varies across issue areas.

Notes

1 I would like to thank Maurizio Carbone, Kelly Kollman, John Peterson, Mark Pollack, Anke Schmidt-Felzmann, Myrto Tsakatika, Steve Woolcock, and Helen Wallace for comments on earlier versions of this chapter. This chapter draws upon and contributes to research funded by the Economic and Social Research Council (RES-062-23-1369).

2 Drawing on both comparative politics and international relations approaches to explain policy-making is a strong, if largely implicit, theme of Moran et al. (2006).

3 In his 1972 article Lowi includes a fourth type of policy 'constituent', which includes set-ting up new agencies, propaganda, but this is less commonly used.

4 Sabatier and Jenkins Smith (1993: 17) use the term 'policy subsystem' to capture the same political phenomenon.

5 This inference, however, is based on the analysis of only roll-call votes, which are used only about a third of the time, and on inferring MEP's ideological preferences from specific votes, which might be strategic or contingent (McElroy 2007: 180).

6 For a fuller discussion of the literature see Hayes-Renshaw and Wallace (2006: 314–17).

7 In the context of external policies, implementation often means getting others to accept the EU's preferences (as in multilateral trade or environmental agreements) or change their behaviour in line with the EU's preferences (as with regard to human rights). The EU's ability to influence others, which Laatikainen and Smith (2006) have dubbed its 'external effectiveness,' has received relatively little scholarly attention (Jørgensen 2007), except with regard to its 'near abroad' (see Chapter 17).

8 Although these authors are formally discussing 'institutions', their definitions cover most policies save one-off decisions (Streeck and Thelen 2005: 10; Hall and Thelen 2009: 3).

FURTHER READING

Moran et al. (2006) provide an extensive overview of the analysis of public policy-making in general. With respect to agenda-setting in the EU see Peters (1994). For a sympathetic discussion of the policy network literature in the EU see Peterson (2004). Zito (2001) provides a nice case study of an epistemic community's impact on EU policy-making. For an overview of lobbying in the EU, see Coen and Richardson (2009). On voting behaviour in the European Parliament see Hix et al. (2007) and McElroy (2007), and on decision-making in the Council see Hayes-Renshaw and Wallace (2006) and Schneider et al. (2006). For a review of the literature on implementation in the EU see Treib (2008). On judicial politics in the EU see Conant (2007a). On political feedback loops in general see Hall and Thelen (2009) and Streeck and Thelen (2005).

Coen, D., and Richardson, J. (2009) (eds.), *Lobbying the European Union: Institutions, Actors, and Issues* (Oxford: Oxford University Press).

Conant, L. (2007*a*), 'Review Article: The Politics of Legal Integration', *Journal of Common Market Studies*, 45/s1: 45–66.

Hall, P. A., and Thelen, K. (2009), 'Institutional Change in Varieties of Capitalism', *Socio-Economic Review*, 7/1: 7–34.

Hayes-Renshaw, F., and Wallace, H. (2006), *The Council of Ministers*, 2nd edn. (Basingstoke: Palgrave Macmillan).

Hix, S., Noury, A., and Roland, G. (2007), *Democratic Politics in the European Parliament* (Cambridge: Cambridge University Press).

McElroy, G. (2007), 'Legislative Politics', in K. E. Jørgensen, M. A. Pollack, and B. Rosamond (eds.), *The Handbook of European Union Politics* (London: Sage), 175–94.

Moran, M., Rein, M., and Goodin, R. E. (2006) (eds.), *The Oxford Handbook of Public Policy* (Oxford: Oxford University Press).

Peters, B. G. (1994), 'Agenda-Setting in the European Community', *Journal of European Public Policy*, 1/1: 9–26.

Peterson, J. (2004), 'Policy Networks', in A. Wiener and T. Diez (eds.), *European Integration Theory*, 1st edn. (Oxford: Oxford University Press), 117–35.

Schneider, G., Steunenberg, B., and Widgrén, M. (2006), 'Evidence with Insight: What Models Contribute to EU Research', in R. Thomson, F. N. Stokman, C. H. Achen, and T. König (eds.), *The European Union Decides* (Cambridge: Cambridge University Press), 299–316.

Streeck, W., and Thelen, K. (2005), 'Introduction: Institutional Change in Advanced Political Economies', in W. Streek and K. Thelen (eds.), *Beyond Continuity: Institutional Change in Advanced Political Economies* (Oxford: Oxford University Press), 1–39.

Treib, O. (2008), 'Implementing and Complying with EU Governance Outputs', *Living Reviews in European Governance*, 3/5, available *at: http://www.livingreviews.org/lreg-2008-5* (accessed 3 March 2009).

Zito, A. R. (2001), 'Epistemic Communities, Collective Entrepreneurship and European Integration', *Journal of European Public Policy*, 8/4: 585–603.

CHAPTER 4

An Institutional Anatomy and Five Policy Modes

Helen Wallace

Summary

This chapter sets the European Union's (EU) policy process in its institutional context, in a period when enlargement since May 2004 to twenty-seven members has posed new challenges. Since the EU is part of, and not separate from, the politics and policy processes of the member states, the institutions that are relevant include national (and infranational, i.e. local and regional) institutions, as well as those created by the EU treaties. Features of the national processes pervade the EU, and differences among member states pervade EU policies and the way in which they are applied. The institutional design of the EU is explained, especially the Commission, Council, European Council, European Parliament, and the European Court of Justice. Some quasi-autonomous agencies, such as the European Central Bank and Europol, also play important roles. EU and national institutions interact differently in different policy domains. Five variants of the EU policy process are identified: the classical Community method; the EU regulatory mode; the EU distributional mode; the policy coordination mode; and intensive transgovernmentalism. The last two of these are particularly strong in some newer areas of active EU policy development.

The institutional design of the European Union

The EU has grown out of three originally separate Communities (ECSC, EEC, and Euratom), each with its own institutions. These were formally merged in 1967. The main elements originally consisted of: a collective executive of sorts—the European Commission; a collective forum for representatives of member governments—the Council (of Ministers); a mechanism for binding arbitration and legal interpretation—the European Court of Justice (ECJ); and a parliamentary chamber—the European Parliament (EP, originally 'Assembly'), with members drawn from the political classes of the member states, and later by direct election. In addition the Economic and Social Committee (ESC) provided a forum for consulting other sectors of society; later, in the 1990s the Committee of the Regions (CoR) was created to allow for consultation with local and regional authorities. The powers and responsibilities are set out in the treaties, and have been periodically revised (see Table 1.1).

In the 1990s the European Community (EC) became the European Union, a term which serves two different purposes. One is to imply a stronger binding together of the member states. The other is to embrace within a single framework the different Communities and the other arenas of cooperation that have emerged, in particular following the Treaty on European Union (TEU) the two 'pillars' of 'intergovernmental cooperation': the 'second pillar' for common foreign and security policy (CFSP; see Chapter 18); and the 'third pillar' for justice and home affairs (JHA; see Chapter 19). The Treaty of Lisbon (ToL), ratified in November 2009, will draw these pillars within a more unified institutional and procedural framework (FCO 2008). The institutional design is subject to periodic revision, latterly with increasing contention. The relative powers of and relationships among the Commission, Council, and EP have changed a good deal across the years. The key elements of the institutional arrangements follow—readers already familiar with these can move on to the section dealing with the five policy modes in the EU policy process.

The European Commission

The Commission is both secretariat and proto-executive in the EU's institutional system. In its earliest version, as the High Authority of the European Coal and Steel Community (ECSC; agreed in 1951), it leaned more towards being executive in nature, with considerable autonomy. This experiment generated the term 'supranational'. When the European Economic Community (EEC) was created in 1958, some member governments had second thoughts about the consequences of creating a strong autonomous institution, thus altering the 'balance' between the Commission and the Council, endowing the Commission with strong powers in some fields and weaker powers in others. The onus was left on the Commission itself to develop credibility, expertise, and the bases for a political power of its own.

The Commission exercises its responsibilities collectively, in that the Commissioners, from 2007 one from each of the now twenty-seven member states, constitute a 'college'. Their decisions and proposals to the Council and EP have to be agreed by the entire college, voting, if necessary but rarely, by simple majority, at its weekly meetings. The Commission is chaired by a President, chosen under the Treaty of Nice (ToN) by qualified majority vote (QMV) in the European Council and subject to approval by the EP. Five other commissioners act as vice-presidents. Commissioners, each responsible for a policy portfolio, are nominated by member governments, endorsed by the Council, and subject to approval by the EP as a body, which can lead to names being withdrawn. Those chosen are senior politicians or high officials from member states, but they swear an oath of independence on taking office for a five-year term to coincide with that of the EP. The College of Commissioners is accountable to the EP, which has the power to censure the College with a two-thirds vote. In March 1999 the College, presided over by Jacques Santer, was forced into resignation by the EP on a charge of financial mismanagement (see Chapter 9). The ToN envisaged a reduction in the size of the College, which the ToL specified will be two-thirds of the number of member states on a rotation system on the grounds that enlargement risked producing too large and too segmented a Commission. This provision, which provoked strong opposition in the Irish referendum campaigns is set to be revoked.

The Commission as an institution is organized into Directorates-General (DGs), named after their main areas of policy activity, and historically known by their numbers. Table 4.1 illustrates the structure under the Barroso Commission (2004–2009). The staffs of the DGs form the European civil service, recruited mostly in competitions across the member states, and supplemented by seconded national experts and temporary staff. Since May 2004 the emphasis has been on recruiting people from the new member states. The powers and 'personalities' of the DGs vary a good deal, as do their relationships with 'their' commissioners. New DGs have been added as new policy powers have been assigned to the EU, not always tidily. The commissioners have their own private offices, or *cabinets*, which act as their eyes, ears, and voices, inside the 'house' and vis-à-vis other institutions, including those of the member states. One DG leads on each policy topic, as *chef de file*, but most policy issues require coordination between several DGs, sometimes masterminded by the Secretariat-General and often by the *cabinets*. Though the Commission is supposed to operate collectively, in practice there are sometimes disagreements among commissioners and their DGs, such that contradictory lines of policy can be observed. Specialist services provide particular expertise, most importantly the Legal Service, and the linguistic and statistical services.[1]

The Commission's powers vary a good deal between policy domains. In competition policy (see Chapter 6) it operates many of the rules directly; in many domains it drafts the proposals for legislation, which then have to be approved by the Council and the EP; it defines, in consultation with the member governments, the ways in which spending programmes operate; it monitors national implementation of EU rules and programmes; in external economic relations it generally negotiates on behalf of the EU with third countries or in multilateral negotiations;

TABLE 4.1   The organization of the European Commission, 2008

Commissioner and area of responsibility	Old no. where relevant	No. of staff in all categories
President		
Cabinets (CA)		489
Secretariat General (SG)		596
Bureau of European Policy Advisers (BEPA)		43
Legal Service (SJ)		402
Spokesperson's Service (see DG COMM)		
Vice-President: institutional relations and communication strategy Communications DG COMM and Spokesperson's Service[a]		979
Vice-President: enterprise and industry		
DG ENTR	III, XXIII	1,002
Vice-President: justice, freedom and security		
DG JLS		547
Vice-President: administrative affairs, audit and anti-fraud		
Personnel and Administration DG ADMIN	IX	764
Informatics DG DIGIT		1,039
Infrastructure and Logistics DG Bx(OIB)		1,123
Lux(OIL)		295
Office for Administration and Payment (PMO)		572
European Personnel Selection Office (EPSO)		160
European Anti-Fraud Office (OLAF)		463
Internal Audit Service (IAS)		105
budgetary discharge (see DG BUDG)		
Vice-President: transport		
Transport [and Energy] DG TREN[b]	VII	[1,178]
Commissioner: energy		
[Transport and] Energy DG TREN[b] Euratom Supply Agency	XVII	[1,178]
Commissioner: competition		
DG COMP	IV	822
Commissioner: agriculture and rural development		
DG AGRI	VI	1,135
Commissioner: maritime affairs and fisheries		
DG MARE	XIV	288
Commissioner: information society and media		
DG INFSO		1,214

Commissioner: internal market and services	XIII	
DG MARKT	XV	537
Commissioner: taxation and customs union		
DG TAXUD	XXI	493
Commissioner: science and research		
Research DG RTD	XII	1, 970
Joint Research Centre (JRC)		2, 862
Commissioner: education, training, culture and youth		
DG EAC	X	725
Commissioner: economic and monetary affairs		
Economic and Financial Affairs DG ECFIN	II	556
Statistical Office 'Eurostat' (ESTAT)		816
Commissioner: environment		
DG ENV	XI	717
Commissioner: health		
Health [and Consumers] DG SANCO[c]		[919]
Commissioner: consumer protection		
[Health and] Consumers DG SANCO[c]		[919]
Commissioner: financial programming and budget		
DG BUDG		592
Commissioner: employment, social policy and equal opportunities		
DG EMPL	V	842
Commissioner: regional policy		
DG REGIO		718
Commissioner: external relations and ENP		
DG RELEX	I/IA	878
RELEX external delegations		1,824
Europe Aid (AIDCO)[d]		[1,080]
Commissioner: trade		
DG TRADE	I/IB	547
Commissioner: enlargement		
DG ELARG		416
Commissioner: development and humanitarian aid		
DG DEV	VIII	347
Europe Aid (AIDCO)[d]		[1,080]
Humanitarian Aid Department (ECHO)		241
Commissioner: multilingualism		
Translation DGT		2,448
Interpretation DG SCIC		803
Office of Official Publications (OPOCE)		661

TABLE 4.1 (Continued)	
Total staff	34,344
established	23,079
temporary	1,855
contractual agents	5,764
national experts	1,113
agency	461
technical and administrative assistance	2,072

Source: author compiled from Commission website pages

Notes:
[a] The Commission Spokesperson acts under the authority of the President and is in charge of the Spokesperson's service. The Spokesperson's service is attached to DG COMM.
[b] DG TREN is to be divided into two separate DGs.
[c] DG SANCO provides services for both commissioners.
[d] AIDCO provides services for both commissioners.

in some areas one of its key functions is to develop cross-EU expertise, on the basis of which national policies can be compared and coordinated; and in yet other areas the Commission is a more passive observer of cooperation among member governments. Recent enlargement has generated more work and made the process more anglophone.

Broadly, within the classical areas of Community cooperation the Commission has a jealously guarded power of initiative, which gives it the opportunity to be the agenda- setter (see Chapter 3). For this reason it is a target for everyone who wants to influence the content of policy. However, as we shall see, in many areas of policy the Commission has a less entrepreneurial role, either because it is not able to exploit the opportunities available to it, or because the nature of the policy regime allows less room for the Commission to play a central role. A key question is therefore how the Commission exploits the opportunities available to it. Its resources include: the capability to build up expertise; the potential for developing policy networks and coalitions; the scope for acquiring grateful or dependent clients; and the chance to help member governments to resolve their own policy predicaments. Versions of all of these are the subject of debate in the theoretical literature, and are addressed throughout the case studies in this volume.

In addition there is a broader problem of capacity. The Commission is a quite small institution, with only some 23,000 or so staff in 2008 (with 11,000 more on non-tenured contracts), not very many to develop or implement policies across twenty-seven different countries. Hence a great deal depends on how the Commission works with national institutions, which in practice implement most Community rules and programmes. Over the years this feature of the policy process has become more explicit, as several of our case studies illustrate (see e.g. Chapters 6, 10, and 12).

Partnership between the national and the European levels of governance has become one of the marked features of EU policy-making. One key mechanism for this is the clumsily-named system of 'comitology'. In essence this is very straight-forward. Both to prepare policy proposals and to implement agreed policies the Commission needs regular channels for consultation and cooperation with relevant national officials. A dense network of advisory, regulatory, and management committees has grown up to provide these channels, much the same as happens in individual countries. In the case of the EU these committees are the subject of procedural, legal, and political debate. Most of the committees are governed by legally specified arrangements, which vary according to the policy, and which strike different balances of influence between national representatives and the Commission. Insights into the workings of these committees appear in several of our case studies (see e.g. Chapters 6, 14).

The Commission has had several high points of political impact, especially in the early 1960s and the mid-1980s, under the presidencies of respectively Walter Hallstein and Jacques Delors. It has also had low points, after the 1965–6 Luxembourg crisis (when President de Gaulle withdrew French ministers from Council meetings), in the late 1970s, and the late 1990s. More recently the Commission has been the subject of criticism, as regards weak internal management and coordination, overstretched staff, and lacklustre leadership. The Prodi Commission (1999–2004) embarked on an administrative reform programme, led by Vice-President Neil Kinnock. The Barroso Commission (2004–9) came into office pledged to improve the performance of the Commission by emphasizing the aim of doing 'less but better'. The Commission has continually to compete for influence with other EU institutions and the member governments.

The Council of the European Union

The Council of the EU is both an institution with collective functions and the creature of the member governments. In principle and in law there is only one Council, empowered to take decisions on any topic, though its structures are more complex (see Figure 4.1). Its members are usually ministers from incumbent governments in the member states, but which ministers attend meetings depends on the subjects being discussed, and on how individual governments choose to be represented. Time and practice have sorted this out by the Council developing specialized configurations according to policy domains, each developing its own culture of cooperation.

Historically foreign ministers comprised the senior configuration of the Council, reflecting the prominence of foreign ministers as coordinators inside the member governments. However, in practice foreign ministers cannot always arbitrate and prime ministers have become much more involved at home and through the European Council. In recent years foreign policy as such has become the priority for foreign ministers, although on some cross-cutting issues foreign ministers remain leading decision-makers (see Chapters 9, 10, 16, and 17). Reforms implemented in 2003 introduced a General Affairs and External Relations Council (GAERC) with

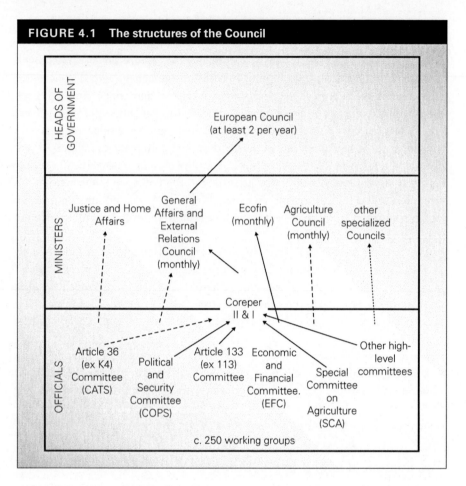

FIGURE 4.1   The structures of the Council

two streams, one to handle coordination across internal policies and the other to deal with external policies (see Chapter 18). As economic and monetary union (EMU) has taken shape, so the Council of Economic and Financial Affairs (Ecofin) has grown in importance (see Chapter 7). As other new policy areas became active, so corresponding formations of the Council emerged—JHA is a striking example (see Chapter 19), and defence policy may well be the next. The multiplication of Council configurations has bred criticism about the fragmentation of work, leading to an effort to reduce the number of distinct configurations. Box 4.1 summarizes the current configurations and their patterns of activity.

Meetings of ministers are prepared by national officials in the committees and working groups of the Council. Traditionally the most important of these has been the Committee of Permanent Representatives (Coreper), composed of the heads (Coreper II) and deputies (Coreper I) of the member states' permanent representations in Brussels. These both meet at least weekly to agree items on the Council agenda and to identify those that need to be discussed (and not merely endorsed) by ministers. In some other policy domains (trade policy, agriculture, EMU, JHA,

BOX 4.1	Council configurations

The Council is in law a single entity, irrespective of which ministers take part in it. It developed several specialized formations reflecting the growth of policy activities and with varying frequencies of meetings. This led to a highly segmented structure, with over twenty formations in the 1990s. From 2000 onwards efforts were made to streamline the Council into first sixteen, and then nine, configurations. However, some of these in practice meet in several parts. As of autumn 2009 the configurations were as follows, numbers of meetings in 2004 and 2008 in brackets:

General Affairs and External Relations (GAERC)
- general affairs, and coordination (2008: 12, 2004: 10)
- external relations (2008: 12, 2004: 9), plus one official and two informal meetings of defence ministers in 2008

Economic and Financial Affairs (Ecofin)
- economics and finance (2008:11 (one as heads of government), 2004: 9), usually back-to-back with Eurogroup meetings)
- budget (2008: 2, 2004, 2)

Agriculture and Fisheries (2008: 12, 2004: 9)

Cooperation in the fields of Justice and Home Affairs (JHA) (2008: 7, 2004: 9)

Competitiveness (internal market, industry, research) (2008: 4, 2004: 7)

Transport, Telecommunications and Energy (TTE) (2008: 7, 2004: 5)

Environment (2008: 3, 2004: 3)

Employment, Social Policy, Health and Consumer Affairs (EPSCO) (2008: 4, 2004: 4)

Education, Youth and Culture (EYC) (2008: 3, 2004: 3)

The *European Council* met five times formally in 2008 (seven times in 2004), once informally, and heads of government of Eurogroup countries met twice, also with UK.

CFSP) similar senior committees of national officials prepare many of the ministerial meetings; often they act as the main decision-makers.

The permanent representations collectively contain some 1,500 national officials, whose job is to follow the main subjects being negotiated in the Council, to maintain links with all the other EU institutions, and to keep in close touch with national capitals. Numerous (250 or so) working groups constitute the backbone of the Council and do the detailed negotiation of policy. Their members come from the permanent representations or national capitals—practice varies. Something like 70 per cent of Council texts are agreed in working groups, another 10–15 per cent in Coreper or other senior committees, leaving 10–15 per cent to the ministers themselves. These patterns mirror the normal practice in a national government, where typically national cabinet meetings are prepared by committees of officials.

National governments work in parallel to the Council (Bulmer and Lequesne 2005). National officials follow each level of Council discussion and each area of Council debate, preparing ministerial positions and coordinating national policies. National ministers are involved in much of this work; how and when depends on national practices and on the degree of political interest in each subject within individual countries. Much of this involvement is at the level of individual ministries, where the relevant officials in turn consult the other branches of central, regional, or local government, public agencies, and relevant private-sector or non-governmental organizations. Aggregating national positions is the responsibility of the coordinating units in each member government. Here again, practices vary between countries, some more centralized and some more decentralized in their approaches. A comprehensive view of how the deliberations of the Council work needs to recognize the continuous engagement of national administrations.

What does the Council do in its various configurations? Mostly it negotiates over detailed proposals for EU action, very often on the basis of a draft from the Commission. Often the Council will have indicated earlier to the Commission that it would welcome a draft on a particular subject. On most of the topics where the Commission has been the primary drafter, the EP is now co-legislator with the Council (see below). In these areas of policy the decision-making outcome depends on the interactions among these three institutions. The dynamics of the process rest on the way in which coalitions emerge within the Council and between the Council members and members of other EU institutions.

In some other areas the Commission and the EP play more marginal roles, and the Council is more in charge of its own agenda—CFSP and JHA are examples. Here more reliance is placed on the Council's own General Secretariat. This has not historically been an organ of policy-making, but rather a facilitator of collective decision-making. However, the growth of work related to CFSP and JHA has prompted the considerable expansion of the Council Secretariat over recent years. Following the Treaty of Amsterdam (ToA) the Council Secretariat was strengthened to deal with JHA (see Chapter 19) and the important initiative was taken to designate Javier Solana as the Secretary General of the Council and the High Representative of the Union to represent the EU externally and to develop firmer policies, with the aid of a bigger staff (see Chapter 18). In parallel a Deputy Secretary General was appointed to oversee the regular work of the Secretariat. As a result we now need to consider the Council Secretariat as much more of an actor in the policy process than hitherto (Beach 2005). These arrangements will be further modified after implementation of the ToL, when an EU 'foreign minister' will be appointed, combining the current High Representative role with that of the Commission's Vice-President for external affairs.

The proceedings of the Council are managed by its presidency (Tallberg 2006, 2008; Warntjen 2008). This rotates between member governments every six months. The Council presidency chairs meetings at all levels of ministers and officials, except for a small number of committees which have elected chairs, including the Eurogroup of finance ministers. Under the ToL, however, the new Foreign Minister will chair the GAERC when it deals with external affairs. The role of the presidency involves the preparation of agendas, as well as the conduct of meetings. The presidency speaks on behalf of the Council in discussions with other EU institutions and with outside partners on issues other than CFSP. Often the Council and the Commission presidencies have to work closely together, for example in external negotiations where policy powers are divided between the EU and the national levels. In the legislative field the Council and EP presidencies have to work together to reconcile Council and parliamentary views on legislative amendments. A recurrent question is how far individual governments try to impose their national preferences during the presidency or whether the experience pushes them towards identifying with collective EU interests. As EU policy cooperation has developed directly between governments, rather than at the promptings of the Commission and through formal procedures, so it has fallen to successive presidencies to act as the main coordinators. This has historically been a particular feature of CFSP and JHA. There are some doubts as to how well the rotating presidency can continue to function within an EU27, and the ToL gives more emphasis to 'team' presidencies.

The important point to bear in mind is that the Council is the EU institution that belongs to the member governments. It works the way it does, because that is the way that the member governments prefer to manage their negotiations with each other. Regularity of contact and a pattern of socialization mean that the Council, and especially its specialist formations, develop a kind of insider amity. Sometimes clubs of ministers—in agriculture, or dealing with the environment, and so forth—are able to use agreements in Brussels to force on their own governments commitments that might not otherwise have been accepted at the national level. Nonetheless the ministers and officials who meet in the Council are servants of their governments, affiliated to national political parties, and accountable to national parliaments and electorates. Thus, generally their first priority is to pursue whatever seems to be the preferred objective of national policy.

The Council spends much of its time acting as the forum for discussion on the member governments' responses to the Commission's proposals. It does so through continuous negotiation, mostly by trying to establish a consensus. The formal rules of decision-making vary according to policy domain and over time—sometimes unanimity, sometimes qualified majority voting (QMV), sometimes (albeit rarely) simple majority. The decision rules are a subject of controversy and have been altered in successive treaty reforms, in particular under the ToN and potentially the ToL to bring the voting weights more in line with the different population sizes of individual member states. Broadly speaking, QMV has become the formal rule in areas where Community regimes are fairly well established, while unanimity is a requirement either in areas in which EU regimes are embryonic or in those domains where governments have tenaciously retained more control of the process. In an average year some 30 per cent of Council decisions deal with topics subject to the unanimity rule, with 70 per cent subject to the QMV rule, and a tiny number of decisions subject to a simple majority rule (see Figure 4.2).

There is a great deal of misunderstanding about how the process works in practice. Habits of consensus-seeking are deeply ingrained, and explicit voting is relatively rare, even when technically possible—votes are explicitly contested on only around 20 per cent of eligible decisions. Under QMV the knowledge that votes may be called

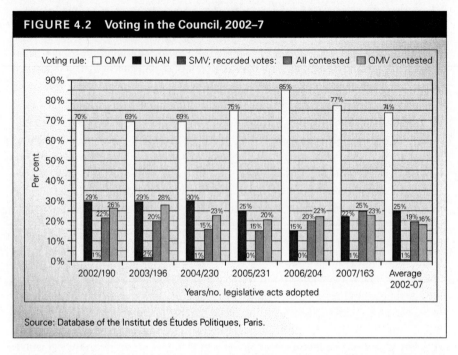

FIGURE 4.2   Voting in the Council, 2002–7

Source: Database of the Institut des Études Politiques, Paris.

often makes doubting governments focus on seeking amendments to meet their con-cerns, rather than on blocking progress altogether. Formally registered 'no's and ab-stentions seem mainly to be signals to domestic constituencies. Under unanimity rules governments are generally much more likely to delay or obstruct agreements, or to exercise blocking power until their views are accommodated, typically on major budg-etary and spending decisions (see Chapters 9 and 10). In practice explicitly contested votes at ministerial level are concentrated in a few areas of policy: around half are operational decisions on agriculture and fisheries; and the rest scattered on regulatory issues, especially the single market and public health (for further details see Hayes-Renshaw and Wallace 2006; Thomson et al. 2006; and Naurin and Wallace 2008).

The Council used to be the main legislator on EU policies. However, as the EP has acquired powers over legislation, the system has become more bicameral. Thus the Council now reaches 'common positions' which have to be reconciled frequently with amendments to legislation proposed by MEPs in a 'conciliation' procedure. This has meant that the Council is now more explicitly required to make a public justification for its collective preferences, which is an important change in the process.

In some policy domains the Council remains the decision-maker of last resort. Interestingly this includes some established areas, such as agriculture (see Chapter 8), where the EP still has little opportunity to intervene (although this would change under the ToL), and some new policy domains—notably JHA and CFSP—where the member governments, through the Council, retain the main control of policy. EMU provides a different contrast—here the main control of the single currency has been assigned to the ECB, leaving Ecofin and the Eurogroup (ministers only from member governments whose currencies are part of EMU) pushing to gain influence over decision-making (see Chapter 7).

It is hard to track the patterns of alignments or 'coalitions' in the Council. Often governments share preferences for issue-specific reasons. There is also evidence of two recurrent cleavages: one between richer, more northern, member governments and poorer, more southern and more eastern, members; and the other between the more and the less market-minded governments (the former typically including the new member governments). The evidence of a recurrent left/right cleavage is less clear in contrast to the pattern in the EP, although governments' positions do vary according to their party political affiliations.

What is the style of the Council—more bargaining or more deliberation? In some policy areas there are sharp disagreements and tough strategic bargaining, in particular when new regimes are at issue (see Chapters 7, 8, 9, 10, 15, 18, and 19). In other policy areas, as policy-making becomes more routine or where the issues are more technical, there is evidence of a more deliberative style (see Chapters 5 and 13).

Lastly, it is with regard to the Council's work that concerns about the adverse impact of enlargement to EU27 have been most vehemently expressed, with prognoses of gridlock. The evidence so far simply does not support this—the Council works pretty much in the same way after enlargement as it did before (Best et al. 2008; H. Wallace 2007), with similar strengths and weaknesses: no gridlock. However, as will be shown in some of the case studies the increased heterogeneity of preferences in an EU27 complicates the Council's work (see Chapters 9, 13, 15, 18, and 19).

The European Council

The European Council began life in the occasional 'summit' meetings of heads of state (France and Finland have presidents with some policy powers who attend meetings) or government (i.e. prime ministers). Two especially important meetings, in The Hague in 1969 and Paris in 1972, were agenda-setters and package-makers for several succeeding years. From 1974 onwards, under the prompting of Valéry Giscard d'Estaing, then French President, European Councils were put on a regular footing, meeting at least twice a year. Successive treaty reforms have put the European Council on a more formal basis, although it operates to an extent outside the main institutional structure: it would be fully incorporated under the ToL. The European Council would then acquire a full-time president, an individual chosen for a renewable term of two-and-a-half years. The preparation of its meetings and drafting of its conclusions depend essentially on the presidency-in-office of the Council, and its agendas are much influenced by the preferences of the government in the chair. Historically one meeting of each semester was held in the country of the presidency but under the terms of the ToN sessions have been held in Brussels since the 2004 enlargement. By custom and practice national delegations in the room are restricted to the president or prime minister and the foreign ministers, and sometimes finance ministers. Increasingly large cohorts of other ministers and officials have parallel meetings where the topics discussed depend on the preoccupations of the moment.

Conceived of initially as an informal 'fireside chat', the European Council became in the 1970s and 1980s a forum for resolving issues that departmental ministers could not agree, or that were subjects of disagreement within the member governments. By tradition it is the European Council that has been left to resolve the periodic major arguments about EU revenue and expenditure (see Chapters 9 and 10). In addition the European Council became, from the negotiations over the Single European Act (SEA) in 1985, the key forum for determining treaty reforms in the closing stages of Intergovernmental Conferences (IGCs).

From the late 1980s the European Council increasingly became the venue for addressing what Peterson (1995) calls the 'history-making decisions' in the EU, namely the big and more strategic questions to do with the core new tasks of the EU and those that define its 'identity' as an arena for collective action. Some of our case studies, especially Chapters 7, 9, 17, 18, and 19, record European Council pronouncements as the main staging posts in the development of policy. The level of activity has expanded, reflecting a sharply increasing concern on the part of the most senior national politicians to take control of the direction of the EU, including at the 'Spring' European Councils which chart progress with the Lisbon Strategy. Their offices have a direct electronic link (Primenet), and within their national settings they are strongly engaged in framing national European policies. Overall the European Council has come increasingly to exercise explicit political leadership in the EU process, despite its weak organizational foundations. The ToL aims to strengthen the European Council notably by the appointment of a full-time president.

The European Parliament

The EP elected in June 2004 and including from 2007 Bulgarian and Romanian members had 785 members (MEPs), elected directly on a basis of proportional representation from across the twenty-seven member states. Elections in June 2009 under the ToN produced 736 members (754 under the ToL). Originally it was composed of national parliamentarians, but in 1978 a treaty amendment provided for direct elections, of which the first were in 1979. Its location, for reasons of member-state sensitivities, is divided among Luxembourg, Strasbourg, and Brussels. MEPs vary in their backgrounds, some having been national politicians, other bringing different professional experience, and a few having made the EP their primary career. The EP is organized into party groupings, of which by far the largest and most important are the European People's Party, a centre-right grouping, and the European Socialists on the centre-left. Smaller party groups include coalitions of liberal, Green, far-right, far-left, and 'Euro-sceptical' or nationalist MEPs. These groupings have gained in importance over time, with most MEPs voting with their party groups rather than by nationality. Much of the work of the EP is carried out in its specialist committees, which have become increasingly adept at probing particular policy issues in detail, more so than in many national parliaments.

BOX 4.2	Powers of the European Parliament

Consultation

Commission proposals to Council are passed to EP for an Opinion. EP may suggest alterations, delay passing a resolution to formalize its Opinion, or refer matters back to its relevant committee(s).

Applies to: agriculture, and those (increasing in number) JHA topics that fall within the 'Community' framework.

Cooperation (Art. 252 TEC, ex Art. 189c EEC)

Commission proposals passed to Council for a 'common position' and to EP for a first reading, in which it may propose amendments. The EP may at its second reading seek to amend the Council's common position, or by an absolute majority reject it. Council can override the EP's rejection only by unanimity. Alternatively, the EP and Council try to negotiate agreement in a conciliation procedure.

Applies to: limited aspects of economic and monetary union.

Co-decision (Art. 251 TEC, ex Art. 189b EEC)

A bicameral legislative procedure in which the Council and EP adopt legislation by common agreement. Council and EP may both agree a proposal at first reading (in 2008 almost three-quarters of relevant issues). If they disagree at second reading, the EP may by an absolute majority reject the proposal, which then falls. Or the EP may amend the Council's common position by an absolute majority, in which case conciliation takes place between the Council (usually Coreper I) and the EP. The results of conciliation must be approved in third reading by both Council (QMV) and EP (majority of votes cast). Proposal falls if not agreed.

Applies since ToA to: most areas of legislation, unless otherwise specified as exempted, or falling under one of the other procedures; ToL extends its application.

Assent

On certain issues the EP must, in a single vote, give its assent by an absolute majority of its members.

Applies to: certain international agreements, enlargement treaties, and framework agreements on the structural funds.

Budget (Arts. 272–3, ex Arts. 203–4 EEC)

EP may try to modify 'compulsory' expenditure, or to amend 'non-compulsory' expenditure. It must approve the budget as a whole, and subsequently 'discharge' the accounts of previous year's actual expenditure (see Chapter 9).

Installation of Commissioners (Art. 214(2) TEC, ex Art. 158(2) EEC)

Since the ToA EP has the right to approve nomination of the Commission President. It holds individual hearings with nominated commissioners and passes a vote to approve the whole college.

Censure of Commission (Art. 201 TEC, ex Art. 144 EEC)

EP may censure the college of commissioners by a two-thirds majority of its members.
Note: the ToL would extend some of these powers.

In the early years of the EU the EP had a marginal role in the policy process, with only consultative powers, apart from its power to dismiss the Commission in a censure motion. During the 1970s the EP gained important powers *vis-à-vis* the EU budget, and especially over some areas of expenditure (although significantly not over most agricultural expenditure) (see Chapter 9). In the 1980s and 1990s the role of the EP was transformed, as it acquired legislative powers in successive treaty reforms. These were rationalized under the ToA into: co-decision with the Council across a wide range of policy domains; cooperation with the Council in some other domains, especially on EMU-related questions; and consultation in those areas where member governments have been wary of letting MEPs into the process, including agriculture and JHA. In addition the EP must give its formal assent on some issues: these include certain agreements with third countries and enlargement (see Box 4.2 on page 83). The ToL subjects more legislative domains (including some agricultural issues) to co-decision and streamlines procedures.

The net result of these changes is that the EP is a force to be reckoned with across a wide range of policy domains. It is in important respects a necessary partner for the Council, although one with a contested electoral authority, because of the rather low participation rate in European elections in many member states. On many areas of detailed rule-setting the EP has a real impact, as some of the case studies in this volume show, and therefore it too is the target of those outside the institutions who seek to influence legislation (see, for example, Chapters 8, 13, 14, and 15). However, there are other areas—JHA, CFSP, and oddly enough, so far the CAP—where its voice is muted.

In 1999 the EP acquired greater political prominence as a result of its role in provoking the resignation of the European Commission on the issue of financial mismanagement. In 2004 the EP delayed the installation of the new Commission, because of criticisms of its composition. This increased political standing of the EP is likely to enable it to influence the policy process as a whole rather more in the future. In 2009 the EP took its time to endorse the Commission President.

The European Court of Justice

Early on it became clear to close observers of the EU that the role and rule of law were going to be critical in anchoring EU policy regimes. If the legal system could ensure a high rate of compliance, a way of giving authoritative interpretation to disputed texts, and a means of redress for those for whom the law was created, then the EU process as a whole would gain a solidity and a predictability that would help it to be sustained. The ECJ was established in the first treaty texts; these have been virtually unchanged since then, except to cater for the increasing workload and successive enlargements of the EU membership.

The ECJ, sited in Luxembourg, is composed of twenty-seven judges, as well as eight advocates-general, who deliver preliminary opinions on cases. The ECJ is somewhat like a supreme court, able to provide an overarching framework of jurisprudence, and to deal with litigation, both in cases referred via the national courts and those brought directly before it. The SEA in 1986 established a second court, the Court of First Instance (CFI) (the General Court under the ToL), composed now of twenty-seven judges, to help in handling the heavy flow of cases in certain specified areas, notably competition policy. The Courts' sanctions are mostly the force of their own rulings, backed up in some instances by the ability to impose fines on those (usually companies) found to have broken EU law. The TEU gave the ECJ power to fine member governments for non-application of European law. Moreover, as a result of its own rulings (especially one of the *Factortame* cases on fisheries; Lequesne 2005), damages can be claimed against governments that fail to implement European law correctly. The Courts hear their cases in public, but reach their judgments in private by, if necessary, majority votes; the results of their votes are not made public, and minority opinions are not issued.

Since the early 1960s a series of key cases has established important principles of European law, such as: the supremacy of EC law over the law of the member states; the direct effect of EC law in national legal orders; a doctrine of proportionality, and another of non-discrimination on the basis of nationality among nationals of EU member states. In so doing the ECJ has gone further in clarifying the rule and the role of law than had specifically been laid down in the treaties and periodically its jurisprudence challenges the policies of this or that member government. In some policy domains court cases have been one of the key forces in developing EU policy regimes (see Chapters 5, 6, and 11).

Appendix 1 (at the end of this volume) summarizes the pattern and volume of cases before the two Courts. This very thorough overview, collated specially for this volume, of cases before the ECJ by policy sector gives us a very full picture of the pattern of litigation. The case load is impressive, reaching 400 cases before the ECJ in the 1980s, and rising to over 500 from 1999 onwards, with a substantial CFI caseload as well, though in both cases the volume of EU staff cases should be discounted. There appears to be an increase in the number of cases following each enlargement of the EU. Agriculture is in 'gold medal' position cumulatively, with strong numbers for free movement of persons, of establishment, and of goods, which generate many cases, as do taxation issues, although with some variations over time. Competition and state aid cases remain important. Environmental and consumer cases have also become latterly more numerous, reflecting a growth of policy activities in these fields. Further commentary on the roles of the Courts follows in our case studies.

This strong legal dimension has a marked influence on the policy process. Policymakers pay great attention to the legal meaning of the texts that they devise; policy advocates look for legal rules to achieve their objectives, because they know that these are favoured by the institutional system; policy reformers can sometimes use cases to alter the impact of EU policies; and in general there is a presumption that rules will be more or less obeyed. Hence policy-makers have to choose carefully between treaty articles in determining which legal base to use, and to consider carefully which kind of legislation to make.

The EU makes three main kinds of laws. Regulations are directly applicable within the member states once promulgated by the EU institutions. Directives have to be transposed into national law, which allows some flexibility to member governments, but within limits set by the ECJ. Decisions are more limited legal instruments applied to specific circumstances or specific addressees, as in competition policy (see Chapter 6). All three kinds of law may be made either by the Commission (under delegated powers), or by the Council, or jointly by the Council and EP (under co-decision). And all are subject to challenge through the national and European courts.

The vigour of the European legal system is one of the most distinctive features of the EU. It has helped reinforce the powers and reach of the EU process, although in recent years the ECJ has become a bit more cautious in its judgments. We should note also that in some policy domains member governments have gone to considerable lengths to keep the ECJ out of the picture. Part of the reason for the three-pillar structure of the TEU was to keep both CFSP and JHA well away from the reach of the European legal system. Even though the ToA went some way towards incorporating parts of JHA and Schengen more fully within the system, it remains contested how far they will be brought within the jurisdiction of the ECJ. The adoption of the Charter of Fundamental Rights, initially on a declaratory basis, adds an important new dimension, though its legal implications are disputed even under the ToL. This to some extent draws it together with the other European legal order, based on the European Convention on Human Rights attached to the Council of Europe.

The wider institutional setting

The EU institutional system includes a number of additional organizations that have an impact on, or provide instruments for, EU policies. Some are consultative. Some provide control mechanisms. And some provide autonomous operating arms.

Consultation and lobbying

The founding treaties established the Economic and Social Committee (and the Consultative Committee for the ECSC), as a point of access to the policy process for socio-economic groups. Its creation borrowed from the corporatist traditions in some of the founder member countries. It has not, however, become an influential body in the policy process. Instead socio-economic groups have found their own more direct points of access since the 1960s, both through EU-level federal associations and through sector-specific trade and producer organizations. These became even more active in the period around the development of the single European market. Individual large firms have also taken pains to develop links with the EU institutions, again some since the 1960s, but many more and with more vigour since the early 1980s. A more recent development has been the increased activity of groups and lobbies representing societal interests, consumers, environmentalists, women's groups, and increasingly a range of other advocacy groups and non-governmental organizations (NGOs). Illustrations of the activities of these different kinds of groups can be found in many of our case studies.

The TEU introduced a second consultative body, the Committee of the Regions (CoR), in response to the extensive involvement of local and regional authorities in seeking to influence those EU policies that impacted on them. The CoR provides regional and local politicians from the member states with a multilateral forum, and an opportunity to enhance their local political credibility. At least as important, however, is the direct lobbying by infranational (local and regional) authorities, many with their own offices in Brussels. These same infranational authorities also engage in efforts to influence national policy positions and the implementation of Community programmes. Chapter 10 comments on this in relation to the structural funds.

Control and scrutiny

In the mid-1970s concern started to be voiced that the EU policy process was subject to few external controls. The EP at the time had few powers, and national parliaments paid relatively little attention to EU legislation and programmes. It was the growing scale and scope of the EU budget and spending programmes that spearheaded the arguments about the inadequacy of scrutiny. This led to the creation of the European Court of Auditors by the 1975 Budget Treaty. Since 1978 it has, from its seat in Luxembourg, endeavoured to evaluate systematically both revenue-raising and spending (see Chapter 9). Both in its Annual Reports and in specific reports it has drawn attention to various weaknesses in the budgetary process, as handled by the Commission and national agencies. Around four-fifths of EU budgetary expenditure is disbursed by national agencies. Many of its criticisms fell for many years on deaf ears—member governments that were reluctant to face up to some of the issues, an EP that had other preoccupations, and a Commission which repeatedly undervalued the importance of sound financial management. In late 1998 this situation was reversed by the row over alleged financial mismanagement by the Commission.

Another new instrument of post hoc control is provided by the European Ombudsman, attached to the EP, under the provisions of the TEU. The aim, borrowed from Nordic practice, is to provide a channel for dealing with cases of maladministration *vis-à-vis* individuals. This office has been responsible for modest improvements in the operations of the policy process at the micro level.

Some control and scrutiny of policy depends on national institutions, both parliamentary and financial. National parliaments had no official recognition in the institutional system until the early 1990s. Each member state had developed its own, mostly rather limited, procedures for national parliamentary scrutiny of EU policy. The same discontent that had led to some strengthening of European procedures started to provoke a debate on national scrutiny. Both the TEU and the ToA mention the importance of encouraging this, and the ToL provides a mechanism for national parliaments to hold up a 'yellow card' to proposals judged to be overly intrusive.

EU-level policy-makers, especially in the Commission, are under increasing pressure to pay increased attention to national parliamentary discussions and appear more readily before national parliamentary committees of inquiry. This heightened sensitivity to country-level preoccupations is becoming a more marked feature of the EU policy process. Indeed as of October 2009 national parliaments from all member states except Malta and Spain had established offices in Brussels to track EU policy. Some see more cooperation between the EP and national parliaments as a promising way forward. Others argue that to date experience, for example through COSAC (Conférence des organes spécialisées aux affaires européennes), which twice a year brings together representatives from the EC scrutiny committees of national parliaments, has been disappointing.

Other agencies and banks

The longest established autonomous agency is the European Investment Bank (EIB), established by the Treaty of Rome (EEC). Its task was, and is, to generate loans for agreed investments in support of EU objectives, both within the EU and in associated third countries. It operates like a private bank, with triple-A credit rating in money markets. Its work is to varying degrees coordinated with programmes directly administered by the Commission, such as the structural funds. It had its potential 'big moment' in the early 1990s after the breakdown of the communist system in central and eastern Europe. However, a decision was taken to establish a new and separate European Bank for Reconstruction and Development (EBRD), with the reforming post-communist countries and other western states as stakeholders.

One other phenomenon should be noted. Over the past decade or so there has been a trend in the EU to contract out some policy implementation activities to agencies, mirroring practice that was becoming more common in many of the member states. One group of executive agencies has been set up to administer programmes for which the Commission lacked either the staff or the inclination, for example the Humanitarian Aid Office (ECHO) and the office which administers the Socrates programme for educational interchange. Another group of agencies handles regulatory functions, such as the European Food Safety Authority (EFSA) (see Chapters 8 and 13), or operating functions, such as Europol (see Chapter 19). A third group provides direct services for the EU institutions, such as the translation centre. There has been some discussion on whether this process could be taken even further, for example by setting up a European Competition Office clearly separate from the Commission or through networks of national regulators (see Chapters 6 and 15).

The most important example of a new and autonomous operating agency is the European Central Bank (ECB) in Frankfurt (see Chapter 7). The battle in 1998 over who should be its first president was an indication of the anticipated importance of an agency that was to exercise considerable independence in a crucial policy domain with high political salience. The ECB has made an impressive start in developing its own functional and operational identity. Quite what the extent of the ECB's autonomy will be in the longer term remains to be seen; several finance ministers have already made it clear that they want their own hands on the tiller.

Thus, we note the proliferation of agencies for operating EU policy regimes and programmes. This diffuseness of arrangements for policy operation and programme delivery has increased in recent years. It seems set to be a persistent feature of the policy process, especially as regards policy implementation, and thus likely to fragment the institutional structures. This should lead us to modify the notion of the Commission as a centralized and centralizing policy executive.

National institutions

The institutions in the member states are also fundamental elements in the EU institutional architecture and partners in the EU policy process (Bulmer and Lequesne 2005). The European dimension is not just an add-on to the work of national governments; in a real and tangible sense national governments, and other authorities and agencies, provide much of the operating life-blood of the EU. After all, in some senses what the EU system does is to extend the policy resources available to the member states. The case studies in this volume illustrate a variety of ways in which this is so. Learning how to manage this extra dimension to national public policy has been one of the most important challenges faced by national governments in the past fifty years.

Much of that challenge has had to be faced by the central governments in each member state, and the patterns of response have varied a good deal from one to another. As a broad generalization we note that the experience has been somewhat different from what many commentators had expected. The trend has been not so much a defensive adjustment to the loss of policy-making powers, but rather in most member states an increasingly nuanced approach to incorporating and encapsulating the European dimension. This has not, however, meant that central governments can operate as gatekeepers between the national and the EU levels. The points of cross-border access and opportunities for building cross-national networks and coalitions have steadily proliferated for both public agencies and private actors. National actors play important and influential roles at all stages of the EU policy process.

Opportunities for access and influence are, however, not evenly distributed within member states. Economic agents and non-governmental organizations (NGOs) seem the most flexible in operating at both EU and national levels. Infranational authorities have become more adept, though how much influence they exert is still open to question. National parliaments have been much slower to adapt, and indeed are among the national institutions most displaced by the emergence of a strong European dimension to policy-making.

One Community method or several policy modes?

Central to our approach to policy-making in the EU is the view that it includes several different policy modes, which are illustrated by the empirical case studies in this volume. These policy modes—we identify five—are the product of: evolution and experimentation over time in the EU; changes in national policy-making processes; and developments in economic and social behaviour. We can observe important rearrangements in the roles and behaviour of the various key actors, in the approaches to policy dilemmas, and in the instruments used to address these. There is a persistent debate about where to strike the balance between delegating policy powers to the EU and retaining those of the member states, increasingly in the shadow of the globalization phenomenon and challenges to the 'western' economic model. There is contestation, both as regards the 'high politics' of the EU and as regards the 'functional appropriateness' of one or other policy mode. Also of critical importance is the issue of how the EU has adapted from its original small membership of only six relatively similar countries to a large membership of twenty-seven rather more heterogeneous countries with diverse legacies, practices, and socio-economic characteristics.

EU policy-making never takes place in a vacuum, but, on the contrary, in a context of multiple locations for addressing policy issues, ranging across levels from the local to the global and with both formal and informal processes. Figures 4.3 and 4.4 illustrate two pictures of policy-making across multiple locations. European policy-makers have to manage the connections between these different locations, and sometimes make choices ('forum-shopping') as to which they prefer for addressing a particular issue.

We set out five variants of the modes through which the EU policy process handles 'day-to-day' policy-making:

- the classical Community method;
- the EU regulatory mode;
- the EU distributional mode;
- policy coordination; and
- intensive transgovernmentalism.

These modes do not include the domain of constitutive politics or system-shaping as regards the overall political and institutional architecture of the EU. They are identified here as a typology of ideal types with the deliberate objective of escaping from the either/or dichotomy between 'supranational' and 'intergovernmental' ways of proceeding. Our central argument is that the patterns of policy-making in the EU are diverse not only because of the continuing arguments about which policy powers to transfer from national to European processes, but also because of functional differences between policy domains and changing views about how to

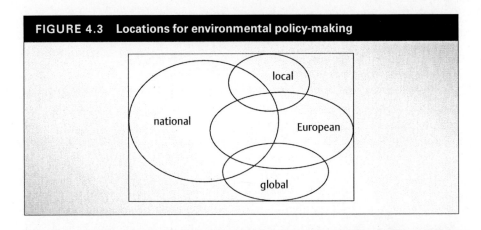

FIGURE 4.3   Locations for environmental policy-making

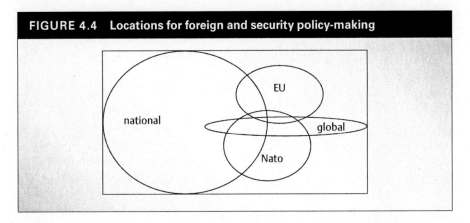

FIGURE 4.4   Locations for foreign and security policy-making

develop contemporary government and governance. Table 4.2 summarizes the key characteristics that delineate them. Most individual policy areas do not fall neatly within a single policy mode and there is strong variation over time, both within policy sectors and in response to events and contexts. As we shall see across the case studies in this volume the variations persist and hybridization across these ideal types is prolific. We return to this in Chapter 20.

The classical Community method

Much of the literature on west European integration and the EU took as its starting point that a single predominant Community method of policy-making was emerging. As an early priority on the agenda of the original EEC, the common agricultural policy (CAP) set the template, defined by the late 1960s roughly as follows:

- a strong role delegated to the European Commission in policy design, policy-brokering, policy execution, and managing the interface with 'abroad';
- an empowering role for the Council of Ministers through strategic bargaining and package deals;

TABLE 4.2 EU policy modes in brief

	Community method	Regulatory mode	Distributional mode	Policy coordination	Intensive transgovernmentalism
Degree of centralization	High	Varies	High, but narrow	Low to moderate	Low
Role of European Council	Rare (overcoming log jams)	Rare (overcoming log jams)	Sets parameters in major bargains	Limited	Sets direction
Role(s) of Commission	Extensive delegation—agenda-setting, implementation, and external representation	Agenda-setting and policing	Agenda-setting and implementation	Developer of networks	Marginal
Role of Council of Ministers (decision rule)	Decision-making (QMV)	Co-legislator (QMV)	Decision-making (mainly unanimity)	Deliberation	Predominant (agenda-setting and decision-making)
Role of EP	Limited consultative impact	Co-legislator	Limited impact	Limited dialogue	Excluded
Impact of ECJ	Occasional, but significant	Significant	Marginal	Excluded for 'soft' law provisions	Excluded
Member governments	Subordinated implementation of common policy	Implementation and enforcement (regulatory networks)	Paymasters and beneficiaries	Laboratories and learners	Key players

Engagement of other actors	Lock-in of stakeholders (policy community)	Policy networks and some self-regulation	Sub-national governments and some other agencies	Epistemic communities	Excluded
Resources	Common	No budgetary costs	Focus on inter-regional transfers, sectoral support, and limited 'public goods'	No budgetary costs	Increasing importance of funding for 'public goods'
Period of pre-eminence	Late 1960s–1970s	Late 1980s	Early 1970s	Late 1960s Late 1990s use of OMC	Early 1970s
Prime examples	Particularly traditional CAP; traditional trade policy	Competition, single market, environment, increasingly CAP, new aspects of trade policy, aspects of social and employment policies	Budget, cohesion	Employment, fiscal policy, aspects of JHA, economic reform	CFSP, JHA

- a locking-in of stakeholders, in this case the agricultural interests, by their co-option into a European process which offered them better rewards than national politics;

- an engagement of national agencies as the subordinated operating arms of the agreed common regime;

- a distancing from the influence of elected representatives at the national level, and only limited opportunities for the EP to impinge;

- an occasional, but defining, intrusion by the ECJ to reinforce the legal authority of the Community regime; and

- the resourcing of the policy on a collective basis, as an expression of sustained 'solidarity'.

The template was labelled as a form of 'supranational' policy-making, in which powers were transferred from the national to the EU level. It was structured by a functionalist logic, in which those concerned with a particular policy sector could be encapsulated and build cross-national allegiances, but mediated by a form of politics in which political and economic élites colluded to further their various, and often different, interests. Within the operation of the Council, Scharpf (1988) identified a 'joint-decision trap', which set high obstacles to the revision of common policy once agreed because of the power of veto-players.

How far this template ever accorded with reality, even in the case of agriculture, is a matter for debate. Chapter 8 suggests that the real story of the CAP may be different, and one in which national politics determined rather more of the outcomes. Interestingly, the fisheries regime, which was intended to imitate the CAP regime and which included strong delegation of powers to manage quotas, does not fit the template very well either (Lequesne 2005). Aspects of EU trade policy have some features of this approach, given the considerable delegation to the Commission for managing trade instruments and trade agreements (see Chapter 16). It had been expected in the early years that this mode would apply in other policy sectors with a strong functionalist character. This version of the Community method came to set many reference points for both practitioners and commentators.

There are strikingly sparse examples of further common policies being introduced according to this classical Community method, with a centralized and hierarchical institutional process, with clear delegation of powers, and aimed at 'positive integration'. The single currency is perhaps the closest-fitting example. However, in this case, as we see in Chapter 7, the delegated institutional powers are centred on the ECB rather than on the Commission, and they apply only to the monetary strand of EMU and not to its economic strand. Delegation to function-specific agencies in other fields is much weaker. Overall, then, the classical Community method has been little replicated.

The EU regulatory mode

As the competition regime took root (see Chapter 6) and the single European market developed (see Chapter 5), so an alternative policy mode emerged. Its roots lay in the ambition of the Treaty of Rome to remove barriers between the national economies of the member states. Much of its driving force came from changes in the international economy, which began to induce new forms of regulation in some west European countries. It turned out that the EU arena was especially amenable to the further development of a regulatory mode of policy-making (Majone 1996). The strength of the European legal process, the machinery for promoting technical cooperation, and the distance from parliamentary interference were all factors that encouraged this further, namely by removing national barriers to the creation of the single market (see Chapter 5). The negotiation process, in and through the European Commission and Council of Ministers, and anchored by the EU legal system, helped national policy-makers to escape some of the constraints of politics that had built rigidities into national policy-making. The EU was particularly well fitted for generating an overarching regulatory framework that could combine transnational standards with country differences. Indeed, so successful was its implantation that this European approach has sometimes been promoted as a model for the development of broader global regulation. Examples can be found in Chapters 13, 14, and 16.

This regulatory mode provides the framework for numerous micro-level decisions and rules. It has shaped relationships with member governments and economic actors within the EU, and for those involved in relevant international regimes. It has been characterized by:

- the Commission as the architect and defender of regulatory objectives and rules, increasingly by reference to economic criteria, and usually working with stakeholders and communities of experts, and often mobilizing the EU legal system;
- the Council as a forum (at both ministerial and official levels) for agreeing minimum standards and the direction of harmonization (mostly upwards towards higher standards), to be complemented by mutual recognition of national preferences and controls, operated differentially in individual countries;
- the ECJ and the CFI as the means of ensuring that the rules are applied reasonably evenly, backed by the national courts for local application, and enabling individual entrepreneurs to have access to redress in case of non-application or discrimination;
- the EP as one way to prompt the consideration of non-economic factors (environmental, regional, social, and so forth), with increasing impact as its legislative powers have grown, but little leverage on the implementation of regulation;

- the important role of regulatory agencies, both European and national; and
- extensive opportunities for stakeholders, especially economic actors, but sometimes other societal actors, to be consulted about, and to influence, the shape and content of European market rules.

EU regulation mode has been described by some commentators as a form of 'negative integration' (Scharpf 1999), although case studies in this volume reveal regulation being used prolifically to promote 'positive integration'. This regulatory mode has shaped the development of the single market (Chapters 5 and 15), and the application of competition rules (Chapter 6). EU industrial policy has been developed in recent years mostly by using regulatory prompts and the competition regime to leverage industrial adjustment. Insofar as the EU has a social policy (Chapter 11), it is mainly constructed through legal regulation and market-making. Employment policy (see Chapter 12) also uses some regulatory instruments. Much of what the EU has done in the environmental domain (Chapter 13) has been by regulating industrial processes. Chapter 14 illustrates the case of biotechnology and food safety. Interestingly, Chapter 8 indicates the increasing impact of the regulatory mode on the operation of the CAP as reforms are introduced. The EU's interactions with the rest of the world, including with neighbours and membership candidates, mirror its internal approach to regulation and industrial adjustment, as is made evident in Chapter 16 on trade policy, and Chapter 17 in relation to central and eastern Europe.

During the 1990s, regulation displaced the CAP as the predominant policy paradigm for many EU policy practitioners. It had the advantage of being focused on a modernization trajectory, through which the rigidities of the 'old' west European political economy would be replaced by more flexible, mainly legal, instruments of market encouragement, and through which different, and less corporatist, relationships could be forged with socio-economic actors. The literature emphasizes the role of interest groups, lobbying, and corporate actors (firms rather than trade associations) (Coen and Richardson 2009), and the networks, coalitions, and alliances that they form.

Two decades of experience in developing the single market reveal changes in and limits to this regulatory mode. Thus it appears to have been particularly successful in dealing with product regulation, and less robust in dealing with process standards, where difference either in levels of economic development or in societal preferences intervene, sometimes with sub-national as well as country variations (see Chapters 13, 14, and 17). The mode has also had rather less purchase on the regulation of services, financial markets, and utilities, where instead we see moves towards more decentralized, less hierarchical versions of regulation (see Chapter 15). Here we see across the member states, and indeed in the global economy, the emergence of more-or-less independent regulatory agencies at arm's length from governments, as well as emerging forms of self-regulation (Coen and Thatcher 2008a). Within the EU there are experiments with:

new quasi-independent regulatory agencies, such as the European Food Safety Authority (see Chapter 14); steered partnerships of national agencies working with the Commission, notably in the case of competition policy (see Chapter 6); transnational consortia of national regulatory bodies, for example in the energy sector (see Chapter 15); and looser networks of self-regulation, notably as regards the operation of financial markets or corporate governance. It is thus becoming much harder to identify the contours of a single coherent EU regulatory mode. Pending issues include how this regulatory mode will respond, first, to the arrival of member states with less advanced economies, and, second, to the stresses of widespread economic recession.

The EU distributional mode

Persistently over the years the EU policy process has been caught up in distributional issues, that is, the allocation of resources to different groups, sectors, regions, and countries, sometimes explicitly and intentionally, and sometimes as a by-product of policies designed for other purposes. The framers of the original treaties included some elements of distribution in the policy repertoire to be exploited. The CAP was funded from a collective base and for a long time accounted for the lion's share of the EU budget. Farmers became both the clients of European funding and the beneficiaries of high prices, gaining transfers of resources from both taxpayers and consumers. It is to the early years of the EEC that the language of 'financial solidarity' owes its origins. 'Cohesion' was added to the policy vocabulary from the mid-1980s, as the European arena was used to protect social groups or regions that were being marginalized in the domestic economy and rendered uncompetitive by global markets, albeit at a cost to other social groups. Fierce arguments over the distribution of budgetary burdens and benefits of participation in the EU meant that distributional policy-making was often highly politicized (se Chapters 8, 9, and 10). Enlargement was always a complication.

This distributional mode of policy-making is characterized by:

- the Commission attempting to devise programmes, in partnership with local and regional authorities or sectoral stakeholders and agencies, and to use financial incentives to gain attention and clients;
- member governments in the Council and often the European Council, under pressure from local and regional authorities or other stakeholders, bargaining fiercely over a budget with some redistributive elements;
- some additional pressure from MEPs based on territorial politics in the regions;
- local and regional authorities benefiting from some policy empowerment as a result of engaging in the European arena, many of them with their own offices in Brussels, with, from 1993 onwards, the Committee of the Regions modestly also articulating their concerns;

- some scope for other stakeholders to be co-opted into the EU policy process; and

- recasting of the EU budget to devote more money to cohesion or to embryonic collective goods, and proportionately less to agriculture.

It was the opening for direct contacts between the European and the infranational levels of government, and the politics that developed around them, that provoked the term 'multi-level governance' to characterize the EU process more generally (Marks 1993) (see Chapter 2). This shifted attention away from the Brussels-centred and entrepreneur-oriented images of, respectively, the Community method and the regulatory mode. The question that follows is where the balance of the evidence lies. Chapter 10 argues that central governments from the member states have remained in the driving seat of the bargains about EU spending and that infranational activity should not be confused with impact. Chapter 8 also indicates that discussions about reshaping the EU budget to cater for an enlarged membership are disturbing the inherited distributional mode. The impact on public budgets of the Maastricht criteria to govern EMU adds a further constraint (see Chapter 7), accentuated by the banking crisis.

The idea of an EU distributional mode focused on deliberate redistribution is under attack for another reason: a shift towards the idea of funding collective goods, both internal and for external responsibilities. Collective goods are being developed through spending to promote innovation, research and development, and through measures to support JHA policies and CFSP actions. EU spending on 'competitiveness', including research and development, accounted in 2008 for some 8 per cent of the EU budget, to back up the Lisbon Strategy for economic reform, adopted by the European Council in March 2000 (Sapir et al. 2004). Meanwhile, preoccupations with internal security and the impacts of migration have generated calls for spending on collective border-control measures and so forth (see Chapter 19). There is also an increase in EU spending as a result of its foreign policy activities, which (depending on how one counts) is now running at 8–10 per cent of the EU budget, in this case with a limited role for the EP (see Chapter 18).

All in all therefore the distributional mode of policy-making is in flux. Agricultural spending is under tighter reins. Internal spending priorities are altering. External demands are increasing. The patterns of policy-making on spending are increasingly differentiated (see Chapter 20).

Policy coordination

An old contrast in the study of European collaboration has been drawn between the EU policy modes outlined above and what in shorthand might be described as the 'OECD technique'. The Organization for Economic Cooperation and Development, the Paris-based club of western industrialized countries, has since the early 1960s provided a forum within which its members could appraise and compare each other's ways of developing public policies.

In its early years the Commission used this technique to develop light forms of cooperation and coordination in fields adjacent to core EU economic competences in order to make the case for clearly assigned policy powers. Thus, for example, in the 1970s the Commission promoted increasingly systematic consultations among member governments on environmental issues, and eventually made a persuasive case for the SEA to give the EU formal legislative powers. Similar efforts were made to develop coordination of macro- and microeconomic policies, as well as in domains such as research and development or aspects of education policy. Policy coordination was intended as a mechanism of transition from nationally rooted policy-making to an EU collective regime. For the advocates of a strong EU, policy coordination might be a useful starting point, but it used to be seen as very much a second-best resting point.

The typical features of policy coordination are:

- the Commission as the developer of networks of experts or epistemic communities, or of stakeholders and/or civil society, and accumulating technical arguments in favour of developing a shared approach to promote modernization and innovation;
- the involvement of 'independent' experts as promoters of ideas and techniques;
- the convening of high-level groups of national experts and sometimes ministers in the Council and occasionally the European Council, in brainstorming or deliberative rather than negotiating mode;
- the development of techniques of peer pressure, 'benchmarking', and systematic policy comparisons in order to encourage policy learning;
- dialogue (sometimes) with specialist committees in the EP, as the advocates of particular approaches; and
- outputs in the form of 'soft law' and declaratory commitments rather than 'hard law' and binding commitments, oriented at gradual changes in behaviour within the member states.

Latterly we can see this coordination approach being developed not as a transitional mechanism, but as a policy mode in its own right. Some argue normatively (Scott and Trubek 2002) that there is a case for understanding this development as the emergence of a new form of postmodern governance. Three factors have served to emphasize policy coordination as a technique. One was the move to a form of EMU with a single monetary policy but only a 'coordinated' macroeconomic policy, with an effort being made to move on from the looser form of pre-EMU policy coordination to forms of more intense and more structured policy coordination through the Broad Economic Policy Guidelines and so forth (see Chapter 7).

A second impulse came from the Lisbon Strategy adopted in March 2000, which specifically identified and elevated the 'open method of coordination' (OMC) as a distinctive policy technique, using 'soft' policy incentives to shape behaviour, rather than 'hard', often legally binding, methods to require compliance. This was to be used specifically in those fields of socio-economic (mainly microeconomic) policy-making where the EU lacked—and was unlikely to gain—strong delegated policy powers. OMC, it was argued, could be a way of engaging member governments, relevant stakeholders, and civil society in iterative comparison, benchmarking, and continuous coordination as ends in themselves (Sapir et al. 2004; Kok 2004).

A third factor was the increasing recognition of cross-country variations in policy and economic performance, which made it harder to argue for uniform policy templates that would be applicable across the whole of the EU, especially an EU that would become even more diverse after enlargement.

The employment policy domain (see Chapter 12) illustrates particularly well the debates and features that have propelled OMC as a technique. Here the main thrust of EU involvement is to compare national, local, and sectoral experiences of labour market adaptation. The object is not so much to establish a single common framework, but rather to share experience and to encourage the spread of best practice. In the now extensive literature and commentary on OMC we find hugely varying assessments of its effectiveness. These range between considerable scepticism as to the value of so 'soft' a form of joint policy-making, as argued in Chapter 12, and great enthusiasm for its success—and further potential—as a mechanism for extending EU influences into parts of the domestic policy processes of the member states where there remain deep obstacles to formal transfers of policy competences to the EU. Judging between these competing assessments is especially hard against the backcloth of a sluggish European economy where causality and outputs are particularly hard to pin down, and where some of the changes being sought are to social behaviour in the hope of improving economic performance. Here too enlargement impinges, since the heterogeneity that it adds to the range of comparisons and indicators of socio-economic reforms makes the notion of common EU-wide policy templates particularly implausible—and perhaps inappropriate. A complication of these policy coordination techniques is that they diffuse and disperse political responsibilities among the relevant policy actors, making it harder to pin down where political 'ownership' rests or how to exercise political accountability.

Intensive transgovernmentalism

Throughout the history of the EU some examples of policy cooperation have depended mainly on interaction between the relevant national policy-makers, with relatively little involvement by the EU institutions. This has been especially so on issues that touch sensitive issues of state sovereignty, and which lie beyond the core competences of the Union for market-making and market-regulating. Generally such cooperation has been described as 'intergovernmentalism'—by both practitioners and commentators. Generally it has been regarded as a weaker and much less fruitful form of policy development. In the early 1960s General de Gaulle was instrumental in promoting the controversial Fouchet Plans, which aimed to shift delicate areas of cooperation well away from the then EEC into a firmly intergovernmental framework. This was vigorously resisted by some of the more integration-minded governments. Nonetheless, in the early 1970s policy cooperation did develop on money and foreign policy, largely outside the EU institutional framework. In both domains, heads of state or government were important actors, and often their preferences were developed in groupings smaller than the whole EU membership. Franco-German bilateral cooperation was at some moments an important catalyst of policy advancement. In the 1980s, and more intensively in the 1990s, some EU countries chose to develop policy cooperation outside the EU framework so as to establish a common external border with liberalized internal borders through the Schengen Agreements, deliberately excluding some EU partners from the initial regime.

The term 'intergovernmental' does not, however, really capture the character of this policy mode in the EU. It resonates too much of cooperation between governments in many other international organizations, in which the intensity of cooperation is quite limited. We therefore prefer the term 'transgovernmental', to connote the greater intensity and denser structuring of some of our examples, where EU member governments have been prepared cumulatively to commit themselves to rather extensive engagement and disciplines, but have judged the full EU institutional framework to be inappropriate or unacceptable, or not yet ripe for adoption.

Intensive transgovernmentalism is characterized by:

- the active involvement of the European Council in setting the overall direction of policy;
- the predominance of the Council of Ministers (or an equivalent forum of national ministers), in consolidating cooperation;
- the limited or marginal role of the Commission;
- the exclusion of the EP and the ECJ from the circle of involvement;
- the engagement of a distinct circle of key national policy-makers;
- the adoption of special arrangements for managing cooperation, in particular the Council Secretariat;
- the opaqueness of the process, to national parliaments and citizens; but
- the capacity on occasion to deliver substantive joint policy.

It might be tempting to dismiss such intensive transgovernmentalism as simply a weak form of cooperation. However, two factors challenge such a conclusion. First, this is the preferred policy mode in some other strong European regimes. Nato is one obvious example; the European Space Agency is another, and very different, case. In both instances quite extensive and sustained policy collaboration has been achieved, albeit with evident limitations. Secondly, within the EU this mode has sometimes been a vehicle for developing more extensive and cumulative cooperation, gradually and with elements of a treaty foundation, even if with arrangements aside from most of the main EU institutions.

In the case of EMU (see Chapter 7 and earlier editions of this volume), since the early 1960s the European Council, national finance ministers and officials, and central bankers produced such sustained intensity of cooperation that the idea of managing a single currency became feasible and eventually acceptable. The development of EMU then bifurcated between, on the one hand, strong delegation to a collective regime for monetary policy, with the ECB as the collective agent (Community method), and, on the other hand, processes of policy coordination. Thus, a period of intensive transgovernmentalism can lead to another policy mode. In the sphere of foreign policy (Chapter 18), foreign policy cooperation developed through coordination within the EU, while defence cooperation continued within Nato and the Western European Union (WEU). Since 1998 these frameworks have gradually been drawn together, albeit still influenced by the Nato mode of policy cooperation. This process of intensive transgovernmentalism has proved more resilient, less voluntarist, and more cumulative than appears at first sight.

In JHA (Chapter 19), two transgovernmental processes have converged. On the one hand, informal policy consultations, both bilateral and multilateral, have bred habits of increasingly intensive transgovernmental cooperation since the early 1970s. On the other hand, a wittingly separate treaty framework was constructed with ad hoc institutions under the Schengen Agreements, and later incorporated within the EU under the ToA. Thus these different processes of cooperation are being drawn together, with the transfer since January 2005 of some JHA issues to a form of Community method, as well as persistent features of transgovernmentalism.

These three domains have been among the most dynamic areas of EU policy development since the late 1990s. In each case the EU framework has become in a broad sense more accepted, but the detailed institutional arrangements are untypical. In all three the European Council plays a key role and the Commission has mainly a light role, apart from the communitarized parts of JHA. Similarly the EP and the ECJ remain largely out of the loop. These three cases suggest that an important systemic change may be under way within the EU policy process. New areas of sensitive public policy are being assigned by EU member governments to forms of collective or pooled regimes, but using institutional—formats over which they retain considerable control. These regimes have been built through 'soft' institutions, though the arrangements for EMU have gone the furthest in hardening the institutional arrangements. These soft institutions seem capable sometimes of developing 'hard' policy, or on occasion of being transmuted into hard institutions.

As we can see, therefore, the EU operates through a variety of different methods, with different patterns of institutional practice, and changing over time. These have evolved organically, and continue to evolve in response to both internal and external factors, both procedural and functional. These five policy modes provide a typology—a set of ideal types—for exploring the shifting patterns of EU policymaking. The case studies should be read in the light of these evolutionary and experimental features of EU policy-making, providing examples of policy successes and of policy failures, of innovation, and of atrophy.

Note

1 In 2007 DG Translation of the Commission produced an output of 1,541,518 pages, of which almost 72 per cent had been drafted in English (up from 60 per cent in 2003), 14 per cent from French (around 28 per cent in 2003), almost 3 per cent from German, and almost 11 per cent from the other twenty languages (Commission 2007*e*).

 FURTHER READING

There is a huge literature on the institutions of the EU and their development. Peterson and Bomberg (1999) provide a dynamic analysis, as well as detailed illustrations of policy cases, while Peterson and Shackleton (2005) provide an overview. Scharpf (1999) offers an excellent and critical overview, linking national and European processes. Hix (2005) stresses the politics of the process. Nugent (2006) gives a thorough catalogue of the EU institutions, while Dinan (2004) sets them into their historical context. Among the many studies of the Commission, Spence (2005), and Page (1997) provide valuable explanation and insights. On the Council and European Council see Hayes-Renshaw and Wallace (2005*b*), Naurin and Wallace (2008) and Westlake and Galloway (2005). Jacobs, et al. (2007) provide a comprehensive account of the European Parliament, to which Hix et al. (2007) provide a nuanced complement. The ECJ and the European legal system are covered by Dehousse (1998), and Mattli and Slaughter (1998). On the national dimension see Cowles et al. (2001), and Bulmer and Lequesne (2005). These academic texts should be supplemented by primary sources, including the extensive material available on the website of the EU institutions, for which the point of access is *http://europa.eu*.

Bulmer, S., and Lequesne, C. (2005) (eds.), *Member States and the European Union* (Oxford: Oxford University Press).

Cowles, M. G., Caporaso, J. A., and Risse, T. (2001) (eds.), *Transforming Europe: Europeanization and Domestic Change* (Ithaca, NY: Cornell University Press).

Dehousse, R. (1998), *The European Court of Justice* (Basingstoke: Palgrave Macmillan).

Dinan, D. (2004), *Europe Recast: A History of European Union* (Basingstoke: Palgrave Macmillan).

Hayes-Renshaw, F., and Wallace, H. (2006), *The Council of Ministers*, 2nd edn. (Basingstoke: Palgrave Macmillan).

Hix, S. (2005), *The Political System of the European Union*, 2nd edn. (Basingstoke: Palgrave Macmillan).

Hix, S., Noury, A., and Roland, G. (2007), *Democratic Politics in the European Parliament* (Cambridge: Cambridge University Press).

Jacobs, F., Corbett, R., and Shackleton, M. (2007), *The European Parliament*, 7th edn. (London: John Harper).

Mattli, W., and Slaughter, A.-M. (1998), 'Revisiting the European Court of Justice', *International Organization*, 52/1: 177–210.

Naurin, D., and Wallace, H. (2008) (eds.), *Unveiling the Council of the European Union: Games Governments Play in Brussels* (Basingstoke: Palgrave Macmillan).

Nugent, N. (2006), *The Government and Politics of the European Union*, 6th edn. (Basingstoke: Palgrave Macmillan).

Page, E. C. (1997), *People who Run Europe* (Oxford: Clarendon Press).

Peterson, J., and Bomberg, E. (1999), *Decision-Making in the European Union* (Basingstoke: Palgrave Macmillan).

Peterson, J., and Shackleton (2005) (eds.), *The Institutions of the European Union*, 2nd edn. (Oxford: Oxford University Press).

Scharpf, F. W. (1999), *Governing in Europe: Effective and Democratic?* (Oxford: Oxford University Press).

Spence, D. (2005) (ed.), *The European Commission*, 3rd edn. (London: John Harper).

Westlake, M., and Galloway, D. (2005) (eds.), *The Council of the European Union*, 3rd edn. (London: John Harper).

PART II

Policies

CHAPTER 5

The Single Market

Deregulation, Reregulation, and Integration

Alasdair R. Young

▌ Summary

The single European market programme marked a turning point in European integration. Its roots, however, stretch back well before 1985. Detailed harmonization had proved a frustrating approach to market integration, especially as external competition challenged European industry. New ideas about market regulation permeated the EU policy process and, supported by ECJ judgments and Commission entrepreneurship, facilitated legislative activism and important changes in the policy-implementing processes. Although the task of 'completing' the single market remains unfinished, it has moved to the heart of European integration and altered the pattern of state–market relations in Europe.

Introduction

The plans to complete the single market induced an explosion of academic interest in the European Union (EU). Before 1985 the theoretical debate on political integration had stalled, studies of EU policy-making were sparse, and few mainstream economists devoted themselves to the analysis of European economic integration. In the late 1980s all that changed, as competing political analyses proliferated and the economic consequences of the single market programme, which aimed to realize the free movement of goods, services, capital, and labour among the EU's member states by 1992, were examined. Indeed, many new theoretical approaches to the study of European integration have taken the single market as their main point of reference, just as many earlier theorists had taken agricultural policy as their stimulus. For many the single European market (SEM) programme constitutes the critical turning point between stagnation and dynamism, between the 'old' politics of European integration and the 'new' politics of European regulation.

This chapter re-examines the renewal of the single European market as a major turning point in European policy-making. In essence, it presents the argument that many of the analyses that proliferated in response to the Single European Act (SEA) and the SEM overstated their novelty and understated some of the surrounding factors that helped to induce their 'success'. Thus, accounts in the late 1980s emphasized the newness of the SEM programme, but in retrospect we can observe a significant degree of continuity with what had come before. Nonetheless, the incorporation of the SEM programme represents a very significant redefinition of the means and ends of policy. It enabled the European integration process to adapt to new constellations of ideas and interests and produced a different policy mode that has permeated many other policy areas (Majone 1994).

The SEM is also important for its impact on the European public policy model *within* the member states. Thus, market regulation at the supranational level of European governance jostles, often uneasily, with other issues on the political and economic agendas of the EU member states. There are also tensions between supranational regulation for transnational markets, engaging transnational regulators and large market operators, and encapsulated national politics, engaging those responsible for, and dependent on, the reduced domestic political space, smaller-scale entrepreneurs, local regulators, and national or regional politicians.

These repercussions have not been confined to the member states that accepted the SEA and the SEM. The formal and informal extraterritorial impact on neighbours, partners, and competitors has been powerful. The SEM has been extended formally to neighbouring countries through the European Economic Area (EEA) and various forms of association with candidate and non-candidate countries and to many eventually by full accession (see Chapter 17). More informally, the SEM has changed the conditions under which goods- and service-providers from third countries may enter the world's largest market. The economic, social, and political costs of adjustment within the single market have also generated rearguard action, sometimes focused on other EU policies that might provide compensation to internal operations or displacement costs to external competitors.

Establishing the single market

The objective of establishing a single market started with the Treaty of Rome (see Box 5.1). It set targets for creating a customs union and the progressive approximation of legislation, as well as for establishing a 'common market', complete with free movement for goods, services, capital, and labour (the 'four freedoms'), all within a single regime of competition rules (see Chapter 6). The path was more clearly defined for the customs union than for the common market (Balassa 1975; Pelkmans 1984), reflecting the greater preoccupation of policy-makers in the 1950s with tariffs and quotas than with technical barriers to trade (TBTs) and trade in services.

In the 1960s and 1970s, however, new technologies, new products, new concerns with consumer welfare and environmental protection, and pressure from domestic firms to curb competition all contributed to the adoption of new national rules and regulations, which, whether intentionally or not, impeded trade. Thus, as tariffs among the member states were removed through the creation of the customs union, other barriers were revealed, and even reinforced. Local market preferences, as well as national policy and industrial cultures, became increasingly divisive.

BOX 5.1	The treaty base of the single market (Treaty of Rome)
Art. 28 TEC (ex Art. 30 EEC)	Prohibition on quantitative restrictions on imports and all measures having equivalent effect
Art. 39 TEC (ex Art. 48 EEC)	Free movement of workers
Art. 43 TEC (ex Art. 52 EEC)	Right of establishment
Art. 49 TEC (ex Art. 59 EEC)	Freedom to provide services
Art. 56 TEC (ex Art. 67 EEC)	Free movement of capital
Art. 94 TEC (ex Art. 100 EEC)	Procedure for the approximation of laws that directly affect the common market

Harmonization and its increasing frustration

In the early 1960s the Commission began to tackle the negative impact of divergent national rules on trade. These efforts gathered pace after the complete elimination of customs duties between member states on 1 July 1968 (Dashwood 1977: 278–89). Initially the Commission tended to regard uniform or 'total' harmonization—the adoption of detailed, identical rules for all the member states—as a means of driving forward the general process of integration. After the first enlargement, however, the Commission adopted a more pragmatic approach and pursued harmonization only where it could be specifically justified. That is, it only insisted on uniform rules when an overriding interest demanded it, using 'optional' rather than 'total' harmonization.

The principal instrument of the original European Economic Community (EEC) for advancing the four freedoms was the directive, in principle setting the essential framework of policy at the European level and leaving the 'scope and method' of its implementation to the member states. In the case of TBTs harmonization was based on Article 94 (ex Art. 100 EEC). Other articles provided the legal foundation for the freedom of movement for services, capital, and labour and for aligning many other national regulations (see Box 5.1).

Harmonization measures were drafted by the Commission in cooperation with sector-specific working groups, composed of experts nominated by member governments. The Commission also regularly invited comments on their drafts from European-level pressure groups (Dashwood 1977: 291–2). Beginning in 1973 with the 'Low-Voltage Directive' the Commission, where possible, incorporated the work of private standard-making bodies—primarily the Committee for European Norms (Standards) (CEN) and the Committee for European Electrical Norms (Standards) (CENELEC)—into Community measures by 'reference to standards' (Schreiber 1991: 99).

Different national approaches to regulation and the pressures on governments from domestic groups with an interest in preserving the status quo made delays and obstruction frequent (Dashwood 1977: 296). The need for unanimity in the Council of Ministers gave those most opposed to change a veto over harmonization. The Commission exacerbated this problem by over-emphasizing the details and paying too little attention to the genuine attachment of people to familiar ways of doing business and buying goods (Dashwood 1977: 297). As a result, only 270 directives were adopted between 1969 and 1985 (Schreiber 1991: 98).

The slow pace of European harmonization could not keep pace with the proliferation of national rules as the member states increasingly adopted measures to protect their industries and to respond to new concerns about consumer and environmental protection in the late 1970s and early 1980s (Dashwood 1983; Commission 1985b). As a consequence, some of the earlier progress in harmonization was undone, contributing to a decline of intra-EU imports relative to total imports (Buigues and Sheehy 1994: 18), and sharply increasing the number of ECJ cases concerning the free movement of goods.

The ECJ's jurisprudence, however, began to bite at the heels of national policy-makers. In 1974 the *Dassonville* ruling established a legal basis for challenging the validity of national legislation that introduced new TBTs. The famous *Cassis de Dijon* judgment in 1979 insisted that under certain specified conditions member states should accept in their own markets products approved for sale by other member states (Dashwood 1983: 186; Alter and Meunier-Aitsahalia 1994: 540–1). There was cumulative frustration in the Commission and in the business community at the slow pace of progress and the uncertainties of reliance on the ECJ, whose rulings apply only to the cases lodged. The high level of economic interdependence within the EU made these TBTs costly and visible (Pelkmans 1984; Cecchini et al. 1988).

In the early 1980s the governments of western Europe were facing an economic crisis. The poor competitiveness of European firms relative to those of their main trading partners in the US and, particularly, Japan contributed to large trade deficits (Pelkmans and Winters 1988: 6). Transnational companies proliferated and often squeezed the profit margins and markets of firms confined to national markets. The sharp increase in oil prices following the revolution in Iran in 1979 helped to push western European economies into recession. Inflation and unemployment both soared during the early 1980s. Business confidence was low and investment, both foreign and European, began to turn away from the Community (Pelkmans and Winters 1988: 6).

The emerging reform agenda

While the crisis was clear, the response was not (see e.g. Tugendhat 1985). Large trade deficits and high inflation constrained the ability of member governments to use expansionary economic policies to bring down unemployment. Economic interdependence further reduced the efficacy of national responses to the crisis and provided an incentive for a coordinated response to the region's economic problems.

The prospects for a collective response were enhanced by changes within the member states. These are widely described in the political-integration literature as a convergence of national policy preferences during the early 1980s (Sandholtz and Zysman 1989: 111; Moravcsik 1991: 21, 1998; Cameron 1992: 56). This conver-gence, it is claimed, reflected widespread acceptance of neo-liberal economic ideas, which stress that markets are better than governments at generating economic growth. Neo-liberal ideas thus advocate that governments should interfere less in economies by privatizing state-owned industries and removing regulations, particu-larly those governing economic competition.

Although new government policies certainly did emerge in the early 1980s, closer examination reveals that these differed substantially between countries in terms of their origins, motivations, and intensities. Political parties advocating neo-liberal economic policies came to power in the UK, Belgium, The Netherlands, and Den-mark, in part due to a rejection of the parties that had overseen the economic decline of the late 1970s (Hall 1986: 100). The rejection was less marked in Germany, where the underlying strength of its economy preserved an attachment to the established 'social market' framework. In France the 'policy learning' was explicit. Expansionary fiscal policies had led to increased inflation and unemployment, exacerbated the trade deficit, and swelled the public debt (Hall 1986: 199). By 1983 the French government had started to look for European solutions, reversing the threat it had made in autumn 1982 to obstruct the common market (Pearce and Sutton 1985: 68). The Spanish government sought to link socialist modernization at home with transnational market disciplines abroad. Convergence is thus something of a misnomer—European market liberalization served quite different purposes for different governments and different economic actors.

New ideas about markets and competition thus started to be floated in response to the problems of the European economy. The appeal of these ideas was influenced by the wave of deregulation in the US in the late 1970s and early 1980s (Hancher and Moran 1989: 133; Sandholtz and Zysman 1989: 112; Majone 1991: 81). Furthermore, the ECJ's 1979 *Cassis de Dijon* judgment provided the Commission with a lever with which to pursue greater market integration (Dashwood 1983).

From the early 1980s European Council communiqués repeatedly expressed concern about the poor state of the single market (Armstrong and Bulmer 1998: 17) and in December 1982 it created an Internal Market Council. Throughout 1983 support for revitalizing the single market continued to grow. In April the heads of some of Europe's leading multinational corporations formed the European Round Table of Industrialists (ERT) to advocate the completion of the single market (Cowles 1994). The Union of Industrial and Employers' Confederations of Europe (UNICE) added its voice to calls for greater market integration.

The single European market programme

Meanwhile the Commission began to look for ways to attack barriers to market access, both by systematically identifying them and by exploring ways of relaxing the constraints on policy change. It suggested the 'new approach' to regulatory harmonization, which advanced 'mutual recognition' of equivalent national rules and restricted much of harmonization to agreeing only 'essential requirements'. It thus built on the jurisprudence of the ECJ, notably the definition in *Cassis de Dijon* of essential safety requirements (Schreiber 1991). It also built on British support for deregulation and French and German efforts to coordinate the activities of their national standards bodies (H. Wallace 1984). Towards the end of 1983 the Commission privately persuaded the British, French, and German governments to accept this new approach, which was formally adopted by the Council in May 1985 (*Bulletin of the European Communities*, 5/1985).

The 'new approach' limits legislative harmonization to minimum essential requirements and explicitly leaves scope for variations in national legislation (subject to mutual recognition). Under the 'new approach' responsibility for developing detailed technical standards is delegated to CEN and CENELEC. It is paralleled in financial services by 'home country control', which sets minimum standards for national regulation of financial service providers, but then allows them to operate throughout the single market regulated by the government of the country in which they have their headquarters (home country). A similar approach was adopted with respect to mutual recognition of professional qualifications once common minimum standards were agreed.

In 1985, after consultations with the member governments, the new president of the Commission, Jacques Delors, decided that a drive to 'complete the single market' was perhaps the only strategic policy objective that would enjoy any sort of consensus. In his inaugural speech to the European Parliament (EP), Delors committed himself to completing the single market by the end of 1992. The Milan European Council in June 1985 endorsed the White Paper (Commission 1985*a*) drawn up by Lord Cockfield, the Commissioner for the single market, containing 300 (later reduced to 282) measures (see Table 5.1).

During this same period, but outside the Community framework, the French and German governments in 1984 agreed the Moselle Treaty in order to mitigate the impact of border controls. In 1985 it was converted, at the insistence of the Benelux governments, into the first Schengen Agreement (see Chapter 19).

The Single European Act

The development of the SEM programme coincided with the most significant reform of the European Community's institutions since the Treaties of Rome. In June 1984 the meeting of the European Council in Fontainebleau cleared the way for institutional reform by resolving the question of Britain's budget rebate and the outstanding issues of the Iberian enlargement. At this meeting the Commission tabled the 'new approach' and the British government tabled a memorandum that called *inter alia* for the creation of a 'genuine common market' in goods and services (Thatcher 1984). The meeting established the Ad Hoc Committee on Institutional Reform (Dooge Committee) to consider reforms to the Community's decision-making procedures, with the Iberian enlargement in mind. Earlier that year in its Draft Treaty on European Union, the EP had sought to focus attention on institutional reform, calling *inter alia* for increased parliamentary powers and greater use of qualified majority voting (QMV) in the Council of Ministers (European Parliament 1984).

By December 1985 a remarkably quick and focused Intergovernmental Conference (IGC) had agreed the terms of institutional reform that became the SEA. In addition to its important focus on accommodating enlargement, the SEA specifically endorsed the '1992 programme' to complete the single market and altered the main decision rule for single-market measures (with the exceptions of taxation, free movement of persons, and the rights and interests of employed persons) from unanimity to qualified majority voting. It also enhanced the powers of the EP by introducing the cooperation procedure for single-market measures. Thus, a strategic policy development and institutional reform were linked symbiotically and symbolically.

TABLE 5.1   The White Paper on the single market: a taxonomy

Markets / Measures	Products	Services	Persons & labour	Capital
Market access	• Abolition of intra-EC frontier controls • Approximation of: – technical regulations – VAT rates and excises • Unspecified implications for trade policy	• Mutual recognition & 'home country control', removal of licensing restrictions (in banking and insurance) • Dismantling of quotas and freedom of cabotage (road haulage) • Access to inter-regional air travel markets • Multiple designation in bilaterals (air transport)	• Abolition of intra-EC frontier checks on persons • Relaxation of residence requirements for EC persons • Right of establishment for various highly educated workers	• Abolition of exchange controls • Admission of securities listed in one member state to another • Measures to facilitate industrial cooperation and migration of firms
Competitive conditions	• Promise of special paper on state aid to industry • Liberalization of public procurement • Merger control	• Introduction of competition policy in air transport • Approximation of fiscal and/or regulatory aspects in various services markets	• European 'vocational training card'	• Proposals on takeovers and holdings • Fiscal approximation of: – double taxation – security taxes – parent-subsidiary links
Market functioning	• Specific proposals on R&D in telecoms and IT • Proposals on standards, trade marks, corporate law, etc	• Approximation of: – market & firm regulation in banking – consumer protection in insurance – EC system of permits for road haulage – EC standard for payment cards	• Approximation of: – income tax provisions for migrants – various training provisions – mutual recognition of diplomas	• European economic interest grouping • European company statute (2001) • Harmonization of industrial and commercial property laws • Common bankruptcy provisions
Sectoral policy	• CAP proposals: – abolition of frontiers – approximation and mutual recognition in veterinary and phytosanitary policies • Steel: – call to reduce subsidies	• Common crisis regime in road transport • Common air transport policy on access, capacity, and prices • Common rules on mass risks insurance	• Largely silent on labour-market provisions	• Call to strengthen EMS

Source: Pelkmans and Winters (1988: 12)

This linkage was crucial. First, it locked together institutional change and substantive policy goals. Secondly, the agreement to proceed with the single market was embedded in a broader set of agreements. This was connected with the accommodation of new members and budgetary redistribution, but a number of flanking policies—such as the environment and technology policy—were also included to assuage the concerns of some member governments about the liberalizing dynamic of the SEM programme (Armstrong and Bulmer 1998: 14).

Squaring the theoretical circle

Theoretical accounts of the SEM and SEA fall into two main approaches: one that emphasizes the role of supranational actors (neo-functionalism), the other that stresses the importance of the member governments (liberal intergovernmentalism). Comparisons of the two approaches are complicated by the fact that some observers focus on the SEM, whilst others concentrate on the SEA.

Those analysts that concentrate on the SEM programme tend to stress the role of supranational actors. Cowles (1994) and van Apeldoorn (2001, 2002) emphasize the importance of transnational business interests in shaping the EU agenda in favour of the completion of the single market. Sandholtz and Zysman (1989) also give pride of place to supranational actors, although they cast the Commission in the leading role, with big business lending support. Garrett and Weingast (1993) contend that it was the ECJ's idea of mutual recognition that provided a focal point for agreement among member governments that favoured liberalization. Alter and Meunier-Aitsahalia (1994) recognize the importance of the idea of mutual recognition, but stress the Commission's entrepreneurial exploitation of this idea as a formula for liberalization.

There was not one unambiguous understanding of the single market programme, however (van Apeldoorn 2001, 2002; Jabko 2006). In addition to the neo-liberal vision of boosting economic efficiency by freeing trade among the member states and thus increasing competition, there was also a more competitiveness-oriented vision, in which the creation of the single market, not least through enabling European firms to take advantage of greater economies of scale, would make European firms more competitive internationally. Jabko (2006) contends that the Commission strategically exploited the ambiguity about the meaning of the market in order to advance European integration. By contrast, van Apeldoorn (2001, 2002) argues that the clash between competition and competitiveness factions within the ERT was won by the competitiveness faction, which wanted the removal of internal barriers to trade to be accompanied by higher barriers to imports from outside the EU and by a European industrial policy, but this agenda was thwarted by opposition from neo-liberal member states (see also Parsons 2008). Despite differences of emphasis, accounts of the SEM programme tend to emphasize the role of supranational actors and are thus at least compatible with neo-functionalism.

Analysts who focus on the SEA, by contrast, stress bargaining among the member governments (intergovernmentalism), although their preferences were influenced by domestic economic pressures (Cameron 1992; Moravcsik 1991, 1998). Moravcsik (1991, 1998), in particular, argues that the SEA was the product of interstate bargaining, principally between the British, French, and German governments, and that traditional tools of international statecraft, such as threats of exclusion and side payments, explain the final composition of the '1992 programme' and the SEA. Garrett (1992) argues that the member-state governments were willing to accept limits on their policy autonomy because they were engaged in an extended cooperative project and wanted to be able to ensure that their partners would comply with agreements. Parsons (2008), however, argues that proponents of the SEM, most notably the British government, accepted institutional reform only as the price demanded by those states less enthusiastic about liberalization, but more committed to integration, not because they considered institutional reform necessary for realizing the project. Thus, while there is broad agreement that the contours of the institutional bargain were defined by bargaining among self-interested governments, precisely why they accepted the outcome they did is contested.

As the neo-functionalist and intergovernmentalist approaches seek to explain distinct, albeit related, events, both may be broadly accurate. The Commission, transnational business interests, some member governments, and to an extent the ECJ, played the lead role in shaping the SEM programme, while bargaining among the member governments primarily determined the outcome of the SEA (Armstrong and Bulmer 1998: 19). This account is consistent with different types of actors having different impacts on different types of policy (Cowles 1994; Peterson 1995). When it comes to 'history-making' decisions, such as the SEA, the member governments are the crucial actors. When dealing with policy-framing decisions, of which the SEM is a particularly weighty example, the supranational institutions, and their allies, tend to be important.

Subsequent institutional reform

The SEA in effect set the institutional framework for the single market programme, and its broad parameters remain largely unchanged. The most significant subsequent change has been the introduction of the co-decision procedure in the Maastricht Treaty on European Union (TEU). The Treaty of Amsterdam established clearer guidelines about when member governments might adopt national rules stricter than agreed common rules. The Treaty of Lisbon makes only modest changes to the single market programme by increasing the EP's role in legislation to liberalize specific services (Amendment 58) and by establishing a formal mechanism for establishing European intellectual property rights (a new Article 97a). More strikingly, the institutional reforms—qualified majority voting, the cooperation and co-decision procedures—first introduced with respect to single-market measures have been subsequently extended to other areas of policy-making; the Treaty of Lisbon even renamed the co-decision procedure the 'ordinary legislative procedure'.

The politics of policy-making in the SEM

The SEM and SEA fundamentally changed the politics of market integration within the European Community. First, the SEM revived 'negative integration', that is, the removal of national rules that impede economic exchange. This is most obvious in the mutual recognition principle, the abolition of frontier controls, and the elimination of exchange controls. Secondly, the SEA changed the institutional framework for 'positive integration'—agreeing common rules to replace national ones—by extending and activating QMV and enhancing the powers of the EP. In addition, with respect to the 'new approach' and 'home country control', the SEM blurred the distinction between positive and negative integration by setting only minimum common requirements. These different modes of integration have profound political implications as they both affect who the key actors in the policy process are and shape their relative influence (see Table 5.2).

TABLE 5.2	The significance of different modes of market integration		
Type of integration	**Mode**	**Description**	**Estimated share of intra-EU trade accounted for by affected products**
Negative	mutual recognition principle	different national standards assumed to be equivalent in effect	50%
Positive	'new approach'	common objectives with reference to voluntary standards	20%
	approximation	common detailed rules	30%
	common authorization	common approval of individual products required	pharmaceuticals, GM crops and food[a]

Source: adapted from Holmes and Young (2000), and Commission (2002c)
[a] No percentage available for 'pharmaceuticals, GM crops and food'.

Negative integration

Negative integration is the elimination of national rules that impede economic exchange. It can occur as the result of political agreement among the member governments on the basis of a proposal from the Commission, as was the case with eliminating border procedures and abolishing exchange controls and the Commission's 2004 proposal for the Services Directive (see Box 5.2). In such instances, negative integration, for all intents and purposes, looks much like positive integration (see below). More commonly, however, negative integration occurs as the result of a national measure being found incompatible with the treaties as the result of a judicial process. In such instances firms are usually the initiators, and the courts (ultimately the ECJ) are the decision-makers.

The principle of mutual recognition is at the heart of negative integration. It is deceptively simple. The basic idea is that all member-government regulations, whatever their differences in detail, should be considered to be equivalent in effect. Consequently, products produced legally in one member state should be considered equally safe, environmentally friendly, etc. as those produced legally in any other member state. If one member government prohibits the sale of a product produced legally in another member state, the producing firm can challenge that prohibition under European law. If successful, the importing member government must accept the product, and negative integration has occurred.

Under EU law, however, member governments have the right, albeit within limits, to enforce strict national rules despite the principle of mutual recognition. Crucially, the principle applies only when the assumption holds that the national rules are equivalent in effect. This is not always the case, and Article 30 TEC (ex Art. 36 EEC) permits restrictions on trade for a number of public policy reasons, including public morality and the protection of human, animal, and plant health and safety. It is, therefore, possible that a government's more stringent regulation will be upheld by the courts if there is a legal challenge.

As a consequence, there are incentives for its trading partners to negotiate a common rule in order to eliminate the disruptive impact on trade of different rules (Vogel 1995; A. R. Young and Wallace 2000). This is one of the reasons why mutual recognition applies primarily to relatively simple products. It also means that strict-standard governments, particularly those with valuable markets, can play an important role in setting the agenda for positive integration.

Positive integration

Because different countries, for a wide variety of reasons, adopt different regulations and because those regulations serve public policy goals and usually impede trade only as a side effect, it is frequently not possible simply to eliminate national rules ('negative integration'). In such cases, in order to square the twin objectives of delivering public policy objectives and liberalizing trade it is necessary to replace different national rules with common European ones ('positive integration'). Given the relative importance of 'positive integration' in the EU's market integration project (see Table 5.2), it is more appropriate to describe the SEM as *re*regulatory, than *de*regulatory.

The policy cycle and institutional actors

Formally the Commission is the agenda-setter for positive integration, as only it can propose new measures. The reality is somewhat more complicated. Member governments can request that the Commission develop proposals and, as noted above, can indirectly shape the agenda by pursuing policies that disrupt the free flow of goods or services within the single market. In addition, member governments, as part of compromises on legislation, often build in 'policy ratchets' requiring that an issue be reconsidered by some specified time in the future. Lastly, the Maastricht Treaty gave the EP the right to request that the Commission propose legislation.

As discussed earlier, the SEA introduced two important changes to the legislative process on single market measures: QMV and the enhanced role of the EP. According to data gathered by Hayes-Renshaw et al. (2006), none of the nineteen definitive legal acts concerning the single market that were adopted during 1998–2004 was adopted unanimously.[1] It is difficult, however, to assess how significant QMV has been to the single market programme as measures are put to a vote only when they are sure to pass. Votes against measures might, therefore, be more to appease domestic constituencies or to signal potential implementation problems than to express strong opposition.[2]

By increasing the power of the European Parliament, the SEA and subsequent treaties have made the adoption of single-market measures more complicated (Parsons 2008). Through the cooperation procedure, the SEA gave the EP the power to reject or amend proposals, but these could be ignored or overturned under most circumstances. The introduction of the co-decision procedure in 1993 under the TEU, particularly strengthening its ability to reject proposals, made the EP more of a co-legislator with the Council, and caused many more of its amendments to be accepted by the Commission and Council (Hix 1999: 96). The EP's increased influence, formally in decision-making and informally in proposal shaping, has affected policy outcomes by enhancing the representation of civic interests, such as consumer and environmental groups (Peterson and Bomberg 1999; A. R. Young and Wallace 2000).

As the vast majority of the SEM legislative programme is in the form of directives, the member states have a central role in implementation. The transposition of directives into national law is a necessary, but not very visible, process, since in most cases it occurs through subordinate legislation that is not much debated. Criticisms of 'Brussels bureaucracy' often relate to rules that had been transposed into national law without debate and with little attention from national parliamentarians, but then 'Brussels' is always an easy scapegoat for unpopular changes.

Although the Commission formally has a role in enforcing the single market, its staff is too small and its policy remit too broad for it to engage actively in policing all nooks and crannies of the single market. Instead, the job of ensuring compliance is decentralized and relies heavily on firms and non-governmental organizations identifying issues and either bringing them to the Commission's attention or addressing them directly through the courts.

The policy players

The SEM is about regulation, and, in keeping with Theodore Lowi's (1964) characterization of regulatory politics, interest-group competition characterizes the politics of single-market measures. 'Brussels' had for a long while attracted pressure groups and lobbyists from the 'cognoscenti' among the would-be influencers of Community legislation, but the SEM contributed to both a dramatic expansion of such activity and some changes in its form.

In part, the increase in the number of 'Eurogroups' was a simple reaction to the range and quantity of sectors and products affected by the SEM programme and the speed with which they were being addressed. Organizations (pressure groups, firms, local and regional governments, and NGOs) that had previously relied on occasional trips to Brussels started to establish their own offices there or to hire lobbyists on retainer. This shift to Brussels was in part a response to the looming shadow of QMV, which meant that firms and interest groups could no longer count on 'their' member government being able to defend their interests. Building alliances with like-minded groups from other countries, other member governments, and within the Commission became crucial, and that meant having a presence in Brussels. The Commission, with limited staff and pressed for expertise, readily opened its doors to these actors.

Another change following the SEA and the launch of the SEM was the increase in the number of civic interest groups, although they found it much harder to exercise effective political muscle. The consumer and the purchaser had been the intended beneficiaries of the SEM programme and the 'minimum essential requirements' of harmonizing and liberalizing directives were often to help them or their assumed interests. However, it is easier to discern consumers as objects of policy than as partners in the process, although they are often sporadic participants (A. R. Young 1997; A. R. Young and Wallace 2000).

In addition to changes in the volume and types of interest groups active in Brussels, the SEM also contributed to changes in the form of interest-group participation in policy-shaping. Individual firms and direct-member associations came to rival the previously dominant conventional peak and trade associations in the consultative processes. Another change was greater reliance on consultancy (an import from the United States), which started to erode the old distinctions between public policy-making and private interest representation. The Commission, member governments, and firms all found themselves relying increasingly on consultants to inject 'expertise'.

Although 'Brussels' is much more important, firms and interest groups retain close contacts with their national governments as important players in the SEM policy process. Rather than consistently preferring national or European policy, the SEM contributed to a rise in 'forum shopping', with non-state actors pursuing their policy objectives at whichever level is considered more likely to deliver the desired result.

In this process the Commission plays a pivotal role. Its sole right of initiative ensures that, but what really matters is how the Commission has chosen to use it. Although *re*regulatory rather than *de*regulatory, the SEM did have the effect of liberalizing markets and increasing competition among firms from different member states. In such circumstances, the costs of policy change (liberalization) are concentrated on the protected firms and the benefits tend to be disbursed thinly across a wide range of actors (consumers and users), although some particularly competitive firms are likely to benefit. In such circumstances, a policy entrepreneur is required to champion change and galvanize support—a role that the Commission has grasped with gusto.

Opening up the policy space

In addition to the institutional changes introduced by the SEA, the sheer reinvigoration of European policy-making also affected state–market relations in Europe. It did so in two principal ways: increasing governments' autonomy from society and opening up existing policy networks. Participation in any international negotiation privileges governments with respect to societal actors (Putnam 1988; Moravcsik 1993*b*). In particular, governments may be able to use an international (including European) agreement or external pressure to push through desired domestic reforms that have been blocked by powerful domestic interests.

In addition, the policy networks surrounding the SEM—both because they involve actors from multiple member states and because the participants are not directly involved in implementing policy decisions—tend to be more open than those in individual member states. As a result, a large number and wide variety of interests have access to the policy process. Furthermore, if there is to be a European regulation, producers tend to want their national rules to provide the template. As a consequence, powerful business interests often compete with each other in the European policy process, thereby undermining the 'privileged position' of business *vis-à-vis* other, less organized actors.

Hence, SEM regulations are usually contested by 'advocacy alliances', tactical, often loose groupings of diverse proponents and opponents of particular policies (A. R. Young and Wallace 2000: 3). Such 'advocacy alliances' bring together combinations of member governments, supranational European institutions, producer and civic interests. Thus, these alliances bridge the agenda-setting, policy-formulation, and policy-decision phases of the policy cycle.

A greater focus on services

Legislative activity in the 1980s and through the 1990s concentrated primarily on the free movement of goods (Vogt 2005; see Figure 5.1). With respect to the free movement of capital, there was the crucial 1988 Directive 88/361 that scrapped all remaining restrictions on capital movements between residents of the member states from 1 July 1990. There were also efforts to galvanize the free movement of labour by removing disincentives to relocating to another member state (see Chapter 11). Services, despite their economic importance—they account for about 70 per cent of EU GDP and employment (Commission 2009a)—however, were relatively neglected until the turn of the century.

What single-market legislation there was on services focused primarily on eliminating quantitative restrictions on service providers, for example in air transport, and road haulage, or on introducing competition in sectors dominated by public monopolies, such as electricity and telecommunications (see Chapters 6 and 15). A version of the 'new approach' with mutual recognition explicitly underpinned by agreement on common minimum principles for national regulation was applied to financial services, where 'home country control' was introduced, and a number of professions in which mutual recognition on the basis of agreed common qualifications was established. The provision of services within the EU has therefore

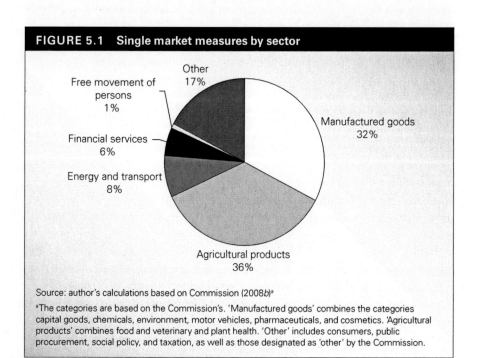

FIGURE 5.1   Single market measures by sector

Other
17%

Free movement of
persons
1%

Manufactured goods
32%

Financial services
6%

Energy and transport
8%

Agricultural products
36%

Source: author's calculations based on Commission (2008b)[a]

[a]The categories are based on the Commission's. 'Manufactured goods' combines the categories capital goods, chemicals, environment, motor vehicles, pharmaceuticals, and cosmetics. 'Agricultural products' combines food and veterinary and plant health. 'Other' includes consumers, public procurement, social policy, and taxation, as well as those designated as 'other' by the Commission.

been governed primarily by the right of establishment and the freedom to supply cross-border services enshrined in the Treaty of Rome (see Box 5.1 above). As a consequence, the provision of services within the EU has been regulated primarily by national rules (Langhammer 2005).

The provision of services between states, however, is particularly prone to barriers. Many services require (or are at least greatly facilitated by) physical proximity, which can be achieved through the establishment of a branch of the service provider (e.g. retail), the temporary posting of workers (e.g. construction) or the movement of the consumer (e.g. tourism). Moreover, services are often subject to more stringent regulations than goods because they are intangible and tend to be complex (Commission 2002c; Vogt 2005). Consequently, different national rules—such as quantitative restrictions, residency requirements, and multiple authorizations—even if not applied discriminatorily, can impede trade in services (see Commission 2002c: 14–42). There are also cultural and language barriers, including consumer and firm habits and preferences (Commission 2002c: 42–5). In part because of such barriers, intra-EU trade in services has only increased very slightly as a share of GDP since the launch of the single market (Ilzkovitz et al. 2007: 49), reaching only 5 per cent of GDP in 2007, compared to 17 per cent for intra-EU trade in goods (Commission 2009a: 8).

Given the importance of services in the European economy and the shortcomings in the single market for services, the 2000 Lisbon European Council identified removal of barriers to services as a key component to boosting the EU's competitiveness. The 2006 Services Directive, which was the response to this challenge, pitted neo-liberalism versus 'social Europe', saw the European Parliament play a major role, and essentially divided the old and new member states (see Box 5.2). Thus, the Services Directive (2006/123), which was the first major piece of single-market legislation adopted after the 2004 enlargement, indicates how politically fraught liberalization within the EU can be.

The financial crisis that deepened in mid-2008 prompted renewed attention to the regulation of financial services at the EU level, not least because of the implications of the failure of financial institutions with operations in more than one member state. These efforts coincided with the Commission monitoring public assistance to banks (see Chapter 6) and seeking to enhance banking supervision (see Chapter 7). The Commission advanced proposals for approximating and raising the level of bank deposit guarantees and strengthening the regulation of banks' capital requirements in October 2008 (Commission 2008c) and for regulating credit rating agencies in December 2008. In January 2009 the Commission adopted decisions aimed at improving supervisory cooperation and convergence among the member states by clarifying and enhancing the roles of committees that supervise the securities, banking, and insurance sectors (Commission 2009b).[3] The financial crisis, therefore, gave a new impetus to European financial regulation.

BOX 5.2	**The Services Directive**

The Commission's 2004 proposal for the Services Directive was radically liberalizing in that it sought to formalize mutual recognition in services through the 'country of origin' provision, under which a service provider would be able to operate throughout the EU in accordance with the regulatory requirements of its country of origin. It was also potentially very broad in scope. Strikingly, the labour market implications were not flagged in internal Commission consultations or in preliminary discussions in the Council. It was only when the draft was leaked that the controversy erupted. The most controversial aspect of the proposal was that it might undermine enforcement of the 1996 Posted Workers Directive (96/71/EC), which specifies that host-country labour and wage laws, where they exist, apply. This issue became much more sensitive after the 2004 enlargement because of the much larger wage differentials between the new and old member states. Playing on this aspect of the proposal, its opponents, notably labour unions in the old member states, managed to frame the directive as permitting a particularly inequitable kind of social dumping, as workers working side by side would be paid different wages and foreign workers would face host-country prices while being paid home-country wages. This concern took corporeal form in the mythic 'Polish plumber'.

The European Parliament responded to these concerns by adopting, over the votes of many MEPs from central and eastern European countries, a substantially modified version of the draft directive that replaced the concept of 'country of origin' with 'freedom to provide services' and exempted a number of sectors. Most of the central and eastern European member states, Finland, and the UK preferred the Commission's proposal, but the Commission, in the face of entrenched opposition to radical liberalization, accepted most of the Parliament's amendments. The Council adopted this version with only minor, slightly liberalizing changes, with only Belgium and Lithuania abstaining. The directive, which is due to be implemented by the end of 2009, will therefore not create a true single market for services and will create conditions only slightly more liberal than the status quo ante.

Sources: Hay 2007; Howarth 2007a; Nicolaïdis and Schmidt 2007.

The regulatory policy mode

The SEM policy process, therefore, combines high levels of interest group engagement with Commission entrepreneurship, Council bargaining, and parliamentary deliberation over common rules. These rules are subsequently often enforced through the courts by private actors. As such the SEM is the exemplar of the EU's regulatory policy mode (see Chapter 4).

It is, however, important to recognize that the regulatory mode actually contains two distinct dynamics: one that promotes market liberalization, the other more stringent regulation. These different dynamics apply to different types of regulation and broadly mirror patterns in other polities. With regard to economic regulations—such as controls on prices or competition—the SEM has been liberalizing. With regard to social regulations, such as consumer safety or environmental product standards, the SEM has tended to increase competition among European firms, but by producing relatively stringent common rules (Sbragia 1993; Peterson 1997; Scharpf 1999; A. R.Young and Wallace 2000).

There are two keys to these different dynamics. The first concerns policy ideas. While neo-liberalism has expounded the benefits of removing restrictions on competition (Majone 1991), post-material values and more recent ideas such as the 'precautionary principle' have supported more stringent social regulations (Vogel 1989; Weale 1992). The second key concerns how the potential for negative integration affects the bargaining power of the member governments within the Council under the shadow of QMV. With regard to economic regulations, the prospect of negative integration is pronounced, putting those member governments with restrictions in a weak position to do more than slow the pace of liberalization (Holmes and McGowan 1997; Schmidt 1998; A. R. Young and Wallace 2000).With regard to social regulations, however, the Treaty establishing the European Community accepts, within limits, the right of member governments to adopt social regulations that impede trade. In addition to putting such issues on the agenda, as noted above, this puts the stricter-standard country in a stronger bargaining position; its firms are protected and its citizens are content, while foreign goods or services are excluded. The cost of no agreement, therefore, falls more heavily on its partners. Under QMV no individual government can hold out alone for stricter standards, but there is usually an 'advocacy alliance' of civic interest groups, stringent-standard producers, several member governments, the Parliament, and often the Commission in favour of more stringent standards. As a consequence, the SEM has tended to contribute to 'trading up' (Vogel 1995).

Outputs and assessment

The legislative output of the SEM programme has been impressive, with over 1,500 measures adopted by 2008 (Commission 2009a: 7).[4] In addition, the proportion of EU directives that have been transposed into national law was very high, so that by November 2008 only 6 per cent of EU directives (92 measures) had not been transposed in all twenty-seven member states, compared to 27 per cent in November 2004 (Commission 2009a: 14).[5] The legislative output of the single market programme is estimated to have translated into significant economic impacts (see Box 5.3).

There are, however, persistent gaps in the legislative programme, especially company law. In addition, the correct transposition and adequate implementation of SEM directives remain a pressing concern (Commission 2002b: 11, 2009a: 17). As of the end of November 2008 the Commission had more than 1,300 infringement proceedings—concerning the incorrect transposition of directives or the incorrect application of single market rules—open against the member states: an average of 49 each, with Italy having the most (112) and only Poland among the new member states above the average (Commission 2009a: 19). Further, despite the SEM programme, there is still significant variation in national

BOX 5.3	The estimated impact of the single market programme

- EU GDP in 2006 was 2.15% higher due to the single market (an increase of €518 per head);
- about 2.75 million more jobs have been created since 1992;
- intra-EU trade relative to GDP rose 30% between 1995 and 2005;
- price dispersion decreased —the coefficient of variation of comparative price levels of final consumption (including indirect taxes) across the EU15 decreased from 20% in 1991 to 13% in 2005;
- intra-EU cross-border investments increased (the share of foreign direct investment among the ex-EU15 rose from 53% in 1995 to 78% in 2005);
- more open and competitive public procurement has led to savings of 10 to 30%;
- 73% of respondents consider the single market to have contributed positively to the range of goods and services on offer and 53% indicate that single market rules have increased consumer protection.

Source: Commission 2007c, Ilzkovitz et al. 2007.

regulation of services (discussed above) and even goods (inference from WTO 2008: Annex D). Thus the single market is not complete, and in many respects never will be, insofar as it is an ongoing project requiring constant updating (Commission 2002c: 4).

Beyond these problems with regulatory approximation, differences in member states' regulations disrupt the effective functioning of the single market because of problems with applying the mutual recognition principle. These problems are most pronounced with regard to technically complex products (such as buses, lorries, construction products, and precious metals), products that may pose a threat to safety or health (such as foods), and services, although the principle works quite well when applied to relatively simple products (Commission 2002b: 2). These problems stem in part from significant underlying cultural differences among the member states. Furthermore, consumers in different markets may prefer different product characteristics or may feel more comfortable doing business with established local firms (Müller 2003). Thus, cultural differences also have a bearing on whether the removal of legal and physical barriers is sufficient to create a single market.

The problems of translating legislative activism into results on the ground are reflected in European consumers' and firms' views of the single market. Majorities of firms in the EU15 report that the SEM, beyond the elimination of customs documentation and abolition of border controls, has had no impact on their activities (Eurobarometer 2006a: 3). Although firms from the new member states tend to be slightly more positive about the single market, sizeable proportions indicated that many aspects of the single market were not of concern to them (Eurobarometer 2006*b*: 5). The wider public has been even less impressed by the single market, with expectations of benefits beginning to wane from 1990 onwards (Franklin et al. 1994; Reif 1994) and public antipathies emerging in response to the apparent efforts of 'Brussels' to remove differences of local taste (food standards being a particularly emotive issue). The Commission (2007*a*: 4) thus concludes that the single market 'needs to deliver better results and tangible benefits for consumers and SMEs'.

The single market came under additional strain from late 2008 as the financial crisis began to impact on the 'real economy'. There were wildcat strikes in the UK in January and February 2009 over jobs at an oil refinery construction project going to Italian and Portuguese workers, a manifestation of the concerns that affected the Services Directive (see Box 5.2). British, Greek, and Spanish politicians suggested that banks that received public funds should lend first to domestic firms and households. French President Nicolas Sarkozy hinted that state aid to French automakers should be made conditional on their keeping production in France. As of late 2009, however, the challenges to the single market had been more rhetorical than real, although notable exceptions include the German government's intervention in the sale of Opel (see *The Economist*, 22 October 2009: 58).

Better regulation of the single market?

Recognizing persistent problems with realizing the economic benefits of the SEM programme, the maturation of the programme—the bulk of the legislative agenda has been adopted—and its outdated emphasis on goods, the Commission (2007*a*) launched an initiative in 2007 on 'A Single Market for 21st Century Europe', which was endorsed by the March 2008 European Council. This renewed initiative aims to place greater emphasis on implementation and enforcement and to rely less on legal measures to remove cross-border barriers. The intention is to make use of a '"smarter" mix' of policy instruments (Commission 2007*a*: 12), including competition policy (see Chapter 6); self-regulation; and other non-binding instruments, such as recommendations (i.e. 'soft law') (Commission 2007*b*). The Commission also wants to enhance cooperation among and with national authorities responsible for single market rules. Where regulation is still considered necessary, it should be flexible enough to adapt over time and to accommodate differences among the member states (Commission 2007*b*). Thus the Commission (2007*a*: 4) contends that this new initiative represents 'a new approach to the single market'.

This new approach builds on the 'better regulation agenda', which has its roots in the Commission's 2001 White Paper on Governance and became a particular concern of the Barroso Commission following advocacy by the British, Dutch, and German governments and reflecting concerted pressure over six presidencies of the Council—Ireland, The Netherlands, Luxembourg, the UK, Austria, and

Finland—during 2004–6. The 'better regulation' agenda is an effort to reduce the adverse impact of regulation on the competitiveness of European firms. It involves efforts to 'modernize' existing legislation by making it simpler through consolidation, codification, or repeal (by the end of the 2005–9 simplification programme the *acquis* should be reduced by about 10 per cent; Commission 2009c: 3). There are also efforts to reduce administrative burdens (on which the Commission is advised by a High Level Group of Independent Stakeholders chaired by Edmund Stoiber), for example by reducing reporting requirements. Moreover, the Commission is required to conduct impact assessments of all proposed EU legislation and the Council and EP must do likewise for any substantive amendments they propose (see Commission 2008a). The new approach to the single market emphasizes that the EU should act where it will have the greatest impact, which will require more systematic monitoring of key goods and services markets; that proposals will go through rigorous impact assessment; and that the Commission will continue to 'roll back' legislation where it no longer achieves desired goals or has been superseded (Commission 2007a).

Given its antecedents in earlier policy initiatives, the new approach to the single market is more a shift in emphasis than a radical change. Nonetheless, it reflects policy learning and adaptation in the wake of assessments of the effectiveness and/or adverse consequences of previous legislative activities. It is also a response to the maturation of the SEM programme: with most legal barriers to trade amongst the member states removed at least formally, the emphasis has shifted to making sure they are eliminated in practice and to encouraging private actors—firms and consumers—to take advantage of the new opportunities.

Policy linkages

The elimination of legal barriers to cross-border exchange has also shifted attention to the processes and conditions under which they are produced and provided. Irrespective of other arguments for European policies on environmental and social issues (see Chapters 11 and 13), the preoccupation of entrepreneurs with operating on a level playing field turned attention to the relevance of such rules for costs, competitiveness, and profitability. Moreover, the Commission seems to consider addressing the social and environmental impacts of increased competition as necessary for maintaining support for the single market project (Commission 2007a: 10).

In addition, the single market was invoked to build support for the two big policy initiatives that followed it: economic and monetary union (EMU) (see Chapter 7); and justice and home affairs (see Chapter 19). It also has implications for the EU's external policies. It has affected the terms on which third-country goods and services enter the EU (see Chapter 16; A. R. Young 2004) and, as a consequence of the 'doctrine of implied powers', it has enhanced the EU's capacity to participate effectively in international trade negotiations (see Chapter 16; A. R. Young 2002). It has also provided a core framework for relations with the EU's 'near abroad,' the members of the European Economic Area, current and former candidate countries, and states participating in the European Neighbourhood Policy (see Chapter 17; A. R. Young and Wallace 2000). Moreover, the new approach to the single market advocates 'expanding the regulatory space of the single market' by *inter alia* 'ensuring that European norms are a reference for global standards' (Commission 2007a: 7).

Conclusions

The SEM programme represents an approach to policy different both from that within the EU prior to the mid-1980s and from that found in most member states. It is an explicitly regulatory mode of policy-making. As a consequence, new relationships have been established between public and private actors at the EU level and between actors operating at the national and European levels. This has tended to open up the policy process, although business groups, especially large firms, have a 'privileged position', as they do at the national level. There is, however, more likely to be competition among such privileged actors than in member states.

The SEM has also reduced the dependence of many economic actors on national policy. The scope for national policy-makers to control economic transactions on their territories has become more limited and will remain limited as long as the transnational legal regime of the EU holds together. That is not to say, however, that the political turf has been won by EU-level policy-makers, since the new regulatory mode involves a diffusion of policy authority rather than its concentration at the European level. This inclination is likely to be reinforced by the imperatives of regulating an enlarged, and more diverse, single market.

Although the Commission has been heavily engaged in promoting the single market, its own net gain in authority is open to debate, not least since it has also become the butt of residual criticism about the downside effects of market liberalization. Moreover, the member governments—as participants in decision-making, the enforcers of most EU legislation, defenders of the losers from the single market, and the proponents of subsidiarity—remain key players in the regulatory process.

Because liberalization, at least in the short run, creates losers as well as winners, the single market programme has to be seen as an important element of the legitimacy test faced by the EU since the early 1990s and vividly illustrated by the interaction between the Services Directive and the French referendum on the Constitutional Treaty. The new emphasis on delivering tangible benefits to consumers is in part a response to these concerns about legitimacy. The political implications of the financial crisis of autumn 2008 may well undermine the idea that less regulation is better and provide even greater impetus for reregulation rather than deregulation.

Notes

1 Author's calculations based on data available at *http://www.councildata.cergu.se/council%20 Data/Wallace/Wallace.htm* (accessed 16 September 2008).

2 I am grateful to Helen Wallace for this observation.

3 Respectively, the Committee of European Securities Regulators (CESR), Committee of European Banking Supervisors (CEBS), and Committee of European Insurance and Occupational Pensions Supervisors (CEIOPS).

4 Author's calculation based on number and percentage of measures not implemented in all member states. This total includes 'energy and transport', 'environment', and 'social policy'.

5 The good transposition performance of the new member states—only Cyprus and Poland exceeded the 1.5 per cent transposition deficit target as of November 2008—underlines that the pre-accession process prepared the new member states well for membership.

FURTHER READING

On the original development of the 1992 programme, see Cockfield (1994) and Pelkmans and Winters (1988). For recent economic evaluations, see Commission (2007c), Ilzkovitz et al. (2007), and the Commission's biennial Internal Market Scoreboard and website at *http://ec.europa.eu/internal_market/*. The introduction to the Commission's (1995) 'pre-accession strategy' summarizes the SEM and its development. For the theoretical debate, see Armstrong and Bulmer (1998), Cowles (1997), Jabko (2006), Majone (1996), Moravcsik (1991), and Sandholtz and Zysman (1989). For discussions of the political dynamics of the SEM, see Armstrong and Bulmer (1998), Scharpf (1999), Young (2007a), and Young and Wallace (2000).

Armstrong, K., and Bulmer, S. (1998), *The Governance of the Single European Market* (Manchester: Manchester University Press).

Cockfield, Lord (1994), *The European Union: Creating the Single Market* (London: Wiley Chancery Law).

Commission (1995), *Preparation of the Associated Countries of Central and Eastern Europe for Integration into the Internal Market of the Union*, White Paper, COM (95) 163 final.

Commission (2007c), *The Single Market: Review of Achievements*, SEC (2007) 1521, 20 Nov.

Cowles, M. G. (1997), 'Organizing Industrial Coalitions: A Challenge for the Future?', in H. Wallace and A. R. Young (eds.), *Participation and Policy-Making in the European Union* (Oxford: Clarendon Press), 116–40.

Ilzkovitz, F., Dierx, A., Kovacs, V., and Sousa, N. (2007), 'Steps Towards a Deeper Economic Integration: The Internal Market in the 21st Century', *European Economy Economic Papers 271* (Brussels: European Commission).

Jabko, N. (2006), *Playing the Market: A Political Strategy for Uniting Europe, 1985–2005* (Ithaca, NY: Cornell University Press).

Majone, G. (1996) (ed.), *Regulating Europe* (London: Routledge).

Moravcsik, A. (1991), 'Negotiating the Single European Act: National Interests and Conventional Statecraft in the European Community', *International Organization*, 45/1: 19–56.

Pelkmans, J., and Winters, L. A. (1988), *Europe's Domestic Market* (London: Royal Institute of International Affairs).

Sandholtz, W., and Zysman, J. (1989), '1992: Recasting the European Bargain', *World Politics*, 42/1: 95–128.

Scharpf, F. W. (1999), *Governing in Europe: Effective and Democratic?* (Oxford: Oxford University Press).

Young, A. R. (2007*a*), 'The Politics of Regulation and the Internal Market', in K. E. Jørgensen, M. A. Pollack, and B. Rosamond (eds.), *The Handbook of European Union Politics* (London: Sage), 373–94.

Young, A. R., and Wallace, H. (2000), *Regulatory Politics in the Enlarging European Union: Balancing Civic and Producer Interests* (Manchester: Manchester University Press).

CHAPTER 6

Competition Policy

Towards an Economic Constitution?

Stephen Wilks

▌ Summary

European competition policy has steadily increased its effectiveness in controlling restrictive practices, abuse of dominant position, mergers, state aid, and the liberalization of utilities. Its success rests on the free-market approach now predominant in all European Union (EU) countries including the new member states. The central dominance of the Directorate-General for Competition (ex DGIV, now DG COMP) in the Commission has been perpetuated, although it now shares enforcement with the national competition authorities (NCAs) in the member states. The exceptionally powerful treaty provisions and apparatus of legal enforcement mean that competition policy has become a supranational policy competence which can be regarded as an 'economic constitution' for Europe. Two recent developments have been: first, the decentralization of antitrust enforcement to the national agencies and courts through the 'Modernization Regulation' of 2003; and, second, a 'turn to economics' in which economic analysis has been substituted for legal tests to move towards an 'effects-based' (effect on competition) interpretation of the law. This is part of a process of Americanization in which the senior decision-makers in DG COMP have embraced US competition economics and have also adopted US-style enforcement mechanisms. This turn to economics and to US enforcement methods has been criticized as a shift to a more Anglo-Saxon, or 'neo-liberal', interpretation of competition policy, which is regarded with suspicion by supporters of a 'social market' approach in continental Europe. Suspicion was manifest in President Sarkozy's 2007 removal of competition from the treaty objectives in Article 3(1)(g) of the Treaty of Lisbon and it will be radically reinforced by the international financial crisis that descended on Europe in October 2008. This question of how to interpret and regulate the market promises to be a new ideological battleground as policy evolves in a more challenging, recessionary European economic environment.

Introduction: competition policy and the European market

Competition policy is concerned with setting standards of conduct rather than with obtaining tangible goals, and is anchored in the principles of free-market capitalism. The character and role of competition policy have therefore been controversial across the EU and in individual member states. Its enforcement has a differential effect across the very varied economic systems ranging from highly liberalized markets to those where the state has played an important role in the economy, to the post-socialist states which started to embrace capitalism only in the 1990s (V. Schmidt 2002). European competition policy is broad and includes antitrust, merger control, and the control of state aid (subsidies to industry). Its overall thrust has been to press on every front for the liberalization of markets.

Competition policy draws its importance from the central role that economic factors and market principles have played in the evolution of the EU. The vision in 1958 was of a common market which would generate benefits for all participants through market integration. This was a liberal economic vision, then controversial, which rested on a faith in traditional market capitalism. The vision was the natural alternative to the centrally planned economies of central and eastern Europe, but it was also regarded sceptically by many west European business and policy élites. It became a dominant principle only as a result of the neo-liberal revolution of the 1980s and the single market programme of 1992 (see Chapter 5). This vision was consolidated by the collapse of Soviet communism and the remodelling of the economic systems of control in central and eastern Europe in alignment with the capitalist norms of the Union. Under free-market capitalism competition is the central dynamic of entrepreneurial activity and the means of energizing the economic system to deliver welfare benefits. Those aspects of economic life which hinder competition—monopoly, oligopoly, cartels, restrictive practices, market-sharing, subsidies, and state protection—also prevent it from generating and distributing wealth efficiently. Just as the European Central Bank (ECB) guarantees a sound currency and low level of inflation, so the EU competition rules guarantee a free market and economic efficiency, providing an 'economic constitution' for Europe.

This emphasis placed upon the market and economic integration means that competition policy has been of central importance in the EU. The Commission has expanded competition policy as one of its key EU competences. It has drawn on powerful treaty provisions, received support from the European Court of Justice (ECJ) and the Court of First Instance (CFI; see below), and entrusted policy to DG COMP, one of the most effective Directorates-General (DGs) in the Commission, directed by a series of able commissioners. Competition policy has taken on con-stitutional characteristics, thus taking precedence over less developed policy areas (such as research and development (R&D) or environmental policy), or framing specific sectoral policies (such as media or telecoms). Indeed, competition policy has been used to discipline governments as well as companies, so that all economic actors must understand it and treat it with respect.

The salience of competition policy

Competition policy is about protecting and expanding competition as a process of rivalry between firms in order to win customers, and also as a process of creating and protecting markets. There are both political and economic rationales for competition policy. The prior, political rationale comprises a commitment by governments to allow economic actors freedom to compete in the market, and to protect consumers from exploitation by powerful companies. The US is the home of competition policy, where it is still called 'antitrust', which reveals its origins in the late nineteenth century as a commitment to protect 'the little man' from the power of the big industrial 'trusts'. The more recent, economic rationale is becoming an orthodoxy. It is based on the standard neo-classical theories of market competition, which affirm that competition creates wealth through the generation of economic efficiency, both productive efficiency (making more goods for the same cost), and allocative efficiency (giving consumers what they want). Accordingly Motta (2004: xvii) defines competition policy as 'the set of policies and laws which ensure that competition in the market place is not restricted in such a way as to reduce economic welfare'. There are criticisms of the 'consumer welfare' orthodoxy (Budzinski 2008), but wider agreement that economies where competitive pressure is intense will be more efficient than those where it is restrained. This argument was reinforced at the 2000 Lisbon European Council which laid out a new economic reform and competitiveness agenda, which has had limited success but remains a central plank in the European economic policy portfolio.

The impact of EU competition policy is evident on a day-to-day basis, as it increasingly affects how we do our jobs, how benefits are distributed, and how and what we consume, from football to cosmetics, the price of cars, and the proximity of supermarkets. This means that a policy area which was traditionally regarded as specialist and arcane makes the headlines. This applies to the big merger cases, such as *Nestlé/Perrier* in 1992, *GE/Honeywell* in 2001, and *Ryanair/Aer Lingus* in 2007,[1] which also stretch beyond intra-EU cases to those with a global or extraterritorial dimension. In the *GE/Honeywell* case the European Commission prohibited a merger between these huge US companies due to an adverse impact on the EU market. The US was outraged and media coverage was intense. Competition issues also surface in some of the big state aid cases, such as the Commission's demand that the French electricity monopoly, EdF, be required to repay €900 million in unlawful tax breaks to the French government (*Times*, 17 October 2002). 'Big name' cases also attract great public interest, such as the Commission's findings that Microsoft abused its near-monopoly and acted illegally in bundling its Media Player software into its Windows operating system. The Commission ruled that Microsoft share details of its software design with competitors and in March 2004 Mario Monti, the then Competition Commissioner, announced a fine of €497 million, the highest ever against a single company, which produced headlines such as 'Mario Monti's Broken Windows', and even 'The Full Monti' (*Financial Times*, 25 March 2004).

Such headlines dramatize the key element in assessing the impact of competition policy, and the way in which it structures the business environment for companies across Europe. EU competition policy has a 'direct effect' on companies, but until the mid-1990s most companies treated competition policy as an afterthought, to be taken into account when drafting a major agreement, entering a joint venture, or contemplating a merger, but not at the heart of decision-making. By contrast, today, the 'competition rules' are a dominant regulatory constraint when companies formulate their corporate strategy or consider their competitive behaviour. They employ legal expertise to advise on the impact of the rules and most big firms will have an in-house 'compliance programme' to train their staff to avoid breaching the competition provisions.

This shift in corporate awareness is partly due to the steady refinement and expansion of the law and the activism of the competition authorities. For corporate executives European law does not yet allow prosecution of individuals, which is commonplace in the US. But the UK law does include a 'criminal cartel offence' and criminal penalties, including imprisonment, have been discussed as a possible European penalty. In practice the most dramatic threat is the increasingly frequent 'dawn raids' when competition officials swoop in on factories, offices, and private residences across several countries to seize papers and computers in order to find evidence of secret agreements, or 'cartels', to manipulate markets. Some raids arise from the successful adaptation by the Commission of a US-style leniency programme, a system of exemptions for 'whistle-blowers' who provide information about a cartel in which their firms are involved. The intensification of action, in particular against 'hard core' cartels, has resulted in a huge escalation of fines. In 2001, the Commission fined fifty-six companies a total of €1,836 million, more than the cumulative total of all fines previously levied in the history of EU competition law. In the three-year period 2005–7 a massive €5,863 million was levied against participants in twenty cartels. The biggest fines were against companies found guilty in the 2007 *Elevators and Escalators* case, including the largest fine ever levied of €480 million against the ThyssenKrupp group (Commission 2008*o*: 10). Policies that pack this sort of punch simply cannot be ignored.

It is worth remembering that competition policy was not always regarded with such approval, and competition was once regarded as wasteful and destructive. The use of cartels was widespread and not regarded as essentially illegitimate until the late 1960s (Harding and Joshua 2003). The industrial policies of many west European countries rested upon nationalization, selective intervention, indicative planning, encouragement of concentration and economies of scale, and the support of 'national champions'. Although these industrial policies became discredited, they still attract some support among trade unions and national politicians and have re-emerged in response to the 2008–9 recession. Thus, there remains a tension between competition policy and company support, as well as with policies to encourage regional economic development, science and technology, and small and medium-sized enterprises. In all these areas competition is being distorted by governments for alternative policy goals.

The move from planning and intervention to the liberalization of markets and competition has a particular contemporary dimension *vis-à-vis* the enlargement of the EU in 2004 and 2007. For over forty years, ten of these twelve new member states had centrally planned economies in which competition was an alien concept and capitalism was condemned. These countries have telescoped the post-war years of west European economic evolution into ten years as they have adopted the EU competition policy embodied in the *acquis communautaire*, as part of the Europe agreements (see Chapter 17). All these countries now have competition laws, competition agencies, and a commitment to competition. Competition policy thus emerges as an essential component for making enlargement work and ensuring that diverse economic systems converge with the market principles that unify the EU economy.

The substance of policy

There are five components of European competition policy, each of which relies on specific legal powers:

- a prohibition on agreements between firms that limit competition (Art. 81 TEC; ex Art. 85 EEC);
- a prohibition on the abuse of a dominant position by one or more large firms (Art. 82 TEC; ex Art. 86 EEC);

- the control of mergers which create a dominant position (Regulation No. 4064/89);

- the control of aid given by a member state to a firm or category of firms (Arts. 87 and 88 TEC; ex Arts. 92 and 93 EEC); and

- the liberalization of measures by member states to favour domestic utilities, and infrastructure industries (Arts. 31 and 86 TEC; ex Arts. 37 and 85 EEC).

The sophistication and effectiveness of these components have grown over time to create a complex agglomeration of principles and powers enshrined in practice and case law. Effective control of state aid began only in the late 1980s, control of mergers in the early 1990s, and liberalization of utilities in the late 1990s. At the heart of competition policy, however, is the prohibition on anti-competitive agreements. The first major decision taken by the Commission under Article 81 (TEU) (ex Art. 85 EEC) came in 1964 and Box 6.1 sets out the subsequent development of policy.

BOX 6.1	Stages in the development of EU competition policy				
	1960s	**1970s**	**1980s**	**1990s**	**2000s**
(1) Antitrust: agreements	Regulation 17; cases	develop principles	first fines	enforcement intensified	stress cartels; modernization
(2) Antitrust: abuse of dominance	dormant	first cases	develop principles; first fines	idea of collective dominance	moderate application; modernization
(3) Merger control	not in Treaty	no action[a]	regulation in 1989	early enforcement	intensified and reform
(4) State aid	dormant	gradual development	becomes priority; first survey 1988	tighter sectoral regimes	Lisbon Agenda reinforces; steady progress
(5) Liberalized utilities	ignored[b]	ignored	more transparency; action on telecoms	becomes priority; systematic challenge	continued pressure; mixed progress

[a] 'no action' means that the problem was recognized but could not be acted on without legal powers.
[b] 'ignored' means that the problem was not recognized.

The first three components of policy affect private sector companies, while the last two, state aid and liberalization, are unique to the EU because they are targeted at the governments of the member states. The following sections review each area, concentrating on the private-sector components.

Antitrust: restrictive practices

Policy on anti-competitive agreements, or restrictive practices, is specified in Article 81 which 'prohibits' all agreements and concerted practices between firms that affect trade between member states and 'have as their objective or effect the prevention, restriction or distortion of competition within the common market'. The Article also specifies exemptions from the prohibition in cases where an agreement 'contributes to improving the production or distribution of goods or to promoting technical or economic progress' (Art. 81(1) TEC, ex Art. 85(1) EEC; and Art. 81(3) TEC, ex Art. 85(3) EEC). These provisions raise extraordinary problems of interpretation. Taken literally, virtually every agreement will 'restrict or distort' competition: that is what agreements are for, and every business spends much of its time and energy in foiling its competitors. On the other hand, some agreements foster competition, although interpretation will often depend on the theoretical biases of the economic analysis involved. In practice, implementation has allowed extensive discretion to the case officials in DG COMP; their interpretations of the rules have usually been confirmed in appeals to the ECJ or more recently to the CFI, and only occasionally overturned.

On the basis of case law and accepted economic theory some practices are presumed to be illegal (Goyder 2003: 97). These include resale price maintenance, horizontal price fixing, export bans, and market sharing. Such practices tend to be administered through cartels among competitors in an industry so as to create or protect a collective monopoly and to make excess profits. Cartels still proliferate across Europe and the Commission has put the attack on cartels at the heart of its enforcement effort. Evidence secured by the Commission reveals astonishing illegal practices by leading companies and senior executives meeting in secret, using codes and subterfuge to outwit the authorities, which in 2007 alone prosecuted cartels in calcium carbide, switchgear, beer, exotic fruit, and videotape (Commission 2008o: 10). In 2002 the Commission also concluded its first cartel case in the world of banking when it found in the *Austrian Banks* case that Austrian banking was organized by a cartel known as 'The Lombard Club', which covered all banking products, services, and advertising 'down to the smallest village' (Guersent 2003: 55). Its action was largely upheld by the ECJ in September 2009.

At the other end of the spectrum the majority of agreements will be perfectly legal. This applies to most distribution agreements, supply agreements (including discounts), and the many small agreements that affect only a small section of the market. Many agreements will also be exempt because they aid efficiency and 'economic progress'. In order to provide certainty the Commission has issued about a dozen 'block exemptions', which define acceptable agreements in areas such as technology, R&D, maritime transport, and insurance (Goyder 2003: 114–15). Similarly, principles have evolved to define the legality of agreements relating to intellectual property (where it can be pro-competitive to cooperate), and in respect of 'vertical agreements', that is, agreements between enterprises at different stages in the supply chain, which are now generally regarded as acceptable. This is in contrast to the horizontal agreements between competitors at the same level in the supply chain which often have cartel-like qualities and are regarded with suspicion.

Antitrust: abuse of dominance

While the control of restrictive practices is regarded as a Commission success story, the same cannot be said of the second component of competition policy, controlling the abuse of dominance. This is covered by Article 82 (TEC) (ex Art. 86 EEC) which prohibits 'any abuse by one or more undertakings of a dominant position within the common market'. This prohibition is aimed at monopolies or, since full monopoly is rare, at oligopoly, where a small number of firms dominate a market. European governments are decidedly ambivalent about the control of oligopoly, the law itself has several significant flaws, and the Commission has been hesitant about exploiting this aspect of its powers. Cini and McGowan (1998: 94) go as far as to assert that 'the Commission's monopoly policy has been largely ineffective'. This is an overstatement, but implementation is indeed impeded by the complex dynamics between the Commission and the member states.

For member states large companies have several attractive features. They enjoy economies of scale, they have financial muscle, and are representative of national industrial prowess, but most of all they can fund high technology and may operate as powerful multinationals able to compete directly with Japanese and US multinationals in global markets. These are the classic features of 'national champions', and many governments, including those of France, Germany, Italy, and The Netherlands, have been loath to see these benefits eroded by active attack from the competition authorities, particularly since Article 82 (TEC), unlike Article 81 (TEC), does not provide for an efficiency defence. This in part explains the hesitancy of the Commission. Article 82 (TEC) is, however, also unsatisfactory in that it requires that the authorities first establish dominance (usually taken as at least 40 per cent of the market as indicated in the 1978 *United Brands* judgment; Whish 2008: 177); and only then can they establish 'abuse'. The law is also weak in attacking oligopolies. The Commission has attempted to establish a principle of 'collective dominance' (several companies working together in an oligopoly), but it was not until the *Italian Flat Glass* case in 1992 that it received any encouragement from the CFI, and even now the concept remains ambiguous (Clarke 2006: 44). If successful in establishing illegal abuse the Commission has powers to fine, to issue a 'cease and desist' order, and under the 2003 Modernization Regulation (see below) it now has powers to break up companies by forcing divestiture. This last option is the anti-trust equivalent of a nuclear strike and has never been imposed by the Commission. There have been a few high-profile cases, such as the 2004 action against *Microsoft*, but very few actions have been taken against the bigger companies operating across Europe.

Merger control

The third component of policy is the control of mergers and acquisitions that have the potential to generate monopolies. This is the dramatic, and often controversial, face of competition policy since its main target is big firms. It attracts huge media attention and frenzied political lobbying so that big mergers present theatrical shows of Shakespearean proportions. They affect thousands of jobs, transform household name companies, make or break fortunes in financial markets and establish or destroy the reputations of captains of industry. In most EU countries, unlike the UK, 'hostile' takeovers (i.e. without the agreement of the management of the target company) are unusual and provoke acute opposition. DG COMP has, for example in 2003, approved (with conditions) the *Pfizer/Pharmacia* merger to create the largest pharmaceutical company in the world, and the *Pechiney/Alcan* merger (again with conditions) to create the largest aluminium company in the world. This constitutes a huge deployment of economic power and the Commission is playing on a global stage. When it blocks an international merger, as with *GE/Honeywell* in 2001, the conflict extends to the highest possible level. In this case the *GE/Honeywell* merger was the largest proposed merger in history and was approved by the US antitrust authorities. The Commission's rejection resulted in the merger being abandoned, but only after furious lobbying by US politicians amidst a blaze of publicity, threats of retaliation, and deterioration in US–EU relations.

The Merger Regulation (Regulation 4064/89 replaced by Regulation 139/2004) emerged as a result of a decade of pressure from DG COMP and came into effect in September 1990. It was regarded as the crowning triumph of Sir Leon Brittan's highly successful period as Competition Commissioner and established the prestige and influence of the DG, prompting the conclusion that, by the early 1990s, the European competition regime had become globally pre-eminent (Wilks with McGowan 1996: 225). The Merger Regulation created a 'one-stop shop' which permitted the Commission to control the largest mergers above a high threshold (mergers below the threshold continue to be dealt with under national legislation). The current threshold is set at an aggregate turnover of €2,500 million (Whish 2008: 829), which catches over 300 mergers a year. Companies are in favour of the EU process, which is rapid, transparent, and avoids having to seek approval from every state in which they operate. Cases can, however, be transferred. Compromises reached during the passage of the Regulation introduced Article 9, the 'German clause', so called because it was demanded by the German authorities which wanted the opportunity to control large national mergers. It allows the Commission to transfer jurisdiction to a member state where the market is mainly national. On the other hand, Article 23, the 'Dutch clause', was demanded by the Dutch authorities and allows a member state to request the Commission to act on its behalf, and also (in the most recent reforms of 2004) allows the merging parties themselves to request that the Commission handle the case. The Commission has pressed for greater flexibility in case-handling and, in a spirit of subsidiarity, regularly transfers jurisdiction to national competition authorities (NCAs).

DG COMP implements a logical two-stage process in which most mergers are cleared within one month and only the difficult cases are examined in more depth through the 'phase two' procedure. The objective is to block or amend mergers which threaten to create a dominant position which might then be abused. The wording of the test is of vital importance and in 2003 the Commission persuaded the Council to pass a reformed Merger Regulation which introduced an adaptation to the wording of the test (Regulation 139/2004: 59–68). This retains the dominance test, which has been extensively criticized by the US and the UK (which both now use the 'substantial lessening of competition' test; Vickers 2003: 102), but it now prefaces it by attacking 'a concentration which would significantly impede effective competition'. This change may tighten European merger control, although it will continue to be based on an economic test rather than on public-interest or non-economic considerations.

Throughout the 1990s the Commission gained confidence, won court cases, and became gradually more interventionist. It is still very unusual for a merger to be blocked completely (Table 6.1 indicates that only twelve mergers were blocked outright in the last ten years), but it is becoming increasingly normal to accept or impose conditions before approving the merger (often divestiture of part of the merged entity). On this basis the Commission built up to a crescendo of activity in 2007 when it received 402 notifications.

Since 2000, merger policy has suffered some major setbacks. In 2001 the prohibition of the *GE/Honeywell* merger precipitated a torrent of criticism from the US accusing the Commission of arrogance, poor economics, outdated thinking, and incompetent analysis. The 'hammer blow' came in June 2002 when a CFI judgment overturned the Commission's prohibition of the *Airtours/First Choice* merger, the first appeal that DG COMP had lost. The shock was compounded by two further defeats in the *Schneider Electric* and *Tetra Laval* cases later in 2002. The CFI was damning. It criticized the Commission processes, its use of evidence, its reasoning, the quality of its economic analysis, and stated that the Commission had committed 'manifest errors of assessment' (Veljanovski 2004: 184). This led US critics to renew their allegation that the Commission was defending 'competitors not competition', or, in other words, protecting big European companies and not the interests of consumers (which is now the main declared objective of US antitrust policy).

In response the Commission reformed the merger regime and reinforced economic analysis across the DG. This was symbolized by the creation of a new post of chief economist, held since 2004 by the Belgian economist Damien Neven (see Neven 2006). Mario Monti, Director-General of DG COMP for 2000–4 and himself an economist,

TABLE 6.1   Merger regulation cases, 1998–2007

Year	Phase 1		Phase 2		
	Notifications	Approved	Approved No Conditions	Approved with Conditions	Refused
1998	235	219	3	4	2
1999	292	255	0	8	1
2000	345	321	3	12	2
2001	335	312	5	10	5
2002	279	250	2	5	0
2003	212	223	2	6	0
2004	247	240	2	4	1
2005	313	308	2	3	0
2006	356	346	4	6	0
2007	402	392	5	4	1
Total	3016	2866	28	62	12

Source: Whish (2008: 887)
Note: lines do not add up due to notifications withdrawn or settled the following year.

noted revealingly that 'to develop an economic interpretation of EU competition rules was… one of my main objectives when I took office' (Monti 2003: 7). Where the balance is struck between law and economics and, indeed, what sort of economics is employed, has a marked effect on the development of policy in mergers and across the entire policy area.

State aid

With the fourth component of policy, state aid, the style and focus of policy takes on a very different form. Here the treaty powers are less clear, the processes of implementation are less powerful, and the Commission typically enjoys less cooperation from national governments, which are themselves the targets of control. In this area (as with the liberalization of utility regulation) the Commission is more than the agent of the member governments; it transcends national interests and aspires to be truly 'supranational'. Despite national hesitation the state aid regime has become a central plank in the EU competitiveness strategy launched in the 2000 Lisbon Agenda.

Article 87 (TEC) (ex Art. 92 EEC) affirms that aid to business, whether private or state-owned, that distorts competition is 'incompatible with the common market'. This applies most blatantly to direct state subsidies to companies. However, the concept extends to all forms of assistance, including tax breaks, preferential purchasing, loans, and even loan guarantees. Some forms of aid, and especially large subsidies, were a major tool of industrial policy as recently as the 1980s. Periodic crises in industries such as shipbuilding, coal, aerospace, and the motor industry persuaded governments to grant massive rescue subsidies. Until 2008 these had virtually been eliminated under the tightening state aid rules, but other aspects of aid may, as Cini and McGowan (1998: 137) point out, 'be a very good thing' in areas such as R&D, small enterprise, or backward regions, where it may help create competition and guarantee social benefits. All aid must be notified to the Commission, which assesses its compatibility and has developed frameworks to examine sector-specific and regional aid. A particular problem exists with the new member states, where the use of state aid is still widespread, as has been the case vis-à-vis the eastern *Länder* in Germany following reunification. The initial emphasis was on transparency rather than abolition. The intention was steadily to reduce aid levels, and it was recognized that, like drug withdrawal, it was dangerous to cut the dose overnight.

In respect of all state aid there was no Council regulation until 1999 when Regulation 659/1999 was enacted to allow exemptions and streamline monitoring. Thus, the Commission is still developing its enforcement apparatus through a 'State Aid Action Plan' launched in 2005 and culminating in a general block exemption in 2008 (Regulation 800/2008). The Action Plan introduces a series of elements which have become familiar on the antitrust side such as:

- a more economic assessment of the competitive effects of aid;
- block exemptions and specific provisions to allow aid for the environment and R&D&I (Research and Development and Innovation);
- regional exemptions and an agreed regional aid map;
- direct challenge to member states through the ECJ;
- recovery of illegal aid, €8.2 billion of which had been recovered by the end of 2007; and
- action in the national courts and discussion of ways to encourage private actions from parties damaged by state aid to competitors (Commission 2008*o*: 35).

The aim is for less and better-targeted state aid which pursues 'horizontal' objectives of common interest, such as environmental protection. But, although these aims are laudable, there are still crude political confrontations to be dealt with such as the Commission decision in July 2008 to reject plans by the Polish Government to grant over €2 billion in subsidies and guarantees to two unprofitable shipyards (Europa, press release, 15/7/2008).

A useful technique, developed first when Peter Sutherland was Competition Commissioner in the late 1980s, has been to 'name and shame' governments and reveal the sheer scale of state aid through periodic surveys. This was reinforced after the 2000

Lisbon Agenda through the creation of a state aid register and an on-line 'scoreboard' in 2001. The Commission found itself frequently working with the grain as national governments, especially the UK, made greater efforts to reduce the use of subsidies. In 1988 state aid accounted for about 10 per cent of public expenditure or 3–5 per cent of GDP, in other words, a hugely distorting degree of cross-subsidy from the taxpayer to industry. By 2002 the figure had fallen to about 1.2 per cent of public spending and 0.6 per cent of GDP and by 2006 to 0.4 per cent of GDP (see the Scoreboard on the DG COMP website, *http://europa.eu/competition*). This is considerable progress, although the figures are still large at €48 billion in 2008 and state aid still proliferates. The Commission is notified of over 500 aid schemes a year and takes over 400 decisions granting approval, often after the negotiation of amendments.

The 2007–8 'credit crunch' and the subsequent recession are testing the state aid regime to the limits. State guarantees and subsidies to the banking sector were only the first of further national steps to protect and subsidize whole sectors and national champions which the Commission found it impossible to resist. In December 2007 DG COMP approved the nationalization of the troubled British bank Northern Rock, but was then faced with a series of further rescues and guarantees which persuaded the Commission to create a crisis regime. In December 2008 the Commission adopted a 'temporary framework' allowing rescue aid, loans, guarantees, and risk capital over the two years to the end of 2010 (Europa Press Release, 17 December 2008). It has approved substantial banking state aid with minimum delay and accepts that broader aid to formerly healthy companies will be inevitable.

The liberalization of utilities

The fifth and final component of competition policy concerns competition in the public sector and the privatized utilities. As with state aid, the primary target is the national governments which may own nationalized industries, grant monopoly powers to state or private utilities, or operate regulatory regimes which suppress competition. The industries in question are the key utility and infrastructure sectors, such as telecoms, energy, water, post, transport, and airlines, although the issues of state control also extend to the financial sector, insurance, and the media. State ownership of these industries had become the norm from the 1950s onwards and the fact that they were often 'network' industries was often used to justify them as 'natural monopolies', on the grounds that the need for maximum efficiency through a single network (as for electricity distribution) required operation by a single company. Moreover, since these industries performed public services they were deemed to operate in the public interest, and thus to be potentially exempt from competition law (see Chapter 15). In many countries exemptions were incorporated into national legislation. In the 1990s this immunity was challenged by technological change, by a shift towards market solutions, and by manifest evidence that such industries were inefficient, inflexible, and far too costly (Cini and McGowan 1998: Ch. 9).

The case for liberalization in these sectors, in the interests of efficiency and European competitiveness, was underlined by the single market programme of 1992 (see Chapter 5), and by the example of the UK where privatization also showed how much change could be achieved. Despite its powers under Article 86(3) (TEC) (ex Art. 90(3) EEC) to require member states to liberalize utilities, the Commission recognized how delicate and political such moves could be in areas of such vital importance to the quality of life, which often excited great public support and were typically heavily unionized and politically powerful. The Commission did not feel politically confident enough to challenge member states until the late 1980s, when it began to focus on those anti-competitive practices created mainly by governments through ownership and regulation. Considerable progress towards liberalization was made, especially in telecoms, but slowed down in the late 1990s and continues to be slow and difficult. The Commission has designed complex packages of measures, including directives, restrictive practices, and merger cases, in order to liberalize sectors such as electricity, gas, postal services, and air transport. DG COMP has cooperated closely with the sectoral DGs as seen in the energy sector, where a new device was used in 2006 involving a sectoral study of competition in the EU energy market (see Chapter 15). The sheer scale of activity illustrates both the dedication of DG COMP in pursuing competitive markets in every setting, and the political limits to what is achievable.

Thus, European competition policy has gone through a process of incremental development (see Box 6.1) including a legal foundation of accumulation of jurisprudence and the creation of a cadre of career competition specialists in big international law firms. Competition policy also needs to be assessed against the economic cycle. In boom periods merger activity increases, state aid work decreases, and on the whole DG COMP faces less opposition. In recession, companies and governments feel more vulnerable and the interventionist voices within the Commission and its other DGs begin to prevail. There has also been a cycle of economic theory and European competition enforcement has ridden on the wave of post-Thatcher neo-liberalism. In exploiting these stages of development the single most important element lies in the nature, leadership, and competence of the responsible agencies and their staff.

Agencies and implementation: DG COMP

The development and implementation of competition policy is centred in the Commission in a Directorate-General, formerly DG IV, now DG COMP. It is a small organization, which employs 719 staff (at April 2009) of whom 429 are senior administrative officials who make decisions and contribute to policy. The senior ranks were traditionally dominated by lawyers, though economists are now playing a greater role. Its political head is the Commissioner, from 1999 to 2004 Mario Monti, an experienced Italian economist, and from 2004 to 2009 Neelie Kroes, a Dutch businesswoman in the Barroso Commission. DG COMP is regarded as one of the most attractive postings both for the Commissioner and for the Director General, and the relationship between them is of key importance. In 2002, Philip Lowe (British) who had also been the first head of the Merger Task Force, became Director General (due to be succeeded by the Dutchman Alexander Italianer towards the end of 2009). Until Lowe's appointment all Directors General had been German, giving the DG a distinctively German feel and perhaps some influence with the traditionally powerful German competition agency, the *Bundeskartellamt* (BKA). The DG was reorganized in 2004 in a surprising move which abolished the Merger Task Force and distributed merger control across five sectoral directorates. The current structure of nine directorates includes one dealing with state aid, one dealing with cartels, two with planning, strategy, and international links, and five organized to engage with sectors of industry (Morgan 2006: 100).

The sectoral approach is usual amongst competition agencies and is the model used by the BKA and the British Office of Fair Trading (OFT). It was argued that the reorganization would enhance staff flexibility and speed up the handling of cases by exporting the rapid response developed in the Merger Task Force to the rest of the organization, where severe delays have been routine (*Financial Times*, 23 February 2004). One feature of DG COMP is that many of its senior officials have spent their entire careers in its ranks. This brings benefits of continuity but at the same time carries the risk of insularity. The Commission does not practise the 'revolving door' exchange of lawyers between the private and government sectors so typical of the US (Cini and McGowan 1998).

A key question when assessing DG COMP is its level of independence. Decisions affecting competition are made by the entire college of Commissioners, who are expected to reach agreement as a collective body. Nevertheless, the Competition Commissioner must expect opposition to controversial policies and decisions: member governments often press 'their' commissioner to influence policy and decisions can rest on political negotiation and compromise, and will—albeit rarely—go to a vote, especially in cases of state aid. Observers often therefore point to 'the politicized nature of European competition policy' (Cini and McGowan 1998: 214), and 'the lack of independence of the Community competition law enforcement mechanisms' (Laudati 1996: 230). This critique has prompted periodic calls for the creation of a more clearly independent European Cartel Office (Wilks 2005b: 128). The extent of its vulnerability to industrial lobbying is less clear, although Wigger (2007) argues that the European Round Table of Industrialists (ERT) has had a great influence on the development of policy.

On the other hand, DG COMP is relatively free from control from the Council and the Parliament, for two main reasons. First, in implementing specific treaty articles it enjoys unambiguous legal authority. Secondly, in 1962 the Council delegated to the Commission extensive procedural powers to implement the relevant articles. These delegated powers were set out in Regulation 17/62 and effectively renewed through the Modernization Regulation 1/2003. Independence is far from absolute, but can be compared with the great independent regulatory agencies of the US, such as the Federal Trade Commission (FTC) (Wilks with Bartle 2002; Wilks with McGowan 1996), and is a prized feature of competition agencies the world over. It is regarded as essential to protect the absolute values of economic competition, to avoid improper influence by business, and to avoid self-interested influence by other government departments or agencies (and, in the EU, by national governments who are among the targets of implementation).

The theme of independence serves to underline the claim that DG COMP is the most powerful competition authority in the world. There are now over 100 competition agencies worldwide and they are ranked annually on a peer-reviewed basis by the *Global Competition Review*. In 2007 the three 'élite' agencies, ranked at a maximum of five stars, were the US Federal Trade Commission, the EU's DG COMP and the UK Competition Commission (which is smaller and more specialized). DG COMP was ranked above the US Department of Justice (DoJ) Antitrust Division; on this measure it therefore has a globally pre-eminent position. The scale of its competence is unique, embracing not only the standard competition areas, but also state aid and the liberalization of utilities. In the US there are two powerful authorities (the FTC and the Antitrust Division of the DoJ), and there much of the dynamism is due to private actions in the courts, which are still very unusual in the EU. The BKA and the OFT are also highly effective, but both are overshadowed by Brussels, and the BKA is losing prestige, while the OFT has yet fully to exploit its new powers under the 1998 Competition Act and the 2002 Enterprise Act. With a mere 429 senior administrative officials to police a market of 490 million consumers DG COMP was, and remains, acutely understaffed. The only plausible explanation for under-resourcing is that the member states see resources as one of the few pragmatic ways in which to restrain the ambitions of the DG.

There has been repeated criticism of DG COMP from both businesses and legal firms for its lack of accountability. It is said that the Commission is 'prosecutor, judge, and jury' or, to extend the metaphor, it is 'policeman, arbitrator, prosecutor, judge, jury, and prison officer'. This criticism arises essentially from the Article 81 (TEC) restrictive practices procedure. A case is opened either following a complaint or as a result of an in-house investigation ('policeman'). The case is handled by one senior member of staff, the *rapporteur*, who investigates the abuse and often negotiates with the companies involved to change their practices ('arbitrator'). If this fails, the *rapporteur* constructs a case, argues it in the office, discusses it with the Legal Service, and presses for a decision ('prosecutor'). Senior staff of the DG decide ('jury'), and settle on a penalty ('judge') which is then imposed or negotiated with the companies ('prison officer'). Not all of this is done by the same person, but much rests in the hands of the *rapporteur* and the whole process takes place within one organization, albeit with attention to natural justice and arrangements such as access to the file and information meetings, as well as the involvement of a neutral 'Hearings Officer' to ensure fair play. Despite efforts to improve accountability, and despite the independent sanction of the courts, there is some truth in the accountability criticism. As DG COMP has become more powerful so the problem has become more acute.

DG COMP in context

How DG COMP operates has also to be seen in a broader EU institutional context, as well as within its network of NCAs. These constrain DG COMP, but can also be employed as sources of strength. No sector of industry is excluded from the competition rules, although there are some exemptions, particularly in agriculture. Thus, all the sectoral DGs such as Transport or Energy need to cooperate with DG COMP. As regards competitiveness and market integration, DG Internal Market and DG Industry are key partners. Historically, DG COMP and DG Industry were often at loggerheads, but today relations are less tense, and DG Industry has accepted the argument that strong competition enhances productivity and competitiveness. The Lisbon agenda, with its emphasis on growth, jobs, and reducing regulatory burdens, acts as a vehicle for coordination and gives prominence to competition policy.

A constraint on DG COMP is the EU legal apparatus. Within the Commission the Legal Service has to be consulted about all legally binding acts and is therefore in constant contact with the DG. The Legal Service represents the Commission before the ECJ and the CFI, and is inherently risk-averse, which at times causes serious tension. The European courts themselves are very important. The ECJ and the CFI, created in 1986, provide the cement of European integration and are the most 'federal' of the European institutions. The ECJ was originally the venue for litigation and appeals in competition matters, and issued a series of key judgments, which not only supported the Commission, but defined market integration as a central goal of European competition policy (a goal unique to the European regime).

The overload of complex and detailed competition cases led to the creation of the CFI as a junior court under the 1986 Single European Act. The CFI has a less formal procedure and is more specialist; it hears the majority of competition cases in small panels of five judges and in some cases (such as mergers) can operate rapidly through an 'expedited process'. The CFI has been less forgiving than the ECJ, which had been accused of being too lenient to DG COMP, especially over procedural inadequacies. In contrast, the CFI has been rigorous and has reinforced the need for procedural correctness over matters such as giving a fair hearing, defining the exact case to be answered, and setting out key evidence. In more recent cases the CFI has also challenged the substantive content of decisions, challenged the reasoning and the interpretation of the evidence, and emphasized the need for more rigorous economic analysis. Thus, we are seeing a shift to a more adversarial stance in the relationship between the Commission and the Court. But the key point remains—that competition policy is being taken forward through a framework of European law within which policy developments are discussed, enacted, and resolved in a legal environment and using a legal discourse.

A third contextual factor in the Commission's ability to develop competition policy lies in its relationship with the NCAs in the member states, which may include executive agencies, courts, tribunals, or government departments. In 1958 there was virtually no competition machinery in the member states, making it easier for policy to be centralized in Brussels. Over the ensuing years every member state has created its own competition agencies and appeals system. Some member states, such as the UK, Ireland, and Austria, had their own antitrust traditions, embodied in laws and agencies which predated their EU membership. There is thus a pattern of long-established agencies, such as the BKA and the OFT, followed by creation or reform of established agencies in the remaining member states up to the late 1990s. In each case the legislation and the agency roles have converged on the model of European law and DG COMP (Drahos 2001; van Waarden and Drahos 2002). The twelve new members post-2004 were not given any choice: acceptance of the competition rules and the entire weight of European jurisprudence as part of the *acquis* were conditions of accession, as was the allocation of reasonable resources to support active competition agencies and courts.

The creation of twenty-seven competition regimes across the EU underlines the success of the Commission in embedding competition as a constitutive element of economic regulation, but also highlights the under-resourcing of DG COMP. In 2007 it had a budget of €97 million and employed 380 'A grade' staff (429 by 2009). In contrast, the competition agencies of the four biggest member states (Germany, France, Italy, and the UK) had a collective budget of about €134 million and employed 693 professional staff (*Global Competition Review* 2007). DG COMP has therefore had administrative as well as legal motives to enlist the cooperation of the NCAs.

From European to transatlantic convergence

The face of EU competition policy has been changed radically since the introduction of the Modernization Regulation (1/2003). Previously, the enforcement of the antitrust rules had been undertaken by the Commission alone. By contrast, the new system empowers the NCAs of the member states to make decisions, grant exemptions, and hear appeals. This was a once-in-a-generation reform which carried the risks of incoherence, inconsistency, and conflict in the application of Articles 81 and 82 (see Wilks 2005a; 2007). In practice, modernization has proved very successful from the point of view of the Commission, which has replaced national laws with EU law (for all cases that involve trade between member states) and has established supervision over the NCAs. It has achieved effective control by a remarkable exercise in policy innovation built on normative agreement over the merits of competition, and administrative coordination through the European Competition Network (ECN) (Wilks 2007). As a result, DG COMP now sits at the heart of a distinctive regulatory network that binds together the twenty-seven competition agencies of the member states. These range from the large, élite, well-resourced agencies of France, the UK, Germany, Italy, and The Netherlands to small and under-resourced agencies such as those of Austria, Belgium, and Estonia (Wilks 2007). These agencies share information through the ECN, allocate cases, engage in cooperative enforcement, and develop policy options. This constitutes a striking model of regulatory cooperation by more-or-less independent agencies which converge around the economic and legal acceptance and enforcement of the treaty competition rules.

The harnessing of the NCAs to implement antitrust has freed resources in DG COMP to engage in defining and pursuing fresh priorities. It has given some priority to control over state aid but put its major effort into the attack on 'hard core cartels'. Here the Commission's rhetoric has been fearsome and Mario Monti referred to them as 'cancers' afflicting the economy (McGowan 2005). In 1998 the Commission created a dedicated cartel unit and has increased international cooperation with the US and Canada in particular to attack cartels globally. The key to success within Europe has been a US-style leniency programme which rewards whistleblowing companies by either exempting them from fines or imposing reduced fines in return for cooperation. First introduced in 1996, the leniency policy has been revised to make it more compelling. Through this route, and via international collaboration with the US authorities, the anti-cartel policy has become startlingly successful, to the point that the Commission has almost been overwhelmed. It has therefore pursued two further aspects of US antitrust: private actions and settlements.

On private actions the Commission issued a Green Paper in 2005 exploring ways in which private parties injured by illegal behaviour could sue in the courts without the involvement of the authorities. This is the typical mode of enforcement in the US but is far less attractive in Europe owing, for instance, to the absence of class actions and triple damages. On settlements the Commission issued in 2008 a Notice allowing settlement of cartel cases through paying an agreed fine but avoiding a formal procedure or appeal. Here the similarity is with the 'consent decrees' by which the majority of US cases are settled. In these initiatives we see a procedural convergence with American antitrust to complement the European convergence evident in modernization and the ECN.

For some observers this procedural Americanization is a symptom of a deeper-seated ideological Americanization. In fact, the shift of EU competition enforcement towards US antitrust is no secret; it is a consensus among practitioners and is applauded by officials (Wilks 2007). What are more controversial are the implications of this shift. First is the proposition that Anglo-Saxon-style competition enforcement embeds neo-liberalism and threatens traditional German-style neo-corporatist or 'Rhenish' capitalism (Wigger 2007: 497–500). Second is the suggestion that the move to US-style economic tests favours large transnational corporations and that this policy stance has been lobbied for by large European corporations. The result is that large corporations are tolerated and even encouraged by EU policy (Lowe 2006; Freyer 2006: 303). This is an important emerging debate, which confirms European convergence in competition policy, but convergence on a model that in its principles, procedures, and effects is encouraging European industry to move towards an Anglo-Saxon liberal market economy.

Competition policy as regulatory policy

Competition policy displays significant features of two of the policy models outlined in Chapter 4—the Community method and regulatory policy—and shows virtually no similarity with the transgovernmental and distributional modes. However, recent reforms also indicate a limited move towards the policy coordination mode. It is not surprising that two of the policy modes are exemplified in competition policy. This policy area is both a leading example of the success of the Community method and provides much of the raw material that allowed Majone (1996) to develop his analysis of European regulation.

The main alignment of competition policy with the traditional Community method lies in the strong role for the Commission in designing and enforcing policy, especially over the period in which policy has been highly centralized and dominated by DG COMP. In competition policy the Commission has enjoyed exceptional freedom from the Council and the member governments. Its key partners are the courts, and so long as its actions are legally defensible the Commission has been able to act assertively and directly. In line with the Community method the Commission has pursued the goal of 'positive integration' with great determination. It has therefore sought to create a market without frontiers and has strongly attacked measures by firms (or governments) that segment markets, limit trade, or apply different practices in different geographical areas. Following modernization this strong version of centralized policy has continued.

Competition policy exhibits an even closer resemblance to the regulatory mode of policy-making. This draws on the exceptionally fertile theories advanced by Majone (1996: 55, 287) about the position of the EU as a 'regulatory state', specifying behaviour in legislation and ensuring compliance through the legal system (Majone 1996: 63), where its ability to undertake regulatory policy is almost limitless. The legal process based on the treaty is enhanced by the legal apparatus of regulations and decisions, supplemented by the 'soft law' of guidelines, frameworks, opinions, and notices, and has been reinforced by supportive judgments of the ECJ which have provided the foundation of Community competence. The primacy of Community law and the supremacy of the European courts mean that, as long as the Commission can win appeals in them, its decisions become binding on companies and governments across the EU—and sometimes extraterritorially. Moreover, this process is extremely inexpensive, at least in terms of its burden on the EU budget. The administrative costs of regulation are borne by the courts, the legal systems of the member states, and the clients of law firms, whilst the substantive costs of compliance and alterations of business practices are hidden and borne by firms.

The freedom of the Commission to regulate is enhanced by the weakness of the European Parliament, a feature shared in this field with national systems. Its legitimacy therefore rests on the acceptance of its market-economy approach and ultimately on how far it succeeds in creating greater efficiency and ensuring some degree of equitable access to benefit from the wealth created. Majone (1996: 296) has argued, subtly and provocatively, that regulation does not need to be legitimized by control through the institutions of popular democracy, but can be legitimized through debate and deliberation among experts, observing due process and pursuing objective standards of efficiency. His analysis has stimulated a wider debate about 'non-majoritarian' agencies, and about the values of independence and expertise embodied in regulatory agencies. DG COMP of the Commission provides the classic example of independent European regulation (Wilks with Bartle 2002), perhaps as an extreme case of law-driven policy-making, conducted with a legal discourse through a network of legal institutions, courts, and law firms across the EU. Indeed, the recent process of modernization may perhaps best be understood as the mobilization of ideas through a legal community spreading across the member states.

The modernization reforms have changed the face of European competition policy and have created a new mode of policy formulation and implementation in the form of the ECN. This invites an evaluation of whether modernization and reform of merger and state aid policy can be seen as an example of the new policy mode of 'policy coordination'. The creation of independent competition agencies in all the member states since the mid-1980s means that the future implementation of policy will depend to a far greater extent on negotiation, coordination, and networking, as the coordination model both predicts and celebrates.

Conclusion

This chapter argues that competition policy has a special place in the European policy matrix because it defends the essential mobilizing principle of the EU, the collective interest in economic efficiency secured through the creation of a common market. In its pursuit of integration the Commission has employed a shrewd strategy of using the market and appealing to free-market principles. Its success has produced what Jabko has called a 'quiet revolution' which has created a truly European political economy. The European economy has grown in parallel with institutions of European economic governance. The most widely studied institution is EMU, led by the ECB, but of equal importance are the competition rules and DG COMP. In these areas 'the European Union has become a real *federal power*' (Jabko 2006: 183). We can argue therefore that, as Europe converts its treaties into a constitution, so the economic provisions of those treaties become constitutional principles underpinning the operation of the European economy, in other words the competition rules can be analysed as an 'economic constitution'. This proposition is explored at greater length elsewhere (Wilks, 2010). It underlines the importance and influence of the competition rules and has three further implications.

First, it emphasizes the independence of the agencies and especially DG COMP. Implementation of constitutional principles makes DG COMP doubly insulated from national political pressures. Second, it identifies the deepening of a process of legalization of economic regulation and an expansion of economic law which could be termed 'juridification' of the economic sphere. The economic constitution protects certain economic rights but at a cost of legal process. Thirdly, and most speculatively, the constitutional perspective suggests that certain market principles have become embedded in European institutional practice and constitutional provisions. Clearly Europe is based on market principles but what sort of market? Jabko (2006) has argued that the Commission integrationists have employed a brilliant market rhetoric but have never defined what sort of market Europe was working towards. It is the argument of this chapter that the competition rules have moved towards a free market which is in fact more neo-liberal, more purely market-oriented, than many in Europe would be inclined to accept. This raises the political stakes and, in terms of the focus of this book on policy-making, it suggests that competition policy has transmuted into a still poorly understood mode of constitutional politics.

The institutional perspective stressed above argues that the independence, confidence, and competence of the Commission and DG COMP remain the key factor in determining the direction of policy-making. The Commission's power will be increased if economic growth recovers, if companies regard the modernized system positively, if NCAs continue to cooperate willingly, and if neo-liberalism remains the dominant economic doctrine. Assessment of the future shape of policy will depend on how these four elements—of growth, compliance, cooperation, and economic doctrine—evolve.

Note

1 For complete references to these and other Commission merger and antitrust decisions, see the Tables of Cases and Legislation at the front of this volume.

 FURTHER READING

The best guide to the evolution of European competition policy is the Commission's annual report which provides a review of Commission and Court activities over the previous year, highlights strategic policy priorities, the Commission's own rationale, and, to some extent, the debates surrounding new initiatives. These latter aspects are also covered in the quarterly *Competition Policy Newsletter*, published by DG COMP. Both publications are available on the DG COMP website (*http://ec.europa.eu/competition/*). More critical accounts of EU and member-state policy can be found in the *European Competition Law Review*.

A good introduction can be found in Cini and McGowan (2009). An excellent introduction to the broader political context is provided by Amato (1997). Wilks (2010) offers a comprehensive overview of the subject area whilst further analysis of the Commission and modernization appears in Wilks (2005*a* and 2007). Wigger (2007) and Wigger and Nölke (2007) provide an excellent critical perspective. There is an extensive legal literature which is accessible to the general reader. Especially valuable are the opening and closing chapters of Goyder (2003), the study by Drahos (2001), and the more technical sixth edition of Whish (2008). The best introductions to the economic basis of policy can be found in Motta (2004) and Budzinski (2008).

Amato, G. (1997), *Antitrust and the Bounds of Power* (Oxford: Hart).

Budzinski, O. (2008), 'Monoculture versus Diversity in Competition Economics', *Cambridge Journal of Economics*, 32/2: 295–324.

Cini, M., and McGowan, L. (2009), *Competition Policy in the European Union*, 2nd edn.; 1st edn.1998 (Basingstoke: Palgrave Macmillan).

Drahos, M. (2001), *Convergence of Competition Laws and Policies in the European Community* (Duventer: Kluwer).

Goyder, D. (2003), *EC Competition Law*, 4th edn. (Oxford: Oxford University Press).

Motta, M. (2004), *Competition Policy: Theory and Practice* (Cambridge: Cambridge University Press).

Whish, R. (2008), *Competition Law*, 6th edn. (Oxford: Oxford University Press).

Wigger, A. (2007), 'Towards a Market-Based Approach: The Privatization and Micro-economization of EU Antitrust Law Enforcement', in H. Overbeek et al. (eds.), *The Transnational Politics of Corporate Governance Regulation* (London: Routledge), 98–118.

Wigger, A., and Nölke, A. (2007), 'Enhanced Roles of Private Actors in EU Business Regulation and the Erosion of Rhenish Capitalism: the Case of Antitrust Enforcement', *Journal of Common Market Studies*, 45/2: 487–513.

Wilks, S. (2005*a*), 'Agency Escape: Decentralization or Dominance of the European Commission in the Modernization of Competition Policy?', *Governance*, 18/3: 431–52.

Wilks, S. (2007), 'Agencies, Networks, Discourses and the Trajectory of European Competition Enforcement', *European Competition Journal*, 3/2: 437–64.

Wilks, S. (2010), 'Competition Policy', in W. Grant, D. Coen, and G. Wilson (eds.), *The Oxford Handbook of Business and Government* (Oxford: Oxford University Press), 730-56.

CHAPTER 7

Economic and Monetary Union

An Experiment in New Modes of EU Policy-Making

Dermot Hodson

▌ Summary

Economic and monetary union (EMU) provides the European Union (EU) with a major role in macroeconomic policy-making. The sixteen members of the euro area have exchanged national currencies for the euro and delegated responsibility for monetary policy to the European Central Bank (ECB). Member states have also agreed to coordinate their budgetary policies and structural reforms and to speak with one voice on international macroeconomic issues. EMU is a high-stakes experiment in new modes of EU policy-making in so far as both economic and monetary decision-making rely on alternatives to the traditional Community method. This experiment has suffered a number of setbacks during the first decade of the euro, but it looks set to continue for the foreseeable future.

Introduction[1]

The macroeconomy is a province of public policy that has traditionally been closely guarded by national politicians, civil servants, and central-bank officials. It typically entails the setting of short-term interest rates (monetary policy) and decisions related to government expenditure and taxation (fiscal policy) and can include measures designed to influence the external value of the currency (exchange-rate policy). Macroeconomic policies and structural reforms are closely intertwined, with the latter including regulatory changes aimed at improving the functioning of product, labour, and financial markets.

EMU entails a radical shift in macroeconomic policy-making in the EU. As of November 2009, 16 euro-area countries—Austria, Belgium, Cyprus, Finland, France, Greece, Germany, Ireland, Italy, Luxembourg, Malta, The Netherlands, Portugal, Slovakia, Slovenia, and Spain—have exchanged their national currencies for the euro and delegated responsibility for monetary policy to the ECB. Member states have retained control over the other aspects of macroeconomic policy, although they have agreed to coordinate these policies within the Council of Ministers for Economic and Financial Affairs (Ecofin). To this end, member states have imposed limits on government borrowing under the Stability and Growth Pact (SGP) and agreed to coordinate structural reforms through the Broad Economic Policy Guidelines (BEPGs).

EMU has a threefold significance for students of EU policy-making. Firstly, the single currency is among the most tangible symbols of European integration for the 328 million people who live in the euro area. Secondly, with the euro now a leading international currency, EMU is central to the EU's ambitions to become a leading player on the world stage. Thirdly, and critically for the themes of this volume, EMU is a high-stakes experiment in new modes of EU policy-making. As discussed in Chapter 4, the traditional Community method involves the delegation of key responsibilities to the Commission. Under EMU, monetary policy has been delegated to a new kind of supranational institution, the ECB, while economic policy-making, with its reliance on legally non-binding measures, is a pioneering attempt at policy coordination among national governments.

This chapter explores the origins and evolution of EMU as the euro enters its second decade. The first section puts EMU in historical context and looks at the economic and political rationale for the creation of the euro. The second and third sections look at monetary and economic policy-making respectively. The fourth section discusses the euro from a global standpoint and the fifth section offers a euro-area perspective on the crisis in global financial markets that emerged in 2007–8.

Historical development and rationale

The 1957 Treaty of Rome (EEC) contained few references to macroeconomic policy and no reference to EMU. Its most significant macroeconomic provisions were Article 105, which called on member states to coordinate their economic policies with a view to achieving equilibrium in their balance of payments, and Article 108, which allowed the Council to provide mutual assistance in the event of a balance-of-payments crisis. One reason why the Treaty did not go further in the macroeconomic domain was that the Keynesian consensus that held sway among economists at the time stressed the need for national control of macroeconomic policy instruments. Specifically, governments were expected to trade off higher inflation for lower unemployment and, in the event of an economic downturn, to stimulate aggregate demand through a combination of tax cuts, expenditure increases, and interest-rate reductions. Also, at the moment of the EEC's creation, member states' currencies were not yet convertible, meaning that there were legal limits on the exchange of one currency for another (Eichengreen 2007: 73). Another relevant factor was that member states had little incentive at this time to challenge the Bretton Woods Agreement of 1944, which secured exchange-rate stability among industrial countries by linking the US dollar to gold and linking national currencies to the dollar (see Maes 2004).

At a summit in The Hague in December 1969, EEC leaders agreed to work out a plan for EMU. The principal reason for this change lay not in shifting macroeconomic paradigms but in the decline of the Bretton Woods system, which had come under increasing strain as the USA struggled to maintain the dollar's link with gold amid the spiralling costs of the Vietnam War. There were also concerns at the time that a switch from fixed to floating exchange rates would disrupt trade relations within the common market and add to the cost of financing the common agricultural policy (Commission 1969).

The Werner Plan for EMU, which was presented in October 1970, fell at the first hurdle. Bretton Woods collapsed in August 1971 and was replaced four months later by the Smithsonian Agreement, which permitted wider bands of fluctuation vis-à-vis the US dollar. In March 1972, the Six (joined by the acceding Denmark, Ireland, and the UK) established the 'snake in the tunnel', an exchange-rate system in which member states agreed to narrower bands of fluctuation for EEC currencies ('the snake') within the wider bands of the Smithsonian Agreement ('the tunnel'). After oil prices surged in 1973, EEC member states were divided on the question of whether to sacrifice the Keynesian priorities of growth and employment for low inflation. This lack of consensus led to macroeconomic divergences within the EEC, most notably between France and Germany, and dealt a fatal blow to the EEC's fledgling exchange-rate regime.

TABLE 7.1	Chronology of EMU
July 1944	Bretton Woods Agreement signed
Mar 1957	Treaty of Rome signed
Dec 1969	Hague summit calls for a plan for EMU
Oct 1970	Werner Group adopts its final report
Mar 1971	Member states agree to three-stage plan for EMU
Aug 1971	Collapse of the Bretton Woods System
Dec 1971	Smithsonian Agreement signed
Mar 1972	Launch of the snake in the tunnel
Feb 1973	Collapse of the Smithsonian Agreement
Mar 1979	Launch of the EMS
June 1988	European Council in Hanover establishes the Delors Committee
Apr 1989	Delors Committee adopts its final report
July 1990	Stage 1 of EMU begins
Feb 1992	Treaty on European Union signed at Maastricht
Sept 1992	Italy and the UK exit the ERM
Aug 1993	Reform of the ERM
Jan 1994	Stage 2 of EMU begins; European Monetary Institute established
June 1997	European Council in Amsterdam adopts the SGP
Dec 1997	European Council in Luxembourg creates the Eurogroup
May 1998	Council of Ministers decides that 11 member states have met the convergence criteria; ECB established
Jan 1999	Stage 3 of EMU begins and the euro area is created
Mar 2000	European Council in Lisbon adopts the Lisbon Strategy
Jan 2001	Greece joins the euro area
Jan 2002	Changeover to euro notes and coins
Mar 2005	European Council in Brussels revises SGP and Lisbon Strategy
Jan 2007	Slovenia joins the euro area
Jan 2008	Cyprus and Malta join the euro area
Jan 2009	Slovakia joins the euro area as the euro marks its 10th anniversary

In 1979, EEC member states made a fresh attempt to coordinate their macro-economic policies with the establishment of the European Monetary System (EMS). The centrepiece of the EMS was the exchange-rate-mechanism (ERM), a regime designed to minimize fluctuations in bilateral exchange rates. A weighted basket of EEC currencies, the European currency unit (ecu), was used as the denominator for this system. The EMS fared better than the snake in the tunnel, helping to promote exchange-rate stability and to reduce inflation, especially in the second half of the 1980s when national governments resorted less frequently to the practice of devaluing their currencies.

McNamara (1998) links the creation and comparative success of EMS to a growing commitment to monetarism among EEC member states from the mid-1970s onwards. Monetarism challenged Keynesianism's approach to macroeconomic policy, rejecting the existence of a long-term trade-off between growth and employment and calling on policy-makers to prioritize the pursuit of low inflation by restricting money-supply growth. Although monetarism typically supports flexible exchange rates, EEC member states, McNamara argues, viewed the ERM as a commitment device for achieving monetarism's primary objective of price stability. A case in point was France, where President François Mitterrand used the ERM to reinforce his efforts to reduce inflation and restore macroeconomic credibility after abandoning his unsuccessful experiment in Keynesianism in 1983.

The European Council in Hanover in June 1988 asked the Commission President, Jacques Delors, to draw up a fresh plan for EMU. On the basis of this blueprint, EU leaders adopted a three-stage transition to EMU that was enshrined in the Treaty on European Union (TEU), signed at Maastricht in 1992. Stage 1 (1990–4) included the removal of the remaining barriers to the free movement of capital and the granting of political independence to central banks. Stage 2 (1994–8) required member states to demonstrate their commitment to macroeconomic discipline by meeting convergence criteria (see Table 7.2) and established the European Monetary Institute (EMI) to oversee the transition to EMU. Stage 3 (1999 onwards) included the irrevocable fixing of exchange rates and the creation of the ECB. In keeping with the new classical economics, the intellectual successor to monetarism in the 1980s, the Treaty tackled concerns about the ability of short-sighted governments to make the right long-term choices for the economy. It did this, firstly, by guaranteeing the ECB's independence from political control (Art. 108 TEC) and, secondly, through the excessive deficit procedure, which prohibits member states from running budget deficits in excess of 3 per cent of gross domestic product (GDP) (Art. 104 TEC).

European integration scholars are divided as to the rationale for resuscitating plans for EMU at this time (see Sadeh and Verdun 2009). Neo-functionalists emphasize the importance of spill-over from prior stages of economic integration. Padoa-Schioppa (2000), for example, argued that member states' commitment to fixed exchange rates under the EMS and the free movement of capital under the single European

TABLE 7.2	Summary of the convergence criteria (Art. 121 TEC)	
What is measured?	**How is it measured?**	**Convergence criteria**
Price stability	Harmonized index of consumer prices (HICP)	Not more than 1.5 percentage points above the three best-performing member states
Sound public finances	Government deficit as % of GDP	Reference value: not more than 3%
Sustainable public finances	Government debt as % of GDP	Reference value: not more than 60%; if above this reference value, government debt should have sufficiently diminished and must be approaching 60% at a satisfactory pace
Durable convergence	Long-term interest rates	Not more than 2 percentage points above the three best-performing member states in terms of price stability
Exchange-rate stability	Deviation from a central rate	Participation in ERM II for two years without severe tensions

Source: Commission (2008d: 8)

market programme (see Chapter 5) rendered national control over monetary policy unworkable and forced them to choose between either flexible exchange rates or full monetary union. Intergovernmentalists, in contrast, explain EMU as the outcome of interstate bargaining. In a variation on this theme, Moravcsik (1998) views EMU as an attempt by national governments, motivated primarily by economic interests, to lock in the benefits of macroeconomic stability at the EU level. The benefits of this enterprise, he argues, were modest for Germany, in part because of the privileged position of the Deutschmark in the EMS. For Moravcsik, this explains why Maastricht enshrined macroeconomic principles that enjoyed a high degree of support among German policy-makers, especially the overriding importance attached to price stability.

Economists have generally been more circumspect than political scientists about the *ex ante* economic rationale for EMU. Following Mundell (1961), the prevailing view in the 1980s and 1990s was that European countries would struggle to form an optimum currency area (OCA) because of the prevalence of asymmetric shocks (economic disturbances that affect different member states in different ways) and the perceived lack of flexibility in product and labour markets. Of course, the logic of OCA theory is not undisputed. Mundell himself warned that floating exchange rates could be a cause of, rather than a cure for, macroeconomic instability when capital flows freely between countries (De Grauwe 2006). Furthermore, the macroeconomic costs of giving up national exchange rates must be weighed against the microeconomic benefits of monetary union, which include the elimination of exchange-rate uncertainty, the transaction cost savings of doing business in one currency, and the competitive gains from increased price transparency between countries (De Grauwe 2007).

In the early 1990s, preparations for EMU hit a stumbling block when falling economic growth and rising unemployment generated significant strains within the EMS. This problem was compounded by the economic consequences of German unification, which created sustained inflationary pressures and forced the Bundesbank to increase interest rates. Other EEC members responded by raising interest rates, a move that helped to stabilize their currencies against the Deutschmark but worsened the effects of the recession. When Danish voters rejected the TEU in June 1992, member states' commitment to EMU and, by implication, the ERM was cast into doubt. Following intense currency speculation, Italy and the UK were forced to suspend their membership of the ERM in September 1992.

The EEC soon weathered this economic and political storm. Danish voters, assuaged by the guarantee of an opt-out from Stage 3 of EMU, voted for the TEU in a second referendum in June 1993. The ERM was effectively dismantled in August 1993, when the remaining member states adopted extra-large margins of fluctuation between their currencies. A sustained economic recovery during the remainder of the decade enabled member states to make significant progress towards meeting the convergence criteria. In May 1998, the Council of Ministers, meeting in the composition of heads of state or government, agreed that eleven member states—Austria, Belgium, Finland, France, Germany, Ireland, Italy, Luxembourg, The Netherlands, Portugal, and Spain—fulfilled the criteria and could proceed to Stage 3 of EMU. The inclusion of Belgium and Italy on this list was politically controversial since public debt in these countries, though it was diminishing in line with the treaty requirements, exceeded 100 per cent of GDP.

The euro was duly launched on 1 January 1999 along with the ERM II, an exchange-rate regime in which member states aspiring to adopt the single currency have agreed to minimize fluctuations between their currencies and the euro. Greece joined the euro area in January 2001, twelve months before the changeover to euro notes and coins. In January 2007, Slovenia became the first of the EU's 'new' member states to join the euro, followed by Cyprus and Malta in January 2008 and Slovakia in January 2009.

The European Council took a number of steps around the time of the euro's launch to strengthen economic policy coordination, including the creation of an informal body of euro-area finance ministers, the Eurogroup, in December 1997 and the unveiling of an ambitious programme of product-, labour-, and financial-market reforms, the so-called Lisbon Strategy, in March 2000. Perhaps the most economically and politically controversial initiative of this period was the signature of the SGP in June 1997. Politically, this agreement signalled the EU's determination to impose limits on government borrowing by speeding up and clarifying the implementation of the excessive deficit procedure. Economically, the SGP provided a medium-term focus for fiscal policy under EMU. In this respect, its aim was to allow member states to use fiscal stabilizers in the event of an economic downturn without breaching the excessive-deficit ceiling by first achieving budgetary positions of close to balance or in surplus (Artis and Buti 2000). In this respect, the SGP's attempt to reconcile the need for short-term fiscal stabilization with the long-term sustainability of public finances reflected one of the key tenets of New Keynesianism, an economic paradigm that has dominated since the 1990s (see Iversen and Soskice 2006).

Only the UK and Denmark have formal opt-outs from Stage 3 of EMU, secured in the negotiations over the TEU. These opt-outs are likely to remain in place until euro membership has been approved by popular referendums. In the UK, the Labour Party, mindful of lukewarm public support for EMU, is committed to euro membership 'in principle' but not until the economic conditions are right, while the Conservatives, scarred by their experience in government during the ERM crisis of 1992, remain strongly opposed to the single currency. In spite of such differences, the political salience of EMU has been low since a study by HM Treasury in June 2003 concluded that the economic case for adopting the euro had not yet been met (HM Treasury 2003). Danish voters roundly rejected euro membership

TABLE 7.3   State of play for non-euro area members

	Participating in ERM II	Official target date for euro adoption
Bulgaria	No	As soon as possible
Czech Republic	No	None
Denmark	Yes	None
Estonia	Yes	As soon as possible
Latvia	Yes	As soon as possible
Lithuania	Yes	As soon as possible
Hungary	No	None
Poland	No	None
Romania	No	Not before 2014
Sweden	No	None
UK	No	None

Source: based on ECB (2008a: 84)

in a referendum in September 2000. The larger Danish political parties continue to support EMU, however, and the government is expected to put this issue to the vote once again by 2011.

The remaining EU member states are formally required under the Treaty to join the euro area if and when they meet the convergence criteria. In practice, member states retain a degree of discretion over the questions of whether and when to apply for membership of the euro area. Sweden, for example, voted against euro adoption in a referendum in September 2003 and has yet to participate in ERM II. For their part, EU policy-makers have been fairly cautious about letting new members into the euro club, especially those countries making the economically and financially turbulent transition from central planning to a market economy. Lithuania's application for euro adoption, for example, was rejected in May 2006 after it was deemed to have missed the Maastricht inflation criterion by just 0.2 per cent. As of spring 2009 most of these member states had not set an official target date for joining the euro area (see Table 7.3), although this situation could change as a result of the global financial crisis (see below).

Monetary policy-making under EMU

Prior to the euro's launch, monetary policy in the EU was determined by national central banks (NCBs). Under EMU, NCBs have, along with the ECB, become members of a new monetary authority, which is known as the Eurosystem. The Eurosystem, in turn, is a subset of the European System of Central Banks (ESCB), which also includes the NCBs of EU member states whose currency is not the euro (Art. 107 TEC). The primary responsibility of the Eurosystem is to define and implement euro-area monetary policy (Art. 105 TEC). It also holds and manages the official foreign reserves of the member states, promotes the smooth operation of the European payments and settlements system and plays a central role in euro-area exchange-rate policy. The Eurosystem's overarching objective is to maintain price stability and, without prejudice to this goal, to support the general economic policies of the Community (Art. 105 TEC). The precise meaning of 'price stability' is not defined in the Treaty (see below for the ECB's own definition). The Treaty states that neither the ECB nor the NCBs should seek or take instructions from Community institutions, national governments, or any other body, thus ensuring a high degree of political independence for euro-area monetary policy (Art. 108 TEC).

The responsibility for financial supervision in the euro area falls not to the Eurosystem but to the individual member states, which have agreed to build a single market for financial services and to coordinate their supervisory practices (see Quaglia 2008). The Eurosystem is required under the Treaty to contribute to 'the smooth conduct of policies pursued by the competent authorities relating to the prudential supervision of credit institutions and the stability of the financial system' (Art. 105). To this end, the ECB monitors and regularly reports on financial stability in the euro area. Responsibility for other aspects of financial crisis management and resolution in the EU rests with the national supervisory authorities, central banks, and finance ministries. To deal with cross-border financial crises, the relevant parties have signed a Memorandum of Understanding, which sets out non-binding principles for cooperation, information exchange, and communication.

The Eurosystem is governed by two conjoined bodies: the Governing Council of the ECB, which formulates monetary policy for the euro area, and the Executive Board of the ECB, which prepares meetings of the Governing Council and implements monetary policy decisions (Art. 107 TEC). The Governing Council includes members of the ECB Executive Board and the NCB governors of euro-area member states. When it comes to the setting of short-term interest rates, each member of the Governing Council possesses one vote and decisions are based on a simple majority, although in practice consensus usually applies. The ECB Executive Board has a President, a Vice-President, and four other members. Members of the ECB Executive Board are appointed for an eight-year, non-renewable term of office on the basis of a common accord by member states following consultation with the European Parliament (EP) and the ECB Governing Council (Art. 11, Protocol 18 TEC).

The ECB has legal personality (Art. 107). It can litigate and be litigated against before the European Court of Justice (ECJ) (Protocol Art. 35). Only the ECJ, and only then with the prior approval of the ECB Governing Council, can request the compulsory retirement of an ECB Executive Board member who is guilty of serious misconduct or otherwise in breach of the requirements for the performance of his or her duties (Art. 11, Protocol 18 TEC). As regards other aspects of accountability, the ECB is required to present an annual report on its activities to the Council of Ministers and the EP (Art. 113 TEC). The ECB President is also required to appear before the relevant committees of the Parliament if requested to do so (Art. 113 TEC).

The ECB as an economic actor

Political independence is commonplace for modern central banks, but certain aspects of the ECB's institutional design and approach to monetary policy are not. Firstly, the ECB arguably enjoys a higher degree of independence than many other monetary institutions. Whereas the US Federal Reserve Act (1993), the Bank of Japan Act (1997), and the Bank of England Act (1997) can all be revised by an act of parliament, the statutes of the ECB are embedded within a treaty that can be changed only with the consent of the EU member states subject to the usual process of ratification. Secondly, the ECB's definition of price stability—a rate of inflation of below but close to 2 per cent over the medium term—arguably makes it more transparent than the Federal Reserve and the Bank of Japan, which do not have quantitative definitions of price stability, but less transparent than the Bank of England, which has a simpler inflation target of 2 per cent. Thirdly, the ECB is a comparatively conservative central bank insofar as its statutes attach overriding importance to the pursuit of price stability. In contrast, the US Federal Reserve is required to 'maintain long run growth of the monetary and credit

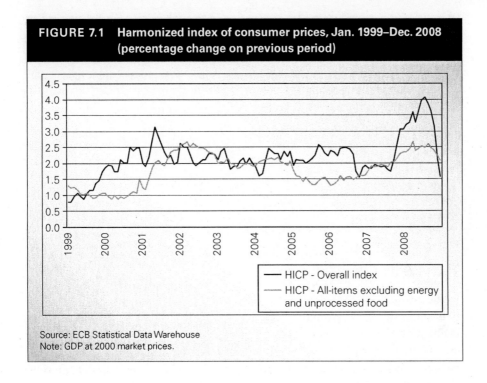

FIGURE 7.1 Harmonized index of consumer prices, Jan. 1999–Dec. 2008 (percentage change on previous period)

— HICP - Overall index

— HICP - All-items excluding energy and unprocessed food

Source: ECB Statistical Data Warehouse
Note: GDP at 2000 market prices.

aggregates commensurate with the economy's long run potential to increase production, so as to promote effectively the goals of maximum employment, stable prices, and moderate long-term interest rates' (Federal Reserve Act, sect. 2a).

The ECB was broadly successful in achieving its objectives during EMU's first decade. The annual rate of consumer price inflation between 1999 and 2008 was 2.2 per cent, which is very close to the ECB's own definition of price stability (see Figure 7.1). Prices were relatively stable throughout this period, with the exception of a temporary surge in inflation in early 2008 due to high oil and food prices. The euro area's growth performance during this period was more disappointing. GDP growth averaged 2.1 per cent between 1999 and 2008, which is low by historical standards and compared with the performance of other industrialized economies (Table 7.4).

The ECB has sought to distance itself from developments in the real economy, blaming the euro area's disappointing growth performance on member states' reluctance to embrace structural reforms that would, *inter alia*, make it easier to adjust to changing economic conditions and to reap the productivity gains associated with new technologies (ECB 2008a: 68). For the most part, political leaders in the EU have largely refrained from public criticism of the ECB out of respect for its political independence. A notable exception has been Nicolas Sarkozy, who courted controversy before and after his election as French President in May 2007 by repeatedly accusing the ECB of paying too much attention to price stability and not enough to the economic situation and the external value of the euro.

TABLE 7.4	Gross domestic product at 2000 market prices (average annual percentage change)				
	1961–1970	**1971–1980**	**1981–1990**	**1991–1998**	**1999–2008**
Euro area	5.3	3.4	2.4	2.2	2.1
UK	2.8	2.0	2.7	2.3	2.6
USA	4.2	3.3	3.2	3.1	2.6
Japan	10.2	4.5	4.0	1.2	1.4

Source: European Commission AMECO Database

The ECB as a political actor

Of the five modes of EU policy-making set out in Chapter 4, monetary policy-making in the euro area is closest to the traditional Community method. The most striking similarities lay in the delegation of significant policy-making powers to the EU level and the creation of a powerful supranational actor, the ECB. Like the Commission, the ECB has a legal personality and the right to formulate opinions, deliver recommendations, and make regulations on certain policies that fall within its sphere of competences. Even more so than the Commission, the ECB's political authority is closely linked to its credibility and technocratic expertise due, in part, to the intense scrutiny of monetary-policy decisions by financial markets.

There are also some major differences between monetary policy-making in the euro area and the traditional Community method. The ECB is a different kind of supranational actor from the Commission. In the first place, the importance attached to central bank independence in the Treaty means that there are fewer checks and balances on the ECB. The EP can force the resignation of the college of Commissioners but, as noted above, it can do little more than invite the ECB President to appear before its committees. In this sense, the EP's formal role in EMU is minor compared to some other areas of EU policy-making. Another distinctive feature of the ECB is its comparatively decentralized decision-making structure, which allows NCB governors and members of the ECB Executive Board to decide on monetary policy in the ECB Governing Council.

A striking feature of the ECB's evolution as a political actor over the last decade has been its uneven and at times uneasy relationship with other EU institutions. A surprising development has been the ECB's dealings with the EP's 'monetary dialogue'. Under this informal arrangement, the ECB President (or other members of the Executive Council) appears before the EP's Economic and Monetary Affairs Committee four times per year to discuss the economic situation and policy challenges facing the euro area. Although expectations concerning the monetary dialogue were low, it has proved to be an institutional win-win, giving the ECB an opportunity to

TABLE 7.5   Overview of ECB Governing Council rotating voting system

| | | No. of NCB governors in the ECB Governing Council | | | | | | | | | |
| | | Stage 1 (22 members) | | | | Stage 2 (22–7 members) | | | | | |
		18	19	20	21	22	23	24	25	26	27
ECB Executive Board	No. of voting rights/ no. of governors	6/6	6/6	6/6	6/6	6/6	6/6	6/6	6/6	6/6	6/6
NCB governors 1st group	No. of voting rights/ no. of governors	5/5	4/5	4/5	4/5	4/5	4/5	4/5	4/5	4/5	4/5
NCB governors 2nd group	No. of voting rights/ no. of governors	10/13	11/14	11/15	11/16	8/11	8/12	8/12	8/13	8/13	8/14
NCB governors 3rd group	No. of voting rights/ no. of governors	n/a	n/a	n/a	n/a	3/6	3/6	3/7	3/7	3/8	3/8
Σ NCB voting rights		15	15	15	15	15	15	15	15	15	15
Σ total voting rights		21	21	21	21	21	21	21	21	21	21

Source: based on ECB (2003)
Note: NCB governors are ranked according to a weighted average of a member state's share in euro-area GDP at market prices and its share of the total assets of the aggregate balance sheet of monetary financial institutions and divided into groups on this basis. For example, the NCB governors of the top 5 ranking economies join the first group.

demonstrate its respect for the EU's directly-elected chamber and the EP a chance to (be seen to) hold the ECB to account.

A low point in the ECB's inter-institutional relations occurred in 2000 when the ECJ overturned the bank's decision to establish its own internal anti-fraud scheme rather than leave this matter to the European Anti-Fraud Office (OLAF), which monitors the financial dealings of other Community bodies, offices, and agencies. In its defence, the ECB had argued, firstly, that it had a legal personality that was distinct from bodies, offices, and agencies of the Community and, secondly, that opening its doors to OLAF contravened the ECB's independence, as guaranteed by Article 108 TEC. The ECJ's OLAF judgment of 2003 rejected both arguments, concluding that the ECB's legal personality was not distinct from that of the Community and that the Treaty's provisions on independence related specifically to monetary policy and did not 'have the consequence of separating it entirely from the European Community and exempting it from every rule of Community law'. As Goebel (2006) argues, this judgment is a landmark one for EMU as it establishes the principle that the ECB is an intrinsic part of the Community and not, as some have argued, legally separate from it. The 2007 Lisbon Treaty (ToL), will reinforce this point by including the ECB under the list of EU institutions (Art. 18 ToL).

The relationship between the ECB and the NCBs has also evolved during the first decade. As the euro area enlarges, more and more NCB governors will join the ECB Governing Council. Fears that this might drown out the voices of the ECB Executive Board prompted member states to agree on a new voting system for monetary policy decisions, based on rotation. This agreement, which was ratified in May 2004 but which is unlikely to enter into force until euro-area membership exceeds eighteen countries, will cap the total number of votes on the ECB Governing Council at twenty-one. Executive Board members will retain their six voting rights permanently, with the remaining fifteen voting rights being rotated among NCB governors according to a formula described in Table 7.5.

It remains to be seen whether this new voting system will suffice. Making monetary policy by committee can lead to better-informed and less ideologically driven decision-making (Blinder 2007) but it can also slow the speed at which a central bank reacts to crises (Gros 2003). With twenty-one voting members, the ECB Governing Council will still be considerably larger than its counterparts: the US Federal Reserve Open Markets Committee has twelve voting members, compared with nine on the Bank of England's Monetary Policy Committee and eight on the Policy Board of the Bank of Japan.

Economic policy-making under EMU

As discussed in Chapter 4, economic policy-making in EMU is at the forefront of the EU's efforts to promote policy coordination. In contrast to the monetary sphere, there has been no significant delegation of economic policy-making powers to the

EU level under EMU. Instead, it falls to Ecofin (and, as discussed below, the Euro-group) to build consensus on the priorities for economic policy in the euro area and to the individual member states to decide how they plan to meet these priorities. The Treaty's principal instrument of coordination is the BEPGs, which take the form of non-binding guidelines from Ecofin to member states on macroeconomic policies and structural reforms. The Commission's modest but nonetheless important role in this set-up is to evaluate member states' economic-policy plans and to monitor their implementation on behalf of Ecofin. In the event of non-compliance, the Commission can sound the alarm but it ultimately falls to Ecofin to issue legally non-binding recommendations for corrective action against the country in question. These recommendations can be understood as a form of peer pressure that is designed to name, shame, and blame the member state into reversing its economic policies.

The Treaty prohibits member states from running excessive budget deficits (Art. 104 TEC), defined as annual government borrowing in excess of 3 per cent of GDP and general government debt in excess of 60 per cent of GDP (Protocol 20 TEC). The Commission has primary responsibility for monitoring member states' budgetary policies, although it ultimately falls to Ecofin to decide by qualified majority vote, on the basis of a Commission recommendation, whether an excessive deficit exists. As in the case of the BEPGs, Ecofin applies peer pressure in the form of legally non-binding recommendations against member states that fail to correct an excessive deficit. In the case of euro-area members, Ecofin can also impose financial penalties and fines but such measures can only be used *in extremis*. The timetable for enforcing the excessive deficit procedure is set out in the 'corrective arm' of the SGP. The 'preventive arm' of this agreement encourages member states to pursue balanced budgets over the medium term.

EMU and policy coordination

How can we explain member states' reluctance to apply the traditional Community method to economic policy-making under EMU? For some scholars, the explanation lies in the desire of the framers of the Treaty to protect the political independence of the ECB by keeping economic decision-making on a decentralized footing (Dyson 2000). Buti et al. (2003: 101) emphasize sovereignty concerns, arguing that the EU's current provisions on economic-policy coordination reflect the limits of what can be achieved given member states' limited desire for deeper integration in this field. On a similar note, Hix (2005: 38) argues that 'if member states were serious about policy reform in a particular area, then the classic EU method would probably be the most efficient way of achieving the policy goals'.

An alternative viewpoint is that new modes of EU governance may be functionally suited to EMU (Hodson and Maher 2001). From an economic perspective, a decentralized approach to policy coordination may be desirable if it gives member states greater leeway to use national budgetary policy to adjust to country-specific shocks. Likewise, allowing member states to tailor specific reform measures to the institutional specificities of national product, labour, and capital markets may be preferable to a one-size-fits-all approach. From a legal perspective, soft law may be preferable to hard law when policy goals lack precision and when the probability of revising these objectives in the future is high (Hodson and Maher 2004).

How has EMU's experiment with new modes of EU governance fared over its first decade? From a bird's eye perspective, the early years of EMU coincided with a sustained improvement in the euro-area's public finances, with a budget surplus being recorded in 2000 for the first time since the early 1970s. In the structural domain, EMU has acted as a powerful catalyst for financial integration. As regards product- and labour-market reforms, member states implemented a series of measures to make employment protection legislation less stringent, to raise average retirement ages, and to introduce greater competition in some sectors, most noticeably telecommunications (see Chapters 6, 11, and 16). These reforms contributed to rising labour-force participation rates, falling unemployment, and, in some sectors, falling prices (ECB 2008a). Progress in product- and labour-market reform has also been matched by significant progress in financial-market integration. In spite of these achievements, serious difficulties were encountered with the implementation of the SGP and the BEPGs in their original incarnations.

The problems with the SGP began when some member states failed to reduce their government borrowing sufficiently during the economic upturn of the late 1990s in spite of periodic pleas to do so by the Commission and Ecofin. As a consequence, several governments, including those of France and Germany, entered the economic slowdown of 2001–2 without having first achieved medium-term budgetary positions of close to balance or in surplus. This deficiency in the preventive arm of the pact soon caused problems for the corrective arm, as rising expenditure and falling revenues brought government borrowing in these countries in excess of 3 per cent of GDP. This put Ecofin in the awkward position of encouraging member states to reduce their government borrowing so as to comply with the SGP in the knowledge that such measures could prolong the economic slowdown by further dampening aggregate demand.

The resulting tensions came to a head in November 2003 when Ecofin met to consider a set of Commission recommendations against France and Germany under Article 104 of the Treaty. The first recommendation noted French and German failure to take effective action to correct excessive deficit in spite of earlier recommendations (Art. 104(8) TEC). The second recommendation called on Ecofin to 'give notice' to France and Germany to undertake specific deficit reductions within a specified time frame (Art. 104(8) TEC). These recommendations were significant because if adopted they would have raised the distinct possibility that the pecuniary sanctions set out under Article 104(11) of the Treaty would be employed for the very first time. After lengthy negotiations, a group of mainly smaller member states with a reputation for fiscal discipline, including Austria, Belgium, The Netherlands, and Spain, that favoured the recommendations was outvoted by a coalition of mainly large member states, which included four countries that were themselves in a state of excessive deficit, France, Germany, Italy, and Portugal. Having failed to find a qualified majority in support of the Commission's recommendations, Ecofin voted to leave disciplinary procedures against France and Germany 'in abeyance' for the time being. The ECJ's *Stability and Growth Pact* judgment in July 2004 overturned this decision, but the damage to the credibility of EMU's fiscal rules was already done (Maher 2004).

Member governments pushed through a number of important structural reforms during the early years of EMU but the overall pace of reform was insufficient to allay concerns about the adaptability of euro-area product and labour markets. These concerns were compounded by the slow response of relative prices and wages to economic conditions in the euro area and the persistence of cross-country inflation and growth differentials (Commission 2006a). The BEPGs were partly to blame for this slow pace of structural reform. Policy-makers at the EU and national level were reluctant to use the guidelines as an instrument to name, shame, and blame reform laggards and the accumulation of an excessive number of guidelines made it difficult to establish clear reform priorities (Deroose et al. 2008).

The March 2005 reforms to the SGP and Lisbon Strategy continued rather than abandoned the EU's experiment with new modes of EU policy-making. The revised pact is a 'softer' version of the original agreement in two key respects. Firstly, the importance of peer pressure over pecuniary sanctions has been increased by allowing Ecofin more time to issue non-binding recommendations for corrective action before resorting to financial penalties and fines. This makes it highly unlikely that financial penalties will be imposed on euro-area member states, thus reducing the possibility of a budgetary stand-off between the EU and national governments of the kind that led to the collapse of the original pact in November 2003. Secondly, greater flexibility has been introduced into the pact's preventive arm by replacing the common goal of achieving a budgetary position of close to balance or in surplus with country-specific medium-term budgetary objectives. Both the revised SGP and the relaunched Lisbon Strategy promote a more decentralized approach to peer pressure. In the case of the former, the European Council encouraged national parliaments to pay closer attention to member states' stability programmes. In the case of the latter, the European Council invited member states to involve national parliaments and other relevant stakeholders in the preparation of annually updated national reform programmes.

Initial reports that the March 2005 reforms had irretrievably weakened the SGP were overstated (Feldstein 2005). France and Germany recorded a marked improvement in their fiscal positions in 2006, allowing Ecofin to revoke the excessive deficit procedure against these countries in the first half of 2007. Buoyant economic growth undoubtedly played a role here but so too did a renewed commitment to the corrective arm of the pact, particularly in Germany which increased value-added tax (VAT) in January 2007 in an effort to gets its budgetary house in order. The relaunched Lisbon Strategy also fared better than some had expected (Pisani-Ferry and Sapir 2007). In December 2007, the Commission (2007d) reported modest increases in potential growth and the lowest unemployment since the mid-1980s as tentative evidence that the EU's economic-reform agenda was beginning to bear fruit.

The emergence of the Eurogroup

A key piece of EMU's governance jigsaw is the Eurogroup. This informal body brings euro-area finance ministers in advance of the Ecofin to discuss the economic situation and shared policy challenges. One finance minister and one adviser from each euro-area country attend the Eurogroup along with the President of the ECB and the Commissioner for economic and monetary affairs. Meetings are confidential and, aside from the occasional communiqué, the Eurogroup produces few visible policy outputs.

The Eurogroup's unusual institutional design reflects a Franco-German compromise on the need for economic policy coordination under EMU (Pisani-Ferry 2006). In advance of EMU, France repeatedly made the case for a *gouvernement économique* to steer economic decision-making under EMU and provide a political counterweight to the ECB (Howarth 2007*b*). Germany consistently opposed such proposals for fear that they were intended as a covert attack on the independence of the ECB. In a deal struck at the European Council in December 1997, member states agreed that euro-area finance ministers could meet informally among themselves but that this body would meet behind closed doors and have no decision-making powers. The Eurogroup's working methods have been described by Puetter (2006) as a form of 'deliberative intergovernmentalism'. He argues that, in the absence of formal decision-making responsibilities, the Eurogroup can exchange information on shared policy challenges and reflect on national policy positions in a way that would not be possible in a busy bargaining chamber such as Ecofin.

Over the past decade, the Eurogroup has emerged as a powerful caucus within the Ecofin (Pisani-Ferry 2006). Today, it is the Eurogroup, not Ecofin, which takes the lead in monitoring euro-area members' compliance with the SGP. The Eurogroup also takes a keen interest in the Lisbon Strategy, structuring its regular discussions of structural-reform challenges around the European Commission's annual progress report on growth and jobs. In some circumstances Eurogroup discussions have had implications for the EU as a whole, thus adding to the political costs of remaining outside the euro area. A case in point is the March 2005 reform of the SGP, which was adopted in Ecofin on the basis of a deal that had been brokered in the Eurogroup.

The switch from a rotating to a permanent chair has been a key factor in the Eurogroup's development. In the early years of EMU, the chair was filled by the President of Ecofin or the finance minister of the next euro-area member in line for this post in cases where a non-euro-area country held the EU Council presidency. In 2005, the Eurogroup elected Jean-Claude Juncker for a two-year term of office, which was renewed in 2007 and again in 2009. Though his penchant for provocative public statements has caused controversy on occasion, Juncker has arguably increased the political profile of the Eurogroup thanks to his considerable political experience (he was a signatory of the TEU and combines the roles of finance minister and prime minister of Luxembourg).

The Eurogroup's track record as a deliberative body is mixed. On some issues, such as fiscal responses to high oil prices, euro-area finance ministers have managed to pursue a relatively coherent line (Pisani-Ferry 2006). On other issues, including the external value of the euro, policy lines have been agreed but not always adhered to by euro-area finance ministers (van den Noord et al. 2008). Furthermore, periodic public criticism of ECB monetary policy by some euro-area finance ministers over the past decade shows that the Eurogroup has not always succeeded in its efforts to keep discussions of the macroeconomic policy mix behind closed doors. The enlargement of the euro area may also have reduced the intimacy of the Eurogroup by adding five new ministers (each with his or her own adviser) to the circle since 2001. There may also be a link between the formalization of the Eurogroup and its limitations as a deliberative body since, as Begg (2008*a*) argues, the dynamics of debate and the value of peer pressure will change as the Eurogroup expands.

The formalization of the Eurogroup is likely to continue for the time being. Under the ToL, the Eurogroup will be officially recognized, although its precise legal status will not be defined (Protocol on the Eurogroup, ToL). The Treaty will also recognise the role of the Eurogroup President, whose term of office will be extended from two to two-and-a-half years. The Eurogroup will also be given de-facto decision-making powers by allowing the finance ministers of member states whose currency is the euro to adopt those aspects of the BEPGs that relate generally to the euro area (Art. 139(2) ToL). The fact that the ToL did not go further in this area is no surprise: its framers were content to 'cut and paste' the Constitutional Treaty's provisions on economic-policy coordination, which in essence sought to preserve the status quo in this highly sensitive area of policy-making (see Puetter 2007; and Hodson 2009).

The euro area as a global actor

The euro is a major global currency that is second only to the US dollar. In 2007, for example, the euro accounted for 27 per cent of the foreign-exchange reserves held by the world's central banks compared with 64 per cent for the US dollar, 4.7 per cent for the British pound and 2.9 per cent for the Japanese yen (ECB 2008*b*). The euro also serves as anchor or reference currency for the exchange-rate policy of forty countries (Commission 2008*e*). Although economists are divided on whether the euro will ever overtake the dollar, the euro area has already become a major presence on the global economic stage (Cohen 2003; Menzie and Frankel 2008).

The Treaty says little about the euro area's global economic role. Perhaps the most important provision concerns the formulation of exchange-rate policy, which is a shared responsibility of the Ecofin and the ECB (Art. 111 TEC). This arrangement gives the ECB a more powerful role in exchange-rate policy than many other central banks; the US Federal Reserve and the Bank of Japan must defer to their respective finance ministries on such matters. Interventions in exchange-rate markets have been a rare occurrence under EMU. In September and November 2000, the ECB intervened to boost the euro following a sustained depreciation in the value of the currency, but it resisted attempts to take action in response to the euro's marked appreciation against the US dollar after mid-2002.

In December 1998, the European Council in Vienna acknowledged the 'global responsibilities' of the euro and the necessity of speaking with one voice on international issues. In spite of this commitment, the euro area's representation in multilateral financial institutions remains fragmented and incoherent. A case in point concerns euro-area representation at the International Monetary Fund (IMF). Whereas economic giants such as the United States appoint a single Executive Director to the IMF Executive Board, the body that runs the IMF on a daily basis, euro-area countries send national representatives only. This picture is further complicated by the fact that only France and Germany make direct appointments to the IMF Executive Board, with the remaining euro-area members represented by an Executive Director who speaks for a constituency of countries from both inside and outside the EU. The Netherlands, for example, belongs to a constituency that includes Ukraine and Israel, while Spain is grouped with Mexico, Venezuela, and several other Latin American countries. The complexity of these arrangements makes it difficult for euro-area countries to exert collective influence in the IMF in spite of the global significance of the single currency.

EMU and the global financial crisis

The world economy experienced financial turmoil in 2007 and 2008 on a scale that had not been witnessed since the Wall Street Crash of 1929. The trigger for this turmoil was the collapse of the US sub-prime-loan market in August 2007 after borrowers who had been granted loans in spite of their poor credit ratings struggled to make repayments as house prices plummeted. Global losses from this crisis—around $1.4 trillion according to the International Monetary Fund (2008: 14)—sowed the seeds for a global credit crunch as inter-bank markets froze and loans to businesses and individuals dried up. These events took their toll on the real economy, with global growth experiencing a sharp slowdown in 2008 while the USA, Japan, and, for the very first time, the euro area entered recession.

Although the global financial crisis had not run its course at the time of writing (summer 2009), the turmoil illustrated some of the strengths and weaknesses of the EU's system of economic and financial governance. Above all, it demonstrated Europe's vulnerability to global economic developments in an age of financial globalization. The credit crunch that began in the USA in August 2007 claimed a number of European casualties, including Northern Rock, the first British bank to experience a run since 1866. Similarly, the banking crisis that took hold in the USA in September 2008 spread to the EU within a matter of days, prompting authorities in Belgium, France, Germany, Luxembourg, The Netherlands, and the UK to rescue distressed financial institutions.

The crisis also laid bare the limitations of policy coordination among sovereign governments. In September 2008, the Irish government unexpectedly announced a 100-per-cent guarantee of deposits in the country's six largest banks. Although this move helped to restore confidence in Irish banks in the short term, it temporarily destabilized the British banking system after tens of thousands of savers in the UK and Ireland transferred their deposits from British-owned to Irish-owned banks to benefit from the more generous guarantees. Fearful of such beggar-thy-neighbour policies, several EU member states, including Austria, Denmark, Greece, and Slovenia, moved quickly to guarantee bank deposits. Germany's decision to do likewise was especially controversial, coming as it did within hours of a summit at which the leaders of the four largest EU economies had called on member states to 'ensure that potential cross-border effects of national decisions are taken into consideration' (European G8 members 2008).

In spite of these limitations, the EU showed a surprising capacity for coordination in relation to other aspects of financial crisis management. In October 2008, the heads of state and government of the euro area invited the UK Prime Minister, Gordon Brown, to an emergency summit to agree a rescue plan for EU banks. Under this plan, which was later endorsed by the full European Council, member states agreed to recapitalize and, if necessary, take shares in European banks. Although in summer 2009 it is too early to tell whether the EU's bank bail-out plan will work as intended, it was widely praised at the time of its launch as an innovative and decisive policy response. The plan also emboldened the EU's efforts to find a global solution to the financial crisis. Within days of the European Council, Nicolas Sarkozy and José Manuel Barroso flew to Camp David to meet with US President George Bush to agree plans for a series of international summits on the future of the global financial architecture.

The EU was less sure-footed in its initial response to the real-economy effects of the global financial turmoil. The European Recovery Plan, adopted at the European Council in December 2008, committed the EU and its member states to an immediate budgetary stimulus equivalent to 1.5 per cent of EU GDP. Although the European Recovery Plan broke new ground in some respects (it is the first joint attempt by EU member states to stimulate aggregate demand) it fell short in others (the proposed fiscal stimulus is small when compared to the efforts of other countries, such as the United States, and it makes little attempt to share the burden of fiscal adjustment among member states). A source of significant political tension in this regard was Germany's reluctance to consider significant tax cuts and expenditure increases. Although such reluctance is understandable in view of Germany's efforts to reduce government borrowing following the breakdown of the original SGP, it left the euro area's largest economy open to accusations of fiscal free-riding on the recovery pro-grammes of others countries. An open question at this juncture concerns the fate of the revised SGP. To date, member states have stood by the March 2005 reform, but the flexibility of the new-look SGP will be stretched to its limit as budget deficits rise sharply in response to worsening economic conditions.

In the monetary sphere, the ECB moved quickly in August 2007 to inject liquidity into monetary markets. This was followed in October 2008 by the first in a series of interest-rate cuts that took the ECB's base rate to 1%, its lowest ever level. The ECB also under took unconventional monetary policies, including a scheme launder in June 2009 to purchase €60 billion worth of covered bonds (debt securities backed by mortgages or public sector loans). Time will tell whether the ECB's monetary policies during the global financial crisis were appropriate but this judgement is sure to have a significant impact on the credibility and reputation of this fledgling monetary authority.

The global financial turmoil is likely to serve as a catalyst for change in the area of EU financial-market policy. In March 2009, a high-level group convened by the European Commission and led by Jacques de Larosière, a former Managing Director of the IMF, called for a radical overhaul of the EU's financial architecture. The Com-mission, and later Ecofin, endorsed the thrust of these recommendations, agreeing *inter alia* to create a European Systemic Risk Board (ESRB) to oversee financial stabil-ity in the EU as a whole. The work of the ESRB will be overseen by a General Board, which will include the NCB governors of the 27 member states and the President and Vice President of the ECB. Although the five details of this reform is to be worked out, the EU's involvement in financial-market supervision is likely to increase in the coming years.

It is premature in mid-2009 to assess the long-term impact of the global financial turmoil on EMU. On the one hand, a prolonged period of economic underperform-ance by the euro area could damage the project's credibility and fuel political tensions between euro-area members. On the other hand, a heightened period of instability in the global economy could increase the attractiveness of EMU as an economic and financial safe haven among EU member states that have not yet joined the euro and among European countries that have not yet joined the EU, such as Iceland.

Conclusions

The traditional Community method, as argued in Chapter 4, has waned as EU member states have sought alternatives to centralized and hierarchical modes of policy-making. Nowhere is this more evident than in relation to EMU, where member states have delegated monetary policy to a new type of Community insti-tution, the ECB, and pioneered the use of policy coordination in the area of fiscal policy and structural reform. This chapter has taken stock of this experiment after a decade of EMU.

In the monetary domain, the ECB's generally impressive but occasionally idiosyncratic performance as a central bank shows that autonomous operating agencies can make an important contribution to EU policy-making. However, concerns that such agencies could fragment the EU's institutional structures are reflected in the ECB's occasionally strained relationship with the EU's legal order. In the economic domain, EMU's experiment with policy coordination continues, with March 2005 reforms 'softening' rather than 'hardening' the SGP and the Lisbon Strategy. The Eurogroup is slowly moving in the opposite direction of travel, having emerged from the shadows of Ecofin to become an influential and increasingly formalized institution. In the external domain, euro-area members have agreed to speak with one voice but their representation in financial institutions and forums remains fragmented.

Looking to the future, ToL is of limited relevance for EMU as it will introduce only minor changes in the macroeconomic domain. A more serious concern relates to the global financial turmoil triggered by the collapse of the US sub-prime-loan market in 2007. The after-effects of this shock in the global financial system and in the real economy provided the sternest test to date of EMU's system of monetary and economic policy-making.

Note

1   Thanks to Deborah Mabbett, Ivo Maes, Imelda Maher, Helen Wallace, Mark Pollack, and Alasdair Young for helpful comments on a draft of this chapter. The usual disclaimer applies.

 FURTHER READING

For an introduction to the economics of EMU, see De Grauwe (2007). Dyson and Featherstone (1999), Moravcsik (1998), McNamara (1998), and Jones (2002) explore the political dynamics underpinning EMU's creation. Schelkle (2006) revisits some of the seminal contributions to the debate on euro-area governance. Dyson (2006) explores the enlargement of the euro area. Hodson and Quaglia (2009) consider the impact of the global financial crisis on EMU and the EU.

De Grauwe, P. (2007), *The Economics of Monetary Union*, 7th edn. (Oxford: Oxford University Press).

Dyson, K. (2006) (ed.), *Enlarging the Euro Area: External Empowerment and Domestic Transformation in East Central Europe* (Oxford: Oxford University Press).

Dyson, K., and Featherstone, K. (1999), *The Road to Maastricht: Negotiating Economic and Monetary Union* (Oxford: Oxford University Press).

Hodson, D., and Quaglia, L. (2009) (eds.), 'European Perspectives on the Global Financial Crisis', *Journal of Common Market Studies*, 47/4: 939–1128 (special issue).

Jones, E. (2002), *The Politics of Economic and Monetary Union: Integration and Idiosyncrasy* (Boulder, CO: Rowman & Littlefield).

McNamara, K. (1998), *The Currency of Ideas: Monetary Politics in the European Union* (Ithaca, NY: Cornell University Press).

Moravcsik, A. (1998), *The Choice for Europe: Social Purpose and State Power from Messina to Maastricht* (Ithaca, NY: Cornell University Press).

Schelkle, W. (2006) (ed.), 'Economic Governance in EMU Revisited', *Journal of Common Market Studies*, 44/4: 669–864 (special issue).

CHAPTER 8

The Common Agricultural Policy

The Fortress Challenged

Christilla Roederer-Rynning

▌ Summary

Today's common agricultural policy (CAP) is a policy in flux. While still absorbing a large slice of the European Union (EU) budget, the CAP today bears little resemblance to the arcane and highly segmented system of market support of the 1960s. Many agricultural policy issues have become so tied up with trade, environmental, public health, and now energy issues that the CAP is losing its narrow sectoral character. The machinery producing CAP legislation has become more differentiated and open as competing logics of intervention increasingly drive the policy process, and the core character of farm issues and sometimes even farm players is changing. The serial reform of the CAP in the past two decades has highlighted the pivotal role of direct payments to producers, making the CAP less market-distorting and better able to channel the changing expectations of European consumers. The CAP is still a fortress; but its walls are lower.

Introduction

The CAP was established in a European Economic Community (EEC) of only six member states, which were recovering from severe post-war food shortages and were worried about the sustainability of food production.[1] In its classic version, which remained essentially intact until the late 1980s, the CAP was a system of market support based on guaranteed prices within the Community, and import levies and export subsidies *vis-à-vis* the rest of the world. This system turned the EEC into a leading agricultural power in the world. It also bred tremendous dissatisfaction, as it became very expensive to sustain, had an economically perverse impact on European agriculture and world agricultural markets, and grew out of touch with the expectations of European taxpayers and consumers.

The five enlargements that the EU has undergone since the 1970s have further added dimensions of controversy and issues of appropriateness. The accession of the UK in 1973 enabled this long-standing critic of the CAP to advocate reform from within and setting new policy priorities on the EU agenda. Since the European Free Trade Association (EFTA) enlargement in 1995, it has received support from Sweden in its quest for agricultural trade liberalization. The enlargement to Spain and Portugal in 1986 revealed the regressive bias of the CAP (which is centred on northern products such as cereals or milk) and raised issues of budgetary redistribution as the structural funds doubled to meet the needs of the new members (see Chapter 9). These issues have become pressing today as the poorer central and east European members(CEECs) are significant recipients of EU regional-policy subsidies.[2] The EU is now a union of twenty-seven member states, whose agricultural structures, social make-up, and basic views on economic policy differ greatly. It is therefore not surprising that, while greeted as a bridge to bring the European peoples closer together, the CAP today is often chastised in the public debate as a monument to economic irrationality and a stumbling-block in the enlarged EU.

The primary objective of this chapter is to understand the processes that make the CAP. The chapter pays special attention to how the Community method (see Chapter 4) functions in agriculture and how it upheld the walls of fortress CAP. Policy substance will also receive attention, though primarily with a view to highlighting how policy shapes politics and how the process of change has affected the type of policy outputs.

It is clear from this perspective that, contrary to widespread popular perceptions, the CAP is a policy in flux. Change has occurred in steps, first in the McSharry reform in 1992, then in Agenda 2000 (1999) and the Midterm Review of the CAP (2003), and lately in the so-called Health Check of the CAP (2008). Today's CAP bears little resemblance to the system of the 1960s, if only because the controversial device of price support has been largely replaced by direct payments to producers. Introduced in 1992 as a compensation for price cuts, these payments now represent the bulk of EU support in agriculture under the label of single farm payments. They are *the* instrument through which the demands of the non-farm world are channelled into agricultural policy: whether to 'green the CAP', to 'decouple' farm support from production, or to 'simplify the CAP'. Under these farm payments, EU expenditure related to traditional farm concerns has been stabilized while the total EU budget has increased: total CAP spending (including newer rural development concerns) thus represented 43 per cent of the EU budget in 2008, down from over 70 per cent in 1980 (see Chapter 9),[3] and CAP support has become less market-distorting.

Less obviously, but perhaps more important for the purpose of the present volume, the policy-making processes underpinning the CAP have changed too. Descriptions of the CAP as a closed policy community powered by a single logic of market intervention are no longer accurate. The CAP has evolved into a complex policy regime driven by competing logics. Internally, policy-making is now bifurcated between traditional market concerns and emerging rural-development concerns (the latter represented about one-fifth of the CAP budget in 2008; see funding for pillar 2 measures in 2008 in endnote 3). Externally, an increasing number of linkages to other policy domains urge CAP policy-makers to integrate, and respond to, an ever-broadening variety of challenges. CAP issues, which once were agricultural in the narrow sectoral sense, have become tied up with trade issues (see Chapter 16), environmental issues (see Chapter 13), health and safety issues (see Chapter 14), and more recently with energy issues (see Chapter 15). This means that the CAP now reflects a combination of heterogeneous policy-making processes, which only partly rely on the Community method and have altered the way in which the Community method itself is conducted in the core CAP concern areas.

Building fortress CAP: from fragmentation to compromise

The CAP was not set in stone from the beginning. It was born against a background of legal ambiguity and political fragmentation. A compromise nevertheless emerged in the 1960s in the course of protracted intergovernmental negotiations. It arose at the crossroads between ideas and power, where the modernizing ambitions of new European élites met the political and economic realities of post-war Europe. This compromise set the political parameters within which the Community method developed in agriculture, to become the foundation of fortress CAP.

Implausible origins

The 1957 Treaty of Rome (EEC) called for EEC policy-makers to establish a common agricultural policy with a view to ensuring fair incomes for farmers and reasonable prices for consumers, by establishing common market organizations (CMOs) and applying the principles of: market unity (i.e. single agricultural prices within the

Community); community preference (i.e. common market products protected against low-price imports); and financial solidarity (i.e. collective responsibility of member states for the financial consequences of the CAP). The Treaty thus envisaged a combination of negative integration ('extension of the Common Market to agriculture and trade in agricultural products', Art. 38.1 EEC), and positive integration ('establishment of a common agricultural policy among the member states', Art. 38.4 EEC).

Observers have often noted the ambivalence and open-endedness of the parts of the EEC Treaty devoted to agriculture (e.g. Neville-Rolfe 1984: 194). On one point, however, the Treaty was clear: this concerned the institutional rules to be followed in agriculture. There was no doubt that member states would be the protagonists of the common agricultural policy. The Treaty called on member states to formulate the guidelines of the common agriculture policy in a post-ratification conference to be convened by the European Commission (Art. 43.1 EEC). The legislative procedure applying to agriculture, consultation (Art.43.2 EEC), also highlighted the preponderance of intergovernmentalism by making the Council of Ministers sole legislator. Potential competitors like the European Parliament (EP) or national parliaments were excluded from policy-making: the former was granted only a consultative role, while the use of regulations directly applicable in the member states deprived national parliaments of any role in the policy-making process.

Beyond these procedural issues, ambiguity characterized treaty provisions on the substantive objectives of the CAP. The Treaty called on policy-makers: to restructure the farm sector in order to free resources for the rest of the economy *while* stabilizing markets; and to protect farm income *while* securing reasonable prices in supplies to consumers (Box 8.1). It further identified the need to take account of 'the particular nature of agricultural activity, which results from the social structure of agriculture and from structural and natural disparities between the various agricultural regions' (Art. 39.2). Two policy tasks were thus sketched out for the CAP: first, to organize common agricultural markets (market policy measures); and second, to promote modern farm structures, to support the professionalization of farmers, and to remedy regional disparities (structural policy measures). Yet, how these tasks should be accomplished remained a perplexing issue and reconciling competing objectives placed policy-makers in a situation where they had to square the circle.

The authors of the EEC Treaty were not sloppy or badly informed; they just recorded the reality of political fragmentation in late 1950s western Europe. In a key country like France, the formidable farm lobbies that later became so intimately involved in European farm policy-making were embroiled in internecine conflicts (Wright 1953). Jealousies and conflicts regarding farmers' status, political ideology, commodity specialization, and specific market situations aroused scepticism about the mobilization potential of peasantry. There was no consensus either among the founding member states as to what the EEC should do in agriculture. The EC6 differed greatly in terms of their export orientations, their degrees of self-sufficiency, and the political clout of their national farm constituencies; and while all six founding members used market control, the forms, degrees, and objectives of national intervention

BOX 8.1	The five objectives of the CAP, Art. 33 TEC (ex Art. 39 EEC)

- To increase agricultural production by promoting technical progress and by ensuring the rational development of agricultural production and optimum utilization of the factors of production, in particular labour;
- *thus*, to ensure a fair standard of living for the agricultural community, in particular by increasing the individual earnings of persons engaged in agriculture;
- to stabilize markets;
- to assure availability of supplies; and
- to ensure that supplies reach consumers at reasonable prices.

Note: I am indebted to Rob Peters and Robert Ackrill for pointing out to me that the second objective starts with 'thus' (emphasis mine). This may suggest that the authors of the Treaty did not foresee objective 2 (to ensure a fair standard of living for the agricultural community) as a stand-alone objective, but as one linked to, and to be achieved through, the promotion of technical progress and the modernization of farm structures (objective 1). This point is important to remember in light of the subsequent evolution of the CAP into a system of price support, which paid only lip-service to farm modernization.

in the farm sector varied significantly from one country to another (Tracy 1989). Legal ambiguity thus reflected the absence of political consensus.

Modernization co-opted

A policy regime nonetheless emerged in the course of the 1960s.[4] In accordance with treaty requirements, a conference took place in Stresa in June 1958 to discuss policy guidelines where the EC6 broadly reasserted the dual mission of the CAP. In the following years, however, a series of intergovernmental negotiations set the CAP onto a quite different course, whose essence is encapsulated in three main points:

- first, a policy of price support: intergovernmental deals in 1962 and 1964 guaranteed European farmers high prices for their produce while keeping world competitors away from the European markets through a system of variable import levies and export subsidies;
- second, a downgrading of structural policy: Commissioner Mansholt's 1968 plan to develop an ambitious policy to restructure European agriculture was watered down and structural policy remained safely anchored at the national level with the exception of a handful of relatively modest measures; and
- third, a ring-fencing of CAP guarantee expenditure: the decision in 1970 to regard agriculture guarantee expenditure for market support as 'compulsory expenditure' (i.e. expenditure necessarily resulting from the treaties or from acts adopted in accordance with them) de facto removed the new agricultural policy budget from the purview of the EP (see Chapter 9).

Clearly, far from a balanced mix of policy considerations, a single logic of market intervention prevailed in the 1960s. The protection of farm incomes had won over other considerations such as consumer concerns (insofar as prospects of 'reasonable prices for consumers' were forsaken) or the restructuring of the farm sector. Thus, European farm affairs underwent an 'agrarian turn' in the 1960s, which must be properly acknowledged (Roederer-Rynning 2003*a*).

What explains this turn of events? There is evidence that Germany's influence was decisive in securing high prices on cereals—and through knock-on effects on dairy and meat products (Pinder 1991; Fennell 1997; Moravcsik 1998). It is less clear, however, why European leaders committed themselves one-sidedly to a policy of market intervention. A policy belief in the 'exceptionality' of agriculture may have justified a high degree of state assistance in this sector (Coleman et al. 1997; Skogstad 1998; Moyer and Josling 2002). European élites may have wished to avoid the repetition of interwar political turbulences by reducing the gap between urban and rural incomes and thus the potential support for extremist political movements from rural areas (Majone 1995*b*; Rieger 2005; Knudsen 2009). National politicians may have been happy to use EEC institutions to shield essentially clientelistic relations from public scrutiny (Vaubel 1986), without intending ever to cede core structural policy competences.

Conflicts among farmers and swords-crossing between national politicians and farm groups suggest yet another interpretation: the CAP of the 1960s also represented the price that modernizing European élites had to pay for securing the support of ordinary farmers and reluctant rural notables. In the 1950s, agriculture was limping behind manufacturing (Tracy 1989). Post-war European élites had tended to neglect the agricultural sector in their haste to tackle more pressing economic and financial problems. European cooperation presented a unique opportunity to reduce bottleneck effects linked to a backward farm sector and to generate wealth for the economy as a whole. Yet, if the establishment of the EEC offered the proper framework and resources to carry out this agenda, the political mandate to advocate and implement the coming policy had to be forged at home, within the politics of individual member states, out of a fragmented political base where rural notables often did not see eye-to-eye with modernizing élites. Initially, these élites were committed to a policy of modernization featuring a European common market accompanied by a moderate price policy *and* a policy of modernization of farm structures. Eventually, they had to settle for much less to rally the support of farmers. Modernization intentions were co-opted by conservative forces in what Selznick (1984 [1949]: 260) once called 'the shadowland of informal interaction'.

Clearly, the CAP of the 1960s resulted from complex compromises: between heterogeneous member states' preferences, but also between policy ideals and political realities. Divergent interests coalesced under the banner of a high-price policy and cemented two 'iron pacts' in western Europe: an agrarian pact between states and farmers now federated in formidable national lobbying groups; and an intergovernmental pact around the Franco-German axis. Views crystallized of the farming world as a special sector of the economy, necessitating special assistance from the state. All these factors created long-term impediments to the efficient modernization of agriculture. They also raised high political and institutional obstacles in the path of advocates of change.

At the service of fortress CAP: the community method in agriculture

An abundant literature has documented how the community method provided the foundation of fortress CAP. It created joint-decision-trap effects (Scharpf 1988), entrenched agrarian worldviews (Fouilleux 2003) and closed policy networks (Daugbjerg 1999), strengthened the political clout of domestic farm interests (Roederer-Rynning 2002), and promoted rent-seeking (Vaubel 1986; Nedergaard 2006). This literature breaks away from a long tradition of research treating institutions as 'the resultant of economic, social and political interactions' (Scharpf 1988: 266). By contrast, this section highlights how the particular economic and political context specific to the agricultural sector coloured the way the Community method worked in practice.

Agrarian nationalism institutionalized

Whereas on paper the Community method grants the Commission a more important role compared with other policy modes, the case of agricultural policy shows that the role of the Commission cannot be appreciated on the sole basis of the formal rules of the game in isolation from politics. Indeed in a context of increasingly nationalized politics, the Commission worked very much as the alter ego of the Council of Ministers, thereby consolidating the grip of agrarian nationalism.

The power of EU institutions in agriculture is specified by the consultation procedure (Art. 43.2 of EEC Treaty), thus called because that grants the EP a merely consultative role. The Commission possesses the exclusive right of initiative, a prerogative that is key to setting the substantive agenda and that is difficult to trump legally. The Council may request legislation, but it cannot draft concrete proposals; nor can it adopt any decision in the absence of a proposal from the Commission. The Council may modify the Commission's draft by a majority of its members, but the Commission still may oppose these modifications, necessitating the Council to act unanimously to override its opposition. In this way, it is not just 'formally, but also materially' that 'the Commission proposal is the basis of the subsequent negotiations' (Meester 1999: 2). The Council, as far as it is concerned, is sovereign in the decision-making phase. Competing law-makers are excluded by law, with the EP having to deliver an opinion before legislation acquires the force of law, but the Council not being obliged to take this opinion into account. National parliaments have even less to say, for CAP legislation, once passed in the form of regulations, is directly applicable in the member states. Thus, on paper at least, Commission and Council enjoy a neatly symmetric relation of power in the CAP, whereby Commission proposes and Council disposes.

Yet, this relation must be evaluated in light of the context within which the CAP was consolidated in the 1960s and 1970s, a context in which member states secured extraordinary channels of influence beyond their treaty-enshrined prerogatives. This occurred first as a result of the six-month 'empty chair crisis' triggered by France on 1 July 1965 in response to a Commission proposal on the financing of the CAP. The Luxembourg compromise of 29 January 1966, which ended the crisis, led to the de-facto recognition of a veto power for the members of the Council, whenever 'very important interests of one or more partners are at stake'. Later, the institutionalization of the European Council secured member states further influence by giving them all the right of initiative (Meester 1999). These informal developments qualified the power of the Commission, not only because they institutionalized the norm of consensus within the Council and introduced a competing right of initiative, but also because they induced a certain degree of nationalization of the Commission itself (Averyt 1977: 88). Thus, in reality, Council–Commission relations in the age of the classic CAP were symbiotic rather than competitive, and failed to reveal the full potential of autonomy that the treaty granted the Commission. Member states influenced legislation already at the agenda-setting phase. The Commission anticipated national positions. Many of its proposals were thus already agreed in sub-formations of the Council when reaching the Council proper (so-called 'A items').

Farm interests were locked in within this policy tandem in both formal and informal ways. Formal segmentation in EU institutions shielded agricultural policy from the pressure of counter-interests. A separate formation of the Council—the Council of Agriculture Ministers—discussed agricultural affairs from the beginning, assisted from May 1960 by the Special Committee on Agriculture (SCA) (a sub-formation of the Council composed of senior civil servants of member states) (Pearce 1981; Swinbank 1989). Furthermore, the 1970 decision to regard guarantee expenditure as compulsory expenditure effectively removed the CAP from the scrutiny of MEPs, paradoxically at a time when the EP began to acquire more substantive powers. On a less formal basis, the routine consultation of farm groups to the exclusion of other interests reinforced institutional closure at all levels and phases of policy-making. At the supranational level, the *Comité des Organisations Professionnelles Agricoles* (COPA) was the main device for channelling the input of farmers, a Euro-farm lobby created at about the same time as the EEC with the active support of the Agriculture Commissioner, Sicco Mansholt. Agricultural interests made themselves felt again at the implementation stage at the national level, where farm groups often received important delegated powers and seats in the myriad national agencies and commissions set up to implement the CMOs.

Unique and less unique features

Many features of this closed policy process could be attributed to characteristics of the agricultural sector. The use of a highly technical form of regulation (market policy) in a fragmented policy environment consisting of millions of production units did generate distinctive features at the EU level, notably:

- a density of social interaction among the various actors involved in the policy-making process (Council, Commission, farm groups, national agencies) unmatched in other policy areas. Here, the CAP stands in clear contrast with regional policy—another redistributive policy—where the Council meets on very rare occasions, thus offering a very low degree of socialization among member governments, and between member governments and members of the Commission (see Chapter 10). The density of social interaction characterizing the CAP has provided a solid basis for building confidence among policy actors, exchanging information, and discovering common interests;

- an unparalleled asymmetric representation of interests, perhaps with the exception of fisheries policy (Lequesne 2005). Asymmetry does not just reflect the fact that counter-CAP constituencies have been notoriously difficult to organize (consumer constituencies are diffuse; most environmental groups have been present on the European scene for fewer than thirty years; their staffs are small and their resources modest (see Chapter 13); finally, the food-processing industry, which otherwise might have been a driver for reform, has heterogeneous interests), but also the technical character of the CAP's market-intervention policy (Keeler 1987), which almost by nature necessitates the intervention of a farm client (Sheingate 2001);

- a particular devotion to the consensual style of policy-making. This feature is enhanced in agriculture by the unusually high level of socialization characterizing CAP policy-making as well as the segregation of producers' and consumers' concerns on an EU level; and

- a regressive form of redistribution whereby affluent farmers receive a disproportionate share of CAP payments.

On the other hand, there are limits to what can be explained with reference to the special characteristics of the farm sector. Notwithstanding descriptions of the CAP as a uniquely Europeanized regime, one must recognize the vigour of national interests and the ability of national governments to resist the pooling of competences at the supranational level. Entire areas of agricultural policy-making thus remained under the partial or exclusive competence of member states: the bulk of structural policy, of course, but also social security provisions for farmers, the regulation of the working conditions and wages of agricultural workers, and the regulation of land tenure—all representing, in contrast with market policy, important levers of agricultural modernization.

Exclusive EU competence applies only to a specific sub-field of agricultural policy—the market pillar of the CAP. Even there, member governments could intervene in favour of the commodities not encompassed by EU legislation and influence commodity prices by intervening at the retail and distribution stages. While it might be exaggerated to view the CAP as little more than a 'co-ordination of national policies' (Pearce in Snyder 1985: 62), the delegation of power to EU institutions proceeded only so long as it enabled a common financing of market policy never to encroach upon the politically sensitive area of modernization policy.

There is no doubt that the equilibrium 'discovered' at the end of the 1960s contributed to reconstructing and sustaining the power of national agrarian blocks while postponing the 'hollowing out' of the state (Milward 1992; Grant 2005). As some have put it, 'the paradox of the CAP is that, in creating a European agricultural block, it has strengthened the place of agriculture in national politics out of all proportion with the sector's economic importance' (Lowe et al. 2002: 14)—and the Community method provided the foundation of this fortress.

CAP challenged: towards multiple logics of intervention

Since the mid-1980s, developments in the CAP present a baffling picture to the observer of European farm affairs. The global General Agreement on Tariffs and Trade (GATT)/World Trade Organization (WTO) trade negotiations (see Chapter 16), internal negotiations on the EU budget (see Chapter 9), and the serial enlargement of the EU (see Chapter 17) have exerted considerable pressures on the CAP. No fewer than six reforms have been passed in the past twenty-five years (Table 8.1). Not all reforms have proved significant in terms of their own premises. Together, however, they have brought about a significant and lasting change with the introduction of direct payments; they have also durably changed the policy mode in agriculture.

Two processes of change

Two main processes have brought about change: they may be labelled 'breaking the farm policy community open' and 'bypassing the farm policy community'. In the first path, 'breaking open the policy community', farm élites are the protagonists: it is they who initiate and adopt change, acting out of ideological conviction and political necessity. This trajectory necessitates the strategic intervention of farm policy insiders, using their institutional prerogatives in combination with new political

TABLE 8.1 From market support to decoupled payments: twenty-five years of CAP reform

Reform	Main points	Context	Implication
Reform of the dairy sector (March 1984)	• production quotas on dairy products	Row on the EC budget; Prime Minister Thatcher secures an automatically-delivered yearly budget rebate for the UK	First binding control on production
Budget ceilings and stabilizers (February 1988)	• *agriculture guideline* limits annual growth of agriculture expenditure to 74% of the annual growth rate of the Community GNP • *production thresholds* trigger automatic price cuts	1986 enlargement to Spain and Portugal leads to doubling of structural funds	CAP placed under general budget discipline though technically CAP spending may still exceed the figures set out in the financial perspective
McSharry reform (May 1992)	• *price cuts* on cereals (30% within three years) and beef and veal (15%) • *compensatory payments to producers* are coupled to production, as only farmers growing the eligible commodities may receive these payments • *accompanying measures* include: aid to the early retirement of farmers; agro-environmental schemes; support for the reforestation of agricultural land; set aside of 15% of their arable land for farms beyond agreed size	Uruguay Round of the GATT focuses on agricultural goods and treats negotiations on goods as single undertaking (i.e., forming a single package)	Farm payments become chief support instrument; make CAP less market-distorting; limits on farm-payments spending place CAP expenditure effectively under control

TABLE 8.1 (Continued)

Reform	Main points	Context	Implication
Agenda 2000 agreement on agriculture (March 1999)	market and income support becomes *first pillar* of the CAP: • *prices are cut by 15% on cereals, 20% on beef and veal, and 15% on dairy products* • *cross-compliance* allows member states to condition the disbursement of payments, now called direct payments, in respect of environmental criteria rural development becomes *second pillar* of the CAP: • *modulation* enables member states to strengthen pillar 2 funds by up to 20% of the total amount of direct payments to which they are entitled	Eastern enlargement: CEECs are poorer and more rural than EU15	New rural development pillar sharpens multifunctionality of the CAP; opens up for 'greening' of direct payments
Fischler reform, also called Midterm Review of the CAP (MTR), June 2003	*partly decouples* farm income support from production by replacing direct farm payments to producers with a *single farm payment* (SFP) • *compulsory 5% modulation* of the single farm payment with a franchise of €5,000: savings generated by compulsory modulation are to a large extent retained in the source country, where they can be used to increase rural development funds; single farm payment subject to *compulsory cross-compliance*, now extended in respect of EU rules on the protection of animal welfare, and public, animal, and plant health—besides the environmental criteria;	Doha Round of the WTO	Farm payments become largely decoupled

	• *national envelopes* enable member states to retain up to 10% of the maximum total amount of income subsidies they receive and spend it as new pillar 1 payments to enhance environmentally-friendly farming, the quality and marketing of farm products • market intervention mechanisms (for intervention, storage, and export restitutions) turned into *safety nets*	
Health Check of the CAP (November 2008)	• payments still coupled become *decoupled* (with some exceptions) • national envelopes (now *'article 68 measures'*) become more flexible as money no longer has to be used in same sector as generated • further phasing out of *market intervention mechanisms* (pig meat, barley, sorghum) • abolition of set–aside • compulsory 10% *modulation* by 2012 with extra cut for payments above 300,000 • cross-compliance simplified	Doha Round of the WTO Pursuit of liberalization of CAP

realities to effect change. A precondition has been the existence in the agricultural services of the European Commission of a circle of reform-minded officials willing to introduce reform proposals and exploiting alternative policy-making venues to shield them. Given that it is farm practitioners themselves who sponsor (in the Commission) and control (in the Council) this process, change comes in the guise of CAP reforms, which, while sometimes far-reaching in their policy consequences, are unlikely to tackle the overarching institutional context of CAP policy-making. Indeed, change of this type takes place on the premises of farm policy-makers.

Global trade talks have provided the main levers of change for this type of process by enabling the Commission to exploit its powers of international negotiation (by virtue of Art.133 TEC, see Chapter 16) and fragmentation in the Council to steer a reformist course. This explains how it was possible for the EU to adopt a radical reform of the CAP in 1992 (McSharry reform 1992), and to follow it up in the 2003 Midterm Review (2003) and the (limited) Health Check of the CAP (2008) (Table 8.1). These reforms marked milestones in the history of the CAP by phasing out the output-geared system of price support and turning farm payments into the main instrument of intervention.

The effects of these reforms have been considerable. Support has become decoupled from production, and the CAP has become less market-distorting (although such support can still distort international trade). It has also become 'greener' as payments have been made conditional upon meeting environmental criteria. The CAP has also been modulated to finance rural-development programmes (the CAP has become more 'multifunctional'). Yet, these reforms have failed to transform the overarching objectives of the CAP and its framework of institutional segmentation.

In the second path, 'bypassing the policy community', change is sponsored and controlled by non-farm élites; it involves the strategic entrepreneurship of actors located *outside* agriculture. Change of this type does not lead to CAP reforms, because the actors are not CAP stakeholders, but rather to a reconfiguration of the macro-institutional and political parameters of policy-making. Crises or quasi-crises generated by CAP externalities provide the main levers of such change. These levers are ineffectual, however, unless entrepreneurs mobilize non-farm constituencies for change and develop institutional solutions to the problems.

EU budget discussions and food scares such as the 'mad cow crisis'[5] provide two good examples of this path of change. In the former case, change materialized in the form of new institutional procedures (inter-institutional budgetary procedure) (see Chapter 9), which durably constrained the CAP through the establishment of a so-called 'agricultural guideline' (Figure 8.1). In the case of the mad cow crisis, change materialized first and foremost through the divestiture from the CAP policy community of veterinary and phytosanitary policy competences (now lodged in the Directorate-General for Health and Consumers (DG SANCO) in the Commission and in the Environment Committee of the EP) and the adoption of the co-decision procedure to settle these issues (Roederer-Rynning 2003b). The point is that change in both cases was driven by actors, especially in the European Parliament, perceived

FIGURE 8.1   Evolution of CAP expenditure 1980–2007

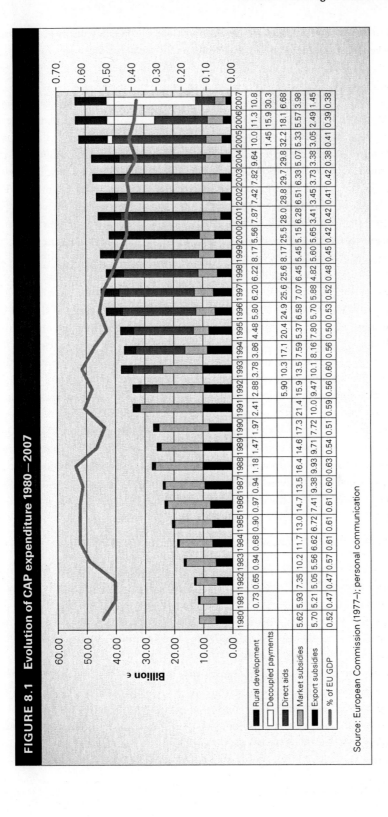

	1980	1981	1982	1983	1984	1985	1986	1987	1988	1989	1990	1991	1992	1993	1994	1995	1996	1997	1998	1999	2000	2001	2002	2003	2004	2005	2006	2007
Rural development	0.73	0.65	0.94	0.68	0.90	0.97	0.97	0.94	1.18	1.47	1.97	2.41	2.88	3.78	3.86	4.48	5.80	6.20	6.22	8.17	5.56	7.87	7.42	7.82	9.64	10.0	11.3	10.8
Decoupled payments																										1.45	15.9	30.3
Direct aids													5.90	10.3	17.1	20.4	24.9	25.6	25.6	8.17	25.5	28.0	28.8	29.7	29.8	32.2	18.1	6.68
Market subsidies	5.62	5.93	7.35	10.2	11.7	13.0	14.7	13.5	16.4	14.6	17.3	21.4	15.9	13.5	7.59	5.37	6.58	7.07	6.45	5.45	5.15	6.28	6.51	6.33	5.07	5.33	5.57	3.98
Export subsidies	5.70	5.21	5.05	5.56	6.62	6.72	7.41	9.38	9.93	9.71	7.72	10.0	9.47	10.1	8.16	7.80	5.70	5.88	4.82	5.60	5.65	3.41	3.45	3.73	3.38	3.05	2.49	1.45
% of EU GDP	0.52	0.47	0.57	0.61	0.61	0.61	0.60	0.63	0.54	0.51	0.59	0.56	0.60	0.56	0.53	0.50	0.53	0.52	0.48	0.45	0.42	0.41	0.41	0.42	0.38	0.41	0.39	0.38

Billion €

Source: European Commission (1977–); personal communication

to be powerless in agricultural policy. Farm policymakers were cast in a defensive position, and had minimal control over agenda-setting and decision-making.

Enlargement as a lever of change?

This interpretation leaves open the question of the impact of the various enlargements. As a 'composite policy', enlargement cuts across all policy areas while calling for negotiated compromises between policy-makers at the sectoral and at the macro-level (see Chapter 17). Enlargement may trigger agricultural change in two main ways: before accession, by tightening the grip of finance ministers on the CAP (as in the 'bypassing the policy community' path); after accession, by introducing a new range of policy preferences in the Agriculture Council (as in the 'breaking the policy community open' path). As mentioned above, the Mediterranean and the eastern enlargements undeniably tightened the budgetary grip on the CAP through the establishment of the agricultural guideline (see Chapter 9). Likewise, the accession of the poorer CEECs (Table 8.2) went hand-in-hand with the freezing of 2000–6 pillar 1 farm expenditure at the 1999 level (€40.5 billion yearly). Though having little impact on the first pillar of the CAP,[6] these constraints have highlighted the political salience of structural and rural development policy measures.

Regarding the political impact of EU enlargement on fortress Europe, both arguments can be made. There is a striking contrast, for example, between Sweden, which had embarked upon an ambitious deregulation of its agricultural policy in the 1990s and was forced to backtrack upon accession, and Hungary, a pro-free-trade member of the Cairns group of agricultural exporters before its accession to the EU. Since accession Sweden has vigorously advocated agricultural liberalization while Hungary has adopted a more status-quo-oriented outlook, having received unhindered access to the EU market. On the whole, however, evidence suggests that majorities for CAP reform are more difficult to assemble in an enlarged EU.

Between old and new: the CAP as a bifurcated policy regime

Assessing the impact of change remains a debated question (Garzon 2006; Swinbank and Daugbjerg 2006). Considered in terms of policy mode, the discussion must take account of two aspects: first, the trends that are making the Community method in agriculture a more competitive and politicized process; and second, the institution-alization of a parallel policy mode in the so-called rural development pillar of the CAP established in Agenda 2000.

In pillar 1, devoted to market policy, the Community method persists, albeit in a modified version. Six trends are particularly noteworthy and likely to become more pronounced in the future: the consensual style is under strain; the character of national farm administrations is changing; the cohesion of traditional farm clients has

TABLE 8.2   Basic agricultural structures in the EU15, new member states, EU25, and USA (latest year available unless otherwise specified)

	Agricultural land	Number of holdings	Average size	Employment		Value of agricultural production	
	(million ha)	(000s)	ha	('000 annual work units)	% of population[a]	million euros[b]	% of GDP[a]
EU15	**141.1**	**6,520**	**21.6**	**6,382**	**4.2**	**245,289**	**1.7**
Cyprus	0.1	52	2.3	14	-	-	-
Czech Republic	4.3	37	117.1	148	-	3,176	-
Estonia	0.8	37	21.6	38	-	375	-
Hungary	5.9	773	7.6	526	-	5,286	-
Latvia	2.5	127	19.7	141	-	477	-
Lithuania	3.5	272	12.9	222	-	1,150	-
Malta	0.01	11	1.0	5	-	118	-
Poland	18.4	1,886	9.7	2,867	-	12,101	-
Slovak Republic	2.4	72	33.5	119	-	1,456	-
Slovenia	0.5	77	6.3	95	-	933	-
New member states (NMS)	**38.4**	**3,343**	**11.5**	**4,174**	**13.2**	**25,072**	**3.1**
EU25	**179.5**	**9,863**	**18.4**	**10,556**	**8.7**	**270,361**	**2.4**
Share of NMS in EU25 (in %)	21.4	34		40	-	9	-
USA[a]	**376**	**2,158**	**174.4**	**3,480**	**2.5**	-	**1.4**

[a] Data reflect the situation before the eastern enlargement of the EU (Rieger 2005: 182).
[b] Period 2002–4.
Source: OECD (2007:87)

weakened; the Commission has demonstrated greater autonomy; the Commission's consultations have become more transparent and confrontational; and there is more flexible implementation within a simplified policy framework. These trends are explored below.

The consensual style of policy-making is coming under strain, because reforms have coincided with increasingly polarized positions in the Council of Ministers. Until now, divergences have crystallized along a rather simple cleavage between pursuing liberalization at home and abroad (the United Kingdom, Sweden, Denmark, and The Netherlands) and maintaining a strong community preference (France and the Latin countries, Germany with some exceptions, and many of the CEECs).

This cleavage ties in with budgetary disputes: proponents of market liberalization stand to gain most financially from a liberalization of the CAP, while the 'countries who defend the CAP typically do well financially from the policy' (Ackrill and Kay 2004: 16). Consequently, this cleavage is highly politically charged and has meant that majority voting has made inroads into consensual decision-making, while agricultural policy as a whole has become the least consensual EU policy (Hayes-Renshaw et al. 2006: 165).

In the future, issues associated with new technologies, such as genetically modified organisms (GMOs) and animal cloning, may complicate this picture (see Chapter 14). Powerful forces impact on these issues: technology; regulatory pressures from abroad; and not least the sudden reversal of global market outlooks fuelling widespread insecurity about food supply. Difficult dilemmas await the EU: for example, should the EU relax the precautionary principle or abandon the production and consumption of meat where GMO-free feed is unavailable? Such issues often pit the broader public against political élites. They may generate alliances that cut across traditional divisions between free-traders and proponents of a strong community preference (e.g. the convergence of France and The Netherlands on sanitary issues in the WTO).

Polarization in the Council has occurred at a time when traditional agricultural administrations in several countries have been reorganized into broad ministries incorporating issues sometimes as diverse as food, consumer protection, the environment, forestry, water management, etc., *changing the character of national farm administrations*. In Germany, food, agriculture, and consumer protection have coexisted within the same ministry for some time. In Austria since 2000, a large *Lebensministerium* has brought together agriculture, food, forestry, water management, and environmental issues. These changes are quite important as they break up the traditional farm ministers' club in the EU and contribute to reframing agricultural policy issues.

'As long as price support was the major agricultural policy instrument, large and small farmers shared the same interests … Reinstrumentation of agriculture policy towards direct payments makes this coalition weaker and redistributional conflicts among different groups of farmers more pronounced' (Rabinowicz 1999: 405), consequently the *cohesion of traditional farm clients has weakened*. Under a policy of farm payments, the pursuit of pragmatism is threatened on two fronts: within the farm community, visible disparities of support across sectors are pitting commodity sectors against one another; in the broader public, the more transparent budgetary consequences of direct payments are challenging policy-makers to articulate clear objectives that can stand the test of public scrutiny. This means that the political clout of farmers' peak organizations has diminished.

While the 1960s and the 1970s featured a 'nationalized' Commission (Averyt 1977: 88), which worked in tandem with the Agriculture Council and national farm interests, the CAP reforms of the 1980s and 1990s have bequeathed a legacy of political activism in the Commission, which has demonstrated *greater autonomy*. With Commissioner McSharry, the Commission substituted in the early 1990s a more selective and ad-hoc consultation of interests for the once closed consultation of farmers' peak organizations. But already in the 1980s, commodity groups nego-tiating outside of umbrella farm organizations were able to influence CAP reform (Culpepper 1993: 311; Petit et al. 1987). The more selective and ad-hoc consulta-tion of societal interests has increased the Commission's room for manoeuvre in preparing CAP reforms; it also explains how it has been possible to pass complicated reforms in a relatively short time. In the years to come, however, the Commission might have to negotiate this new-gained freedom with the EP and to open up the phase of preparation following ratification of the Lisbon Treaty (Box 8.2).

The Commission has sought to institutionalize a more transparent and confrontational style of consultation. These efforts are responses to two main developments in the 1990s: first, the 'mad cow' crisis, which highlighted the negative consequences of institutional segmentation; and, second, the lack of progress in institutional reform, which lent appeal to the idea of improving regulation within existing institutions. This

---

BOX 8.2	Co-decision in agriculture—what will change?

Under the Lisbon Treaty, co-decision will replace the consultation procedure for the 'bigger' political issues of the CAP while consultation will continue to govern the more 'technical' farm issues. This means that the EP will have a greater say in agriculture, although it is unclear what type of division of labour this distinction implies and whether it is realistic and feasible to uphold such distinction in practice. Co-decision will affect the politics of agriculture within the EP and between the EP and other EU institutions. New rules can be expected to bring new people into the EP's committee on agriculture (COMAGRI), until now perceived as a conservative forum welded to the defence of vested interests; they might also lead to reinforced EP control over COMAGRI. The broader CAP policy process will likely become more open but also more protracted due to the technical and political requirements of co-decision. The paradox is thus that, while potentially making the CAP accountable to a wider constituency, co-decision might also slow down the pace of reform by placing new technical and political constraints on the Commission's right of initiative.

TABLE 8.3   Flexible implementation within a common framework: the case of the 2003 midterm review's Single Farm Payment Scheme (SFPS) in the EU27

Countries	Calculation of SFP	Partial decoupling
Belgium	Historical	Yes
Ireland	Historical	No
Greece	Historical	Yes
Spain	Historical	Yes
France	Historical	Yes
Italy	Historical	Yes
Malta	Regional	No
The Netherlands	Historic	Yes
Austria	Historic	Yes
Portugal	Historic	Yes
Denmark	Dynamic hybrid	Yes
Germany	Dynamic hybrid	Yes
Luxembourg	Static hybrid	Yes
Finland	Dynamic hybrid	Yes
Slovenia	Regional	Yes
Sweden	Static hybrid	Yes
United Kingdom	Dynamic hybrid (but static hybrid in Northern Ireland)	Yes

Note: following accession, the new member states could opt for a different type of aid from the direct payments disbursed in the EU15 and not open to the EU15 member states, the so-called 'single area payment scheme' (SAPS) or 'simplified scheme' consisting in a flat payment per hectare of agricultural land up to a national ceiling. Ten new member states chose SAPS. Malta and Slovenia opted instead for the SFPS in force in the EU15. The SFPS must be implemented between 2005 and 2007. Finland, France, Greece, The Netherlands, and Spain began implementing the reform in 2006. In all other member states, implementation started in 2005. Member states have two basic choices when introducing the SFPS: the first concerns the method of calculation of payments; the second concerns exemptions from full decoupling.

Three methods of calculation and disbursement of payments:

- in the *historical approach,* each farmer receives a payment which is based on the payments (s)he was entitled to during a reference period (reference amounts) and the number of eligible hectares (s)he was farming during the reference period; this approach does not entail any redistribution among farmers;

- in the *regional approach*, all farmers in a given region receive a flat-rate entitlement which reflects the reference amounts pooled at the regional level and then divided by the number of eligible hectares declared by the farmers of the region in the year of introduction of the SFPS; this approach entails some redistribution of payments among farmers;

- in the hybrid approach, member states may, under some conditions, either apply different systems of calculation in different regions of their territory, or mix the two approaches in the calculation of SFPs. *Static* forms of implementation of the hybrid approach do not vary over time while *dynamic* implementations of the hybrid approach may enable member states to transit gradually from the historic to the regional, flat-rate approach.

Two exemptions from full decoupling:

- *Partial decoupling* opens up the possibility for member states to maintain a proportion of product-specific direct aids in their existing form, notably where they believe there may be disturbance to agricultural markets or abandonment of production by moving to the SFPS. Member states may choose between several options, at national or regional level, but only under well-defined conditions and within clear limits. There is no time limit on continuing partial decoupling. Amounts paid out in partially decoupled form come from within national ceilings.

- *Additional payments*, using up to 10% of the funds available nationally for the SFPS, may support agricultural activities that encourage the protection or enhancement of the environment or improve the quality and marketing of agricultural products. Additional payments reduce the funds available for basic SFPS payments and product-specific direct aids.

Source: based on Commission (2006*e*) and Commission (2008*h*)

resulted in the 'impact assessments' (IA) initiative, which now compels the Commission to ensure that important policy proposals take account of impacts in the economic, environmental, and social fields and are based on an evaluation of the advantages and disadvantages of each option.[7] As a consequence, important policy proposals are subject to inter-service consultation within the Commission to secure the involvement of all affected interests. In agriculture, the Commission tested the method in the sugar-regime reform, and is now extending it to broader CAP reforms.

Talk of the renationalization of the CAP has popped up with each reform initiative, and this theme has permeated the two dimensions of the debate: the budgetary dimension, with its discussion of the partial or total repatriation to the national level of farm expenditure, and the regulatory dimension, with issues about where to locate policy competences. The budget debate exploded during the Agenda 2000 negotiations as a result of demands by individual countries to introduce co-financing of the CAP. In the absence of a general agreement on the co-financing of the CAP, a renationalization of farm expenditure has taken place mainly through the development of the 'rural development' pillar 2 of the CAP, which is co-financed. The fact that pillar 2 has developed slowly in spite of its broad degree of acceptance and legitimacy in the EU attests to the amount of resistance to the renationalization of farm expenditure in today's Agriculture Council. There seems to be less political debate about the regulatory aspects of renationalization, as there is a general consensus among EU practitioners that the development of parallel market regulation at the national level would create market distortions. The creation of 'national envelopes' and flexibility in the implementation of reforms repatriate some competences to the national level (Table 8.3). Yet, the administrative and political intricacies associated with pursuing differentiated strategies, sometimes within the same territory, have supported the Commission's case for pursuing simplification of CAP support and the adoption of a single system of flat payments (see Health Check of the CAP in Table 8.1).

Simultaneously, the establishment of a second pillar devoted to rural development has introduced a new policy mode into the CAP, much more akin to the 'distributional mode' (see Chapter 4). Accordingly, the policy process is decentralized in pillar 2: the EU defines priorities; then national and regional authorities specify these priorities in national strategy plans and rural development programmes. Pillar 2 measures are co-financed by the EU and member states. This policy mode has opened up the policy process to a broader set of societal concerns and economic interests traditionally excluded from the CAP. In some cases, regions have also become active in agricultural policy-making both as the key target of European programmes (due to the new objectives introduced by pillar 2) and a close planning partner of the Commission (owing to the import of the distributional style of policy characterizing regional policy). If pillar 2 has not given birth to a Europe of agricultural regions, it has provided regional and local peripheries with a lever of political negotiation vis-à-vis traditional centres (Ieraci 1998; Perraud 1999; Genieys et al. 2000; Ward and Lowe 2004). The result has been *flexible implementation within a simplified policy framework*.

Institutional differentiation has increased competition for resources within the CAP. In a context of budgetary discipline, the pie must be shared even as the size of the pie is diminishing; rural development measures cannot grow unless more money is switched from pillar 1 to pillar 2 (so-called 'modulation' of payments). This compels agricultural policy-makers to justify better the *raison d'être* of CAP subsidies. Why should one continue to support farm income in the twenty-first century? How should this be done? Who should pay? Experience from previous budget rows shows that, in spite of broad public legitimacy, pillar 2 payments are the first to be cut when money must be saved. Yet as the changes described above suggest, the battle will increasingly play itself out in the open with the broader public as the eventual legitimating authority.

Conclusions

The CAP long conjured up images of medieval strongholds. Traditionally in the hands of a closed policy community, it invariably took on the guise of an impenetrable fortress built by farmers for farmers on the promontory of national sovereignty. This chapter has shown that the CAP today more fittingly summons up images of early modern European fortified cities. Society has moved inside the walls while becoming ever more connected to the outside world by a dense web of ties. This new construction must find its place in changing patterns of political consolidation at the local, regional, national, and global levels. The walls are still there—but they are lower.

Production surpluses, blatant income gaps among farmers, and repeated food scares eroded the foundations of the old regime. Budget discipline and the emergence of new policy priorities on the EU agenda depleted the resources available for the defence of traditional farm concerns. Global trade talks and successive enlargements provided venues for change. These developments contributed to shedding the outdated system of price support and asserting direct payments as a pivotal instrument of support, linking farmers' concern for income support to changing public expectations regarding global trade liberalization, food safety, environmental protection, animal welfare, or balanced regional development.

As EU negotiations approach on the post-2013 financial perspective, proponents of change have been concerned that current energy pressures, the fashion for bio-fuels, and the rash of food price rises might help status-quo players reverse the changes of the last decades. Yet as this chapter shows, it is not just policy that has changed, but also the very machinery through which CAP regulations and directives are produced at the national and the EU levels. In today's complex setting, some CAP policy areas have shifted hands and are now regulated by non-farm actors operating under completely different institutional rules. Core agricultural concerns have become so tied up with issues larger than the CAP that they are losing their narrow sectoral character. Sometimes, the very core CAP players have changed character, as illustrated by the opening up of traditional agriculture ministries in several EU member states—and all of this makes rather implausible a return to the old days of price support and generalized market intervention.

Today's CAP is always under pressure from new developments and changing hierarchies of issues, and this challenges deterministic views of a CAP caught in an institutional straightjacket. Various versions of path-dependency arguments have highlighted the independent impact of institutions. The CAP indeed provides vivid illustrations of the power of institutions to create 'sticky legacies' that place a premium on the status quo once procedures are established and policy is decided. Even so, institutions cannot be praised or blamed for everything. The CAP originated in a mix of sector-related strictures, political realities, and modernizing ambitions, and its evolution cautions us, again and again, against downplaying the role of national interests and the ability of member states to control the supranational delegation of powers.

Notes

1 Thomas Falslund Johansen provided fine research assistance. I would like to thank the persons I interviewed at the European Commission and in various national permanent representations in spring 2008. Robert Ackrill, Carsten Daugbjerg, Wyn Grant, Johannes Michelsen, Mogens N. Pedersen, and Rob Peters read an earlier version of the chapter. I would like to thank them, together with the editors of this volume, for their helpful comments.

2 With a population representing 30 per cent of that of the EU15, the ten CEECs generated a GNP of only 5 per cent of that of the EU at the time of accession.

3 In 2008, CAP expenditure represented €52.5 billion (€4.3 billion devoted to market measures; €36.8 billion devoted to direct payments measures, and €11.4 billion devoted to pillar 2 measures) in a total EU budget of €120.3 billion (Official Journal of the European Communities L71-2008).

4 This section builds in large part on Rieger (2005: 189)

5 The 'mad cow crisis' took place in 1996 in connection with the epidemic development of bovine spongiform encephalopathy (BSE)—a fatal, brain-wasting disease leading to the mass destruction of cattle in several member states.

6 The main impacts were: the abandonment of market intervention for rye and maize and a very gradual introduction of the direct payments in the new member states.

7 See e.g. the Commission's web page on impact assessment:

   http://ec.europa.eu/governance/impact/index_en.htm.

 FURTHER READING*

For a detailed history of the CAP, see Tracy (1989), Grant (1997), and Ackrill (2000). Milward (1992: Ch.5) provides the best account of the prehistory. Fennell (1997) offers the most detailed, historically oriented policy analysis of the CAP. For a view of US agricultural politics and policies, see Orden et al. (1999) and for a comparison of agricultural policy reform in the EU and in the US, see Moyer and Josling (2002). Greer (2005) offers a detailed account of how national governments influence the CAP at all levels of the policy cycle. Daugbjerg and Swinbank (2009) provide an up-to-date and detailed account of the impact of WTO trade liberalization on the CAP. On the BSE crisis and its regulatory implications, see Zwanenberg and Millstone (2005). For an account of the CAP as a 'welfare state of farmers' see Sheingate (2001) and Knudsen (2009). Those interested in current developments should consult *The Agricultural Situation in the European Union*, an annual publication by the Commission (Commission 1977–).

Ackrill, R. (2000), *The Common Agricultural Policy* (Sheffield: Sheffield Academic Press).

Commission (1977–), *The Agricultural Situation in the European Union*, DG AGRI (previously *The Agricultural Situation in the Community*).

Daugbjerg, C., and Swinbank, A. (2009), *Ideas, Institutions and Trade: The WTO and the Curious Role of EU Farm Policy in Trade Liberalization* (Oxford: Oxford University Press).

Fennell, R. (1997), *The Common Agricultural Policy: Continuity and Change* (Oxford: Clarendon Press).

Grant, W. (1997), *The Common Agricultural Policy* (Basingstoke: Palgrave Macmillan).

Greer, A. (2005), *Agricultural Policy in Europe* (Manchester: Manchester University Press).

Knudsen, A. C. Lauring (2009), *Farmers on Welfare: The Making of Europe's Common Agricultural Policy* (Ithaca, NY: Cornell University Press).

Milward, A. (1992), *The European Rescue of the Nation-State* (London: Routledge).

Moyer, H., and Josling, T. (2002), *Agricultural Policy Reform: Politics and Processes in the EU and in the US in the 1990s* (Aldershot: Ashgate).

Orden, D., Paarlberg, R., and Roe, T. (1999), *Policy Reform in American Agriculture: Analysis and Prognosis* (Chicago, IL: University of Chicago Press).

Sheingate, A. (2001), *The Welfare State for Farmers: Institutions and Interest Group Power in the United States, France, and Japan* (Princeton, NJ: Princeton University Press).

Tracy, M. (1989), *Government and Agriculture in Western Europe* (New York, NY: Harvester Wheatsheaf).

Zwanenberg, P. van, and Millstone, E. (2005), *BSE: Risk, Science, and Governance* (Oxford: Oxford University Press).

CHAPTER 9

The Budget

Who Gets What, When, and How?

Brigid Laffan and Johannes Lindner

Summary

The budget is a focus for repeated negotiation among the European Union (EU) member states and institutions, following firmly established rules. In 1988, after several years of bruising annual negotiations, the EU moved to multi-annual 'financial perspectives', or package deals, for which the Commission makes proposals and the 'Budgetary Authority'—the Council, particularly the European Council, and the European Parliament (EP)—negotiates agreement. This has concentrated budgetary politics into periodic strategic bargains, linking national costs and benefits, reform of the common agricultural policy (CAP), regional imbalances, and enlargement. This pattern was reinforced by subsequent budget packages in 1992 (Delors-2), in 1999 (Agenda 2000), and in 2006 (the Financial Perspective for 2007–2013). Over these years the structure of the budget changed only slightly; agricultural and regional expenditure remain the two large spending blocks. The Treaty of Lisbon confirmed the existing practice of budgetary decision-making by giving treaty status to the system of multi-annual financial planning and by abolishing the distinction between compulsory and non-compulsory expenditure. The camps of net contributors and net beneficiaries are more pronounced than ever in the Union. Thus, the EU struggles to shift budgetary priorities to embrace new challenges within the Union and internationally.

Introduction[1]

Historically, budgets have been of immense importance in the evolution of the modern state and they remain fundamental to contemporary government. This chapter enters the labyrinth of EU budgetary procedures in an attempt to unravel the characteristics of budgetary politics and policy-making. Where EU money comes from, how it is spent, and the processes by which it is distributed are the subjects of intense political bargaining. Budgets matter politically, because money represents the commitment of resources to the provision of public goods and involves political choices across sectors and regions.

The politics of making and managing budgets has had considerable salience in the evolution of the EU because budgets involve both distributive and redistributive politics. Budgetary issues have inevitably become entangled with debates about the nature of the EU, the competences of individual EU institutions and the balance between the European and the national levels of governance. Budgetary flows to the member states are highly visible so that 'winners' and 'losers' can be calculated with relative ease. As a result, budgetary politics are more likely to become embroiled in national politics and national electoral competition than rule-making. Questions about the purpose of the budget and the principles that govern the use of public finance in the Union are linked to wider questions about the nature of the EU and its evolution as a polity that goes beyond the set-up of a traditional international organization. In that context, the budget is also a useful yardstick with which to measure a type of integration that differs from the creation of a single market and the harmonization of rules and regulations. The size and scope of the EU budget have implications for the operation of a vast range of policies.[2]

The existence of the EU budget has often been justified and explained by its different functions: (a) as a means of side-payments that are necessary to gain the overall consensus and political cement on further economic, particularly market, integration; (b) as the source for financing European public goods that benefit not only individual member states but European citizens at large; or (c) as the basis for redistribution from richer to poorer parts of the Union which—following the value of European solidarity—fosters economic convergence towards a higher standard of living across the EU; and (d) as a means of financing Europe's role in the world.

The process of managing, rather than just formulating, budgets raises questions about the management capacity of Commission, but also about that of national authorities. All EU institutions and bodies, in particular the Court of Auditors, are paying increasing attention to the impact of fraud on the budget and searching for better ways to protect the financial interests of the EU.

A thumbnail sketch of the budget

In the early years of the Community, the budget was a financial instrument similar to those found in traditional international organizations. The budget treaties of 1970 and 1975 led to a fundamental change in the framework of budgetary politics and policy-making. These treaties established the constitutional framework for the finances of the Union in a number of important respects (see Box 9.1). The treaties created a system of 'own resources' which gave the EC an autonomous source of revenue, consisting of three elements: customs duties; agricultural levies; and a proportion of the base used for assessing value-added tax (VAT) in the member states, up to a ceiling of 1 per cent. The 1970 agreement on own resources was subsequently altered a number of times. One basic principle was that this revenue base should apply to all member states, regardless of their size, wealth, the pattern of EC expenditure, or their ability to pay. This was to cause increasing difficulty in the years to come.[3]

The 1970 and 1975 Budgetary Treaties altered the institutional framework for reaching decisions on the budget. The EP was granted significant budgetary powers, including the rights to increase, to reduce, or to redistribute expenditure in areas classified as 'non-compulsory' expenditure (essentially not agricultural spending); to adopt or reject the budget; and to give annual discharge, through a vote of approval, to the Commission for its implementation of the budget. The 'power of the purse' gave the EP leverage in its institutional battles with the Council of Ministers and allowed it to promote its autonomous policy preferences. The 1975 Budgetary Treaty provided for the creation of the independent Court of Auditors to enhance accountability in the budgetary process.

After 1970, the emergence of the budget as a real instrument of European public policy was constrained by a basic factor which still shapes EU finances. The EU budget was, and remains, small in relation to Community gross national income (GNI), and to the level of public expenditure in the member states. In 2008, EU spending amounted to around €130 billion. This was 1.03 per cent of EU GNI and thus, much less than domestic budgets which represent between 30 and 40 per cent of GNI in Europe. However, although the budget has little macroeconomic significance for the Union as a whole, it is very important for those member states that receive extensive transfers from the structural funds. For example, net receipts from the EU budget amounted in 2007 to 2.95 per cent of GNI for Lithuania, 2.55 per cent for Latvia and 2.43 per cent for Greece. EU spending programmes mobilize constituencies within the member states, such as farmers (see Chapter 8) and regional groups (see Chapter 10), which have a material interest in the maintenance of their receipts. The small overall size of the budget masked impressive increases

BOX 9.1	The budgetary cycle, rules, and practice prior to the Treaty of Lisbon

Articles 268–280 TEC lay down the financial provisions governing the EEC Treaty, with Article 272 TEC establishing the timetable and procedure for making the budget each year. An inter-institutional agreement between the EP, the Council, and the Commission specifies the exchanges and interaction between the EP and the Council. This agreement was the key reference point in budgetary decision-making prior to the Treaty of Lisbon.

- The Commission initiates the budgetary cycle by presenting the Preliminary Draft Budget to the Council.
- The Council adopts a Draft Budget by 5 October of the year preceding its implementation. The EU financial year starts in January.
- The Council meets with the EP in a conciliation meeting before actually adopting the Draft Budget.
- The EP has forty-five days to complete its first reading of the Draft. It is entitled to propose modifications to compulsory expenditure, that is, expenditure needed to meet the Community's legal commitments defined as 'expenditure necessarily resulting from this Treaty and from acts adopted in accordance therewith' (Art. 272(4) TEC) (essentially agriculture guarantee spending), and amendments to non-compulsory expenditure. Its control over non-compulsory expenditure is limited to increases within a 'margin of manoeuvre', which is equal to half the 'maximum rate of increase', a percentage determined each year by the Commission on the basis of the level of economic growth, inflation, and government spending.
- The Council has fifteen days to complete its second reading of the Draft Budget. The Council has the final word on compulsory expenditure but returns the Draft to the EP, indicating its position on the EP amendments to non-compulsory expenditure. The Council meets with the EP in a conciliation meeting shortly before the second reading.
- At its second reading, the EP has the final word on non-compulsory spending within the limits of an agreed maximum rate of increase. After its second reading of fifteen days, the EP adopts or rejects the budget. If adopted, the EP President signs it into law.
- If there is no agreement on the budget by the beginning of January, the Community operates on the basis of a system of month-to-month financing, known as 'provisional twelfths', until agreement is reached between the two arms of the budgetary authority.
- The Commission then has the responsibility for implementing the budget. The Court of Auditors draws up an annual report covering the year in question, and on the basis of that report the EP decides whether or not to give a discharge to the Commission in respect of the implementation of the budget. The discharge is normally given in the second year following the year in question.

in financial resources in the Delors-1 (1988–92) and Delors-2 (1993–9) budgetary agreements (see Figure 9.1). The Berlin Agreement (1999–2006) and the Brussels Agreement (2007–13) did not include increases of a similar magnitude to those of Delors-1 and Delors-2.

The slenderness of EU budgetary resources highlights an important feature of the emerging European polity, namely the significance of regulation as the main instrument of public power in the Union (see Chapter 5), and reflected a view which limited the role of public finance in European integration. This view was not always dominant. In the 1970s the acquisition of sizeable financial resources

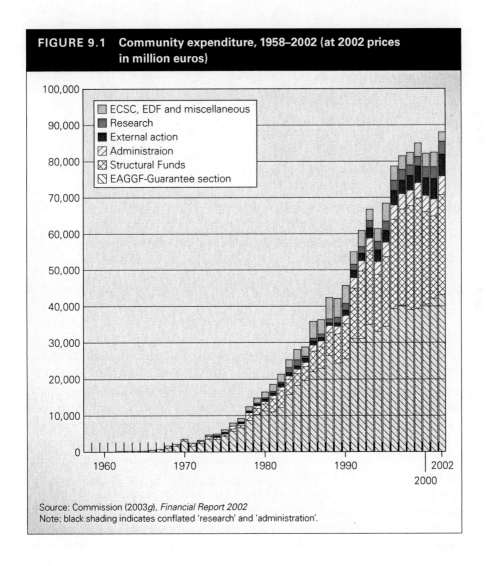

FIGURE 9.1   Community expenditure, 1958–2002 (at 2002 prices in million euros)

Source: Commission (2003*g*), *Financial Report 2002*
Note: black shading indicates conflated 'research' and 'administration'.

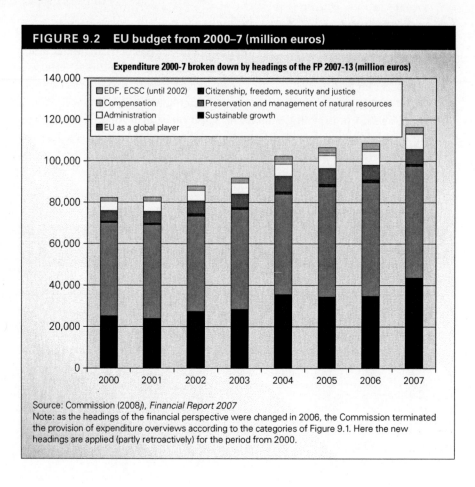

FIGURE 9.2   EU budget from 2000–7 (million euros)

Source: Commission (2008j), *Financial Report 2007*
Note: as the headings of the financial perspective were changed in 2006, the Commission terminated the provision of expenditure overviews according to the categories of Figure 9.1. Here the new headings are applied (partly retroactively) for the period from 2000.

for the budget was widely seen as essential to integration, especially to economic and monetary union (EMU) (see Chapter 7). It was anticipated that a larger budget would be necessary to deal with external shocks and fiscal stabilization, which member governments could no longer deal with through management of their own currencies. In contrast, the view that there could be strong Community government focused on liberalizing and opening-up national markets, with limited financial resources, gained ground in the 1980s, as Keynesian economic policies (with a strong distributive role for the state) were discredited in favour of monetarist approaches (stressing the efficiency of free markets). The capture of the EU budget by agricultural interests in the 1970s made it difficult for arguments in favour of a stronger distributive role for the European centre to win political ground (see Chapter 8).

Since the mid-1990s, the constraints set by the fiscal framework of EMU and other pressure on national expenditure have made many member states reluctant to accept significant transfers of financial resources to the EU level. Enlargements in 2004 and

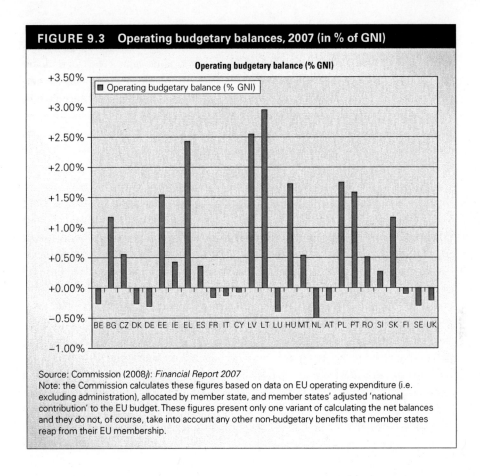

FIGURE 9.3   Operating budgetary balances, 2007 (in % of GNI)

Source: Commission (2008*j*): *Financial Report 2007*
Note: the Commission calculates these figures based on data on EU operating expenditure (i.e. excluding administration), allocated by member state, and member states' adjusted 'national contribution' to the EU budget. These figures present only one variant of calculating the net balances and they do not, of course, take into account any other non-budgetary benefits that member states reap from their EU membership.

2007 have further intensified this trend. In the Union of twenty-seven, economic diversity among member states has increased significantly (see Chapter 17); yet, an expansion of the Union-wide redistribution of funds is strongly opposed by the wealthier member states.

The major players

Budgetary policy-making in the Union rests on 'history-making decisions', i.e. big multi-annual package deals, an annual budgetary cycle, and thousands of management decisions within each expenditure area. 'History-making decisions', taken periodically since 1988, in which the European Council is the dominant player, shape the annual budgetary cycle. The management of the budget engages many layers of government, from the Commission to central, regional, and local governmental agencies in the member states. The Commission has responsibility for establishing the draft budget each year, and for proposals intended to shape the 'grand bargains'. The Commission has traditionally been an advocate of a bigger EU budget in order to fund policy integration, but in the 1990s it was forced to pay more attention to managing EU spending. In addition, the Commission tries to play the role of honest broker in budgetary battles, charged by the member governments with drafting reports on sensitive issues, such as 'own resources' and net flows to the member states.

Different configurations of the Council play a central role in budgetary negotiations. The Budget Council, consisting of representatives from finance ministries who approve the annual budget, has well-established operating procedures and decision-making rules. The General Affairs and External Relations Council (GAERC), the Economic and Financial Affairs Council (Ecofin), and the Agricultural Council each play a key role in negotiating the big budgetary deals. The GAERC attempts to coordinate across different negotiating chapters and, not least, to contain the Agricultural Council. Ecofin tries to exert budgetary discipline and has an important role in monitoring the Maastricht budgetary criteria (see Chapter 7), whereas the Agricultural Council has tended to be locked into a clientelist relationship with farmers and generally favours higher agricultural spending (see Chapter 8). Other Council configurations that develop spending programmes have to face tough negotiations about money when their programmes are reviewed and altered. However, the European Council, where heads of state or government broker the final stages of the 'history-making' bargains, still provides the most important forum for striking the big budgetary deals. Agreed by unanimity, these big bargains set the frame for EU budgetary politics for a seven-year period—thus, limiting the degree of flexibility but also the scope for potential conflict in the decision-making process for the annual budgets.

Since it was granted budgetary powers in 1975, the EP has regarded EU finances as one of its key channels of influence vis-à-vis the Council. The EP has tried to influence what happens at both the macro and the micro levels. As was seen in March 1999, it was an intervention by the EP, criticizing financial management, which provoked the unprecedented resignation of the whole college of commissioners. In the annual cycle of determining detailed appropriations, the EP frequently intervenes to alter the sums assigned to specific programmes and projects. For member governments, the budget is a crucial element of EU policy.

Budgetary politics over time

Since the first enlargement in 1973 there have been two distinct, different phases of budgetary politics and policy-making in the EU. The first phase (1973–88) was characterized by intense conflict about the size and distribution of EU monies, and by institutional battles between the Council and the EP. The second phase (since 1988) has been one of relative budgetary calm as member governments succeeded in negotiating the four big budgetary bargains, known as Delors-1, Delors-2, Agenda 2000, and the 2007–13 framework, and the Council and the EP cooperated closely in annual budgetary decision-making. Both phases correspond to a specific set of rules and procedures, and a distinct budgetary paradigm.

Phase 1: the dominance of budgetary battles

The first enlargement disturbed the budgetary bargain established by founder member governments. In particular, between 1979 and 1984 the member governments and EU institutions were locked into a protracted dispute about revenue and expenditure, which contributed in no small way to a wider malaise and lack of political impetus in the Union during the early 1980s. The 1970 treaty was designed to fix the rules before the UK became a member. The revenue sources suited the six founder countries, and the main spending would flow 'automatically' to support the common agricultural policy (CAP) (see Chapter 8). The package was essentially a French achievement, won in return for starting accession negotiations with the UK and the other applicants. The rules of the budgetary game were fixed to the advantage of the incumbents, above all France, making confrontation with the UK more or less inevitable (see H. Wallace 1983). Moreover, with the 1970 budgetary treaty member states half-heartedly delegated budgetary powers to the EP, introducing a complex annual procedure with a number of ill-specified rules. The mismatch between the limited desire of member states to involve the EP and the high expectations from the use of their newly acquired political powers on the part of members of the EP (MEPs) soon became apparent. The considerable scope for interpretation left open by the vaguely defined treaty provisions intensified this tension. In short, both the UK and the EP entered a budgetary stage that was characterized by a 'de Gaulle budget'.

After accession, successive British governments struggled to get the budget issue onto the agenda and slowly managed to alter the terms of the debate to ensure that distributional issues were taken seriously. Despite being one of the 'less prosperous' member states, the UK was set to become the second largest contributor after Germany. In trying to address the problem, a key concern of British governments was the dominance of CAP expenditure (constituting 70 per cent of the EC budget), from which the UK with its small agriculture sector benefited very little. The European Regional Development Fund, which was set up in 1975 to stimulate economic development in the least prosperous regions (see Chapter 10), brought only little relief.

Against this background, it became clear to the British government that the UK problem was structural rather than the result of chance consequences. Hence in 1979, the new British Prime Minister, Margaret Thatcher, began to demand a rebate system, which would guarantee the UK a better balance between contributions and receipts. The Commission and the other member governments were loath to concede the British case at the outset. The Commission had always been reluctant to engage in discussion of the net financial flows to the individual member states, lest this encourage too narrow a calculation of the benefits of Community membership, and lead states to seek *juste retour*, i.e. to extract. from the Community budget more or less what they put in. The key 'orthodoxy' regarding the budget at this time was that receipts flowed from EU policies and were thus automatic. This orthodoxy was challenged by the problem of UK contributions. Although Mrs Thatcher's confrontational approach was regarded as non-*communautaire*, she finally succeeded. At the Fontainebleau European Council in June 1984, the British government traded its consent to an agreement for increasing the VAT ceiling from 1 to 1.4 per cent against the establishment of a 'rebate' mechanism for dealing with excessive British contributions on a longer-term basis. The mechanism was designed to deal with the British problem and could not be generalized to other member states, even though other states became significant net contributors.

While the member governments were engaged in restructuring the budget, the EP and the Council were involved in a continuing struggle over their respective powers on budgetary matters. The EP rejected the 1980 and 1985 draft budgets, and the annual budgetary cycle was characterized by persistent struggle between the two institutions, the 'twin arms' of the budgetary authority. The EP actively exploited the broad scope for interpretation that the ill-specified treaty provisions offered. By contrast, the Council sought to limit the level of power-sharing with the EP as far as it legally could. In 1982 (case withdrawn), and again in 1986 (Case 34/86), the Council of Ministers brought an action in the European Court of Justice (ECJ) to annul the budget signed by the President of the Parliament as it disagreed with the EP's interpretation of the treaty provisions on the classification of expenditure (compulsory versus non-compulsory expenditure). Repeated attempts to solve the disputes over the interpretation of the treaty provisions through joint declarations and agreements failed.

Against a Council that displayed little willingness to take the EP seriously, the Parliament was determined to use the budgetary powers which it had acquired in 1975 to enhance its position in the Community's institutional landscape and to further its policy preferences. This was done in three ways. First, the Parliament attempted to use its budgetary powers to gain some leverage in the legislative field by introducing expenditure lines in policy areas where no legal bases existed. Secondly, the Parliament used its amending power to increase expenditure in order to promote Community policies of interest to it, notably regional policy, transport, social policy, and education. Thirdly, the Parliament used the annual budgetary cycle to expand the areas considered as non-compulsory expenditure, which meant it had a larger volume of expenditure where it could apply its margin for manoeuvre (see Box 9.1). In view of these priorities, the EP tended to pay more attention to authorizing expenditure than to monitoring how it was spent, a priority reflected in the importance of the EP's budget committee, and the assignment of budgetary control to a sub-committee (Lindner 2006).

Phase 2: ordered budgetary decision-making

The year 1988 marked a turning point. After the accessions of Greece, Portugal, and Spain and the adoption of the Single European Act (SEA) (see Chapter 5), it became clear that the intense budgetary battles and the constant shortage of revenue could not continue. Following a proposal by the President of the Commission, Jacques Delors, the EC embarked on a far-reaching political and institutional reform in the budgetary field. On the institutional side, it introduced the multi-annual financial perspective, which balanced revenue and expenditure and constrained the ballooning CAP by dividing the budget into different headings and setting annual ceilings for spending categories across a five-to-seven-year period. Although established by member states in the European Council, the financial perspective acquired its binding nature from the inter-institutional agreement between the Council, the European Parliament, and the Commission. The EP accepted the constraint on annual budgetary decision-making, because of the distributive component of the reform. The new financial perspective guaranteed a significant increase of resources and established regional spending as the second-largest part of the budget, both long-standing EP priorities.

Overall, the 1988 reform changed the rules of the game by supplanting the budget treaty with a set of superior soft-law arrangements among the budgetary actors. Annual decision-making lost its place in the inter-institutional spotlight and became the domain of budgetary experts, who cooperated closely and developed a routine of adopting annual budgets on time and without major tensions. Moreover, the 1988 reform transformed the CAP-centred 'de Gaulle budget' into the 'Delors budget' that, due to its strong regional policy dimension, was more redistributive and less CAP-oriented. In subsequent renewals of the financial perspective and inter-institutional agreement, the main institutional and distributive structure established in 1988 persisted. The requirement for unanimity did not change. The Delors-1 package and subsequent budgetary deals required the agreement of all member states. The veto made it very difficult to challenge entrenched budgetary gains such as the British budgetary rebate or the French demands on agriculture. The introduction of the multi-annual framework did not mean that conflict and disputes disappeared. However, tensions among member states or between the EP and the Council were kept at a manageable level during the annual procedures and channelled towards the renegotiation points of the large budget packages every five to seven years. At these renegotiation points, all players were assured that the unanimity requirement would allow them to block a package that would run contrary to their fundamental interests. This had not been the case in pre-1988 times: key players, such as the UK government, had to fight long and

TABLE 9.1 The main elements of the financial perspectives between 1988 and 2013

	Delors-1	Delors-2	Agenda 2000	FP 2007–13
Revenue ceiling	Rise to 1.2 per cent of GNP by 1992 and an extension of the system of 'own resources' to include a new fourth resource based on the relative wealth of the member states as measured by GNP	Unchanged for 1993 and 1994, but rise to 1.27% of GNP by 1999	Unchanged at 1.27% of GNP	Unchanged at 1.24% of GNI (which is a recalculation of the 1.27% of GNP) with average actual spending level of 1.05%
UK rebate and other correction mechanisms	Continuation of the complex Fontainebleau rebate system	UK rebate maintained; slight adjustments for other net contributors	UK rebate maintained; slight adjustments for other net contributors	UK rebate maintained; slight adjustments for other net contributors
CAP	contain the growth of agricultural expenditure at not more than 74% of GNP	Implementation of 1992 CAP reform (no significant change)	Only limited changes in the size and policy structure of the CAP	Implementation of 2003 CAP reform (no significant change in level of expenditure)
Cohesion expenditure	A doubling of the financial resources available to the less prosperous regions of the Community	Significant increase in the flows to the poorer parts of the Community	Flows to cohesion countries were marginally reduced, leaving some scope for flows to the new member states after eastern enlargement	A shift of regional expenditure from old cohesion countries to recently acceded countries

hard until their distributive concerns were addressed, and budgetary disputes continuously prevented the orderly adoption of annual budgets.

Delors-1

The budgetary agreement reached in February 1988 was a classic EC package deal. The fact that, for the first time, all the different elements of the budget were addressed in one reform was instrumental for the agreement. Moreover, the link to the ambitious internal-market project and related institutional reforms (in the form of the SEA) motivated in particular the German Chancellor Helmut Kohl to secure an agreement, even though it meant a significant increase in German net contributions to the budget. Not only was budgetary peace needed to set the Union again on a more integrationist path, for the poorer member states, such as Greece, Spain and Portugal, that did not benefit so much from CAP expenditure, a significant strengthening of cohesion spending was a prerequisite for agreeing to an internal-market project that would put more challenges to their economies than to those of wealthier member states (see Chapter 10).

Delors-2

The pattern established by Delors-1 was replicated in the negotiations on Delors-2. The political link between the SEA and Delors-1 was followed by a similar link between the Treaty on European Union (TEU) and the Delors-2 package. Again, poorer member states established the link between an increase in cohesion spending (i.e. the creation of a new cohesion fund) and further economic integration (i.e. the introduction of EMU).

The debate on Delors-2 was as tortuous and controversial as the earlier debate on Delors-1. The member governments grappled with their desire to reach agreement, on the one hand, and with their determination that the terms of the agreement be as favourable as possible to their own viewpoint, on the other. At the 1992 Edinburgh European Council an agreement was reached (see Table 9.1 for main elements).

Agenda 2000

In the mid-1990s, the balance of forces in the Union on budgetary matters began to change radically. The sizeable expansion in the size of the budget led to the emergence of a 'net contributors' club, an austerity camp concerned about the level of their financial commitments to the EU budget. At the Copenhagen European Council in 1993, the member governments had accepted the principle of an eastward enlargement of the Union. The accession of so many comparatively poor states would generate pressure for more redistribution and a larger budget.

Against these developments it is surprising that the institutional setting and the distributive character of the budget proved so robust. The status quo was by-and-large confirmed, but, in contrast to the significant increases recorded in 1988 and 1992, the Union's budgetary resources were consolidated (see Table 9.1 for the main elements of the final agreement).

The Financial Perspective for 2007–13

The negotiations of the next financial perspective took place against the background of three developments. First, at the Lisbon European Council in 2000 the EU set itself the strategic goal of becoming 'the most competitive economy in the world' by the end of the decade. Heads of state or government committed to take measures that would increase the competitiveness of their economies and raise investments in research and technology. The Lisbon goal was taken up by a report of an independent group of high-level experts headed by the Belgian economist, André Sapir (Sapir et al. 2004). Mandated by the Commission President, Romano Prodi, the group identified a number of measures that would help the EU overcome its problem of sluggish growth. The report criticized the dominance of the CAP spending and suggested refocusing the budget on European public goods, most importantly research and technology. Although fiercely criticized by some in the Commission, the report clearly established a link between the Lisbon goal and the EU budget. Second, most member states, in particular the large euro-area members, Germany and France, were experiencing a period of low growth rates and strong pressures on their national budgets. Their failure, in three subsequent years (2002–4), to meet the terms of the Stability and Growth Pact (SGP), which commit members of the euro area to compliance with the Maastricht criteria (see Chapter 7), further limited their willingness to accept increases in the EU budget. Third, for the first time the ten new member states sat at the negotiation table with high expectations of budgetary transfers and a full veto-right. None of these states had received any mitigation of their budgetary contributions at the moment of accession (see Chapter 17).

The negotiations for the new financial perspective began in early 2004 with a proposal by the Commission. Romano Prodi, then President of the Commission, emphasized the need to give the EU the resources to match its political priorities. Rather than fighting over details of future budget allocations, the Commission sought to engage member states in a debate over the priorities of the EU and wanted to transform the redistributive 'Delors budget' into a more distributive 'Lisbon budget' that would strengthen expenditure for public goods and reduce the focus on redistribution resources to poorer regions/member states or farmers. For the first time since the inception of the financial perspective in 1988, the Commission envisaged an overhaul of the expenditure headings so as to reflect the new policies and priorities of the enlarged EU. The Commission proposed an average spending level of 1.14 per cent of the EU's GNI over the period covered. This was a significant increase compared to the existing spending level of about 1.0 per cent of GNI, but still below the 'own resources' ceiling of 1.24 per cent of GNI.[4] Moreover, the Commission presented a proposal for a generalized correction mechanism, establishing a more transparent and equitable method to correct a budgetary burden deemed excessive in relation to any country's relative prosperity. Such a mechanism would modify and extend the 'UK rebate' to other countries.[5]

Finding an agreement was again not easy. Essentially, three key cleavages dominated the debate. First, net contributors were unwilling to accept an increase in the spending level, while governments from beneficiary member states, such as Spain and Portugal, endorsed the Commission's proposal and stressed the importance of pursuing the objective of 'economic and social cohesion'. Second, among the beneficiaries of regional expenditure, 'old' beneficiaries wanted to prevent an abrupt ending of transfers and demanded compensation, while the new member states feared that these compensation payments would be financed from cuts in transfers to the east. Third, the UK government strongly opposed any attempt to abolish the UK rebate through replacing it with a generalized mechanism, which was naturally favoured by all the other net contributors. Significantly, the Commission's ambition to strengthen expenditure for public goods found very few active supporters, except for Parliament. There was little space left for new spending programmes in fields such as innovation and technology given the fact that agricultural expenditure was excluded from the negotiations (under a Franco-German agreement concluded in 2002) and that regional expenditure was dominated by strong vested interests in the new and old member states. An agreement was finally reached in late 2005 (see Table 9.1 for the main elements).

A new style of budgetary politics?

Although the agreement on the financial perspective for 2007–13 did not alter the established structure of the Union's budget, two subsequent events have given rise to expectations that a new style of budgetary politics might evolve. First, the Treaty of Lisbon incorporated significant changes to the treaty provisions on budgetary decision-making. Second, when adopting the financial perspective for 2007–13 member states agreed to reassess the main budgetary issues in 2008–9 on the basis of a mid-term budget review to be undertaken by the Commission.

The Treaty of Lisbon

Although the Treaty of Lisbon, just as the proposed Constitutional Treaty (CT), includes significant changes to the treaty provisions for the budgetary procedure, a closer look reveals that the main elements of the 'new' budgetary procedure are taken from the rules that are laid down in the existing inter-institutional agreement and that they are therefore already current practice.

Under the Treaty of Lisbon, both arms of the budgetary authority will have equal decision-making power over all components of the EU budget. Similar to the co-decision procedure in legislative politics, a Conciliation Committee will feature as the key forum for brokering a deal between the EP and the Council before their respective final readings. These seemingly innovative features are much in line with the informal arrangements that are in place for the current procedure. Most of the time, the annual budget is de facto adopted in a conciliation meeting between the Council and the EP shortly before the second reading in Council. Given that negotiations at the conciliation meeting cover all areas of the budget, the distinction between compulsory and non-compulsory expenditure has become less relevant over time. The Council and EP both use their budgetary powers over the respective classifications of the budget as bargaining chips to strike a deal for the whole budget. Under the provisions of the Treaty of Lisbon, the Council will be able to prevent an agreement in the Conciliation Committee and thus trigger a new budget proposal by the Commission. The granting of this de-facto right of rejection to the Council upholds the existing balance.

With regard to the financial perspective, the Lisbon provisions will institutionalize the procedures for the multi-annual budget plan (as laid down in the inter-institutional agreement) requiring a unanimous decision in the Council and the consent of the EP. If no agreement is reached, the ceilings of the previous multi-annual budget plan remain in place.

However, it remains an open question whether the Treaty of Lisbon will leave budgetary decision-making unchanged. Although the new provisions largely institutionalize existing rules and procedures, the move from soft to hard law might alter the incentives of the players involved. Under the Treaty of Lisbon, the binding force of the financial perspective, as well as the arrangements between the EP and the Council for the annual procedure, will no longer be based on the political willingness of actors to cooperate but on the legal force of the Treaty. Under the pre-Lisbon set-up, the EP, as well as the Council, can renounce the inter-institutional agreement and return to the treaty provisions (which entail an increase in flexibility as annual budgetary decision-making would be largely unconstrained by spending ceilings and unanimity requirements for revising them). This threat has been a powerful instrument for the EP, in particular when the treaty provisions would have allowed for a higher increase in non-compulsory expenditure than foreseen in the financial perspective. Under the provisions in the Treaty of Lisbon, the EP will no longer have the possibility of renouncing the financial perspective. Once adopted, the multi-annual budget plan will become binding law. Moreover, if the EP does not consent to a new budget plan, the ceilings of the last financial perspective will continue to apply indefinitely until new ceilings were adopted by unanimity. This will reinforce the status-quo bias inherent in the framework of financial perspectives, strengthening in particular those member states in the Council that want to prevent any significant change, and thus making significant reductions in the CAP or structural funds, or any move to a Lisbon-style public-goods budget, extremely difficult and unlikely.

The budget review

When adopting the new financial perspective for 2007–13, member states seemed keen to demonstrate that they were, in principle, open to considering more far-reaching reforms of the budget. This was relevant in particular for those member states that complained about the very incrementalist nature of the agreement. The European Council mandated the Commission to undertake in 2008–9 a review of the EU expenditure and revenue sides, covering all issues including CAP and the UK rebate. The European Council could then take decisions on the basis of the review. The inter-institutional agreement of 2006 confirmed this plan and associated the EP to it.

When starting the review process in 2007, the Commission emphasized that the main objective of the review was to initiate a broadly based public debate on the longer-term challenges facing the EU. This debate should translate into reform proposals for how the EU budget could better help EU policies to address these challenges. The Commission stressed that the review was not aimed at preparing a proposal for a new financial perspective. In line with the focus on public debate and open reflection, a large number of public presentations and conferences, as well as a public consultation, took place.

Although the Commission's initiative did not really lead to a large public debate on the budget and the challenges of the Union, it did spark a number of academic and political contributions advancing new or already known reform proposals (BEPA 2008). On the expenditure side, there were numerous calls for shifting the budget more towards the financing of public goods, such as defence, security, and research and development. Some also recognized the link between CAP and the UK rebate and hoped that reform of the one could lead to the abolishment of the other. On the revenue side, proposals for Union-wide tax based on, for example, air traffic, CO_2 emissions, or financial transactions, gained some momentum, with the former Austrian Chancellor Wolfgang Schüssel, as well as the EP, presenting this as a way to establish a direct link between European taxpayers and the EU budget (Le Cacheux 2007; Schüssel 2007; European Parliament 2007a). Many analyses criticized the strong status-quo bias of the existing institutional arrangement for budgetary decision-making. Some new proposals on how to address this resistance to change without significantly altering the institutional set-up were made. For example, the concept of 'constraint flexibility' foresees the loosening of the constraints set by the categories and annual ceilings of the financial perspective for annual decision-making (Buti and Nava 2008). Sunset clauses for spending programmes sought to prevent the automatic and incremental renewal of expenditure lines (Gros 2008).

Despite these interesting reform proposals it seemed unlikely that the European Council would take concrete decisions that alter the existing budgetary order of the Union. First, it was unclear how much political weight the outgoing Commission and its President really wanted to put behind the budget review given that there would be European elections in 2009 after which Mr Barroso sought and won reappointment as Commission President. Second, in view of the immediate problem stemming from the financial crisis beginning in 2007 and the uncertain economic outlook, member states would be less interested in entering into discussions on the longer-term challenges of the Union and the need to adjust the EU budget accordingly. Third, the institutional set-up of the multi-annual budget plan made significant reforms half-way through the seven-year term unlikely. Although in the past CAP reforms occurred outside the framework of the big budget bargains such as the 1992 and the 2003 reforms (Ackrill and Kay 2006), the pressure to adopt a new package deal would not outweigh the incentives for the member states to wait until 2012–13, i.e. the regular end of term of the financial perspective. Moreover, the budget review could not be linked to significant integration projects that in the past had been instrumental for large-scale distributive reforms.

Managing a larger budget

Agreeing the overall size of the EU budget and how it should be spent is the stuff of distributive and redistributive politics. Managing the EU budget involves a different kind of politics, namely, executive politics and multi-level administration. The struggle for budgetary resources in the Community and the inter-institutional battles about budgetary power initially overshadowed questions of 'value for money' and the quality of the Commission's financial management. These became an increasingly important focus of budgetary politics as the financial resources of the budget grew.

In the 1990s the first attempts were made to improve financial management, but they proved insufficient to prevent financial mismanagement becoming an explosive political issue in 1999 when the Santer Commission was forced to resign. Time and time again the Court of Auditors drew attention to financial mismanagement in the Commission and in the member states, and two senior Commission financial-control staff, Paul van Buitenen and Marta Andreasen, went public about their auditing concerns in 1998 and 2002 respectively.[6]

Managing a budget that involves around 400,000 individual authorizations of expenditure and payment each year is a major challenge, particularly as the management of the EU budget is characterized by a fragmentation of responsibility between the Commission and public authorities in the member states: 80 per cent of the budget is managed on behalf of the Union by the member states. There is a great diversity of public management and public finance cultures across Europe and limits to the auditing capacity of a number of states. The complexity of European rules, particularly in agriculture, the customs union, and regional policy, creates loopholes, which can be exploited by those who are intent on defrauding the EU budget. The sheer number of agricultural subsidy payments and export refunds creates considerable opportunities for abuse. Reports of fraud in olive oil, beef, cigarettes, wine, and fish, running in some cases into millions of euros, undermine the credibility of the Community's policies. Press reports and investigations carried out by the European Anti-Fraud Office (OLAF) have highlighted scams involving the forging of customs documents in order to claim export refunds, avoiding anti-dumping duties, non-payment of excise duties, switching labels on foodstuffs to claim higher refunds, claiming headage payments for non-existent animals, and putting non-existent food into intervention storage. No one knows with any degree of certainty the level of fraud affecting the EU budget: estimates of between 7 and 10 per cent of the budget are often cited, but have never been convincingly proved. Investigations of fraud suggest that some member states are dilatory in following up cases of fraud against the EU budget, as this would, paradoxically, mean devoting additional national resources in order to obtain less money from the EU budget.

Financial management in the Union has been characterized by considerable institution-building, beginning with the 1975 agreement to create the Court of Auditors. In its first report (1978) the Court raised the issue of fraud and it has continued to do so in all subsequent reports. The Court's reports have been consistently highly critical of the Commission's financial management. In the TEU, the Court of Auditors was given additional responsibilities in relation to financial management, notably the need to make a Statement of Assurance (SAD) each year to the Council and the EP to demonstrate that the financial transactions underlying the budget are legal and regular. The Court's report in 2006 on the 2005 Budget was the twelfth successive year that the Court failed to give a positive SAD.

The Commission's management of EU finances became high politics in January 1999. The battleground was a classic parliamentary–executive conflict. It was prompted in part by allegations, in both the EP and the media, of mismanagement of the EU budget and financial irregularities. A motion of censure against the Commission was tabled in the EP, but was voted down by MEPs in January 1999 in return for a commitment from the Commission that it would cooperate with a special inquiry. The report of the five 'Wise Men' (lawyers and auditors), which was presented to the Commission in March 1999, highlighted problems in a number of European programmes. The report (Committee of Independent Experts 1999: 142) concluded that mismanagement in the Commission was:

tantamount to an admission of a loss of control by the political authorities over the administration they are supposed to be running. The loss of control implies at the outset a heavy responsibility for both the commissioners individually and the Commission as a whole.

It went on to say that 'it was becoming difficult to find anyone who has even the slightest sense of responsibility' (Committee of Independent Experts 1999: 142).

The political context in which the report was drafted and its tone left the Santer Commission, after a night of drama, with little option but to resign.

The Prodi Commission that took over in autumn 1999 was given a mandate to reform the Commission services by the European Council. Vice-President Neil Kinnock, who was given responsibility for administrative reform, proposed a White Paper on the Reform Strategy in March 2000 (Commission 2000*e*). Not unexpectedly, reform of financial management and control systems was one of four priorities in the White Paper. The implementation of the White Paper led to a new Financial Regulation (*Official Journal*, L 248, 16 September 2002) and extensive management changes in the Commission services. The Commission is also adopting a stricter approach with the member states, taking the unprecedented step in July 2008 of suspending aid worth over €500 million to Bulgaria because of corruption. The Kinnock reforms have enhanced the regulatory framework and the capacity of EU institutions to practise sound financial management, but the EU budget remains highly fragmented and is dispersed across so many countries and levels of government that problems continue.

Conclusions

Budgetary politics in the EU is marked by both elements of continuity and factors of change. The capture of the EU budget in the 1960s by agricultural interests has proved relatively enduring. France, the main defender of the CAP, has been successful in preserving its interests in this policy domain. However, agricultural support has moved decisively since 1992 from market measures to compensation payments, and the funding has started to shift from consumers to taxpayers (see Chapter 8). Cohesion funding assumed a central role in budgetary politics in the late 1980s with the arrival of Spain and Portugal. At about 30 per cent of total expenditure under the Berlin Agreement, structural funds remain an entrenched part of the budgetary *acquis*. Attempts by the Commission to refocus the EU budget towards European public goods and thus to reduce the redistributive emphasis within the existing 'EU distributional mode' have not met with success.

Agreement in 1988 to the Delors-1 financial perspective represented a step change in how EU budgets were made. Since 1988, multi-annual bargains have become the norm, and are now part of the *acquis*. Although difficult and protracted negotiations have characterized all four budgetary bargains outlined in this chapter, the political process, characterized by a set of integrated Commission proposals, intensive negotiations across a range of Councils, and high-level bargaining in the European Council, demonstrated a capacity to frame an outcome that would enjoy broad consensus. Thus the Union's annual budgetary cycle became successfully locked into a medium-term financial perspective, which in turn reduced the dangers of acrimonious arguments and inter-institutional conflicts.

The system of multi-annual financial planning and big budgetary agreements endured, notwithstanding the significant increase in the number of member states. Since 2004, the new members states have benefited from cohesion expenditure and funds have been shifted away from the 'old' to the 'new' cohesion states (see Chapter 10). Following accession in 2004, the new member states played a very active role in the budgetary negotiations on the 2007–13 financial perspective. Poland, as the largest of the new member states, was particularly significant, siding with Spain at the early stages of the negotiations, then with the UK, and at the end of the negotiations interacting closely with Germany. It also maintained close relations with the other new member states which were more willing to compromise in the closing stages of the negotiations. In the end, even for Poland getting agreement became a priority as it would enable it to draw down additional funds from 2007. The increase in the economic diversity in the Union as a consequence of enlargement suggests that there will be a strong 'cohesion club' in the Union for the foreseeable future. The net contributors' club, however, remains very resistant to endowing the Union with significantly larger financial resources. Hence, there are limits to EU solidarity and to potential transfers to the east.

The small size of the EU budget persists as a key characteristic of the finances of the Union. A strong status-quo bias in EU budgetary politics, in terms of both institutional structures and the preferences of the major actors, makes significant changes in the distributive order of the Union unlikely. This creates a mismatch between the expenditure priorities of the EU budget and key policy priorities facing Europe. The 2008 financial crisis and fears of a large-scale global economic recession brought back some of the macroeconomic arguments in favour of a European stabilization policy and a burden-sharing arrangement for the financial and economic crisis. It will be interesting to see whether these arguments may create momentum for new budgetary policies.

Notes

1 This chapter draws on the EU budget chapter by Brigid Laffan and Michael Shackleton in the fourth edition. Michael Shackleton's consent is gratefully acknowledged. The views expressed in the chapter do not necessarily reflect those of the European Central Bank.

2 For the most comprehensive and detailed treatments of the development of the EU budget and the rules that govern it, see Laffan (1997), and Lindner (2006).

3 This chapter draws heavily on the analysis of Laffan (1997), Lindner (2006), and Shackleton (1990, 1993a, 1993b).

4 The figure 1.24 per cent GNI equals 1.27 per cent GDP. The switch from GDP to GNI reflects a new national accounting methodology that the European Commission adopted in line with the 1993 System of National Accounts.

5 The Dutch government obtained an agreement on a declaration attached to the final act of the Constitutional Treaty stating that The Netherlands would support a move to qualified majority voting only once a decision on the own resource system 'has provided The Netherlands with a satisfactory solution for its excessive negative net payment position *vis-à-vis* the European Union budget'.

6 In the 2004 European elections, Paul van Buitenen was elected as one of two MEPs of his newly founded anti-fraud party 'Europa Transparant'.

 FURTHER READING

A comprehensive volume on the EU budget is Laffan (1997). Lindner (2006) presents a thorough institutionalist analysis of EU budgetary decision-making over the past three decades. For a non-academic, but detailed, account of the finances of the EU see Commission (2008i). For an analysis of the revenue side, see Begg and Grimwade (1998).

Begg, I., and Grimwade, N. (1998), *Paying for Europe* (Sheffield: Sheffield Academic Press).

Commission (2008*i*), *European Union Public Finance* (Luxembourg: Office for Official Publications of the European Communities).

Laffan, B. (1997), The *Finances of the European Union* (Basingstoke: Palgrave Macmillan).

Lindner, J. (2006), *Conflict and Change in EU Budgetary Politics* (London: Routledge).

CHAPTER 10

The Structural Funds and Cohesion Policy

Extending the Bargain to Meet New Challenges

David Allen

▌ Summary

The structural funds are the European Unions's (EU) only explicitly redistributive policy. Moreover, they provide an important part of the empirical foundation for the challenge from the multi-level governance approach to intergovernmentalism. Understanding the structural funds is thus revealing about both the nature of European integration and how we should seek to understand it. This chapter argues that, while the European Commission has played an important role shaping the priorities of the structural funds, the overall development of the policy has been dictated by intergovernmental bargains. The centrality of intergovernmental bargaining has undermined the original redistributive objective of the policy.

Introduction

The structural funds have a distinctive place in European integration because they are the EU's only explicitly redistributive policy. Moreover, analysis of the structural funds was central to the development of the governance approach to European integration (see Chapter 2). According to the 'multi-level governance' approach developed by Gary Marks (1992, 1993), national governments are losing control both to the supranational European Commission and to regional and local governments within the member states.

This chapter argues that, although the Commission and sub-national governments are actively involved in the implementation stage of the structural funds, the development of these funds has been driven by a series of intergovernmental bargains. More specifically, the structural funds have been used to facilitate history-making developments in European integration with respect to both widening (enlargement) and deepening (single market, economic and monetary union (EMU), and the Lisbon Agenda on economic reform). Once these grand bargains have been negotiated and overall structural fund expenditure embedded in the EU's multi-annual financial perspectives (see Chapter 9), the Commission has used its own powers and initiative to shape and to implement the detail of cohesion policy. In part it has aimed to advance the development of what has been described as multi-level governance (Bache 2004, 2008) by encouraging the participation of sub-national (regional and local) governments and of representatives of civil society in detailed programme planning, implementation, and evaluation.

The structural funds grew steadily for twenty years from the 1970s and then stabilized at just over one-third of the EU budget. The original rationale for the structural funds was to remove regional disparities, with EU regions defined and targeted as recipients for different types of assistance. This regional 'logic' gradually became known as 'cohesion policy'. Whilst assistance to regions remained important, funds were also made available to some entire member states, with the Cohesion Fund initially providing money specifically for those member states striving to meet the public spending and debt criteria for participation in the euro (see Chapter 7). More recently the structural funds have been seen as part of the means towards the achievement of the growth and competitiveness goals set out in the Lisbon Agenda, which was intended to make the EU the most competitive economy in the world by 2010 (see Chapters 7 and 12). Other EU objectives have also been associated with the structural funds with the result that, over the years, they have been linked to economic growth, competitiveness, employment, sustainable development, subsidiarity, regionalism, and good governance including the participation of civil society, as well as with bringing the EU 'closer to its citizens'.

In recent years the central governments of some of the older member states (EU15) have sought to retain or regain their 'gate-keeping role' (Bache 1999), whilst many of the new member states have implemented structural fund expenditure in a decentralized manner. Since the 2004 and 2007 enlargements some of the older member states, such as Sweden, The Netherlands, and the UK, have also questioned the need for continuing to provide EU-level funding for regional assistance (Ujupan 2009: 12). They have argued that, in the short term, structural-funds finance should be restricted to new member states, and that, in the longer term, structural funding to deal with regional disparities should be renationalized, with the role of EU institutions confined to the coordination of national programmes.

The 2008 financial crisis will place serious strains on future EU expenditure. It may lead to an increased emphasis on the coordination of essentially national solutions to the problem of regional disparities rather than on the further development of EU-level policies. Nevertheless it seems likely that the structural funds will continue to be an important part of the EU budget, even though their expenditure may be directed at a more diverse set of objectives than is currently the case with cohesion policy. It is likely therefore that the structural funds will continue to play an important role in facilitating the preservation and continuing development of the EU regardless of the fate of cohesion policy as currently construed.

Intergovernmental bargaining: from regional policy to cohesion policy

In the early days, structural funding for a regional policy developed partly because the 1957 Treaty of Rome provided for it, but mainly because, following the 1973 enlargement, there was a determination to reduce the dominant role of the common agricultural policy (CAP) (see Chapter 8) in the evolving European Economic Community (EEC) budget (see Chapter 9) by developing other areas of expenditure (see Box 10.1). In particular it was judged necessary to develop policies from which the UK, a major net contributor to that budget, might be able to benefit through the creation of the European Regional Development Fund (ERDF) (H. Wallace 1977). Thus from the outset regional policy was related to enlargement and was perceived as playing a significant facilitating role when it came to trying to establish a balanced and equitable budget. In these early days, regional funds were allocated to the member states using a quota system rather than one informed by the comparative evaluation and weighting of specific regional needs.

During the 1980s this intergovernmental logic remained significant, even though it was accompanied by moves to impose at least the veneer of economic rationality through the development of principles such as additionality, concentration, programming, and partnership (see below). From 1986 onwards regional policy was rationalized in terms of economic and social cohesion and the reduction of regional disparities was to be achieved predominantly by structural-fund expenditure. In addition, loans from the European Investment Bank (EIB) would

---

BOX 10.1   **Structural funds: financial instruments**

European Regional Development Fund (ERDF)

Established in 1975. Provides funds for investment in companies (especially small and medium-sized enterprises), infrastructure, capital risk funds, local development funds, and technical assistance for the implementation of ERDF projects. Allocated at the regional level.

European Social Fund (ESF)

Established in 1958. Provides funds for the integration into working life of the unemployed and disadvantaged sections of the population, mainly by funding training measures. Allocated at the regional level.

Cohesion Fund (CF)

Established in 1994. Provides funds for member states that have GDPs per capita below 90 per cent of the EU average. Finance is limited to environmental and transport infrastructure. Funding is restricted to those member states whose public deficit is 3 per cent or less of national GDP. Funds allocated at the member-state level.

European Agricultural Guidance and Guarantee Fund — Guidance (EAGGF-Guidance) renamed European Agricultural Fund for Rural Development (EAFRD)

Established in 1962 and renamed in 2007. Finances rural-development expenditure not related to CAP market support. Allocated at the regional level and limited currently to agricultural measures.

Financial Instrument for Fisheries Guidance (FIFG)

Established in 1999. Provides funds for structural measures in fisheries, aquaculture, and the processing and marketing of fishery and aquaculture products. Allocated on a regional basis.

---

improve the working of the single market and member states' regional policies would be coordinated, even though not every member state possessed a national regional-policy framework. It is from this period onwards that 'cohesion' was embedded as a core EU objective, buttressed by its inclusion in the 1986 Single European Act (SEA).

Links to broader policy developments

Regional funding also came to be used to facilitate further EU developments, as first illustrated by the Integrated Mediterranean Programmes (IMPs) (Allen 2005: 218), and repeated with the complex bargain of 1988 that saw the supposed financial 'costs' of the single market programme 'compensated' for in the first financial perspective (see Table 10.1 and Chapters 5 and 9). This doubled the structural funds available to support regional/cohesion policy. A similar development occurred in the early 1990s, when the package on economic and monetary union (EMU) (see Chapter 7) was agreed in Maastricht in December 1991 as part of the Treaty on European Union (TEU). This was financed by the second financial perspective agreed in Edinburgh in December 1992 (Allen 2005: 219–21). The de-facto enlargement which saw the five eastern *Länder* incorporated into a unified Germany in 1990 was also facilitated by an additional allocation of 3 billion ecus of cohesion funding for the 1991–3 period.

TABLE 10.1	**Evolution of the structural funds in relation to spending on the CAP, 1975–2013**			
Year	Structural fund expenditure as percentage of EU budget	CAP expenditure as percentage of EU budget	Structural funds and CAP combined as percentage of EU budget	EU budget as percentage of EU GNP
1975 (establishment of the ERDF)	6.2	70.9	77.1	0.53
1980 (introduction of non-quota allocation of structural funds)	11.0	68.6	79.6	0.80
1985 (further reduction of national quota allocation)	12.8	68.4	81.2	0.92
1988 (start of 1st financial perspective)	17.2	60.7	77.9	1.12
1993 (start of 2nd financial perspective)	32.3	53.5	85.8	1.20
2000 (start of 3rd financial perspective)	34.8	44.5	79.3	1.07
2007 (start of 4th financial perspective)	36.7	47.1	83.8	1.04
2013 (end of 4th financial perspective)	38.1	43.0	81.1	0.93

Source: House of Lords (2008: 19) amended by the author

A similar, albeit less direct, link can be seen between the 1997 Treaty of Amsterdam (ToA) and the Commission's Agenda 2000 proposals (1997), and further consolidated in the third financial perspective, agreed in Berlin in March 1999 (Allen 2005: 222–5; this volume, Chapter 9). This compensation saga was then repeated once again at the end of 2005 when a fourth financial perspective was agreed by the EU25. This included complex plans for cohesion funding for the EU27 up to 2013, and thus made possible the implementation of the plans for further regional policy reform laid out in the Commission's third Cohesion Report (Commission 2004a) and further discussed in the fourth Cohesion Report (Commission 2007l).

TABLE 10.2 Structural fund objectives: progressive concentration		
1988–99 Financial Perspectives 1 and 2	**2000–6 Financial Perspective 3**	**2007–13 Financial Perspective 4**
Cohesion Objective (Cohesion Fund after 1993)	Cohesion Objective (Cohesion Fund)	Convergence Objective (Cohesion Fund, ERDF and ESF) (81.5% of 2007–13 structural funds)
Objective 1 (ERDF, ESF, EAGGF-Guidance)	Objective 1 (ERDF, ESF, and EAGGF)	–
Objective 2 (ERDF, ESF)	Objective 2 (ERDF, ESF, and EAGGF-Guidance)	Competitiveness and employment objective (ERFDF and ESF) (15.9% of 2007–13 structural funds)
Objective 3 (ESF) Combined with Objective 4 after 1993	Objective 3 (ESF)	–
Objective 4 (ESF)	–	–
Objective 5a (EAGGF-Guidance) and 5b (ERDF, ESF, and EAGGF)	–	–
Objective 6 ERDF, ESF, and EAGGF-Guidance) after 1995	–	–
Community Initiatives: INTER-REG, LEADER, REGIS, ADAPT, SME, RECHAR, KONVER, RESIDER, RETEX, URBAN, PESCA, EMPLOYMENT (ERDF,ESF, EAGGF-Guidance)	Community Initiatives: INTERREG (ERDF), LEADER+ (EAGGF-Guidance, EQUAL (ESF) Rural development and restructuring of fishery sector outside Objective 1 (EAGGF-Guidance and FIFG)	European Territorial Cooperation (formerly INTERREG) (ERDF) (2.5% of 2007–13 structural funds)

Throughout this period, both the primary 'historic' decisions about the financial perspectives and the secondary 'distributive' arrangements about the various cohesion objectives (see Table 10.2) were dependent on high-level bargaining among the member governments, in essence an intergovernmental process. It was only subsequently, as the implementation process began, that other actors began to play a role. From 1988 onwards the process of implementation of structural fund expenditure provided some scope for a challenge to the powers of the central governments of the member states, thus opening up a form of multi-level governance.

Some care, however, needs to be taken in specifying how and to what extent state powers were being challenged by the development of multi-level governance. Some member-state governments may have had little interest in the implementation stage once they had secured guarantees of a certain level of structural funding. The member governments that are net contributors to the EU budget may have an interest in a degree of Commission oversight over the spending performance of those that are net recipients. It may also be the case that the member governments are able to control, manipulate, or even cooperate with newly enfranchised sub-national actors so as to consolidate, rather than weaken, their central authority. Thus, the intergovernmental perspective best explains how decisions are made about the overall size of the structural funds and how they are distributed among the member states. The multi-level governance perspective, on the other hand, is a useful way of understanding precisely how the funds are subsequently spent within the member states. By imposing operating principles (see below) and by empowering sub-national actors the European Commission was able to use structural fund expenditure in order to establish a distinct and common 'Community' approach to regional/cohesion policy.

In the shadow of enlargement

The accessions of Sweden, Finland, and Austria in 1995 did not disturb the cohesion funding arrangements, other than to stimulate the invention of what was then known as objective six (see Box 10.2) in order to ensure that these new members would be eligible for regional benefits. The prospect of further enlargement to the east and south necessarily led to a more extensive debate about the future of the structural funds and EU cohesion policy. Decisions on this were postponed while the member governments negotiated the ToA, but immediately afterwards the Commission delivered, as requested, its proposals for managing further enlargement (see Chapters 9 and 17). The Agenda 2000 documents (Commission 1997) made proposals for the third financial perspective and recommended that overall structural funding, in both the EU15 and the enlarged membership, be frozen at 0.46 per cent of EU GDP. This led the Commission to propose structural funding totalling €275 billion, at 1997 prices, for the 2000–6 period. This sum was broken down into €230 billion for the EU15, with an additional €45 billion, to be ring-fenced, for pre-accession aid for all the candidates and post-accession aid for the 'Luxembourg' six states that were assumed at that time to be likely to

---

BOX 10.2   Structural fund objectives

- 1988–99

– Objective 1 intended to cover regions where the GDP per capita is less than 75% of the EU average but the Council reserved the right to include other regions.

– Objective 2 covers regions affected by industrial decline, where the unemployment level is above the EU average. Eligibility negotiated between the Commission and the Council.

– Objective 3 combats long-term unemployment. In 1993 it was combined with Objective 4 to facilitate the occupational integration of young people.

– Objective 4 originally (pre-1993) designed to facilitate adaptation of workers to industrial change.

– Objective 5a earmarked specifically for agricultural and forestry assistance and Objective 5b designed for the development of rural areas, mainly via diversification away from traditional agricultural activity.

– Objective 6 was introduced after the 1995 enlargement for developing sparsely populated Nordic areas.

– Cohesion Objective for states with a GDP of less than 90% of the EU average

- 2000–6

– Objective 1 as above but with stricter application of eligibility criteria, although it also includes regions previously eligible for Objective 6 and phasing out funds for those eligible before 2000 for Objective 1 funding.

– Objective 2 is for regions facing major change in the industrial services and fisheries sectors, rural areas in serious decline, and disadvantaged urban areas.

– Objective 3 covers those regions not covered by other objectives. It is specifically aimed at encouraging the modernization of systems of education, training, and employment.

– Cohesion Objective for states with GDPs per capita of less than 90% of the EU average.

- 2007–13

– Convergence Objective: to support growth and job creation in states using the cohesion criteria and regions using the Objective 1 criteria (above). In addition, this objective provides 'phasing out' funds for those states and regions which would have remained eligible if the cohesion threshold had been set at 90% of the EU15 average GDP per capita and the regional threshold at 75% of the EU15 average GDP per capita and not that of the EU25.

– Regional Competiveness and Employment Objective provides funds for all regions not covered by the Convergence Objective and 'phasing in' funds for those regions which qualified for Objective 1 funding in the 2000–6 period but whose GDP per capita now exceeds 75% of the EU15 average GDP per capita.

– European Territorial Cooperation provides funds for cross-border cooperation for NUTS3 regions that have maritime, national, or EU borders, for trans-national cooperation for 13 Commission-identified EU regional cooperation zones between EU NUTS3 regions, and for inter-regional cooperation and the establishment of networks and the exchange of experience.

join the EU by 2006 (see Chapter 17). In proposing that cohesion funding should remain a high priority, but that its growth should be curtailed, the Commission was constrained by those member states which were committed to freezing the overall budget at a maximum of 1.27 per cent of EU GDP up to 2006 (see Chapter 9), with little prospect that they could agree any significant reductions in other areas of expenditure such as agriculture (see Chapter 8).

The Commission proposed that the cohesion objective, underpinned by the structural funds, should be further concentrated and that their implementation should be simplified. To this end it suggested reducing the number of objectives to just three (see Table 10.2) and reducing coverage of the funding from over 50 per cent of the EU population to between 35 and 40 per cent. It was also proposed that unemployment should become the major criterion for allocating funds in the newly created objective-2 regions. The new rules for determining aid in objective-2 regions and the proposed stricter application of the rules for objective-1 eligibility would mean that many regions that had received aid between 1988 and 1999 would no longer be eligible in the period up to 2006.

After tough negotiations on these proposals, the European Council agreed a deal in March 1999 which reduced the Commission's proposed expenditure from €275 billion (at 1999 prices) to €258 billion, with €45 billion ring-fenced for pre-accession aid and post-accession benefits (for overall outcome see Table 10.1). To secure agreement the Commission had to accept special transitional arrangements for those regions likely to lose out so that no region would lose coverage by EU funding for more than one-third of its previously eligible population, and continuation of the Cohesion Fund for the 'poor four' (Greece, Ireland, Portugal, and Spain), even though three of them had apparently 'converged' enough to join the single currency (see Chapter 7).

The 1999 Berlin agreement was facilitated by continued acceptance of the well-established principle of structural funding that it should provide something for everybody—or, more precisely, for every member state. The persistence of this principle seemed to leave the member governments, especially the net recipients, in a stronger position than before. The Berlin agreement appears to confirm the argument advanced by Bache (1999) that, since the reforms of cohesion policy in 1993, there has been a consolidation of member governments' control of structural fund expenditure, and a subsequent weakening of the Commission's position. This view is contested by Bachtler and Mendez (2007), although they focus on implementation (concentration and programming) rather than on the core funding decisions.

The 1999 reforms, which formally dealt with the immediate problem of the budgetary implications of enlargement, had little serious impact on regional disparities. Politically the new proposals served mainly to facilitate agreement among the member governments, and the Commission may have been wise to respond to the new atmosphere with its proposals to simplify the implementation procedures, and to step back from some of its contacts with sub-national actors. Thus the process of implementing structural fund expenditure moved further and further away from the concept of multi-level governance and much closer to the modified intergovernmentalism that Bache (1999: 37–42) describes as 'extended gatekeeping'.

Strikingly, at a time when the 1999 reforms were devolving budgetary control over the structural funds down to the EU15 member-state governments, the Commission maintained its own tight control over pre-accession funding—the Phare programme (*Pologne, Hongrie: assistance à la restructuration des économies*), the Instrument for Structural Policies for Pre-Accession (ISPA), and the Special Accession Programme for Agricultural and Rural Development (SAPARD) (see Chapter 17): not the best way to prepare the new members for 2004. Similarly, whilst efforts were made to build institutional capacity in the prospective new members, doubts were expressed about the likelihood of institutional capacity being turned into capability in the short time that was available before enlargement (Bailey and De Propris 2004: 90).

Implementation and multi-level governance

As we have seen above, the overall size of the structural funds and their distribution among the EU member states have always been determined by intergovernmental bargaining within the European Council. However, the Commission has fought hard and successfully over the years to establish a set of fundamental principles that have underpinned rules for the EU-wide implementation of, first, regional and, subsequently, cohesion policy. In so doing the Commission has given the policy a true Community dimension aimed at consistency of application across the EU and has quite deliberately involved a number of sub-national actors, as well as the central governments of the member states, in the implementation and evaluation process.

Building on the limited discretion that it had over a small non-quota section of the ERDF in the early 1980s, the Commission seized the opportunity afforded by Jacques Delors's success as Commission president in establishing the concept of cohesion in the SEA. It proposed in 1988 a package of regulations for spending the structural funds allocated under the first financial perspective that amounted to a major reform. The Commission sought thereafter to link reforms of cohesion policy to each successive new financial perspective and developed further packages in 1993, 1999, and 2006. These reforms came to comprise a set of underlying principles—programming, concentration, additionality, partnership, proportionality, subsidiarity, co-financing, and Lisbonization (see below)—for the implementation of structural fund expenditure which enhanced both the coherence and the consistency of EU cohesion policy. They also advanced, to a limited extent, the development of a distinctive policy-making process. This policy-making process involved the supranational EU institutions, the member governments, and regional and local (sub-national) institutions, as well as private citizens and groups, and could be described as 'multi-level' rather than purely intergovernmental.

Programming

After 1988 structural fund expenditure was allocated to specific programmes drawing on one or more of the available funds (see Box 10.1) rather than individual projects. The programmes were mainly (90 per cent) initiated by the member states, which were required to consult with their regional authorities where they existed. These programmes are approved by the Commission after each member state has produced a National Strategic Reference Framework (NSRF) in which it has to demonstrate to the Commission's satisfaction how it intends to implement the priorities established by the Commission in its Community Strategic Guidelines on Cohesion (Commission 2005). Between 1988 and 1999 the remaining 10 per cent of the funding supported 'Community Initiatives' (see Box 10.3). However, after 2006 this category was renamed 'European Territorial Cooperation' and reduced to just 2.5 per cent of overall expenditure. In the 2007–13 period there are 455 operational programmes.

Concentration

The Commission used the objectives it had established for the structural funds after 1988 to impose consistent criteria for their management and thereby to concentrate spending on the most needy regions and states. It thus directly confronted the member governments' preference for maximizing their national 'takes' from the structural funds. As Box 10.2 demonstrates, the number of cohesion objectives has been steadily reduced over the years, thereby increasing the degree of concentration by reducing the percentage of the EU population eligible for structural aid.

Additionality

This principle is designed to preserve the integrity of EU policy by preventing the member governments from reducing national expenditure by the amount gained from the EU structural funds. Bache (1998; 2004) has documented the battles that the Commission, actively supported by many local and regional authorities, has had over this. For Marks (1993) this alliance between the supranational and sub-national institutions supports his thesis that structural fund expenditure has advanced the development of multi-level governance in the EU, although this is disputed by Pollack (1995). The Commission's problem is that additionality is particularly difficult to verify given the varying methods and degrees of transparency in the ways that member states manage and report their expenditure. The Cohesion Fund was used between 1993 and 2006 to promote and to maintain the economic convergence of the poorer member states seeking to qualify for EMU by helping to reduce their public debt (see Chapter 7). This logically required that the additionality principle be suspended.

BOX 10.3	Community initiatives and European territorial cooperation, 1988–2013

1988–99

– INTERREG	– Cross-border, transnational, and inter-regional cooperation
– LEADER	– Rural development
– REGIS	– Support for the most remote regions
– ADAPT	– Adaptation of the workforce to industrial change
– SME	– Small and medium-size firms in disadvantaged areas
– RECHAR	– Adaptation to industrial change in coal-dependent areas
– KONVER	– Adaptation to industrial change in defence-industry dependent regions
– RESIDER	– Adaptation to industrial change in steel-dependent regions
– RETEX	– Adaptation to industrial change in textile-dependent regions
– URBAN	– Urban policy
– PESCA	– Restructuring the fisheries sector
– EMPLOYMENT	– Integration into working life of women, young people, and the disadvantaged

2000–6

– INTERREG	– Cross-border, transnational, and inter-regional cooperation
– LEADER	– Rural development
– EQUAL	– Transnational cooperation to combat all forms of discrimination and inequalities in the labour market

2007–13

– EUROPEAN TERRITORIAL COOPERATION	– Cross-border, transnational, and inter-regional cooperation

Partnership

The Commission has insisted since 1988 that (implementing) decisions about operational programmes (as opposed to financial perspectives and general cohesion principles) be taken in partnership among the Commission, the member governments, their regional organizations, and other public bodies and non-governmental organizations. Those who apply the multi-level governance perspective (Marks 1993; Hooghe 1996; Marks et al. 1996; Peterson and Bomberg 1999; Bache 2004, 2008) put a great deal of emphasis on this, and argue that one core goal of the structural funds was thus a policy made *for* the regions and *by* the regions in that potentially it encouraged not only (administrative) regionalization but also (political) regionalism and regional devolution. During the life of the structural funds the Committee of the Regions (CoR) has been established as a collective EU body with members from local and regional authorities, although it is hard to demonstrate that it has exerted any significant influence (see Chapter 4). Commentators are divided between those (Laffan 1996; Nanetti 1996; Bachtler and Mendez 2007; Baun and Marek 2008) who believe that the partnership principle has facilitated substantial regional and local governmental involvement in the policy process and those (Sutcliffe 2000; Bache and Bristow 2003; Gualina 2003; Hughes et al. 2004*a*; and Bailey and De Propris 2004) who argue that such participation has been mainly symbolic.

Proportionality

Proportionality, which was introduced only in the 2007–13 financial perspective, is designed to place limits on the amount of structural fund expenditure that is devoted to the administration, control, and monitoring of operational programmes. It is a response to criticisms from a number of the older member states that EU-level controls and monitoring involve wasteful and unnecessary expenditure which could be eliminated by 'renationalizing' elements of the structural funds. The problem is that these are the very member states that have over the years been 'careless' in the way that they have spent the structural funds allocated to them, with the result that the European Court of Auditors (COA) has refused to approve EU spending for the past fourteen years. In its verdict on the 2007 budget the COA estimated that 11 per cent of the €42 billion spent on cohesion did not comply with EU rules (Court of Auditors 2008). An additional problem arises from the lack of institutional and administrative capacity in the new member states (Baun and Marek 2008: 252–4).

Subsidiarity

Subsidiarity is a fundamental EU principle that insists that decisions be taken at the lowest practical level, which also provides a justification for the Commission to pursue a multi-level governance approach in alliance with sub-national actors. The UK government is particularly hypocritical about this principle in relation to the structural funds in that it argues in general that as many decisions as possible should be taken at the national rather than the EU level, but resists the further extension of this logic to the regional or local level. This stance was moderated slightly in the arrangements for implementing cohesion policy following devolution in 1997. However, it remains the case that it is the UK government—rather than the devolved administrations from

Scotland, Wales, and Northern Ireland—that participates in the intergovernmental bargaining of the Council (usually composed for these purposes of foreign ministers) and the European Council about the size and composition of financial perspectives.

More generally, the richer member states increasingly support the view that any expenditure from EU funds must 'add value' which the member states acting alone could not achieve. It is much easier to justify structural fund expenditure in the poorer states (normally also net recipients from the EU budget) on the grounds that they are indeed gaining 'added value' from their allocations, whereas this is harder to argue for the net contributors, some of which use the subsidiarity principle to argue the case for renationalization of structural fund expenditure (see Begg 2008*b* for an extended discussion).

Co-financing

Structural funding is also designed to encourage the member states both to stimulate private-sector involvement in appropriate projects and to increase (the additionality principle is there to prevent decreases) public expenditure on regional policy. Thus the maximum contribution that the EU can make to a cohesion project is between 50 per cent and 85 per cent. Logically the EU makes its biggest percentage contributions to the poorest states, but it only rarely entirely substitutes for national expenditure.

Lisbonization

In the current period (2007–13) EU countries which were members before May 2004 are required to allocate 60 per cent of their expenditure under the convergence objective and 75 per cent of that under the regional competiveness and employment objectives in pursuit of the aims of the Lisbon Agenda. In practice all member states have had little difficulty in 'reorienting' their structural fund expenditure towards the Lisbon goals, as detailed by the Commission (2005) (see Box 10.4). Baun and Marek (2008: 257–9) report that, amongst the older member states, only Germany has expressed regrets about any resultant loss of flexibility with regard to the way that the structural funds can be spent. Most of the new member states have willingly addressed the Lisbon Agenda, even though, for them, so far it is a voluntary not a compulsory requirement.

Enlargement, Lisbonization, and beyond

The Treaty of Lisbon (ToL) commits the EU to continue to pursue the objective of economic, social, and territorial cohesion. The implication is that the structural funds would continue to be used in pursuit of a logic according to which regional and national convergence will deliver cohesion in every sense of the term. This in

BOX 10.4	**The Lisbonization of cohesion policy: Commission priorities for cohesion 2007–13**

- Improving the *attractiveness of member states, regions, and cities* by improving accessibility, ensuring adequate quality and level of services, and preserving their environmental potential.
- Encouraging *innovation, entrepreneurship*, and the growth of the *knowledge economy* by research and innovation capacities, including new information and communication technologies.
- Creating *more and better jobs* by attracting more people into employment or entrepreneurial activity, improving adaptability of workers and enterprises, and increasing investment in human capital.

Source: Commission (2005: 12)

turn is intended to deliver growth, competitiveness, employment, and sustainable development, the Lisbon and Gothenburg objectives (see Chapters 7 and 12). There has also been some discussion in response to the 2008 financial crisis of using the structural funds in support of efforts to provide a short-term financial stimulus to the EU economy (Council of the European Union 2009: point 9). The sums allocated to the structural funds for 2007–13 are, in addition, intended to address the impact of recent enlargements, partly by compensating for the concerns of the EU15 and partly by including the allocations deemed appropriate for and acceptable to the states that joined in 2004 and 2007. Achieving this consensus regarding the future of the structural funds and EU cohesion policy required, as previously, that all member states receive something tangible from the funding allocation.

The future of the structural funds after 2014 is under consideration both as part of the general budget review initiated by the Commission in late 2007 (Bachtler et al. 2008; Ujupan 2009; and see Chapter 9) and in response to the Fourth Report on Economic and Social Cohesion (Commission 2007l). Before the extent of the 2008–9 financial and economic crisis became evident the most plausible outcome of both reviews was a budget of roughly similar size, dominated by (around 80 per cent) the combined total of structural-fund and agricultural expenditure. One possible outcome would be a consensus to continue the trend which has seen the percentage of the budget spent on the structural funds increasing slightly at the expense of the percentage spent on agriculture. This trend might be halted if the money spent on agriculture were further directed away from price supports towards 'structural' support for rural development (i.e. effectively returning the 'second pillar' of the CAP to the structural funds) via increased funding for the European Agricultural Fund for Rural Development (EAFRD) (House of Lords 2008: 30–1) (see Chapter 8). A different outcome would emerge if the severity of the economic crisis led to a renewed emphasis on the structural funds as a means of sweetening the pill for those member states under pressure to adapt their short-term crisis-management policies in order to preserve the fundamentals of the single market. This might lead to the structural funds being justified in terms of broader issues such as R&D investment, employment, short-term macroeconomic management, sectoral support, or climate change, rather than the more specific objective of attempting to deal with broad regional inequalities.

Adjusting to enlargement

In the light of the 2004 and 2007 enlargements a number of issues remain as regards the structural funds. The determination to maintain co-financing as a principle begs the question as to how relatively poor states (which in the wake of the financial crisis are under particular stress) can afford to accept and hence to match EU money. Success in developing sophisticated governance institutions may not be enough, even though this is necessary in order to devise and to manage regional programmes according to the administrative standards required by the European Commission (Hughes et al. 2004a; Baun and Marek 2008: 252–4) and to the accountability and transparency standards that the EP and the Court of Auditors should apply. It seems likely that the 'absorption cap' (calculated at around 4 per cent of a member state's GNP) will continue to be used so as to restrict the structural fund entitlement of the poorer member states.

During the pre-accession period there was little chance for the candidates to do anything other than receive instructions from the Commission. There was no real opportunity to shape policy and there was limited understanding that structural funding is designed to change structures, such that the need for such funding should diminish over time. Ireland, for example, had been transformed with the help of structural and cohesion funding to the extent that it became ineligible for them. There was, however, a general raising of expectations that EU receipts and national incomes would rise in the short term. It is being increasingly argued by the richer net contributors to the EU budget that structural funding for the purposes of removing regional inequalities should be necessary for only a limited period of time. In the 2007–13 negotiations several member governments argued that structural funding should be given only to the relatively poor new member states where some of the greatest regional inequalities were to be found (see Table 10.3). The net contributors were motivated both by a desire to maintain the EU budget at its current level of around 1 per cent of EU GNP and by the possible scope to shift funding to other objectives, such as increased investment in R&D or in a low-carbon economy.

We should note the emerging debate in the literature as to the nature of the involvement of sub-national authorities in the new member states. There is some evidence (Baun and Marek 2008) that the arrangements in the new member states for the implementation of structural fund expenditure in the 2007–13 period seems consistent with the multi-level governance perspective. Blom-Hansen (2005), however, challenges this view and warns against the danger of confusing the 'involvement' of multi-level actors with the notion of multi-level governance. Using a principal-agent framework Blom-Hansen argues that as a weak and poorly coordinated 'principal' the Commission loses out to the 'agents', the member states, for which there is little incentive to comply with EU-formulated goals when it comes to structural fund expenditure.

The context for planning the fourth financial perspective was clearly dominated by the 2004 and 2007 enlargements (*European Voice*, 1–7 June 2006), which increased the population of the EU by 20 per cent but its GDP by only 4–5 per cent, with the result that the EU's overall per capita income fell by 10 per cent. In the EU of twenty-seven member states more than one-third of the population live in a member state with an average income less than 90 per cent of the EU average income, compared with just one-sixth in the EU15. In the EU27 the poorest 10 per cent of the population earn just 31 per cent of the EU27 average compared to the 61 per cent of the EU15 average income earned by the poorest 10 per cent in the EU15.

For the first full post-enlargement period (2007–13) covered by the fourth financial perspective the member states eventually agreed at the end of 2005 to a total of €308 billion, having rejected the most radical UK suggestion that a figure of around half that sum be allocated to only the new member states. The new sum represented an 11.5 per cent increase in structural fund spending compared to the previous period to be divided among just three renamed objectives (see above Box 10.2). The Commission produced indicative annual sums per member state for the three objectives, leaving each to decide how to divide these among eligible regions. In this period the new member states will enjoy a 166 per cent increase compared to the funds that they received when they first joined (2004–6) and the original EU15 will receive 30 per cent less.

Links to the Lisbon Agenda

The practice of ensuring that everybody gets something from the structural funds has been maintained, but at least in theory the EU15 are more rigorously constrained by the so-called 'Lisbon restraints'. Once the Commission had agreed the Lisbon strategic guidelines (see Box 10.4) the member states drew up their own NSRFs, followed by a list of operational programmes. All 27 NSRFs and most (302: 96 per cent of those planned for the 2007–13 period) of the operational programmes were agreed by the end of 2007 (Commission 2008*q*: 93), at which point the Commission was able to report the success of the first stage of the strategy for relating structural fund expenditure to the Lisbon goals (Commission 2007*m*). As the member states implement projects in the current period, the Commission will commit the expenditure and hand it over to the member states. It will then monitor progress and produce further strategic reports (see, for instance, Commission 2008*p*) which will support its campaign to retain a major element of structural funding in the EU budget both through the ongoing budget review and the preparations for the fifth financial perspective.

TABLE 10.3   EU member states, regions, and share of structural funds, 2007-2013

Member State	GDP per head in 2005 (€)	GDP per head in poorest region, 2005 (EU27 PPS = 100)	GDP per head in richest region, 2005 (EU27 PPS =100)	Total Structural Funds (million €) 2006–13	Total Structural Funds per capita (€) 2006–13	Structural Funds as percentage of national GDP 2006–13	Share of total structural funds 2006–13 (%)
Luxembourg	59,202	264.3*	264.3*	58	130	0.02	0.0
Ireland	32,197	104.3	158.1	815	207	0.06	0.3
Netherlands	29,374	96.3	164	1,697	105	0.05	0.6
Austria	28,852	88.7	142.7	1,301	161	0.07	0.4
Denmark	28,375	94.9	161	545	101	0.04	0.2
Sweden	27,721	105.4	172.2	1,682	188	0.08	0.5
Belgium	27,135	79.5	240.5	2,020	195	0.07	0.7
UK	26,715	77.4	302.7	9,468	160	0.07	3.1
Germany	25,797	74.2	202.1	23,449	284	0.14	7.6
Finland	25,774	85.3	139.5	1,533	295	0.13	0.5
France	25,077	50.5	172.6	12,736	208	0.10	4.1
Italy	23,474	66.9	136.7	25,647	449	0.25	8.3
Spain	23,069	69.7	133.9	31,536	778	0.49	10.2
Greece	21,589	59.1	131.1	18,217	1,658	1.34	5.9
Cyprus	20,753	92.6*	92.6*	580	812	0.56	0.2

Slovenia	19,462	71.6	104.7	3,739	1,874	1.70	1.2
Malta	17,330	77.4*	77.4*	761	1,922	2.35	0.2
Czech Rep.	17,156	59.8	160.3	23,698	2,323	3.25	7.7
Portugal	16,891	59.8	106.3	19,147	1,847	1.82	6.2
Hungary	14,393	40.9	104.9	22,451	2,210	3.22	7.3
Estonia	14,093	62.9*	62.9*	3,058	2,247	3.31	1.0
Slovakia	13,563	43.1	147.9	10,264	1,904	3.30	3.3
Lithuania	11,914	53.2*	53.2*	6,096	1,757	3.42	2.0
Poland	11,482	35.0	81.2	59,698	1,562	3.43	19.4
Latvia	11,180	49.9*	49.9*	4,090	1,749	3.52	1.3
Romania	7,933	24.2	74.8	17,316	795	3.00	5.6
Bulgaria	7,913	26.9	52.2	6,047	768	3.15	2.0
Not allocated				392			
EU27				308,041			
New member states				158,190			
EU15				149,851			

* Indicates member states treated as a single region.
PPS = purchasing power standard.
Source: House of Lords (2008: tables on p. 11 and pp. 20–1).

Evolving practice in implementation

Day-to-day financial control of structural fund spending is now said to be more proportionate and devolved downwards as much as possible to deal with the charge of excessive bureaucracy against the Commission. The decision to continue funding for all member states has prevented an intensification of the concentration principle. There is currently an increased emphasis on partnership with an enhanced decentralization to partnerships on the ground, underpinned by tripartite contracts among the member states, the regions, and local authorities, all of which will be certainly studied in detail by those seeking evidence for the multi-level governance perspective. European Territorial Cooperation, the third, sparsely funded, objective of the 2007–13 period, has also recently attracted a growing academic interest (Mirwaldt et al. 2009), with new formal arrangements to promote cross-border, transnational and transregional cooperation. This new consolidated programme that has evolved from the INTERREG Community Initiative has given rise to a new legal entity, the European Grouping for Territorial Cooperation (EGTC), whose members can be representatives from member states, regional or local authorities, associations, or other public bodies. The EGTC is designed to enable the grouping together of authorities from various member states without the need for prior international agreements ratified by national parliaments. It remains to be seen whether this new body 'takes off', but its establishment confirms the view that the Commission remains interested in any institution that serves to blur the sharpness of national boundaries within the EU.

It is likely that the process of renationalizing and simplifying the means of delivery, financial management, and evaluation of cohesion funding will continue. In addition, some member states already see the pursuit of best practice and benchmarking with regard to national regional policies as being an attractive alternative to a more interventionist EU-level cohesion policy. The Commission has already made concessions to this tendency with its proposals for the coordination and standardization of national regional programmes as part of its recent regional policy reforms. On the other hand, the regions, in the new member states as well as the old, that benefit from EU financial support may, as suggested above, come to value the role of the structural funds in regional support and financing partly for its medium-term economic reliability, when, especially in the current economic climate, national expenditure might be more likely to be cut at short notice.

Impact assessment: political adjustment vs. economic gain

There is an increased emphasis on the role of national regional policies, which already account for over 75 per cent of regional spending in the EU, although there is also some evidence to suggest that national regional policy has to a minor extent itself been Europeanized over the years. Involvement in EU cohesion and regional policies has impacted on the way that the member states define their regions (Mendez et al. 2006) and it has also led to a greater awareness within the member states of the need to pay attention to regional divergence. EU programmes may have enhanced the visibility of the EU in those regions and localities that have benefited from structural funding, but this does not necessarily constitute evidence that this has enhanced the popularity of the EU in the public imagination.

Opinion also remains divided about the precise extent of the impact of EU funding on regional and national convergence; other factors, such as national regional programmes, other national macroeconomic policies, and globalization, are not easily measurable (House of Lords 2008: 25–7). Attempts to evaluate the impact of EU policy to date have not produced clear results. There has been a great deal of economic modelling and survey-data gathering, but these have not produced any outstanding evidence of structural fund expenditure having a discernible economic impact. At the member-state level, between 1995 and 2004 three of the original cohesion countries—Ireland, Greece, and Spain—experienced growth more rapid than the EU average, although Portugal did not. However, of the fifty lagging regions that qualified for objective-1 funding in 1995, thirty-eight still qualified in 2004, and five additional regions slipped into the category during the decade (House of Lords 2008: 26). Furthermore, as Table 10.3 demonstrates, as of 2005 significant regional disparities remained within both the original EU15 and the new members.

Even the Commission struggles to find clear evidence that structural funding directly enhances EU cohesion, although recent Commission (2007l, 2008p) reports on structural fund expenditure remain positive in their evaluation. This continued optimism conflicts with other assessments (Boldrin and Canova 2001) including those commissioned by the British Parliament (ECOTECH 2003; House of Commons 2004; House of Lords 2008), which suggest that structural fund expenditure in the richer member states is now producing diminishing returns with no visible value added over what might be achieved by national programmes. The use of the Lisbon Agenda criteria to provide further rationalization of this expenditure may also prove premature for those new member states which need more basic assistance before they progress to becoming more competitive.

The Sapir Report (Sapir et al. 2004) noted the compensation function of structural fund expenditure on cohesion, but could find no hard evidence to support either the argument that the funds had made a significant difference to the performance of lagging regions or that they had not. The Sapir Report recommended that providing money only to the new member states and to their national budgets, rather than to their regions (more of a macroeconomic than a regional approach to diversity), would be more effective. This was politically too challenging for the Commission to take on board in the current period. It remains to be seen whether the 2008 financial crisis will prompt a rethinking of whether, when, and how to draw on the structural funds as a short-term fiscal stimulus.

In practice, structural fund expenditure on EU cohesion policy is judged more by political than by economic criteria. This is partly because, whilst the economic evidence of positive impact is unconvincing, survey evidence about the visibility and popularity of the policy seems more positive (despite its nebulous character). It is also the case that political considerations seem to prevail in enabling the member states to reach the necessary consensus on the periodic financial perspectives. This is why the structural fund expenditure continues as it does, albeit underpinned by a constantly changing set of strategic rationalizations, of which the Lisbon goals are but the latest and almost certainly not the last.

The relationship between the structural funds, cohesion policy, regional policy, and regionalism also touches on the issue of whether and how the EU interacts with questions of regional identity. In particular, the aspiration to create a Europe of the regions is not always shared by member states anxious to preserve their own national identity. The Commission's enthusiasm for partnerships with sub-national partners in the pursuit of cohesion serves to present an alternative potential framework for those who aspire to detach Scotland from the UK, Bavaria from Germany, Northern Italy from the rest of Italy, Flanders or Wallonia (and Brussels!) from Belgium, the Basque country or Catalonia from Spain—within the all-embracing haven of the EU. It remains to be seen whether similar reactions emerge within the new member states.

Conclusions

This chapter takes issue with the argument that the manner in which the structural funds have been implemented has had a significant impact on the development of multi-level governance. Despite the initial thrust of the 'partnership' provisions of the 1988 reforms, the central governments of both the old and new member states have 'gatekeeping' capabilities that allow public and private, regional and local interests to participate, but just that. Multi-level participation should not be confused with multi-level governance. There is slender evidence that regional and local actors are more effective because of cohesion policy, just as their contribution to EU governance collectively through the CoR is limited. The extent of sub-national participation in the broad decisions about the size of the structural funds (financial perspectives) or about the objectives of cohesion policy is extremely limited and depends primarily on constitutional arrangements within individual member states.

To be sure, Commission rules require the active participation of sub-national institutions and actors in the production and implementation of individual operational programmes. This process can be argued both to meet the subsidiarity criterion and perhaps to contribute towards the legitimization of EU cohesion policy and the structural funds. Bachtler and Mendez (2007) would further argue in support of the multi-level governance approach that, whilst the European Council continues to dominate the fundamental decisions about structural fund expenditure, it is the supranational Commission which has been mainly responsible, via its brokering role among the member states, for crucial reform measures. This has been in particular so when it comes to the implementation of the two cohesion-policy principles of concentration and programming.

Nevertheless it is argued here that over the years the Commission has been forced to accept a growing and increasingly decisive role for the member states both in decision-making about and in the implementation of the structural funds (Pollack 1995; Hooghe and Keating 1994; Bache 1998; Peterson and Bomberg 1999; Allen 2000; Hooghe and Marks 2001; Pollack 2003; Allen 2005; Manzella and Mendez 2009), even if this does not amount to a full scale 'renationalization'. It seems likely that the structural funds will, in the future, be directed at much wider and more diverse objectives than the removal of regional inequalities and the encouragement of overall EU competiveness and growth (House of Lords 2008; Baun and Marek 2008: 268–9; Bachtler et al. 2008; Ujupan 2009). Insofar as the structural funds have encouraged the member states to value their participation in the EU, they are likely to continue to absorb a significant percentage of overall EU budgetary expenditure beyond 2014. That expenditure may well, however, be in pursuit of broader objectives, such as increased R&D, the low-carbon economy, or energy security, rather than those currently associated with EU cohesion policy in the current period.

 FURTHER READING

For an excellent overview of the early development of the EU structural funds and regional policy see Bache (1998) and Hooghe (1996) and for the current situation, as well as a useful summary of reform proposals, see UK House of Lords (2008) and its accompanying oral and written evidence. For a recent discussion of the relationship between EU structural fund expenditure and the multi-level governance perspective see Bache (2008). Baun and Marek (2008) contains a good overview of the impact of the most recent enlargements on EU cohesion policy and Bachtler et al. (2008) comprehensively summarize the contemporary debate about the future role of the structural funds in the ongoing EU budgetary review. Commission (2007l) provides a starting point for the next re-evaluation of cohesion policy.

Bache, I. (1998), *The Politics of European Union Regional Policy: Multi-level Governance or Flexible Gatekeeping?* (Sheffield: Sheffield Academic Press).

Bache, I. (2008), *Europeanization and Multi-Level Governance: Cohesion Policy in the European Union and Britain* (Lanham, MD: Rowman & Littlefield).

Bachtler, J., Mendez, C., and Wishlade, F. (2008), *Ideas for Budget and Policy Reform: Reviewing the Debate on Cohesion Policy 2014+*, European Policy Research Paper 08/04 (Glasgow: University of Strathclyde; European Policies Research Centre).

Baun, M., and Marek, D. (2008), *EU Cohesion Policy after Enlargement* (Basingstoke: Palgrave Macmillan).

Commission (2007*l*), *Fourth Report on Economic and Social Cohesion*, COM (2007) 273 final.

Hooghe, L. (1996) (ed.), *Cohesion Policy and European Integration: Building Multi-level Governance* (Oxford: Oxford University Press).

House of Lords (2008), *The Future of EU Regional Policy,* European Union Committee, Nineteenth Report of Session 2007–08, HL paper 141 (London: TSO).

CHAPTER 11

Social Policy

Left to the Judges and the Markets?

Stephan Leibfried

▌ Summary

Though many assume that the European Union (EU) is minimally involved in social policy, the dynamics of market integration have spilled over substantially into the EU social arena. Resistance by national governments to loss of autonomy, and conflicting interests between rich and poor regions, or between employers and employees, present formidable obstacles to EU policies. However, in the 1980s and 1990s, the EU accumulated significant regulatory mandates in social policy, reaching out more recently to anti-discrimination politics. Yet under the pressures from integrated markets member governments have lost more control over national welfare policies than the EU has gained in transferred authority, although this development may have stopped. The resultant multi-tiered pattern is largely law- and court-driven, marked by policy immobilism at the centre and by 'negative' market integration, which significantly constrains national social policies. The increase in heterogeneity with eastern enlargement marked the highpoint of *traditional* twentieth-century EU social policy, and points to *new* regulatory horizons for the twenty-first.

Introduction[1]

Accounts of European social policy typically report a minimalist EU involvement (Collins 1975; Falkner 1998). The EU is seen as 'market-building', leaving an exclusive, citizen-focused, national welfare state, its sovereignty formally untouched, though perhaps endangered by growing economic interdependence. 'Welfare states are national states' (de Swaan 1992: 33; Offe 2003), and, at first sight, the European ones indeed look national. There are no EU laws granting individual entitlements against Brussels, no direct taxes or contributions, no real funding of a 'social budget' for such entitlements, and no significant Brussels welfare bureaucracy. Territorial sovereignty in social policy seems alive and well. However, an alternative view has become plausible: European integration has eroded both the sovereignty (legal authority) and autonomy (regulatory capacity) of member states to conduct their own social policies. What began as a parallel universe turned into a single conflict arena (Becker 2004*a*). National welfare states remain the primary institutions of European social policy, but they are built into an increasingly constraining multi-tiered polity (Pierson and Leibfried 1995).

While there have been extensive barriers to an explicitly collective European social policy (Obinger et al. 2005), the dynamics of the single market have made it increasingly difficult to exclude social issues from the EU's agenda. The emerging multi-tiered structure, however, results less from the ambitions of Eurocrats to build a welfare state than from spill-overs from the single market process, which has invaded the domain of social policy (Falkner 1998). In the 1980s the single market initiative (see Chapter 5) to ensure the free movement of goods, persons, services, and capital was based on a version of regulation that assumed that the single European market could be insulated from social policy issues, which would remain the province of member states. This assumption runs directly contrary to central tenets of political economy, which stress that economic action is embedded within dense networks of social and political institutions (North 1990; Hall 1999). The neat separation between supranational 'market' and national 'social issues' appears unsustainable. To be sure there have been 'high politics' struggles over proposals to strengthen treaty provisions on social policy and to develop social charters. Yet it is rather the movement towards market integration that gradually erodes national welfare states' autonomy *and* sovereignty, and increasingly situates them in a complex, multi-tiered web of Europeanized public policy.

This transformation occurs through three processes (see Table 11.1). *Positive integration* results from policy initiatives taken at the 'centre' by the Commission and the Council, increasingly pushed by the European Parliament (EP), along with the often expansive interpretations of the European Court of Justice (ECJ). In the 1990s the treaty mandate was strengthened, providing a Euro-corporatist anchor, drawing European trade unions and employer organizations towards

TABLE 11.1   European integration transforms national welfare states: processes, key actors, and examples

Pressures and processes	Key actors	Examples
Direct policy pressures of integration —> *positive* initiatives to develop uniform social standards at EU level	Commission, expert committees, ECJ, and since 1992 institutionally entrusted corporate actors (UNICE, CEEP, ETUC) (background actors: EP, ESC; diverse lobbies)	*Old politics*: national and gender equality; health and safety; Social Protocol 'corporatism' since 1992, generalized 1997, with expansion of competences and of QMV; 1989 EC Social Charter, 'incorporated' in ToA; extending notion of European citizenship
		New politics: expanding anti-discrimination law beyond nationality and gender to 'any ground such as' *race*, colour, *ethnic* or social *origin*, genetic features, language, *religion or belief*, political or any other opinion, membership of a national minority, property, birth, *disability, age or sexual orientation'* (items in italics already in Art. 13 TEC; others Art. 21 EU Charter of Fundamental Rights)
Direct policy pressures of integration —> *negative* policy reform imposing market compatibility requirements at EU level	ECJ, Commission; Council (national governments), national legal institutions	Labour mobility, since late 1980s freedom to provide and consume services, combined with impact of the European Treaty's 'competition regime'
Indirect pressures of integration —> adaptation of national welfare states	market actors (employers, unions; sensitive sectors: private insurance, provider groups), Council, individual national governments in fields outside social policy	Further 'social dumping' accented by Eastern enlargement, EMU, and Maastricht criteria; harmonization of tax systems; single market for private insurance; since the 1980s, dispensing with the 'public utilities state' the traditional outer mantle of the welfare state

that centre. Since then a softer version of policy-making has evolved via the open method of coordination (OMC) (see Chapter 12), which might amplify positive integration—as in modernizing social protection systems—or step in where the EU would otherwise have little competence, or even turn into hard law despite the many obstacles to achieving this (Heidenreich and Zeitlin 2009). *Negative* integration occurs as the ECJ imposes market-compatibility requirements via the four freedoms (Barnard 2007)—especially free movement of labour and of services—that restrict member states' social policies. Both positive and negative initiatives create direct, mostly *de jure*, pressures on national welfare states through new instruments of European social policy. Finally, European integration creates an escalating range of *indirect de facto* pressures that encourage adaptations—convergence (see Starke et al. 2008)—of national welfare states. These pressures strongly affect national welfare states, but they are not directly derived from EU social policy instruments.

Positive initiatives from the centre have generally prompted major social conflicts, and have been attempted since the foundation of the European Community. The 1957 Treaty of Rome, for instance, met stiff resistance in the French National Assembly in part because weak social clauses were seen to endanger the well-developed French welfare state, making French industry less competitive. Negative integration efforts were, at first, less visible, but are just as old. The coordination of rules governing labour mobility was enshrined in one of the earliest EC legislative acts (1958), whereas similar action on services dates only from the mid-1980s, reaching a high plateau at the end of the 1990s. Indirect pressures are more recent in response to the development of economic integration. Under the ascendance of centre-right parties the primacy of economic integration was locked firmly into the EU policy-making level from 1957 onwards. In contrast, the social democrats in their two phases of ascendance in the 1970s and late 1990s, were unable—and often unwilling—to lock in a similarly effective social integration perspective (Manow et al. 2004); they invented OMC instead. With eastern enlargement these trajectories seem frozen into place, though this may be challenged in the course of the financial and economic crisis that began in 2007.

The limited success of activist social policy

Discussions of social policy generally focus on prominent actors like the Council, the Commission (and the responsible Directorate-General (DG)), and increasingly the EP (and its committees), and the representatives of business and labour interests in an emerging corporatist policy community. The Commission has been a central actor in attempting to construct a 'social dimension' for its 'European social model' (Commission 1994, 2000d, 2003c, 2008f)—areas of European social policy with uniform or at least minimum standards. These attempts have occurred in fits and starts during the past decades, with high aspirations and modest results, marked by plenty of cheap talk, produced in the confident knowledge that unanimous—or even qualified-majority—voting in the Council would block all ambitious blueprints (Streeck and Schmitter 1991; Lange 1992). The main point here is that the focus on the efforts of Euro-federalists to foist a social dimension on a reluctant Council has been somewhat misleading. European integration did indeed alter European social policy-making, but largely through mechanisms operating *outside* the welfare dimension proper. The obstacles to an activist role for Brussels in social policy development are formidable, increasing, and twofold (Pierson and Leibfried 1995).

Institutional constraints

The EU process makes it much easier to block than to enact reforms. Only narrow, market-related openings for social legislation have been available (see Table 11.2) and reform requires at least a qualified majority. Member governments are jealous gatekeepers for initiatives requiring Council approval and protect their prerogatives. Since the second world war the scope of national sovereignty has gradually diminished. The welfare state remains one of the few key realms where national governments have usually resisted losses of policy authority, not least because of the electoral significance of most social programmes.

Until the early 1990s legislative reform was limited to a few areas where the Treaty of Rome, or the single-market project, allowed more latitude, mainly the gender-equality provisions and health and safety in the work place. In the 1970s the Council unanimously agreed to a number of directives which gave the equal-treatment provision some content. Over the past thirty years, the ECJ has played a crucial activist role, turning Article 119 (EEC) and the directives into an extensive set of requirements and prohibitions related to the treatment of female, and occasionally male, workers (Ostner and Lewis 1995; Hoskyns 1996; Mazey 1998; Walby 2005; Costello and Davies 2006). These rulings have required extensive national reforms. The Single European Act (SEA) in Art. 118a allowed qualified majority voting (QMV) on health and safety and QMV on gender equality followed in the 1990s (now all gender directives are recast in Directive 2006/54/EC). Surprisingly, policy-making has produced neither stalemate nor lowest-common-denominator regulations in health and safety, but rather high standards. Furthermore, European regulators moved beyond regulating products to production processes (Eichener 1997, 2000).

The shifting balance of power among relevant social interests

The 'social democratic' forces most interested in a strong social dimension are relatively weak and often Euro-sceptical (Manow et al. 2004). Across most of the EU, unions and social democratic parties had become weaker since the 1980s; in the second half of the 1990s, social democracy—bent less on traditional social than on 'new' employment policy ('activation')—had grown again, although union power did not. Meanwhile, business power had grown considerably, partly fostered by European- and OECD-wide capital markets. This shifting balance of power has further hindered efforts to deal with institutional blockages, limited fiscal resources, and widely divergent and deeply institutionalized national social policies.[2]

TABLE 11.2   Assignment of explicit social policy mandates to the EU up to the Treaty of Lisbon

Field of mandate	European Economic Community EEC	Single European Act SEA	Treaty on European Union TEU	Social Protocol SP	Treaty of Amsterdam ToA	Treaty of Nice ToN	Treaty of Lisbon ToL
	1957 (1958)	1986 (1987)	1992 (1993)	1992 (1993)	1997 (1999)	2000 (2003)	2007 (2009)
1 Discrimination on grounds of nationality	Unan 7	No ref	QMV 6	No ref	QMV 12	QMV 12	QMV 18
2 Basic principles of anti-discrimination incentives, harmonization excluded	No ref	No ref	No ref	No ref	QMV 13 (2)	QMV 13 (2)	QMV 19 II
3 Free labour movement	Unan 48–50	QMV 48–50	QMV 48–50	No impact	QMV 39–40	QMV 39–40	QMV 45–46
4 Gender equality in pay[b]	Unan 119	Unan 119	Unan 119	Unan 6	QMV 141	QMV 141	QMV 157
5 Gender equality for labour force[b]	No ref	No ref	No ref	QMV 2 (1) v	QMV 137 (1) v	QMV 137 (1) i	QMV 153 (1) i
6 Working environment	No ref	QMV 118	QMV 118a	QMV 2 (1) i	QMV 137 (1) i	QMV 137 (1) a	QMV 153 (1) a
7 Working conditions (outside former Art.118a, line 6)	No ref	No ref	No ref	QMV 2 (1) ii	QMV 137 (1) ii	QMV 137 (1) b	QMV 153 (1) b

8	Worker information and consultation	No ref	No ref	QMV 2 (1) iii	QMV 137 (1) iii	QMV 137 (1) e	QMV 153 (1) e
9	Integration of persons excluded from labour market[c]	No ref	No ref	QMV 2 (1) iv	QMV 137 (1) iv	QMV 137 (1) h	QMV 153 (1) h
10	Combating of social exclusion	No ref	No ref	No ref	No ref	QMV 137 (1) j	QMV 153 (1) j
11	Modernization of social protection systems	No ref	No ref	No ref	No ref	QMV 137 (1) k	QMV 153 (1) k
12	Public health	No ref	QMV 129	No ref	QMV 152	QMV 152	QMV 168
13	Social security coordination	Unan 51	Unan 51	n. a.	Unan 42	Unan 42	QMV 49
14	Anti-discrimination measures	No ref	No ref	No ref	Unan 13 (1)	Unan 13 (1)	Unan 19 (1)
15	Social security and protection of workers	No ref	No ref	Unan 2 (3) i	Unan 137 (3) i	Unan 137 (1) c	Unan 153 (1) c, (3)
16	Protection of workers (employment contract termination)	No ref	No ref	Unan 2 (3) ii	Unan 137 (3) ii	Unan 137 (1) d	Unan 153 (1) d, (3) If not QMV 153 (2) last para

TABLE 11.2 (Continued)

Field of mandate	European Economic Community EEC 1957 (1958)	Single European Act SEA 1986 (1987)	Treaty on European Union TEU 1992 (1993)	Social Protocol SP 1992 (1993)	Treaty of Amsterdam ToA 1997 (1999)	Treaty of Nice ToN 2000 (2003)	Treaty of Lisbon ToL 2007 (2009)
18 Employment of third-country nationals	No ref	No ref	No ref	Unan 2 (3) iv	Unan 137 (3) iv	Unan 137 (1) g	Unan 153 (1) g, (3) If not QMV 153 (2) last para
19 Funding for employment policy[c]	No ref	No ref	No ref	Unan 2 (3) v	Unan 137 (3) v	No ref	No ref
20 Pay	No ref	No ref	No ref 100a (2)	Excl 2 (6)	Excl 137 (6)	Excl 137 (5)	Excl 151 (5)
21 Right of association	No ref	No ref	No ref 100a (2)	Excl 2 (6)	Excl 137 (6)	Excl 137 (5)	Excl 151 (5)
22 Right to strike and to impose lock-outs	No ref	No ref	No ref 100a (2)	Excl 2 (6)	Excl 137 (6)	Excl 137 (5)	Excl 151 (5)

		(128) 140	(128) 140	(148) 156 1st dash
23	Mandates for the Open Method of Coordination (OMC)d	Employment		
		Labour market and working conditions	140	156 2nd dash
		Professional education and training	140	156 3rd dash
		Social security	140	156 4th dash
		Prevention of occupational accidents and diseases	140	156 5th dash
		Protection of health at work	140	156 6th dash
		Law of coalitions and collective agreements between employers and employees	140	156 7th dash

Notes: years for treaties refer to the signing and (in parentheses) the ratification of the treaty. Numbers listed in the table refer to articles in each treaty.

Unan = unanimity required; QMV = qualified majority voting; No ref = no reference to mandate; n.a. = not applicable; Excl = mandate explicitly excluded.

Medium shading denotes weaker mandate. Heavy shading shows explicit denial of mandates, anchored in the treaties only since 1992 in these areas.

[a] As a rule the table refers to *explicit* powers mentioned in the treaties, in contrast to *unspecified general* powers, as under Arts. 100 and 235 EEC (now Arts. 95 and 308 TEC (now Arts. 114 and 352 TFEU = Treaty on the Functioning of the European Union = *part* of ToL), or to *non-enabling* norms (on an exception see note b).

[b] Between the original Treaty of Rome and the 1992 Social Protocol, the ECJ had interpreted gender equality ever more widely. Art. 119 EEC (now Art. 141 TEC) contained no express enabling clause; respective directives were based on Art. 100 or 235 EEC, which required unanimous decisions. In the end Art. 141 (3) TEC in 1997 brought the first special mandate and QMV.

[c] From 1992 to 1997 this QMV-mandate excluded the one for *funding*, where *unanimity* was required according to Art. 2(3) of the Social Protocol and then Art. 137(3) TEC, thus maintaining anti-poverty spending programmes as highly veto-prone.

[d] The term 'open method of coordination' is not mentioned in any of the treaties.

Source: Falkner (1998: 82), supplemented by the author, with special thanks again to Josef Falke, University of Bremen, for his continuous help in updating and legal advice.

The historical trajectory is one from noisy public policy fights since the 1980s, with a consolidating high point in the Treaty of Amsterdam (ToA) in 1997, to a slow slide into the sounds of silence of the twenty-first century, though with new frontiers in sight. At least until the 1993 Social Protocol, annexed to the Maastricht Treaty on European Union (TEU), was agreed with a British opt-out, UK opposition rendered serious initiatives impossible (Kleinman and Piachaud 1992), leaving member governments, European officials, and interest groups free to make rhetorical commitments to a grand social dimension (Ross 1995*a*, 1995*b*; Streeck 1995). Since the 1980s, noisy fights over initiatives to increase EU social policy mandates had regularly far exceeded the true implications of the proposals made and the results achieved. The struggle over the Social Charter in the 1980s was typical (Falkner 1998), although in the meantime the 1989 Community Charter of the Fundamental Social Rights of Workers and the 1961 European Social Charter of the Council of Europe were both silently incorporated into the 1997 ToA through a reference in the preamble, carried forward in the 2000 Treaty of Nice (ToN). These rights reappeared in the Charter of Fundamental Rights of the EU, proclaimed in Nice on 7 December 2000 by the European Council, which Art. 6 of the Treaty of Lisbon (ToL) would incorporate.

The high point of these developments was the 1997 ToA with its Social Chapter, accepted at last by the UK as a hard 'constitutional' achievement. Two mandates—health and safety in the 'working environment' and gender equality 'in pay'—were kept, the first broadened to all 'working conditions' and the second to all 'labour force' issues; all were placed under QMV, new for gender equality. Two additional mandates were introduced under QMV: worker information and consultation; and integration of persons excluded from the labour market, but without EU financing. Five new topics were introduced subject to unanimous decision-making: social security and worker protection; protection of workers when employment contract is terminated; collective interest representation; employment of third-country nationals; and financing measures to integrate the excluded. Three topics were declared off-limits: pay, right of association, and right to strike or to impose lock-outs. Agreement was also reached on applying more widely the powers of the 'social partners' (i.e. the unions and the employers) to adopt quasi-legislative agreements. The ToA included a new Title VIII Employment, Articles. 125–30, based on a Swedish initiative, mainly about coordinating national employment initiatives via OMC (Johansson 1999; Tidow 2003; Zeitlin et al. 2005). Since then OMC has been extended to pensions, social inclusion, health, and migration, and in 2005 was 'streamlined' beyond recognition (Commission 2003*b*; Casey 2003; Daly 2008; this volume, Chapter 12).

In principle, the revised Social Chapter (Arts. 136–45 ToN) facilitates efforts to expand EU social policy. First, a country's capacity to obstruct legislation has diminished. By 1992, the four cohesion states—Greece, Ireland, Portugal, and Spain—no longer commanded enough votes to block reform under QMV. This minority status became more pronounced after the northern expansion to the EU15 in 1995, bringing in advanced industrialized economies with strong welfare states. The obstruction that had met the 1989 Social Action Programme (Falkner 1998) had been made impossible. Several directives were passed (Working Time 93/104/EC, Young Workers 94/33/EC, European Works Council 94/45/EC, Parental Leave 96/34/EC, Part-time Work 97/81/EC, Burden of Proof in Sex Discrimination Cases 97/80/EC, Fixed-term Contracts/Temporary Work 99/79/EC; see Falkner et al. 2005) and became successes for a form of Euro-corporatism endowed with legislative powers. The social partners seemed ready to negotiate, now 'in the shadow of the [Council] vote', and based on their own experience. But no other major directives followed; instead, the social partners side-stepped this with a 2002 Framework Agreement on Teleworking. For the first time the social partners committed their own members to direct implementation, and sought no ratification through the Council of Ministers; this was seen as having greater political promise—but also the risk of having little effect (UNICE et al. 2006).

All these directives belong to the *acquis communautaire* and thus are also becoming legally effective in the twelve countries that joined the EU in 2004 and 2007. As yet little is known of how effective they are on the ground (Kvist 2004; Falkner et al. 2008; Maydell et al. 2006), though we know that large differences in wages, atypical employment, hours worked, and in the role of the informal economy plus the collective bargaining situation may make implementation a problem (Vaughan-Whitehead 2007). Also, twelve additional member states with less interest in Social Europe have made QMV harder to achieve on new legislation.

While most aspects of the Social Charter have moved forward, further initiatives have been modest and 'consolidating', as the Social Action Programmes since 1998 indicate. From the early 1990s the Commission has continued to engage in intensive soul-searching on its proper social policy role (Ross 1995b). Efforts to combat stubbornly high levels of European unemployment moved centre stage during the mid-1990s (Commission 1994, 2003a, 2003c), as reflected in the ToA in 1997, and combined in the 2000 ToN with efforts to 'modernize social protection systems' and to 'combat social exclusion' (Art. 137(1) (k, j))—these two QMV mandates were the only new ToN contributions to social policy. The Commission seemed to have accepted at least some of the British case for the need to promote 'flexibility' (Commission 1993b: 116ff). This trend has intensified, with 'slimming down' of national welfare states now a regular and prominent topic on the agenda of Ecofin, the European Council, and the Commission—and with the Employment and Social Policy Council and the corresponding Commission DGs mostly on the defensive. Member governments seem unlikely to allow the Commission to take the lead here, thus leaving the immediate prospect as consolidation, with the completion of some current agenda items, but few new initiatives.

Less noted has been the *silent revolution* to promote anti-discrimination in the treaties. While the 1992 TEU held to the old politics of prohibiting labour discrimination by nationality and gender, the 1997 ToA Article 13 added 'racial and other origins, religion or belief, disability, age or sexual orientation', and Article 21 of the 2000 EU Charter of Fundamental Rights amplified this by adding 'any' further 'ground such as' colour, social origin, genetic features, language, political or any other opinion, membership of a national minority, property, birth, and disability. There followed the 'Article 13 Package' of two Directives (Anti-Racism 2000/43, Framework 2000/78), and an Action Programme in 2000 (Eichenhofer 2004), also ratcheting up gender equality standards by feedback (Gender Directive 2002/73; Costello and Davies 2006: 1567f; Husmann 2005). In a more heterogeneous and veto-prone EU this may well become the regulatory route for social policy in the twenty-first century.

US experience may be relevant here. After the 1960s civil rights reforms there was a burst of anti-discrimination regulatory politics which burdened third parties only, promised well-being whilst by-passing burdens on public budgets, and relied mainly on legal strategies (Kochan et al. 2001; Nivola 1998). Similarly, anti-discrimination might also develop into an apparent European panacea for a welfare-guaranteeing state, especially in an increasingly heterogeneous EU (Franzius 2003), especially given eastern enlargement (Heidenreich 2003). One example is the struggle over unisex private insurance tariffs with repercussions across all branches of insurance (Schwark 2003; House of Lords 2004; Boecken 2005; Rothgang 2007). Such a transformation would emphasize employment with a 'citizenship-consumer' focus, which might accommodate the very different welfare traditions in Europe as well as echo US consumer welfare (Rieger and Leibfried 2003). A slow legal convergence and harmonization might emerge, with anti-discrimination leaders like the UK and The Netherlands taking the lead (House of Lords 2000).

To sum up, to focus on the highly politicized and widely publicized struggles in the EU over positive, centre-imposed social policies is to miss the point. Devices such as the Social Charter in the 1980s and the Social Protocol in the early 1990s are probably much less pertinent than measures such as the 1992 Maternity Directive 92/85/EEC, or directives under the Social Protocol (1992) and the 'constitutionalized' Social Chapter of 1997. EU legislative activity is now at least as extensive as federal social policy activity was on the eve of the US New Deal in the 1930s (Robertson 1989; Pierson 1995a; Leibfried and Obinger 2008)—and it moves in great strides to match the US anti-discrimination era dating since the 1970s.

European integration and direct market compatibility requirements

Lost amidst the noisy fights has been the quiet accumulation of constraints on national social policy by market integration. The last four decades have witnessed a gradual expansion of EU-generated regulations and court decisions that have seriously eroded the sovereignties of the national welfare state and overlaid it with a new mobility- and competition-friendly regime. Rather few political scientists (Falkner 1998; Falkner et al. 2005; Hantrais 2007; Conant 2007*b*) paid attention to the 'low politics'—let alone the judicial politics—of what was happening, since most were entranced by the 'high politics' in treaty bargaining. The topic was left to European labour and welfare lawyers and the scholars who monitored the courts (Burley and Mattli 1993; Shapiro and Stone 1994; Stone Sweet and Caporaso 1998; Weiler 1999; Chalmers 2004; Eichenhofer 2006; Barnard 2007; Bercusson 2007; Conant 2007*b*).

Since the 1960s the ECJ has delivered more than a thousand decisions (*output*) on social policy topics (see Table 11.3), with free movement for workers and their (plus third-country migrants') social security amounting to about two-thirds and other social policy matters to one-third (within the scope of now Arts. 136–45 ToN). Also, the Commission brought to court treaty violations by member governments concerning social policy. The social-policy caseload (*input*) (see Table 11.3 and Appendix 1) was second only to agriculture, and on a par with environmental and consumer issues, which puts social policy in second place for demand of ECJ decisions—staying firmly in the ECJ's major league. These statistics do not include freedom of services cases, and those of all other categories that may occasionally impact upon national welfare states.

There have been in addition many law suits initiated by EU staff for whom the ECJ serves as a labour and social security court (see Appendix 1, Tables A.1–2), a huge demand on ECJ resources, which was partly the reason for the founding of the Court of First Instance (CFI) in 1989 (Emmert 1996; Forwood 2008), with the ECJ now serving only as a court of appeal. But the social status of EU civil servants does not serve as a welfare model for EU citizens—as it had in some member states, such as Germany and France—so these cases do not affect the harmonization of national social policies. Nor do the statistics include some 100 decisions of the CFI on social policy issues (see Appendix 1, Table A.3), which mostly address conflicts over distributive criteria in the European Social Fund (ESF). Already in the period from 1971 to 1991 social policy cases were on a par with competition cases, slowly overtaking them almost to double the caseload by 2003 and matching the caseload on the free movement of goods.

The thousand or so social-policy cases (*output*) come unevenly from member states (see Table 11.4). The most active have been Germany (on free movement of persons), Belgium and The Netherlands (on social security of migrant workers), and the UK (on workers' protection and equal treatment). France and Italy have consistently produced few cases (Stone Sweet and Brunell 1998). Small countries with few cases may nevertheless trigger big consequences as the 1998 *Kohll* and *Decker* cases from Luxembourg show (see below). Since plaintiffs usually may not appeal to the ECJ directly, the national legal profession and its activist stance play a critical intermediary role in feeding cases to the ECJ (Conant 2007*b*).

The EU's social dimension is often advocated as a corrective to market-building, but in practice seems to have been part of it, as free movement and increasing competition have prompted court cases and thus expanded the bite of European

TABLE 11.3 Distribution of ECJ judgments on social policy by functional subcategories, 1954–2007

Period	Sum Total ECJ judgments — All TEC articles — cases — No. (= 100%)	Freedom of movement for workers — Arts. 39–41 TEC (ex Arts. 48–50 EEC) — cases — %	— No.	Social security of EU migrant workers[a] — Art. 42 TEC (ex Art. 51 EEC) — cases — %	— No.	Social security of third-country migrant workers[b] — Arts. 300 and 310 TEC (ex Arts. 228 and 238 EEC) — cases — %	— No.	Workers' protection and equal treatment — Arts. 136–45 TEC (ex Arts. 117–22 EEC) — cases — %	— No.	Social policy (all) — cases — %	— No.
1954–60	50										
1961–65	52			15.4	8					15.4	8
1966–70	45	2.2	1	44.4	20					46.6	21
1971–75	249	4.4	11	15.7	39			0.4	1	20.5	51
1976–80	462	2.4	11	14.7	68			0.6	3	17.7	82
1981–85	657	2.4	16	6.7	44			3.2	21	12.3	81

1986–90	855	3.4	29	6.7	57	0.2	2	4.6	39	14.9	127
1991–95	929	4.4	41	7.6	71	0.6	6	6.7	62	19.3	180
1996–2000	1,084	4.2	45	5.1	55	1.6	17	8.9	96	19.8	213
2001–5	1,317	3.3	44	3.2	42	0.5	7	7.2	95	14.4	189
2006	294	4.1	12	2.0	6	0.0	0	6.5	19	12.6	37
2007	254	5.5	14	2.4	6	0.0	0	4.3	11	12.2	31
1954–2007	6,248	1.4	224	6.6	416	0.5	32	5.5	347	16.3	1,020

Source: the data on the distribution of ECJ decisions for the years 1954–2003 were obtained by Andreas Obermaier from the analytical indices of the *Reports of Cases before the Court of Justice and Court of First Instance* (Luxembourg: ECJ), and verified by inspecting the individual cases (available on-line at *http://curia.eu.int*); data from 1998–2003 were corrected by Josef Falke. Decisions concerning the staff of the European Communities and appeals were not included. The data for the years 2004–2007 were obtained by Josef Falke with the search-form provided by the ECJ and verified by inspecting single cases.

On the cases deemed most important by the ECJ see the yearly reports, for 2007: *http://curia.europa.eu/en/instit/presentationfr/rapport/pei/07_cour_activ.pdf*.

[a] This column reports the decisions based on Regulations 3/58, 1408/71, 574/72 (and amendments). These regulations are based on Art. 51 EEC, now Art. 42 TEC.

[b] This column reports the decisions based on Association and Cooperation Agreements with third countries (like Turkey, Algeria, Morocco, Slovakia), insofar as they address social security concerns of third-country migrant workers.

TABLE 11.4 ECJ rulings on social policy by functional subcategories and EU member states, 1954–2007*

Countries	AU	BE	DK	FI	FR	DE	GR	IE	IT	LX	NL	PT	ES	SW	UK	All (%)
Freedom of movement for workers																
1 Referral under Article 230																1
2 Referral by European Commission		13	2		6	3	5		13	6	2	1	7			59
3 Preliminary rulings	8	23	1	1	17	39	5		16	7	21	1	3	4	21	168
4 All	9	**36**	3	1	**23**	**42**	10	1	**29**	13	**23**	2	10	4	**21**	228 (15.2)
Social security of EU migrant workers																
5 Referral by European Commission		5			5	1	1	1		1	2				1	16
6 Preliminary rulings	9	125	1	3	42	101	2		10	6	71		11	2	20	403
7 All	9	**130**	1	3	**47**	**102**	3		10	7	**73**		11	2	21	419 (28)
Social security of third-country migrant workers																
8 Preliminary rulings	2	**4**			1	**18**					**5**					30 (2)

Workers' protection and equal treatment

	1	2	3	4	5	6	7	8	9	10	11	12	13	14	15	All
9 Referral under Article 230																3
10 Referral by European Commission	8	6	1	1	8	4	3	2	15	8	2	2			6	66
11 Preliminary rulings	13	19	18	3	12	72	7	6	18	1	31		14	4	61	279
12 All	21	**25**	19	4	20	**76**	10	8	**33**	9	**33**	2	14	4	**67**	350 (23)

Social policy—all

	1	2	3	4	5	6	7	8	9	10	11	12	13	14	15	All
13 Referral under Article 230																6
14 Referral by European Commission	9	24	3	1	19	8	9	2	28	15	5	3	7	0	7	141
15 Preliminary rulings	30	167	20	7	71	212	14	7	44	14	123	1	28	10	102	850
16 All	39	**191**	23	8	90	**220**	23	9	**72**	29	**128**	4	35	10	**109**	997 (66)

Source: see Table 11.3. All across the table higher than average summary values per country are in bold.

* As of the end of 2007 no cases from the member states which joined in 2004 and 2007 had been decided by the ECJ, but cases may be pending. The cases reported here are hence from only the EU15. The number of cases per member state should be seen in proportion to the duration of its membership (see Chapter 1).

law on national social provisions. Only cases dealing with European citizenship (Bieback 2003; Besson 2007; Shaw 2007) or legitimate residency (Eichenhofer 2003) would generate a social dimension separate from market-building. We can already see signs of this as regards Union citizenship (Art. 17 ToN), as the heated exchanges over the *Grzelczyk* decision of 2001 (C-184/99) indicate (Hailbronner 2004*a*, 2004*b*; Epiney 2007), a decision that granted access to Belgian welfare benefits to a French citizen studying at the Catholic University of Louvain-la-Neuve based on Union citizenship. More broadly the ECJ in its jurisprudence increasingly cites citizenship provisions in undoing, revising, or adjusting secondary European law (Besson and Utzinger 2007).

Freedom of movement for workers

Over a period of fifty years a complex patchwork of regulations[3] and court decisions has partially eroded national sovereignty over social policy in pursuit of European labour mobility, now Articles 39–42 EC (Slaughter et al 1997; Jorens and Schulte 1998; Eichenhofer 2006; Schulte 2008). These constrain national capacities to limit eligibility for social transfers 'by territory' (Maydell 1991: 231; Maydell et al. 2006) and to shape autonomously welfare-state reform trajectories (Conant 2002):

- A member state may no longer limit most social benefits to its citizens. As regards non-nationals from within the EU, the state of legal residence no longer has any power to determine whether they are entitled to benefits. Benefits must be granted to all—or withheld from all. This development is remarkable, since 'citizen-making' through social benefits—demarcating the 'outsider'— was a watershed in the history of state-building on the continent, especially in France and Germany. This restriction encourages attempts to develop innocent-looking, but devious, discrimination mechanisms at the national level, many of which reach the ECJ in due course (as does the German private-pension Riester-subsidy, C-269/07 in 2009).

- A member state may no longer insist that its rights and benefits only apply to, and can only be provided within, its territory. Today states can exercise such a power to determine the territory of benefit consumption to only a limited extent—basically when providing in-kind or universal means-tested benefits, and in unemployment insurance (see Husmann 1998), though the latter may change with the modernization and simplification of coordination regulation (with implementing Regulation EC 883/04 replacing EEC 1408/71).

- A member state is no longer entirely free to prevent other social policy regimes from directly competing on its own territory. This is a problem for many states, and conflicts have been reported across the EU (Dølvik 2006) over posted construction workers from other EU countries, who work for extended periods at their national wage level, while covered by many of their home country's social regulations. Cases arising in 2007 from Scandinavia like Viking (C-438/05) and Laval (C-341/05), and in 2008 from Germany like Rüffert (C-346/06), in which national wage minimums were undercut by the free movement of enterprises, have had major political reverberations in a time where Europe's social dimension came under additional stress due to the economic crisis of 2007 and beyond; the court kept to its course in Commission v. Luxembourg (C-319/06) in 2008 (see Chapter 12). Thus, the state has lost some of its exclusive power to determine how the people living within its borders are protected, though there have been successful attempts since the 1990s (Directive 96/71/EC) to contain such losses through obligatory minimum wages and holidays (see Streeck 1998; Eichhorst 1998, 2000; Menz 2003; Boeri and Brücker 2006).

- Member states have no exclusive right to administer claims to welfare benefits from migrants. Instead, the authorities of other states may also have a decisive say in adjudicating benefit status—as controversial cases that seemed to imply unstoppable receipts of fraudulent benefits as in the Paletta cases of 1992 and 1996 (C-45/90, C-206/94) (stating that a doctor's certificate from the country of abode entitled a worker to sickness benefit in the country of employment) revealed repeatedly in Germany and elsewhere.

Compared with the US, intra-EU migration has been small, and member states have quite different migration profiles (see Chapter 19). Prior to the 2004 enlargement only about five million workers in the EU, including their dependants, exercised this freedom, far outnumbered by third-country migration into the EU (Angenendt 1997; Mau and Verwiebe 2009: 111ff; Recchi and Favell 2009). Eastern enlargement has changed this situation, a factor that could generate a good deal of ECJ litigation. For the law to bite does not require a quantum leap in the volume of intra-EU migration, but only a few individuals as litigants and national courts which refer cases to the ECJ, as has been the pattern since 1959. Similarly, third-country migrants have prompted important cases, and concerns about irregular labour migration has been one of the driving forces behind the development of justice and home affairs (see Chapter 19).

Complete national legal authority has ceased to exist in the EU. Supranational efforts to broaden access to social policy and national efforts to maintain control go hand in hand, are recalibrated from conflict to conflict, and are moving piecemeal into a new, albeit sketchy, system. Member governments have resisted this transformation. Individually, they have baulked at implementing some facets of coordination, although the ECJ has often taken them to task for this. Collectively, they sought to roll back some aspects of coordination in the early 1990s, unanimously agreeing to revisions that would allow them to restrict portability in a somewhat broader range of cases following proper 'notification' (Schuler 2005).

Arguably the result is an incremental, rights-based homogenization of social policy. Neither supranationalization nor harmonization describes this dynamic: each implies more policy control at the centre than currently exists. The ECJ is central to this process by applying a light, but far-reaching, hand, reshaping the boundaries of national autonomy. The process structures the interfaces between twenty-seven national social-policy systems with potentially far-reaching implications for the range of national policy options available.

Freedom of services and the European competition regime

The EU's agenda on market integration has covered the freedom to provide services since 1957 (now Arts. 49–55 ToN). The Treaty's signatories were aware that an explicitly coordinated social policy would affect their national welfare states (Romero 1993), but saw no connection between this and the freedom of services, for which they only had the financial-services markets in mind (see Chapter 5). But developments since the mid-1980s under the 1986 SEA have shown that implementing this freedom could entail far-reaching consequences for national social-policy regimes. Several ECJ judgments, notably *Kohll*, a case about a Luxembourg citizen who obtains dental treatment in Germany without prior authorization (C-158/96), and *Decker*, a case about a Luxembourg citizen buying his prescription glasses in Belgium without authorization (C-120/95), have ruled that freedom of services includes both the freedom of movement for consumers 'of social policy' to shop in other EU countries and the right of service providers to deliver their services 'across the border' in another country, redrawing the demarcation line between the national welfare state and the EU-wide market (Becker 2004b, 2005a; Kingreen 2007).[4] Notably, since 1998 this spill-over has generated European conflicts over social policy—especially health—reform (Maydell 1999; Becker 1998, 2005b), though its precise effects are disputed (Obermaier 2008). These developments have potentially wide ramifications, not least since 5–10 per cent of the national labour forces are involved in the delivery of national social policies, a growing sector in an ageing continent.

This understanding of a free market for services has three general implications for the sovereignty of national welfare states. First, the treaty provisions set up a tension between 'economic' activity and 'solidaristic' action, which now frames the welfare state but contains two polarized trajectories (Schulz-Weidner 1997). They protect some core components of the 'old' welfare state (redistribution, pay-as-you-go, etc., which belong to the 'social security provider monopoly'); but, as redistribution measures contract, the welfare state (in whole or in part) moves over the borderline into the sphere of 'economic activity', thus becoming subject to the freedom of services and establishment (see Chapter 5) and the competition regime (see Chapter 6). Thus, slowly a single European 'social security' *market* is emerging, with a level playing-field for private actors (Giesen 2005); for example, several member states already allow for private competitive provision in accident insurance. There is no general exemption from the treaties' market freedoms for welfare state activity per se (Becker 1998, 2007a). This continuous redrawing of the fine line between 'economic' and 'solidaristic' action is what much of the legal conflict is about, as evidenced by *Sodemare* 1997 (C-70/95) and many other cases: that is, whether the state may allow non-profit-making private operators to participate in running its social welfare system by concluding contracts which entitle only them to be reimbursed by public authorities for the costs of their healthcare services. Only at the end of a long process will we know the real contours of this interface between European law and national welfare states (Graser 2004).

Second, consumer and provider rights in services have come to the fore since the mid-1990s, also challenging the closed shops of the welfare state. Member governments may no longer exclusively decide who provides social services or benefits. They may no longer exclusively organize social-service occupations, since the mutual recognition of degrees and licences from other member states intervenes. And their capacity to protect their national service organizations from the competitive inroads of service organizations in other member states has shrunk radically.

Third, the health area has become a crucial, Europe-wide testing ground for the turf battle between national welfare states and the EU-cum-market, as represented by private insurance, producers, etc. (Mossialos and McKee 2002; Commission 2004c: section 4.4; Mossialos et al. 2002; Thomson and Mossialos 2007). Compared with pensions, health insurance has more 'market traces' in most national systems, is more fragmented by provider groups already operating in markets (medical instruments, pharmaceuticals), or quasi-markets (doctors in private practice), and has been traditionally exposed to substantial private provision in most countries. Some producers are more likely to take the European route than others, especially private international service organizations involved in hospitals, medical drug markets, and the provision of medical equipment (Bieback 1993: 171). They are likely to become strong actors at the EU level, *vis-à-vis* the Commission or in the courts. National reforms have pointed increasingly to 'market cures', opening themselves to particular single markets, like a single drug market (Woolcock 1996; Schwarze 1998; Kotzian 2002, 2003). As health is a general concern for Europeans, a European Health Insurance Card was introduced in 2006 and is seen by some already as the health-policy equivalent of the euro.

The single market for private insurance provides a telling example. Since 1994 national private insurance has been drawn into the European single market, as the Commission has actively sought to establish a single occupational pensions market, among others with a Pension Funds Directive 2003/41/EC, also supported by the ECJ (see decisions *Danner* (2002) and *Skandia* (2003); Schulz-Weidner 2003). The proliferation of cross-border mergers and acquisitions is creating a heavily interlocked insurance sector operating at the Europe-wide level (Vauhkonen and Pylkkönen 2004: 105–10; Klumpes et al. 2007). Integrated European insurance markets allow for a greater differentiation of policy-holders by risk groups, and thus for cheaper policies with lower operational costs. This integrated private sector confronts twenty-seven national, internally segmented, public insurance domains, often themselves caught up in spirals of deregulation and thus already exposed to challenges from these private markets. Insurance providers with the option of relocating to more lenient member states will gain a growing influence over national social regulation. At the same time, the clash between particular national regulatory styles and the different traditions of competing insurers from other member states is likely to intensify.

For some time there has been considerable evidence from studies of national welfare states that the reform of private-sector markets can have dramatic effects on the provision of public services (Rein and Rainwater 1986). Public and private insurance compete mainly in areas such as occupational pensions (Pochet 2003; Pedersen 2004), life insurance, and supplemental health insurance (Thomson 2007; Thomson and Mossialos 2007). Permanent turf battles seem likely concerning where 'basic' (public) coverage should end and 'additional' (private) insurance begin. Private (or competing 'out-of-state' public) actors may arm themselves with the 'economic action' approach. The welfare state, which has traditionally been important for demarcating the lines between public and private, is bound to be affected by such a redrawing of boundaries (Hagen 1998).

The balance between a market and institutionally autonomous national welfare states, both embedded in the EU treaties, is not static but has become dynamic, with national reforms heading for privatization-cum-deregulation and the single market regime both feeding into each other in a race towards 'marketization' (Bieback 2003). Brussels finds a wide-open terrain here, with a large potential for restructuring welfare-state delivery regimes. The Commission's *White Paper on Services of General Interest* (Commission 2004c) and the December 2006 Services (Bolkestein) Directive 2006/123/EC, 'the legislative hot potato of the early twenty-first century' (Barnard 2008a: 323; Commission 2004b; Neergard et al. 2008; Hendrickx 2008; Koeck and Karollus 2008), and street demonstrations in 2005 may foreshadow a much more prominent role for the Commission here than in the coordination arena, despite the fact that the directive currently excludes social and health services, which may become the subject of a special directive. The Commission took the initiative with a 2007 Commission White Paper, *Together for Health: A Strategic Approach for the EU 2008–2013* (Commission 2007f), but two months later the stalled progress on a framework directive for cross-border healthcare (Commission 2008g) already showed the rough road lying ahead.

So, even if we focus exclusively on issues of freedom of movement for workers and to provide services, we see a wide range of market-compatibility requirements, through which either EU regulations or ECJ decisions impact on the design and the reform of national social policies. Examples of other welfare-state effects of single-market measures could easily be multiplied—e.g. restrictions related to subsidies for economic activities in regional policy (Schulz-Weidner 2004) or to state aid for services (Becker 2007b). The broader point is clear: a whole range of social policy designs that would be available to sovereign welfare states—and belong to the traditional policy 'toolkit'—are prohibited, or made more costly, to member states within the EC's multi-tiered polity.

European integration and indirect pressures on national welfare states

The EU intervenes directly in the social policies of member states in the two ways outlined above. In addition, European integration indirectly affects national social policies significantly, as the economic policies of the EU, and the responses of social actors to those policies, restrict national welfare states. Indirect effects are hard to measure; nonetheless they exert supranational influence on the design of national social policy. While, as shown by the Services Directive, so-called social dumping may generate greater fears than current evidence warrants (see Chapter 12), the opposite could hold for the many other ways in which economic and monetary union (EMU) (see Chapter 7) creates pressures on national social policy systems:

- *Social dumping*: this refers to the prospect that firms operating where 'social wages' are low may undercut the prices of competitors, forcing higher-cost firms out of business, or to relocate to low-social-wage areas, or pressure their governments to reduce the social wage. The surge of Polish plumbers into France, alleged to have happened just before the French referendum on the EU Constitutional Treaty, epitomizes this expectation. In extreme scenarios, still trendy in countries bordering on the eastern enlargement, these actions fuel a downward spiral in social provision, eventually producing rudimentary, lowest-common-denominator, welfare states. These kinds of pressures may have restricted social expenditure in the US, where labour—and capital—mobility is traditionally far greater than in the EU (P. E. Peterson and Rom 1990). The evidence that European integration will fuel such a process remains limited (Majone 2005). The 'social wage' is only one factor in investment decisions, and firms will not invest in low-social-wage countries unless worker productivity justifies such investments. Even in eastern enlargement a huge wage disparity only leads to a relatively small productivity disparity to the advantage of the east (Vaughan-Whitehead 2003; Guillén and Palier 2004). Neo-classical trade theory suggests that high-social-wage countries should be able to continue their policies as long as overall conditions allow profitable investment. A sign of the ambiguous consequences of integration is that northern Europe's concerns about 'sunbelt effects' are mirrored by southern, and now eastern, Europe's concerns about 'agglomeration effects' in which investment flows towards the superior infrastructures and high-skilled workforces of Europe's most developed regions.

- *EMU and Maastricht criteria*: EMU, with its tough requirements for budgetary discipline, may also encourage downward adjustments in welfare provision (see Chapter 7), although the economic crisis has led to a (temporary?) relaxation of these tough requirements. To participate in EMU, for example, Italy had to reduce its budget deficit from 10 to about 3 per cent of GDP by the end of the 1990s (Ferrera and Gualmini 2004; della Sala 2004). This legitimated efforts by successive governments to make cuts in old age pensions and other benefits in 1994/95. Although not all would-be euro members have faced such radical adjustments, the Maastricht convergence criteria present formidable problems for most of them and have increased the level of reform pressures (Martin and Ross 2004: 316–21; Townsend 2007: 270–3). These constraints are of particular weight in the context of the current economic recession and bear heavily on the economies of central and eastern Europe, described by some as a 'bill that could break up Europe' (*Economist*, 2 February 2009: 13). Governments would have faced austerity pressure anyway (see Pierson 2001) and this has simply become more acute. The convergence criteria do not require budget reductions, as tax increases could also reduce overall budget deficits—but they strengthened the hand of those seeking cuts. A backlash against the Maastricht criteria, however, has built up since 2002, and this can be read under the heading 'national welfare states strike back'. EMU could prod the EU into a more active role in combating unemployment (see Chapter 12). Historically the prospects for EMU were seen as coupled with the need for social policies to address emerging regional imbalances (Ross 1995b). EMU would strip national governments of macroeconomic policy levers, and an EU-wide macroeconomic stance would create significant regional unemployment. Flexible exchange rates allowed national adaptations to economic conditions. Once these instruments were dismantled, combating pockets of regional unemployment at the national level became more difficult (Eichengreen 1992). What the global economic crisis will do to reconfigure this general constellation is still unclear.

- *Harmonization of tax systems*: the single market is encouraging a movement towards a narrowing band of value-added tax rates (Uhl 2008); in March 2009 additional exemptions from the minimum standard rate of 15 per cent were allowed for labour-intensive services at the minimum reduced rate of 5 per cent, a step which encourages the downward movement in harmonization. In theory, governments whose VAT revenues are lowered can increase other taxes. Because it is politically easier to sustain indirect taxes, however, this movement may create growing constraints on member-state budgets, with clear implications for some national social policies (Hibbs and Madsen 1981). This is a problem for countries like Denmark, which relies on high indirect, rather than payroll, taxes to finance its generous welfare state (Petersen 1991, 2000; Hagen et al. 1998) and resists 'upper limits' for value-added taxes.

- *Dispensing with the 'public utilities state'*: a further pressure on national welfare states stems from the consequences of the dismantling of the 'public service state', which happened partly for EU reasons, but partly for purely national, endogenous rationales. Trains, mail, air transport, electricity, gas and other utilities, together with local services, used to be public enterprises, financed by tariffs that ensured equal service across the nation, urban and rural, often cross-subsidizing poor with rich services. Since the mid-1980s, branch after branch of these public structures has been privatized (Schneider et al. 2005; Tenbücken 2006). Supranational prodding via EU regulation based on competition law (S.K. Schmidt 2004a, 2004b) and privatization/deregulation in the UK and US were exacerbated by domestic cuts in state spending and the levelling of the playing field for different kinds of enterprises, and resulted in radically increased competitive pressure in newly internationalized markets (see Chapter 6). Private, multinational companies formed in branches of public service that had been national or regional. The welfare state, in a sense, is the last domino of the public-service state that has not fallen, but since most other dominoes already did, the burden of proof for its legitimacy has now shifted to the last fully standing one. We have seen a transnationalization of the public-service state and a national lock-in of welfare-state change (Leibfried and Zürn 2005)—and thus the loss of the welfare state's protective outer skin (Leibfried 2001). The principles established here may now well be applied to the welfare state proper.

What are the consequences of these indirect pressures for welfare states? Many of the potential problem areas lie in the future, and some of the others are difficult to measure. One has to weigh the reform pressures against the welfare state's powers of resilience (Pierson 2001). The picture that emerges is of national governments with diminished control over many of the policies that traditionally supported national welfare states—the currency, macroeconomic policies, public finance, tax policies, the public services, and also industrial-relations systems (Hurrelmann et al. 2008).

Europe's emerging multi-tiered social policy

Attention has focused on the Commission's efforts to establish a social dimension. These efforts have modified national social policies in relatively few areas like labour law (see e.g. Burley and Mattli 1993; Stone Sweet and Caporaso 1998; Weiler 1999; and Bercusson 2007). But the expansion of EU mandates and QMV indicate that an 'activist' threshold may have been reached. Important, but less visible, have been the policy effects of the single market's development itself: some of these occurred directly, as the Commission, national courts, and the ECJ have reconciled national policy autonomy with the creation of a unified economic space, and others indirectly, through contextual pressures on national welfare states.

We are living through an epoch of transformation in the relations between states and an increasingly global market system (Leibfried and Zürn 2005; Hurrelmann et al. 2008; Leibfried and Mau 2008; Castles et al., forthcoming), and that transformation is hastened in unforeseen ways by the global economic crisis, strengthening the nation states' hands for the time being. In the EU, both member-state sovereignty and autonomy have diminished (Leibfried 1994; Pierson 1996*b*), with eastern enlargement having greatly enhanced territorial inequality and probably lastingly so (Heidenreich 2003), especially as exacerbated by the economic crisis. The process is subtle and incremental, but member governments find their revenue bases attacked, welfare-reform options circumscribed, delivery regimes threatened by competition, and administrators obliged to share implementation control. What is emerging is a distinctive multi-tiered social-policy system, with three distinctive characteristics:

- *A propensity towards joint-decision traps and immobility*: European policy-makers are hemmed in by the Council's scepticism, dense social-policy commitments within countries, and limited fiscal or administrative capacities. Compared with other multi-tiered systems the EU's social policy-making apparatus is bottom-heavy (Pierson and Leibfried 1995; Obinger et al. 2005). The weak centre's capacity for positive social policy is limited. Policy evolves rather through mutual adjustment and accommodation. The centre generates various constraints on social-policy development, rather than producing clear mandates for positive action. But member states' capacity to design their own welfare states has weakened considerably (Pierson 1995*b*), and authority, albeit of a largely negative kind, has gravitated towards the EU level. Loss of autonomy and sovereignty occurred without member governments paying much attention. Sometimes—as when Italy pushed for labour mobility in the Treaty of Rome—they actively sought erosion of sovereignty. Resistance to some of the single market's implications jostles with fears of jeopardizing benefits from integration. Resistance is further checked by a ratchet effect. Within the EU, a member state is bound by all ECJ rulings, and can pursue reforms only subject to complicated EU procedures. Diminished member-state authority combined with continued weakness at the EU level restricts the room for innovative policy. Member governments still choose, but from an increasingly restricted menu. As control over social policy increasingly means announcing unpopular cuts, governments are sometimes happy to be constrained in their options. Moving towards a multi-tiered system opens up new avenues for a politics of 'blame avoidance' (Weaver 1986). This dynamic may strengthen national executives against domestic opponents (Milward 1992; Moravcsik 1998). Yet, in escaping from domestic constraints, executives have created new ones. Decision-makers at both levels face serious restrictions of their regulatory capacity, since they have 'locked themselves in' through previous steps towards integration.

- *A prominent role for courts in policy development*: the requirements which develop from the centre are normally law- or court-driven.[5] A series of ECJ rulings and Commission–Council initiatives is the source of new social policy. While the latter are stasis-prone, the ECJ's design fosters activism. Faced with litigation, the ECJ cannot avoid making what are essentially policy decisions. The Court relies on secret simple-majority votes, sheltering it from political immobility, which is a common feature of the EU legislative process. Only a unanimous vote of the Council can generally undo ECJ decisions on European primary law. The EU system therefore places the ECJ centre stage. Attempts at corporatist policy-making generated much drama surrounding Europe's social dimension, but until recently (Falkner 1998) businesses and unions had little direct involvement in making legally binding requirements for member states' policies. Today, the ECJ's backsliding on balanced corporatism (in *Laval* etc.) delegitimizes that whole policy-making effort. Generally, legal strategies have the advantage of leaving taxing, spending, and administrative powers at the national level—even more so, as they are regulatory in nature. But a court-led process of social-policy development has its own logic. Legal decisions reflect demands for doctrinal coherence more than substantive debates about policy outcomes. The capacity of reforms built around a judicial logic to achieve substantive goals is limited. Furthermore, courts heed political constraints in prescribing solutions less and may exceed the tolerance of important political actors within the system. In this sense the scope for a more explicit form of EU policy-making was made difficult because ECJ activism may generate resentment. This is one aspect of the disquiet over the 'democratic deficit'.

- *An unusually tight coupling to market-making*: the EU system of social policy is tightly connected to a process of market-building. Social policies intersect in a variety of ways with market systems. In the past, social policy had generally been seen as a spontaneous 'protective reaction' against market expansion (Polanyi 1994), as an outcome of politics *against* markets. In the EU case, however, even in areas like gender where the EU has been activist, policies have been directly connected to labour-market participation. As the centrality of decisions on labour mobility and free service markets reveals, EU social policy has been an *integral part of* the process of market-building itself. Never before in the world has the construction of markets so visibly and intensively shaped the trajectory of social policies.

The overall scope of EU influence has been crucial: national welfare states are now part of a larger, multi-tiered system of social policy. Member governments influence this structure, but no longer fully control it. Such governance occurs at multiple levels, although the EU processes differ from classical federal states: a weak policy-making centre, court-driven regulation, and strong links with market-making—a pattern radically different from any national European welfare state (Streeck 2000). One stalemate increasingly needs breaking: 'the policy-making capacities of the union have not been strengthened nearly as much as capabilities at the level of member states have declined' (Scharpf 1994: 219; Offe 2003). While the latter process is a permanent feature of globalization and Europeanization, the former process is an optional one, one which can be shaped politically. Perhaps the current economic crisis will be a catalyst for a reconfiguration of this constellation.

Notes

1 This chapter is based on, but substantially revises and updates, Leibfried and Pierson (2000) and the more elaborate Leibfried (2005). I am indebted to the editors and to Eberhard Eichenhofer, Bernd Schulte, Dieter Wolf, and especially to Josef Falke, for their help.

2 Recommendations 92/441 (Common Criteria Concerning Sufficient Resources and Social Assistance in Social Protection Systems, 24 June 1992), and 92/442 (Objectives and Policies of Social Security Systems, 27 July 1992) reflect these difficulties and point to social policy convergence (Maydell 1999). In contrast, in the 1970s harmonization was still the major focus (see Fuchs 2003).

3 The first regulations were EEC 3/58 and 4/58; later EEC 1408/71 and 574/72. These were extended to third-country nationals in Regulation EC 859/03. After 29 April 2004, all coordination regulation was modernized under Regulation EC 883/04.

4 Much welfare state activity falls under 'services' in the terms of the treaty, not only 'social services'. Private insurance is a matter of financial services. So is the (monetary) 'transfer state', when considered as 'economic' activity rather than 'true welfare state activity', as, for example, when public pensions are shorn of all their redistributive elements in welfare state reform.

5 Falkner (personal communication 2004) pointed us to a budget-driven factor which shapes national thinking on some social problems and policies, insofar as national agencies tailor their projects to specific EU programmes as a way of obtaining complementary EU-funding.

 FURTHER READING

For the main contours of the subject, see Leibfried and Pierson (1995); the first and last chapters provide a guide to theoretical explanations, and the second chapter details the core contours of social policy. For more recent analyses see Castles et al. (forthcoming), Hantrais (2007), and Offe (2003). For an outspoken UK view, see Kleinman (2001). For a broad 'continental' view, see Scharpf (1999: Ch. 4). On eastern enlargement expectations see Kvist (2004). For an overview of the legal dimension on labour law see Bercusson (2007), on welfare law see the comprehensive German contributions by Eichenhofer (2006), Schulte (2008), and Fuchs (2005). On health law, see Mossialos and McKee (2002), and on health policy, see Mossialos et al. (2002). On the withering away of the services (public utilities) mantle of the welfare state due to EC competition law, see Leibfried and Starke (2008). Recent ECJ cases may be consulted on the web under *http://www.curia.eu.int/*. For a comprehensive analysis of the new corporatist perspectives, see Falkner (1998). Both the *Journal of European Social Policy* (1991–), and the *Journal of European Public Policy* (1994–) contain useful articles. Since 1993 regular policy news is reported monthly in the German bulletin, *Eureport social* (until Feb. 1995 entitled *Eureport*), published by the European representation of the German social insurance (*http://dsv@esip.org*) in Brussels, which is a member of the network European Social Insurance Partners (ESIP; *http://www.esip.org*). No equivalent English source exists.

Bercusson, B. (2007), *European Labour Law*, 2nd edn. (London: Butterworths).

Castles, F. G., Leibfried, S., Lewis, J., Obinger, H., and Pierson, C. (forthcoming), *Oxford Handbook of Comparative Welfare States* (Oxford: Oxford University Press).

Eichenhofer, E. (2006), *Sozialrecht der Europäischen Union*, 3rd edn. (Berlin: Erich Schmidt).

Falkner, G. (1998), *EU Social Policy in the 1990s: Towards a Corporatist Policy Community* (London: Routledge).

Fuchs, M. (2005) (ed.), *Nomos Kommentar zum europäischen Sozialrecht*, 4th edn. (Baden-Baden: Nomos).

Hantrais, L. (2007), *Social Policy in the European Union*, 3rd edn. (Basingstoke: Palgrave Macmillan).

Kleinman, M. (2001), *A European Welfare State? European Union Social Policy in Context* (Basingstoke: Palgrave Macmillan).

Kvist, J. (2004), 'Does EU Enlargement Start a Race to the Bottom? Strategic Interaction among EU Member States in Social Policy', *Journal of European Social Policy*, 14/3: 301–18.

Leibfried, S., and Pierson, P. (1995) (eds.), *European Social Policy: Between Fragmentation and Integration* (Washington, DC: The Brookings Institution).

Leibfried, S., and Starke, P. (2008), 'Transforming the "Cordon Sanitaire": The Liberalization of Public Services and the Restructuring of European Welfare States', *Socio-Economic Review*, 6/1: 175–82.

Mossialos, E., and McKee, M. (2002), *EU Law and the Social Character of Health Care* (Brussels: PIE-Peter Lang).

Mossialos, E., Dixon, A., Figueras, J., and Kutzin, J. (2002) (eds.), *Funding Health Care: Options for Europe* (Buckingham: Open University Press).

Offe, C. (2003), 'The European Model of "Social" Capitalism: Can It Survive European Integration?', *Journal of Political Philosophy*, 11/4: 437–69.

Scharpf, F. W. (1999), *Governing in Europe: Effective and Democratic?* (Oxford: Oxford University Press).

Schulte, B. (2008), 'Supranationales Recht', in Baron Maydell and F. Ruland (eds.), *Sozialrechtshandbuch (SRH)*, 4th edn. (Baden-Baden: Nomos), 1611–76.

CHAPTER 12

Employment Policy

Between Efficacy and Experimentation

Martin Rhodes

▌ Summary

Attempts to put in place an employment policy for the European Union (EU) have been bedevilled by a complex and long-standing regulatory conundrum: how to accommodate member-state diversity in employment-regulation and industrial-relations practices while also resolving conflict between member states over both the direction of labour-market reform and the assignment of policy powers to the EU. Nevertheless, by the early 2000s, the EU had acquired an extensive regulatory system for employment based on three different modes of policy-making and governance: EU legislation and ECJ hard law that promotes employment rights; 'law via collective agreement' between the EU-level social partners; and the adoption from the late 1990s of a 'soft-law' process, the European Employment Strategy, which aims to promote rather than just protect employment. All three have seen ongoing contestation of the form, substance, and level of regulation, as well as persistent power games between member states and the supranational institutions. Yet all three venues are now used concurrently, providing a multi-layered opportunity structure for further policy innovation.

Introduction

In recent years, employment policy has moved close to the centre of EU policy preoccupations, after several decades of policy initiatives, institutional and treaty innovations, and experimentation with negotiated and 'new' modes of governance. Employment policy is not, as is sometimes assumed, coterminous with the European Employment Strategy (EES)—a rather recent innovation, with as yet unclear potential—but consists of a massive corpus of European law and legislation. Employment policy is actually formulated and implemented via several parallel policy modes, including the Community method of legislating and the case law of the European Court of Justice (ECJ); a unique hybrid of the Community method and the regulatory approach in the post-Maastricht method of 'making law via collective agreement'; and softer modes of intervention through policy coordination and benchmarking in the EES. Their coexistence reveals the instability and frequent renovation of the EU's employment policy architecture, triggered by the changing nature of the employment 'problem', the diversity of European labour-market organization and industrial relations, and the 'essentially contested' nature of employment regulation.

Innovation and contestation come from three directions. First, the European employment policy-making agenda has shifted over time, following the end of full employment after the 1970s, the emergence of a crisis of 'welfare without work' in the 1990s, and newer challenges created by post-industrial, service-sector employment creation. As many countries have discovered, if service-sector employment is to be generated in the private sector, then labour-market regulations may have to be more flexible than hitherto. This has complicated policy-making, producing new national strategies that seek to rebalance flexibility for firms and security for employees (Hemerijck et al. 2006). It has also provided a major impetus in the late 1990s and 2000s for the European Employment Strategy and the EU's adoption of the so-called 'flexicurity' paradigm, which seeks to facilitate more temporary and part-time work by loosening employment regulation, while mitigating the income insecurity that might result with tax and social-policy innovations.

Second, the diversity of European industrial relations and labour-market regulation complicates and frustrates attempts to tackle both employment protection and its promotion at the EU level. Employment regimes are coupled closely with national social security, pensions, and unemployment benefit arrangements (see Chapter 11), and employment-regulation and industrial-relations rules differ considerably across countries. They range from those in which the state plays a central role through the constitutional provision of workers' rights and comprehensive labour-market legislation (for example, in Belgium, France, Germany, The Netherlands, Luxembourg, Italy, Spain, and Greece), through those where the state has traditionally abstained from regulating industrial relations (the UK and Ireland), to those where many rules have been and are still set by corporatist-type agreements between employers and

FIGURE 12.1   The 'double cleavage' in EU employment policy

Level of policy-making

		National	European
Nature of regulation	less/ flexible	market liberals UK government employers' organizations	advocates of the EES/ OMC
	more/ rigid	most national unions	European unions socialists/social democrats

unions (Denmark and Sweden). Enlargement to the east has complicated the mix further still by adding a fourth model, one in which state intervention is combined with weak levels of unionization and firm-level representation.

Third, EU employment policy-making in the Commission, the Council, and the European Parliament (EP) has always been riven by a two-way conflict, or double cleavage: that between supporters and opponents ('federalists' versus 'subsidiarists') of an EU 'social dimension', which would elevate social and employment policy-making to the European level; and that between competing conceptions (socialists/ social democrats versus market liberals) of how labour markets and social systems should be organized (M. Rhodes 1992). Actors (politicians, trade unionists, and public officials, both national and European) can be found in various locations across this dichotomous space of political contestation (see Figure 12.1). Although often considered a 'technocratic' part of the EU system, as discussed below, the ECJ—part of the standard Community method of policy-making—has also been subject to the same political currents and pressures, as it has attempted to deal with the often competing claims and priorities of EU economic rights (the freedom of movement of enterprises) and state-level social and employment protection.

The three modes of policy-making and governance

Three modes of policy-making and governance in European employment policy, each entailing quite different policy instruments, have been developed since the 1960s (Figure 12.2 provides a summary). The first is that of legislated 'rights', based on the classical Community method, and used in fits and starts for employment issues from the 1960s onwards. This mode of policy-making has been based on both unanimity and (after the Single European Act (SEA)) qualified majority voting (QMV) in the Council and implemented via directives, in which scope for variation in implementation has (at least in principle) been restricted. The second mode of 'law via collective agreement' has its roots in the social dialogue promoted by the Commission between European-level employer and trade union confederations in the 1980s. It was backed by Article 118b (EEC) (now Art. 138 TEC), and formally institutionalized in the social-policy agreement (Art. 4; now Art. 139 TEC) of the Maastricht Treaty on European Union (TEU). This allows the social partners to request a Council decision on an employment policy agreement, or alternatively the implementation of directives via collective bargaining and 'national practice'. The third mode is the more recent and more experimental European Employment Strategy (EES)—a 'new' mode of governance, using the 'open method of coordination'—and dependent for implementation on persuasion via benchmarking and peer review.

The first mode—legislated rights—employs binding legal instruments (directives) and a rather rigid form of implementation via labour law, backed by the courts (both national and European). This is the most coercive form of governance in this domain of policy. However, treaty requirements insist that employment legislation respect variations in industrial-relations and labour-law systems. Employment directives therefore typically avoid harmonizing objectives and aspire instead to 'partial harmonization' or 'diversity built on common standards' (Kenner 2003: 30–1). Legislation sets *minimum* and not lowest-common-denominator standards; and there is nothing to prevent member states from implementing more stringent rules.

The second mode—'law via collective agreement'—produces binding but flexible instruments (e.g. framework legislation that offers a menu of alternatives for member states to choose from), as well as non-binding but rigid instruments, such as targeted recommendations that contain explicit rules of conduct for workers and employers. This approach relies heavily on negotiation between social actors at both

---

FIGURE 12.2   Policy instruments and modes of governance

		Legal instrument	
		binding	non-binding
Implementation	rigid	I. coercion (Mode one)	III. targeting (Mode two)
	flexible	II. framework regulation (Mode two)	IV. voluntarism (Mode three)

Source: derived from Treib et al. (2007: 14)

the European and national levels. This is a flexible form of governance, but one still potentially conducive to effective implementation. Nonetheless, the impact of directives produced in this pillar has been rather weak, owing to political opposition to upward harmonization and the institutional fragility of this form of law-making.

The third mode—the EES and the open method of coordination—uses non-binding and flexible instruments. This is a 'voluntarist' form of governance with still weaker implementation capacities, and uncertain links between policy inputs and outputs. Open-ended experimentation, in both the form and substance of policy-making, takes priority over the search for efficacy as such (Citi and Rhodes 2007).

Over time, the second and third modes of policy-making and governance have been added to the first, due largely to the efforts of the European Commission and pro-integration élites to work around member-state vetoes and to neutralize the operation of the double cleavage between 'federalists' and 'subsidiarists' and socialists/social democrats and market liberals. However, 'new' and experimental modes of governance and policy instruments have not even begun to replace the old. As a result of an ongoing process of experimental 'venue-shopping' (Baumgartner and Jones 1993) by the pro-integration employment advocacy coalition, searching for the best institutional venue, with the least powerful vetoes, for policy innovation, each of the three policy-making and governance modes remains important in different ways in promoting and implementing European employment initiatives.

Employment policy-making before Amsterdam

Mode one: the 'Community method' and the EU regulatory model

The history of EU employment legislation has been a tortured one. The Commission has acted as tireless promoter of new regulatory objectives and rules, often in the face of intense political opposition; the Council has forged agreements on minimum standards, to be implemented differentially in individual countries; and the ECJ has provided backing for those standards, but has typically refrained from over-zealous judgments where the treaty basis is unclear. Use of the Community method proper has been restricted to those few areas where there has been a sound treaty basis for legislation (some aspects of health and safety, for example, and gender equality at work), or where the original legal base for employment directives has, in certain limited cases, been replaced by a stronger treaty alternative.

The Treaty of Rome (EEC) made only highly ambiguous provision for EU social or employment policy. Articles 117–122 (EEC) (social provisions) conferred few real powers upon the EU institutions. Under Article 117 (EEC) working conditions and standards were intended to flow from the functioning of the common market, as well as from law, regulation, or administrative action, thus providing the basis for the ensuing conflict between pro-integration forces which relied on the first, and their opponents who invoked the second. Article 118 (EEC) simply required the Commission to promote cooperation between the member states through studies, opinions, and consultations. Given the market-oriented nature of the Treaty of Rome, social and employment policies were to be used for correcting obvious market failures, not for creating a supranational welfare state (see Chapter 11). National welfare states, it was assumed by the founding philosophy of the European Community, would 'embed' the new economic area in systems of social protection that would remain distinct from one another.

But there was early conflict among member governments over whether and when European rule-making could be used to defend national systems from regulatory competition. Whereas the French believed that social security harmonization would protect their high social charges from creating competitive disadvantage, and that gender-equality provisions in the French constitution should be transferred to the Treaty, the Germans were opposed to any legal competence for the supranational authorities in this area (M. Rhodes 1999). The only substantial concession made to the French position was Article 119 (EEC) on the principle of equal pay.

As a result, many of the employment-policy advances from the 1960s onwards were based on alternative articles. In the early 1970s, for example, the Council of Ministers made use of Articles 100 (EEC), the internal market provision, and 235 (EEC), the 'flexible clause' that allowed the Council to adopt by unanimity any provisions directly related to the aims of the Community. These empowered the Council to issue directives and regulations for the 'approximation' of national regulatory systems, including laws, insofar as they directly affected the establishment and functioning of the common market, and led to directives on dismissals (in 1974) and workers' rights in the event of mergers (1975).

Subsequent treaty revisions sought to strengthen the basis for employment policy, but only meagre steps were taken, and each time only after major clashes and compromises between member states. In the SEA, Community competences were bolstered, but only for health and safety issues where regulation could be justified as preventing potential market distortions. Article 118a (EEC) thus granted the Commission the right of initiative in health and safety legislation after consultation with the Economic and Social Committee, gave the EP a second reading of proposals through the new cooperation procedure, and allowed the Council to act under QMV. Yet such directives were constrained by the proviso that small and medium-sized firms should be protected from excessive regulatory burdens. Elsewhere in the SEA, although Article 100a (EEC) introduced QMV for measures essential for the construction of the single market, British and German opposition ensured that those relating to the free movement of persons and rights and interests of workers were explicitly excluded (M. Rhodes 1992; Majone 1993).

By the time of the TEU, there was a broader coalition of member states in favour of European employment rules to prevent a regulatory 'race to the bottom' as the single market deepened and the prospect of currency union came closer. Yet opposition from the British government placed a major constraint on any new supranational transfer of powers, as did the reinforced subsidiarity principle in the

TEU. The ambition, especially of northern member states (apart from the UK), was to resolve procedural disputes by bringing most areas of labour-market policy under QMV, and to extend Community competence to contractual rights as well as workers' representation and consultation. In the final agreement adopted as a 'Social Protocol' to the Treaty by eleven member states (the UK opted out), only health and safety, work conditions, and equality at work fell under QMV. In the revised Articles 117–118 (TEC) (Arts. 1–2 of the Social Agreement), there was also bolstered reference to the need to respect member-state differences and avoid new regulatory burdens on small and medium-sized firms.

Only with the Treaty of Amsterdam (ToA) in 1997—when the UK also revoked its opt-out under a New Labour government—was QMV extended to worker information and consultation and the integration of persons excluded from the labour market. But most areas of employment policy remained under the unanimity rule, while pay, the right of association, and the right to strike and impose lock-outs were excluded from Community competence altogether (Art. 137(6) TEC).

Given these constraints, the Commission set out to exploit the fragile treaty bases to the maximum, sometimes backed up by ECJ case law, sometimes by undertaking 'soft law' initiatives. Thus, it put forward recommendations and codes of practice to strengthen the application of existing laws; it also issued 'solemn declarations', such as the 1989 Social Charter, or 'social action programmes', designed to further its coalition-building efforts and set the agenda for future EU initiatives. In this way, in the mid-1970s, the Commission's Social Action Programme, adopted by a Council Resolution, provided the 'soft-law' basis for negotiation and coalition-building around a new series of employment policy directives (see Kenner 2003: Ch. 2)—a practice that continues to this day.

During the period of acute conflict among member governments over social policy, between the SEA and Maastricht, the Commission also proposed a series of employment initiatives by playing the 'treaty-base game'. This tactic sought to stretch as far as possible the interpretation of 'health and safety' to include directives affecting the workplace, thereby allowing the use of QMV to minimize member-state (especially UK) opposition (M. Rhodes 1995)—a broad definition backed up by the ECJ when the UK challenged the Commission's strategy in 1996 (Barnard and Deakin 2002: 405–8). Thus, although the 1989 Social Charter on the basic rights of workers was vague and non-binding, and efforts to introduce 'harder' instruments, including a framework directive on rights and a binding workers' statute, were defeated, much to the dismay of the more powerful of Europe's trade unions (especially the Germans), the Commission's policy activism promoted a raft of legislative proposals in the early 1990s and gave powerful impetus to the social-policy advances achieved at Maastricht and Amsterdam (M. Rhodes 1991).

None of this, however, produced a more solid legal basis for EU legislation, and a considerable difference in the nature and quality of regulation emerged between those areas of policy where there were firm legal foundations and those where the Commission resorted to 'creative regulation'.

The firm treaty-based measures emerged from the Social Action Programme of the 1970s. Making use of Article 100 (EEC) (now Art. 94 TEC), designed for single-market-related laws, and Article 235 (EEC) (now Art. 308 TEC), which provided for law-making in areas not covered specifically in the Treaty, the Council produced Directive 75/129 on procedural rights under collective redundancies, Directive 77/187 on rights of employees under changes of ownership of undertakings, and Directive 80/987, which guaranteed state compensation to employees of insolvent companies. All were deemed appropriate in an era of extensive industrial restructuring, and received ECJ support—even when the worker representation clauses of Directive 75/129 clashed with the 'voluntarist' tradition of UK industrial relations (Barnard and Deakin 2002: 404–5).

Spurred on by the ECJ, which had linked direct effect with the supremacy of community over national law in key judgments (*Van Gend & Loos*, 1963; *Costa*, 1964; *Van Duyn*, 1974), a half-dozen directives on equal pay and equal treatment in the 1970s and 1980s were based on the more solid Article 119 (EEC) (now Art. 141 TEC), which requires unanimity in the Council. ECJ jurisprudence on equal pay and equal treatment also helped ensure the implementation of these directives (Barnard and Deakin 2002: 402–3). Using Article 118a (EEC) (now part of Art. 137 TEC), the first framework directive (80/1107) on health and safety at work produced a series of 'daughter directives' on specific hazards, plus the 'soft-law' Council Recommendation on a forty-hour week and four weeks' annual paid holiday (a forerunner of the later working time directive). A second framework directive on health and safety (89/391) laid down general objectives and obligations on employers and workers, while leaving scope for varied application at the national level, and ultimately produced fourteen daughter directives and a series of action programmes.

Legislation produced in the late 1980s and early 1990s via the 'treaty-base game' was less successful. The effort to define workers' rights as a health and safety issue to avoid a British veto during the Thatcher, then Major, Conservative governments severely weakened the impact of the directives. Thus, the Pregnancy and Maternity Directive (92/85) has ensured health protection, but has been less effective with regard to employment discrimination. The Working Time Directive (93/104)—which provides workers with minimum daily and weekly rest periods, a maximum forty-eight-hour working week, and a minimum of four weeks' annual leave—was innovative in allowing some elements to be implemented through collective agreements, but it excluded a number of sectors, and allowed important derogations for member states, such as the UK opt-out for individual workers. The Young Workers Directive (94/33) created rights for workers under the age of eighteen, and banned work under the age of fifteen, but contained many derogations, such as the UK's special entitlement to delay implementation (Kenner 2003).

As such, they indicated the limits to hard-law harmonization across an increasingly diverse set of member states after enlargement to the UK, Ireland, and Denmark in 1973 (countries with very different traditions of employment regulation and industrial relations from the original six), and to Greece (1981) and Portugal and Spain (1986). However, they did succeed in placing a floor of minimum standards under national systems to prevent a process of competitive deregulation, creating conditions for the further consolidation of such regulations dependent on the political dynamics of individual member states—a form of what EU lawyers refer to as 'reflexive law' and aspired to in slightly different form in the second mode of employment policy-making and governance: 'law via collective agreement'.

Mode two: the social dialogue and law via collective agreement

One of the key innovations of the Maastricht TEU regarding social policy was its creation of an alternative mode of law-making—an 'inter-professional social dialogue'—involving the European social partners, employers, and trade unions. Several forces converged behind this reform. For European unions, especially the powerful German unions, it would strengthen the weak European Trade Union Confederation (ETUC), and bolster their influence after their defeat in the dilution of the 1989 Social Charter. For the European Commission and a number of member states, it would provide an alternative means for counteracting obdurate British opposition to further EU employment legislation. And for those seeking to defend national sovereignty, a shift to directives produced at EU level, but implemented via negotiation in the member states, would better accommodate the diversity of European industrial relations.

Europe's employers, acting through the Union of Industrial and Employers' Confederations (UNICE; since 2007 Business Europe: The Confederation of European Business) and the European Association of Craft, Small and Medium-sized Enterprises (UEAPME) had tried to keep the social dialogue in check, and consistently opposed both EU-level collective bargaining and any legislative enhancement of workers' participation rights in transnational companies. But by 1991, even they had accepted the procedural importance of rule-setting at the EU level through the social dialogue, and had discovered a potential channel for diverting Commission initiatives away from the standard legislative path.

The role of Commission entrepreneurialism and institution-building in gaining this concession was central. Article 118b (EEC) obliged the Commission to promote dialogue between management and labour, and it worked hard to promote discussions between UNICE/UEAPME, the public employers' association—the European Centre of Enterprises with Public Participation and of Enterprises of General Economic Interest (CEEP)—and the ETUC through joint union–employer working parties on the economy, employment, social dialogue, and new technologies. Originally launched in the Val Duchesse talks in 1985, after 1989 this process became more focused, prioritizing education and training, and producing four joint opinions on the promotion of labour mobility, education, vocational guidance, and management–labour partnerships, which, in turn, provided the groundwork for two key agreements: the September 1990 framework agreement, signed by the CEEP and the ETUC, on improving vocational training and health and safety via social dialogue; and, most importantly, a joint submission to the Intergovernmental Conferences, which in 1991 negotiated the TEU, proposing a new role for the social partners in making and implementing EC policy (M. Rhodes 1995; Falkner 1998).

This submission was inserted almost verbatim into the Social Protocol of the TEU (later integrated into the ToA), creating a complex set of procedures for the pursuit of law via collective agreement: all directives, whether adopted by QMV or by unanimity, could henceforth be entrusted to 'management and labour' at their joint request for implementation via collective agreement; the Commission was now obliged, before submitting social-policy proposals to the Council, to consult management and labour on the possible consequences of Community action, to which the social partners could respond with an 'opinion' or a 'recommendation'; and, most importantly, the social partners could now negotiate directly the content of Commission proposals, proceeding, given consensus, to a collective agreement. Such agreements could then be implemented by a further negotiation in the member states in accordance with their own procedures and practices, or via a Council decision on a proposal from the Commission.

The negotiation procedure was first used in 1993, when the Commission presented a modified version of a legislative proposal on the creation of European works councils that had previously failed by the normal legislative route. In the event, the social dialogue channel also failed, and the directive—under which management must institute forums for informing and consulting employees in all companies with more than 1,000 employees and more than 150 in at least two member states—was finally passed under the Social Protocol, using the standard legislative process, in 1994 (Directive 94/45/EC) and then extended to the UK (97/74/EC) in 1997. But several other proposals were successfully translated into social framework agreements, also after failing under the standard legislative route, including three intersectoral agreements, which led to Directives 96/34 on parental leave, 97/81 on part-time work and 99/70 on fixed-term work, and two sectoral agreements which led to Directives 99/95 on working-time provisions in maritime transport and 2000/79 on the working time of mobile workers in civil aviation.

The limited use of this new channel prior to the Treaty of Amsterdam has been described by some as "a derisory outcome" for those who worked hard to break the EU social-policy impasse at Maastricht (Kenner 2003: 291). The legislation does provide real regulatory added value, but its critics argue that its minimal standards and flexibility have limited its impact to the least well-regulated countries. The directive on parental leave has been criticized as a 'lowest common denominator' agreement; the directive on part-time work has been regarded as weak, consisting of a series of non-obligatory provisions unlikely to remove discrimination against this category of workers; and the directive on fixed-term work has been called a 'missed opportunity' to regulate one of the most insecure forms of agency work: in most member states little or no change was required to existing law (Kenner 2003: 290). Cross-sectoral accords on 'joint opinions'—such as those agreed to by the EU-level social partners in March 2005 on a 'framework of actions' in four priority areas of gender equality in the workplace, or in October 2007 on 'guidelines for defining 'flexicurity'—are really statements of good intent and therefore obviously even weaker.

A more optimistic interpretation argues that 'this mode of governance can act as a catalyst for mutual learning' (Deakin 2007: 18ff), a favourable view of the utility of 'soft' policy influence based on the notion of 'reflexive law' or 'reflexive govern-ance' and usually reserved for the OMC (see below). Deakin points out that the part-time and fixed-term work directives have stimulated policy innovations that have strengthened contract requirements in the UK, and loosened them in more highly regulated Germany, while in both countries, the parental-leave directive has created the parameters for a new debate on the subject, and the definition of a new consensus.

Nevertheless, even if the gradual shift towards negotiated and 'non-coercive' framework agreements facilitated political agreement in a period of intransigent opposition to European employment-policy initiatives, from employers, the British government, and other member states—such as Germany—that were committed to enhanced subsidiarity, at its best negotiated framework legislation has variable and unpredictable effects from one country to the next.

Importantly, however, such legislation does provide the opportunity for subse-quent 'hardening' by ECJ case law as, for example, in the July 2006 judgment in *Adeneler* (Case-212/04) and the April 2008 ruling in *Impact* (Case C-268-06), both of which bolstered the implementation of Council Directive 99/70 on fixed-term work (following the social partners' framework agreement), regarding the defini-tion of successive fixed-term employment contracts, its coverage of both public and private-sector workers and the importance of national law in preventing the abuse of such contracts.

But the relative weakness of the social partners at the European level and the determination of employers to dilute the impact of this mode of governance have clearly prevented a major leap forward (Smismans 2007). For the same reasons, and regardless of a commitment by the social partners at the European Council in Laeken in 2001 to a new and more autonomous bipartite social dialogue (backed by a Commission Communication on the future of the social dialogue in 2002, reiter-ated in the presentation of the social partners' work programme for 2003–5, and reaffirmed in 2005 at the twentieth-anniversary social dialogue summit), progress is still heavily dependent on the Commission acting as an entrepreneurial prime mover, typically by threatening (and taking) recourse to hard law in the absence of social partner agreement (Keller 2008; Smismans 2008*a*).

Employment policy innovations post-Amsterdam

Mode three: the EES and the OMC

The launch in 1997 of the European Employment Strategy (EES)—a broad, multi-faceted job-creation strategy, based on the non-binding, soft-law instruments of peer review, benchmarking, and persuasion—marked a radical departure from the existing two policy modes, adding employment creation to European policy ambitions and seeking to extend EU influence to jealously guarded areas of national sovereignty.

In part, the EES was a political response by pro-social dimension élites and interest groups to economic and monetary union (EMU), which prevented individual countries from using expansionary monetary and fiscal policies to boost employment and which, at least in the view of many of its critics, represented a major threat to national welfare states (see Chapters 7 and 11). But importantly it was also a response by the same coalition to failures and blockages in the two existing policy modes, and a further attempt to overcome the enduring 'double cleavage' in the politics of EU social and employment policy.

Origins and institutional development

How did the notion of a common European policy for employment promotion arrive on the agenda for the Treaty of Amsterdam? In essence, the Commission, operating once again in full entrepreneurial mode, managed to exploit a new political opportunity in the mid-1990s to mobilize a coalition of like-minded social-democratic governments in support of the initiative (Arnold 2002; van Riel and van der Meer 2002).

But the EES originally began to take form much earlier, following the Delors Commission's White Paper on *Growth, Competitiveness and Employment* in 1993 (Commission 1993b) and the Essen European Council of 1994. Attempting to blend the priorities of European social democrats, Christian democrats, and liberals, the tactical aim of this initiative was to strike a new political balance between notions of solidarity and competitiveness behind the EU's 'social dimension'. But due to counter-pressures from several member states, including Germany and the UK, there was little real progress at the time (Goetschy 2003; Mosher and Trubek 2003). A stronger interpretation of the Delors vision emerged via member-state bargaining at the European Council meetings in Madrid in 1995 and in Dublin in 1996. The Commission spurred progress along by striking alliances with key European political groups (most importantly the Party of European Socialists) and by organizing peer pressure on the most reluctant member states.

An agreement to create a formal European Employment Strategy was reached at the Amsterdam European Council in 1997. The goals and procedures of the EES are set out in Title VIII (later XI) of the ToA (Arts. 125–30 TEC) on employment. The main objective was a high level of employment, to be achieved by promoting a 'skilled, trained and adaptable workforce and labour markets responsive to economic change'. Under Article 126 (TEC), the Community should contribute to that end 'by encouraging cooperation between member states and by supporting, and if necessary complementing, their action'. The guidelines are not binding—an essential feature for the compromise that eventually brought all member states on board. But by its inclusion in the ToA, the EES became part of the processes in which member states are obliged to participate.

The process of policy deliberation envisaged was put into effect at the Luxembourg European Council in November 1997, since when it has been repeated on a yearly basis. The first set of (nineteen) European Employment Guidelines (EEGs) was also adopted, based on four 'pillars': employability, entrepreneurship, adaptability, and equal opportunities, each containing between three and seven guidelines. The 2000 Lisbon European Council confirmed its support for the EES and committed the member states to striving for 'full employment', coupled with new quantitative objectives: a 70 per cent overall employment rate and a 60 per cent female employment rate by 2010. At Lisbon, and then at the Nice and Stockholm European Councils, successive Council presidencies, held by social-democratic governments, acted closely in alliance with the Commission and the EP to sustain the coalition, propel the EES forward, and extend the 'open method of coordination' (or OMC) to other areas of policy such as social exclusion (van Riel and van der Meer 2002). Nevertheless, the EES remained contested terrain, both ideologically and in power games between the Council and the Commission.

The EES as a 'new mode of governance'

When first launched, the EES had a relatively low profile. It was only after the OMC was formally endorsed and given greater political weight by the European Council at Lisbon in 2000, and extended beyond the EES to other areas of policy-making, that it became a topic of intense interest and debate as a 'new mode of governance' different in its core characteristics from both the traditional Community method and older hard- and soft-law procedures: the heterarchical participation of actors; a 'new' problem-solving logic based on deliberation and 'policy learning'; and the use of benchmarking and reference to 'best practice' (Scott and Trubeck 2002; Cohen and Sabel 2003; Borrás and Jacobsson 2004). All are considered advantages over traditional modes of policy-making by the advocates of the EES/OMC, in addition to its purported capacity to neutralize the conflict over national versus European, and flexible versus more rigid forms of labour-market regulation by allowing national policy-makers to interpret European guidelines, and by promoting 'flexicurity' in employment regulation. But regardless of these theoretical advantages, ultimately, the EES is a political strategy and its success or failure is determined by hard political realities. We can assess those realities first by considering the formal EES policy system and second by examining the ways in which the tensions and political conflicts found in the other two modes of European employment policy have also emerged in this new mode of policy-making and governance.

Formally, the roles of the EES actors and relations between them can be set out in terms of the EES 'policy coordination' cycle. This cycle was reformed substantially at the Brussels European Council in June 2003, not only to 'mainstream' the EES within the Lisbon Agenda, but also in response to complaints from the member states over the excessive complexity and high level of detail in EES guidelines, the considerable overlap between the EES and other processes, and the duplication of work for national officials (see Jacobsson 2004).

From 1997 to 2002, the annual policy cycle began with agenda-setting, in which both the rotating presidency of the Council and the Commission have considerable influence, the latter providing the 'support team' as well as analytical and pre-paratory documents. The Commission draws up the guidelines, which are then endorsed by the Council via QMV. Policy objectives are then decided: before 2002 they took the form of twenty or so guidelines, organized around the four pillars of employability, entrepreneurship, adaptability, and equal opportunities, but thereaf-ter were reduced to ten 'results-oriented' priorities structured around three objec-tives: full employment, quality and productivity at work, and social cohesion and inclusion. In 2004–5 those objectives were further reformed under member-state pressure via the 'European Employment Taskforce' (EET), chaired by Wim Kok, to focus more closely on 'jobs and growth' and the Commission's new 'flexicurity' agenda (see below).

In parallel, the Commission makes individual recommendations, endorsed by the Council, to each member state. The recommendation tool, as defined in the ToA, is a key element of influence distinguishing the EES from other OMCs. Member govern-ments then prepare their National Action Programmes (NAPs) in response to the rec-ommendations. These are then 'peer reviewed' in the so-called 'Cambridge process'—a closed two-day meeting of the Employment Committee (EMCO), which has two dele-gates from each member state and two members from the Commission, followed by bilateral meetings on the NAPs between the latter and government representatives.

In theory, this process is given an important infusion of democracy and legitimacy by involving political and interest-group representatives. According to the ToA, the EP has to be consulted on the EES, although in practice its role was somewhat mar-ginal during the first five years due to time constraints. However, the timetable of the EES was modified in 2003, creating additional time for the EP to prepare its opinion for the annual June European Council where the EES is discussed (Table 12.1).

Efficacy versus experimentation

It was hoped that the EES would reduce political conflict over employment policy, given its soft-law character and acceptance of member-state diversity. Indeed, much literature on the EES has focused on its deliberative, consensus-seeking qualities. But a closer analysis reveals ongoing contestation reminiscent of the history of the other modes of EU employment policy-making: conflict between the Commission's 'competence-maximizing' aspirations and the concern of member states to contain them; related sovereignty disputes within the EES policy-making system; and tensions between the EES's deliberative 'network governance' pretensions and its tendency in reality to replicate traditional top-down policy hierarchies.

TABLE 12.1 The European Employment Strategy: key characteristics

Features/Process	European Employment Strategy (EES) 1997–2002	After adaptations—2003
Started	1997	2003
Cycle	Yearly	Tri-annual; synchronized with Broad Economic Policy Guidelines (BEPGs)
Policy objectives	+/– 20 guidelines organized around four pillars.	10 'result-oriented' priorities around three overarching aims
Number of cycles undergone	Five	Two
Key participants—those who make the actual decisions	Ministers of social affairs and employment (in Council formation) in close collaboration with the European Commission	Ministers of social affairs and employment (in Council formation) in collaboration with the European Commission
Final veto point—through qualified majority voting	Ministers of social affairs and employment (in Council formation)	Ministers of social affairs and employment (in Council formation)
Mandatory consultative participants	European and national social partners, European Parliament, ESC, Committee of Regions (CoR)	European and national social partners, European Parliament, ESC, CoR
Legal basis of process	Employment Chapter of Amsterdam Treaty, 1997	Employment Chapter of Amsterdam Treaty, 1997
Technical Indicators and targets	99 indicators in 2002—35 key indicators and 64 context indicators; 70% overall employment rate (2000) to be reached 2010, 60% female employment rate (2000) to be reached 2010; 50% older workers employment rate (2001) to be reached 2010	64 indicators in 2003—39 key indicators and 25 context indicators.
Peer review (or in-built incentive structures for 'learning')	Yearly peer review of the National Action Plans (NAPs) ('Cambridge process')	Yearly peer review of the NAP ('Cambridge process'); peer review programme of active labour market policies (from 1999 onwards); political aim to focus the 'Cambridge process' on only one objective to render it more effective

All three conflicts have characterized the functioning of the Employment Commit-tee (EMCO), which lies at the core of the process. EMCO has been characterized as a kind of 'deliberative institution' located between the Commission and the member states. In reality it is driven more by intergovernmental, interest-driven bargaining (Jacobsson and Vifell 2003) and has become increasingly politicized as member gov-ernments have sought to use it to shape the policy agenda.

In an early 'sovereignty dispute' in the late 1990s, many member states reacted with hostility to the Commission's use of recommendations, and were dismayed at the secretive way in which it prepared and publicized them to exert peer pressure on governments. After intense debate, the Commission and EMCO agreed to refrain from being polemical, accept amendments, and treat member states equally rather than according to their employment performance.

A second such dispute took place in 2002–3, preceding the transformation of the EES guidelines (Jobelius 2003). While the Commission sought out new channels of influence over the member states, the latter actively resisted, a conflict resolved only when the Commission abandoned its new quantitative targets in all areas except for education and measures to 'activate' the unemployed. A Commission injunction on member states to ensure that adequate financial resources were deployed to meet its employment guidelines was replaced by a call for more 'transparent and cost-effective' financing (Watt 2004: 131).

In both cases the Council fiercely resisted a de facto extension of Commission in-fluence (Borrás and Jacobsson 2004). A third such instance was evident in the 2003 EES reform. The earlier social-democratic coalition had fragmented and right-wing governments dominated the Council, revising employment priorities: liberal market concerns were evident in the shift from the four-pillar approach to the three 'core objectives' structure, as well as in an increasingly tortured EES policy discourse that sought to reconcile social-democratic solidarity with liberal market flexibility.

A more liberal policy orientation was further evident in 2004–5 when the 'Euro-pean Employment Taskforce', chaired by Wim Kok, radically shifted the 2003 core objectives (which focused on: full employment; raising the quality and productivity of work; and promoting social cohesion and inclusive labour markets) in a liberal, supply-side direction, placing a major new emphasis on the adaptability of workers and enterprises, including more flexible contract arrangements. From 2005, the EES was integrated into the Broad Economic Policy Guidelines, and in 2006 the 'renewal' of the Lisbon Strategy by the Barroso Commission downgraded social protection priorities in favour of growth and job creation.

As Zeitlin (2008: 438) argues, these changes have reduced the visibility of employment-policy coordination at both EU and national levels, producing a greater unevenness in national employment-policy reporting and, as a result, an even lower degree of European-level monitoring capacity than hitherto. For its fiercest critics (e.g. Raveaud 2007), the EES is now mostly concerned with developing flexible labour contracts, jeopardizing earlier goals of gender equality and 'social inclusion', and undermining rather than rein-forcing the so-called 'European social model'.

As for the supposed experimental—'heterarchic' and 'network-governance'—character of the EES, the participation of labour and management has been widely recognized as weak (Smismans 2008b). The EES policy cycle is actually rather closed, élitist, and arguably much less democratic and accountable than the standard Community method of legislating (Syrpis 2002). In particular, parliamentary influence (whether national or European) is very limited (though see Duina and Raunio 2007), and there is no form of judicial review. The Council and the Commission are in practice the key decision-makers.

Nor is the EES especially effective as a means of shaping policy reform. The most authoritative accounts conclude that NAP procedures have been insufficiently integrated into national decision-making structures and budget allocations to make them matter (Jacobsson and Vifell 2003). Less a deliberative process of policy-learning or best-practice diffusion, the EES can best be described as a 'double standards game' in which governments endorse European guidelines, but frequently fail to take responsibility for their implementation at home. For Deakin (2007), the danger of the EES is that its deliberative, soft-law pretensions provide little defence against the risks of regulatory competition and little in the way of counterweight to the forces of negative integration—especially at a time when the ECJ has begun to prioritize market access rules over national social protection regulation (see below).

At best, it seems, the EES has encouraged better coordination among certain government ministries, as well as between administrations and interest groups, in a limited number of member states (Jacobsson and Vifell 2007). But even that conclusion is qualified by evidence that such influence is limited to a small group of actors, leading to little by way of institutional innovation, and figuring hardly at all in public discourse or inter-party competition (Meyer and Kunstein 2007).

Moreover, as demonstrated above, there is no real political support base for a hardening or upgrading of the rules for employment-policy coordination, as evident in fierce divisions in the discussions of the Economic Policy Working Group of the Convention on the Future of Europe in 2002–3, and in the more general opposition to constitutionalizing the OMC. Further changes in 2004–6 revealed a steady shift away from social-democratic federalism towards a more liberal—and 'subsidiarist'—member-state-led labour-market strategy. In sum, far from neutralizing the 'double cleavage' generating political conflict in European employment policy, the EES has clearly fallen victim to it.

A new source of contestation: social versus economic rights in EU law

As noted at numerous points above, the European Court of Justice has been a central actor in EU employment policy. It has played an important role in extending the influence of employment-related legislation by building up a powerful body of jurisprudence and by striking down numerous challenges to the Commission's broad interpretation of sometimes ambiguous treaty foundations. More generally, the ECJ's case law has largely reinforced the view that stems from the Treaty of Rome and justifies the provision of a floor of minimum EU social policy provisions, rather than an extended upward harmonization of member-state social and employment policy— that the pursuit of the four freedoms (the free movement of goods, persons, services, and capital) should not undermine national social and employment protection.

Nevertheless, the position of the ECJ regarding the balance between freedom of movement and national social and labour market regulations has shifted over time, as it has sought to respond to political pressures from other Community institutions and the member states in interpreting the treaty and refining its earlier jurisprudence (see also Chapter 11). In a neo-liberal phase that followed the landmark free-trade-promoting judgments in *Dassonville* (1974) and *Cassis de Dijon* (1978) that radically reformulated the prohibition of quantitative restrictions on imports in Article 28 TEC (formerly Art. 30 EEC) to include domestic regulations, the Court struck down a series of national laws that it deemed to impede free trade, including (in *Macrotron*, 1990) the German Federal Employment Office's monopoly of job placement (Eliasoph 2007–8).

Yet in light of the broader developments in EU social policy discussed above, both prior to and after the Maastricht Treaty, the Court's deregulatory enthusiasm was dampened by the prospects of a major political clash over state sovereignty that threatened to undermine the ECJ's legitimacy. In 1991, in both *Keck* (regarding a French law prohibiting the resale of commercial goods for lower than their purchase price) and *Poucet and Pistre* (in which a French insurance fund for the self-employed was claimed to contravene Community competition law), the ECJ sided with the national regulators, and applied the principle of 'solidarity' to protect social welfare schemes from competition law. In 1999, in *Albany*, the Court took a cue from the new social provisions in the Amsterdam Treaty to exclude from competition Article 81(1)—which prohibits agreements that restrict or distort competition—a supplementary pension scheme negotiated by Dutch social partners in the textile industry. In all of these cases, the protection of national social regulations was privileged above competing claims on behalf of market freedoms (Eliasoph 2007–8; Barnard 2008b).

However, it would be wrong to imagine that the balance of ECJ case law sided with national regulation in all cases. In 1990, in *Rush Portuguesa*, the Court ruled against a requirement imposed by the French state on a Portuguese service provider that it obtain work permits for its Portuguese employees. But at the same time it reassuringly stated that Community law does not prevent member states from extending their legislation or collective labour agreements to any person employed—even temporarily—within their territory, no matter in which country the employer is established. This seemed more consistent with *Keck* and *Poucet and Pistre* (and their accommodation of national regulations) than with the free trade judgments made in *Cassis* and *Dassonville* (Syrpis 2007). But in 1991 in *Säger*—the source of current controversy in recent employment-related ECJ rulings—the Court ruled that only an 'imperative' reason relating to 'the public interest', could justify a 'proportionate' discrimination or restriction against a provider of services based in another member state. This—and other Court judgments in the early 2000s—extended the market-access priority the ECJ had applied to cross-border services to the sphere of employment. The implication was that a business wishing to set up in another member state could justifiably claim that complying with that state's employment laws would restrict its freedom of movement (Barnard 2008*b*).

It is precisely this claim that has triggered a series of more recent Court judgments. Together they threaten a new clash with the other Community institutions over the balance between economic freedoms and social rights and have raised new concerns regarding the legitimacy of Court decisions that overturn the social and employment laws and practices of member states.

Much recent EU legislation has in fact sought to protect national systems of employment regulation from deregulatory pressures stemming from greater freedom of movement, in large part in response to earlier ECJ rulings that might endanger such regulations. Thus, at the end of 1996, in an effort to clarify *Rush*, the Posted Workers Directive (96/71/EC) set out to ensure that workers posted to another member state in the framework of the transnational provision of services are guaranteed the working conditions and pay in effect in that state, including collectively agreed provisions and arbitration awards declared universally applicable. Equally, ten years later, when the Services Directive (2006/123/EC) (see Chapter 5) was adopted by the Parliament and the Council, from the outset—and well before the controversy that led to the removal from the legislation of the 'country of origin' principle (under which service providers operating in a member state other than their own would only be subject to the laws of their own state)—all matters coming under the Posted Workers Directive were exempted, and the final draft explicitly stated that the Services Directive does not affect national labour law, social security legislation, or the exercise of fundamental rights (Syrpis 2007; Barnard 2008*b*).

And yet, between 2005 and 2008, three highly controversial ECJ judgments resurrected the market-access priority and the principle established in *Säger* that only an 'imperative' reason relating to 'the public interest', could justify a 'proportionate' discrimination or restriction against a provider of services based in another member state. As such they have renewed the debate on when and under what circumstances national systems of employment regulation and social standards are truly insulated from single-market pressures.

In *Viking* (2007) a strike by the Finnish Seaman's Union against a Finnish company that flagged a ferry operating out of Helsinki as Estonian was judged to be an interference with the company's rights under Article 43 TEC preventing restrictions on the freedom of establishment. In *Laval* (2007) Swedish union action against a Latvian company building a school in Sweden, using Latvian workers who were paid 40 per cent less per hour than locally bargained wage rates for Swedish workers, was judged unlawful under Article 49 TEC on the freedom to provide services. And in

Rüffert (2008) a decision by the state of Lower Saxony to terminate a contract with a German firm employing Polish workers at wages 46 per cent lower than the locally applicable collectively bargained wage was similarly judged to violate Article 49. In both *Laval* and *Rüffert*, the ECJ argued that the Posted Workers Directive sets out maximum rather than minimum protection of workers, and that in all three cases the regulations being defended by national actors were 'disproportionate' and 'unjustified'. All three judgments raise important questions about the robustness of numerous social rights in the EU, including the right to strike and the right to establish national standards by collective bargaining if and when subject to a strict application of the Court's proportionality test.

Interestingly enough, neither the ratification of the Lisbon Treaty nor its attribution of legally binding status to the EU Charter of Fundamental Rights (2000), which defends the right to collective bargaining and action (including the right to strike), is likely to have any impact on the direction recently taken by the ECJ, or on employment policy-making in the EU more generally, as those rights are already acknowledged by the Court—it is simply their 'proportionate use' that is at stake. But Syrpis (2008) argues that accession to the European Convention for the Protection of Human Rights and Fundamental Freedoms, provided for in Article 6(2) TEU, might well make a difference in cases like *Viking*, *Rüffert*, and *Laval* under Articles 10 and 11 regarding freedom of expression and assembly and association. For unlike the ECJ, which takes the economic goal of free movement as its starting point and then assesses the proportionality of any restrictions placed on it, the European Court of Human Rights does the reverse: it begins with Convention rights and assesses the proportionality of restrictions on those rights. One should be sceptical, however, that the Charter—which explicitly guarantees neither the right to collective bargaining nor the right to strike, and has a poor record in protecting such rights—will matter nearly as much in protecting national employment regulations against incursions based on the freedom of movement as will political pressure from member states and national and EU-level organized labour and the new threat to ECJ legitimacy that such pressure will create.

Assessment: employment policy in the 2000s—a multi-layered opportunity structure

This chapter began by noting that employment policy poses some of the most difficult regulatory problems in the EU, precisely because both the assumption of Community competences and the nature of regulation itself have been so fiercely contested. But over time, an EU employment advocacy coalition, spanning the member states and the European Commission, has kept the issue alive. Opposition has been evaded or diffused by shifting the parameters of the regulatory system and, via a process of 'venue-shopping', by seeking alternative institutional channels conducive to the integrationist project in employment policy, including a creative interpretation of the treaty base, transferring legislation to the 'inter-professional dialogue', and, finally, by shifting emphasis to the wholly soft-law-based EES. Each mode of policy-making and governance remains firmly in place, however, creating what could be considered either a barely legitimate layering of institutional innovations (Wendler 2004) or a multi-layered opportunity structure, holding out the possibility of a complementary or integrated use of policy instruments and governance modes.

In contrast to claims made on behalf of a major shift to the soft-law, voluntarist EES/OMC, the Community method of legislation remains highly active and is far from being replaced by non-binding instruments (Arnold et al. 2004). Recent employment legislation includes the framework equal-treatment directive to combat employment discrimination on the grounds of religion, disability, age, or sexual orientation (2000); the regulation governing the creation of a European Company Statute (2001) and an accompanying directive on worker involvement (2001); a controversial directive on national information and consultation rules, under which firms over a certain size must put in place mechanisms for informing and consulting employees (2002); agreement on a directive implementing equal treatment between men and women outside the workplace (2004); the merging of seven directives on equality for men and women in employment into a single coherent instrument (2005); and the approval of a directive to regulate temporary agency work, and agreement in the Council to amend and strengthen the Working Time Directive, in the second half of 2008. The ECJ continues to play a critical role in enforcing such directives, as when in December 2004 five member states—Austria, Finland, Germany, Greece, and Luxembourg—were referred by the Commission to the ECJ for failing to transpose the 2000 framework equality directive.

The second mode—the more experimental social dialogue—has appeared to weaken over time. With the exception of more limited sectoral dialogues and related directives, such as the 2008 agreement and directive to improve working conditions in the maritime industry, the transfer of draft directives from the first legislative mode has dried up and the focus of the social dialogue has shifted to 'new generation' framework agreements. The latter include agreements on 'teleworking' (2002), 'work-related stress' (2004), and 'harassment and violence at work' (2007). These agreements are well-intentioned but (very much in line with Europe's employers' associations' preferences) do not have the force of a directive, are not subject to threats by the Commission to proceed with directives, and their implementation is heavily shaped by ongoing national power games between social partners and the state (Larsen and Andersen 2007; Keller 2008).

However, the Commission has not become any less entrepreneurial in promoting this and related forums for exerting influence in employment policy, especially in using unions and employers as a sounding board for future legislative proposals, to help set its agenda for future policy initiatives, and to police the implementation of existing legislation. Examples include the Commission's 2005 call on social partners to begin negotiations on promoting and monitoring best-practice guidelines for industrial restructuring and the operation of European Works Councils, which helped in the adoption of a recast Works Councils Directive in December 2008 (2009/38/EC); the Commission's consultation of the social partners after 2007 on the issue of the cross-border transfer of undertakings; its use of unions to report on the implementation of employment guidelines in member states; and the mobilization of social partners across Europe behind the new (post-December 2006) integrated Commission programme for employment and social solidarity, *Progress*. *Progress* replaces previously separate action programmes on anti-discrimination, gender equality, the fight against social exclusion and employment measures, and promotes network creation, projects, and partnerships between governments, NGOs, employers' and workers' organizations to help bring national policy reforms into line with European guidelines. Such initiatives that foster the creation of national advocacy coalitions provide the Commission with a degree of access to and influence over member-state policy-making that it would not otherwise enjoy.

As for the EES, as observed by Jacobsson and Vifell (2003), it has had three principal aims: cooperation among actors, the coordination of national employment policies, and convergence in outcomes. However, as noted above, there is no clear consensus or institutional commitment to any of these goals across the EU member states, or to developing further more effective means for achieving them. One should note in this context the narrowing of employment objectives to 'flexicurity' in recent Commission documents—such as the 'Strategic Report on a Renewed Lisbon Strategy for Growth and Jobs' (Commission 2007*h*) that was presented to the 2008 Spring European Council—a trend that mirrors the parallel narrowing of priorities in the EES noted above. Both the ETUC and the European Parliament have lobbied against such developments, seeking a more 'balanced' approach that would strengthen the 'social dimension' of EU employment guidelines within the Lisbon strategy.

'Flexicurity' has become the *leitmotiv* of European employment policy-making in recent years, the core elements of which were defined in a Commission communication in June 2007 (Commission 2007*g*) and placed alongside the notions of 'decent work' and the 'reconciliation of economic competitiveness with social justice'. A similar discourse appears in the Commission's Green Paper on modernizing labour law (Commission 2006*d*), which has been criticized for its vagueness, obsession with non-standard forms of employment, and lack of attention to core labour standards (Sciarra 2007). Such critiques reinforce the view of other critics (e.g. Raveaud 2007 and Deakin 2007) that the danger of the EES/OMC lies precisely in its potential shift of policy attention away from 'hard' to 'soft' governance, based on imprecise policy goals, at a time when developments elsewhere (as in the ECJ's *Viking*, *Laval*, and *Rüffert* judgments) demand a new emphasis on treaty-based legislation, both to underpin existing forms of employment protection and the exercise of fundamental rights, and to firmly establish the boundaries between the freedom of movement and national systems of employment regulation.

One solution to the trade-off between efficacy and experimentation in favour of the former in both the social dialogue and the EES would be to strengthen the links between these 'softer' modes and the still vigorous first mode of policy-making, either by using instruments of soft law (e.g. peer review and benchmarks) to facilitate the implementation of hard law, or by using hard law to ensure the implementation of soft-law initiatives. Examples of such combinations have been referred to above, and point to the potential for deploying the Community method, European social agreements, and the coordination mechanisms of the EES together in pushing the employment-policy agenda forward, creating scope for regulatory innovation across the several existing modes of employment policy-making and governance. Even so, the history of EU employment policy suggests that these processes, as well as the substance of employment measures, will remain highly contested, and their operation far from smooth. Indeed, the battle has only just begun regarding the challenges posed by recent ECJ cases to the fragile balance that has been struck until now between advancing the 'four freedoms' and the protection of core elements of national social compacts and sovereignty.

FURTHER READING

Employment policy is a constantly moving target. For ongoing developments, the European industrial relations observatory on-line (*http://www.eiro.eurofound.eu.int/index.html*) is an indispensable resource. For a legal perspective, see the authoritative contribution of Kenner (2003), and the studies in Shaw (2000) and Sciarra (2001). Syrpis (2007) provides a rare conceptual analysis of EU intervention in national labour law. As for political science approaches, Falkner et al. (2005) provide the best analysis of EU employment regulation and compliance. For in-depth analyses of the EES, see Foden and Magnusson (2003) and Zeitlin and Pochet with Magnusson (2005); Heidenreich and Zeitlin (2009) contains the most recent and most comprehensive account. Borrás and Greve (2004) and Heidenreich and Bischoff (2008) provide a more general analysis of the OMC. On new modes of economic governance more generally, see Linsenmann et al. (2007).

Borrás, S., and Greve, B. (2004) (eds.), 'The Open Method of Coordination in the European Union', special issue, *Journal of European Public Policy*, 11/2: 181–336.

Falkner, G., Treib, O., Hartlapp, M., and Leiber, S. (2005), *Complying with Europe: EU Harmonisation and Soft Law in the Member States* (Cambridge: Cambridge University Press).

Foden, D., and Magnusson, L. (2003) (eds.), *Five Years' Experience of the Luxembourg Employment Strategy* (Brussels: European Trade Union Institute).

Heidenreich, M., and Bischoff, G. (2008), 'The Open Method of Coordination: A Way to the Europeanization of Social and Employment Policies?', *Journal of Common Market Studies*, 46/3: 497–532.

Heidenreich, M., and Zeitlin, J. (2009) (eds.), *Changing European Employment and Welfare Regimes: The Influence of the Open Method of Coordination on National Reforms* (London/New York: Routledge).

Kenner, J. (2003), *EU Employment Law: From Rome to Amsterdam and Beyond* (Oxford: Hart).

Linsenmann, I., Meyer, C., and Wessels, W. (2007) (eds.), *Economic Government of the EU: A Balance Sheet of New Modes of Policy Coordination* (Basingstoke: Palgrave Macmillan).

Sciarra, S. (2001) (ed.), *Labour Law in the Courts: National Judges and the European Court of Justice* (Oxford: Hart).

Shaw, J. (2000) (ed.), *Social Law and Policy in an Evolving European Union* (Oxford: Hart).

Syrpis, P. (2007), *EU Intervention in Domestic Labour Law* (Oxford: Oxford University Press).

Zeitlin, J., and Pochet, P. with Magnusson, L. (2005) (eds.), *The Open Method of Coordination in Action: The European Employment and Social Inclusion Strategies* (Brussels: PIE-Peter Lang).

CHAPTER 13

Environmental Policy

Contending Dynamics of Policy Change

Andrea Lenschow

▌ Summary

Environmental policy has become a well-established field of European Union (EU) en-gagement over the years. Its development was characterized by institutional deepen-ing and the enormous expansion of environmental issues covered by EU decisions and regulations. From its typical regulatory policy mode follow some challenges for policy makers, including the choice of appropriate instruments, improvement of imple-mentation performance, and better policy coordination at all levels of policy-making. This chapter points to the continuing adaptations that have been made in these areas. It also highlights some more recent challenges. First, recent enlargements brought a number of countries into the Union that were expected to resist further intensifica-tion of environmental policy efforts due to the financial implications this might have for them. Interestingly, however, no rolling back of the policy can be observed so far. Second, the international dimension of environmental policy is amounting to an ever greater challenge for the EU. While its institutional role in participating in international negotiations is now widely accepted, the EU is struggling to become a credible leader. In this regard the climate change issue is causing a great deal of mobilization internally and externally. Whether 'climate' will even become the next 'big idea' of the European

Union, giving it greater presence both *vis-à-vis* the citizens of the EU and on the international scene, or whether this idea will vanish once other problems preoccupy the European leaders, cannot yet be answered. Nonetheless, it illustrates the substantial profile that EU environmental policy has gained among other policy objectives of the Union.

Introduction

We can now look back at half a century of environmental policy-making in the EU, during which time the policy has become solidly institutionalized. Since the adoption of the Treaty of Amsterdam (ToA) most environmental policy decisions are taken by qualified majority voting (QMV) in the Council and with co-decision rights for the European Parliament (EP). During that period, the environmental-policy activities of the Commission, the Parliament, and the Council have grown dramatically, and EU environmental policy itself has grown from its initially marginal status to become one of the most active areas of EU policy-making. This chapter will begin by briefly tracing the history of this institutional 'success story'. It will continue by providing a deeper understanding of the role of the primary policy actors in the EU, highlighting their role in the environmental-policy process and in the expansion of the policy over time.

The chapter will proceed by illuminating some challenges that emerged with the rise of the EU's regulatory agenda, on the one hand, and with the development of an international role for the EU in environmental policy, on the other hand. With the growth of the regulatory output, questions about the effectiveness of the policy gained in saliency. The EU has responded to this challenge by increasing attention to the implementation process, addressing the issue of better policy coordination (both horizontally across policy fields and vertically across levels of governance), and diversifying its portfolio of policy instruments. The enlargement of the Union is introducing new issues and triggering new dynamics in these ongoing reforms. While there is little evidence of a slowdown or of a lowering of environmental standards so far, the financial burden of regulatory policy and the issue of adequate administrative capacities acquired new weight in recent debates.

Over the years, the EU has become an important actor in international environmental policy. After a period of establishing the EU as a formal participant in international organizations and environmental regimes, the EU is now claiming a leadership role for itself. The challenge of giving credibility to this claim will be discussed in this chapter. Focusing on the issue of climate change, I note that international commitments have introduced new dynamics on regulatory policy-making inside the EU.

History

The evolution of environmental policy in the EU can be characterized as a steady deepening in institutional terms as well as expansion in substantive responsibilities. Many authors (e.g. Zito 1999; Knill and Liefferink 2007) distinguish three phases in order to point to some characteristic institutional and political features in this evolution. The first phase (1972–87) followed some earlier incidental policy-making in the environmental field (Hildebrand 1993: 17) and established the institutional and normative core for a fast-growing new policy area in the EEC and its member states. Environmental policy during this period followed primarily trade-related motivations and was legally based on the single-market provisions in the treaties. Common environmental standards for products and the regulation of production processes in order to protect air, water, and soil or ensure the safe treatment of hazardous waste during industrial activity were decided in order to level the playing field for economic actors and to remove non-tariff barriers to trade emerging from different regulatory practices at the national level.

Generally, in the 1970s the time for environmental policy seemed ripe at the national, European, and international levels, and pioneering states (Andersen and Liefferink 1997) pushed for an increasing range of measures at a high level of environmental protection. These leading states, supported by a proactive Commission (see below), began establishing a new policy field at Community level, building linkages to the market-building task of the Community and pointing to transboundary effects of environmental pollution. Despite the need for unanimity, states lagging in environmental protection policy agreed to common European standards in order to secure market access—and to maintain legitimacy in a 'greening' European and international discourse.

The Single European Act (SEA) initiated the second phase, lasting from 1987 to 1992, codifying EC competence in this policy area and laying down the objectives, principles, and decision-making procedures. More specifically, the SEA provided an explicit legal basis for environmental regulation, introduced qualified majority voting in the Council for some areas of environmental policy, and increased the powers of the EP in decision-making. During the following years the EC witnessed a steep rise in activities in this field. Its third Environmental Action Programme (EAP) laid out the general objectives and strategies of European environmental policy for this period, declared 'high levels of protection' a principle of EU policy, and emphasized the role of prevention as well as the need to integrate the objective of environmental protection in other policy areas. This period also witnessed a trend to more specific and emission-oriented regulation aiming at controlling environmental pollution at the source (Johnson and Corcelle 1989; Jordan 2002a).

The third phase of EU environmental policy began with the Maastricht Treaty on European Union (TEU) coming into force in 1993 and strengthened EU competence still further. Knill and Liefferink (2007: 20–4) identify two opposite trends as characteristic of this phase. On the one hand, the legal and institutional basis for environmental policy-making was consolidated and improved. In the Maastricht and Amsterdam treaty reforms the EP gained co-decision powers and QMV was introduced for almost all aspects of environmental policy in the Council (important exceptions being environmental taxes, the choice of energy sources (see Chapter 15) and spatial planning). Yet, on the other hand, the momentum in the policy expansion slowed and attention shifted to reform the European regulatory agenda in this field. The fifth EAP, covering the period 1993 to 2000, announced the 'new governance' approach to environmental policy, emphasizing (a) the need for greater participation of all addressees of environmental policy during decision-making and implementation and (b) the advantages of more flexible and context-sensitive policy instruments. The ongoing sixth EAP (2001–10) follows this spirit in calling for improved regulatory policy and deeper collaboration with industry and EU citizens.

Yet, despite the increasingly cautious tone with regard to further expanding the coverage of EU environmental policy, this period also witnessed the formulation of a number of significant environmental policies designed to tackle critical problems—such as water pollution, chemicals control, and climate change—and employing new regulatory approaches (see below). The enlargement of the EU in 2004 and 2007 did not, as anticipated by some, result in a retrenchment of the policy, and hence a new phase. Due to the high level of institutional consolidation, on the one hand, and the ability of European policy-makers to programmatically adjust—even reframe—European environmental policy to changing circumstances and demands, on the other hand, the new members have been absorbed into policy-making without greater disruptions. Box 13.1 provides an overview of the development of the legal basis for environmental policy over time and corresponding procedural and substantive characteristics of the policy.

Key players

This section introduces the main actors in EU environmental policy-making, namely the four main EU organs, Commission, EP, Council of Ministers, and Court of Justice (ECJ), and outside the institutional set-up of the EU, environmental interest groups. It highlights intra-institutional relations—including the conflicts between proponents and opponents of more or stricter environmental standards within each institution—and procedures. It also places specific emphasis on the inter-institutional relations that are characteristic of this policy field.

The European Commission

The general structure and functions of the Commission correspond to those in other policy areas in the 'first pillar' of the EU (see Chapter 4). The following discussion will

BOX 13.1	**Key treaty changes and associated characteristics of environmental policy**

Treaty base	*Characteristics of environmental policy*

1957: Treaty of Rome

- Article 100 (EEC) on the single market (new: Art. 94)
- Catch-all Article 235 (EEC) on general functioning of the Community (new: Art. 308)
- Article 2 on living and working conditions in the Community

- *Decision rules:* Unanimity, EP consultation
- *Substantive implication:* Environmental policy needed to be linked to the completion of the single market and the general economic mission of the Community

1987: Single European Act (SEA)

- Article 100a (EEC) (new: Art. 95) on the single market cites environmental regulation explicitly
- Article 130r-t (EEC) (new: Art. 174-6) on environmental policy

- Environmental policy established as an official task of the Community
- *Decision rules:* (a) Art. 130r-t calls for unanimous voting in the Council, (b) Art. 100a follows new 'cooperation procedure', allowing for QMV and extending the EP's participation rights
- *Substance:* Objectives and principles of environmental policy are defined, building the basis for policy expansion and fairly high standards of protection

1993: Treaty on European Union (TEU)

- Modification of Articles 100a (new: Art. 95) and 130s (new: Art. 175)
- Article 2 (TEC) introduces the concept of 'sustainable growth respecting the environment'

- *Decision rules:* (a) QMV is extended to most areas of environmental policy, (b) Art. 100a introduces co-decision-making with the EP
- *Substance:* Formal commitment to a high level of protection and the integration of environmental policy objectives into other policy areas

1999: Treaty of Amsterdam (ToA)

- Article 2 (TEC) and Preamble establish concept of sustainable development and strengthened commitment to integration principle

- *Decision rules:* Co-decision (Art. 175 TEC) for measures adopted under Art. 174 TEC (ex Art. 130r TEC)

2003: Treaty of Nice (ToN)

- *Decision rules:* Adjustments to QMV raise the threshold for reaching qualified majority

2009: Treaty of Lisbon

- *Decision rules:* Revision of the system of QMV (replacing weighed voting in the Council)
- *Substance:* Introduction of an Energy Title (prospectively strengthening climate policy)

therefore highlight some of the specific challenges characterizing environmental policy-making, namely the challenge of horizontal policy coordination and the balancing act of establishing a European profile for a policy field that emerged as a flanking policy to the core economic functions of the Community, on the one hand, and responding to member-state preferences (i.e. acting as their agent), on the other hand.

First, part and parcel of the development of a European environmental policy was its institutionalization as a more or less discrete sector, with its own legal basis (after the SEA), a dedicated Directorate-General (DG) within the Commission, a specialized 'Environment Council' within the Council of Ministers, and so on. Yet environmental policy is also a 'horizontal' policy, affecting economic sectors ranging from agriculture to transportation and requiring coordination among a diverse set of DGs within the Commission. The often conflictual relationship among DGs poses problems for coordinated and coherent policy formulation. These conflicts became widely acknowledged with the adoption of the fifth EAP in 1993, which introduced a new consensual rhetoric pointing to win-win solutions and joint responsibility for environmental and economic objectives. Specific coordination arrangements were decided, responding to the principle of environmental policy integration laid down in the treaty, such as the designation of 'environmental correspondents' in various sectoral DGs, a Consultative Forum for Sustainable Development and a (now suspended) 'Green Star' system to identify proposals with likely environmental impacts. However, these initiatives went against a tradition of respecting 'turf' boundaries in the Commission (A. Jordan et al. 2008: 166). They both underestimated their organizational implications and lacked high-level political support (cf. A. Jordan and Schout 2006), and especially in the presence of potent economic interests inside the Commission or among the policy addressees they proved rather ineffective.

The regulation of automobile emissions has been such an area, where cross-DG turf battles and even conflict within the College of the Commissioners prevented coordinated and effective environmental policy. In the 1990s the problems of divided responsibility were the reason for an interesting regulatory experiment in the car industry—the so-called Auto-Oil Programme. In this exercise, DG Environment and DG TREN (responsible for energy), against the initial opposition of DG Industry, invited the car and the oil industry to think jointly about the most cost-effective solutions for tackling air pollution from cars by combining measures to improve fuel quality and to advance motor technologies. Based on such coordinated industrial input the leading DGs hoped to be able to introduce an innovative—and cross-sectoral—solution for the problem of rising auto emissions after internal fragmentation and opposing preferences between DG Environment (in charge of environmental motor technology) and DG Industry (controlling the fuel issue) had previously prevented the preparation of such a cross-issue proposal. The attempt to effectively delegate coordination functions to industry, however, proved to be of limited success, not least due to coordination problems between the two different industries, each of which understandably hoped to shift the adaptive burden to the other (Friedrich et al. 2002). More recently, in

2008, conflicts between the Commissioner for the Environment, Stavros Dimas, and the Commissioner for Enterprise, Günther Verheugen, about regulating car emissions of greenhouse gases became public. While Verheugen failed to take full control of the dossier, he (and the auto industry) succeeded in watering down significantly the initial proposal developed under Dimas' leadership. Such a public fight between two Commissioners may be unusual, but it revealed the challenge of complying with the principle of environmental policy integration even inside the Commission.

Second, the Commission needs to balance its ambition as the 'motor of integration' with the need to be responsive to the member states, and hence raise the chances of successful decision-making and implementation. Especially during the 1970s and 1980s, when the institutional and normative position of environmental policy was still weak at the EU level, the Commission had used the policy formulation stage to advance its role as a supranational actor and to promote tough environmental rules exceeding the status quo in the member states. From an inter-institutional perspective, this role put the Commission in almost natural opposition to many member states and the Council. While developing a profile in environmental policy, it invited long-winded negotiations and poor implementation due to national resistance. But even during the early phases of EU environmental policy-making, the above description risks being a caricature. As indicated above, in the 1970s several member states began developing an interest in environmental protection policy and—partly in order to reduce the risk of competitive disadvantages—sought to 'upload' national regulation to the Community level. Hence, the Commission regularly responded to national demands for European policy in developing its proposals. Here, with a small staff of about 500 A-grade officials, the Commission was dependent on national expertise and regularly sought the opinion of the national ministries to ensure the feasibility of its proposals and to anticipate the conflicts that might otherwise hamper decision-making.

This attentiveness to the member states' points of view increased further during the last decade due to a re-ordering of the Commission's priorities. Deficient implementation led the Commission to improve its relations with the implementers 'on the ground', namely the relevant agencies in the member states, during the policy design stage. Beginning with the fifth EAP, the Commission began to speak of the member states as partners; formal and informal dialogue networks were created to put this cooperative approach into practice (Commission 1993a: 113–16). Supranational entrepreneurship seemed more promising in such cooperative settings than within a confrontational modus operandi.

Latest evidence of the Commission's policy-shaping activities can be observed in climate policy. It has framed the climate change problem as the next big integrative project of the Union—relevant for jobs and competitiveness and environmental protection as well as its credibility as a 'world partner' (see also Chapter 15). Environmental measures related to the climate change issue were presented with much verve and with demanding standards, sometimes surprising even the Commission's usual allies in the Parliament (author interviews, EP, June 2008), but never failing to make reference to prior commitments of the EU member states.

The Council of Ministers

The Council of Ministers, like the Commission, is characterized by segmentation. There is little coordination between the Environment Council and the various other Councils. Similarly, the Secretariat General of the Council and the pyramid of Council committees follow by and large a sector-specific approach. This 'insularity' allows the environment ministers some escape from domestic constraints. At some distance from influential colleagues in charge of the economy, finance, or agriculture, environment ministers may seek the opportunity to give support to an agenda that would stand little chance domestically, although this depends also on how tightly national positions are coordinated across ministries. Back home, controversial decisions may then be blamed on 'Brussels' or a too-powerful alliance of environmental leader states. Enhanced transparency of Council negotiations, as well as the greater accountability of governments as regards their previously agreed mandates, may reduce this informal leeway of national policy-makers in Brussels and the resulting dynamism—with its sometimes rather unpredictable consequences.

At first sight a single cleavage, separating leaders from environmental laggards, runs through the Council of Ministers. Simply put, the leaders appear to be countries like Germany, The Netherlands, Sweden, and Denmark, i.e. the richer, northern states, whereas the laggards are the poorer, southern states like Greece, Spain, Portugal, and the new member states, which have other investment priorities and do not face electorates pushing for tougher environmental standards. The United Kingdom, given its insular location (protecting it from some transboundary effects), and the legacy of its heavy industry sector, was long considered the 'dirty man' of Europe, although this has changed in the past decade (A. Jordan 2002b). The existence of this north–south, rich–poor cleavage was visible in previous rounds of enlargement. The southern enlargements in 1981 and 1986 were accompanied by a substantial increase and refocusing of the Communities' financial support schemes for environmental investments. In 1993 the Cohesion Fund, spending about 50 per cent of its monies on environmental projects, was launched. The 'northern' countries which joined in 1995, in turn, negotiated a treaty revision that allows them to exceed EU environmental standards under certain conditions.

The impact of enlargement has emerged starkly with the addition of twelve mostly central and east European countries (CEECs) in 2004 and 2007. Unlike previous accession countries, these new members have had to adopt the entire environmental *acquis* with very few exceptions and without comparable side-payments.[1] While a distinct CEEC 'block' of opposition to strict environmental policy cannot be identified generally, there are issues where the new member states ally to fight against financial burdens imposed on them. The negotiations over the climate change package, which was agreed in Parliament and among the EU leaders in December 2008, with the final legislation being adopted in April 2009, were such an example, where special treatment of the new member states has been successfully fought for in the context of EU-internal 'effort-sharing' arrangements as well as within the emissions trading scheme (see Chapter 15). These countries justified such special treatment by pointing to the massive transformation processes in the past two decades which inadvertently had led to significant reductions in greenhouse gas emissions (EurActiv 2008). Demands for additional conciliations were successfully voiced in the final stages of the negotiations in the light of the financial crisis. Yet, the kind of slowdown in environmental policy that can be attributed to the financial crisis shows no clear-cut east–west pattern as so-called environmental-leader states like Germany or the UK also shy away from imposing extra costs on industry.

In fact, the cleavage structure in the Council has never been quite as two-dimensional as suggested above. Three reasons account for this greater complexity. In the first place, member states face different environmental problems. Highly industrialized countries are likely to be more concerned with air quality, waste treatment, and noise, while countries with a larger rural sector and dependence on tourism place greater value on the quality of soil, nature protection, and sufficient quantities of water. Second, countries differ in their regulatory philosophies and styles (Richardson 1982; Vogel 1986). Hence, their governments argue not only about the level of standards, but also about the type of policy instrument, the amount of administrative or regional flexibility, and the required scientific certainty before agreeing to EU measures. Third, member governments alter their positions over time, if either the economic and environmental conditions change or a new government with different policy priorities comes to power.

The European Parliament

As indicated above, the EP has gained decision-making power over the years. Today the co-decision procedure applies to most aspects of environmental policy—making the EP the equal partner of the Council. But even earlier the EP had left its mark.

Traditionally, the EP has been the 'greenest' of the three main environmental policy-making bodies. In the case of the 1979 Wild Birds Directive, for instance, the EP had been petitioned by several animal rights groups concerned with the hunting of migratory birds, and in 1971 requested the Commission to take up this issue. The Commission responded in the first EAP and, after consulting numerous experts, presented a draft directive in 1976 (Haigh 2004: 9.2). In the 1990s, the EP brought the issue of implementation in environmental policy to the fore and pushed the Commission to engage more systematically with societal and administrative actors on the ground (Collins and Earnshaw 1992; European Parliament 1996); regular Commission reporting and modifications of implementation strategies (see below) were initiated under EP pressure. More directly, the EP contributes to implementation in passing on citizens' petitions to the Commission and in regular implementation meetings with the Commission. In 2007, the EP sent 146 petitions related to the field of environment to the Secretariat General of the Commission; this was around one-third of all the petitions sent by the EP, up from 25 per cent in 2006 (Commission 2008*m*: 16).

The effects of co-decision on the nature of environmental policy decisions are hard to generalize. While a 'green' EP may push the passage of stringent rules, some argue that conciliatory behaviour may replace previous vigorous advocacy because the EP can now be held accountable for decisional failure (Holzinger 1994: 114–16). It is important to note that the EP committee on the environment is one of the committees most involved in legislative procedures (Maurer 2003*b*), creating an enormous workload on the committee members and increasing the incentive to reach early compromises. Also, the often technical and presumably apolitical nature of environmental proposals, especially if they are effectively amendments of earlier legislation, may lead to a moderation in the negotiation style and to agreement in first reading. However, a study by Anne Rasmussen (2007)—though not focusing on environmental policy-making specifically—highlights two other, seemingly more significant, factors influencing the nature of co-decision-making: working relationships with the other institutions and party politics.

Regarding the working relationships, especially with respect to larger policy dossiers, such as the climate package, chemicals, or waste regulation, the informal trilogue between EP, Commission, and Council plays an important role for identifying and agreeing on compromises outside the formalized 'ping-pong' during the official readings and reconciliation procedures. With regard to the overall political composition of the EP, compared to most national parliaments the green faction is quite large and despite the dominance of the Socialist and the European People's Party (EPP) groups it has contributed to the green image of the EP in playing a strong environmental advocacy role. Yet, compared to the fifth term (1999–2004) when 7.7 per cent of the seats went to the Group of the Greens/European Free Alliance (EFA), this proportion dropped to 5.4 per cent after the 2004 elections (forty-two members, including two independents), not least due to the arrival of the ten new member states, with different political preferences (only Latvia elected one EFA MEP). While this may have contributed to a certain moderation in style, the European Parliament is still considered 'environmental' in its overall orientation, although this does not apply across the board and is issue-dependent (author interview, EP, May 2008). Here, it certainly matters that the MEPs in the European multi-level governance system are some steps removed from the operational level (and demands of accountability) and hence prone to articulate more general programmatic ideas.

Finally, bargaining style is also related to personalities[2] and committee relations. The policy driver inside the EP has been its Committee on the Environment, Public Health and Food Safety (ENVI).[3] A proactive and often uncompromising attitude characterized the operations of this committee in the 1980s and 1990s under the chairmanship of Ken Collins (1979–99),[4] a Scottish Labour MEP (Sbragia 2000). His successors, Carolyn Jackson (1999–2004) and Karl Heinz Florenz, were both members of the EPP and politically less prone to radical environmental views. But, as long-time active members of the committee, they contributed to continuity and expertise in its work, ensuring its influence despite some moderation in style. The subsequent chairman of the committee (2004–9), Miroslav Ouský (EPP) of the Czech Republic, gained this position not due to his personal interest in the field, but due to the complex and therefore unpredictable system of assigning such posts to party and member-state delegations in the EP. Especially after enlargement the assignment of posts in the EP revealed a number of surprises—not only to external observers. Ouzký led this large committee in a professional manner, but was person-ally sceptical when it came to developing new or more demanding environmental measures. For instance, he was one of the fundamental opponents to the climate change package, questioning the scientific basis of this policy, and therefore voted against adopting the Interim Report on the scientific facts of climate change which pointed to its man-made origins (European Parliament 2008*b*), produced by the temporary committee on climate change. Chairmanship of the panel switched once again, however, in July 2009 following the most recent EP elections, when Socialist MEP Jo Leinen was named as the incoming chair of the Committee. Leinen, a former regional environment minister in his native Germany, was expected to take a more proactive role as chair (*EUobserver.com*, 16 July 2009).

The climate package—as many other large environmental dossiers—is also shaped by complex inter-committee relations within the EP. Here the so-called Hughes procedure (and its 'enhanced' variant) empowers other non-environmental committees—such as the Industry, Research and Energy Committee (ITRE) or Internal Market and Consumer Protection (IMCO)—with the aim of providing a procedural solution for lengthy internal conflicts and rationalizing policy-making by reducing the number of amendments presented by various committees to the plenum. While the procedure tackles committee turf battles between committees, it does not (intend to) silence party politics within the Parliament.

The European Court of Justice

In the history of EU environmental policy, the ECJ through its case law has played a crucial role in establishing the legitimacy of environmental measures at the EU level and in insisting on participatory procedures. In the *Danish bottle* case it ruled that the principle of free movement of goods can be overridden if this serves to achieve common environmental objectives (*Commission v. Denmark* C-302/86 [1988] ECR 4607). The ruling confirmed a Danish recycling law, which had limited the range of containers that could be used to bottle beverages. In the *Titanium Dioxide* case (C-300/89 *Commission v. Council* [1991] ECR I-02867), the Court eased the way towards delineating the decision-making procedures in the environmental field and supported further empowerment of the Parliament. Here the Court found that the objectives of the directive to harmonize and eventually eliminate waste from the titanium dioxide industry were compatible both with Article 100a (single market) and with Article 130s (environment) of the treaties and ruled that under such conditions that legal base should be chosen which best reflects the fundamental democratic principle that the peoples should take part in the exercise of power through the intermediary of a representative assembly. It thereby legitimated the choice of Article 100a for solely procedural reasons as it provided for cooperation rather than mere consultation with the EP. In the medium term this ruling induced the harmonization of procedures in environmental policy-making.

The main responsibilities of the Court in the later, legally consolidated phase of environmental policy relate to implementation and enforcement. First, in infringement proceedings usually initiated by the Commission against member states (Art. 226 TEC), the Court ensures compliance with EU law. Under the Article 228 TEC procedure it may impose pecuniary sanctions in cases of prolonged non-compliance or poor compliance. Although the total number of cases initiated under Article 228 is significant (approximately thirty per year) and amounts to the largest share across policy areas (see Figure 13.2 below), the length of the procedure, with three steps each under Articles 226 and 228, usually allows member states to reach compliance before the ECJ reaches a penalty ruling. So far there have been three environmental cases where the Court ordered fines against member states; in the latest, against France, regarding the transposition of Directive 2001/18 on the deliberate release of genetically modified organisms (C-121/07), the Court imposed a fine of 10 million euros.

Under Article 234 TEC, if an individual argues before a national court that a national law or policy conflicts with EU law, the national court may seek guidance from the ECJ by making a preliminary ruling reference. This procedure operates analogously to an enforcement mechanism, as individuals or groups are able to bring legal action against national authorities that have failed to transpose or comply with EU law.[5] Between 1976 and 2007 the Court made 108 preliminary rulings in environmental matters, almost 50 per cent of all cases being introduced by Italian (27) and Dutch (20) courts (Krämer 2008: 6–7). The otherwise low numbers seem to reflect either reserved attitudes or limited familiarity of the national judiciaries with EC environmental law.

Environmental interest groups

Environmental policy is influenced by a wide range of interest groups representing environmental, consumer, or industrial interests. Among the environmental groups, the European Environmental Bureau (EEB) has the longest history in Brussels. It was set up in 1974 with the help of the European Commission, which had an interest in garnering societal support for expanding European competencies to the environmental field and in establishing a counterweight to the strong industrial associations. Today the EEB is a federation of 143 organizations from thirty-one European countries. Together with the Friends of the Earth (FoE), Greenpeace International, and the

World-Wide Fund for Nature (WWF), which established their Brussels offices in the late 1980s, the EEB founded the 'Gang of Four' in 1990, an informal coalition of leading environmental NGOs active at the European level. Since then this coalition has expanded to ten and has been joined by Climate Network Europe (CNE), the European Federation for Transport and Environment (T&E), BirdLife International, Health and Environmental Alliance, International Friends of Nature, and, as the latest addition, the CEE Bankwatch Network. Both enlargement and the adoption of new policy priorities by the EU have led to new arrivals. For instance, the CEE Bankwatch Network, founded in 1995 and joining the group of environmental NGOs in 2005, consists of central and eastern European NGOs concerned about unsustainable practices sponsored by international finance institutions.

Given the volatile nature of membership and public campaigning contributions, nine of the 'Green Ten' also rely on Commission funding for their regular operations.[6] Based on Decision No 466/2002/EC laying down a Community action programme promoting non-governmental organizations primarily active in the field of environmental protection, an annual amount of €8.4 million has been made available to Brussels-based as well as member-state- or candidate-country-based environmental NGOs. This decision has formalized and made transparent[7] previous regular contributions from the Commission to environment groups. In addition, other budget lines of the Commission such as those focusing on development assistance or the build-up of civil society have been tapped by these NGOs as they match some of their goals and activities. The relative dependence on EU funding varies greatly between zero (Greenpeace) and more than 60 per cent (EEB); it depends on both the philosophy and the organizational structure (e.g. membership) of the groups.

Differing philosophies become visible also in the activities of the NGOs. Generally, the Brussels-based staffs concentrate activities on the policy formulation phase. Yet, some emphasize their role as pressure group while others operate also as advisors, offering expertise and information to the Commission. With the exception of Greenpeace, the Green Ten seek to be consulted in this phase, while during the decision-making phase all NGOs resort to the classical tools of the environmental movement and use public campaigns to create awareness and seek direct contacts with member governments and MEPs to ensure the desired majorities. The range of activities is reflected in today's professional operations and the increasingly diversified environmental policy expertise present in Brussels.

Compared to national industrial federations or firms, which may also get involved in the policy-formulation and decision-making stages, national NGOs (which may also be members of the Brussels-based groups) are crucial during the implementation and enforcement phases of policy-making. In addition to national legal action, environmental groups can use the complaints procedure to inform the Commission of any gap in implementation that is found in the member states.[8] Especially to detect the non-application of EU legislation this procedure can offer valuable information to the Commission given the absence of an EU inspectorate in the member states. In 2006–7, the Commission introduced a 'pilot problem-solving mechanism', which transmits citizens' inquiries concerning the application of EU environmental legislation

BOX 13.2   The making of the REACH chemicals package

The REACH (Registration, Evaluation and Authorization of Chemicals) package resulted in a consolidation and renewal of the EU chemicals policy, which has a history going back to the late 1960s and covered over 100 pieces of EU legislation. The initial critics of REACH disapproved of (a) its complexity, (b) insufficient protection of the environment and human health from hazardous chemicals (especially from the vast amount of already existing chemicals), and (c) the lack of guidelines or incentives for the substitution for hazardous chemicals of less harmful substances.

Policy initiation was dominated by 'green states' (Austria, Denmark, Germany, The Netherlands, Sweden, and the UK), hoping to export their ambitious national goals to the European level (Selin 2007: 78) and leading the Environment Council in 1999 to request the Commission to develop a new chemicals policy. These green states were joined by DG Environment in the Commission (and the new Swedish Commissioner Margot Wallström), which presented a White Paper on a Strategy for a Future Chemicals Policy in February 2001, as well as the majority of the Environment Committee in the EP and many environmental NGOs. Opposition to the initiative was led by CEFIC (European Chemical Industry Council), representing 27,000 chemical companies across Europe, who mobilized support in DG Enterprise as well as the EP Committees on Industry, Research and Energy (ITRE) and the Internal Market and Consumer Protection (IMCO).

The policy-formulation and decision-making stages were characterized by heavy consultation of stakeholders and policy experts aiming to raise awareness of insufficient regulation (spectacular in this context was the DetoX campaign led by the WWF) and improve acceptance of regulation among industrial actors. Furthermore, decision-making was exemplified by a high degree of institutional 'depillarization' (Hey et al. 2008: 439f). This involved (a) joint responsibility assigned to DG Environment and DG Industry in the Commission, (b) the Council negotiations taking place in the horizontal Competitiveness Council where both economic and environmental ministers (and experts at the working group level) met, and (c) the enhanced Hughes procedure forcing the leading ENVI committee to cooperate closely with the IMCO and ITRE committees in producing the committee report. From the environmental point of view, both the participatory and the institutional strategies strengthened the industrial position by extending access beyond the initial small 'green' alliance. Not surprisingly, therefore, the Commission proposal presented in October 2003 envisaged weaker registration, information, and substitution requirements, as well as some exemptions compared to its earlier White Paper. Also, the Council common position agreed in December 2005 under the British presidency departed from the earlier demands formulated in the Environment Council in acknowledging the need to protect the competitiveness of European chemical industry.

Interestingly, while depillarization in the Commission and Council was introduced with the dual aim of renewing the regulatory framework for chemicals and fostering a more cooperative climate, the situation in the EP was characterized by open antagonism. Industrial and environmental lobbies had successfully polarized the debate; in particular, industry opponents of REACH kept delaying the process hoping for more favourable majorities in the EP and in the Council after European (2004) and German (2005) elections. In the end the ENVI committee was forced to move toward a compromise with the industrial coalition by agreeing to relaxed information and testing requirements for chemicals produced in small volumes and relaxed conditions for substitution, in order to avoid the collapse of the negotiations (Pesendorfer 2006; M. P. Smith 2008).

Finally, the REACH package was passed in second reading in December 2006. It introduced a mix of instruments, with obligatory procedural standards limited to hazardous substances, self-regulatory information, and risk management of industry being the core of the new system, accompanied by new rules of transparency to allow for bottom-up pressure. The new European Chemicals Agency (ECHA), which was inaugurated in June 2008, shares with national regulatory agencies responsibility for the implementation of REACH, ensuring uniform practices. In short, the final decision reflects a compromise both in substance and in the choice of governance mechanisms. In sum, this case study prominently shows the strong and yet highly contingent impact of intra- and inter-institutional arrangements, rendering a simple assessment of who are the losers and who the winners of the negotiations unviable.

[a] The regulatory framework for the management of chemicals and the establishment of the European Chemicals Agency consists of: (a) Regulation (EC) No 1907/2006 of the European Parliament and of the Council of 18 December 2006 concerning the Registration, Evaluation, Authorisation and Restriction of Chemicals (REACH), establishing a European Chemicals Agency, amending Directive 1999/45/EC and repealing Council Regulation (EEC) No 793/93 and Commission Regulation (EC) No 1488/94, as well as Council Directive 76/769/EEC and Commission Directives 91/155/EEC, 93/67/EEC, 93/105/EC, and 2000/21/EC; and (b) Directive 2006/121/EC of the European Parliament and of the Council of 18 December 2006 amending Council Directive 67/548/EEC on the approximation of laws, regulations, and administrative provisions relating to the classification, packaging, and labelling of dangerous substances in order to adapt it to Regulation (EC) No 1907/2006 of the European Parliament and of the Council concerning the Registration, Evaluation, Authorisation and Restriction of Chemicals (REACH) and establishing a European Chemicals Agency.

back to the member states to encourage an immediate response (Commission 2008n: 7). Arguably this will erase a valuable source for the Commission's 'top-down' control, however (Krämer 2008: 14).

Regulatory policy-making at the crossroads

Years of EU environmental activism had not significantly improved the state of the environment (EEA 1999). Some critics condemned the cost of environmental regulation, and the EU's tendency toward ad hoc and 'wild' regulatory expansion. Others deplored the apparent lack of coordination between environmental and other EU policy areas, such as transport, energy, agriculture, or the single market, and wished to see better integration of environmental objectives into general policy-making in the EU. Furthermore, despite some justified concerns about the quality and comparability of the Commission's own data (Börzel 2001), EU environmental policy appears to suffer from an implementation deficit exceeding that of other policy areas such as the single market, industry, and consumer affairs (see Figure 13.1). At the level of infringement proceedings as well as court referrals (see Figure 13.2) and court rulings (Krämer 2008: 3–5), environmental cases amount to the largest policy grouping (although the proportion seems to be decreasing).

EU policy-makers responded to these challenges in several ways. First, the Commission started several initiatives to improve implementation and enforcement. The European Network for the Implementation and Enforcement of Environmental Law (IMPEL), made up of Commission officials and representatives of relevant national (or local) authorities, has become an important forum for considering the feasibility of EU proposals early in the game, as well as for improving the capacity and willingness of local implementers through the exchange of experiences. In order to tackle structural problems in some outstanding areas, such as waste, water, air, nature protection, and impact assessment, DG Environment formed implementation task forces. The Commission also introduced a more 'rational handling of complaints and infringements' (Commission 2006c: 7), prioritizing structural and costly problems as well as intensifying proactive measures by offering guidelines, interpretive documents, and training initiatives to increase implementation capacities on the ground. Importantly, both the total and the relative drop in environmental infringement cases after 2004 is primarily related

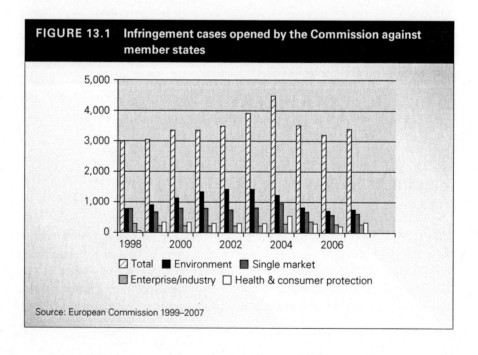

FIGURE 13.1   Infringement cases opened by the Commission against member states

Source: European Commission 1999–2007

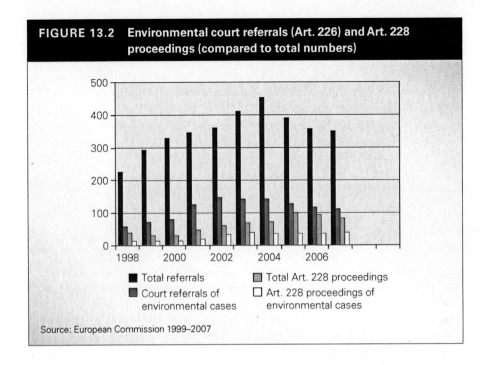

FIGURE 13.2   Environmental court referrals (Art. 226) and Art. 228 proceedings (compared to total numbers)

Total referrals

Court referrals of environmental cases

Total Art. 228 proceedings

Art. 228 proceedings of environmental cases

Source: European Commission 1999–2007

to the 'rational handling' as well as to changes in the treatment of complaints (see above) under Commissioner Dimas, i.e. to an apparent turn towards the management approach to implementation (Tallberg 2002), focusing on building states' capacity and expertise to implement policies, rather than punishing lack of implementation; these numbers should not be mistaken as an indication of better implementation.

Second, the Commission has started reforms in the choice of proposed policy instruments. Since the turn of the century the EU has adopted a number of *environmental framework* directives that aim both to avoid overregulation and to generate greater coherence of EU legislation. The Water Framework Directive of 2000, for instance, consolidates previous regulatory output by replacing seven of the 'first wave' water directives. By requiring all member states to cooperate in the management of river basins, the EU brought the hitherto neglected cross-boundary and cross-media effects of water pollution into focus (Grant et al. 2000: 167–75). The so-called waste framework directive (2006/12/EC) merely serves to consolidate the waste directive of 1975 with its numerous amendments. The new Air Quality Directive (2008/50/EC), which entered into force in June 2008, merges four existing directives and one Council decision on air quality and adds new standards and targets on fine particles while giving the member states more flexibility in complying with these rules. Though not presented as a framework directive, the climate and energy 'package' proposed in January 2008 by the Commission also aimed to achieve an overarching goal, namely to cut carbon dioxide emissions in the EU by 20 per cent by the year 2020 (see Box 13.3).

BOX 13.3	The internalization of external pressure: the EU climate change package

In January 2008 the *European Commission* responded to the European Council decision establishing the 20-20-20 target with a package of four proposals on climate and energy. The proposed measures included:

- an *improved emissions trading system (ETS)* covering more emissions and allowing firms in one EU country to buy allowances in any other country;
- an *emissions reduction target for industries not covered by the ETS* (e.g. buildings, transport, waste);
- *legally enforceable targets for increasing the share of renewables* in the energy mix— taking into account each country's individual needs and potential, but amounting to an overall increase of 20 per cent; and
- new rules on *carbon capture and storage (CCS)* and on *environmental subsidies*.

Negotiations in the *European Parliament* were conducted under enormous time-pressure, as it was the declared aim to reach an agreement within the EU before the next European elections in June 2009 and far in advance of the Copenhagen meeting at the end of that year. Relations between the involved committees (most notably ENVI and ITRE) were shaped by the perceived need to reach a compromise. This tamed the free exchange of views and restrained open conflict otherwise typical for the first reading stage (author interviews, EP, May 2008).

Similar time pressure was felt at *Council* level. In October 2008, in the midst of the financial crisis, the European Council declared its commitment to stick to the ambitious climate and energy targets agreed in 2007 and 2008 (Council of the European Union 2008). The financial crisis induced some heavy attacks (see Chapter 15) on the ETS dossier in particular by east European countries, with other countries adding their demands for special treatment. Also, energy-intensive industry fought for leniency during economically tough times, and argued, for instance, against the auctioning system for receiving emission permits. Yet, the French Presidency negotiated a compromise which was agreed at the European Council in December 2008, i.e. on schedule for the Copenhagen agenda. The compromise did indeed considerably water down the initial Commission proposal, but the 20-20-20 target was maintained. On 17 December 2008 the package was endorsed in the EP and by April 2009 all related EU legislation was formally adopted in the Council of Ministers. Further discussions took place at the European Council of 29/30 October 2009.

Hence, despite softening the environmental measures and corresponding heavy criticisms among the environmental NGO community, the EU was set to appear on the international scene as a leader sticking to its core commitments even in tough economic times. Turning the perspective inward, the enormous dynamic triggered by the EU in international negotiations has been remarkable. The issue of climate change was effectively utilized by environmental policy-makers to push internal decisions on difficult issues such as energy consumption and industrial and car emissions. At a more general level, 'climate change' was used to give the Union a more visible profile internally and to enhance its public image.

The climate package, which was agreed by the EU leaders and endorsed by Parliament in December 2008, is a visible example of a compromise between the member states that takes account of their different economic structures, histories, and capacities as well as policy preferences even at difficult economic times. In addition, it is characterized by an innovative *instrument mix* with regulatory, market-based, and investment tools.

Such diversification of policy instruments, with an emphasis on more context-oriented and flexible approaches, represents a change in regulatory philosophy first announced in the fifth EAP. In this context, new information-based instruments aim at raising awareness and triggering learning effects; economic instruments attach a price (in the form of fees, taxes, or withheld subsidies) to environmentally harmful activities or create a market for permits or allowances; and voluntary agreements with private actors complement this toolbox of 'new' instruments. Compared to the total legislative output of the EU in environmental policy, these new policy instruments are still limited (Héritier 2002) though growing in numbers (Holzinger et al. 2008). Considering the level of political contestation—related to very different patterns in the choice of policy instruments in the member states (see A. Jordan et al. 2005)—the repertoire of EU environmental policy tools has become surprisingly varied.

Third, EU policy-makers are aiming at better policy integration in two senses. On the one hand, several measures pay attention to the combined effects of pollution on different environmental media (air, water, and soil), and the interdependency between these media. The two latest EAPs have pursued this perspective by following thematic strategies, e.g. the focus is now on climate change, biodiversity, or the connection between environment and health. The directives on environmental impact assessment (revised in 1997), on strategic impact assessment (extending the impact perspective from individual projects to policy programmes, effective since 2004), and on integrated pollution prevention and control (adopted in 1996) facilitate pollution control beyond the initial medium affected by discharge.

Policy integration in a second sense applies to policy coordination. In June 1998 the Cardiff European Council appeared to represent a breakthrough for the policy integration principle. Most configurations of the Council, ranging from agriculture to Ecofin, were called on to develop an environmental integration strategy, and member governments were supposed to exchange 'best practice' models (Lenschow 2003). Some first improvements can be detected, for instance in the reform of the CAP in 2003 and agreements on cross-compliance, meaning the attachment of environmental conditions to agricultural support policies. But the commitment of the EU's political leadership to environmental integration remains volatile, especially during difficult economic times. Ultimately, the economic preoccupations of the EU may trump its environmental agenda and the historical policy-making mode of opportunistic 'niche-seeking' may turn out to be far from obsolete for policy-makers dedicated to environmental objectives (see A. Jordan and Lenschow 2008).

With respect to all three policy challenges discussed above—implementation, diversification of instruments, and integration—eastern enlargement had been expected to slow down the renewal owing to limited financial and administrative capacities as well as insufficient mobilization of civil society in the new member states. The Commission's infringement data, however, suggest that the implementation record in eastern Europe outperforms the average 'old' member state, which may be attributable to a greater susceptibility of the new member states to shaming, the institutional investment into legislative capacity during the pre-accession period (Sedelmeier 2008), and the post-accession threat of the Commission to punish non-compliance with the withdrawal of funding from the structural funds. The good record of the new member states might change with regard to the actual application of EU legislation—a stage that is poorly reflected in the Commission data and that might anyway be too early for related infringement proceedings. Available research points to deficient administrative capacities, poor coordination between the branches of government, and poor enforcement in order to protect vulnerable industry. But it also highlights that societal environmental groups have been successfully mobilized during the pre-accession phase both through financial support and in empowering them through procedural instruments. These NGOs use both conflictual and cooperative strategies to ensure compliance on the ground (see Buzogány 2008).

The EU as an international actor

So far EU environmental policy has been presented as being largely internally motivated, either to facilitate the internal market or to deal with European transboundary effects. A significant number of EU environmental measures, however, can be traced back to international agreements related to water, the atmosphere, waste, wildlife, etc. (Baker 2003: 25). The EU is a member of over forty multilateral environmental agreements[9] and uses both bilateral relations and its neighbourhood policy to bolster environmental standards at international, regional, and national levels. As international conventions are usually formal agreements among sovereign states, and as the EU obviously is not a state, this process involved the establishment of new procedures and routines, both internationally and within the EU, challenging traditional multilateral practices.

The question of whether to accept the Community as a party to a convention at the international level had to be answered and is controversial both internally and externally. Non-EU states are not always ready to accept the EU as a signatory, unless it is made sufficiently clear how the agreed obligations will be implemented internally. The Convention on International Trade in Endangered Species (CITES) from 1973 still prohibits the Community from acceding, while the Vienna Convention on the Ozone Layer (1985), and the subsequent Montreal Protocol (1987) included—

after heated arguments—both the Community and the member states. This form of a 'mixed agreement' has also been chosen for the United Nations Framework Convention on Climate Change (UNFCCC), which entered into force in March 1994. But also within the EU, the form of representation is controversial, since it has to be clarified whether the EU has the legal competence to deal with the problem under consideration. Prior to the SEA and the establishment of a legal base for European environmental policy this was evidently contested. But even now the exact policy competences are never quite clear, and hence the practice of mixed—member-state and EU—representation. A second and related issue is who should speak on behalf of the EU—the Commission or the presidency of the Council of Ministers? Despite these persisting ambiguities, EU member governments have become increasingly willing to coordinate their positions and act collectively, while international partners have come to expect 'the Union' in some formation at the negotiation table (Sbragia 1998; Bretherton and Vogler 2006).

During this process of institutionalization, the EU evolved from a 'Vienna laggard to a Kyoto leader' in global environmental negotiations (Sbragia and Damro 1999: 53). By the time of negotiating the Kyoto Protocol, in 1997, the EU's member states had not only got used to complex representation structures—in this instance most of the negotiating was done by the Council presidency—but, more importantly, they had become quite used to accepting national restrictions due to European, and now global, rules and even to agreeing on differential treatments among themselves. In the case of Kyoto the intra-EU burden-sharing agreement allocated different commitments for the reduction of greenhouse gases to the member states; this strengthened the EU's negotiation position as it was able to commit itself to the toughest (collective) target of an 8 per cent reduction.[10] This target (together with the burden-sharing agreement) became binding when the Protocol came into force on 16 February 2005.

With the Kyoto targets expiring in 2012, international negotiations are now taking place under the UNFCCC with the goal of reaching a global agreement governing action beyond that date. With its 'independent commitment' of March 2007 to reduce by 2020 the greenhouse gas emissions of the EU by 20 per cent from the 1990 baseline and a promise of a 30 per cent cut if other countries joined in, the European Council 'was a major driving force behind the launch of negotiations on a global post-2012 climate agreement that was agreed by the parties to the UNFCCC in Bali in December 2007' (Oberthür and Roche Kelly 2008: 2).

In order to conclude these negotiations successfully in Copenhagen in 2009 the EU had to strengthen its claim to be a *credible* leader. Hence, it needed to show its capacity to meet its Kyoto commitments. With the CO_2 emission reductions stagnating and the implementation of crucial policies, such as the emissions trading scheme, the renewable energy directive, and the voluntary agreement with the automobile industry, showing serious problems, doubts had been getting louder (see Chapter 15). Furthermore, the EU needed to present concrete proposals for how to achieve the ambitious targets of reducing greenhouse gas emissions and boosting renewable energy production by 20 per cent by 2020. The prospect of losing credibility among the international partners spurred the internal policy developments related to climate change and at the end of the French Presidency in December 2008 it underpinned the deal among the member states and the endorsement of Parliament (see Box 13.3).

Conclusions

What—in a nutshell—are the key features of EU environmental policy-making? Empirically, it is a story of policy expansion, deepening, and institutionalization, which has been traced back to pragmatic and adaptive policy-makers in the Commission, a competitive dynamic between the member states, and the facilitating role of the Court, the EP, and societal interests. Processes of gradual institutionalization moved environmental policy principles from the status of programmatic statements into the formal *acquis* and finally into prominent treaty provisions. This prevents a rolling back, even at times of little political enthusiasm for new initiatives and rising criticism about high degrees of interventionism, excessive costs, and poor records of implementation especially during periods of economic recession. In this field, which is dominated by a regulatory policy mode, not contraction but adaptation and some experimentation with new or softer regulatory formats appear as the pattern of change, with the critics of yesterday becoming the reformers of tomorrow.

While the 2000s were not characterized by great enthusiasm inside the EU for environmental protection in general—not least due to the cautious approach adopted by the new member states—the climate change issue has the potential to rise to the next big idea in the Union. Not only in environmental policy, but also in areas such as energy, transport, agriculture, industry, international development, and neighbourhood policy, climate change has been responsible for enormous mobilization. In the issue area of climate change, EU environmental policy has become embedded in a larger project of policy coordination. Policy coordination across issue areas, which otherwise continues to be an unresolved problem in environmental policy, is helped by the presence of overarching policy targets and political will to act on at least one of the many dimensions of the climate issue—be it the implications for the environment, energy security, industrial modernization, or the EU's international profile. With regards to the latter, the EU now faces the challenge of providing credibility for its status of international 'actor' and its claim to leadership. Although the threat of economic crisis and negative competitive implications are proving to be a serious constraint to developing—and mainstreaming—environmental policy, the impact of the Union's reputational interest has been remarkable in both internal and external negotiations over the climate change package.

Notes

1 The new member states have received between three (Czech Republic) and ten (Poland) transitional arrangements; the transition periods vary between countries and environmental sectors (the longest periods apply to industrial pollution). Complete data can be accessed at the Commission website: *http://europa.eu.int/comm/enlargement/ negotiations/*.

2 Besides the committee chairmen, the *rapporteurs* assigned to individual policy proposals also play an important role in shaping the discussions within and between committees.

3 Its earlier name was Committee on the Environment, Public Health and Consumer Protection. Consumer protection has now moved to the Internal Market and Consumer Protection Committee (IMCO).

4 Ken Collins was chairman from 1979 until 1984 and 1989 until 1999, and vice-chairman from 1984 until 1989.

5 For both individuals and environmental NGOs this is effectively the only way to take legal action against the breach of EU law unless they are directly affected by the breach. This issue of access to the ECJ, which depends on the *'locus standi'* of the plaintiff, has created some public and legal controversy over the years, but it continues to be handled restrictively.

6 The Commission relies on the expertise of national as well as interest-group representatives in developing its policy proposals. In order to counterbalance the well-resourced industry influence it has actively contributed to the presence of environmental or consumer protection groups at the European level.

7 See the Commission's website at: *http://ec.europa.eu/environment/funding/finansup_arch.htm*.

8 The process of implementation can be described as (a) the formal transposition of the EU legislation (in the case of a directive), (b) notification of transposition, and (c) the actual application of the law 'on the ground'.

9 A complete list, dated 27 October 2006, can be found on the Commission homepage: *http://ec.europa.eu/environment/international_issues/pdf/agreements_en.pdf*.

10 Compared to 7 per cent for the US (albeit still hypothetical in the absence of a US signature), and 6 per cent for Japan.

 FURTHER READING

The regularly updated manual of EU environmental policy (Pallemaerts/IEEP) provides a brief overview of all EU environmental legislation and its political development; it pays particular attention to the British role in decision-making as well as implementation. Knill and Liefferink (2007) provide a good overview of EU environmental governance, including several case studies. A. Jordan (2005) puts together core articles on this topic. Jordan (2002*b*), Knill (2002), as well as Liefferink and Jordan (2004) look at the interplay between (selected) member states and EU policy-making—a topic only alluded to in this chapter. A useful overview of the EU's international role in environmental policy can be found in Bretherton and Vogler (2006). On new policy instruments in the EU and in the member states, see Jordan et al. (2003) and for implementation, Knill and Lenschow (2000). For an overview of the contributions all this research has made to our understanding of European integration, policy-making, and governance see Lenschow (2007).

Bretherton, C., and Vogler, J. (2006), *The EU as a Global Actor* (London: Routledge).

Jordan, A. (2005) (ed.), *Environmental Policy in the European Union: Actors, Institutions and Processes*, 2nd edn. (London: Earthscan).

Jordan, A. (2002b), *The Europeanization of British Environmental Policy: A Departmental Perspective* (Basingstoke: Palgrave Macmillan).

Jordan, A., Wurzel, R. K. W., and Zito, A. R. (2003), *'New' Instruments of Environmental Governance: National Experiences and Prospects* (London: Frank Cass).

Knill, C. (2002), *The Europeanisation of National Administrations: Patterns of Institutional Change and Persistence* (Cambridge: Cambridge University Press).

Knill, C., and Lenschow, A. (2000) (eds.), *Implementing EU Environmental Policy: New Directions and Old Problems* (Manchester: Manchester University Press).

Knill, C., and Liefferink, D. (2007) (eds.), *Environmental Politics in the European Union: Policy-making, Implementation and Patterns of Multi-level Governance* (Manchester: Manchester University Press).

Lenschow, A. (2007), 'Environmental Policy in the European Union: Bridging Policy, Politics and Polity Dimensions', in K. E. Jørgensen, M. A. Pollack, and B. Rosamond (eds.), *Handbook of European Union Politics* (London: Sage), 413–32.

Liefferink, D., and Jordan, A. (2004) (eds.), *Environmental Policy in Europe: The Europeanisation of National Environmental Policy* (London: Routledge).

Pallemaerts, M. (2009, continuously updated), (ed.), *Manual of Environmental Policy: The EU and Britain*, Institute of European Environmental Policy (IEEP) (Leeds: Maney Publishing).

CHAPTER 14

Biotechnology Policy

Between National Fears and Global Disciplines

Mark A. Pollack and Gregory C. Shaffer

▌ Summary

Over the past two decades the institutions of the European Union (EU) have emerged as the primary European regulators of genetically modified (GM) foods and crops, one of the most controversial and complex policy issues facing the EU today. Agricultural biotechnology presents three special challenges to the EU. It is multi-sectoral (cutting across multiple 'issue areas'); multi-level (cutting across national, supranational, and global levels of governance); and inherently concerned with risk regulation (which raises both scientific and ethical challenges). The EU adopted its first binding regulations on GM foods and crops in 1990. The implementation of these regulations proved controversial, provoking a revolt among member governments that responded with a de facto moratorium on the approval of new GM varieties. Faced with widespread governmental and public calls for a stricter and more comprehensive approach, after 2000 the EU engaged in a root-and-branch reform of its policies, setting out detailed rules on labelling for GM foods and the traceability of GM crops 'from farm to fork'. EU regulations have not developed in isolation, however. Instead, EU policies have been shaped by international pressures from the United States (US) and the World Trade Organization (WTO), which in 2006 ruled against the EU for 'undue delay' in its approval process and against member-state safeguards. The Commission has, since 2004, resumed approvals of selected GM foods and crops, but the issue remains one of the most deeply politicized and difficult of all EU policies.

Introduction[1]

Few issues of European law and policy excite as much attention and concern as the creation and marketing of genetically modified organisms (GMOs). Lauded by many scientists, policy élites, and members of the biotech industry as a scientific and economic step forward, GM foods and crops have also been rejected as unsafe or undesirable by many environmentalists and consumer advocates, and by the greater part of the European public. Into this controversy have stepped the institutions of the EU, which increasingly play the leading role in establishing the regulatory framework for the growing and marketing of GM foods and crops in the EU's twenty-seven member states.

In this chapter, we examine EU policy and policy-making in the area of biotechnology, with a specific focus on agricultural biotechnology—namely, the development and marketing of GM crops and foods. More specifically, the chapter summarizes both the *content* of the EU's rapidly evolving regulations, and the *process* whereby these regulations have been promulgated, disputed, comprehensively reformed, and imperfectly implemented over the past two decades. EU policy in this area is predominantly regulatory in character, setting the increasingly detailed regulatory framework within which GM foods and crops may be developed, introduced into the environment, and work their way into the food supply.

This chapter begins by examining the specific challenges of regulating biotechnology. It then provides a historical background to EU biotech policy, followed by a section on the problems of implementing the EU's early regulations. The chapter next examines the reform of the EU regulatory framework after 2000, the impact of international pressures from other states and from international institutions such as the WTO, and the tentative and deeply politicized resumption of approvals since 2004. The concluding section assesses EU biotech policy in relation to the typology of modes of governance discussed in Chapter 4, and in particular the 'regulatory mode'. The chapter does not deal with other issues associated with biotech policy, such as approving pharmaceuticals developed using genetic modification, developing patenting rules for new and controversial inventions, or the funding of biotechnology research.

Regulating GMOs: three challenges

GMOs pose three fundamental regulatory challenges, which are particularly pronounced in the EU. Biotechnology is an issue that is inherently *multi-sectoral*, requiring horizontal coordination across a range of issue areas; inherently *multi-level*, requiring vertical coordination across the national, supranational, and international arenas; and inherently concerned with *risk regulation,* requiring difficult, highly contested decisions about the role of science and politics in the assessment and management of risk to modern European societies.

A multi-sectoral challenge

The regulation of biotechnology is a complex and multi-sectoral policy, having implications for the single market, the common agricultural policy, the environment, consumer protection, trade policy, industrial policy, and research and technological development. The regulation of GMOs is viewed differently from the perspective of each of these issue areas. Moreover, different actors engage in the policy process in each of these areas. Thus each issue addresses the regulation of GMOs distinctively:

- With respect to the *internal market* the primary concern is the free movement of GM seeds, crops, and food within the EU. Indeed, the need to complete the internal market was claimed by the Commission as the primary legal basis of much of the EU's GMO legislation (see Chapter 5).

- From the perspective of industrial policy the Commission and others have sought to secure a regulatory environment conducive to the development of a European biotech industry able to compete with that of the US.

- In terms of the EU's research and technological development policy biotechnology has long been a priority area for collaborative cross-national scientific research.

- From an *environmental policy* perspective the concern is with potential negative environmental effects from growing GM crops, such as affecting related wild plant species or harming insects and birds. Largely for this reason, the Commission's Directorate-General for the Environment has played a leading role in the formulation of EU biotech policy, which has been negotiated and adopted predominantly by the Environment Council. This concern also played an important part in galvanizing the European Parliament's (EP) engagement with the issue.

- Marketing GM foods also raises questions of *food safety and consumer protection*, insofar as EU consumers worry about the safety of GM foods or simply insist on the right to know whether the foods they buy are genetically modified. Consumer concerns about food safety have played a key role in the controversies regarding the regulation and marketing of GM foods.

- From the perspective of the *common agricultural policy* (CAP; see Chapter 8) the key issues are how EU regulations affect which crops can be grown and feeds used and what procedures govern the production of GM crops.

- Finally, because the EU's GM regulations affect imports as well as local production, there is a significant *international trade policy* dimension to the policy. Indeed, the need to justify EU policies within the legal framework of the WTO has led to substantial reforms of EU biotech policy over the past decade, although it is controversial whether these changes constitute a 'watering down' or a 'trading up' of EU regulations (A. R. Young 2003).

As a multi-sectoral issue, the regulation of GMOs raises the challenge of coordinating policy-making horizontally among a large number of actors with diverse perspectives on the aims and the context of EU regulation. Not surprisingly, it has proven difficult for the Commission and the other EU institutions to coordinate policy-making across so many issue areas. The Commission has established, and repeatedly reformed, multi-sectoral working groups to coordinate policy across all DGs with an interest in the issue. The multi-sectoral nature of GMOs has also rallied a range of individuals and interest groups in organized opposition to GMOs from a variety of perspectives (environmental, food safety, and anti-globalization). From this hybrid mix of politics, GMO policy-making has emerged as a volatile issue.

A multi-level process: three arenas

The regulation of biotechnology has also been marked by a multi-level process which involves overlapping and sometimes conflicting regulations promulgated at the national, EU, and global levels. EU policy-makers, therefore, face not only the challenge of horizontal coordination across issue areas, but also the vertical coordination of EU policies with a diverse and politically sensitive set of national policies, and a growing body of international trade and environmental law governing GMOs. In fact, as we shall see, EU policy has faced sharp political and legal challenges from below (in the form of national revolts against the licensing of individual GM foods and crops) and from above (in the form of challenges from other countries within the WTO).

Prior to the adoption of the first EU regulations in 1990, biotech research and development (R&D) in Europe was regulated entirely at the national level. These national regulations varied across the member states, with countries such as Denmark and Germany imposing tight restrictions on genetic engineering research, with others, such as the UK and France, being more permissive, and relying mainly on self-regulation, and a large third group which had not yet adopted any regulations (Cantley 1995). The first binding EU directives on the contained use and deliberate release of GMOs featured substantial roles for the member governments, playing an important part in the initial approval of GM foods and crops, and retaining the ability to impose national-level safeguards against GMOs authorized at the EU level.

National and EU regulation of biotechnology, while aiming primarily at environmental protection, consumer protection, or food safety, also has important implications for international trade, since these regulations can serve as non-tariff barriers impeding the import of GM foods and crops into the EU. The question of biotech regulation as non-tariff barriers became an important political and legal issue from the late-1990s when US farmers rapidly adopted GM foods and crops only to find themselves unable to export them to the EU, where many fewer varieties had received regulatory approval (see below). The US placed increasing pressure on the Commission to rectify the situation, culminating in a WTO legal dispute and a judicial ruling against the EU in 2006. Within Europe, however, US pressure prompted a backlash from environmental, consumer, and agricultural groups, and from some member governments, further politicizing an already sensitive issue. Caught between these conflicting national and international pressures, the Commission sought, albeit with limited success, to reconcile the political demands of European citizens and national governments, on the one hand, with the legal obligations and political pressures from the international arena, on the other.

Risk regulation and legitimacy

The regulation of biotechnology also intersects with two broader, vitally important, and interrelated questions for the EU, namely the regulation of risk and the legitimacy of EU governance. In particular, risk regulation raises fundamental normative questions about the roles of science and politics in the management of risk, calling into question the legitimacy of EU decision-making in a context in which democratic control of EU institutions is widely considered to be inadequate (Scharpf 1999; Greven 2000).

In modern societies, governmental actors are frequently called upon to adopt regulations regarding the acceptable degree of risk posed to society by products or by industrial processes. Risk, in this context, refers to 'the combination of the likelihood (*probability*), and the harm (*adverse outcome*, e.g. mortality, morbidity, ecological damage, or impaired quality of life), resulting from exposure to an activity (*hazard*)' (Wiener and Rogers 2002: 320, emphasis in original). In principle, regulators faced with a novel product or process—such as the genetic modification of foods and crops—need to ascertain the potential harm caused by such activities, as well as the probability of such harm, before deciding on the legality or illegality of a product or process.

In practice, risk regulation frequently requires regulators to act in the face of *uncertainty* regarding the nature and extent of the risks posed by new products and processes. Frequently, regulators take *precautionary* measures, regulating or even banning products or activities, in the absence of complete information about the risks posed (Majone 2003).

Risk regulation in Europe took place largely at the national level until the 1980s, when EU institutions began to play an increasing role in harmonizing risk regulation across the member states. The EU's approach to risk regulation has evolved quite differently from that of the US (Vogel 2001). Whereas the former began with highly precautionary legislation in areas such as the environment, consumer protection, and worker health and safety, only to adopt scientific risk assessment and cost-benefit analysis more recently, regulators in the EU have become more precautionary and more risk-averse over time. Vogel and others argue that a key cause has been a series of European regulatory failures and crises over the past decades, including the BSE or 'mad cow' crisis, which have weakened public trust in EU regulators and scientific risk assessments, increased support for highly precautionary regulations, and called into question the *legitimacy* of EU regulations and EU institutions in European public opinion. Responding to this crisis of legitimacy, EU institutions have moved aggressively to overhaul EU risk regulation across a range of areas (see e.g. Commission 2000c; Wiener and Rogers 2002; and Majone 2002). Other scholars dispute Vogel's characterization, noting that the purported 'flip-flop' in US and EU approaches to risk regulation draws disproportionately on a few controversial issue areas, of which the regulation of GMOs is one (Wiener and Rogers 2002). Crucially for our purposes here, the issue of risk regulation in general—and the regulation of GMOs in particular—poses serious challenges to the EU's regulatory capacity and legitimacy (see e.g. Neyer 2000; Vos 2000; Joerges 2001b; Vogel 2001; Chalmers 2003; and Majone 2003).

Historical origins of EU biotech policy

The 1957 Treaty of Rome (EEC) made no explicit mention of environmental protection or food safety, let alone biotechnology. Since the late 1970s, however, the EU has developed de facto policies on biotechnology as policies on R&D, agriculture, food safety, and the internal market have 'spilled over' into the regulation of the content and labelling of GM foods and crops.

Genetic engineering is a technology used to isolate genes from one organism, manipulate them in the laboratory, and inject them into another organism. This technology, also known as recombinant DNA (rDNA) research, first emerged as a concern for national and international regulators in the 1970s, as biological scientists began making crucial advances in rDNA research (Cantley 1995; Patterson 2000). During this period, from the 1970s through to the mid-1980s, the development and marketing of GM foods and crops was a distant goal, and regulators in

Europe and elsewhere focused primarily on issues relating to laboratory research and the development of a competitive biotech industry. In 1978 the DG for Science, Research and Development (then DG XII) proposed a Community R&D programme in molecular biology, together with a draft directive requiring notification and prior authorization by national authorities for all biotech research. This latter proposal was withdrawn by the Commission in 1980, in favour of a non-binding 1982 Council Resolution calling for notification of rDNA research to national authorities. Commission concerns about the competitiveness of the EU's biotech industry remained, however, and in 1983 it incorporated biotechnology into its multi-annual Framework Programme for research and technological development (for a chronology of EU GMO regulation, see Box 14.1).

By the mid-1980s, with the rapid development of genetic engineering and the early efforts to regulate biotechnology among the member governments, the Commission began to explore more actively the development of a Community framework for biotech regulation. The Commission created inter-departmental coordinating bodies, notably the Biotechnology Steering Committee (1984) and the Biotechnology Regulation Inter-service Committee (1985), to determine a new regulatory approach (Patterson 2000: 324–32). Within these groupings, the centre of gravity gradually shifted away from DG XII, and towards other DGs, particularly Environment (DG XI), which became involved in the late 1980s, as biotechnology moved increasingly out of the laboratory and toward releases into the environment and the marketing of GM foods and crops. With DG Environment taking the lead the Commission in 1986 released 'A Community Framework for the Regulation of Biotechnology', which laid out the Commission's rationale for a European regulatory regime and its plans for specific EU regulations (Commission 1986).

The 'Deliberate Release' Directive 90/220

In May 1988 the Commission proposed two new directives, which ultimately became Directive 90/219 on the Contained Use of Genetically Modified Micro-organisms and Directive 90/220 on the Deliberate Release into the Environment of Genetically Modified Organisms (Commission 1988). The former relates primarily to the safety procedures for laboratory research involving genetic modification, whereas the latter concerned the release of GMOs from the laboratory into the environment, including field trials and the cultivation and marketing of GM foods and crops. We concentrate on Directive 90/220 because it emerged during the 1990s as the primary, and most controversial, piece of legislation governing the approval and marketing of GM foods and crops.

Under Directive 90/220, a manufacturer or importer seeking to market a GMO or release it into the environment had to apply for permission to the competent national authority of an EU member state, providing an extensive scientific risk assessment for the GMO in question. The member state considered the application, either rejecting or accepting it. In the case of a favourable opinion, the dossier was forwarded to the Commission and to the other member governments, each of which

BOX 14.1	Key events in EU biotech regulation, 1978–2008
1978	Commission proposes Directive requiring prior notification and authorization of GM research (withdrawn 1980)
1983	Biotechnology included in EU Framework R&D Programme
1984	Commission forms Biotech Steering Committee
1986	Commission report, *A Community Framework for the Regulation of Biotechnology*
1988	Commission proposes twin directives on Contained Use and Deliberate Release of GMOs
1990	Council adopts Directives 90/219 and 90/220, establishing legal framework for the approval and marketing of GM foods and crops
1996 (March)	Start of BSE Crisis, questioning of EU food safety regulation
1997 (Jan)	Council adopts Novel Foods Regulation
1997 (Jan)	Commission approves sale of GM maize; three member states invoke safeguard clause
1998 (Oct)	Start of de facto moratorium on approval of new GM varieties
1999 (June)	Declaration of moratorium on GM approvals by five member states
2000 (Jan)	White Paper on Food Safety
2000 (Jan)	White Paper on the Precautionary Principle
2000 (Jan)	Cartagena Protocol on Biosafety Adopted
2001 (March)	Council and EP adopt Directive 2001/18, replacing 90/220, on deliberate release of GMOs
2002 (Jan)	Establishment of European Food Safety Authority
2003 (May)	US launches WTO complaint over EU regulation of GMOs
2003 (Sept)	Council and EP adopt Regulation 1830/2003 on Traceability and Labelling of GMOs
2003 (Sept)	Council and EP adopt Regulation 1829/2003 on Genetically Modified Food and Feed
2004 (Apr)	Entry into force of Regulations 1829/2003 and 1830/2003
2004 (May)	Commission ends moratorium with approval of Bt-11 maize
2005 (May)	Commission 'orientation debate', decision to press ahead with new approvals, challenge member-state bans
2005 (June)	Environment Council rejects Commission effort to overturn national safeguard bans
2006 (Sept)	WTO ruling in EC-Biotech dispute
2007 (July)	Member states fail to agree on approval of GM potato for cultivation
2007 (Nov)	EU Environment Commissioner Dimas proposes to deny approval of two GM maize varieties for cultivation
2008 (Jan)	France announces new national ban on MON810
2008 (May)	Removal of Austrian safeguard ban on sale of two GM varieties
	Commission delays approval of seven new GM varieties pending new studies
2008 (July)	French EU Presidency announces creation of group to consider strengthening EU regulations on GMOs.

could raise objections. If no objection was raised, then the member state carrying out the original evaluation formally approved the product, which could be marketed throughout the EU.

If one or more member states raised an objection, however, a decision would have to be taken at the EU level. The Commission, acting on the basis of an opinion from its scientific committees, adopted a draft decision. This draft decision was forwarded to a regulatory committee of member-state representatives, who could approve the decision by a qualified majority vote. If the committee did not approve the decision, however, it would be sent to the Council of Ministers, which could approve the Commission decision by QMV or reject it by a *unanimous* vote. If the Council failed to act within three months, the directive provided that 'the proposed measures shall be adopted by the Commission' (Art. 21).

Finally—and significantly in light of later developments—the directive provided that a member state could, on the basis of new evidence about risks to human health or the environment, 'provisionally restrict or prohibit the use and/or sale of that product on its territory'. The member state in question would be required to inform the Commission, which could approve or reject the member-state measures, again after consulting a regulatory committee of member-state representatives. Such restrictions, referred to as 'safeguard bans', would later become an important, and controversial, feature of EU regulation in this area.

The Novel Foods Regulation

In 1997 Directive 90/220 was supplemented by Regulation 258/97, the so-called Novel Foods Regulation, which created an authorization procedure for 'novel foods', similar to that of Directive 90/220. It defined 'novel foods' as all foods and food ingredients that had 'not hitherto been used for human consumption to a significant degree within the Community', which included foods that were genetically modified and foods produced from, but not containing, GMOs (e.g. oils processed from GM crops, but no longer containing any traces of GM material). The regulation also imposed requirements for novel foods that were authorized for marketing, including the labelling of foods containing GMOs or derived from GMOs, provided that the latter were deemed 'no longer equivalent' to their conventional counterparts. Significantly, however, the regulation created a simplified procedure for foods derived from, but no longer containing, GMOs, provided these remained 'substantially equivalent' to existing foods in terms of 'their composition, nutritional value, metabolism, intended use and the level of undesirable substances contained therein' (Art. 3). In practice, this provision would prove important, as member governments would approve a number of products derived from GMOs as being 'substantially equivalent' to their conventional counterparts. Finally, and significantly in terms of later developments, the regulation (like Directive 90/220) contained a safeguard clause allowing member states, 'as a result of new information or a reassessment of existing information' to 'temporarily restrict or suspend the trade in and use of the food or food ingredient in question in its territory' (Art. 12).

The politics of implementation: member-state revolt and international reaction

To understand successive attempts to regulate agricultural biotechnology in the EU, and the subsequent difficulties of implementation, we need to place these in the context of other developments in the mid-1990s. Central to this political context was the BSE food-safety scandal, which struck in 1996. In March 1996, the British government revealed a possible connection between the human illness, Creutzfeldt–Jakob's disease, and bovine spongiform encephalopathy (BSE), known as 'mad cow disease'. BSE infected some 150,000 cattle in the UK, triggering a wide-scale slaughter of cattle, a European ban on the export of British beef, the collapse of beef sales throughout Europe, and a loss of consumer confidence in regulatory officials. While the ban on British beef was eventually rescinded, the BSE scandal raised the question of risk regulation 'to the level of high politics, and indeed of constitutional significance' (Chalmers 2003: 534–8), generating extraordinary public awareness of food-safety issues and widespread public distrust of regulators and scientific assessments.

It was in this political context that GM crops were first commercially introduced in the US and Europe. In April 1996, within a month of the ban on British beef, the Commission approved the sale of GM soya products over the objections of many member states. In November 1996, GM soy was imported from the US to the EU, spurring widespread protest by environmental groups. Media coverage and public debate about GM foods, therefore, began just as the BSE food crisis struck.

Two other critical events occurred in late 1996. In December, a Scottish scientist announced to the world the first successful reproduction of a cloned mammal, a sheep named 'Dolly'. The announcement spurred ethical challenges to biotechnological research. Also in December, the US and Canada lodged complaints with the WTO challenging the EU's ban on hormone-treated beef, on the grounds that it constituted a disguised barrier to trade and was not justified on the basis of a scientific risk assessment. The WTO subsequently ruled against the EU, and, when the EU failed to comply with the ruling, authorized the US and Canada to retaliate with trade sanctions equivalent to their trading losses, which they did, imposing trade sanctions worth US$116.8 million and CND$1.3 million per year.

The close succession of these events illustrates how the popular understanding of GM products in Europe became associated with consumer anxieties related to food-safety crises, distrust of regulators and scientific assessments, disquiet over corporate control of agricultural production, ethical unease over GM techniques, environmental concerns, and anger over the use by the US of international trade rules to attempt to force 'unnatural' foods on Europeans. A widespread cross-sectoral movement organized to oppose GMOs in Europe, bringing together environmentalists, consumers, and small farmers. The British media dubbed GM products 'Frankenstein' foods, playing on fears that scientists and public agencies could not control the release of GM products. Negative European attitudes toward GM crops and foods rose rapidly. In early 1996, 46 per cent of French respondents opposed GMOs, a figure that rose to 65 per cent in 1999 and 75 per cent in 2002. Similarly, over 80 per cent of Germans expressed negative opinions about GMOs by late 1998 (Gaskell et al. 2003).

In the midst of the fray, in January 1997, the Commission approved the sale of another GM food crop (Bt-maize), over the objection or abstention of all but one of the then fifteen member governments (Commission 1996; Bradley 1998: 212). Member governments did not, however, simply accept the Commission's decision. They undermined its implementation, invoking the safeguard clause of Directive 90/220. Austria was the first to act, promptly prohibiting the cultivation and marketing of the GM maize variety in February 1997. Luxembourg followed suit in March. Member-state deployment of safeguard bans grew, undermining the central purpose of Directive 90/220 to create a single market for GM crops under a harmonized regulatory system. By January 2004, Austria, France, Greece, Germany, Luxembourg, and the UK had invoked nine safeguard bans. Italy invoked an analogous safeguard procedure under Article 12 of the Novel Foods Regulation (Regulation 258/97) to ban the sale of food products containing ingredients from four varieties of GM maize.

Opponents of GMOs not only worked the political process, but also took their battle to the market-place. Under pressure from potential consumer boycotts of their foods, many large European retailers, such as the UK-based Sainsbury, pledged that their foods would be GM-free. Thus, although GM soya and maize varieties had been legally authorized for marketing throughout the EU, they were subject to resistance by both consumers and retailers and were barely commercialized (Vogel 2001: 11).

This widespread resistance to the approval of new GM varieties among both governments and civil society underlines that any account of EU biotech policy-making must address the politics of *implementation* as well as the *legislative* politics. Indeed, in the case of agricultural biotechnology, member-state resistance proved sufficient to stymie the implementation of Directive 90/220 for a period of years. More specifically, in June 1999, responding to the popular backlash against GMOs, Denmark, France, Greece, Italy, and Luxembourg declared the need to impose a moratorium on all approvals of GM products, pending the adoption of a new and stricter regulatory system:

The Governments of the following Member States, in exercising the powers vested in them regarding the growing and placing on the market of genetically modified organisms (GMOs), . . . point to the importance of the Commission submitting without delay full draft rules ensuring labeling and traceability of GMOs and GMO-derived products and state that, pending the adoption of such rules, in accordance with preventive and precautionary principles, they will take steps to have any new authorizations for growing and placing on the market suspended (Council of the European Union 1999*b*).

For nearly six years, from October 1998 (when two GM varieties of carnations were approved) to May 2004, no GM varieties were authorized for sale in the EU market, the only exception being for foods derived from GM varieties deemed 'substantially equivalent' to traditional foods under the 1997 Novel Foods Regulation. Rather, member governments within the Council would obstruct the authorization of any new GM variety, pending the adoption of a revised EU regulatory framework.

The reform of EU policy 'from farm to fork'

By the end of the 1990s, the Commission found itself between a rock and a hard place, or rather between conflicting pressures from the international level above and from EU domestic politics below. Domestically, the Commission faced not only widespread opposition to GM foods and crops, but also a more general backlash from member governments and from the EP, which eventually triggered the 1999 resignation of the Santer Commission (see Chapter 9). Under the circumstances, the Commission did not wish to further provoke the member governments and the EP by using its powers under existing regulatory procedures to approve GM crops over their objections.

At the international level, however, the Commission faced countervailing pressures, not least from the US, which opposed the EU's de facto moratorium and called for a loosening, rather than tightening, of the EU regulatory framework. By contrast with the EU's precautionary approach, US regulatory policy tends to treat GM crops and foods as 'substantially equivalent' to non-GM varieties, and the vast majority of GM research, development, and production occur in the US, where around two-thirds of all GM crops are grown. The EU's moratorium, therefore, led to cries of protectionism and calls for retaliation from US farmers. GMO regulation in the EU faced not only the challenge of multi-sectoral coordination, but also a multi-level one.

Facing pressure on multiple fronts, the Commission pursued a two-part strategy. It sought (first) to tighten and 'complete' the EU's regulatory framework so as to reassure member states and their constituents that adequate controls were in place, which (second) would enable the resumption of approvals and removal of member-state safeguard bans in order to assuage international pressure.

In January 2000, therefore, the Commission (2000*b*) issued a preliminary policy initiative in the form of a White Paper, in which it proposed that the EU overhaul its food safety system and establish a new centralized EU agency, the European Food Safety Authority (EFSA). The White Paper's general approach to risk regulation in the food sector divided 'risk assessment' from 'risk management'. Specialized scientific committees within the new agency would conduct risk assessments, and provide food-safety information to consumers and operate a rapid-alert system in conjunction with member-state authorities to respond to food-safety emergencies. Risk *management*, concerning what level of risk is acceptable, in contrast, would remain under the control of the EU's political bodies. In an annexed 'action plan', the Commission listed over eighty proposed food-safety-related measures to adopt, including amendments to Directive 90/220 and the Novel Foods Regulation.

The following month, the Commission (2000*c*) issued a Communication on the precautionary principle, indicative of a more risk-averse approach in an increasingly politicized domain. The Commission declared that the 'precautionary principle' would be applied whenever decision-makers identify 'potentially negative effects resulting from a phenomenon, product or process' and 'a scientific evaluation of the risk . . . makes it impossible to determine with sufficient certainty the risk in question [on account] of the insufficiency of the data, their inconclusiveness or imprecise nature'. It stressed that 'judging what is an "acceptable" level of risk for society is an eminently *political* responsibility' (Commission's emphasis).

In 1998 the Commission proposed a directive to replace Directive 90/220, which was eventually enacted in 2001. In the wake of the BSE crisis, the Commission had in 1997 reorganized its internal handling of food-safety matters within a recast (and renamed) DG for Health and Consumer Protection (known by its French acronym, SANCO) (Skogstad 2003). Once more, the Commission was divided between those who desired less-restrictive authorization and labelling requirements (DG Industry, DG Research, and DG Trade) and those who sought stricter controls (such as DG Environment and DG SANCO) (Stewart and Johanson 1999: 273). The leading players were DG ENV and DG SANCO, both of which favoured a precautionary approach to risk regulation.

Both the EP and Council pressed the Commission for further regulatory controls. The majority of members of the EP insisted on tighter labelling requirements and lower thresholds for acceptable levels of trace amounts of GMOs in products sold in the EU. The member governments varied in their views, with some determined that no GM crops would be grown in their territories (such as Austria and Luxembourg) and others torn between the demands of GM opponents and those of the biotech sector (such as Germany and the UK).

The resulting legislation, Directive 2001/18, was adopted in March 2001 by co-decision. The need to reassure those member governments that desired stringent regulation led to a ratcheting up of EU regulatory requirements (A. R. Young 2004). The directive tightened requirements on commercial applicants and member governments, requiring more extensive environmental risk assessment, further information concerning the conditions of the release, and monitoring and remedial plans. Although touted by the EP's *rapporteur* David Bowe as 'the toughest laws on GMOs in the whole world,' the directive did not satisfy the most GM-sceptical member governments, which insisted on continuing the moratorium and maintaining national safeguard bans, pending still more stringent EU regulations.

Faced with this continuing resistance, in 2001 the Commission proposed two additional legislative instruments: on the labelling and traceability of GM foods and their use in food and feed. Adopted after drawn-out bargaining between the Commission, Council, and EP, both measures took the form of regulations, and not directives, placing authority predominantly in the hands of EU institutions. Regulation 1829/2003, on the authorization of GMOs in food and feed, replaced the provisions of Directive 2001/18 governing the authorization for marketing and the labelling of GMO foods and crops. Regulation 1830/2003, in turn, created new rules on the traceability of GM products throughout the production and distribution process. Both regulations became effective in April 2004 (see Table 14.1).

Regulation 1829/2003 established a more centralized procedure for authorizing the release and marketing of new GM varieties. In this way, the Commission hoped to manage divergent challenges from member governments and the US. The procedural scheme at the EU level became more centralized in two primary respects. First, although the application process still begins when an operator submits an application dossier to the competent authority of a member government, that authority now immediately provides the dossier to the EFSA, which in turn issues the risk assessment, working in conjunction with the competent national authority and an EU reference laboratory. The remainder of the new authorization procedure is largely similar to that provided under Directives 90/220 and 2001/18 (see Box 14.2). Any authorization of a GM variety, however, is now limited to a term of ten years, although authorizations may be renewed.

TABLE 14.1   EU legislation governing GMOs and GM products as of June 2009

Step-by-step activities in the production process	Applicable EU legislation
GMO research in laboratories	Contained Use Directive 90/219
GMO experimental releases (trials)	Directive 2001/18
GMO environmental releases for crops	Regulation 1829/2003 and Directive 98/95/EC crops (common seed catalogue)
Authorization of marketing of GM seeds (for environmental releases for crops)	Regulation 1829/2003 and Directive 98/95/EC
Authorization of marketing of GM food and feed	Regulation 1829/2003
Labelling of GM seed, food, and feed	Regulation 1829/2003
Traceability and labelling of GM products	Regulation 1830/2003

BOX 14.2	**Authorization process for GM food and feed under Regulation 1829/2003**

1. An operator submits an application to the competent authority from one of the member states.
2. The member state provides the file to new European Food Safety Authority (EFSA).
3. The EFSA provides a copy to the other member states and the Commission, and makes a summary of the file publicly available.
4. Within six months, the EFSA submits its opinion, based on risk assessments, to the Commission, the member states, and the applicant, and, after the deletion of any confidential information, makes it publicly available.
5. The Commission is then to issue a draft decision, which may vary from EFSA's opinion, based on the regulatory committee consisting of member state representatives.
6. The committee is to deliver its opinion on the Commission's proposed decision by a qualified majority. If the committee delivers no opinion or a negative opinion, the Commission must submit its proposal to the Council. If the Council does not adopt (or indicate its opposition to) the Commission's proposal (but this time by a qualified majority vote, as opposed to a unanimous one), then the proposed decision 'shall be adopted by the Commission'.

The second centralizing aspect of the regulation is that it restricts the grounds on which member states may ban GMOs unilaterally as a 'safeguard measure'. A member state may adopt 'interim protective measures . . . where it is evident that products authorized . . . are likely to constitute a serious risk to human health, animal health or the environment', provided it first informs the Commission of the 'emergency' situation and the Commission does not act (Scott 2003: 224).

Regulation 1829/2003 also broadened the scope of product coverage in two ways. First, GM animal feed is covered for the first time. Second, the new regulation also covers food and feed that does not contain, or consist of, GMOs, but nonetheless is 'derived', in whole or in part, from GMOs, or contains ingredients 'derived in whole or in part from GMOs'. The former 'simplified procedure' of the Novel Foods Regulation has thus been eliminated.

One of the most controversial elements of the new regulation was the establishment of thresholds for the 'adventitious' presence of GM ingredients below which labelling requirements do not apply. Recognizing that it is practically impossible to ensure that any shipment is entirely free of GM material because of the way crops are threshed, stored, and transported, the Commission initially proposed a threshold of 1 per cent GM material. Environmental and consumer groups, the EP, and several member governments called for lower thresholds. European biotech companies and the US government, by contrast, criticized the threshold as unrealistic, costly, and scientifically unjustified. These divisions were mirrored in the Council, where the UK favoured the Commission's proposed 1 per cent threshold, while Austria at the other extreme favoured thresholds as low as 0.1 per cent. The final wording, in a compromise, established two distinct thresholds. First, food products would have to be labelled if they contain material from EU-approved GMOs 'in a proportion no higher than 0.9 per cent of the food ingredients considered individually . . . provided that this presence is adventitious or technically unavoidable'. Second, during a three-year transition period, a stricter threshold of 0.5 per cent applied for GMOs not yet approved for environmental release in the EU after which no residues of non-approved GMOs are allowed in food or feed products—the so-called 'zero tolerance' policy.

Regulation 1830/2003, finally, included a more centralized framework for tracing GM products, responsibility for which had previously been left to the member states. The regulation required the Commission to establish a system of unique identifiers for each GMO in order 'to trace GMOs and products produced from GMOs at all stages of their placing on the market through the production and distribution chain'. More specifically, producers must collect and retain data on the GM content of foods and crops one step upstream and one step downstream in the distribution chain for five years. These strict traceability requirements have been bitterly criticized by many US producers, as well as by some European producers. The Commission, however, justified these requirements as vital to the EU labelling system and for any future recalls of GM foods or crops.

By the end of 2003, in sum, the EU regulatory framework for GMOs had been comprehensively reformed, and neither the aborted Constitutional Treaty nor the Treaty of Lisbon, ratified in November 2009, was expected to result in any significant changes to that framework. Once again, however, *implementation* of EU GMO legislation would remain controversial, both domestic and internationally.

The international context

Throughout this period, EU policy was influenced, at least in part, by external challenges, in particular from the US, which exerted bilateral pressure in the shadow of the rules of the WTO. The WTO Agreement on Sanitary and Phytosanitary (SPS) Measures requires that regulatory measures are based on scientific risk assessments and are not disguised restrictions on trade. Starting in 1998—when the EU tightened its labelling requirements for GM foods, stopped approving new GM varieties, and effectively shut down the marketing of varieties that had been approved—the US threatened to lodge a complaint with the WTO. The US government hesitated for years to bring such a case, fearing consumer backlash against GMOs and against the WTO itself. In May of 2003, however, the Bush Administration's forbearance gave way, and the US, joined by Argentina and Canada, brought a WTO complaint against the EU, alleging that its de facto moratorium on new approvals, as well as the national bans on approved varieties, constituted a violation of WTO law and specifically of the SPS Agreement.

Significantly, the US and other complainants did not challenge the EU's legislative framework for GM approvals as such, nor did they challenge (despite loud complaints from producers) the EU's labelling and traceability provisions. Instead, the complaints focused on the EU's implementation of its own regulatory framework, challenging three specific actions: (1) the EU's de facto 'general moratorium' on new approvals; (2) 'product-specific moratoria', or failure to approve particular GM varieties found to be safe by the relevant EU scientific bodies; and (3) the persistent use of 'safeguard provisions' by some EU member states to ban GM varieties that had been approved as safe by the EU's own scientific experts. In all three cases, the complainants argued, the EU had failed to base its regulatory decisions on scientific risk assessments as required under Article 5.1 of the SPS Agreement, and those decisions were therefore inconsistent with EU obligations under WTO law.

The EU, by contrast, denied the existence of any moratorium, maintaining that new approvals needed to wait until after the completion of the EU's regulatory framework. It further argued that the SPS Agreement did not apply (or applied only in part) to the regulation of GMOs, since the EU was concerned with the protection of its environment which fell outside of the SPS Agreement's scope.

In September 2006, the WTO dispute-settlement panel issued its decision (see Pollack and Shaffer 2009: 177–234). The panel expressly avoided examining many controversial issues, and most particularly 'whether biotech products in general are safe or not' and 'whether the biotech products at issue in this dispute are "like" their conventional counterparts'. On the specific questions raised in the complaints, the panel found in favour of the complainants, although largely on procedural rather than substantive grounds. It held that the EU had engaged in 'undue delay' in its approval process in violation of Article 8 and Annex C of the SPS Agreement, which increased pressure on the EU to proceed with specific decisions on the many GMO approval applications already in the pipeline, even though it had resumed approvals prior to the ruling (see below).

Regarding safeguards enacted by EU member states, the panel again found in favour of the complainants, ruling that all of the national safeguard bans violated the EU's and member states' substantive obligations under article 5.1 of the SPS Agreement because they were 'not based on a risk assessment'. It noted in particular that the EU's 'relevant scientific committees had evaluated the potential risks . . . and had provided a positive opinion' on the GM varieties. Thus, while the panel refrained from substantively evaluating decisions at the EU level, it expressly found that the member-state bans were inconsistent with the EU's WTO commitments. In so doing, the WTO panel decision appeared to strengthen the position of the Commission, which had long sought to restart and regularize the approval process and challenge and remove the member states' safeguard bans.

The end of the moratorium—but not of controversy

With the 'completion' of the EU's legislative framework, and in the face of a pending legal dispute with the US, the Commission at long last sought to enforce existing legislation, resume approvals of new GM varieties after the six-year moratorium, and end the national bans on varieties that had been assessed as safe by EFSA. Nevertheless, the implementation of the EU's new rules faced continuing political contestation from both interest groups and member governments, resulting in a pattern of formal voting and deadlock within both the regulatory committee and the Council. Neither the 'completion' of the EU's regulatory structure nor the external pressure generated by the US and the WTO appear to have been sufficient to change the contentious nature of GMO regulation in the EU. If we look at three key developments—the pattern of contested approvals for new varieties for marketing and use as food and feed, the intense controversy over the possible approval of new varieties for cultivation, and the Commission's ongoing efforts to overturn the existing national bans—the story of GM regulation since the WTO decision remains as deeply politicized as ever (Pollack and Shaffer 2009: 245–61).

The resumption of approvals

In May 2004, the EU resumed approvals of new GM varieties. By that time, the Commission had received twenty-two requests for approval of GM varieties—eleven involving import-processing only, and eleven for cultivation. With the completion of the new regulatory framework, the Commission moved to resume approvals of new GM varieties. In November 2003, it proposed approving the importation and marketing (but not the cultivation) of a variety of GM maize (Bt-11 sweet corn), for which EFSA had delivered a favourable opinion. The regulatory committee, however, refused to approve the Commission's proposal, so the matter was referred to the Council, which was given until the end of April to act. On 26 April 2004, a divided Agriculture Council failed to reach agreement on the Commission's proposal with six states voting in favour, six opposed, and three abstaining (Commission Press Release IP/04/663 of 19 May 2004). In the absence of a decision by the Council, the Commission was able to adopt the proposal the following month—the first new approval of a GM variety in nearly six years.

Despite this apparent breakthrough, critics of EU policy noted that the Commission's decision had been taken over the objections of a bloc of implacably hostile member governments, and a chorus of condemnation from European environmentalists and consumer groups, with no guarantee that additional approvals would follow or that EU risk managers would continue to be guided by the scientific risk assessments carried out by EFSA. Subsequent approval procedures appeared to support this cautious interpretation of the 'end' of the moratorium. Also in May 2004, for example, a similar pattern emerged when the Environment Council of the newly enlarged EU of twenty-five states met to consider the Commission's recommendation to approve the importation and marketing of another Monsanto variety, NK603 corn. Again the Council was divided, with nine member states (including four of the new members) reportedly voting against, nine in favour, and seven abstaining (*EUobserver.com*, 29 June 2004). Although the Commission approved NK603 in July 2004, this case once more demonstrated the persistent divisions among the member governments on new approvals.

This pattern would be repeated again and again in the following years. The Commission, after consulting EFSA, would propose a draft decision authorizing the importation and placing on the market of various new GM crops, and in each and every case from May 2004 through the end of 2008, the relevant comitology committees deadlocked (i.e. failed to reach a qualified majority for or against approval), resulting in the submission of the draft decision to the Council. It is worth stressing that such deadlocks are extremely unusual within the EU's expert committees. In its report on the workings of comitology committees for 2005, for example, the Commission noted that out of 2,637 draft decisions submitted to the various EU expert committees that year, only eleven of those decisions (less than 0.5 per cent) were referred to the Council for a decision—and six of these involved the authorization of GM foods and crops (Commission 2006*h*)! The pattern of deadlock, moreover, persisted in the Council (meeting variously in its Environmental and Agriculture formations), which failed repeatedly to reach qualified majorities for or against the approval of one new GM variety after another, leaving the Commission in each case to authorize the new variety, to choruses of condemnation from member governments, members of the European Parliament, and environmental and consumer groups.

Overall, in the years between the resumption of approvals in May 2004 and the end of 2008, the Commission approved some seventeen new GM varieties for use as food and feed (Pollack and Shaffer 2009: 254), marking a clear end to the moratorium of the 1998–2004 period. In each case, however, the decision had been taken by the Commission after both the Standing Committee on the Food Chain and Animal Health and the Council of Ministers had failed to reach a qualified majority either for or against the varieties in question, and each and every approval remained deeply controversial.

These decisions, moreover, seemed to dispel initial expectations that the new member states—several of which were already engaged in small-scale cultivation of GM crops, often without adequate controls—might serve as a 'Trojan horse' for the United States and the biotech industry. Instead, it seems clear that the ambivalence toward agricultural biotechnology in 'old' Europe is shared in the public opinion and governmental positions of the EU's new members as well. A survey of citizens of the EU's ten new members in relation to these countries' pending accession found that 68 per cent held negative views toward GMOs, a result roughly similar to surveys of citizens of the existing members (*The Economist*, 3 April 2004: 5). One of the new member states, Hungary, proceeded to adopt some of the strongest anti-GMO policies in the EU, issuing a safeguard ban on Monsanto's modified YieldGuard corn (MON810) and adopting a strict coexistence law that would require growers of GM crops to establish 400-metre buffer zones between GM and conventional crops and obtain the written consent of neighbouring farmers. In 2006 another new member, Poland, ran afoul of the Commission, when its parliament adopted a strict law forbidding the cultivation and marketing of all GMOs, leading the Commission to initiate infringement proceedings against Poland for violation of EU law. Enlargement, in short, seems to have replicated the EU's existing divisions on a larger scale, rather than changing those divisions in any significant way.

Approvals for cultivation: dividing the member states and the Commission

Even more controversial than the approval of GM varieties for marketing have been applications for the *cultivation* of new GM crops in the EU. In the first of these, the German chemicals firm BASF sought permission to cultivate a potato genetically modified to produce a higher starch content for industrial use in paper. Although BASF's initial application was only for industrial use, and despite a favourable risk assessment by EFSA and a proposed approval by the Commission, the relevant regulatory committee, consulted in December 2006, deadlocked, leaving the decision in limbo (*Financial Times*, 19 December 2006: 19). Seven months later, in July 2007, the Council also failed to reach a qualified majority on the cultivation of the so-called 'amflora' potato, which put the decision once again into the hands of the Commission. As one EU official noted, 'These are elected officials and they have to face general unease at home about GMOs. They are passing the buck to the Commission, which is between a rock and a hard place on this issue' (*New York Times*, 24 July 2007: A3). Indeed, by contrast with previous approvals, the Commission did not move promptly to approve the BASF potato in the following months, raising charges that Environment Commissioner Stavros Dimas was 'prevaricating' (Mortished 2008).

Also in 2007, the Commission received applications for the cultivation of two GM maize varieties—Syngenta's Bt11 and Pioneer/Dow's 1507—that had previously been approved for import and marketing in the EU. The EFSA had issued positive opinions on both varieties in 2005. Rather than adopt a draft opinion for consideration by the member states, however, the Commission asked EFSA in April 2006 to consider more explicitly the potential long-term effects of GMOs on the environment and called on it to review its decision on the two maize varieties in question. In November 2007, Dimas (whose DG Environment was in charge of the file within the Commission) reportedly produced a draft decision for circulation within the Commission that called for the rejection of both varieties. Calling the 'potential damage to the environment irreversible', and citing scientific studies not considered by EFSA in its opinion, the draft concluded that 'the level of risk generated by the cultivation of this product is unacceptable' (*International Herald Tribune*, 22 November 2007).

Dimas's draft decision, widely reported in the media, would represent the first time that a GM crop had been rejected by the Commission, despite a positive opinion from EFSA. It attracted accolades from anti-GMO campaigners and intense criticism from outside and within the Commission, where a number of Commissioners, and their respective DGs, take a more favourable view of biotechnology and were seeking to open up the approval process. Trade Commissioner Peter Mandelson and Agriculture Commissioner Mariann Fischer Boel, in particular, called for regularization of the approval process and for a reconsideration of the EU's 'zero-tolerance' policy toward the adventitious presence of non-EU-approved GMOs in shipments to the EU. While not explicitly proposing a relaxation of the rules, Fischer Boel repeatedly noted the costs of the policy for the EU, which relies heavily on imports of corn and soy for animal feed, the prices of which had risen dramatically as a result of the zero-tolerance policy (*European Report*, 29 November 2007).

Facing controversy on all three decisions, the Commission decided in May 2008 to return all three pending applications for cultivation (the Amflora potato and the Bt11 and 1507 maize varieties) to EFSA for further evaluation, with the expectation that the approval processes would proceed once EFSA confirmed their safety (O'Donnell 2008).

The following year, after EFSA once again affirmed their safety, the Commission did put forward the two GM maize varieties, Bt-11 and Pioneer 1507, for approval for cultivation, only to have the Standing Committee on the Food Chain and Animal Health deadlock yet again, with six member states voting in favour and the rest abstaining or voting against approval, sending the decision for further consideration in the Council of Ministers (*Inside US Trade*, 27 February 2009). By contrast, the Commission made no move to approve the amflora potato more than a year after the Council's formal vote, leading its manufacturer, BASF, to initiate legal proceedings before the EU Court of First Instance against the Commission for 'undue delay' in the approval process (*International Herald Tribune*, 25 July 2008). Given these delays, only one GM crop, Monsanto's MON810 maize, was approved for cultivation in mid-2009, with a number of member states imposing safeguard bans on that variety.

Challenging the national safeguard bans

In addition to the 'undue delay' in new GM approvals, the other major issue raised by the WTO complaint was the various national safeguard bans, which EFSA, the Commission, and the WTO panel had all ruled were not supported by scientific risk assessments. Both before and after the WTO panel decision, the Commission repeatedly expressed its determination to challenge member-state safeguard bans that were not supported by scientific evidence. Its success in overturning these bans, however, has been at best limited.

In June 2005, the Commission submitted to the Environment Council eight draft decisions to overturn the eight national bans on GM varieties that had been declared safe by EFSA. By contrast with the pattern of deadlocks over the approval of specific GM varieties, on this issue the Council delivered lopsided majorities of twenty-two member states *against* Commission proposals—the first qualified majority for or against *any* Commission proposal on GMOs—and thus upheld the continuation of the member-state bans (*European Report*, 29 June 2005). Luxembourg Environment Minister Lucien Lux, who chaired the meeting during the Luxembourg Presidency of the Council, expressed his 'great satisfaction' at the outcome, noting pointedly that, 'We were able to give a clear message to the European Commission' (quoted in *EUobserver.com*, 27 June 2005). Over the next several years, the Commission tried again, challenging two Austrian safeguard bans on GM maize varieties in December 2006, and a Hungarian maize ban in February 2007. In both cases, overwhelming majorities in the Environment Council voted against the Commission.

In light of these overwhelming defeats, the Commission changed its tactics in October 2007, opting initially to challenge only Austria's ban on the use of the two maize varieties (MON810 and T25) for sale as food and feed, while accepting, for the moment, Austria's continued ban on their cultivation. This strategy paid off, to some extent, as the Environment Council failed to obtain a qualified majority against the Commission proposal. Fifteen member states reportedly voted against the Commission's proposal, with only four voting in favour, but a group of eight member states abstained, denying the Austrians a qualified majority (*European Report*, 31 October 2007).

In principle, the failure to reach a qualified majority empowered the Commission to move ahead and at least partially overturn the Austrian ban, yet the contentious nature of the vote and the public protestations of many ministers put the Commission in a politically difficult position. In an unusual press conference, Portuguese Environment Minister Francisco Nunes Correia, who had chaired the meeting and whose country had abstained in the vote, described the discussions as 'intense,' adding that 'this is an uncomfortable position that we're all in'. Many member states had supported Austria, he continued, either out of opposition to GMOs, or because of a belief that member states' positions should be respected. 'The majority of member states are against the Commission's proposal, but the Commission's proposal will prevail against the will of one particular member state,' he concluded, adding that, 'this is something that has to give us pause for thought' (quoted in *EUobserver.com*, 30 October 2007). Finally, after considerable delay, the Commission informed Austria in May 2008 that it was required to lift the ban on the marketing of the two varieties in question, and Austria complied later that month, formally repealing the two bans and informing the Commission of its actions (*Inside US Trade*, 6 June 2008).

Nevertheless, the Austrian and Hungarian bans on *cultivation* of MON810 remained in place, and the Commission's effort to challenge these met once again with failure in March 2009, when only five of the twenty-seven environment ministers backed the Commission's effort to overturn them (*The New York Times*, 3 March 2009). Perhaps more importantly, the trend in recent years has been toward greater national restrictions on GMOs, with a growing number of EU member governments announcing stricter policies—and new safeguard bans—on GM foods and crops. While some governments, such as that of the UK, remained generally favourably disposed toward the promise of genetic engineering (notwithstanding hostile public opinion), a number of governments—such as those of Austria, Italy, Luxembourg, and Greece—remained firm opponents of GM foods and crops, and several member governments adopted more critical positions toward GMOs, even after the 2006 WTO decision.

In Ireland, for example, the June 2007 elections brought the Irish Green Party into the Fianna Fáil-led government, bringing Ireland into the anti-GMO camp. Electoral turnover brought another stark change in France, where incoming President Nicolas Sarkozy indicated a fundamental reappraisal of GM foods and crops. France had been hostile to GMOs in Brussels—calling for the moratorium and often abstaining or voting against new approvals—but had also seen increasing cultivation of GM maize crops, which had grown fourfold to some 22,000 hectares in 2007. Sarkozy's government, however, took a sharp turn against GMOs, announcing a freeze on GM cultivation in late 2007, introducing a formal ban on MON810 maize in early 2008, and using the bully pulpit of its 2008 Council Presidency to call for a further tightening of the EU regulatory framework for GMOs (*Inside US Trade*, 4 January 2008). In March 2009, Germany followed suit, becoming the sixth EU country to ban cultivation of MON810 maize (*The New York Times*, 15 April 2009). Far from being eliminated, the various national bans on GM foods and crops—and national resistance to GMOs more generally—showed signs of spreading still further.

Conclusions

The regulation of biotechnology has presented the EU with a number of challenges. Many of these are common to all EU regulations, but others relate specifically to the nature of biotechnology as a highly politicized case of risk regulation, a multisectoral challenge requiring cross-sectoral coordination, and a multi-level concern in which EU regulations must respond to both national fears and international disciplines. The policy process most closely approximates the 'regulatory mode' of governance set out in Chapter 4. We find all of its five features in the case of biotech regulation, albeit to differing degrees, and with some policy-specific exceptions.

The Commission has acted as the primary entrepreneur in the development and implementation of EU policies. However, member governments retain important prerogatives, including the power to regulate trial releases of GMOs in the environment, to determine liability and coexistence rules, and to impose safeguard bans on GM seed, feed, and food. The creation of EFSA, furthermore, has resulted in a separation of executive functions at the EU level, with EFSA taking primary responsibility for risk assessment, while risk management continues to be shared between the Commission and the member governments.

The Council has played the dominant role in the adoption of framework directives and regulations, with an increasing role for the EP. In the implementation of EU regulations, and the approval (or blocking) of new GM varieties, regulatory committees of member-state officials as well as the Council of Ministers have played unusually active roles, supervising, questioning, and in some cases blocking the Commission's implementation of the regulatory framework. The EP, by contrast, has been essentially an onlooker regarding the implementation of EU legislation. To date the European Court of Justice has not yet been a major player in agricultural biotech, largely because few GMO-related cases (such as a case against France for non-transposition of EU directives) have been brought before it. There are signs, however, that the ECJ may play a greater role insofar as citizens, interest groups, grain traders, and biotech companies seek to challenge, clarify, and enforce the growing corpus of EU biotech regulation in the courts.

Although the EU has been a pioneer and a laboratory for international regulatory harmonization, it is joined in this endeavour by other international organizations, such as the WTO, the disciplines of which increasingly apply to the EU. The relationship between the EU and global regulatory bodies has been twofold, combining both defensive and offensive elements. On the defensive side, international developments and the threat of legal action have repeatedly spurred the EU, and especially the Commission, to restart the approval process and challenge national bans, although in both cases its success has been limited by entrenched domestic opposition. Those same international pressures, however, have increasingly motivated the EU to take an offensive approach, seeking to export its more precautionary principle and its rules to other countries and to 'forum shop' for international regimes—particularly environmental regimes like the UN Convention on Biodiversity—more receptive to EU arguments (Pollack and Shaffer 2009: 113–76).

Most importantly, the case of agricultural biotech regulation points to the limitations of EU supranational policy-making when regulatory issues become highly politicized and subject to public and international challenge. Disputes over risk regulation in this domain risk becoming disputes over the legitimacy of EU law itself.

Note

1 This chapter draws upon research conducted for Pollack and Shaffer (2009), which reflects our effort to explain both the domestic origins of EU GMO policy, as well as the interaction of domestic EU policy with international pressures emanating from other countries (such as the United States) and from various international organizations.

FURTHER READING

The literature on agricultural biotechnology has mushroomed in recent years. Cantley (1995) and Patterson (2000) provide excellent histories of early EU policy-making in this area. Vogel (2001), Bernauer (2003), Jasanoff (2005), Ansell and Vogel (2006), and Tiberghien (2007) all provide sophisticated analyses of EU GMO policy in comparative perspective, while Wiener and Rogers (2002), Chalmers (2003), Sunstein (2005), and Kahan et al. (2006) constitute a sophisticated debate over the use of the precautionary principle. On the transatlantic and global aspects of GMO regulation, see e.g. A. R. Young (2003), Drezner (2007), Fukuda-Parr (2007), and Pollack and Shaffer (2009).

Ansell, C., and Vogel, D. (2006) (eds.), *Why the Beef? The Contested Governance of European Food Safety* (Cambridge, MA: MIT Press).

Bernauer, T. (2003), *Genes, Trade and Regulation: The Seeds of Conflict in Food Biotechnology* (Princeton, NJ: Princeton University Press).

Cantley, M. (1995), 'The Regulation of Modern Biotechnology: A Historical and European Perspective: A Case Study in How Societies Cope with New Knowledge in the Last Quarter of the Twentieth Century', in H. J. Rehm and G. Reed (eds.) in cooperation with A. Pühler and P. Stadler, *Biotechnology*, vol. XII: *Legal, Economic and Ethical Dimensions* (Weinheim: VCH), 506–681.

Chalmers, D. (2003), 'Food for Thought: Reconciling European Risks and Traditional Ways of Life', *Modern Law Review*, 66/4: 532–64.

Drezner, D. W. (2007), *All Politics is Global: Explaining International Regulatory Regimes* (Princeton, NJ: Princeton University Press).

Fukuda-Parr, S. (2007) (ed.), *The Gene Revolution: GM Crops and Unequal Development* (London: Earthscan).

Jasanoff, S. (2005), *Designs on Nature: Science and Democracy in Europe and the United States* (Princeton, NJ: Princeton University Press).

Kahan, D, Slovic, P., Braman, D., and Gastil, J. (2006), 'Fear of Democracy: A Cultural Evaluation of Sunstein on Risk', *Harvard Law Review*, 119/4: 1071–109.

Patterson, L. A. (2000), 'Biotechnology', in H. Wallace and W. Wallace (eds.), *Policy-Making in the European Union*, 4th edn. (Oxford: Oxford University Press), 317–43.

Pollack, M. A., and Shaffer, G. S. (2009), *When Cooperation Fails: The International Law and Politics of Genetically Modified Organisms* (Oxford: Oxford University Press).

Sunstein, C. (2005), *The Laws of Fear: Beyond the Precautionary Principle* (New York, NY: Cambridge University Press).

Tiberghien, Y. (2007), 'Europe: Turning Against Agricultural Biotechnology in the Late 1990s', in S. Fukuda-Parr (ed.), *The Gene Revolution: GM Crops and Unequal Development* (London: Earthscan), 51–69.

Vogel, D. (2001), 'Ships Passing in the Night: GMOs and the Contemporary Politics of Risk Regulation in Europe', Working Paper No. 2001/16, (Florence: European University Institute), available at: *http://www.iue.it/RSCAS/WP-Texts/01_16.pdf* (accessed 14 May 2007).

Wiener, J. B., and Rogers, M. D. (2002), 'Comparing Precaution in the United States and Europe', *Journal of Risk Research*, 5/4: 317–49.

Young, A. R. (2003), 'Political Transfer and "Trading Up"? Transatlantic Trade in Genetically Modified Food and US Politics', *World Politics*, 55/4: 457–84.

CHAPTER 15

Energy Policy

Sharp Challenges and Rising Ambitions

David Buchan

▌ Summary

Energy policy has rapidly gained in importance for the European Union (EU), as it faces the challenges of creating an internal energy market, increasing energy security, and playing an active role in combating climate change. Reform of the energy market has been a constant activity since the late 1980s, although with the adoption of the third package of liberalization the emphasis will move from policy development to policy enforcement to prevent backsliding. Energy security is the area of energy policy to which the EU still adds least value for member states. This may change, as the new member states increase pressure for a collective energy security policy and as repeated interruptions in Russian gas flows push the EU into seeking diversified supplies from elsewhere. Finally, efforts to curb energy use and to develop low-carbon energy are at the heart of Europe's new programmes and targets to combat climate change. These three strands of policy involve different policy-making communities and illustrate a range of different policy modes.

Introduction

Worries about cut-offs of Russian gas supplies, see-sawing oil prices, and energy-driven climate change have brought energy policy to the top of the European Union's agenda in recent years. At the same time, energy-market liberalization, which has remained a constant on the EU agenda for the past twenty years, has been pushed harder than ever by the Commission. This chapter focuses on the EU's three main energy-related preoccupations: the internal energy market, energy security, and efforts to develop a low-carbon economy.

Each of these strands of energy policy has different characteristics and dynamics, involving different circles of policy-makers and stakeholders. These strands also have varied connections to other EU policy domains: liberalization is part of the single market programme (see Chapter 5) and has been heavily affected by competition policy (see Chapter 6); energy security connects to EU foreign and security policy (see Chapter 18), while climate change brings together energy and environmental concerns (see Chapter 13).

As regards the internal energy market, the Commission in particular has, over the past several decades, sought adoption and implementation of several 'packages' of liberalizing legislation, with a controversial third package winning approval by the European Parliament (EP) in April 2009 and by the Council in June 2009. In 2007, dissatisfaction with the lack of competition and frequency of discrimination in the energy market had led the European Commission to make another push to open access to Europe's gas and electricity grids, where the first package and the second package were judged to have largely failed in their aims (see below). The Commission proposed in its third package that energy supply companies should be forced to sell or 'unbundle' the ownership of any networks they owned. In the course of 2008 the Commission compromised in the face of solid opposition from the French and German governments. Before it was forced to do so, however, the Commission managed to use antitrust pressure to get some significant ownership-unbundling in Germany.

Energy security, defined as having adequate access to energy at reasonable prices, has acquired far greater salience, especially because of new member states' concerns about over-reliance on Russia. Nowhere has the Union's 2004 and 2007 enlargements to central and east Europe had more impact than on relations with Russia, given the region's energy dependence on, but political animosity toward, Russia. Yet the twenty-seven member states still seem unsure about how far to go towards having a collective EU energy policy towards Russia, as distinct from national policies and bilateral deals with Moscow. But repeated interruptions in the flow of Russian energy along the traditional transit routes of Ukraine and Belarus have not only spurred Moscow into devising alternative routes to Europe. These disruptions have also encouraged the EU to do more to diversify away from Russian energy altogether. Such diversification received a jolt from Russia's conflict in mid-2008 with Georgia, a main conduit of non-Russian oil—but was nonetheless the main theme of the Commission's second Strategic Energy Review (Commission 2008*l*) in November 2008.

Europe's ambitious climate-change goals are transforming almost every aspect of its energy system, given that energy use accounts for around two-thirds of all greenhouse gases. When the European Council and the EP agreed in December 2008 on the new climate and renewable-energy package, they showed some concern about costs, especially *vis-à-vis* foreign competitors, in an economic downturn. But the same agreements also showed that the perceived urgency of climate action has the potential to develop an integrationist dynamic comparable to that created by the '1992' single-market programme (see Chapter 5).

Scope and history of EU energy policy

The goals of energy policy—ensuring that energy is as cheap, secure, and clean as possible—are the same at EU level as at national level. But the remit for EU policy is narrower, addressing the internal energy market and environmental aspects of energy.

In the early years of European integration coal and nuclear power did figure prominently, in the form of the 1951 Treaty of Paris (European Coal and Steel Community, ECSC) and in the 1957 Treaty of Rome (European Atomic Energy Community, or Euratom). The ECSC was essentially a political scheme to put coal, which had been an economic engine of war-making, under international constraints. That done, the ECSC continued for fifty years as a social instrument to assist, with money and retraining, the run-down of west European coal mining (and steel production). When that task was largely completed, the ECSC Treaty was allowed to expire in 2002. Euratom, which is still in force, had some of the same political rationale, namely to create international supervision over something that could be used as a weapon, although it was also thought that civil nuclear energy could be developed effectively on a collective European basis. In practice Euratom has since functioned more as a technical agency, while EU governments have kept nuclear policy decisions very much in their own hands. The ECSC and Euratom, therefore, were not devised, and have not served in practice, as parts of a common energy policy.

Both coal and nuclear power declined in importance relative to oil, the use of which expanded greatly in the 1950s and 1960s. The first oil crisis in 1973–4 was dealt with largely by the founding in 1974, on United States initiative, of the International Energy Agency (IEA) to organize the holding and sharing of emergency oil stocks among its members (Black 1977). The EU also has legislation on oil stocks, but for the nineteen EU states that belong to the IEA (which also includes Australia, Canada, Japan, New Zealand, and the US) it is essentially secondary to their IEA obligations. To be members of the IEA states must first belong to the IEA's mother institution, the Organization for Economic Cooperation and Development (OECD), and not all EU states yet do. So there was far less to the foundation of EU energy policy than initially meets the eye.

While the treaties contained no separate and specific article on energy policy, over the years policy-makers borrowed legal competence from the economic and environmental parts of the treaties to justify proposing and passing energy measures. Energy's economic importance gained recognition in the 1986 Single European Act (SEA) and the subsequent single-market programme (see Chapter 5). Leaning on the treaties' market-opening and antitrust principles (see Chapter 6), the Commission in 1989 set about the task of liberalizing the electricity and gas markets, a task in which it is still engaged twenty years later. EU policy thus far has such a narrow focus because it concentrates on those energy sources that are especially dependent on fixed, cross-border networks and which are dominated by monopoly suppliers. By contrast, oil and coal have physical characteristics that allow them to be transported fairly flexibly and stored fairly easily. Therefore the EU policy focus on oil relates to security of supply and the level of stocks, and even then the EU plays a secondary role to the IEA.

The 1992 Maastricht Treaty on European Union (TEU) gave the EU competence to improve cross-border energy infrastructure in a programme know as Trans-European Networks (TENs) and increased the EU's ability to act on the environment (see Chapter 13 and Matlary 1996). It is on this legal foundation that the EU's ambitious climate-change programme has been erected.

More recently two factors have combined to push up the agenda the idea of a more ambitious energy policy. On the one hand, the growing concern about climate change has focused attention on the need to reduce the use of carbon and to control emissions more effectively. On the other hand, eastern enlargement has drawn more attention to the issue of security of energy supplies. Hence the Treaty of Lisbon (ToL) will give the EU a bigger role in energy. It states in Article 176A that:

In the context of the establishment and functioning of the internal market and with regard for the need to preserve and improve the environment, Union policy on Energy shall aim, in a spirit of solidarity between Member States, to:

- ensure the functioning of the energy market;
- ensure security of energy supply in the Union;
- promote energy efficiency and energy saving and the development of new and renewable forms of energy; and
- promote the interconnection of energy networks.

But the same article of the ToL goes on to reaffirm that 'such measures shall not affect a member state's right to determine the conditions for exploiting its energy resources, its choice between different energy sources and the general structure of its energy supply'. Thus the ToL would not reduce the autonomy that the member states currently enjoy. France is perfectly free to use nuclear reactors to generate most of its electricity, just as Poland does with its deep coal seams. Likewise the UK has been free to go full steam ahead in extracting its oil and gas, just as The Netherlands has been free to husband its gas reserves carefully. Therefore the EU role in energy policy is weaker than the role of central governments in more developed federations. In the latter, even where fossil fuel reserves are the property of states or provinces or (in the case of the US) private landowners, the federal authorities levy royalties, impose retail taxes, and own all offshore reserves and some onshore reserves. In the EU, national governments decide how to exploit their energy resources, what mix of energy sources they choose to rely on, and, largely, how they tax energy.

Energy security is the weakest side of the EU energy policy triangle. Enlargement has increased the case for strengthening it. New central and east European states are keen for an EU energy security policy to help them avoid over-reliance on Russia, while older and bigger member states in western Europe still prefer to settle energy ties with Russia bilaterally. In the past, EU authorities have had little legal right to involve themselves in securing energy supply. Only with the ToL would they get formal competence 'to ensure security of energy supply'.

Internal energy market

The construction of the internal energy market has been the longest standing of the three strands of the EU's energy policy. It is situated at the intersection of two robust EU policies—the single European market (see Chapter 5) and competition policy (see Chapter 6). Nonetheless, progress to date has been hard fought.

Issues and interests

The Commission has been the champion of liberalization in the European energy market. Knowing the resistance from some governments, it was understandably slow in the 1990s to start its liberalization drive. Yet, once launched in this direction, the Commission has doggedly persisted, even after energy security and climate change began to eclipse liberalization as an issue. Its main goal is to curb the natural monopolies of the gas and power networks by ensuring open, non-discriminatory access for all third parties to these grids. It started with a first package of directives in 1996 (Electricity Directive 96/92/EC) and in 1998 (Gas Directive 98/30//EC), but soon decided these measures were too weak. So it proposed a second package of legislation (Electricity Directive 2003/54/EC and Gas Directive 2003/55/EC) that required the 'legal unbundling' of supply networks from energy generation, causing energy companies to put network grids at arm's length by placing them in separate subsidiaries. Again the Commission soon decided that these measures did not go far enough to liberalize the market. So in 2007 it proposed its third package of measures, incorporating the concept of ownership unbundling (OU), forcing energy companies either to sell their networks outright or to put these networks under entirely independent management. These proposals provoked strong opposition from France and Germany as well as a number of small member states.

Behind the Commission's persistence is its conviction that a competitive and fully interconnected energy market would also help to tackle energy security (by making emergency stocks easily transferable around the EU) and climate change (by maximizing efficient use of energy and minimizing emissions). Another reason is that the Directorate-General for Competition (DG COMP) became heavily involved, when, in response to consumer complaints about rising gas and electricity prices, it started in mid-2005 an in-depth investigation into EU energy markets. This investigation uncovered, according to DG COMP, 'serious shortcomings' (RAPID press release Memo/07/15), particularly with regard to attempts by companies to keep rivals off their grids. As well as paving the way for some antitrust suits (see below), this sector-wide investigation led DG COMP to conclude that grids and networks had to be made stand-alone operations, and the way to do this was new ownership-unbundling legislation. In this, the DG then responsible for energy and transport (DG TREN) concurred.

A large number of member states backed the Commission's proposals on OU. This was not surprising as nearly half the EU members—thirteen to be precise—had already by 2007 taken their own national decisions to introduce a form of OU in electricity. Seven of these countries had done so in gas as well. Some pro-OU countries—for example The Netherlands and Spain (which had OU in both electricity and gas) and Italy (OU only in electricity)—said they wanted the playing field levelled by generalizing the OU regime. Their concern was that their unbundled (and therefore inherently smaller) energy companies and networks would otherwise be left at a competitive disadvantage vis-à-vis vertically integrated (and therefore inherently larger) companies.

The UK also hardened its support for OU within the EU. Although having led the unbundling revolution in the 1980s with the break-up of British Gas, the UK had for a long time paid little attention to the unreconstructed nature of the continental energy industry. But from 2000, as the UK turned from gas exporter to importer, it began to realize that it needed to ensure that the terms on which it imported gas from continental Europe were as competitive as possible.

Arrayed against OU were France, Germany, and six smaller states: Austria, Bulgaria, Greece, Latvia, Luxembourg, and Slovakia. In France, where the energy sector has been dominated by state-owned Electricité de France and Gaz de France, many politicians anathematized OU as forced privatization. In Germany, with its privately owned energy sector and constitutionally guaranteed property rights, many in industry as well as in politics lambasted OU as expropriation. Some smaller member states argued that their energy companies were too small to be unbundled, especially in gas where they must confront foreign suppliers of considerable size. This concern for gas to be treated differently from electricity was shared by many member states in the pro-OU camp.

Internal energy market legislation is a matter for co-decision by the EP and the Council. While there was a clear majority in the EP for OU in electricity, many MEPs shared the reluctance of some governments in the Council to interfere with the structure of a gas industry stretching far beyond the EU. Most MEPs followed the line set by their political groups, rather than their national governments. Particularly vociferous in speaking against their governments' opposition to OU were Green MEPs from Germany and Luxembourg, who claimed that the big utilities had deliberately kept renewable energy off their grids, and urged that they should be broken up.

Significantly, the EU-level body of national regulators, European Regulators Group for Electricity and Gas (ERGEG), endorsed the Commission's OU proposals. Whatever the line taken by their governments, almost every one of the twenty-seven national regulators supports the concept of stand-alone networks because they are clearer and simpler to regulate. Significantly, too, in the face of many governments and MEPs calling for a two-track approach to gas and electricity, ERGEG said there should be no differentiation: 'There is no justification for less unbundling in gas than in electricity, as the potential for discrimination does not differ' (ERGEG 2007).

Lobbying over energy-market reform takes place at several levels—at the member-state level especially in the case of big state-owned producers, in special consultative forums created by the Commission (see below), and through EU-wide associations. Among the latter, it has naturally been energy users who have lobbied for a more competitive energy industry, including OU if necessary. Prominent among these user groups is the European branch of the International Federation of Industrial Energy Consumers, together with its powerful German national affiliate, the *Verband der Industriellen Energie und Kraftwirtschaft* (VIK). The Commission has been receptive to energy users' complaints about over-pricing and anti-competitive practices. Such complaints spurred the Commission into launching its 2005 competition inquiry into the energy sector and its third legislative package of 2007.

On the producers' side, the electricity industry, as represented by its main trade association, Eurelectric, generally responded more constructively to the Commission's third package proposal than did the gas industry, represented by Eurogas. Electricity companies have felt less need to hang on to their networks at all costs, in terms either of ownership or of management, because networks are a relatively small part of their business, which is dominated by power generation. Eurelectric never embraced OU, but was quicker to try to come up with alternative ways of reaching the Commission's goals than Eurogas, whose opposition to OU was more rigid.

In this strand of energy policy the pattern of issues and interests is familiar from many other sectors caught up in the drive to develop the single European market, with persistent arguments between the enthusiasts and the doubters as regards the pace of liberalization. The bias within the EU has been towards a faster pace, although in some member states powerful coalitions of governments and industries have been able to apply the brakes now and then. The energy sector has much in common with experience in other industries.

Third time lucky for liberalization?

In developing the internal energy market, the EU has been acting in classic regulatory or re-regulatory mode—and with considerable success, if the ambition of the
task is taken into account. For the Commission has been trying to open up to cross-
border competition a sector that was historically organized around 'national champion' companies, backed, if not owned, by national governments, as well as to break
up vertical integration in a sector where that structure has been the standard business model. By way of comparison with another federal system, the Commission will
come closer to getting a standard electricity-market design for the twenty-seven EU
member states than the US federal authorities have ever done with the fifty states.

In terms of agenda-setting, a typical role of the Commission, there has been little surprise in recent years. The Commission has essentially been trying for twenty
years to push through the same agenda or to achieve the same goal—open access
on energy networks. The greater power for national regulators that the Commission
sought in 2007 as part of its third package, and the proposal to separate ownership
and operation of networks from other parts of the energy business, was to ensure
that owners and operators of networks do not abuse their monopolies. In terms of
the policy cycle, this raises a question about the implementation and enforcement
of earlier directives, but also the possibility of policy-makers learning from previous
mistakes and adapting to new circumstances.

What has been new in recent years is the close cooperation between the Commission's energy and competition directorates-general, and how competition policy

TABLE 15.1	Re-regulating energy			
	Unbundling of networks	**Access to networks**	**Market opening**	**National regulation**
First legislative package 1996–8	Separate management & accounts	Negotiated or regulated terms of access	Power: 35% open by 2003. Gas: 33% open by 2018	Mechanism for regulation
Second legislative package 2003	Separate subsidiary	Regulated terms of access	Power and gas markets 100% open by July 2007	Specific regulator for energy
Third legislative package 2009	Separate ownership or operator	Regulated terms of access	No change from second package	Upgraded and harmonized powers for national energy regulators

has been brought in to bolster liberalization. It was not like this at the outset. When in 1991 Leon Brittan, the Competition Commissioner, announced his intention to apply competition policy to energy, DG TREN was nervous that this would be 'a very costly political strategy' (Matlary 1996: 272) and might backfire. There was also a view, particularly promoted by France, that energy was special, and that it should be exempted from competition policy because it was a 'service of general economic interest'. The Commission produced a green paper (Commission 2003*d*) and then a white paper (Commission 2004*c*) on services of general interest, but did not find evidence that energy liberalization had failed to serve the general interest.

DG COMP has used the in-depth knowledge it gained as a result of its 2005–6 energy sector investigation in support of liberalization. In May 2006 it launched surprise inspections—or 'dawn raids' as the press likes to call them—on a number of gas company premises across Europe. In December 2006 it did so with several electricity companies. In addition, during the following two years it launched formal antitrust investigations against several companies for allegedly shutting competitors out of their markets or manipulating prices.

On announcing each investigation, the Commission formally maintained that the investigations did not stem from the sector inquiry in order to avoid giving the company under investigation legal ground for demanding access to the huge amount of general data unearthed by the sector inquiry. Yet it more or less confessed that the sector inquiry had showed its inspectors where to look and what to look for. For example, on opening investigations against Italy's Eni and Germany's RWE for allegedly shutting competitors out of their home gas market, the Commission (RAPID press releases Memo/07/186 and Memo/07/187 of 11 May 2007) stated that the inquiry had given it 'an in-depth understanding of the functioning, and in some cases, mal-functioning, of the energy sector'. This understanding, said the Commission, helped it in turn to 'draw conclusions as regards where Commission investigations based on competition law could be appropriate and effective'. But knowledge dates, and the Commission does not always have such current and detailed understanding of the energy sector to draw on.

Nonetheless, in this instance, antitrust pressure provided an interesting interaction with the legislative reform process. The Commission maintained that the scale and nature of the conflict of interest inherent in vertically integrated energy companies required the sort of structural remedy that could be achieved only by legislation requiring 'stand-alone' networks, not through isolated antitrust actions imposing behavioural remedies (usually fines) on individual companies. 'This requires comprehensive structural reform [because] even the most diligent competition enforcement cannot solve all the problems in these markets', noted Neelie Kroes (2007), the Competition Commissioner, launching the Commission's third package.

Antitrust pressure played a dramatic part in concentrating politicians' minds on the need for reform. On the morning of an Energy Council in February 2008, held to discuss ownership-unbundling among other things, Germany's Eon and the Commission announced that they had come to a preliminary agreement in which Eon would sell off its German electricity grid and the Commission would drop its anti-trust investigation into alleged power market manipulation by the German utility. Just before the June 2008 Energy Council, the Commission got Germany's RWE to agree to a very similar deal.

In parallel with the legislative measures over the past decade to equalize network access has been the trend towards more European-wide regulation. The big difference, however, between the two developments is that while there is an agreed goal of creating a single energy market, there is little desire—among governments or even in the Commission—to create a single European regulator. So far, regulation has been discussed in the general sense of how the EU operates in 'regulatory mode' in the internal energy market—making rules, regulations, and laws (see Chapter 4). The Commission plays a central role, but much, as Cameron (2007: 99) has pointed out, is actually 'the function of oversight of the liberalization process'. This is in contrast to the narrower concept of regulation, which we will now concentrate on. This concerns the largely technical decisions on network access, tariffs, rates of return on investment, and so on, that national regulatory agencies make to protect the public interest in energy infrastructure and markets.

Each package of liberalizing legislation has been accompanied by some development in regulation. The first package of 1996–8 was followed by the creation of industry forums. The Florence Forum was set up in 1998 as a twice-yearly meeting of all the stakeholders in the electricity industry—producers, transmission system operators (TSOs), consumers, traders—with national regulators, government officials, and the Commission. In 1999 the Madrid Forum was set up to do the same for the gas industry. The forums have provided a useful process of consultation between the regulators and the regulated. But, lacking any law-making or mandatory enforcement powers, they have been little more than regulation by cooperation. During this period, however, network operators were encouraged, particularly by the Commission, to form themselves into EU-wide associations—the European Transmission System Operators' association (ETSO) for the power grids and Gas Transmission for Europe (GTE)—to make consultation easier. As Cameron (2007: 104) points out, this constituted a form of unbundling at the European level by separating the TSOs out, irrespective of what was happening at the national level.

Moreover, the changing structure and ownership of national industries has required more explicit regulation, leading to the considerable expansion of the roles of national energy regulators. Their role began to acquire a European dimension under the first package of open-access directives of 1996 and 1998, which allowed the option of 'regulated' third-party access to networks on the basis of tariffs approved by national regulators. The second package of directives of 2003 required every member state to have a national energy regulator; by that stage all member states had one except for Germany, which finally set up a network regulator in 2005. National regulators were given a minimum set of powers and an instruction to coordinate with each other and liaise with the Commission. The Commission decided to make a kind of carbon copy of the Council of European Energy Regulators (CEER) (which the regulators had set up in 2000 as their own informal club), to call it the European Regulators Group of Electricity and Gas (ERGEG), and to give it the formal duties of advising the Commission and consulting with industry on regulation.

Despite these developments, the competences and independence of national regulators have remained very uneven. At one extreme is the UK regulator, the Office of Gas and Electricity Markets (Ofgem), which is independent by parliamentary statute and has antitrust as well as standard network regulation powers. At the other end are national regulators in Spain, Portugal, and some new member states, which function more as advisers to government ministries that can, and often do, overrule them. All national regulators, however, are prevented by national statute from taking into account any factors beyond their national frontiers, and at present lack any European mandate to take a broader view.

The Commission's 2007 proposal for the third package, therefore, promised a step-change in the national regulators' European role. It proposed harmonizing up the powers of national regulators. More important, it proposed upgrading the present European Regulators Group for Electricity and Gas into the Agency for the Cooperation of Energy Regulators (ACER), which would have, for the first time, the power to take and enforce binding decisions. This would enable national regulators to exercise some European powers. The Commission has argued that such changes are necessary to ensure that whatever is decided on unbundling should be implemented and enforced. But as far as ACER is concerned, the Commission has not wanted this particular acorn to develop into an oak. In particular it has been reluctant to give ACER power over the European associations of TSOs.

The Commission's stated reason for pulling its punch on ACER's powers is constitutional. The European Court of Justice (ECJ), in its 1958 *Meroni* ruling and other case law, has held that an authority to which power is delegated (like the Commission) cannot confer on another body (like ACER) powers different from those possessed by the delegated authority under the treaty, and that there should be no delegation of powers involving a wide margin of political discretion between different objectives and tasks that would escape democratic control. The Commission's legal service maintained that the Meroni doctrine must limit ACER's powers, while other Commission officials said they were nervous about ACER being used as the thin end of the wedge in a long-standing campaign by some to remove competition powers entirely from the Commission and give them to an independent agency (see Chapter 6). However, the Parliament *rapporteur* claimed (European Parliament 2008*a*) that his proposals for ACER would respect Meroni, because, while the agency would have a prime role on codes of a technical nature, responsibility for network codes on politically sensitive competition and market issues would stay with the Commission. Some MEPs felt the Commission has been inhibited less by a fifty-year-old ruling than by a desire to dominate a weak agency.

To sum up, carrying through the third package of energy-market reform has been the result of unusually close cooperation between the Commission's DG COMP and DG TREN, with antitrust action used as the spearhead for legislative reform.

It may prove the high-water mark of energy-market liberalization, which has become somewhat eclipsed, even compromised, by issues of energy security and climate change that often require non-market rules and mechanisms. If there is a fourth package it is likely to focus less on the highly political issues of network ownership and independence, and more on technical matters of cross-border regulation and energy-market unification.

Energy security

Energy security is the weakest of the EU's three energy policy strands. The 2004 and 2007 enlargements have increased the case for strengthening it. The central and east European member states are keen for an EU energy security policy to help them avoid over-reliance on Russia, while bigger and more established member states generally prefer to deal with Russia bilaterally on energy issues. In the past, EU authorities have had little authority to involve themselves in securing energy supply. Only with the ToL will they get formal competence 'to ensure security of energy supply'.

Issues and interests

The issue of energy security has gone up and down the ladder of salience within the EU depending on how easy it has been for Europeans to gain reliable access to energy supplies and on the variations in energy, especially oil, prices. In the 1970s there were two moments of 'crisis' related to the actions of Middle East oil producers. In subsequent years European consumers relaxed as new sources of oil and gas were discovered, including in Norway and the UK, and supplies seemed to be more reliably available. In recent years, however, concerns about energy security have re-emerged as, on the one hand, reserves in the EU have been depleted and, on the other hand, the doubts about the reliability of foreign suppliers, especially Russia, have increased.

The Commission has historically been a *demandeur* in energy security, seeking a role that has not been granted by the member states, particularly regarding negotiating with any specific supplier country. Its approach has been general: to police the level of emergency oil stocks; to hold energy dialogues with countries or groups of countries (such as the Organization of Petroleum Exporting Countries (OPEC)); and to try to export policy through such mechanisms as the Energy Charter Treaty and the Energy Community (see below).

The weakness of EU energy security policy is commonly put down to the fact that among the older member states, the bigger ones prefer to conduct their own foreign energy policies. In relation to Russia, it should be pointed out that energy is only part of the bilateral foreign policies that countries such as Germany, France, and

FIGURE 15.1   Main gas pipeline projects to Europe up to 2015

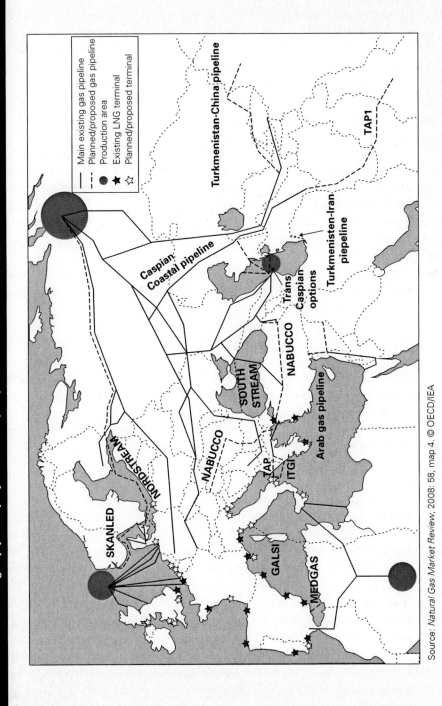

Source: *Natural Gas Market Review*, 2008: 58, map 4. © OECD/IEA

Italy conduct with Moscow. Moreover, the energy element of these foreign policies—though backed by governments—is carried out largely by leading national champion companies, such as Germany's Eon, Gaz de France, and Italy's Eni, which have long-term contracts with Russia's Gazprom, because both sides see this as in their interest. So the weakness of EU energy security policy *vis-à-vis* Russia stems in part from a wider weakness in Europe's common foreign and security policy (see Chapter 18).

It is an open question whether having a major oil or energy company really contributes to a country's feeling of energy security. But the fact is that, while not all large EU states have an oil major, none of the smaller states does. Smaller states are therefore more interested in the EU having a common external energy security policy and speaking with one voice. Where the central and east European member states differ from other smaller states is that they want this voice, when directed at Moscow, to be a tough one. The central and east European member states still carry a strong anti-Russian animus from their days as forced members of Soviet institutions and alliances. Among this group the three Baltic states are in a unique position, because they are still linked to the Russian electricity grid, and not yet connected to the main EU grid.

On energy security and policy towards Russia, MEPs' views have evolved over time. In 2003 the EP adopted a report by a German Christian Democrat, Peter Mombaur, which effectively neutered a Commission proposal to increase the holding of gas stocks (European Parliament 2003). In 2007 the European Parliament approved a report, written by the Polish chairman of its Committee on Foreign Affairs, Jacek Saryusz-Wolski (European Parliament 2007*b*). It called for a stronger and more collective 'common European energy policy, covering security of supply, transit and investment related to energy security', and for the appointment of 'a High Official for Foreign Energy Policy' to coordinate such a policy.

Energy security is not a universal concern for European energy providers. The electricity sector is more concerned about broad issues of network reliability and of the stability of renewable energy sources such as wind power than about energy security. The gas sector, which depends overwhelmingly on foreign (particularly Russian) gas and is tied to inflexible supply lines from abroad, by contrast, is very sensitive about energy security. This concern persists even though shipments by sea of Liquefied Natural Gas (LNG) to Europe are increasing. Concerns about energy security contributed to the gas industry's hostility to the Commission's OU proposals, which threatened to make the companies sell their gas transport and logistics facilities. Not only have the gas companies wanted to hold on to their pipelines, but many of them have also sought to raise the proportion of their gas sales that they can cover with gas from their own upstream assets, as insurance against gas shortages or price spikes. This has tended to incline Europe's gas companies against supporting a collective EU energy security policy, if that were to make it harder for them to compete with each other for the lease of upstream assets from gas-producing states around Europe, such as Algeria, Egypt, Libya, and Russia.

Overall, therefore, the discussion of energy security is marked by an untidy patchwork of different concerns and conflicting interests. These do not easily coalesce around collective and consistent European interests or yield a clear priority list of issues to be pursued.

Driven by events

Energy security is probably the area in which the biggest gap between potential (what EU states could do together) and performance (what they actually do together) lies. It is also difficult to characterize in terms of the EU's usual policy modes. The EU has taken some energy security decisions—for instance, the 2004 Gas Security Directive (2004/67/EC) and the 2005 Electricity Security Directive (2005/89/EC)—in its traditional regulatory mode.

In terms of its grand design, however, EU energy security policy is harder to categorize. It hardly falls into the category of policy coordination, because few member states have formal policies to coordinate. Most, if not all, member states would subscribe to the general desirability of having a diversity of energy types and energy sources. This is particularly the wish of Bulgaria, Estonia, Finland, Latvia, Lithuania, Romania, and Slovakia, which are entirely dependent on Russia for their gas imports. But only Spain has a formal limit (60 per cent) on the maximum amount of gas that it can import from any one country, which was set in 2000 and corresponded to the level of Spain's imports from Algeria at the time (these have since proportionally declined). National energy security policies tend to be just the random result of the accretion over time of decisions on energy mix and sourcing.

Nor can EU decision-making in energy security be remotely described as intensive transgovernmentalism in or outside EU institutions. Until recently member states barely talked to each other about energy security. Nineteen member states can discuss energy security issues in the IEA, but their decisions there on security of supply relate only to emergency oil stocks.

Events have tended to be the driver in energy security. The first measure to address oil security, the 1968 Oil Stocks Directive 68/414/EEC), which required the holding of minimum reserves, was taken well before the build-up to the first oil shock of 1973–4. That price-and-shortage shock prompted further legislation in the 1970s, but this was really to implement the regime for oil crisis management instituted by the IEA. This regime helped the EU weather the second oil shock of 1979–80, which from the mid-1980s was followed by a long period of relative calm, even price decline, in energy markets that lasted until the long run-up in oil prices started from 2000.

The Soviet Union's collapse in 1991 jolted the EU into creating the Energy Charter Treaty (ECT). It was designed to create a legal framework for cross-border investment and trade in the energy sectors of the countries of the former Soviet Union, though it was dressed up as a wider international agreement and has more than fifty signatories. The ECT was an interesting attempt to export EU policy to countries from which the EU imports energy. It has, however, been only a limited success, not least because the most important target country, Russia, has not ratified the treaty or a subsequent protocol on gas transit. Gazprom objected to the transit provisions of

The 2004 Gas Security Directive (2004/67/EC) is an object lesson in how a proposal can be turned on its head during the EU decision-making process and rendered meaningless. With the benefit of hindsight over subsequent repeated interruptions of Russian gas supplies through Ukraine, it showed considerable complacency. Negotiated just before the 2004 enlargement, it failed to cater for new member states' security concerns. It is also an unusual case in which the Parliament outdid the Council in telling the Commission that gas security was best left to member states.

In September 2002 the Commission (2002d) proposed a draft directive on security of gas supply. The Commission recognized that member states could not be asked to hold stocks of gas equivalent to a set number of days' consumption as they could with oil, because gas is far harder to store than oil and not every country has the geology to do it. So it recommended that each member state should ensure, by means either of storage or flexible production or sharing arrangements with neighbouring states, that it would have enough gas to maintain supply to 'non-interruptible' customers with no possibility of switching to other fuels (mainly households) if the single largest source of supply to the country were to be disrupted for up to sixty days. The draft directive also committed member states to gas-sharing arrangements, over which the Commission would have had some discretionary power.

On virtually every count the draft directive was criticized by the EP's Industry and Energy Committee *rapporteur,* Peter Mombaur, as unnecessary, because 'no difficulties in the field of gas supplies have ever arisen which would be comparable to the oil crises', because there was competition rather than a cartel among gas exporters, and because there was mutual dependence between gas exporters and importers based on long-term contracts (European Parliament 2003). Gas storage issues had been largely dealt with by internal market legislation (Directive 2003/55/EC), and any extra gas-security measures should be left to member states 'in the light of their particular national circumstances'. The *rapporteur* said he disagreed with the Commission's assumptions that neither governments nor companies were able to ensure gas security. Mr Mombaur's report, adopted by the committee by twenty-nine votes to four in June 2003 and nodded through by the full Parliament without a roll-call vote in September 2003, deleted any precise storage and reporting requirements and amended the text to ensure the crisis-reaction mechanism at EU level would only be convened in 'restricted, clearly defined cases', and only at member states' request.

The Council had no difficulty in agreeing with the EP's unexpectedly strong defence of member states' interests. One of the few changes made by the Council, in December 2003, was to change the legal base of the directive from Article 95 EC, used for harmonizing single-market legislation and which gave the EP co-decision rights, to Article 100 EC, under which the Council could decide any emergency supply measures and need only inform the EP. Since the EP had so strongly criticized any harmonizing intent by the Commission and so defended member states' rights in this matter, it was ill-placed to disagree. So it acquiesced in the legal base change that cut it, the EP, out of the loop of any subsequent action.

While retaining the EP's imprecision on gas stocks and storage, the Council introduced a definition of the level of 'major supply disruption' requiring a possible EU response. This was set at an interruption of 20 per cent of total EU gas imports for a period of eight weeks, a level that took no account of the imminent enlargement. No fewer than nine smaller member states, mainly those in central and east Europe with small but Russian-dominated gas markets, could have their gas imports totally cut off without this threshold being met.

Although the threshold has never been met, the Gas Coordination Group (composed of member states and the Commission) created by the Directive has met several times, mainly to discuss interruptions in supply from Ukraine. So the Directive has not been totally useless, though the Commission (2008k) set out in November 2008 its intention to revise it. To be fair to Mr Mombaur, the gas supply picture seemed to many people to be stable before the first Russian–Ukrainian gas row of 2006.

the ECT, which it felt threatened its effective monopoly control over the flow of gas in Russia and the flow of gas from central Asia across Russia.

The EU has since exported its energy policy successfully in another direction. In 2005 it set up the Energy Community for south-eastern Europe to include the western Balkan countries of the former Yugoslavia, as well as Albania and, until they joined the EU, Bulgaria and Romania. The original aim of this Community—which obliges its members to accept EU energy market principles and decisions—was to provide a framework for EU financial aid in repairing the shattered grid of the former Yugoslavia and to prepare states for eventual EU membership. Subsequently it has come to be seen by Commission officials in Brussels as a valuable potential bridgehead for exporting EU energy market policy and practice further east, to Turkey and beyond. But the Energy Community has yet to attract more members, in particular Turkey, a key transit country.

The 2004 enlargement was thus a catalyst for policy on energy security. Central and east European states brought with them serious concerns about energy dependence on Russia and high expectations of the EU easing these concerns. These expectations have been largely disappointed. The only advance in gas security, as the result of the 2004 Gas Security Directive (see Box 15.1), was the institutional innovation of the Gas Coordination Group, a committee of national officials who meet to discuss gas security. Russia's 2008 conflict with Georgia, as well as disruption of gas supplies through Ukraine, led to a focus on energy security when the Commission brought out its second Strategic Energy Review in November 2008 (RAPID press release IP/08/1696). A far more modest affair than the first strategic review in 2006 (Commission 2006b), which led to the new EU energy and climate programme, the energy security aspect of this second review proposed revision of the Gas Security Directive, updating of oil-stocks policy to approximate to IEA practice, and greater EU involvement in planning and supporting energy infrastructure, including new pipelines to bring Caspian-region gas to Europe as an alternative to Russian supply. How far such proposals get will hinge less on the impact of the ToL, with its first-time mentions of ensuring 'security of energy supply' in the EU 'in a spirit of solidarity', and more on events, such as Russia's 2008 conflict with Georgia, and repeated disruptions of gas through Ukraine.

To sum up: the EU was ill prepared for the implications of enlargement for its energy security. The EP played a surprising part in previously telling the Commission that responsibility for gas security could be safely left to member states and industry. Events finally forced energy security on to the top of the EU agenda and into the ToL.

Climate change

The third strand of EU energy policy, climate change, is arguably the one in which the EU has shown the greatest ambition. EU policy-makers see themselves as pioneers in developing both international and domestic measures to mitigate climate change, especially through the part they played in negotiating the Kyoto Protocol and its implementing provisions and the role it is playing in the negotiation of Kyoto's successor (Sbragia 2000; Lenschow 2005). Ambition to lead internationally (see Chapter 13) has been translated into a determination to lead by example and thus to ambitious internal targets for reducing greenhouse gas emissions. Because of energy production's significant contribution to greenhouse gas emissions, this has major implications for internal energy policy.

Issues and interests

The Commission has been particularly ambitious and entrepreneurial with regard to climate change. Internally, it managed to reverse some initial European scepticism about using a cap-and-trade system to control carbon emissions, which involves putting a reduced (and gradually declining) cap on emissions, issuing permits for emissions up to that overall cap, and allowing trading of these permits. In 2003 the EU created the Emissions Trading System (ETS) (under Directive 2003/87/EC, known as the directive on 'establishing a scheme for greenhouse gas emission allowance trading withing the Community') and turned it into the central instrument for implementing the EU's Kyoto obligations.

Externally, the Commission exploited the Bush administration's rejection of the Kyoto protocol by effectively taking over leadership of international efforts to combat climate change (see Chapter 13). Most member states share the Commission's desire for EU leadership in the United Nations climate negotiations. Consequently, the member states' governments have by and large acquiesced in the Commission's redesign of climate-change policies, challenging its detail more than its principles. The publication of the Stern Review (2006), which focused on the economics of climate action and showed the pay-off of early action to combat global warming, may have constituted a critical juncture at which there was a paradigm shift to put climate change ahead of other concerns. Indeed in some member states governmental portfolios were rearranged by collocating the relevant energy and environmental ministries under the same minister, as France did in 2007 and the UK in 2008, in order to improve policy-making coherence. The EP, where Greens are well represented, is also strongly committed to combating climate change.

That said, climate-change policies evoke different reactions within governments. Energy or industry ministers tend to want to temper the climate-change enthusiasm of their environment-ministerial colleagues with realism about the competitive effects of making European industry pay for stringent carbon controls. The newer member states have tended to be less enthusiastic about taking radical measures to address climate change, worried about the cost implications for their relatively poor and energy-intensive economies. Moreover, some of them are heavily dependent on coal for electricity generation; coal generates 95 per cent of Polish power, for instance.

Energy-intensive industries—particularly aluminium, cement, and steel—concerned about foreign competition, particularly amid the economic downturn from 2008, are very concerned about the implications of the increased energy costs associated with addressing climate change as they would not be able to pass them on to consumers as their competitors would not face the same costs.

There were two particular drivers to the development of the EU's climate-change-related energy policy in 2008. One was the desire for leadership in the negotiation of a successor agreement to Kyoto, which will set binding emissions targets from 2012. The other concerned problems with the initial phase of the ETS (2005–7). The Commission had no one to blame but itself when its clumsy disclosure of emissions data in spring 2006 caused the price for first-phase allowances to crash to a level from which it never recovered before these allowances expired at the end of 2007. But this was put down to inevitable teething problems in the world's only international emissions scheme. The greater problem was seen to be 'gaming' of the allocation system by national governments for the benefit of their own industries. In order to take the ETS beyond Kyoto, in January 2008 the Commission (RAPID press release IP/08/80) proposed a set of binding targets for reductions in emissions, increased use of renewables, greater energy efficiency, and a more centralized allocation of permits under the ETS.

External ambition and internal compromise

The major feature of the negotiations leading up to the EU's December 2008 climate and renewable energy agreement was the revolt of new member states over its cost for their relatively poor economies. In its January 2008 blueprint the Commission had tried to head off this revolt by proposing that central and east European member states should get: (a) less demanding targets for increases in renewables with several concessions; (b) permission to increase emissions in sectors outside the ETS (mainly transport, building, agriculture, and services), in contrast to emissions cuts for richer, older member states; and (c) a slightly larger share of ETS allowances to auction than their share of economic output would warrant.

But the central and east European member states made clear during the course of 2008 that they wanted more. They organized within the Council and negotiated as a bloc with the French presidency. Eventually they settled after getting two more concessions—a further increase in ETS auction revenue and transitional free allowances for their power sectors. This last concession was a key demand of Poland, the largest and often politically most truculent member state in this group, which, because of its reliance on dirty coal, said it could not accept the Commission plan for electricity utilities to pay for all their ETS carbon allowances from 2013. However, central and east European states will still face adjustment problems to the new climate and green-energy policies that accelerate the adaptation these countries have already had to make from the energy wastefulness of their communist past.

In the December 2008 agreement the Commission did succeed in securing greater centralization of the allocation of carbon permits under the ETS. Under the agreement allocation will move from national governments to a mixture of market auctioning and allocation by the Commission. Finance ministers, however, intervened in the debate in order to ensure that future revenue from auctioning ETS allowances did not escape their control; the December 2008 compromise declared only that governments would be 'willing' to spend half the auction revenue on climate-change remedies.

However, the Commission largely failed in its attempt to design a parallel pan-EU system for trading renewable electricity. This was not totally surprising. While the Commission had a fairly clear field in designing the ETS—only the UK and Denmark had prior national emission schemes—it had, in the trading of renewables, to steer around twenty-seven national support schemes, often dear to their governments' hearts. The EP largely strongly supported the Commission's proposals, but they too disliked the Commission proposal for free cross-border trade in renewable electricity because of its probable effect in disrupting generous green-power subsidies. The opposition of the EP, supported by several key governments in the Council, meant that restrictions on trade in renewables were retained. Nonetheless, the initiative also sets differentiated renewable energy targets for all twenty-seven member states, despite ToL language letting countries keep control of their energy mix. The agreement also sets a common bio-fuels target for all (see Box 15.2), despite MEPs' criticism that this would aggravate food shortages and price surges by encouraging crop-based fuels. MEPs did secure changes to encourage renewable road fuels not based on food crops.

The economic downturn during 2008 also affected the strength of support amongst the old member states, although primarily in the form of seeking special treatment of selected sectors. It caused Chancellor Angela Merkel's German government—with very separate environment and economics departments under ministers from different parties—to insist that major exporting industries, such as

BOX 15.2	**The EU climate change and energy agreements of December 2008**

- 20% reduction in emissions by 2020 compared to 1990; up to 30% in the case of a matching international agreement.

- 20% renewable share in total energy consumption by 2020, based on binding targets for individual member states.

- 10% minimum share for renewable energy in all forms of transport. Second-generation bio-fuels, made from wood and waste and that do not compete with food, and electricity to power cars count extra towards this target.

- 20% improvement in energy efficiency by 2020 compared to business-as-usual projections. This is not a binding target nor will it mean a cut in overall energy use.

Germany's, should continue to have free carbon permits as long as they remained in danger of losing market share to foreign rivals with no carbon constraints. The downturn also fuelled similar demands from poorer central and east European states for free allocations, especially if, like Poland, they were heavily dependent on dirty coal for power generation.

Citing the problems of recession and foreign competition, European industry has lobbied effectively for a gradual phasing-in of paid carbon allowances, under a system whereby companies would have to buy their carbon allowances at auction, instead of being given them for free, in the reform of the ETS. The electricity industry in the old member states accepted early on that it would have to pay for its permits in the future. Not being exposed to competition from outside the EU, the power sector can pass on the cost of permits to its EU customers without fear of losing market share. This of course raises costs for its customers, especially electricity-intensive industries that are exposed to extra-EU competition, and therefore, if they pass on all of their higher energy bills to customers, they risk losing market share or jobs to non-EU competitors. So in the reform of the ETS they lobbied for, and won, the promise that they would continue to receive free allocations of emissions permits. Thus, while most of the broad intent of the Commission's proposal survived in the December 2008 agreement, a number of compromises were made to diminish the economic impact on some actors, be they member states or industries.

To sum up: with regard to climate change, the EU is acting in what might be called a 'revolutionary regulatory mode'—seeking to change the way Europeans live, produce their energy, make their products, heat their houses, and take their holidays, and by taking the lead in climate change negotiations seeking to some extent to change the rest of the world's lifestyle. It could be argued the EU was pre-disposed towards early action on climate change, as the 'precautionary principle', which requires action to avert potential environmental harm even in the absence of scientific certainty, was incorporated into the 1992 TEU in Article 130R dealing with the environment. This principle has been put into effect in a good deal of legislation already, as, for example, in the REACH package on chemicals (see Chapter 13).

The EU showed some capacity to learn from the mistakes in the early phases of the emissions trading scheme (ETS) when it came to designing later stages. But the Commission found it easier to design a pan-EU policy on emissions trading because there were fewer national schemes than exist in renewable energy. Climate-change policy is a trade-off between economic and environmental factors, requiring complex brokering of competing interests within both EU institutions and national governments, a process which is susceptible to economic cycles.

Conclusions

EU energy policy has developed unevenly because it is part economic policy, part environmental policy, and part security policy. Market-making came first, but it took several decades before environmental policy took off, and the EU is still stumbling over security policy. Future energy policy will also develop unevenly, with different policy strands moving at different paces. In the internal energy market, further radical structural reform seems unlikely. The then EU Energy Commissioner, Andris Piebalgs, promised that the third package of liberalization measures would be the last. Rather than policy construction, the internal energy market will mainly require policy maintenance to prevent backsliding.

Climate-change policy-making will probably accelerate, regardless of the economic downturn that has so far led to a questioning of only the costs rather than the principles of the policies. Further in-filling of the policy superstructure is required. The Commission will have to tackle harmonization of renewable energy subsidies; otherwise can an electricity market in which eventually nearly 40 per cent of generation is supported by twenty-seven different (and potentially distorting) national schemes really be called a single energy market? Now that aviation emissions are to be included in the ETS from 2012, why should shipping be excluded? The technical complexity of climate-change mechanisms already puts the Commission in a strong position vis-à-vis member states. Continued centralization of climate-change policy could strengthen the case for the Commission to become the Union's main external negotiator on climate change, as it long has been on trade policy (see Chapter 16).

Far less certain is how policy on energy security will develop. Member states will agree to take single-market-type measures, such as improving grid links and gas storage, to guard against energy cut-offs from outside. But it remains to be seen whether they will be scared enough of Russia to want to join in a collective external energy policy that would actively seek to diversify sources of energy.

FURTHER READING

Black (1977) and Matlary (1996) provide useful background to the development of classic EU energy policy, and Helm (2007) sets the scene for the broadening of energy policy to tackle climate change. On the three main strands of energy policy, Cameron (2007) is comprehensive on the internal energy market, while Barysch (2008) and Skjaerseth and Wettestad (2008) are informative on key aspects of energy security and climate change, and Stern (2006) addresses the economic and policy dimensions of climate change. Buchan (2009) discusses all of these issues in more depth. The best news website for tracking EU energy policy is *http://www.euractiv.com*.

Barysch, K. (2008) (ed.), *Pipelines, Politics and Power: The Future of EU–Russia Relations* (London: Centre for European Reform).

Black, R. E. (1977), 'Plus Ça Change, Plus C'est la Même Chose: Nine Governments in Search of a Common Energy Policy', in H. Wallace, W. Wallace, and C. Webb (eds.), *Policy-Making in the European Communities* (Chichester: John Wiley): 165–96.

Buchan, D. (2009), *Energy and Climate Change: Europe at the Crossroads* (Oxford: Oxford University Press).

Cameron, P. (2007), *Competition in Energy Markets: Law and Regulation in the European Union*, 2nd edn. (Oxford: Oxford University Press).

Helm, D. (2007), 'European Energy Policy: Securing Supplies and Meeting the Challenge of Climate Change', in D. Helm (ed.), The *New Energy Paradigm* (Oxford: Oxford University Press), 440–51.

Matlary, J. H. (1996), 'Energy Policy: From a National to a European Framework?', in H. Wallace and W. Wallace (eds.), *Policy-Making in the European Union*, 3rd edn. (Oxford: Oxford University Press): 257–77.

Skjaerseth, J. B., and Wettestad, J. (2008), *EU Emissions Trading: Initiation, Decision-making and Implementation* (Farnham: Ashgate).

Stern, N. (2006), The *Economics of Climate Change: The Stern Review* (London: HM Treasury).

CHAPTER 16

Trade Policy

A Further Shift Towards Brussels

Stephen Woolcock

▌ Summary

Over the past fifty years, European Union (EU) trade policy has become progressively more comprehensive due to treaty changes, stronger internal policies that provide the basis for common external policies, and the need to respond jointly to external challenges to EU policies. This also implies a steady shift in the focus of debate on trade from the member states to Brussels, a trend which will be confirmed by the Treaty of Lisbon. This strengthening of the EU in trade has not translated into an ability to shape the multilateral trade agenda, given the diffusion of power in a more multi-polar global trading system. As a result EU trade strategy has reverted to the use of preferential agreements as well as the pursuit of a comprehensive multilateral rules-based system to pursue its aims.

The historical development of EU trade policy

Initially trade policy served the primary aim of building Europe. Both the customs union (see Chapter 5) and the common agricultural policy (CAP) (see Chapter 8) liberalized trade among the member states while establishing common policies towards third countries. During the 1960s and 1970s EU trade policy served to defend these preferences and the ability of member-state governments to pursue interventionist industrial policies, as well as the offensive aim of opening markets for the national industries in the EU by reducing third-country tariffs.

During the 1980s the creation of a single European market (see Chapter 5) and the associated strengthening of the *acquis communautaire* resulted in more genuine common policies. This stronger *acquis* then constituted a broader 'domestic' (i.e. EU) base for common EU trade policies and went hand-in-hand with a shift towards a more proactive and liberal trade policy that was also more supportive of a rules-based multilateral trading system. During the Uruguay Round of negotiations within the General Agreement on Tariffs and Trade (GATT) (1986–94), the EU shared leadership with the US and helped to bring about the considerable development of the rules-based, multilateral system, culminating in the creation of the World Trade Organization (WTO) in 1995.

By the mid-1990s the EU was seeking to initiate a new multilateral trade round. But the EU's views on a comprehensive agenda—including negotiations about multilateral rules governing competition policy, foreign investment, environmental provisions, and public procurement standards—were not fully shared by either the US or developing countries. With the rise of China, the growing economic strength of India, and a more cohesive coalition of developing countries led by Brazil and India, the trading system had become multi-polar by the late 1990s. Thus the EU emerged as a leading proponent of a comprehensive rule-based multilateral trading system just as it was becoming harder for any single trading power to shape the trade agenda. Having agreed to lower its tariffs on manufactured goods in previous rounds of GATT negotiations, the EU sought to use agriculture—where it still had relatively high tariffs, provided substantial domestic support, and used export subsidies (see Chapter 8)—as leverage to further its offensive interests in a comprehensive multilateral round. Without active support from the US, however, the EU has not been very successful in shaping the WTO Doha Development Agenda (DDA) negotiations, which were launched in November 2001.

From 2006 the EU has therefore followed the trend, initiated by the US, towards more actively pursuing bilateral free trade agreements (FTAs) in order to realize its commercial and trade-policy objectives. The EU has long used preferential trade agreements but these have mainly served foreign-policy objectives, such as by stabilizing and integrating countries of central and eastern Europe (see Chapter 17) or promoting the development of the former colonies of the member states (the Lomé, Cotonou. and Economic Partnership Agreements (EPAs) with the African, Caribbean, and Pacific (ACP) states). The different dimensions of EU trade policy are discussed in Box 16.1.

BOX 16.1	The dimensions of EU trade policy

There are different dimensions to EU trade policy, the importance of which vary over time. Although EU trade policy is influenced by liberal arguments favouring *unilateral* liberalization, it only unilaterally offers preferential market access or zero tariffs for least developed countries under the United Nations' General System of Preferences (GSP) scheme and its own Everything But Arms (EBA) policy.

EU *bilateral* trade policy takes the form of Association Agreements or free-trade agreements with third countries. Trade and trade-related topics also form the core of efforts, not especially successful, to reach *region-to-region* agreements, such as with Mercosur, which are intended both to open markets for EU exporters and to promote integration within the partner region.

Plurilateral agreements, such as the Agreement on Government Procurement (GPA) and Agreement on Trade in Civil Aircraft under the aegis of the WTO, or various agreements on investment under the aegis of the Organization for Economic Cooperation and Development (OECD) are negotiated by the EU (or its member states) with like-minded or similarly developed countries on specialist topics.

The *multilateral* dimension of EU trade policy centres on the WTO. Major agreements are reached through periodic 'rounds' of negotiation, such as the Doha Development Agenda. There are, however, also a range of WTO committees concerned with implementation, the review of WTO members' trade policies (Trade Policy Review Mechanism), and a binding dispute-settlement mechanism.

EU trade policy includes the application of *commercial instruments*. These include anti-dumping and countervailing duties to counter unfair practices of firms selling into the EU market below the cost of production or being subsidized by their governments. Safeguards may be used to raise tariffs in order to offset sudden, disruptive surges in imports. The EU Trade Barriers Regulation (TBR) provides a mechanism for challenging foreign governments' barriers to EU exports or non-compliance with trade rules.

Towards a comprehensive EU trade policy

Trade policy is an area in which the EU, as opposed to the member states, has considerable influence on the international scene thanks to the EU's largely exclusive authority (competence) for trade policy and the size and depth of the single European market. But it has taken many years to establish a comprehensive policy. This section considers how treaty changes, internal policy developments, and external factors have played a role in the creation of such a comprehensive, common EU trade policy.

Treaty provisions and reform

The 1957 Treaty of Rome, as amended, provides for exclusive EU competence for 'common commercial policy' in Article 133 (TEC) (ex Art. 113 EEC) and sets out the decision-making processes. As is discussed in detail below, negotiations are conducted by the Commission on the basis of a 'mandate' agreed by the member states in the Council of Ministers and in consultation with a special committee of national trade representatives. The results of the multilateral trade negotiations must be adopted by the Council and in certain cases (see below) have the assent of the European Parliament (EP). Ratification by member states is required for agreements that fall outside the exclusive competence of the EU (see below). Bilateral or preferential agreements, such as association agreements, must be adopted unanimously by the Council and have the assent of the EP (Art. 310 TEC; ex Art. 238 EEC).

The Treaty of Rome did not provide an exhaustive definition of the 'common commercial policy.' In 1958 trade policy was essentially limited to tariffs, so these were mentioned, as were agricultural levies and anti-dumping duties. But otherwise the allocation of competence between the EU and the member states has been at issue whenever new topics appeared on the trade agenda. The decision to create a customs union and common agricultural policy did, however, require the original member states jointly to set tariffs and to develop a common trade policy on agriculture as they did in the Kennedy Round of GATT negotiations (1964–7). As the trade agenda expanded, the EU was called upon to negotiate an ever wider range of topics, such as technical barriers to trade (TBTs), subsidies and countervailing duties (SCDs), and public procurement during the Tokyo Round (1973–9); services, investment, and intellectual property in the Uruguay Round (Woolcock and Hodges 1996). In response to what was in effect an external and largely US-driven trade agenda, member-state governments pragmatically accepted that the Commission should act as the negotiator for the EU as a whole and were willing to leave aside the issue of legal competence until the ratification stage of negotiations.

The allocation of competence in trade policy has featured in all of the recent Intergovernmental Conferences (IGCs). In the IGC that led to the Maastricht Treaty on European Union (TEU) of 1992, the Commission pressed for increased EU competence to include services, investment, and intellectual property rights on the grounds that these were part of the package of issues being negotiated in the Uruguay Round, but this was resisted by some member states because they were concerned about the implied loss of sovereignty. The TEU also kept trade policy within the control of the technocratic policy élite of senior national and Commission trade officials, and the EP at arm's length. In the IGC that led to the 1997 Treaty of Amsterdam (ToA), renewed Commission pressure for increased competence led to a modest compromise, which enabled the Council, acting unanimously, to add a specific issue, such as services, to EU competence without having to go through a formal treaty change (Art. 133(5) TEC), but this 'enabling clause' has never been used. The

2001 Treaty of Nice (ToN) added some service activities to EU competence, but excluded sensitive service sectors such as audio-visual, education, and healthcare.

The Treaty of Lisbon (ToL) makes all trade policy exclusive EU competence, dispensing with mixed competence, but member states concerned about the liberalization of audio-visual, health, and educational services secured a provision that unanimity applies to trade agreements that threaten cultural and linguistic diversity or the effective provision of national health, education, and social policies (Woolcock 2008). The formal treaty provisions governing EU trade policy have therefore evolved over the past half a century. They have been concerned with the allocation of competence rather than how trade policy is made. However, the ToL also effects a change in the latter by granting the EP greater powers (see below).

The impact of the *acquis communautaire*

Treaty changes alone, however, afford only a limited understanding of the evolution towards a comprehensive EU trade policy. Developments in 'domestic' EU policies (known collectively as the *acquis communautaire*), including how domestic policies have responded to external factors, have been arguably more important in bringing about a more comprehensive EU trade policy. Domestic policies first and foremost provide the basis for common external policies. The establishment of domestic competence for a topic also establishes implied powers or competence for external relations.

The common external tariff (CET), anti-dumping and safeguard provisions, and the CAP came into effect in the late 1960s, but many other trade and trade-related issues were not governed by common EU policies. In the early 1970s the individual member states used Article 115 (EEC) to maintain national import quotas on textiles and clothing from low-cost developing countries and national 'voluntary' export restraint agreements (VERs) on products such as cars, consumer electronics, and machine tools from Japan and the newly industrializing countries (NICs). Throughout the 1970s member states also pursued policies to bolster the competitiveness of national companies through the use of subsidies, preferential government procurement, technical regulations and standards, and the (non-)application of competition policy (see Chapter 6).

During the 1980s the picture changed considerably due largely to the realization of a genuine single European market (SEM) (see Chapter 5). For example, the elimination of frontier controls within the EU made the continuation of national quotas and VERs impossible and loosened the grip of defensive interests enough to facilitate EU support for a ban on such measures (Hanson 1998). Stricter enforcement of the existing EU rules on national subsidies provided the model for the subsidy rules of WTO Agreement on Subsidies and Countervailing Duties. In the field of government procurement, where the EU had previously blocked US attempts to open the EU electricity, gas, and telecommunications markets, the adoption of a panoply of EU directives (on energy markets see Chapter 15) brought virtually all public procurement under

EU rules and facilitated a more positive EU position in the plurilateral negotiations on a revised Government Procurement Agreement (GPA) in the WTO (Woolcock 2008). The SEM also liberalized the provision of telecommunications and financial services (see Chapter 5), which again facilitated a more proactive EU stance in the Uruguay Round (A. R. Young 2002). Similarly, reforms in the common agricultural policy, starting with the 1992 McSharry reforms and continuing through the Agenda 2000 and July 2003 mid-term review of the CAP, have shaped what the EU can offer in international negotiations. Trade negotiations have in turn also contributed to the reform of EU agricultural policy (see Chapter 8).

The SEM and the development of the *acquis* had a threefold effect on the EU policy process in trade. First, the SEM liberalized trade in goods and services within the EU and thus gave the Commission negotiators more flexibility to seek ambitious reciprocal trade agreements. Second, the deepening of the EU market, combined with widening it through enlargement (including anticipated enlargement) enhanced the economic power of the EU; in trade negotiations, power can be broadly equated with the ability to withhold access to a large market. Third, the adoption of common policies gave EU negotiators an agreed basis for negotiating international rules and obligations.

Beyond the *acquis* there are a number of more general EU values that have shaped its trade policy. First is the belief, based on the European experience, that market integration cannot stop with requiring national treatment (formally treating foreign and domestic firms alike) and removing border measures, but also requires positive integration (agreeing common policies to replace national ones) or at least agreement on a range of trade-related topics. This is reflected in the EU's search for a comprehensive trade agenda in the WTO and—for the most part—in the preferential agreements it negotiates. Second is the belief—again based on the EU experience—that regional economic integration has considerable economic and political benefits. This is why the EU favours region-to-region agreements to promote regional integration in other regions and why the EU has become the 'patron saint of inter-regionalism in international relations' (Aggarwal and Fogarty 2005: 327). Third, liberalization in the EU has taken place within a framework of agreed rules that protect competition, the environment, and other legitimate social-policy objectives. This has also shaped the EU goal of a comprehensive agenda, promoting rules on trade-related topics for reasons of governance, as well as to enhance market access (Lamy 2004; Baldwin 2006).

External factors

External factors have also driven EU trade policy towards greater comprehensiveness. From the origins of the GATT in the late 1940s until well into the 1980s, the international trade agenda, if not always the outcome of negotiations, was shaped by the US. In the 1960s this took the form of pressure for tariff reductions and negotiations on agriculture to limit the impact of the CET and the CAP on US exporting interests. In the 1970s it took the form of adding trade-related topics, such as restrictions on subsidies and government procurement, to the agenda in an effort to extend GATT disciplines to the 'unfair' competition resulting from the use of such instruments by European states and Japan. In the 1980s it took the form of getting services, intellectual property, and investment on the GATT agenda, because these topics reflected the US competitive advantage in financial services, communications, high technology/research-based products, and the media. Thus the international trade agenda has consistently involved issues that did not fall clearly within the EU's exclusive competence as conveyed by the common commercial policy.

Faced with this 'challenge', the EU member states responded pragmatically and agreed that negotiating with one voice through the Commission was in the EU's best interest (Meunier 2005). The Commission was thus given the role of negotiating on a range of topics, but without prejudice to the location of formal, *de jure* competence. Once agreements had been negotiated it was then necessary to resolve the legal-competence question in order to know how the agreements were to be adopted and implemented. At the end of the Tokyo Round a political agreement was reached on joint signature by the EU and the member states (Bourgeois 1982). At the end of the Uruguay Round the General Affairs Council first decided, in March 1994, that the Council Presidency, Commission, and member states should all sign the Marrakesh Agreement that concluded the negotiations. But the Commission, supported by Belgium, was concerned that this would set a precedent that would prejudice the forthcoming (Amsterdam) IGC in which the Commission was seeking increased EU competence. So the Commission referred the issue to the European Court of Justice (ECJ).[1] The ECJ's resulting Opinion 1/94 lent rather more towards the member-state than the Commission position (Devuyst 1995). Crucially, however, because the Commission was given the job of negotiating, it was able to build negotiating capacity, expertise, and institutional memory, which have helped it to progressively establish de facto competence for the wider, comprehensive trade agenda.

The policy process

As a result of all of these pressures and the responses to them, the Commission has emerged as the sole voice for the EU in international trade negotiations, in which it must reflect the interests of the member states. This section examines the nature of the relationship between the Commission and the member states and how, if at all, the EU has responded to the greater pressure for accountability in trade-policy decision-making.

The Council decides on the EU's objectives

In multilateral negotiations, notably within the WTO, the Commission produces a draft mandate, drawing on the positions of the member governments, the views of business and civil society, and resolutions or reports from the European or national parliaments. In developing its mandate the Commission rarely works from a blank sheet. As discussed above, the EU's agreed rules—the *acquis*—provide an obvious point of departure. In addition, trade negotiations are usually part of an iterative process, so that rules agreed and positions adopted in previous rounds will inform the EU's position in the current negotiation. Moreover, trade agreements or positions once adopted in one negotiating context may well affect positions taken in other negotiating contexts. Continuity and consistency in the EU's negotiating positions are facilitated by a strong institutional memory within the Commission and national trade administrations.

The Commission's draft mandate is discussed in the Article 133 Committee, which consists of senior trade officials from each member government, and is chaired by the rotating Council presidency. The formal mandate is then adopted by the General Affairs and External Relations Council (GAERC) (see Figure 16.1). The EP has no formal role in mandating or authorizing negotiations, but it may be able to shape opinion by debating the topics and passing resolutions or adopting reports on specific trade topics. The adoption of the Lisbon Treaty is unlikely to change this as it clearly states that it is the Council that will retain the right to authorize negotiations and determine the mandate (Art. 218(2) ToL). The mandate is not time-limited. For example, the EU negotiated the DDA on a formal mandate adopted in 1999 before the Seattle WTO Ministerial meeting. But the mandate can be and is adjusted as negotiations proceed.

The Commission negotiates

The Commission negotiates on behalf of the EU in consultation with the member governments, mostly through the regular meetings of the Article 133 Committee (Johnson 1998). In negotiations the Commission is the only member of the EU delegation to speak, although national officials from member governments are present in formal negotiations. This is the case for topics on which the EU has competence, as well as in trade negotiations in which there is mixed or member-state competence. The Commission is expected to report to the member governments on important informal contacts with the EU's trading partners to, for example, exchange information. There is a grey area here in the sense that there is no clear dividing line between exchanging information and negotiations. If the negotiations are in Geneva, where the WTO has its headquarters, member states are represented by officials drawn from the national delegations to the WTO or experts from national capitals. At key junctures in negotiations or at WTO ministerial meetings, member governments are represented by ministers.

Before the Commission can act by proposing a particular line of action it must go through inter-service consultation in which the lead Directorate General, DG Trade, consults with other DGs. These other DGs will not always share the same views as DG TRADE. DG AGRI has historically been much more cautious about liberalizing trade in agricultural products. DG ENV is concerned about integrating trade and environmental objectives and how trade commitments may impinge upon the Commission's international environmental policies. Other DGs will also be concerned about the impact of trade agreements on food safety or foreign policy objectives.

The Council can direct the Commission on any issue during negotiations, but in most cases new initiatives or changes result from Commission proposals, which are discussed in the Article 133 Committee. If a Commission proposal does not have sufficient support, the chair will refer the matter back to the Commission. Although qualified majority voting (QMV) is provided for under treaty rules, the Article 133 Committee hardly ever takes a formal vote and favours consensus. The prospect of a vote based on a QMV means, however, that member governments go to considerable lengths to avoid being isolated and thus faced with the possibility of being outvoted.

The central dynamic of EU trade policy lies in the interaction between the Commission and the Council/Article 133 Committee. In this, the member governments not only set the objectives and ratify the results, but can also intervene directly in the negotiating tactics and composition of the final package. This is slightly different from the US system of Trade Promotion Authority (TPA), formerly 'fast track', in which Congress delegates constitutional powers to negotiate commercial policy to the executive and must accept or reject, but cannot in principle amend what is negotiated. Although the United States Trade Representative (USTR) has to be very sensitive to Congressional opinion, because it must have majority support for the final package, it probably has more negotiating flexibility than does the Commission vis-à-vis member governments.

The EU system works well when communication between the Commission and the member governments is effective and when the Commission is seen as a credible, trusted negotiator by the member-state governments. The degree of flexibility will, however, vary from topic to topic, with the Commission tending to have more latitude on detailed technical topics, such as rules of origin or the detail of tariff schedules, than on politically sensitive issues, such as the key modalities for agricultural trade agreements. The Commission will therefore generally wish to deal with issues by means of technical discussions within the Article 133 Committee. Any member state not happy with how the Commission deals with an issue at this level will seek to 'politicize' the issue by pressing for a debate on it in the Council, where the normal practice is for trade issues to be approved without discussion.

The Commission and Council consult the EP, and this has become more formal with the establishment of the International Trade Committee (INTA) in 2004. There is a growing acceptance among policy-makers that 'trade can no longer operate in a hermetically sealed box', but must be more open to scrutiny and debate (Baldwin 2006: 941). Although the adoption of provisions in the Lisbon Treaty formalizes this and requires the Commission to *report* regularly to the INTA on the progress of negotiations, the Article 133 Committee will remain more important and continue with its existing role of *assisting* the Commission in negotiations.

FIGURE 16.1 EU decision-making process for multilateral trade negotiations prior to the Treaty of Lisbon

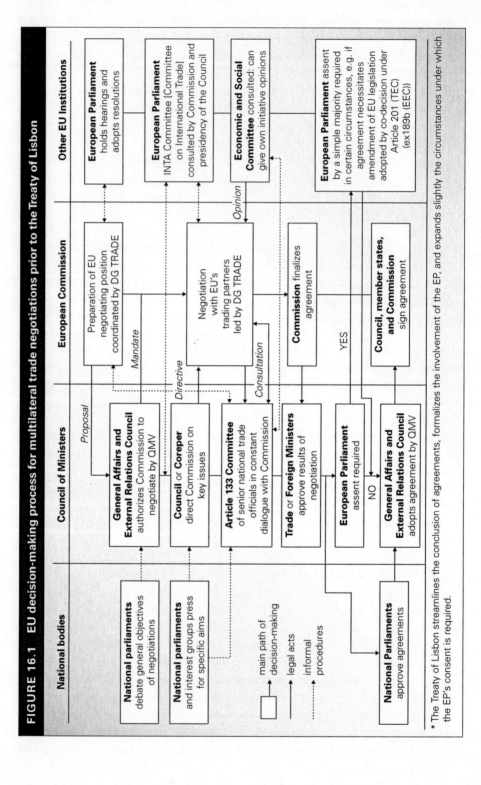

* The Treaty of Lisbon streamlines the conclusion of agreements, formalizes the involvement of the EP, and expands slightly the circumstances under which the EP's consent is required.

The balance of member state positions

The ideological stances of the member states on trade are a factor. But some caution is called for when categorizing member governments as liberal or protectionist. Positions are also significantly shaped by sectoral interests and the party composition of governments, not to mention economic and electoral cycles. For example, Ireland is liberal on trade in manufacturing, investment, and services, but protectionist on agriculture. France is protectionist on agriculture, but liberal on services, except audio-visual services. Germany is generally liberal on trade in goods, but less so on the liberalization of agriculture or services. Generally speaking, Sweden has tended to occupy the liberal end of the spectrum. Denmark, Finland, Germany, The Netherlands, and the UK tend to adopt liberal positions, whereas Italy, Spain, and Portugal are more protectionist, with the other member states in swing positions. France also tends to see itself as providing the backbone for the EU trade policy in the sense of holding out against pressure from third countries, especially the US.

Successive enlargements of the EU have influenced this pattern. UK accession meant that EU policy would in future be shaped by a state that has deep liberal trade traditions. Portuguese and Spanish accession tipped the balance towards a less liberal view, especially in sectors such as steel and textiles, whereas the 1995 enlargement to include Austria, Finland, and Sweden shifted the centre of gravity towards liberal policies. The 2004 enlargement to include central and east European countries, as well as Cyprus and Malta, has on balance proved to be relatively neutral. Whilst Poland and Slovakia have sectors they wish to protect, there are liberal countervailing forces in Estonia, the Czech Republic, Slovenia, and Hungary. There is also not much evidence of enlargement bringing about changes, or making decision-making harder. The smaller new member states tend to be relatively passive except on a few key issues. As they do not have strong views on many issues, these smaller member states tend to support the Commission's proposals. Supporting the Commission on issues where they have no stake has the benefit of preserving their limited political capital for those things that are really of central national importance and on which they want Commission support.

A relatively limited role for outside interests

The EU trade-policy process is shaped by sectoral or interest groups, but such groups, including business groups, generally play less of a role in the EU processes than, for example, in the US, which has had formal channels for representation since the 1970s in the shape of the US Trade Advisory Committees. The European Economic and Social Committee (and Committee of the Regions) are consulted on EU trade policy, but, rightly or wrongly, are not taken very seriously by the policy-makers or stakeholders.

The Commission is happy to hear the views of business. Indeed, the need for private-sector input in order to define the EU's offensive and defensive trade objectives has, on occasion, led the Commission to encourage the creation of new EU-level business representation where it did not previously exist. The Commission, for example, sponsored the creation of the European Services Forum (ESF) in the late 1980s. The Commission tends to favour EU-level representation and can relatively easily fend off lobbying from sectoral interests in one or only a couple of member states on the grounds that they are not representative of the EU-wide interest. The need for representation to take place at the EU level necessitates common positions among national sectoral interests and thus makes for more institutionalized lobbying through EU-level sector bodies, which generally requires compromise and thus dilutes preferences. This may be one of the reasons why European business lobbying on trade policy is relatively less assertive than that in the US (Woll 2009). This does not of course preclude independent lobbying by major firms, which may in any case have a presence across the EU.

An increased sensitivity to civil society non-governmental organizations (NGOs) after the Seattle WTO Ministerial in 1999, among other things, led to the establishment of a semi-formal Consultative Forum with NGOs, including business and sectoral organizations, as well as a wide range of civil-society NGOs. The diverse views in the Consultative Forum mean that, while it enhances policy transparency, it leaves the existing technocratic policy-making machinery of the Commission, the Article 133 Committee, and the Council largely untouched. Civil-society advocacy does, however, have an indirect impact on EU trade policy to the extent that it influences public opinion and has heightened the calls for greater parliamentary scrutiny. The EP is also more open to civil-society lobbying and hence a greater role for the EP looks likely to translate into a larger role for NGOs.

The Council adopts the results but the role of the EP is growing

The Council adopts the eventual results of each negotiation. National ministers are normally present at key stages of a major negotiation to provide final instructions and to endorse last-minute agreements and compromises. Formal adoption then follows in the GAERC under the QMV rule on issues within EU competence, although in practice the Council operates by consensus, at least as far as major issues affecting major member governments are concerned. Smaller member states may be bought off with side payments.

The adoption of provisions that fall within member-state or mixed competence are also subject to ratification at member-state level, including by national parliaments. In practice, if member states delay ratification of trade agreements, it is in order to gain negotiating coinage for other internal EU issues, not because they wish to refuse to ratify an agreement accepted by the Council.

Under existing treaty provisions the EP must give its assent, by a simple majority, if a trade agreement (a) requires changes in EU internal legislation adopted by co-decision-making, (b) establishes specific institutional obligations (such as a joint parliamentary body or committee), or (c) has budgetary implications. Unless a multilateral trade agreement is very limited it is likely to require EP assent under one or more of these conditions. For political reasons it would also be difficult not to seek EP assent. The adoption of the Lisbon Treaty strengthens the powers of the EP by requiring that it give its 'consent' for all trade agreements. As yet, however, the EP has no real credible veto power over multilateral agreements. If all the members of the WTO and all the twenty-seven EU member states have agreed on an outcome, it is difficult to see how the EP could reject such an agreement. To date there has typically been a majority in the EP in favour of a liberal external trade stance.

Association agreements, which have been used for all major bilateral agreements to date, require unanimity within the Council and the assent of the EP.[2] This can clearly affect the policy process by strengthening the position of a member state that wishes to block an agreement and making it more important for the Commission and Council to keep the EP 'on board'. The EP's rejection of a bilateral agreement, such as an EPA between the EU and an ACP state or region, is more likely than that of a multilateral agreement. The EP has shown considerable interest in aspects of bilateral agreements, such as human-rights conditions in the EU's trading partners. But there must still be some doubt that the EP will decline to give its assent to a bilateral agreement that has been negotiated, accepted by all twenty-seven member states, and adopted by the trading partner.

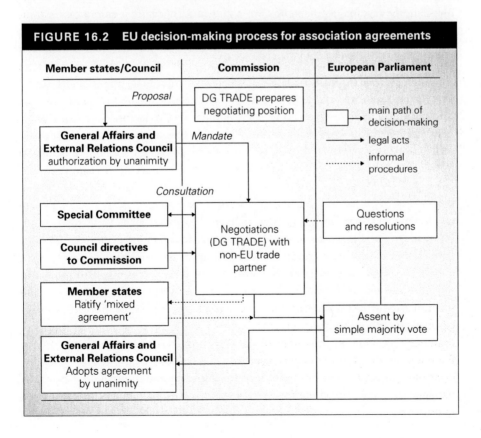

FIGURE 16.2   EU decision-making process for association agreements

Commercial instruments

Anti-dumping has been by far the most important commercial instrument used by the EU. The GATT lays down rules on anti-dumping that are implemented in EU regulations. These regulations are currently adopted by the Council following a proposal by the Commission, in other words not by co-decision-making. An anti-dumping complaint is triggered by a claim from an EU sectoral interest group that imports are being 'dumped' (sold below cost) and are causing—or threatening to cause—'serious injury'. DG TRADE considers the general validity of such complaints. At this stage there may well be informal communications between the industry or lawyers representing the industry and the Commission on the strength of the case. If the Commission is persuaded there is sufficient evidence, it seeks approval from the Anti-Dumping Committee, composed of member-state officials, to begin an investigation. Approval to investigate requires a simple majority of the member states voting.

The Commission is then fully responsible for establishing (a) if dumping has occurred, (b) whether there is serious injury, (c) causality, in other words the injury must result from dumping, and (d) whether the 'Community interest' would be served by imposing duties. As the GATT's requirements are not tightly drawn, the Commission has a good measure of discretion in its evaluations of dumping and injury. This is especially the case for judgments of 'Community interest', which require an assessment of the costs to consumers and other user industries and the benefits for the injured industry of imposing anti-dumping duties. In cases of dumping the Commission imposes provisional duties, which may be imposed for up to nine months after consulting, or in the case of extreme emergency informing, the member states. The Council can overturn the imposition of provisional duties by a qualified majority. The Council, however, must approve definitive duties, which can run for up to five years.

In recent years procedures on anti-dumping have been changed to make it easier to have a definitive duty adopted. In 1994 the threshold for adopting a definitive duty was lowered from QMV to a simple majority of member states (Council Regulation 522/94). When the 2004 enlargement threatened to make it harder to get a simple majority in favour of action due to concerns that smaller new member states would tend to abstain unless directly affected (Molyneux 1999), a further change was made to the effect that a Commission proposal for a definitive duty stands unless there is a simple majority *against* it (Council Regulation 461/2004).

Broader policy issues relating to the use of anti-dumping or other forms of contingent protection, such as whether to exercise restraint in the use of commercial instruments during the international economic downturn following the 2008 financial crisis, may also be discussed in the Commercial Questions Group of the Committee of Permanent Representatives (Coreper), but the Commission has had some success in limiting the role of this committee.

The Commission's responsibility for implementing anti-dumping policy, therefore, gives it considerable discretionary power. In the past this has been criticized as providing scope to use anti-dumping duties as a form of hidden or contingent

FIGURE 16.3   EU decision-making process for anti-dumping measures

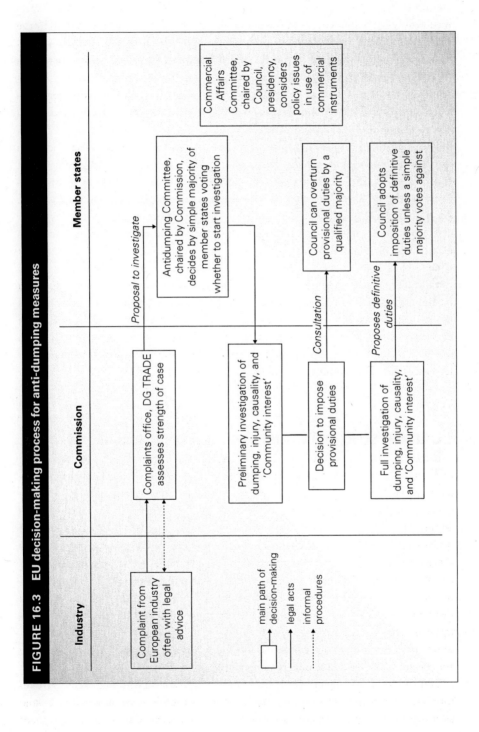

protection. In 2008 DG TRADE was, however, accused by industry of using its discretion to hinder the process of adopting anti-dumping measures. Finally, it is perhaps worth stressing that in contrast to most other decisions on trade it is common practice to take votes on anti-dumping actions. This can lead to active lobbying of small member states without a direct interest in the case by the larger member states with important sectoral interests at stake.

Another crucial aspect of EU trade policy concerns the day-to-day implementation of bilateral and multilateral agreements. This involves work in the various WTO committees and bilateral joint committees or councils, as well as the use of formal dispute-settlement procedures. Most disputes are resolved in consultations between the Commission and the relevant trading partner. However, there is a greater use of adjudication in dispute settlement, especially in the WTO. The EU has won several important WTO cases including against the US's safeguard actions on steel and the Foreign Sales Corporation (FSC) provisions of the US tax code. It has also lost some notable cases, such as those challenging its banana-trade regime, ban on hormone-treated beef, and moratorium on approvals of genetically modified organisms (see Chapter 14). When the EU is accused of non-compliance the Commission submits the EU's case and represents the EU in any hearings. Decisions on whether to bring a case in the WTO are generally taken by the Commission, but with the backing of the Article 133 Committee. Challenging another WTO member under the Dispute Settlement Understanding (DSU) can be seen as an aggressive step, especially when losing the case would require politically or economically costly changes in policy or legislation. In these instances decisions are taken by the Council.

EU trade strategy since the Uruguay Round

This section considers the more substantive question of how the EU has responded to the lack of progress in the multilateral Doha Development Agenda by re-emphasizing bilateral and (at least rhetorically) region-to-region agreements. In 1999 the EU adopted a de facto moratorium on new free-trade agreements (FTAs) in order not to undermine the credibility of its push for a comprehensive multilateral round (Lamy 2004). The EU pursued its aim of a comprehensive multilateral agenda, and WTO Working Groups on competition, investment, public procurement, and trade facilitation were established after the 1996 Singapore Ministerial. In 1998 the Clinton Administration agreed, rather reluctantly, to support the EU proposal for a comprehensive, 'millennium' round, but the attempt to launch this in Seattle in December 1999 failed due in part to opposition from developing countries and civil-society NGOs and in part to a lack of agreement between the EU and US on the negotiating aims. At the WTO Ministerial in Doha in 2001 a new round was launched thanks to the use of the time-honoured GATT device of constructive ambiguity in the agenda, a more supportive US position in the wake of the terrorist attacks on 11 September

2001, and EU work on the Doha Declaration, which provided a waiver from the Trade-Related Intellectual Property Rights (TRIPs) Agreement, concluded as part of the Uruguay Round, for the production of essential medicines, and which was a precondition for developing-country support for a round.

Movement in the EU position on agriculture compared to the 1980s (see Chapter 8) was reflected in the fact that a joint EU–US paper on agriculture could be agreed in the run up to the 2003 Cancun WTO Ministerial meeting (Woolcock 2005). This joint paper, however, provoked developing countries, led by Brazil and India, to form the G20 coalition in order to counter what they saw as an attempt to maintain the US–EU duopoly in the trading system. With India and other G20 members opposing a comprehensive round and seeking more on agriculture than either the EU or US was ready to offer, the Cancun Ministerial collapsed even though the EU took off the agenda both investment and competition, two of the so-called 'Singapore' issues that the EU saw as essential for a comprehensive round, as part of an effort to save the negotiations. Transparency in public procurement, a third Singapore issue, was subsequently dropped, leaving only trade facilitation.

The abandonment of most of the Singapore issues and the lack of progress on other issues was a major setback for the EU. The EU retained a preference for multilateralism, but there was a growing debate within the Commission and among the member states on the option of negotiating new preferential agreements. In a policy statement in November 2003 the Commission (2003f: 16) articulated the view that the DDA remained the priority but FTAs would not be ruled out, if they offered clear economic benefits and, in cases of region-to-region agreements, the EU's partners showed evidence of progress towards regional integration. By March and April 2006 a broad consensus in favour of a more active FTA policy emerged, more as a result of the ongoing dialogue in the Article 133 Committee in response to the problems of the Doha Round than of pressure from any specific sector or lobby (Elsig 2008). This consensus was reflected in the 'Global Europe' strategy paper adopted by the Commission in October 2006 (Commission 2006g).

There were three main reasons for this shift in policy. First, there was the lack of progress in the DDA, both in comprehensiveness and ambition on mainstream topics such as non-agricultural market access (NAMA) (i.e. tariff reductions) and services.

Second, other major WTO members shifted towards more active FTA strategies. In 2000 China approached the Association of South East Asian Nations (ASEAN) with a view to negotiating preferential agreements. Japan and even India began to conclude comprehensive economic cooperation agreements that went beyond eliminating tariffs (Heydon and Woolcock 2009). Perhaps most important of all, the US pursued an active policy of 'competitive liberalization' once the Bush Administration obtained Trade Promotion Authority in 2001 and it was soon negotiating FTAs with Central America, Thailand, Korea, the Southern Africa Customs Union (SACU), as well as seeking to conclude the Free Trade Area of the Americas (FTAA) (Evenett and Meier 2007). These FTAs offered better access to some major markets for the

EU's competitors and therefore led to pressure from European industry and particularly the service sector for the EU to negotiate equivalent access via FTAs if the DDA was not going to deliver. Many FTAs, particularly those negotiated by the US, also included trade-related topics such as investment, government procurement, 'TRIPs Plus' intellectual property rights, as well as elements of labour and environmental protection. This led to a growing concern that the EU's major international competitors would gain better access to third-country markets and thus increased pressure on the member states and Commission to follow suit and ensure matching access.

A third factor was that many EU bilateral trade agreements had been motivated more by foreign policy or development considerations than by commercial objectives. For example, the Stability and Adjustment Agreements (SAAs) with the Balkan states were primarily motivated by a desire to promote economic and political stability in the region (see Chapter 17). Similarly the EuroMed Association agreements were aimed at promoting economic growth to counter the political instability and the rise of fundamentalism in the Mediterranean littoral. The economic partnership agreements (EPAs) with the ACP states, which together accounted for only 4 per cent of EU exports, were prompted for the most part by development aims. Only the FTAs with Mexico and Chile, both of which were negotiated to counter the trade-diversionary effects of US FTAs, and perhaps the Trade Development and Cooperation Agreement with South Africa, could be said to be with emerging markets. The EU therefore shifted to pursue a more active policy of negotiating bilateral trade agreements, for largely commercial reasons.

Conclusions

Until well into the mid-1990s EU trade-policy decision-making could be characterized with confidence as technocratic and rather opaque, with Commission and member-state trade officials in the Article 133 Committee doing much of the work and ministers in the GAERC making key political decisions and providing democratic legitimacy. This technocratic and opaque process facilitated efficiency by keeping trade policy at arm's length from protectionist forces. National and EU policy interests were based on largely informal contacts with private-sector interests.

Since the mid-1990s there has been a consolidation of the 'Brussels-based' decision-making process due to treaty changes, more common internal EU policies, and the growth of de facto competence for trade in the Commission. Pressures for greater transparency and accountability have not significantly impacted on the policy process. In terms of broad trade strategy, the EU moved to adopt a multi-level approach (i.e. bilateral, region-to-region, as well as multilateral), more in common with other WTO members, once its limited ability to shape the multilateral agenda alone became apparent. EU trade strategy in this context is thus dependent on developments elsewhere. If its major trading partners de-emphasize FTAs or do not ratify negotiated bilateral agreements, the pressure on the EU to conclude FTAs will be eased. Progress at the multilateral level will also help to restore EU interest in the WTO, but the expectation must be that bilateral trade agreements will remain a central feature of the trading system for some time to come.[3]

Notes

1 In an effort to head off a formal legal judgment, the German Council presidency along with the British and French governments suggested a political solution in the form of a code of conduct for dealing with negotiations involving issues of mixed competence in the future.

2 Prior to the ToL bilateral trade agreements that fell entirely under EU competence did not require the EP to grant its assent, although again the Commission and Council tended to consider such assent politically necessary for major agreements.

3 See Heydon and Woolcock (2009), who argue that the US will continue to pursue a competitive liberalization strategy, despite the change of administration in 2009.

FURTHER READING

For a general introduction to EU trade policy from a political economy perspective see Elsig (2002). Two good recent compilations of journal articles that provide a range of perspectives on the policy process as well as some excellent contributions on substantive policy are Peterson and Young (2006) and Dür and Zimmermann (2007). On the legal basis for EU trade policy see Eeckhout (2004). On interest group lobbying see Woll (2009). For a discussion of EU trade policy in operation in the Doha Development Agenda from the perspective of a principal–agent analysis of Commission and Council relations see Kerremans (2004).

Dür, A., and Zimmermann, H. (2007) (eds.), 'The EU in International Trade Negotiations', *Journal of Common Market Studies*, 45/4 (special issue).

Eeckhout, P. (2004), *External Relations of the European Union: Legal and Constitutional Foundations* (Oxford: Oxford University Press).

Elsig, M. (2002), *The EU's Common Commercial Policy: Institutions, Interests and Ideas* (Farnham: Ashgate).

Kerremans, B. (2004), 'What Went Wrong in Cancun? A Principal–Agent View on the EU's Rationale Towards the Doha Development Round', *European Foreign Affairs Review*, 9/3: 363–93.

Peterson, J., and Young, A. R. (2006) (eds.), 'The European Union and the New Trade Politics', *Journal of European Public Policy*, 13/6 (special issue).

Woll, C. (2009), 'Trade Policy Lobbying in the European Union: Who Captures Whom?', in D. Coen and J. J. Richardson (eds.), *Lobbying in the European Union: Institutions, Actors and Issues* (Oxford: Oxford University Press), 268–89.

CHAPTER 17

Enlargement

From Rules for Accession to a Policy Towards Europe

Ulrich Sedelmeier

Summary

The founding treaties of the European Union (EU) already contained rules for the accession of new members. They did not, however, amount to an enlargement policy that also managed relations with would-be members that the EU did not yet judge ready for membership. The end of the cold war forced the EU to devise such an enlargement policy, both to respond to the unprecedented demand for membership and to use its attractiveness to influence developments in post-communist Europe. Despite initial strong reluctance both within the European Commission and among the member states, the EU achieved two rounds of eastern enlargement in 2004 and 2007; extended the membership perspective to the countries of south-eastern Europe; opened accession negotiations with Turkey and Croatia; and created an 'Eastern Partnership' for six successor states of the Soviet Union. The Commission maintained the momentum of the policy, and European Council meetings during the presidencies of pro-enlargement member states served as key focal points for policy development. In the process, the EU incrementally developed a framework for its enlargement policy that includes three partly overlapping stages: association agreements; pre-accession alignment based on accession partnerships; and finally accession negotiations. The EU has made each step—and increasingly intermediate steps within these frameworks—conditional on compliance with certain political and economic criteria. In the context of eastern enlargement, this conditionality has given the EU unprecedented influence on domestic politics in its neighbourhood, even if this influence varied considerably over time, and across issues and countries.

Introduction

Few of the policies covered in this volume have seen their importance increase as spectacularly over the past two decades as enlargement. Enlargement has always been an important event for the European Union (EU), but for much of its history, enlargement was restricted to intermittent episodes. During the cold war, membership doubled from the original six founding members, but since the 1990s, the pace of enlargement has accelerated dramatically, with EU membership more than doubling again by 2007, and the queue of would-be members remains long (see Table 17.1). In 1999, the Commission created a separate Directorate-General for Enlargement (DG ELARG), while for most of the Commission's history, enlargement had been one of many tasks of the Directorate-General for External Relations (DG RELEX) and ad hoc task forces. Since the end of the cold war, enlargement has thus become a constant item on the EU's agenda.

According to Lowi's (1972) typology (see Chapter 3), enlargement can be viewed as a major 'constituent policy'. Enlargement affects the EU's institutional structure, and often triggers changes in the rules governing politics and policy-making. Such changes have attempted to compensate for the impact of larger numbers and increased diversity on the effectiveness of collective decision-making, the fairness of representation, and the scope for further integration. Enlargement also has elements of a redistributive policy, especially in policy areas that receive most funding from the EU budget (see Chapters 8, 9, 10). These constitutive and redistributive characteristics have made each enlargement controversial. Such controversies were expressed in the French vetoes of the UK's first two applications; the Commission's negative assessment of Greece's application in 1979; the length of accession negotiations with Spain and Portugal; the Commission's attempts to create an alternative framework to deflect the pursuit of accession by Austria, Finland, Norway, and Sweden; the long reluctance to acknowledge formally the possibility of an eastern enlargement; not to mention the ongoing controversies about Turkish membership. Yet demands for accession also present an opportunity for the EU. New members enlarge the single European market (see Chapter 5) and can increase the effectiveness of common policies. More recently, practitioners and commentators alike have praised enlargement as the EU's most powerful foreign-policy tool (see also Chapter 18).

A distinctive analytical feature of enlargement policy is that although the rules for enlargement identify the member states as central actors, the Commission has played a very significant role. In particular for the eastern enlargement, the Commission has set the agenda by forging incremental agreements on the path to enlargement, managing pre-accession relations with candidates, and monitoring their adjustment efforts. It has shaped the outcome of accession negotiations by brokering compromises. Moreover, through its role in the application of accession conditionality, the Commission has enhanced its role in EU foreign policy. At the same time, enlargement policy also provides evidence that the Commission is not a unitary actor. Debates over enlargement policy often reveal transgovernmental cleavages that cut across member states and the Commission.

This chapter first clarifies what the enlargement policy involves, and how it has broadened significantly since the end of the cold war. It then reviews the main phases of the enlargement policy process—association, pre-accession, and accession—and clarifies for each of these stages the key decisions involved, how they are made, and how policy practice has evolved over time. The chapter then focuses on the use of enlargement as a foreign-policy tool and the development of the EU's accession conditionality. It concludes with a consideration of an 'enlargement fatigue' after the 2007 enlargement and policy towards the other European successor states of the Soviet Union that might lay claim to EU membership.

Rules, procedures, and policy

From its inception, the EU had rules for the accession of new members, but these procedures did not amount to an enlargement policy. The procedures for accession are set out in the treaty (Art. 49 TEU, see Box 17.1). They have remained largely unchanged since the 1957 Treaty of Rome (Art. 237 EEC), although the 1987 Single European Act (SEA) added the requirement that the European Parliament (EP) give its assent, and the 1997 Treaty of Amsterdam (ToA) made the political conditions explicit by inserting the reference to Article 6(1) TEU. In the context of its first

TABLE 17.1   History of EU enlargement: overview

	Association agreement (signed)	Membership application	Commission opinion	Accession negotiations (start/end)	Accession
United Kingdom		Aug. 1961	*(unpublished)*	*French veto Jan. 1963*	
		May 1967	Sept. 1967	*de facto French veto Nov. 1967*	
			Oct. 1969	June 1970–Jan. 1972	Jan. 1973
Ireland		July 1961	*Suspended after French veto of UK Jan. 1963*		
		May 1967	Sept. 1967	June 1970–Jan. 1972	Jan. 1973
Denmark		Aug. 1961	*Suspended after French veto of UK Jan. 1963*		
		May 1967	Sept. 1967	June 1970–Jan. 1972	Jan. 1973
Greece	July 1961	June 1975	Jan. 1976	July 1967–May 1979	Jan. 1981
Portugal		Mar. 1977	May 1978	Oct. 1978–June 1985	Jan. 1986
Spain		July 1977	Nov. 1978	Feb. 1979–June 1985	Jan. 1986
Austria	[EEA 1992]	July 1989	July 1991	Feb. 1993–Mar. 1994	Jan. 1995
Sweden	[EEA 1992]	July 1991	July 1992	Feb. 1993–Mar. 1994	Jan. 1995
Finland	[EEA 1992]	Mar. 1992	Nov. 1992	Feb. 1993–Mar. 1994	Jan. 1995
Cyprus	Dec. 1972	July 1990	June 1993	Mar. 1998–Dec. 2002	May 2004
Hungary	Dec. 1991	April 1994	July 1997	Mar. 1998–Dec. 2002	May 2004
Poland	Dec. 1991	April 1994	July 1997	Mar. 1998–Dec. 2002	May 2004
Czech Republic	Oct. 1993[a]	Jan. 1996	July 1997	Mar. 1998–Dec. 2002	May 2004
Estonia	June 1995	Nov. 1995	July 1997	Mar. 1998–Dec. 2002	May 2004
Slovenia	June 1996	June 1996	July 1997	Mar. 1998–Dec. 2002	May 2004
Malta	Dec. 1970	July 1990[b]	June 1993; updated Feb. 1999	Feb. 2000–Dec. 2002	May 2004
Slovakia	Oct. 1993[a]	June 1995	July 1997	Feb. 2000–Dec. 2002	May 2004
Latvia	June 1995	Oct. 1995	July 1997	Feb. 2000–Dec. 2002	May 2004
Lithuania	June 1995	Dec. 1995	July 1997	Feb. 2000–Dec. 2002	May 2004
Romania	Feb. 1993	June 1995	July 1997	Feb. 2000–Dec. 2004	Jan. 2007
Bulgaria	March 1993	Dec. 1995	July 1997	Feb. 2000–Dec. 2004	Jan. 2007

Croatia	Oct. 2001	Feb. 2003	Apr. 2004	Oct. 2005–	
Turkey	Sept. 1963	Apr. 1987	Dec. 1989	Oct. 2005–	
Norway	[EEA 1992]	Apr. 1962	*Suspended after French veto of UK Jan. 1963*		
		July 1967	Sept. 1967	June 1970–Jan. 1972	*Negative referendum Sept. 1972*
		Nov. 1992	April 1993	Apr. 1993–June 1994	*Negative referendum Nov. 1994*
Switzerland	[EEA 1992]	May 1992	*Application suspended after negative referendum on EEA, Dec. 1992*		
FYROM	Apr. 2001	Mar. 2004	Nov. 2005		
Montenegro	Oct. 2007	Dec. 2008			
Albania	June 2006	Apr. 2009			
Iceland	[EEA 1992]	July 2009			
Serbia	May 2008[c]				
Bosnia-Herzegovina	June 2008				
Morocco	Feb. 1996	July 1987	*no Commission opinion, application rejected by Council (Oct. 1987) since not a European state*		

[a] Agreement with Czechoslovakia: Dec. 1991.
[b] Temporary suspension in Oct. 1996.
[c] Not ratified; interim agreement blocked.

enlargement in the early 1970s, the EU established a more specific practice for the accession process and the conduct of accession negotiations (Preston 1997; Nugent 2004*b*). These procedures are essentially still in place and will be elaborated on in the remainder of the chapter. Of course procedures are no substitute for policy, yet it might require clarification what such an 'enlargement policy' entails.

At a general level, enlargement policy consists of decisions about the conditions under which new members can join the EU. The decisions relate to two distinctive sets of conditions: first, the more general conditions that a country has to meet in order to be considered a candidate for membership; and, second, decisions about the concrete terms of accession. Article 49 TEU covers both decisions. It specifies the

> **BOX 17.1**   **Treaty basis for EU enlargement**
>
> *Article 49 (TEU)*
>
> Any European State which respects the principles set out in Article 6(1) may apply to become a member of the Union. It shall address its application to the Council, which shall act unanimously after consulting the Commission and after receiving the assent of the European Parliament, which shall act by an absolute majority of its component members.
>
> The conditions of admission and the adjustments to the Treaties on which the Union is founded, which such admission entails, shall be the subject of an agreement between the Member States and the applicant State. This agreement shall be submitted for ratification by all the contracting States in accordance with their respective constitutional requirements.
>
> *Article 6(1) (TEU)*
>
> The Union is founded on the principles of liberty, democracy, respect for human rights and fundamental freedoms, and the rule of law, principles which are common to the Member States.

general conditions, and leaves the accession terms to negotiations. Until the 1990s there appeared no need for an enlargement policy beyond the rules of Article 49 and case-by-case bargaining among the member states and between existing members and candidate countries. Although the preamble of the Treaty of Rome expressed the founders' desire to create 'an ever closer union among the peoples of Europe' and called 'upon the other peoples of Europe who share their ideal to join in their efforts', demand for accession was limited. The Iron Curtain precluded one half of Europe from contemplating EU membership. The remainder of western Europe was either sceptical about deeper integration (and instead created the European Free Trade Association, EFTA) or under authoritarian regimes. Enlargement was therefore restricted to fairly discrete episodes, and ad hoc bargaining.

However, the end of the cold war confronted the EU with the challenge of formulating an enlargement policy that went beyond the procedures for accepting new members to managing relations with those that wanted to join. In the immediate wake of the end of the cold war, apart from the EFTA members already engaged in membership bids, the great majority of potential applicants were post-communist countries at various stages of a transition towards market economies and liberal democracies. A key challenge for the EU was therefore how to manage relations with countries that desired to join, but were not yet ready to enforce the body of EU legislation—the *acquis communautaire*. Enlargement policy became part of a broader challenge to devise a general policy towards the rest of Europe for the first time in the EU's history (Smith and Wallace 1994).

One key element of a policy towards post-cold-war Europe was a decision on how to provide support for the transitions to market economies and democracy, and specifically whether to use the prospect of eventual EU membership to support such reforms. Another question was to what extent and how to help the would-be members' efforts to adjust to the more specific membership conditions. Moreover, EU policy-makers did not only consider successful reforms in the countries of central and eastern Europe (CEECs) as intrinsically desirable. They also recognized the broader value to them of having as neighbours prosperous and democratic states that respected minority rights, which would be less likely to engage in interstate conflicts or to generate refugees and economic migrants. Thus a successful transition provided the EU with an opportunity to further a broader foreign-policy objective of fostering stability in its European neighbourhood. This prospect raised the question of how the EU could use enlargement to shape domestic changes actively in the direction most suitable for creating stability. The challenges that the EU's post-cold-war enlargement policy thus has had to confront go much beyond reaching ad hoc agreements between the member states about whether a specific candidate country can join and on what terms.

Since 1989, the EU has incrementally developed a policy framework for enlargement. It goes far beyond the procedures specified in Article 49 TEU, as the enlargement policy comes into play long before a country officially applies for membership and accession negotiations are only the final stage of a much longer process. In broad terms, we can distinguish three phases in the enlargement process (see Table 17.2). The first phase is an associate status. Association agreements provide the legal framework for pre-accession relations with potential candidate countries until accession. The second phase starts with a country being recognized as a (potential) candidate for accession; it consists of a policy framework for accession preparations. The final phase is accession negotiations. After an accession treaty is signed, a candidate has the status of an acceding country. Each phase includes separate decisions by EU actors (see Table 17.3) and specific policy instruments. Conditionality permeates all of these phases: the EU links progress from one phase to the next, and to intermediate steps within each phase, to the fulfilment of certain conditions (see the bottom row of Table 17.2). Rather than following a single policy mode, enlargement policy follows different modes at each of the three stages.

Association agreements

A country's application for membership is no longer the first stage of the accession process. During the cold war, it usually marked the start of the process, just as Article 49 TEU seems to suggest. The reason is that the candidates up to the EFTA enlargement of 1995 were mostly judged to be already in a position to apply and to enforce the *acquis* if they chose to (although doubts were expressed about this in the cases of Greece and Portugal). However, latterly (with the exception of the application in July 2009 from Iceland, a long-standing

TABLE 17.2 Key stages of the accession process

	Country expresses desire to join the EU	Association agreement	Pre-accession alignment	Official application	Commission opinion	Accession negotiations	Ratification of accession treaty	Accession
Key stages in the accession process in sequence								
Legal framework of relations		association agreements (Europe agreements, stabilization and association agreements)						
Policy framework			European partnership			accession partnership		
Aid		Phare, CARDS	IPA (ISPA, SAPARD)					
Conditional EU decisions	- granting/ suspending aid	- opening negotiations - initialing agreement - signing agreement - implementation of Interim Agreement	granting potential candidate status			granting candidate status - opening negotiations - opening/ closing negotiations on specific chapters - suspending/ closing negotiations	confirmation/ postponement of accession date	cooperation and verification mechanism: - suspension of aid - non-recognition of judicial decisions

TABLE 17.3   Formal decision rules for EU enlargement policy

Issue	Legal basis	Commission	Council	European Parliament	Other actors?
Association agreements	Art. 310 TEU	proposal	QMV	assent	national ratification by EU member states for 'mixed competence' agreements (non-trade-related aspects)
EU objectives for accession partnerships (European partnerships)	Council Reg. 622/98 (Council Reg. 533/04)	proposal	QMV	assent	
Opening accession negotiations	Art. 49 TEU	opinion (non-binding)	unanimity		
Conduct of accession negotiations	None. Precedent established in first accession negotiations	proposal for common position	unanimity (common position, opening/closing negotiation chapters); conduct of negotiations: Council presidency		
Agreement on accession treaty	Art. 49 TEU	recommendation	unanimity	assent	national ratification by accession country and member states (parliament ± referendum)

member of EFTA) formal membership applications have been submitted at a much later stage of the actual process, given that the post-communist countries decided to pursue the goal of membership after the regime changes of 1989/90, when they were not yet in a position to apply the *acquis*. Although most declared their foreign-policy goal of joining the EU very early in their transition processes, even the front-runners waited at least some five years until they formally applied. This time lag resulted from the Commission dissuading applications for which it was unlikely to recommend opening accession negotiations in the medium term.

As a consequence, the first step in the accession process is now usually the declaration of a country's desire to join, not the formal membership application. Such dissuasion does not always work. Montenegro applied on 15 December 2008 and Albania on 28 April 2009, despite being told that 'the time was not yet ripe' and that political circumstances in the EU made a favourable response and the opening of accession *negotiations* unlikely (*Agence Europe*, 30 October 2008). In an unprecedented move, several member states, led by Germany and The Netherlands, subsequently blocked the Council's request for the Commission's opinions on these applications (which had hitherto been considered an automatic, technical act) for several months (*Agence Europe*, 18 February 2009).

In the EU's emerging enlargement practice, the first stage in establishing closer relations is an association agreement (see Table 17.2). Association agreements are a long-standing instrument for the EU's external relations (based on Art. 310 TEU; see also Chapter 16), and are not limited to countries aspiring to membership. In Europe, the EU concluded association agreements with Greece and with Turkey in the early 1960s. Although the 1961 Athens Agreement with Greece and the 1963 Ankara Agreement with Turkey contained references to eventual membership, the original six member states had not appreciated the implications of their rash commitment that has since caused them much embarrassment in relations with Turkey. In the light of this the EU signed a more limited 'trade and cooperation' agreement with Franco's Spain in 1970, indicating that by then the EU saw association as an expression of close relations (see also Thomas 2006). The association agreements with Cyprus and Malta foreshadowed customs unions but not membership. On a separate track in 1972 the EU signed free trade area agreements with the EFTA states (see Table 17.1).

Over recent years, the EU has explicitly made association agreements—and a good record of implementing them—a necessary step on the path to membership. For example, in the above-mentioned negative reaction to Montenegro's plans to apply for membership, the Commission commented that the very recent signing of the association agreement made it premature to assess its correct implementation. Likewise, in 2008 the Commission stressed that Serbia could expect a positive evaluation of a future membership application only after it had demonstrated the correct application of its interim association agreement (*Agence Europe*, 6 November 2008).

European Economic Area Agreement

The European Economic Area (EEA) Agreement is an example of an agreement that EU policy-makers specifically intended as an alternative to accession. It became for some EFTA countries a stepping stone to membership (Phinnemore 1999), while for some it remained a more persistent framework. The EEA, floated by Commission President Jacques Delors in 1989, was negotiated with all the then EFTA countries. The agreement was signed in 1992 and entered into force in 1994. It is to date the closest form of economic relationship between the EU and non-member states and enables the EFTA states to participate (with some voice but no votes) in the EU's internal market—with the exception of agriculture—through their unilateral legal alignment with EU policies, and includes payments from EFTA countries into EU funding programmes. The Commission had intended the EEA as a long term framework for relations with all the EFTA countries, because it was concerned that the membership applications by Austria, Finland, Norway, Sweden, and Switzerland were motivated by the economic benefits of membership, and that the neutrality of most of them and their scepticism about political integration might present obstacles to further integration, especially in foreign and security policy. By offering them what the Commission had assumed they were primarily interested in—participation in the internal market—Delors hoped that the EEA would ease the pressure for enlargement.

However, most of the EFTA countries considered the EEA from the start only as a transitional regime on the way to full membership (E. Smith 1999). The notion of the EEA as a stable long-term framework for relations between equals was further undermined through the European Court of Justice's (ECJ) Opinion 1/1991. Initially, the EEA had envisaged an EEA Court, consisting of ECJ judges and EFTA judges, but the ECJ held that such a participation of EFTA judges was incompatible with EC law. This opinion prevented a more symmetrical relationship between the EU and EFTA in the EEA. Instead, the EEA's two-pillar structure requires EFTA and the EFTA Surveillance Authority to handle the EFTA countries' side of the relationship, including decisions on competition policy and associated litigation. The lack of symmetry reduces the EEA's appeal as an alternative to membership.

With the accessions of Austria, Finland, and Sweden in 1995 the EEA became a residual arrangement for Iceland, Liechtenstein, and Norway, in the last case because of the negative referendum on accession. Switzerland did not ratify the EEA following a negative referendum and negotiated instead a number of 'thick' bilateral agreements, and its membership application is dormant. The Commission has also mentioned the EEA as a possibility for closer relations with some countries included in the European neighbourhood policy (ENP) (discussed below). However, since participation in the EEA presumes sophisticated regulatory and administrative capacities to apply and enforce the *acquis*, it is unlikely that it will become a practicable framework for relations with further would-be members that are not advanced industrialized countries. Instead, the main template for association agreements with countries desiring membership became the 'Europe agreements' that the EU first devised for the CEECs in the early 1990s.

Europe agreements

After the fall of the communist regimes in eastern Europe in 1989, the EU moved quickly under the leadership of the Commission to conclude bilateral trade and cooperation agreements (TCAs) and to support economic reform through the Phare (*Pologne, Hongrie: aide à la restructuration des économies*) programme (Pelkmans and Murphy 1991; Sedelmeier and Wallace 1996: 357–62; Mayhew 1998: 138–50). As the TCA merely provided for a normalization of relations, a consensus emerged around association agreements as the appropriate framework for relations with the CEECs (Kramer 1993). In December 1989 the European Council in Strasbourg agreed to devise 'an appropriate form of association' and the Commission's Directorate-General for External Relations quickly sketched a broad framework. The European Council in Dublin in April 1990 agreed to create 'Europe agreements' (EAs), a 'new type of association agreement as a part of the new pattern of relationships in Europe', to be offered to the leading reformers, Hungary, Poland, and Czechoslovakia.

The EAs consisted mainly of the gradual establishment of a free trade area for industrial products, in which the EU liberalized faster than the CEECs, supplemented by a 'political dialogue' on foreign policy, and backed by technical and financial assistance (through Phare) and economic and cultural cooperation. The Commission conducted the negotiations with the CEECs, based on negotiation directives that it proposed and the Council adopted by unanimity. The Council working group on eastern Europe (rather than the Art. 133 Committee of national trade officials that usually oversees trade negotiations, see Chapter 16) monitored the negotiations. The Council had to approve the final agreement unanimously and the EP had to give its assent (see Table 17.3). The inclusion of provisions for political dialogue made the EAs 'mixed agreements' involving both Community and member states' competence and required ratification by all members. The trade component, subject to only Community competence, could enter into force earlier through interim agreements.

The main controversies in the EA negotiations concerned, first, the link between the agreements and eventual EU membership, and second, the extent of the EU's trade liberalization. Given that association agreements are now considered the first step towards membership, it is maybe surprising that the CEECs' key criticism was that the EAs did not establish a clear link to future membership of the EU. Although the label 'Europe' Agreements played to the symbolism of a 'return to Europe' through closer relations with the EU, most member states and most Commissioners opposed raising the question of membership at this early stage. The Commission (1990) had attempted to pre-empt argument by stating that there was 'no link either explicit or implicit' between association and accession, and while 'membership is not excluded when the time comes', it was 'a totally separate question'. The Council's decision on the negotiation directives specified that if the CEECs raised the issue during the negotiations, the Commission should simply refer to their right under the treaty to apply for membership.

The other key area of contestation concerned trade liberalization. While the EU offered to open its market to industrial products over a period of five years, special protocols and annexes covering 'sensitive' sectors—notably agriculture, textiles, coal, and steel—offered slower and more limited liberalization. These sectors accounted for the bulk of CEEC exports and reflected their medium-term comparative advantages. Furthermore, provisions for contingent protection (anti-dumping, safeguards, and anti-subsidy measures—see Chapter 16) provided EU producers with instruments to limit competition.

The dissatisfaction of the CEECs led to two periods of deadlock in the negotiations. On each occasion, the Commission successfully persuaded the Council to amend the negotiation directives in order to take better account of CEEC demands (Sedelmeier and Wallace 1996: 370–2). As a consequence, the EU accepted greater market access than it had initially proposed, and the preamble of the EAs noted that 'this association, in the view of the parties, will help to achieve [the CEECs'] objective [of eventual membership]'. This latter concession in particular fell short of the firm commitment that the CEECs had hoped for, and they were far from enthusiastic about the final outcome of the negotiations.

Stabilization and association agreements

The EU drew on a very similar template for relations with the countries of the 'Western Balkans', namely Albania and most of the successor states of Yugoslavia (Slovenia concluded an EA, see Table 17.1). Following the violent break-up of Yugoslavia and the US-brokered Dayton agreement that stopped the fighting in Bosnia (see Chapter 18), the EU agreed a 'regional approach' towards the countries of south-eastern Europe in February 1996. In the aftermath of Nato's military intervention in Kosovo, the European Council in Cologne in June 1999 endorsed an initiative by the German Presidency for a stability pact for south-eastern Europe (Friis and Murphy 2000). The Commission elaborated proposals for a 'Stabilization and Association Process' (SAP) that included not only the aim of supporting economic and democratic transition but also regional cooperation, as well as explicit preparation for eventual accession.

The key element of the SAP was a specific type of association agreement— 'stabilization and association agreements' (SAAs)—as well as financial assistance through CARDS (Community Assistance for Reconstruction, Development, and Stabilization). The SAAs were largely modelled on the EAs as regards substance, but included much more detailed political conditionality (Phinnemore 2003; Pippan 2004; Gordon 2008). In contrast to the EU's reluctance to establish a link between the EAs and eventual membership, the European Council in Feira in June 2000 affirmed the status of the south-east European countries as 'potential candidates' even before the first SAAs were signed.

Association agreements with European successor states of the Soviet Union

The EU initially offered less preferential partnership and cooperation agreements (PCAs) to the European successor states of the Soviet Union (apart from the Baltics). Latterly policy has shifted a bit with the decision to negotiate an association agreement with Ukraine and subsequently to make them the core of the Eastern Partnership (EaP) (see below). This decision emerged from a tricky discussion among EU member states in the wake of the Russia–Georgia conflict in 2008 and raised the same debate about the link between association and membership as previously in the EA negotiations. Ukraine—with support from the Czech Republic, Poland, Sweden, and the United Kingdom—pressed for confirmation of the country's membership prospects in the agreement's preamble. Other member states, particularly Belgium and The Netherlands, as well as Austria, Luxembourg, Portugal, and Spain, argued that it would go too far even to acknowledge that Ukraine was a 'European' country with the right under the treaty to apply for membership. Instead, the agreement should clearly stipulate that it did not in any way 'prejudge the future of EU/ Ukrainian relations' (*Agence Europe*, 5 September 2008). The joint declaration of the EU–Ukraine summit in September 2008, reflecting a French presidency proposal, 'recognized that Ukraine as a European country shares a common history and common values with the countries of the European Union', and that the future association agreement 'leaves open the way for further progressive developments in EU–Ukraine relations'. Although the EU did not offer the prospect of membership, it 'acknowledge[d] the European aspirations of Ukraine and welcome[d] its European choice' (*Agence Europe*, 10 September 2008).

Pre-accession alignment and (potential) candidate status

Association agreements provide the legal framework for relations with would-be members until accession, even after they achieve the next step towards accession: potential candidate status and pre-accession alignment. The pre-accession policy runs in parallel to association, rather than replacing it. The point at which a would-be member enters the second main stage of the accession process is not clear-cut. Generally, it starts once a country has been recognized by the EU as a potential candidate country. EU practice about such an acknowledgement has also changed. For the ten CEECs concerned in the 1990s, this acknowledgement happened only at the European Council in Copenhagen in 1993, after sustained lobbying from the candidates and from within the EU (Sedelmeier 2005b). By contrast, the European Council in Feira in 2000 acknowledged that the south-eastern European countries were 'potential candidates' at a rather early stage in the process. Pre-accession policies thus now sometimes start even before the conclusion of association agreements, in line with the more extensive and detailed conditionality.

Origins of the EU's pre-accession policy

The need for a pre-accession policy as an element of enlargement policy reflects the specific characteristics of most membership candidates since the end of the cold war, namely that they are not ready to apply the EU's single-market legislation at the time of application. The EU faced the challenge of whether and how to support candidates' efforts to meet the conditions of membership through regulatory alignment. The EU's response was a pre-accession strategy. The first time the Commission had suggested such a strategy was the accession of Greece, which it did not consider ready for full membership, and proposed a pre-membership programme of structural adjustment and economic convergence (Preston 1997: 51–2). However, the Council rejected the Commission's suggestion, deciding unanimously to open accession negotiations, despite Belgian, British, and Danish reservations.

In the context of eastern enlargement, the pre-accession strategy resulted from an initiative of the Commission's Directorate-General for External Relations and the *cabinet* of Sir Leon Brittan, the Commissioner for External Economic Relations. Following the general endorsement of the possibility of enlargement at the European Council in Copenhagen in June 1993, these policy advocates in the DG and the Brittan *cabinet* were keen to use the momentum for a follow-up initiative that placed accession preparations on a concrete working footing that would keep enlargement firmly on the EU's agenda. The cornerstone of their strategy to prepare the relevant CEECs for accession was a regulatory alignment with the *acquis communautaire*. Progress with alignment would dispel fears that the CEECs were insufficiently prepared for membership and make it difficult for the EU to justify dragging its feet. Moreover, as long as the CEECs remained sufficiently flexible to set their own priorities, alignment could also be beneficial to them within the broader process of economic restructuring and in reducing the scope for the EU to use trade defence measures.

Despite initial reluctance both inside the Commission and among the member states, this particular strategy also appealed to those reluctant about enlargement; an explicit programme of legislative alignment could provide a checklist of necessary preparations that would make it easier to argue against premature accession until all the measures were in place. The double-edged nature of the pre-accession strategy—that it could be interpreted as a means both to accelerate and to postpone enlargement—as well as the support from the German presidency for the policy advocates in the Commission led to the announcement of the EU's pre-accession strategy at the European Council in Essen in December 1994.

The core element of the pre-accession strategy was a White Paper (Commission 1995) that set out key elements of the internal-market *acquis* that the CEECs had to adopt as a preparation for membership, and the necessary legal and institutional framework for transposing them into national legislation and applying them. It suggested a logical sequencing of measures in each issue area (but not priorities across areas). In addition, the Commission would set up an office—the Technical Assistance Information Exchange Office (TAIEX)—to provide assistance for regulatory alignment. One of its main tasks became to organize a 'twinning' of seconded experts from the member states with their counterparts in CEEC national administrations to assist with the implementation of specific measures of the *acquis*. The pre-accession strategy would involve the CEECs establishing national programmes for the adoption of the *acquis* (NPAAs), which would set out priorities and specific timetables for adopting EU legislation.

The Commission White Paper's presentation of the key parts of the *acquis* might appear a merely technical exercise—and was deliberately presented by the Commission as such—but in fact it was profoundly political (see also A. R. Young and Wallace 2000: 118–19; Sedelmeier 2005b: 141–7). Given the massive amount of EU legislation, the policy advocates in the Commission argued for a selective approach that would accord the CEECs maximum flexibility in their alignment. The basis for selection would be a distinction between legislation that is 'essential' for the functioning of the single market (by eliminating trade barriers) and measures aimed at achieving other EU objectives (e.g. environmental and social-policy standards for production processes). Such a distinction raised extremely sensitive questions about the status of those measures left out. In the Commission, especially DG EMPL (employment, social affairs, and equal opportunities) was concerned that the choices of the White Paper would imply a ranking of EU policy areas. The Commission still largely managed to avoid controversy with, and among, the member states, by presenting the White Paper as a technical exercise, which avoided alerting interest groups that could otherwise have lobbied for the inclusion of specific measures. As a result, the White Paper largely excluded process regulations, which do not impede trade, notably in environmental policy (Commission 1995). The European Council in Cannes in June 1995 agreed it without much discussion.

Accession partnerships and European partnerships

The Commission's approach to regulatory alignment as a pre-accession strategy backfired with the member states when it advanced a 'reinforced pre-accession strategy' in July 1997. As the main instrument for the management of legislative alignment, the Commission proposed bilateral 'accession partnerships' (APs). In the APs, the candidate countries would commit themselves to clear programmes for alignment by setting 'short term' and 'medium term' priorities for measures to be adopted. The CEECs would then set out clearly the timetables in NPAAs. Pre-accession aid would be targeted more directly at investment necessary to adopt the *acquis* through a revamping of Phare into two new financial support instruments: ISPA (Instrument for Structural Policies for Pre-accession, along the lines of the cohesion fund) and SAPARD (Special Accession Programme for Agriculture and Rural Development). Although the speed of alignment was in principle left to the candidates, the EU tied progress both to financial assistance and the speed of accession negotiations, which created pressures for rapid and far-reaching adjustments.

The Council re-asserted control over the process. The Council decides by QMV the priorities and objectives contained in individual APs submitted to candidate countries, as well as subsequent adjustments (upon a Commission proposal and with EP assent) (Council Regulation 622/98 of 16 March 1998; see Table 17.3). The more rigid approach of the APs compared to the original pre-accession strategy resulted from the member states' concern that if the Commission negotiated the APs with the candidates, it could prejudge eventual accession negotiations. This approach left little scope for the candidates themselves to shape the pace and content of the APs, causing considerable criticism that the language of partnership disguises rather thinly the imposition of EU priorities (see also Grabbe 2006: 14–18).

Still, the Commission maintained a considerable influence on the pace of the accession process and the selection of candidates through its role in the evaluation of the candidates' progress on alignment. It monitored progress through annual Regular Reports, which involved it in the domestic politics of applicant countries far more than in previous enlargement rounds (and in monitoring existing member-state compliance with the *acquis*).

The EU essentially maintained this framework for pre-accession alignment in the context of south-eastern Europe. The European Council in Thessaloniki in June 2003 agreed to a Commission proposal that introduced new instruments within the broader framework of the SAP. It adjusted financial support by replacing the CARDS programme with the Instrument for Pre-accession Assistance (IPA). The main instrument for accession preparations was new 'European partnerships', which essentially copy the APs. They identify each country's priorities in their preparations for further integration, and progress is monitored through the Commission's Regular Reports. Once a country moves from the status of 'potential' candidate country to 'candidate country', its European partnership is replaced by an AP.

The EU's procedures for granting 'candidate' status are not very explicit. The first time that the EU formally acknowledged a country as a 'candidate state' was when the European Council in Helsinki in 1999 designated Turkey as such in order to reward progress made, although it did not yet envisage opening accession negotiations. In the case of the former Yugoslav Republic of Macedonia (FYROM), the

Commission proposed granting candidate status in its opinion on the country's formal membership application, despite otherwise recommending that accession negotiations should not be opened yet.

Accession

Commission opinions

The Commission's opinion remains a key element in proceeding to the accession stage, although it has lost some of its distinctive character as the main document containing the Commission's assessment and recommendation through the practice of regular monitoring reports both before and after the official opinion. The college of commissioners adopts the Opinion with a majority vote, which was necessary in the case of Greece (Preston 1997: 50). Voting aside, another indicator of controversy is the time the Commission takes to prepare its opinion, as in the cases of Turkey, Cyprus, and Malta, and the first CEEC applicants (see Table 17.1). The Commission's opinion is not binding on the Council, which decides unanimously on whether to open accession negotiations with an applicant. Yet so far only in the case of Greece did the Council not follow the Commission's recommendation.

A key novelty in the opinions on the CEECs was that the Commission did not assess their preparedness at the time (except for the political conditions), but explicitly their *prospective* readiness, since none of the candidates met all the conditions when the opinions were published. In this case, there was genuine uncertainty about which countries the Commission would recommend for accession negotiations and which the European Council would endorse. There was considerable debate within both institutions. One side argued for a strict application of a merit-based approach to starting negotiations. The other suggested a more inclusive approach in which all candidates started negotiations (but might conclude them at different times) to avoid hampering reform efforts in the countries left out. The European Council in Luxembourg in December 1997 endorsed the Commission's recommendation of starting accession negotiations initially with only Cyprus, the Czech Republic, Estonia, Hungary, Poland, and Slovenia, which has been interpreted as evidence for the Commission's agenda-setting powers (Friis 1998).

The desire in parts of the Commission and the Council to maintain incentives for domestic reforms in the other applicant countries led to agreement that the Commission should regularly assess their progress and possibly recommend opening accession negotiations. The Commission's Regular Reports, usually published in October/November each year, are similarly structured to the Opinions. They assess in a fairly standardized manner the progress made with regard to political and economic conditions, and with legislative alignment in the various policy areas. So far, the European Council has always followed the Commission's recommendations:

the 1999 Regular Reports proposed starting accession negotiations with Bulgaria, Latvia, Lithuania, Malta, Romania, and Slovakia, and the 2004 Regular Report with Turkey. In recent policy practice *vis-à-vis* south-eastern Europe, Regular Reports no longer only follow the Commission's opinion, but already assess potential candidate countries even prior to their official application.

Accession negotiations

The procedures for accession negotiations were essentially set in the first enlarge-ment negotiations with Denmark, Ireland, Norway, and the UK. In contrast to external trade negotiations (see Chapter 16), they are not conducted by the Com-mission, but by the Council presidency on behalf of the member states (see Table 17.3). Although the Commission does not have a formal role in the negotiations, it has often been able to broker compromises and identify solutions (Avery 2004). Negotiations occur through bilateral 'accession conferences' that can run in parallel with more than one candidate. Prior to opening official negotiations, the Commis-sion conducts a 'screening process' with the applicant countries. In multilateral and bilateral sessions, the Commission assesses whether an applicant is able to apply the *acquis*, and identifies possible challenges for the negotiations. After the screening, the candidates submit their negotiation positions. The Commission drafts a com-mon EU position that requires unanimous agreement by the Council.

The Council then decides unanimously to open, and subsequently to close pro-visionally, negotiations on specific 'chapters' of the *acquis* (relating to specific pol-icy areas, plus budgetary provisions, and institutions: thirty-one in the case of the CEECs and thirty-five in the case of Turkey, where additional chapters include 'judi-ciary and fundamental rights', and 'food safety'). In the 2004 enlargement round, the procedure led to a 'chapterology' among commentators, especially in the candidate countries: a tendency to assess relative progress towards membership in terms of chapters opened and closed.

The guiding principle of accession negotiations—that the *acquis* is not negotia-ble—was established in the first enlargement round. Many aspects of the *acquis*, such as the financing of the CAP, created problems for the UK. Although Article 49 TEU does not preclude a renegotiation of the founding treaties, this was precisely what the incumbents wanted to avoid. The Commission's (unpublished) Opinion on the UK's first application stated the key guiding principle for accession negotiation that has been repeatedly reaffirmed since then (Preston 1997: 28): the EU expects can-didates to adjust unilaterally to existing EU law, even if established policies and practices do not fit their specific situation. What is negotiable is rather limited: a timetable for adopting the *acquis*, rather than permanent derogations. The best that candidates can hope for are transition periods after accession during which they do not have to apply specific elements of the acquis. Conversely, the member states might seek to reduce their own adjustment costs through transition periods during which new members will not enjoy the full benefits of membership. New members' rights to market access and involvement in the CAP and structural funds can increase economic competition for the incumbents, or reduce their budgetary receipts. If interest groups in threatened sectors cannot prevent enlargement, they may seek to delay granting these rights after accession.

In the history of enlargement, EU concessions have been rather limited. Such exceptional cases include the EFTA enlargement in 1995, when the EU allowed the new members to maintain certain higher standards of environmental protection, even though they could constitute trade barriers (A. R. Young and Wallace 2000), and the long transition periods of ten years or more that the CEECs obtained for certain investment-intensive environmental regulations that did not affect product standards. The preservation of existing rules imposed notoriously harsh accession terms on the UK, particularly with regard to budget contributions. These remained contested until Prime Minister Margaret Thatcher negotiated the UK rebate in 1984 to 'get her money back' (see Chapter 9). Spain and Portugal had to wait ten years after accession before certain Mediterranean agricultural products enjoyed full market access in other members, as well as to accept restrictions on free labour movement for their citizens.

The accession agreements with the CEECs are also striking examples of discrimination against new members in key areas of membership. The incumbents could decide to restrict the movement of workers from the new members for up to seven years after accession. Direct payments from the CAP are to increase only gradually from a quarter of the level paid to farmers in the old member states, to equality only after ten years. In addition, receipts from structural funds were capped at 4 per cent of the recipient's GDP (see also Avery 2004). Nonetheless, the candidates all still found membership, even under such disadvantageous conditions, preferable to remaining outside. It was the strength of their preference for membership that enabled the incumbents to shift adjustment costs so heavily to new members (see also Moravcsik and Vachudova 2003). Yet the cases of the UK and Spain show that adverse terms of accession can create disgruntled new members that attempt to redress these bargains once on the inside.

Once the member states and the candidate have reached an agreement, and the EP has given its assent, the accession treaty is signed by all governments and the candidate becomes an 'accession country'. The accession country and all the member states have to ratify the treaty. Ratification referendums have failed twice in Norway in 1972 and 1994. France is the only incumbent so far to hold a referendum to ratify an accession treaty, which succeeded in the case of the UK. Following constitutional amendments in 2005 and 2008 the French president can choose between a referendum and parliamentary ratification, if it is approved by three-fifths of the two houses of parliament convened in Congress (*Agence Europe*, 25 July 2008). In addition to national ratification, a further hurdle before full membership was introduced in the accessions of Bulgaria and Romania. A novel provision allowed the Commission to assess the accession countries' progress even after the signing of the accession treaties, and to recommend a postponement of accession by one year.

Conditionality and enlargement as a foreign policy tool

Since the final stages of the EU's 2004 enlargement, it has become increasingly common for academic commentators and EU officials alike to refer to enlargement as the EU's 'most powerful foreign policy tool' (see Commission 2003*e*: 5; K. Smith 2003: 66). There are two distinct ways in which enlargement can be understood as a foreign-policy tool. The first relates to anchoring fragile democracies that have emerged from authoritarian rule within a prosperous and democratic international community. This notion did not only emerge in the context of post-communist transition, but was already highly salient in the Mediterranean enlargements of the 1980s after Greece, Portugal, and Spain emerged from dictatorships.

The second way in which enlargement is a foreign-policy tool is the EU's strategic use of the incentive of membership in order to induce or preserve specific policy changes in non-member states. Accession conditionality—tying the ultimate reward of membership to certain conditions—can change the incentive structure for candidate countries in such a way as to trigger domestic changes that the existing member states desire (K. Smith 1998; Jacoby 2004; Kelley 2004; Pridham 2005; Schimmelfennig and Sedelmeier 2005*a*, 2005*b*; Vachudova 2005; Grabbe 2006; Schimmelfennig et al. 2006). Accession conditionality has developed dramatically in the context of its eastern enlargement and goes far beyond the conditions of 'Europeanness' specified in Article 49 TEU and even the more recently included principles of Article 6(1). It now underpins every step of pre-accession relations virtually up to the day of accession and even beyond in the cases of Bulgaria and Romania (see also last row in Table 17.2).

Evolution of accession conditionality

The EU made the first reference to political membership conditions beyond what is now Article 49 TEU in the context of the Mediterranean enlargements. The 'Declaration on Democracy' at the European Council in Copenhagen in April 1978 stated that 'respect for and maintenance of representative democracy and human rights in each Member State are essential elements of membership'. Although the declaration related formally to the first direct elections to the EP, it was also 'intended to strengthen the Community's leverage against any future member which might slip towards authoritarian rule' (W. Wallace 1996: 16)—which was not inconceivable in view of the attempted putsch in Spain in 1981.

The EU's use of conditionality with regard to human rights and democracy increased significantly in the context of eastern enlargement. Phare aid was provided only once countries had achieved progress in democratic transition. The EU suspended aid to Romania (along with trade negotiations) in 1990 after the government organized the violent repression of post-election demonstrations; to Yugoslavia in 1991 after the breakout of war following the secession of Slovenia and Croatia; and to Croatia in 1995 after the military offensive to establish government control over the Serb-held Krajina region. The start of EA negotiations also reflected differences in democratization. In the context of negotiations with Romania, EU concerns about democratic developments led the Council to agree in May 1992 that *all* cooperation and association agreements with members of the Conference on Security and Cooperation in Europe (CSCE) should include a clause that would allow the suspension of agreements in the event of violations of democracy and human rights. In May 1995, the Council extended the suspension clause to agreements with any non-member state. While these measures generally expanded the use of conditionality in the EU's external relations, the first direct statement of accession conditions stems from the European Council in Copenhagen in June 1993.

At this meeting, the European Council declared for the first time that the CEECs that so desired might eventually become members. Many member states had been reluctant about this step, and a key debate in the run-up to the declaration concerned the criteria that potential members had to fulfil. Some opponents as well as proponents of early enlargement argued for quantitative criteria, such as a specific level of GDP per capita, in order to reduce the scope for politically motivated decisions for or against enlargement. However, the Council accepted the Commission's proposal for qualitative conditions that included not only the ability to apply the *acquis* after accession, but also political and economic criteria (see Box 17.2). A further condition related to the EU's ability to absorb new members, which the CEECs feared would allow the incumbents to stop enlargement even if the candidates fulfilled all the conditions. Concern about the EU's absorption capacity resurfaced after the 2007 enlargement (see below).

The subsequent application of political conditionality by the Commission and the European Council was considerably broader than that set out at Copenhagen (see Box 17.2). The vague reference of the European Council in Madrid in 1995 to the CEECs' administrative structures has since been widely interpreted as the basis of assessing administrative and judicial capacities, and the fight against corruption. The EU's emphasis on such issues that affect a country's ability to apply the *acquis* became particularly pronounced in the accessions of Romania and Bulgaria. In the EU's relations with the Western Balkans, the political conditions expanded further to include issues related to the ethnic conflict and the violent break-up of Yugoslavia, such as cooperation with the International Criminal Tribunal for the former Yugoslavia (ICTY), the return of refugees, and setting a threshold of 55 per cent for approval of the independence referendum in Montenegro.

By setting political conditions that are not covered by the *acquis* (despite the inclusion of Art. 6 TEU), the EU has entered new territory. Accusations of double standards in the treatment of candidate and full members strengthened calls for EU competences in these areas. It also provides scope for actors other than member-state

---

BOX 17.2   Accession conditionality

'Copenhagen criteria' (European Council, Copenhagen, 1993):

- stable institutions guaranteeing democracy, the rule of law, human rights, and respect for and protection of minorities;

- a functioning market economy, as well as the capacity to cope with competitive pressure and the market forces within the Union;

- ability to take on the obligations of membership, including adherence to the aims of political, economic, and monetary union;

- the EU's capacity to absorb new members, while maintaining the momentum of European integration.

European Council in Madrid, 1995 (adding administrative capacity)

' ... create the conditions for the gradual, harmonious integration of those States, particularly through the development of the market economy, the *adjustment of their administrative structures* and the creation of a stable economic and monetary environment' [emphasis added].

Example of expanding political criteria: Commission 'benchmarks' for opening accession negotiations with FYROM (March/June 2008):

- implementation of the SAA;
- improved dialogue with political parties;
- police reform;
- reform of legal sector;
- reform of public administration;
- fight against corruption;
- employment policy and improving investment environment;
- electoral law reform.

---

governments to exert influence. The Commission plays a key role by setting conditions and assessing compliance, even if the ultimate decision on whether a country has met the conditions is the Council's. The conditions also reflect lobbying by actors such as the EP. For example, following the persistent advocacy by Emma Nicholson, the EP's *rapporteur* on Romania, the EU insisted on improvements of the standards of state-run orphanages and changes to practices for international adoptions. More recently, the High Representative for the common foreign and security policy (CFSP) has also attempted to influence the EU's application of conditionality, for example by pressing for the implementation of the interim SAA with Serbia, which The Netherlands blocked due to Serbia's failure to cooperate fully with the ICTY.

Other international organizations also acquire a role in the EU policy process. Since the EU lacks rules in most areas of political conditionality, it demanded compliance with the rules of organizations such as the Council of Europe, the Organization for Security and Cooperation in Europe (OSCE), or the ICTY. The above example of Serbia and the ICTY underlines the tensions that can arise from an international organization's strict assessment of compliance in cases in which the majority of member states prefer a more flexible approach that would allow the EU to proceed with the accession process.

Conditionality and foreign policy

Most studies agree that conditionality has provided the EU with a highly effective means to influence policy change in applicant countries. It was particularly powerful in bringing about adjustment to the *acquis*. Nonetheless, such adjustment was not uniform across issues and countries; it depended for example on the nature of the *acquis* in an issue area and the constellation of domestic actors (Jacoby 2004). Compliance with the EU's political conditions, such as democracy and human rights, particularly depended on favourable domestic conditions. In countries with strongly nationalist and/or undemocratic governments—such as Belarus, Slovakia under Vladimir Mec̆iar, and Croatia under Franjo Tudjman—political conditionality was ineffective. However, it had a certain lock-in effect in the latter two cases, once nationalist and authoritarian parties lost elections to a coalition of liberal democratic parties (Vachudova 2005; Schimmelfennig et al. 2006). The EU did not cause their electoral victories, but once the new governments carried out political reforms that brought the country closer to accession, even an eventual return of the previous governing parties did not lead to a reversal of the reforms.

If governments did not perceive adjustment costs as prohibitively high, as was generally the case with regard to the *acquis*, then the EU's influence depended on the credibility of conditionality. Such credibility was undermined if EU actors sent out contradictory signals about the requirements for accession (Hughes et al. 2004a, 2004b; Sissenich 2005), or if a candidate country had reasons to doubt that the member states would agree to accession, even if it met all the conditions. In the context of its eastern enlargement, the EU's main instrument for making the prospect of membership credible was the opening of accession negotiations (Schimmelfennig and Sedelmeier 2005b).

In the case of Turkey, however, the opening of negotiations has lost much of this significance. The argument by some member states and some in the Commission that negotiations might not necessarily lead to accession—a clear break with previous policy—and the possibility of a French referendum to ratify its accession have made it less credible that the EU would grant accession even if Turkey meets the conditions. The EU's application of conditionality faces similar circumstances with regard to Ukraine or other successor states of the Soviet Union. Given the high domestic adjustment costs of its political conditions, the EU either has to make an unambiguous commitment to the possibility of membership, or abandon any ambitious attempts to influence domestic politics in would-be member states.

Other changes in the EU's application of conditionality include the specification of additional intermediate steps on the path to accession as rewards for compliance (see bottom row of Table 17.2). The EU also identified additional incentives, such as lifting visa requirements, which, however, presumed that additional criteria would be met, such as the signing of a Readmission Agreement for asylum seekers. Moreover, the EU has extended conditionality both beyond the signing of accession treaties, and even after accession itself. First, after the signing of accession treaties with Bulgaria and Romania, the Council asked the Commission to continue its monitoring and to recommend a postponement of the accession date if necessary. In the 2004 enlargement, Article 38 of the accession treaties allows the Commission to take 'appropriate measures' even after accession, if a new member caused within the first three years of membership 'a serious breach of the functioning of the internal market' or if there is an 'imminent risk of such breach'. The accession treaties with Bulgaria and Romania went a step further: a 'cooperation and verification mechanism' without a fixed expiry date authorizes the Commission to monitor reforms of their judicial systems and measures against corruption and organized crime, and to recommend the suspension of the obligation for other member states to recognize and implement judicial decisions. An example of post-accession sanctions was the Commission's decisions in July and November 2008 to freeze a total of €520 million in aid for Bulgaria for suspected fraud.

The Commission has also initiated a shift in the strategy of demanding strict compliance with conditions prior to awarding the promised benefits, towards making these benefits more tangible before full compliance is achieved. For example, the EU suspended negotiations of an SAA with Serbia over the government's failure to cooperate fully with the ICTY on the arrest of the Bosnian Serbs Ratko Mladić and Radovan Karadžić. Although no progress occurred, the EU signed the agreement just prior to the parliamentary elections in 2008 to bolster support for the pro-EU party of President Boris Tadić, but made the ratification of the agreement (and implementation of the interim agreement) still conditional on further cooperation with the ICTY. Likewise, the EU initialled the SAA with Bosnia in December 2007 in return for the mere promise of constitutional and police reform in the hope that making the benefits of the SAA more tangible would reduce domestic opposition to reforms. This strategy may have had some success in the case of Serbia: Tadić's party won the elections and Karadžić was arrested and extradited, although the interim SAA remained blocked by The Netherlands over the failure to arrest Mladić. There has been much less to show for the EU's inducements in Bosnia: a police reform bill was passed in April 2008 prior to the signing of the SAA in June, but did not envisage the unification of police forces demanded by the EU, and constitutional reform had not yet begun.

The 'Eastern Partnership' and enlargement fatigue

The perceived success of accession conditionality has led the EU to extend this practice to relations with neighbours that it does not currently consider potential candidates (see also Kelley 2006). In March 2003, the Commission (2003*e*) proposed a European neighbourhood policy (ENP) as a new framework for relations with the EU's eastern and southern neighbours. In this framework, the Commission strategically adapted the key tenets of its conditionality policy to expand its role in EU foreign policy. Bilateral relations were then organized around 'action plans' that are very similar to APs, and regular reports that assess a country's alignment. One obvious flaw in this mechanical policy transfer from enlargement is that the EU does not offer its greatest reward—membership—but only the rather vague incentive of 'closer relations'. Thus the ENP appears better equipped to achieving issue-specific objectives—such as the fight against illegal immigration, organized crime, human trafficking, or money laundering—through issue-specific rewards like abolishing visa requirements, than to broader objectives such as democratic reforms.

The EU developed relations with the eastern European countries of the ENP in the framework of the 'Eastern Partnership'. The initiative by French President Sarkozy that led in July 2008 to the launch of the 'Union for the Mediterranean' with the southern neighbours of the ENP (and the remaining Mediterranean non-members) prompted a Polish–Swedish initiative to strengthen relations with Armenia, Azerbaijan, Belarus, Georgia, Moldova, and Ukraine. The European Council in June 2008 asked the Commission to prepare a proposal and in September 2008 urged it to accelerate its work after the fighting between Russia and Georgia in August 2008 prompted new attention to the region, amidst a broader debate about what kind of relationship to develop with Russia (see Chapter 18). The cornerstones of the Commission's proposal are: association agreements to replace the existing PCAs (a move already under way with Ukraine); the creation of a free trade zone (possibly leading to a 'Neighbourhood Economic Community', inspired by the EEA, which ignores the high demands that the EEA makes on the regulatory capacity of participating states); and gradual visa liberalization. Since the initiative excludes what most eastern neighbours value most—military security and eventual membership—it remains unclear whether the EaP will allow the EU to promote its broader foreign-policy objectives any more effectively than the ENP. The European Council in December 2008 referred the proposal to the Council for examination with the aim of endorsing it in March 2009. The EaP was formally launched on 7 May 2009.

The EU's ability to use accession conditionality for foreign-policy objectives is further undermined by evidence of 'enlargement fatigue' after the 2007 enlargement and the emphasis that opponents of further enlargement put on the EU's 'absorption capacity'. The Commission's 2006 Enlargement Strategy Paper (Commission 2006*f*) suggested that absorption capacity concerned the impact of enlargement on the EU's budget and its ability to implement common policies, and on effective and accountable decision-making. So far, however, there is no evidence that the EU sets tougher thresholds for current candidates than in earlier enlargements (Schimmelfennig 2008). The belief in some member states that the Bulgarian and Romanian accessions were premature, coupled with the Commission's freezing of funds for corruption and maladministration, nonetheless, fed the reluctance to envisage additional candidates in the medium term.

Moreover, the uncertainty surrounding ratification of the Treaty of Lisbon (ToL), combined with the economic and financial crisis of 2008, made the member states and the Commission more reluctant to accelerate the ongoing enlargement processes. After the Commission's report in November 2008 suggested that Croatia should be able to conclude accession negotiations by the end of 2009, France, Germany, and Luxembourg sought to link its accession to the prior entry into force of the ToL. The Commission referred to the economic crisis when cautioning Albania and Montenegro against early formal membership applications. On the other hand, however, the Commission indicated that the application submitted in July 2009 by Iceland—where the new government viewed accession, as a means to EMU membership, as more attractive in the wake of its deep financial crisis—could be processed rather quickly, possibly leading to an accession at the same time as Croatia.

In sum, after the 2004 and 2007 enlargements the conditions for the EU's use of enlargement as a foreign-policy tool have become less favourable. The member states are less able to agree on using membership as an incentive and the domestic adjustment costs of the EU's political conditions for governments in the target countries are generally higher than in the previous accession rounds.

Conclusions

The EU's enlargement policy has developed considerably since the end of the cold war. It is no longer synonymous with accession negotiations, but sets the longer-term framework for relations with countries desiring membership and specifies how they can proceed towards accession. This framework includes three overlapping stages—association agreements, pre-accession preparations, and accession negotiations—each underpinned by more extensive and demanding conditionality. EU enlargement policy illustrates several policy modes (Chapter 4), in that policy within each of these three stages follows diverse procedures and dynamics.

The association framework exhibits many elements of the 'Community method', albeit with a strong oversight by foreign ministers that has on occasion constrained the influence of defensive economic interests. The framework follows largely a template forged in the early 1990s in the negotiations of the first generation of 'Europe agreements' with the CEECs. These negotiations were characterized both by an intergovernmental disagreement about the link between association and potential membership, and by bargaining along transgovernmental lines about the trade component between sectoral policy-makers across the member states and the Commission on the one hand, and foreign policy-makers on the other.

The pre-accession alignment phase also displays characteristics of the 'Community method'. The Commission plays a key role in formulating conditions, monitoring and assessing compliance, and making recommendations for further steps towards accession on the basis of its assessment. The European Council still has the final say, and political considerations about the desirability of closer relations and enlargement play a prominent role, but so far the Commission has largely been able to set the agenda through its role in applying conditionality.

Accession negotiations, however, are mainly the domain of 'intensive transgovernmentalism'. The member states play a key role in determining the EU's negotiation position and the shape of accession treaties, often mindful of national economic or regional interests. The Commission's informal role in identifying compromises can carry the negotiations forward and make unfavourable deals more acceptable to new members. On the other hand, the EU's use of enlargement as a foreign-policy tool has allowed the Commission to play a more important role in EU foreign policy, the traditional realm of 'intensive transgovernmentalism' (Chapter 18).

FURTHER READING

For overviews of the EU's enlargement rounds, see Preston (1997) and Nugent (2004*b*). For accounts of the evolution of eastern enlargement, see Baun (2000), Mayhew (1998), and Sedelmeier (2005*b*). For theoretical approaches to enlargement, see the contributions in Schimmelfennig and Sedelmeier (2005*a*). For the EU's impact on candidate countries and the effectiveness of conditionality in the context of eastern enlargement, see Grabbe (2006), Hughes et al. (2004*b*), Jacoby (2004), Kelley (2004), Kubicek (2003), Pridham (2005), Schimmelfennig and Sedelmeier (2005*b*), Schimmelfennig et al. (2006), and Vachudova (2005).

Baun, M. (2000), *A Wider Europe: The Process and Politics of EU Enlargement* (Lanham, MD: Rowman & Littlefield).

Grabbe, H. (2006), *The EU's Transformative Power: Europeanization through Conditionality in Central and Eastern Europe* (Basingstoke: Palgrave Macmillan).

Hughes, J., Sasse, G., and Gordon, C. (2004*b*), *Europeanization and Regionalization in the EU's Enlargement to Central and Eastern Europe: The Myth of Conditionality* (Basingstoke: Palgrave Macmillan).

Jacoby, W. (2004), *The Enlargement of the European Union and NATO: Ordering from the Menu in Central Europe* (Cambridge: Cambridge University Press).

Kelley, J. G. (2004), *Ethnic Politics in Europe: The Power of Norms and Incentives* (Princeton, NJ: Princeton University Press).

Kubicek, P. (2003) (ed.), *The European Union and Democratization* (London: Routledge).

Mayhew, A. (1998), *Recreating Europe: The European Union's Policy Towards Central and Eastern Europe* (Cambridge: Cambridge University Press).

Nugent, N. (2004*b*) (ed.), *European Union Enlargement* (Basingstoke: Palgrave Macmillan).

Preston, C. (1997), *Enlargement and Integration in the European Union* (London: Routledge).

Pridham, G. (2005), *Designing Democracy: EU Enlargement and Regime Change in Post-Communist Europe* (Basingstoke: Palgrave Macmillan).

Schimmelfennig, F., and Sedelmeier, U. (2005*a*) (eds.), *The Europeanization of Central and Eastern Europe* (Ithaca, NY: Cornell University Press).

Schimmelfennig, F., and Sedelmeier, U. (2005*b*) (eds.), *The Politics of EU Enlargement: Theoretical Approaches* (London: Routledge).

Schimmelfennig, F., Engert, S., and Knobel, H. (2006), *International Socialization in Europe: European Organizations, Political Conditionality and Democratic Change* (Basingstoke: Palgrave Macmillan).

Sedelmeier, U. (2005*b*), *Constructing the Path to Eastern Enlargement: The Uneven Policy Impact of EU Identity* (Manchester: Manchester University Press).

Vachudova, M. A. (2005), *Europe Undivided: Democracy, Leverage and Integration after Communism* (Oxford: Oxford University Press).

CHAPTER 18

Foreign and Security Policy

Civilian Power Europe and American Leadership

Bastian Giegerich and William Wallace

▌ Summary

Diplomacy and defence are part of the core of state sovereignty, around which the practitioners of functional integration tiptoed in the formative years of the European Union (EU). The EU developed as a self-consciously 'civilian' power, with European security provided through the North Atlantic Treaty Organization (Nato) under US leadership. Policy cooperation has therefore developed under contradictory pressures. France and intermittently Britain have sought to use the EU to reinforce their international strategies; the Commission has worked to expand its limited competences in external policy; other national governments have welcomed the additional international standing that EU cooperation provides, while resisting providing the resources needed for the projection of power. There is little agreement on what a common foreign policy should be about; national political cultures differ widely on appropriate international roles. Intensive transgovernmentalism therefore remains the dominant mode of policy-making, with institutional development and capability-building emerging painfully from responses to external crises.

Introduction

States have foreign policies; international organizations coordinate national positions. National defence, and the mobilization of national resources for defence, require centralized command and control; concepts of national security and national interest justify strong state authority. Hardly surprisingly, therefore, even the most federalist proponents of European integration have found foreign and security policy peculiarly difficult. Cooperation in this policy field has evolved gradually, often spurred by external events which exposed inadequacies. The structures and underlying assumptions of policy-making in this field today are marked by past struggles over the balance between national sovereignty and effective capabilities. National political cultures differ significantly in assumptions about appropriate roles in international politics, about the projection of power beyond national boundaries, and about the use of force. Such political cultures change slowly. While a Brussels-based set of institutions and procedures has emerged, intergovernmentalism remains the norm in the sense that the predominant actors are the member governments. This in part explains why performance in common foreign and security policy falls so far short of aspirations. None the less the increasing intensity of policy development in this field and its increased importance in the treaties suggest elements of the policy mode of 'intensive transgovernmentalism' (see Chapter 4).

West European integration began under US sponsorship, with the European Economic Community (EEC), as it was then, 'nested' within the broader framework of the North Atlantic Treaty. Consultations on foreign and security policy therefore took place within Nato, which provided the integrated structure for the defence of western Europe against the Soviet-led Warsaw Pact. The Treaty of Rome gave the EEC limited competences for external trade relations (see Chapter 16) and assisting development in former colonial territories. French Gaullists insisted on a clear distinction between 'high' and 'low' politics: the EEC was to be confined to the low politics of commercial diplomacy, leaving the high politics of foreign policy and defence to sovereign states.

Issues of national security and foreign policy were, of course, fundamental to the development of west European integration. The French government had launched the Schuman Plan for a European Coal and Steel Community (ECSC) in 1950 in response to intense US pressure, to contain the reconstruction of West German industry within a supranational framework. The outbreak of the Korean War then led Washington to press for West German rearmament; the Pleven Plan for a European Defence Community (EDC), into which German units might be integrated, was the reluctant French response. The European Defence Treaty, signed in Paris in May 1952, committed its signatories to design the 'political superstructure' needed to give the EDC direction and legitimacy. The resulting draft treaty for a European Political Community would have transformed the six founding member states into a form of federation, with a European executive accountable to a directly elected European

Parliament (EP). The Korean armistice and the death of Stalin in 1953, however, made so direct an attack on the core of national sovereignty less compelling; the French National Assembly rejected the treaty. An intergovernmental compromise, promoted by the British, brought West Germany and Italy, with France and the Benelux (Belgium, The Netherlands, and Luxembourg) states into the Western European Union (WEU), a body which at first served mainly to monitor German rearmament.

Five years later, President de Gaulle chose foreign-policy cooperation as the ground on which to make his double challenge to US hegemony and to the supranational ambitions of the infant EEC. A 'conference of heads of state and government and foreign ministers' of the Six met, at French invitation, in Paris in February 1961 'to discover suitable means of organizing closer political cooperation' as a basis for 'a progressively developing union' (European Parliament 1964). This 'Fouchet Plan' (named after the French diplomat Christian Fouchet) was vigorously opposed by the Dutch, and found little support even within the German government. With Britain applying to join the EEC, and the Kennedy administration calling for a new 'Atlantic partnership', this was an evident challenge to US leadership and to Nato as such. De Gaulle's 1963 veto on British accession negotiations sank the initiative, and the French later left Nato's integrated structures (Cleveland 1966; Grosser 1980). This chapter captures the gradual development of foreign and security policy cooperation among member states by analysing the hesitant moves from European political cooperation (EPC) to a common foreign and security policy (CFSP), and the emergence of European security and defence policy (ESDP) as a part of CFSP. Second, the underlying theme of national sovereignty combined with EU-level capacity is explored through a range of examples.

From European political cooperation to common foreign policy

Foreign-policy consultations among EU members—separately from those within Nato—were agreed as a concession to the French in 1969, after de Gaulle's departure. 'European political cooperation' (EPC) was an entirely intergovernmental process, outside the treaties, steered by foreign ministers and managed by diplomats. The Commission was rigorously excluded in the early years. In sharp contrast to the leaky policy-making processes of the EEC, EPC was managed confidentially, with infrequent reporting to national parliaments and little coverage in the press. The evolution of cooperation in foreign policy since then has moved in cycles: at first hesitant steps to strengthen the framework, followed by periods of increasing frustration at the meagre results achieved, culminating in further reluctant reinforcement of the rules and procedures in the face of external events.

Relations with the US have been the most important factor in these cycles, the Middle East the most frequent and difficult focus for transatlantic dispute. The French government, the most strategic actor in promoting a more autonomous European foreign policy, frequently came up against American opposition. Divergent reactions to the Arab–Israeli War of October 1973, for example, escalated into a bitter Franco-US confrontation, with other west European governments caught in between. European dismay at the drift of US policy in 1979–81, over the coup in Poland and over the revolution in Iran, as well as at their own failure to concert their response to the Soviet invasion of Afghanistan, led to renewed efforts to promote cooperation, this time led by the British.

Western Europe's self-image as a 'civilian power' in the 1970s and 1980s partly reflected the exclusion of security and defence issues, reinforced by the unresolved Gaullist challenge to US security leadership. The concept also implied a claim to normative authority, portraying western Europe as a model of peaceful diplomacy, operating through economic instruments—a self-image with a particular appeal within Germany, whose recent history had led to a rejection of 'power politics' in its domestic culture (Bull 1982; Sjursen 2007). It also appealed to the Commission, which had international capacities in the civilian dimensions of trade and development, but was excluded from the 'harder' instruments of foreign policy. Foreign ministries developed extensive networks for consultation on such harder issues through EPC, but with little policy output and almost no national or European accountability.

The revolutions in central and eastern Europe in the course of 1989, and the rapid moves towards German unification which followed in 1990, nevertheless forced foreign and security policy up the EU's agenda. The end of the cold war brought Germany back to the centre of a potentially reunited continent, and reopened underlying questions about the delicate balance between France and Germany and about American security leadership through Nato. West European governments adjusted slowly and hesitantly to this radical transformation of their strategic environment.

End of the cold war and launch of CFSP

The French and German governments jointly proposed, in April 1990, that the planned intergovernmental conference (IGC) should formulate a common foreign and security policy (CFSP) as a central feature of the EU, alongside economic and monetary union (EMU; see Chapter 7). The two governments, however, had widely different concepts of CFSP, with the French government focused on capabilities and the German on institution-building. Lengthy negotiations followed, with several dividing lines: between defenders of American leadership through Nato (the British, the Dutch and Portuguese, and to some extent the Germans) and supporters of greater European autonomy (Belgium, France, and Italy, and to some extent Spain); between defenders of national sovereignty (Britain, Denmark, and France) and proponents of transfer of foreign policy into the Community framework (Belgium, Germany, Italy, and Luxembourg); between states with the capacity and domestic support for active foreign and defence policies—above all Britain and France—and those like Germany for which international strategy, above all military deployment beyond national borders, was surrounded by political inhibitions (Gnesotto 1990).

The US was an active player throughout this IGC, determined to maintain the primacy of Nato (and thus of US leadership) in post-cold-war Europe. Successful agreement on the conclusions of the post-cold-war Alliance Strategic Review, launched in April 1990, was a precondition for successful agreement among the then twelve member states (Menon et al. 1992). External developments distracted the negotiators from their institutional designs. New regimes to the EU's east were pressing for the promise of membership (see Chapter 17). Iraq invaded Kuwait in August 1990; Britain and France contributed significant ground forces to the US-led coalition, with some dozen or other European countries in supporting roles. The break-up of Yugoslavia began in the summer of 1991, and the Luxembourg president of the Council unwisely declared—as civilian EU monitors were deployed in Bosnia—that 'this is the hour of Europe' (*New York Times*, 29 June 1991). There was also an attempted *putsch* in Moscow in August 1990. The subsequent disintegration of the Soviet Union into fifteen separate states accompanied the final stages of the IGC.

The confident opening statement of Article J of the Maastricht Treaty on European Union (TEU)—'A common foreign and security policy is hereby established'—therefore papered over unresolved differences. CFSP and justice and home affairs (JHA; see Chapter 19) were to remain as the second and third 'pillars' of the EU outside the integrated, Commission-led first pillar. Policy initiative, representation, and implementation were explicitly reserved to the Council presidency, 'assisted if need be by the previous and next member states to hold the Presidency' in what became known as the 'troika.' The Commission was to be 'fully associated' with discussions in this intergovernmental pillar, and 'the views of the European Parliament . . . duly taken into consideration'. Ambiguous language allowed for 'joint actions' in pursuit of agreed common aims, and referred to 'the eventual framing of a common defence policy, which might in time lead to a common defence'.

Much of the CFSP negotiation during the IGC leading to the TEU amounted to shadow-boxing behind the security cover which the US provided, while monetary union and social policy preoccupied heads of government. There was little discussion of the strategic implications of the transformation of European order, or of the balance between civilian and military instruments required for an effective common policy in this new context (Niblett and Wallace 2001). It was only after the IGC was concluded that the WEU secretariat, after negotiations with Nato, persuaded European governments to agree, in the 'Petersberg Declaration' (Box 18.1), to define a range of shared tasks in peacekeeping and peacemaking operations. Most unresolved issues, such as the extent of qualified majority voting in CFSP or how to define the overall institutional link between the WEU and the EU, however, were put off to a further IGC, to be convened in 1996.

BOX 18.1	The Petersberg tasks

Petersberg Declaration, June 1992, Section II, *On Strengthening WEU's Operational Role*, para 4:

'Apart from contributing to the common defence in accordance with Article 5 of the Washington Treaty and Article V of the modified Brussels Treaty respectively, military units of WEU member states, acting under the authority of WEU, could be employed for:

- humanitarian and rescue tasks;
- peacekeeping tasks;
- tasks of combat forces in crisis management, including peacemaking.'

(Western European Union Council of Ministers, Bonn, 19 June 1992, available at: *http://www.weu.int*).

The Treaty of Amsterdam's substantial revisions of the Treaty on European Union's provisions in Title V (TEU) on CFSP incorporated this list, as Article 17(2) (CTEU). The European Security Strategy (ESS) expanded this task spectrum and the Treaty of Lisbon (ToL), which entered into force in December 2009 following ratification by all member states, offered a further revised definition of what the ESDP was to cover. The ToL stipulates that the EU should use both civilian and military means to conduct humanitarian, rescue, and disarmament operations, provide military advice and assistance to third countries, and undertake conflict prevention and peacekeeping. It further specifies that the Union should be able to apply combat forces to crisis-management tasks including peacemaking and post-conflict stabilization. The Treaty observes that all these tasks could also be applied to the fight against terrorism, and that the EU could use ESDP missions to support third countries combating terrorist activity in their territories. Whether or not the ToL enters into force, it is likely that this expanded definition of the task spectrum will guide ESDP in the future.

External events nevertheless drove European governments to cooperate more closely during the course of the 1990s. The United Nations Peacekeeping Force (Unprofor), the initial peacekeeping force in Bosnia, was under French command. The French and the British provided the largest numbers on the ground; the Spanish and Dutch also contributed substantial contingents. Other European countries with troops in Bosnia or Croatia in early 1995 included Belgium, the Czech Republic, Poland, Slovakia, and Ukraine, as well as the Danes, Finns, and Swedes with Norwegians in a joint Nordic battalion. French attitudes both to Nato and to Britain shifted further under the experience of cooperation with British forces in the field, and closer appreciation of the utility of Nato military assets. Another field of closer cooperation arose from pressure exerted by the EU's southern members for Mediterranean programmes, oriented particularly towards the Maghreb, to parallel the eastern-oriented Phare programme (*Pologne, Hongrie: assistance à la restructuration des économies*) and Technical Assistance to the Commonwealth of Independent States programme (TACIS), and with a comparable share of the EU budget. The Spanish presidency convened a Euro-Mediterranean Conference in Barcelona in November 1995, which committed the EU in principle to a generous long-term programme (Barbé 1998).

Nevertheless, the US continued to dominate Nato and overshadowed some of the effects of European governments working closer together. For example, the US, which had insisted in 1991 that Yugoslavia was now a European responsibility, nevertheless intervened to supply and to train Croatian forces, and dominated the negotiations which led to the Dayton Agreement in December 1995 (Neville-Jones 1997). Similarly, the US through Nato continued to define East–West political strategy, although west European governments collectively and individually provided by far the largest proportion of economic assistance to the former socialist states, including Russia. American officials promoted a parallel Nato dialogue with the Maghrebi states. At the Nato summit in Brussels in January 1994 the Clinton administration proposed to enlarge the alliance to Poland, Hungary, and the Czech Republic, ahead of their projected accession to the EU. The accession to the EU in 1995 of three more non-aligned states (Austria, Finland, and Sweden), to join neutral Ireland, further complicated the relationship between the EU and Nato.

Britain, France, and Germany were the key players in moves towards a more effective CFSP. Painful reassessment of post-cold-war German responsibilities was leading to a gradual 'normalization' of German foreign and defence policy. Nevertheless, continuing support for the principle of a conscript 'citizen army' and deep cuts in defence spending left its armed forces poorly structured and ill-equipped. Attitudes in the British and French governments were, however, converging. The French government had explicitly modelled its post-Gulf-War defence review on the British armed forces, ending conscription to focus on a smaller, better-equipped, and more deployable military force. Cooperation on the ground in Bosnia built mutual respect between the French and British military. At the political level the British and French shared similar frustrations over the reassertion of US leadership in the Balkans and the imposition of the Dayton Agreement. All this contributed to a convergence of attitudes between London and Paris, though the strength of Euroscepticism within the British Conservative party and within the British press meant that its implications did not become evident until well after the election of a Labour government in May 1997.

With ratification of the TEU completed only in 1993, there was little enthusiasm for the 'major review' of CFSP in the IGC which was convened in 1996 and stretched through Italian, Irish, and Dutch Council presidencies over eighteen months. Proposals from member governments for this IGC revived the debate from five years earlier. As in 1990–1, intra-European negotiations on security policy and defence moved in parallel with developments within Nato.

The concept of a European security and defence identity (ESDI), agreed at the Brussels Nato summit in January 1994, signalled US willingness to accommodate French sensitivities, as well as US insistence that the European allies should play a larger role in maintaining the security of their own region. In December 1995 the French government announced a formal return to some parts of the Nato structure, although President Chirac made clear that France expected a genuine 'Europeanization' of the alliance in return. His public demand that a French officer should take over Nato's southern command and Washington's predictable refusal, however, dashed hopes that French re-entry into Nato's integrated military structure would permit the emergence of a stronger European pillar within the alliance, closely integrated with the EU.

From CFSP to ESDP: Britain and France as leaders

Given the reluctance of most member governments to clarify the strategic objectives that CFSP should serve, innovations in this field have come more from responses to external crises than from IGCs. The crisis in Kosovo, a Serbian province with an Albanian majority, in 1998 sent another surge of refugees through neighbouring countries into EU member states. The US administration led a bombing campaign against Serbian targets; the British and French were willing in addition to deploy substantial ground forces. Tony Blair, the new British prime minister, was shocked to discover how few troops other European governments could deploy beyond their borders. Over 1,000 German troops were nevertheless posted to the neighbouring former Yugoslav Republic of Macedonia (FYROM), and German troops participated in the later peacekeeping force in Kosovo, after Joschka Fischer, the Green Party Foreign Minister, had passionately argued the case for a change in Germany's attitude to humanitarian crises beyond its borders.

Partly in response to Kosovo and partly to demonstrate the new government's commitment to closer European cooperation, the British now moved from laggard to leader in promoting European defence integration. In the defence realm Britain and France stand apart from the other EU member states. By 2008, between them, they accounted for 45 per cent of defence expenditure in the EU, and 60 per cent of spending on defence equipment; Germany and Italy accounted for a further 15 per cent and 13 per cent of defence spending respectively, though their equipment budgets are much smaller. At a bilateral Franco-British summit in December 1998, Blair and Chirac issued the St Malo Declaration, robustly stating that 'the Union must have the capacity for autonomous action, backed up by credible military forces', with member governments operating 'within the institutional framework of the European Union', including 'meetings of defence ministers'. Intensive Franco-British consultations between political directors and senior defence officials expanded bilaterally to other key EU governments, and then to the US, the Norwegians, and the Turks (as Nato members). Within the EU the Germans and Dutch were most closely drawn in. The Social Democrat–Green coalition government in Berlin found it hard to formulate a coherent response: the concept of Europe as a power for peace, renouncing military ambitions, retained strong support among the German left.

Initial reactions in Washington were mixed. The North Atlantic Council which met in Washington in April 1999 to celebrate the fiftieth anniversary of the Atlantic Alliance and to welcome three new members—the Czech Republic, Hungary, and Poland—declared in its carefully balanced communiqué that 'we reaffirm our commitment to preserve the transatlantic link', but also 'welcome the new impetus given to the strengthening of a common European policy in security and defence' (Nato 1999).

The Franco-British partnership, with the support of the German Council presidency in the first six months of 1999, pushed through some significant innovations. The strategy was to focus on EU military capabilities more than institutional change. They challenged their European partners to reshape their armed forces, in order to enable European states to manage peacekeeping operations outside their region without depending on the US for crucial equipment and reinforcement. Their intention, outlined in the 1999 Cologne communiqué, was to gain stronger commitments from their partners to build deployable European forces, and then to merge WEU into the EU in the further IGC planned in 2000. They achieved the first of these aims at the December 1999 European Council, which adopted the 'Helsinki headline goals', pledging EU governments collectively to constitute a European Rapid Reaction Force of up to fifteen brigades (60,000 troops), 'militarily self-sustaining with the necessary command, control and intelligence capabilities, logistics, other combat support services and additionally, as appropriate, air and naval elements on operations beyond their borders'—and to achieve this aim 'by 2003' (Council of the European Union 1999c).

A follow-up Capabilities Commitment Conference, in November 2000, identified the major shortcomings in weapons and transport systems, and drew up a list of pledges and priorities. The working method was similar to that of the Lisbon economic-reform process, intended to spread 'best practice' from the most advanced to the laggards, and to shame the most deficient governments into improving their performances. Nineteen working groups were set up to consider each target and shortfall in more detail. As so often before, the US was sponsoring a parallel process through Nato, the Defence Capabilities Initiative. Neither process, however, made much impact on most governments. Meetings of EU defence ministers received almost no attention in parliaments or press. Competing pressures on national budgets blocked any reversal in the reduction of defence spending. The German government, after the effort required to persuade the Bundestag to deploy troops to Kosovo, discouraged discussion of whether the Rapid Reaction Force might be sent beyond Europe to Africa or the Middle East. In south-eastern Europe, however, the succession of crises had left behind a much higher level of European political and military engagement. As the Pentagon withdrew US troops from deployments in Bosnia and Kosovo, the number of contributing European countries rose.

Only the British and French governments were yet prepared to project military forces beyond Europe for more than UN peacekeeping operations. A small British force re-established order in Sierra Leone in 2001, after a UN force of over 17,000 had failed to contain civil conflict. French forces intervened in Côte d'Ivoire in 2002. In a gesture of shared commitment to the stability of a continent where Franco-British rivalry had persisted into the 1990s, the British and French foreign ministers travelled round Africa together the same year. Nordic governments, the Irish and Austrians had long contributed to UN peacekeeping operations in Africa and the Middle East. While EU member states have for decades contributed to UN peace-keeping missions, the number of troops deployed rose significantly in the context of the Balkan crises. Today, EU member-state governments sustain between 60,000 and 70,000 troops on international crisis-management operations. While deployments are conducted through many frameworks, including the UN and since 2003 the EU's ESDP, Nato remains dominant.

CFSP in the context of eastern enlargement

The implications of the EU's forthcoming eastern enlargement for the European region preoccupied European governments much more directly. If enlargement is seen as a part of the EU's foreign policy (see Chapter 17), the extension of security, prosperity, and democracy within a strong international framework across eastern Europe must be counted as a major achievement. The Helsinki European Council of December 1999 also saw reluctant heads of state and government accept Tur-key as a formal candidate, under intense US pressure—based on Turkey's strategic importance to western interests across the Middle East. Negotiations with Russia, with which the EU now shared a common border—jointly managed in unwieldy fashion by representatives of the Commission, the High Representative, and the rotating Council Presidency—ranged from relations with Belarus to energy secu-rity (see Chapter 15) to the future of Kaliningrad (the Russian region surrounded by EU member states), to cross-border criminal networks. Nato enlargement, which passed another milestone with the Prague summit of 2002, was relatively straightforward in institutional terms. EU enlargement necessitated delicate adjustments of common policies, financial flows, institutional representation, and voting weights.

Postponement of decision on these issues in the Treaty of Amsterdam (ToA) required a further IGC, ending with President Chirac's mismanaged late-night compromises at Nice in December 2000. This failure, in turn, sparked the proposal for a broader Convention on the Future of Europe, which met from mid-2002 to July 2003, with representatives of thirteen candidate states (including Bulgaria, Romania, and Turkey) as participating observers. Meanwhile the European Commission was attempting to focus the attention of member governments on the implications of enlargement for the wider European periphery, east and south. In early 2003 it floated proposals for a broader European neighbourhood policy (ENP), aimed at providing a framework for economic cooperation and political consultation for the states around the EU's eastern and southern borders: common foreign policy in effect, but defined and managed through civilian instruments (see Chapter 17).

Coordination in Brussels, but decisions in national capitals

The CFSP pillar remains largely in the hands of the member governments, although it is now supplemented by a cluster of Brussels-based institutions. Intensive transgovernmentalism thus has become the dominant policy mode (see Chapter 4), and its character is changing, in particular as a result of the structures created in the wake of the decision to launch ESDP. Heads of state and government remain ultimately responsible for CFSP and its overall direction through the European Council. The General Affairs and External Relations Council (GAERC, up to 2002 called the General Affairs Council), which brings together member states' foreign ministers in monthly meetings, is the main decision-making body in practice. To manage better the ever-growing agenda, GAERC is divided into two sessions. The first, prepared by the Committee of Permanent Representatives (Coreper), deals with internal policy coordination among governments and the second, prepared by the Political and Security Committee (PSC, also known after its French acronym COPS) in coordination with Coreper, addresses the external dimension. While there is still no formal Council of Defence Ministers, they have met in informal sessions under GAERC to discuss military-capability questions since 2002. Furthermore, EU member-state defence ministers serve as the steering board of the European Defence Agency (EDA), which was created in 2004. The European Council and the GAERC are supported by the Council Secretariat, which has acquired a substantial number of foreign affairs officials as well as a military staff.

The Council is formally empowered to appoint 'special representatives' for particular policy issues—generalizing the experiment adopted (with Lord Carrington, David Owen, and Carl Bildt) for the Yugoslav wars. In autumn 2009, the EU had eleven special representatives (EUSRs) in different regions of the world which promote EU policies and seek to contribute to their overall coherence and effectiveness by acting as the 'face' of the Union: Afghanistan and Pakistan, the African Great Lakes Region, the African Union, Bosnia and Herzegovina, Central Asia and Georgia, Kosovo, the former Yugoslav Republic of Macedonia (FYROM), the Middle East, Moldova, the South Caucasus, and Sudan.

The PSC, created on an interim basis in 2000, was formalized in 2001 and is the successor to the Political Committee of EPC. Unlike its predecessor, its members are all based in Brussels, permanent national representatives with ambassadorial rank who meet at least twice a week. Its meetings are also attended by representatives from the Commission's Directorate-General for External Relations (DG RELEX) and Council Secretariat's Directorate-General E for External and Political-Military Affairs and its Policy Unit. The PSC is tasked with monitoring international affairs, drafting policy options for the Council, and overseeing the implementation of adopted policies, thus located at the centre of CFSP/ESDP's day-to-day business.

The creation of the PSC in its current form clearly reflects recognition on the part of member-state governments that coordination at the centre had to be strengthened. However, the PSC is also a good example of the efforts governments undertake to maintain tight control of the Brussels-based institutions that they created in the field of foreign and security policy. Governments had rather diverging views on how senior their representatives in the PSC should be, with some reasoning that more junior ambassadors would be easier to control from capitals. More substantively, the divergent views relating to the 2003 invasion of Iraq illustrate that national governments will not be shy to put the brakes on if the stakes are perceived to be high. Several PSC ambassadors were issued rigid and unequivocal instructions from their respective ministries of foreign affairs to resist discussion in the EU on the issue of Iraq (Howorth 2007).

An important institutional innovation under the ToA was the creation of the post of High Representative for CFSP which was merged with the post of Secretary General of the Council (HR/SG). Its holder is part of the *troika*, consisting since the ToA also of the Council presidency and the Commissioner for external relations, and is assisted by a small Policy Unit to develop policy and assess relevant events. The job description for the High Representative was imprecise, beyond 'assisting' the Council. However, the first High Representative, former Nato Secretary General, Javier Solana, has made himself the external face of CFSP, tirelessly travelling, in and out of Belgrade, Moscow, Washington, and across the Middle East, while carefully avoiding too open a challenge to member-state authority. As in the debate about the seniority of PSC representatives, member governments did not see eye to eye when discussing the desirability of having a political and diplomatic heavyweight like Solana in the HR/SG position. The UK in particular favoured a more junior appointment whereas more integrationist-minded governments and the Commission had argued that the post should be located inside the Commission rather than the Council.

The limited roles played by the European Commission, the EP, and the European Court of Justice (ECJ) further underline the dominance of the member governments through intergovernmental structures. The Commission has only a non-exclusive right of initiative for CFSP and despite involvement through the Commissioner for external relations in the reformed *troika*, it is in a difficult position to exert influence. However, given the multi-faceted nature of most foreign- and security-policy issues, the Commission, in its role of running external economic relations, is sometimes able to exploit cross-pillar linkages to make its voice heard. In response to the creation of CFSP and ESDP it has further adapted its structures, for example through the creation of a Conflict Prevention and Crisis Management Unit (CPCMU) and a further increase of the number of units within directorates-general responsible for aspects of external relations. The EP remains limited to providing running commentary on CFSP. The treaty rules stipulate that the parliament's views on all CFSP matters have to be taken into account, but in practice much depends on the Council providing a steady flow of information and on MEPs, especially in relevant specialized committees, developing the necessary expertise to strengthen the Parliament's voice. The ECJ remains excluded from the CFSP pillar.

Political resistance to the encroachment of the Commission and the EP into the second pillar has lessened through successive IGCs. Duplication of functions between the Commission and the now substantial external DG E of the Council Secretariat was contained by easy personal relations between Solana and Christopher Patten, the then Commissioner for External Relations. Bureaucratic rivalry is nevertheless a constant problem, in particular from those within the Commission who view the expansion of the Council Secretariat as a threat to its powers and privileges. There were turf battles, too, over funding CFSP activities: the Commission and the EP were seeking to use the 1 per cent of external action expenditure (€60 million) allocated to the CFSP to introduce Community procedures and oversight, while governments were torn between seeking additional common funding and defending the intergovernmental approach. Administrative expenditure for the second pillar and non-military operational expenditure can now be charged to the EU budget, leaving 'operations having military or defence implications' to be funded by those states which have not exercised their right of constructive abstention in each case.

ESDP triggered a further raft of institutional engineering in Brussels. The EU Military Committee (EUMC), the Union's highest military body, was created in 2001 (*ad interim* from 2000) and brings together member states' chiefs of defence (CHODs). The EUMC usually meets in the form of the CHODs' military representatives, who are often 'double-hatted' with their nation's representatives at Nato. The EUMC provides unanimous advice and recommendations on military matters of ESDP to the Council, channelled through the PSC. For example, it evaluates different options for ESDP missions, oversees the development of an operations plan, and monitors the conduct of ESDP operations.

The EU Military Staff, now more than 200 strong, was set up at the same time. It works under the political direction of the European Council through the PSC and under the military direction of the EUMC. It constitutes the permanent Brussels-based military expertise that the EU can draw on for early warning purposes, situation assessment (and intelligence cooperation), and strategic planning tasks. It is organized like a directorate-general within the Council Secretariat. It houses a civil-military planning cell and, since January 2007, the nucleus of an operations centre which can, if reinforced through national secondments, run autonomous ESDP missions of up to about 2,000 personnel.

Mirroring these military bodies on the civilian side are: the Committee for Civilian Aspects of Crisis Management (CIVCOM) and the Civilian Planning and Conduct Capability (CPCC). CIVCOM advises and drafts recommendations for the PSC on civilian aspects of crisis management. The CPCC has a mandate to plan and conduct civilian ESDP operations and in general assist the Council with regard to civilian missions. The CPCC Director serves as EU Civilian Operations Commander.

Finally, several agencies play important enabling roles. The EDA is working on defence capabilities development, armaments cooperation, the European defence technological and industrial base and defence equipment market, and research and technology. The work of the EDA does not seek to replace national defence-planning or capabilities-development processes with a European-level equivalent but rather operates as a facilitator and to some degree coordinator of such processes. The EDA suffers from divergent British and French views of its primary objective: whether to focus on raising the effectiveness of national forces and their equipment, or to promote defence procurement from European manufacturers. The agency has attempted to collect comprehensive data on defence programmes underway and defence-spending trends across member states, although some governments have resisted publication of their data (Witney 2008). Its steering board consists of national defence ministers, chaired by the HR/SG: it thus remains firmly in the hands of the member governments. Furthermore, the EU incorporated the WEU's Institute for Security Studies in 2001 and the satellite centre in Torrejon, Spain, which produces and analyses space-based imagery in support of CFSP. To provide training in the field of ESDP, the Council set up the European Security and Defence College (ESDC) in July 2005. The ESDC is a virtual institution organized as a network between national institutes, colleges, and academies.

The institutional set-up clearly shows a growing trend towards more coordination at the EU level in CFSP and ESDP and thus represents a marginal shift from the original and wholly intergovernmental model of EPC towards closer association with the established Brussels institutions and thus with intensive transgovernmentalism (see Chapter 4). The result is a remarkably complex machinery which is intended to make the EU a more effective actor in the security realm through coordination of national policies. However, it is clear that governments are careful not to relinquish control.

From Iraq to the European Security Strategy

The policies pursued by President George W. Bush provided an external shock to the EU's loosely coordinated structures for foreign policy. President Bush's first visit to Europe, for an EU–US summit in Gothenburg in June 2001, was a disaster, when fifteen heads of government repeated criticisms of US policy on climate change, having failed to agree what messages to convey to their most important external partner.

The terrorist attacks of 9/11 followed three months later. European governments expressed their solidarity with the US by invoking for the first time ever Nato's collective defence clause, Article 5. In gathering support for its planned intervention in Afghanistan the US nevertheless ignored both Nato and the EU as consultative forums, working bilaterally with the major European states. Under US command, French, German, and Spanish ships patrolled the Indian Ocean, British air tankers refuelled US planes, and special forces from several European countries, including Denmark and Germany, operated inside Afghanistan— marking a further point of transition in the gradual adjustment of European governments to global commitments.

In moving rapidly on from Afghanistan to Iraq, US policy-makers made even less effort to carry their European allies with them. The flimsy structures of CFSP, weakened further by the deterioration in personal relations between British and French leaders and by the domestic politics of a German election campaign, buckled under the strain. The British offered full public support, in the hope of influencing the direction of US policy, and British troops entered Iraq with the US. The French refused support for an invasion without US concessions, and resisted the British–US efforts to gain authorization from the UN Security Council for military action. The Franco-German claim to represent 'European' opposition to the invasion provoked competing statements by other groups of governments. In April 2003 the Belgian government worsened divisions by convening a summit to discuss an independent European defence headquarters, which only the French, German, and Luxembourg heads of government attended. Washington policy-makers celebrated the division between 'old Europe' and 'new Europe', as Donald Rumsfeld, US Secretary of Defence, dubbed it, playing on transatlantic loyalties of the ten east European countries about to join the EU. Disintegration of a common European foreign policy over the invasion of Iraq, in the winter of 2002–3, revealed the wide gap between a 'common' policy, created out of political negotiations among heads of government and foreign ministries, and a 'single' policy built on integrated institutions and expenditure and on a Europe-wide public debate.

The intervention in Iraq constituted the sharpest crisis in transatlantic relations since 1973–4. The underlying issue for CFSP remained how far European governments should converge towards an autonomous international role, as opposed to one rooted within the Atlantic framework and under US leadership. Bitter words among Europe's political leaders, and across the Atlantic, did not, however, prevent a rapid return to cooperation among EU governments. Here, as after previous crises, the European response to failure was to re-establish collaboration, on a firmer base where possible, following the path set by established institutions.

In June 2003 Solana's Secretariat produced a draft European Security Strategy (ESS), *A Secure Europe in a Better World*, partly as a response to the Bush administration's 2002 National Security Strategy, but also as a means of stimulating an EU-wide debate. A revised version was adopted by heads of government at the December 2003 European Council (Council of the European Union 2003b). Tellingly, the 2003 ESS received scarcely any mention in national media, and little or no attention in national parliaments. National governments, in spite of approving the document, had not wanted to encourage an open debate. Its prominent place in the Brussels-based discourse on security affairs thus served to widen the gap between Brussels and national capitals, where prior assumptions and commitments continued to drive defence policy. The British and French governments were pushing the ESDP agenda forward together only months after the invasion of Iraq (Menon 2004). Frustrated at the failure of other governments in the multilateral capabilities-pledging process to achieve the Helsinki goals, they declared in February 2004 that they would advance in defence through 'enhanced cooperation'; they announced that they would provide 'battle-groups' in response to international crises, and invited those other members (or groups of members) which could demonstrate a comparable capability to join them. The German government announced its commitment to join them the following day (Institute for Security Studies 2004). The battlegroups concept was adopted at EU level in May 2004 within the framework of the military Headline Goal 2010 (see Box 18.2).

Under the pressures of US demands for 'burden-sharing', inhibitions over long-range military deployment were giving way. Every EU member government (except those of Cyprus and Malta) has contributed troops to Afghanistan since the end of 2001. Recognizing their shared interest in a stable outcome in Iraq, despite the divisions caused by the 2003 invasion, no fewer than fifteen governments from the post-2004 EU25 contributed troops to post-conflict reconstruction.

BOX 18.2   EU battlegroups

The Council of Ministers declared in May 2004 that the 'ability for the EU to deploy force packages at high readiness as a response to a crisis either as a stand-alone force or as part of a larger operation enabling follow-on phases, is a key element of the 2010 Headline Goal. These minimum force packages must be military effective, credible and coherent and should be broadly based on the battlegroups concept' (press release, 2,582nd Council Meeting, General Affairs and External Relations, 17 May 2004). Battlegroups can be provided by individual member states or as a multinational force package. High readiness is rotated on six monthly schedules. Since the EU aims to have the capability to conduct two rapid response operations at once, four slots need to be filled each year. An EU battlegroup, a particular military rapid reaction element, has the following characteristics:

- its generic composition is capable of stand-alone operations across all crisis management tasks included in ESDP's remit;
- it is based on a combined-arms battalion-sized force reinforced with combat support and combat service support units leading to a generic strength of about 1,500 troops;
- it can be initially sustained in theatre for 30 days, a period that can be extended to 120 if the battlegroup is resupplied appropriately; and
- it is deployable within 5–10 days of a decision to launch an operation.

At a Military Commitments Conference in November 2004 EU member states agreed to set up the first thirteen battlegroups, with initial operational capability from January 2005 and full operational capability from January 2007. Since 2007 the EU has had a minimum of two battlegroups on standby call at all times. Although the target strength of a battlegroup is set at 1,500 troops, the total involved can exceed 3,000 when all support and enabling capabilities are taken into account.

TABLE 18.1   ESDP missions

Mission	Location	Duration	No. of personnel
Africa			
Operation Artemis	DRC	2003	1,800
EUSEC RD Congo	DRC	2005–	40
EUPOL Kinshasa	DRC	2005–7	30
Mission to support AMIS II (African Union mission)	Sudan	2005–6	50
EUFOR RD Congo	DRC	2006	2,400
EUPOL RD Congo	DRC	2007–	39
EUFOR Chad/CAR	Chad and Central African Republic	2008–9	3,700
EU SSR	Guinea-Bissau	2008–	39
EU NAVFOR (*Atalanta*)	Somali coast	2008 (Dec.)–	1,200
Asia			
AMM	Aceh/Indonesia	2005–6	225
EUPOL Afghanistan	Afghanistan	2007–	230
Balkans			
EUPM	Bosnia-Herzegovina	2003–	182
Concordia	FYROM	2003	400
EUPOL PROXIMA	FYROM	2004–5	200
EUFOR/*Operation Althea*	Bosnia-Herzegovina	2004–	2,500 (initially 7,000)
EUPAT	FYROM	2006	30
EUBAM	Ukraine/Moldova	2006–	69
EULEX Kosovo	Kosovo	2008–	1,900
Caucasus			
EUJUST THEMIS	Georgia	2004–5	10
EUMM Georgia	Georgia	2008 (Oct.)–2009	300
Middle East			
EU BAM Rafah	Palestine	Since 2005	27
EUJUST LEX	Iraq/Brussels	Since 2005	25
EUPOL COPPS	Palestine	Since 2006	31

Source: updated from Giegerich (2008: 9)

ESDP enters the real world

ESDP became operational in 2003, when the EU formally took over command of the modest civil and military operations in FYROM. It took over military responsibility from Nato for the much larger mission in Bosnia in December 2004. By the end of 2008 no fewer than twenty-three missions, almost all small and most of them civilian in nature, had been launched (Table 18.1). The overall deployment of European troops on operations outside the boundaries of the EU and Nato rose from 40–50,000 in the late 1990s to over 70,000 from 2003 on—thus surpassing the target of the Headline Goals even as they missed their formal deadline. The percentage of these actually deployed through the EU nevertheless remained low; most were committed to Nato operations, or were part of UN peacekeeping missions (Giegerich and Wallace 2004; IISS 2008). EU operations were limited to the lower end of the spectrum of military tasks; even then, they relied on Nato assets (and often on Ukrainian air transport) for logistical support, and were deficient in command-and-control and operational-planning capabilities, as well as in tactical airlift.

The EU's decisions to deploy a military mission to the Democratic Republic of Congo (DRC) in 2003 and 2006 under the ESDP heading and the failure to do so at the end of 2008 serve as good illustrations that the EU is in some cases able to deliver substantially, in particular if there is strong leadership from a major player, while differences among capitals continue to throw up obstacles. On 11 May 2003, France indicated that it was willing to deploy a force to Bunia in the DRC following a request from the UN Secretary-General for a stopgap measure to reinforce the UN mission already in country in the face of a deteriorating security situation. Having secured assurances for a UN Chapter VII mandate, with agreement from the relevant regional players including on the limited nature of the operation in terms of time and scope, the French government officially announced its readiness to conduct the operation. French planning for what was then dubbed 'Operation Mamba' was already well underway when then President Chirac recognized this as an opportunity to showcase ESDP 'on operations'. It was only then that Operation Artemis, the ESDP mission, was born—in essence a Europeanized French operation built on the French desire to demonstrate that ESDP could operate autonomously in Africa, which enabled the Council's decision of 12 June 2003 to launch the operation.

When in 2006 the EU was again asked to reinforce temporarily the UN's presence in the DRC to help ensure security around the presidential elections scheduled for 30 July, the absence of such determined leadership proved problematic. France made clear that it would not lead again and was looking to Germany to fill this role. Pressure on Germany rose further after the UK indicated it would not participate in any significant way owing to overstretch in its armed forces, then heavily engaged in Afghanistan and Iraq. Germany, however, found it difficult to form a coherent position, with the Minister of Defence sending confusing signals regarding whether Germany was willing to lead. A lack of available funding, the absence of Africa experience of the *Bundeswehr* (indirectly emphasizing the responsibilities of former colonial powers and those with remaining security and defence obligations in Africa), and overstretch were advanced as obstacles ultimately reflecting the fragile domestic consensus that enables the deployment of German forces abroad in general. The German Minister of Defence, Franz Josef Jung, indicated he did not think Germany should play a leadership role and a leaked memo from the policy planning staff of the Ministry of Defence argued that significant German involvement would be inappropriate because no vital German interests were at stake.

In the wake of growing EU pressure Germany shifted its stance, at first setting out conditions similar to those France secured in 2003, while adding that, if Germany were to lead an ESDP operation, it would need to be truly multinational. Even while this shift was underway, Germany refused officially to take on the role of framework nation as long as other member states did not make unequivocal commitments. This reversal of the process delayed planning efforts. Solana made little headway with other member states and finally asked Germany to organize the force generation process, in response to which Germany arranged for a force contribution conference in late March. The pressure that Solana exerted on the German government to take on this leadership role, while also arguing for a more wide-ranging operation than the German government was ready to support, led to sharp exchanges between Jung and Solana. Some of the German staff in the vicinity of the minister's phone reported a major shouting match.

While EUFOR RD Congo, as the German-led ESDP operation became known, was eventually conducted successfully, the episode nonetheless points to a clash between the centre in the form of Solana pushing ESDP into a prominent role and national capitals' efforts to control carefully how much they might want to invest. As a result it took the EU several months to organize a relatively limited deployment of forces. Furthermore, the successes which the EU claimed in 2003 and 2006 did not have a strategic effect on the crisis in the DRC—indeed they could not have, even though the military personnel deployed implemented with great professionalism and effectiveness the limited mandate given to them by their political masters (Giegerich 2008).

However, when the security situation in eastern DRC deteriorated rapidly in autumn 2008, even a limited deployment proved to be unattainable. While then French Foreign Minister, Bernard Kouchner, insisted the EU 'has to act', including through the provision of troops, his British counterpart, David Miliband, pointed out that responsibility lay with the UN (Xinhua News Agency, 4 November 2008). In December, the UN Secretary-General explicitly called on the EU to send troops as a stopgap measure so that UN reinforcement could be arranged and deployed, not unlike in 2003. The European Council conclusions from its meeting a few days later in December 2008 were notable for their unwillingness to commit the EU. Concerns that had been looming in the minds of national policy-makers harked back to military overstretch and the thought that it would be easier to reinforce the UN mission, Monuc (United Nations Mission in the Democratic Republic of the Congo), than to set up a new ESDP mission. In the event, the UN Security Council authorized an increase of some 3,000 troops for Monuc and extended the mandate of the mission by one year until the end of 2009. Deployment of one of the EU battlegroups was rejected by EU member governments, with some arguing that it would not represent the appropriate force package to fulfil the task at hand, a logic which further undermined the rationale for having battlegroups in the first place.

The dithering over eastern Congo in 2008 contrasts with EU member governments' closely coordinated response to the war between Israel and Hezbollah in Lebanon in summer 2006. Although proposals for an ESDP mission were rejected, the European action in response to the crisis amounts to a fairly successful example of power projection. During and immediately after the hostilities—a UN-sponsored ceasefire ended two months of fighting on 14 August—EU member states could have launched one of several possible ESDP missions: an evacuation mission for European nationals, a humanitarian assistance mission, or a peacekeeping operation. None of these options gathered wide support among member states. In part this has to do with the fact that the UN has had a mission in place for twenty-five years and clearly enjoyed greater legitimacy as an organizational framework for action.

Thus, several EU member states, with France, Italy, and Spain in the lead, chose to contribute troops through national channels to the reinforced UN mission Unifil II (United Nations Interim Force in Lebanon). France, initially tapped to play a leadership role in the UN mission, remained hesitant for several weeks as the government tried to negotiate a more robust mandate and rules of engagement. While France was partially successful in this endeavour, Italy had in the meantime stepped up to fill the vacant leadership role. Among them EU governments provided some 7,000 troops (almost half of Unifil II) and heavy equipment, including main battle tanks, an aircraft carrier, and several other warships. The decision to commit forces was taken in Brussels in the presence of the UN Secretary-General, who had all but begged EU governments to provide the backbone of the UN operation.

In return for doing so, EU governments insisted on an interesting and unprecedented mechanism for control. They pushed through the creation of a special strategic cell at the UN headquarters in New York to direct the operation. While this cell ultimately reports to the UN Secretary-General, nineteen of the twenty-seven officers in the cell were initially seconded from EU member states, thus giving significant direct control to contributing EU governments (Gowan 2007).

It is further interesting to note that, aside from acting outside the ESDP framework, member governments also rejected the opportunity to make the EU formally the clearing house for national contributions to UNIFIL II, even though such a role is foreseen in declarations on EU–UN cooperation. Some, including France, also wanted the HR/SG, Javier Solana, to be empowered to speak on behalf of the EU and its member states during the crisis. However, this proved unacceptable to others, reflecting divisions about the desirable levels of EU and national involvement and also about the tricky question of whether to assign blame to Israel for the escalation of hostilities.

European support for UNIFIL II is nonetheless a positive story. It underpins the observation that intensive transgovernmentalism can indeed deliver substantive outcomes. Not only did EU member states rapidly deploy a sizeable force to a major crisis, they also did so in a spirit that strengthened the UN. The role played by DG RELEX and the European Humanitarian Aid Office (ECHO) proved vital in managing important civilian aspects of the response to this crisis, in particular refugee return and humanitarian aid, and has to be recognized alongside the military contributions by EU member states.

The EU27 collectively were pledged to provide some 39 per cent of the UN regular budget in the period 2007–9, and some 41 per cent of its peacekeeping budget. EU member governments take common positions in over 90 per cent of votes in international organizations, with an effective caucus at the UN and a Commission delegation. Furthermore, EU member states contributed some 60 per cent of net official development assistance disbursed in 2007 by the Development Assistance Committee (DAC) of the Organization for Economic Cooperation and Development (OECD). Yet EU influence over the agendas of the UN and of other international organizations remains much less than that of the USA. Britain and France carefully protect their privileged positions as permanent members of the UN Security Council, alongside the USA, Russia, and China. Other governments defend their rights to participate and speak, even when the Council presidency is presenting an agreed position.

Conclusions

The communiqué of The Hague Summit in December 1969 which had agreed to start EEC member governments on the road towards coordinated foreign policy had spoken of 'paving the way for a united Europe capable of assuming its responsibilities in the world . . . and of making a contribution commensurate with its traditions and mission' (European Union 1969). Thirty-three years later, the European Security Strategy stated in more disillusioned terms that 'the European Union is inevitably a global player . . . Europe should be ready to share in the responsibility for global security and in building a better world' (Council of the European Union 2003*b*). A heavy institutional structure now existed, occupying large numbers of ministers, officials, and military and police officers, yet the output did not measure up to the input of constant activity.

The fundamental weakness of this framework was the lack of obligation to implement agreements made. All too often, member governments have signed up to policies in Brussels that they have neither reported back to their parliaments nor implemented. CFSP has remained a field in which national ministers and officials control the agenda, though assisted by increasing numbers of staff within the Commission and the Council Secretariat. National approaches to foreign policy, filtered through each government's interpretation of its European commitments to parliament and public, remain diverse. The Treaty of Lisbon (ToL) aims to strengthen the institutional structure further, but may do little to overcome persistent national defection from the principle of solidarity (Box 18.3). It is hard to disagree with the bitter conclusion of the first head of the EDA, that 'member states and Brussels institutions have ignored the need for coherent strategies, improvised important operations, and taken refuge in process as an easier option than delivering real-world change' (Witney 2008: 8).

From 1969 onwards, French governments have driven CFSP forward. Their Belgian, German, and Italian counterparts have supported institution-building, though preferring a more supranational framework. They have not, however, shared French strategic objectives, or France's willingness to invest in military instruments to fulfil them. In terms of defence, Britain and France constitute the dominant players; agreement between them launched ESDP. The cooling of the British Labour government towards the project, and the major commitments of British forces to Iraq and Afghanistan, have contributed to the slow pace of progress in the ten years since St Malo. The greatest obstacle has, however, been the reluctance of other governments to invest in the equipment needed, or to reshape their armed forces to be able to operate effectively outside the EU—to the shared frustration of the British and French governments. ESDP has created the as-yet unfulfilled promise of comprehensive (civil and military) crisis management, which adds a crucial building block to CFSP. While ESDP operations so far have been moderately successful within the limitations defined by their parameters on the ground, they in the end are yet another reminder of the difficulties EU member governments face as they try to align their commonly agreed aspirations with actual policy output.

West European integration was built on a revulsion against *Machtpolitik*. Extension of the EU across southern, central, and eastern Europe has created what the head of Solana's CFSP Secretariat called a 'postmodern' state system, from which force has been excluded and across which human rights and civil liberties are enforced (Cooper 2003). Many intellectuals and politicians within European countries would like to extend this 'civilizing process' to the rest of the world, through civilian instruments and moral example—thus justifying the low level of military spending by many west European governments (Linklater 2005; Manners 2008). The EU is now a civilian power in a limited number of fields, which is making some progress towards shared civil–military capabilities. A rising proportion (now approaching 10 per cent) of its common budget is spent on external relations, including nation-building in south-east Europe; further development of neighbourhood policy would increase this further.

The EU punches below its weight in international diplomacy—including in the international institutions through which civilian power might best be exercised. Dependence on the US for hard security and for leadership in managing extra-European security threats betrays idealist claims to distinctively civilian power. The absence of a European public space—of a shared public debate, communicating through shared media, think tanks, political parties, responding to and criticizing authoritative policy-makers—leaves issues of global strategy and external threats to small groups of professionals. A transnational expert community has gradually developed across

BOX 18.3	**Treaty of Lisbon provisions for CFSP**

New foreign policy institutional arrangements in the Treaty of Lisbon:

- The new EU High Representative (EUHR), taking over the functions of Presidency, High Representative, and Commissioner for External Relations and appointed by the European Council and Parliament for up to two five-year terms, will be responsible to the Council for the leadership, management. and implementation of the EU's foreign and security policy.
- The EUHR will at the same time be Vice President of the Commission, responsible for all of the Commission's activities in the external relations field, either directly, or in a coordinating role where other Commissioners have the lead (e.g. enlargement, development, trade, energy, climate change).
- The EUHR will be assisted for the purpose of external representation by an External Action Service (EAS), drawing together officials from the Council Secretariat and Commission engaged in external affairs and diplomats seconded from the diplomatic services of the member states.
- The EU will have a solidarity clause (Art. 222) and a mutual assistance clause (Art. 42.7). The assistance clause calls on EU member states to aid each other in case of 'armed aggression' on a member's territory and to do so with 'all means in their power'. The solidarity clause commits EU member states to support each other in the event of terrorist attacks or natural and man-made disasters. While the clause refers to military assets, it will be left to member states to decide what kind of assistance they would provide.
- The Petersberg tasks are be redefined. Lisbon lists these as 'joint disarmament operations, humanitarian and rescue tasks, military advice and assistance tasks, conflict prevention and peace-keeping tasks, tasks of combat forces in crisis management, including peace-making and post-conflict stabilization ... all these tasks may contribute to the fight against terrorism, including by supporting third countries in combating terrorism in their territories'.
- A 'start up fund' is envisaged through which member states could agree to fund some activities outside the EU budget.
- Further innovations are the provisions regarding permanent structured cooperation (Art. 42.6 and Protocol on Permanent Structured Cooperation) which allows those member states 'whose military capabilities fulfil higher criteria and which have made more binding commitments to one another in this area with a view to the most demanding operations' to set up a leadership group seeking closer cooperation but within the overall framework of the EU.
- A full-time president of the European Council, with a two-and-a-half year mandate, renewable once, is at that level to 'ensure the external representation of the union on issues concerning its common foreign and security policy'.

the EU, communicating through specialist journals and think tanks, such as the EU Institute for Security Studies, but it has developed only weak links with national political debates.

European cooperation in foreign policy has gone beyond the framework of sovereign state diplomacy, but still remains far short of an integrated single policy, with integrated diplomatic, financial, and military instruments. The dominant mode of policy-making (see Chapter 4) is predominantly intensive transgovernmentalism among foreign ministries within the EU and among embassies in third countries. Within its restricted fields of competence for external relations the European Commission pursues the Community method, with national representatives monitoring its ambitions to extend its authority. Variable geometry is a frequent characteristic, both in closer cooperation between Britain and France, often also with Germany in an informal leadership group of states with active international interests, and also across the EU's external boundaries, with Turkey, Norway, and even Switzerland contributing to external actions. ToL proposals for enhanced cooperation might reinforce this trend.

There remain evident tensions between national autonomy and common policy, and (particularly for the smaller member states) between national passivity and the acceptance of the 'global . . . responsibilities' which the European Security Strategy spelled out. Acceptance of shared responsibilities and institutions since 1970 had been driven as much by a succession of external demands and crises, from across the Atlantic and from the USSR (later Russia) and the Middle East, as by competing Gaullist and federalist grand designs. It seemed likely that further development would similarly be driven by external pressures, but with the significant path dependence of established structures and procedures through which to respond.

 FURTHER READING

There is a substantial and growing literature on the various aspects of European foreign and defence policy as well as on the broader field of EU external relations. For a thorough introduction to the field see Hill and Smith (2005). K. E. Smith (2003) and M. E. Smith (2004) examine the gradual development of foreign policy cooperation. Howorth (2007) and Jones (2007) trace the development of ESDP. Carlsnaes et al. (2004) offer a more theoretical approach. The series of Chaillot Papers from the EU Institute for Security Studies provide case studies of CFSP and ESDP, as well as compilations of primary source material, most recently Glière (2008). Journals such as *Survival* and the *European Foreign Affairs Review* are useful on recent developments.

Carlsnaes, W., Sjursen, H., and White, B. (2004) (eds.), *Contemporary European Foreign Policy* (London: Sage).

Glière, C. (2008), *EU Security and Defence: Core Documents 2007, Vol. VIII*, Chaillot Paper No. 112 (Paris: EU Institute for Security Studies).

Hill, C., and Smith, M. (2005) (eds.), *International Relations and the European Union* (Oxford: Oxford University Press).

Howorth, J. (2007), *Security and Defence Policy in the European Union* (Basingstoke: Palgrave Macmillan).

Jones, S. G. (2007), *The Rise of European Security Cooperation* (Cambridge: Cambridge University Press).

Smith, K. E. (2003), *European Union Foreign Policy in a Changing World* (Cambridge: Polity).

Smith, M. E. (2004), *Europe's Foreign and Security Policy: The Institutionalization of Cooperation* (Cambridge: Cambridge University Press).

CHAPTER 19

Justice and Home Affairs

Communitarization with Hesitation

Sandra Lavenex

▌ Summary

The control of entry to, and residence within, national territory, citizenship, civil liberties, law, justice, and order lie very close to the core of the state. Nevertheless, the permeability of borders in Europe has prompted cooperation among governments, and in less than twenty years, justice and home affairs (JHA) have moved from a peripheral aspect to a focal point of European integration. Cooperation among national agencies concerned with combating crime, fighting terrorism, managing borders, immigration and asylum, and with the judicial and legal implications of rising cross-border movement, has thus been gradually moved from loose intergovernmental cooperation to more supranational governance within the European Union (EU). These developments, however, continue to be marked by reservations and arguments about the role of EU institutions, resulting in a hybrid institutional structure, and policy measures which are riddled with delicate compromises and flexible arrangements among the member governments.

Introduction

The ambition involved in creating an 'area of freedom, security, and justice' (AFSJ) within the EU may be compared with that which propelled the single market (see Chapter 5). The 1997 Treaty of Amsterdam (ToA) declared the AFSJ a fundamental EU objective (Art. 2 TEU), and justice and home affairs (JHA) has been one of the busiest policy areas, with the Council adopting an average of ten texts a month in this field since 1999 (Monar forthcoming). In contrast to economic integration, however, which has been at the core of the European integration project, JHA touches on many issues that are deeply entrenched in national political and judicial systems and have strong affinities to questions of state sovereignty: since the seventeenth century, the state has drawn legitimacy from its capacity to provide security for its inhabitants (Mitsilegas et al. 2003: 7). Cooperation in JHA also has direct implications for democratic values and for the balance between liberty and security in the Union and its member states, and security considerations have hitherto received more attention than those relating to 'freedom' or 'justice'.

The development of a common response to immigration and asylum-seekers, the joint management of the external borders, the increasing coordination of national police forces in the fight against crime, the approximation of national criminal and civil law, and the creation of specialized EU bodies such as Europol, Eurojust, and Frontex to deal with these matters thus constitute a new stage in the trajectory of European integration. These processes reflect the increasing involvement of EU institutions in core functions of statehood and, concomitantly, the transformation of traditional notions of sovereignty and democracy in the member states.

Notwithstanding the strong symbolism inherent in the creation of a European area of freedom, security, and justice, the EU is far from having unified, integrated common policies in JHA. As in other areas of EU policy, integration has been incremental, riddled with delicate compromises and reservations by member governments. Reservations about transfers of responsibilities to the EU and the domestic sensitivity of issues such as immigration and organized crime in national political debates and electoral campaigns have sustained transgovernmental governance as the dominant mode in JHA. Transgovernmentalism combines elements of the traditional 'Community method' with more intergovernmental ones: it is characterized by the relative weakness of legal harmonization and a focus on more operational aspects of coordination between national authorities. This has generated a peculiar pattern of shared competences between sub-national, national, and European levels of governance, with the continuity of a significant level of cooperation outside the EU's formal institutions.

This chapter starts with a short review of the emergence and institutionalization of JHA cooperation in the EU treaties, before presenting its key actors and institutional set-up, and discussing the main policy developments in related fields and recent proposals for reform.

The institutionalization of justice and home affairs cooperation

The dynamics of this new area of European integration reside both within and outside the EU and its member states. One important internal motor has been the spill-over from the realization of freedom of movement in the single market (see Chapter 5). The decision in the 1985 Schengen Agreement to extend the elimination of internal border controls that had been in place among the Benelux countries since 1948 to the five contracting member states—Belgium, France, Germany, Luxembourg, and The Netherlands—spurred concern about safeguarding internal security and prompted closer cooperation on questions relating to cross-border phenomena such as immigration, organized crime, and drug trafficking. The surge of asylum-seekers from outside western Europe in the 1980s which followed the closure of legal channels for economic immigration, the phenomena of organized crime and terrorism, and the end of the cold war, which opened the EU's previously closed eastern border to hopeful immigrants and criminal networks, generated external pressures for closer cooperation.

This intensified cooperation could draw on informal cooperation among security services and law-enforcement agencies that had developed since the 1970s. These included the Pompidou Group on drugs, set up in 1972 within the wider Council of Europe, and the Trevi Group created at the December 1975 European Council in Rome to coordinate anti-terrorist work among EU governments faced with Irish, Italian, German, and Palestinian groups operating within and across their borders. After 1985 Trevi's mandate was extended to other issues of cross-border public order and serious international crime such as drug trafficking, bank robbery, and arms trafficking.

In 1990 two important international treaties set the guidelines for future European cooperation. The Schengen Implementing Convention (SIC) devised 'compensatory measures' for the removal of frontier controls, covering asylum, a common visa regime, illegal immigration, cross-border police competences, and a common computerized system for the exchange of personal data (Schengen Information System (SIS)). The Dublin Convention on Asylum, concluded among all EU member states, incorporated the asylum rules also included in the SIC and established the responsibility of the state in which an asylum-seeker first enters for the examination of an asylum claim.

Thus, prior to the formal establishment of cooperation in justice and home affairs in the 1992 (Maastricht) Treaty on European Union (TEU) an extensive network of cooperation had already developed which operated both outside and under the overall authority of the European Council. Cooperation took place on several political and executive levels, ranging from ministers through directors-general of the relevant ministries to middle-ranking civil servants, and representatives of police forces and other agencies. Cooperation among the initially five Schengen states was to turn into a motor for and 'laboratory' of integration and had an influential impact on the subsequent communitarization of cooperation (Monar 2001).

Intergovernmental formalization: Maastricht's third pillar

During the intergovernmental conference (IGC) leading to the TEU, the Dutch Council Presidency's draft, which proposed to bring both the common foreign and security policy (CFSP) and JHA into a single integrated structure, was dismissed, and instead, foreign policy and internal security remained primarily intergovernmental, in separate 'pillars' (on CFSP see Chapter 18). Asylum policy, rules and controls on external border-crossing, immigration policy, and police and judicial cooperation in civil and criminal matters were included as 'matters of common interest' in the third pillar of the TEU. In this way the existing network of committees was formalized without transforming the framework of authority and accountability (see Lavenex and Wallace 2005).

The loose intergovernmental structure did not prevent JHA from becoming the most active field for meetings convened under the Council of Ministers in the late 1990s. The frequency and intensity of interaction, especially in the area of police cooperation and organized crime, induced a transformation of the working practices of interior ministries and of police forces, which had remained among the least internationally minded within national governments, and led to the emergence of an intensive transgovernmental network (see Chapter 4).

By the 1996–7 IGC, the third pillar had developed an extensive set of instruments and institutions. Europol was taking shape as a coordinating agency for cooperation among national police forces, even though the Europol Convention had not yet been ratified by all member states. Four common databases were being set in place: the SIS was already up and running, the Customs Information System was being computerized, and the Europol Information System and Eurodac, the finger-print database for asylum-seekers, were being developed. Ministries of justice were drawn in more slowly; it was not until the revival of the concept of a European Judicial Area, after the ToA, that justice ministries began to be drawn into a similar European network.

Uneasy communitarization: the Treaties of Amsterdam and Nice

The current framework of cooperation in JHA was shaped by the treaties of Amsterdam and Nice. This framework, which shifted parts of JHA to the Community pillar while maintaining a 'streamlined' third pillar on police and judicial cooperation in criminal matters (PJCCM), reflects the delicate compromise between intensive transgovernmental cooperation, on the one hand, and the incremental consolidation of supranational structures, on the other (see Box 19.1). The 2007 ToL introduces significant changes to JHA, more far-reaching than the changes which that treaty makes to any other areas of EU law (see section, 'The agenda for reform' below).

BOX 19.1	Changes to JHA in the Treaty of Amsterdam and the Treaty of Nice

Title IV, Articles 61–9 TEC

- Articles 62–3 TEC list 'flanking measures' to be adopted within five years (by May 2004) to compensate for free movement within the EU, including common procedures for controls on persons at the EU's external borders, common visa policy, common measures on asylum seekers, 'temporary protection' of refugees, and immigration policy.

- Articles 64, 67–8 TEC maintain the intergovernmental decision-making procedures (shared right of initiative, consultation procedure with the EP, unanimity voting) until the end of the transition period in 2004 and impose strict limits on reference to the ECJ.

- Different opt-outs for Denmark, the UK, and Ireland.

Title VI, Articles 29–42 TEU

- Articles 29–34 TEU provide more detail on 'common action' in police and judicial cooperation in criminal matters, including references to 'operational cooperation' among law enforcement agencies, and collection and storage of data. The ToN specified in Article 31 TEU the functions of Eurojust.

- The opaque legal instruments of the TEU were replaced by well-established, legally binding legal instruments, but some of these, the framework decisions, are excluded from direct effect.

- Articles 35–9 TEU reflect parallel unresolved disputes on the involvement of the EU institutions (Commission, EP, ECJ) in this field; a lengthy section on the ECJ reflects sensitivity of extending cooperation in legal administration and law enforcement without providing for judicial review.

- Article 40 TEU extends provision for 'closer cooperation' among smaller groups of member states and registers the integration of the Schengen *acquis* 'into the framework of the European Union' (set out in more detail in an attached protocol).

The 'Amsterdam' reforms were motivated by widespread dissatisfaction with the working of the intergovernmental procedures. Three weaknesses, in particular, stood out: ambiguity about the legal and constitutional framework, evident in the frequency with which institutional issues were entangled with policy proposals; the low democratic accountability and political visibility of this essentially bureaucratic framework for policy, which allowed the practice of cooperation to develop far beyond what was reported to the European and the national parliaments or to national publics; and the absence of mechanisms for ensuring national ratification or implementation. The prospect of eastern enlargement added to the political salience of the policy fields covered by JHA cooperation and exacerbated the limits of decision-making structures based on unanimity.

Influenced by these considerations, the Westendorp Reflection Group preparing the 1996 IGC agenda stressed the importance of JHA reform by framing it as one aspect of 'making Europe more relevant for its citizens' (Monar 1997; McDonagh 1998). These ideas inspired the phraseology of the Amsterdam Treaty, which framed JHA in terms of establishing an 'area of freedom, security, and justice'. The justification of integration with reference to citizens' concerns has remained a major argument behind recent reforms, as evident in the Constitutional Convention and the IGC that prepared the ToL.

The ToA contained substantial changes to the framework for JHA (see Box 19.1). A new Title IV transferred migration and other related policies to the first pillar. Police cooperation and judicial cooperation in criminal matters remained in a revised and lengthened Title VI TEU, and the Schengen *acquis* was integrated into the treaties. It is important to note that the treaties do not provide for comprehensive competences in the sense of creating 'classic' EU 'common policies', even in the case of the 'common visa policy' or the 'common asylum system', which come closest to this idea.

While preparing the ground for a greater involvement of supranational actors in JHA, the ToA broke with the traditional doctrine of the Community method by introducing important intergovernmental elements into the first pillar while intergovernmental procedures persisted in the third pillar, though the Commission was now given a right of initiative shared with the member states.

National sensitivities about sovereignty encouraged a high degree of flexibility in the application of common rules. Denmark, for example, is a Schengen member and participates in the free movement area, but is free to adopt relevant European provisions as international law rather than EU law (thereby avoiding its direct effect and European Court of Justice (ECJ) jurisdiction). Ireland and the UK maintain their opt-out from Schengen and the lifting of internal frontier controls, but adhere, on a selective basis, and subject to unanimous agreement by 'insiders', to the flanking measures of the JHA *acquis* such as asylum, police and judicial cooperation in criminal matters (PJCCM), and the SIS (Kuijper 2000: 354).

Apart from these voluntary exemptions from the JHA *acquis*, the conditionality of the Schengen accession mechanisms adds a more compulsory form of flexibility. Notwithstanding their obligation to adopt the JHA *acquis* including the Schengen provisions in full, the twelve new member states have to first prove their capacity to implement effectively these tight border-management provisions before being recognized as having achieved what is often referred to as 'Schengen maturity' by the old members. At the end of 2008 nine of the twelve new member states had passed the test, but Bulgaria and Romania (because of capacity deficits) and Cyprus (because of problems relating to the partition of the island) currently remain outside of the integrated border control system.

Existing opt-out provisions and extended opportunities for enhanced cooperation under the Treaties of Amsterdam and Nice have not prevented individual member states from engaging in selective forms of intergovernmental cooperation outside the provisions of the treaties. The most prominent example is the Prüm Treaty concluded on German initiative with Austria, Belgium, France, Luxembourg, The Netherlands, and Spain in 2005. Facilitating and widening the conditions for the exchange of data included in the various JHA databases (see below) and intensifying operational cooperation between police, law enforcement, and immigration offices, this treaty is also sometimes referred to as 'Schengen III', a laboratory for deeper police cooperation among a vanguard of a few member states. As with the integration of Schengen into the Treaty of Amsterdam, the German Council Presidency in 2007 succeeded in extending these intensified forms of cooperation to the rest of the member states by incorporating the Prüm provisions into EU legislation.

The association of non-member states exacerbates the variable geometry of the 'area of freedom, security, and justice'. Norway and Iceland, as members of the pre-existing Nordic common travel area, have been included within the Schengen area, and are fully associated with the Schengen and Dublin Conventions. Switzerland, entirely surrounded by Schengen members, but not (like Norway and Iceland) a member of the wider European Economic Area, has negotiated a bilateral agreement which entered into force in March 2008. Liechtenstein ratified a Schengen/Dublin association treaty in 2008.

Key actors

The fragmentation of cooperation in JHA is also reflected in the multiplication of actors dealing with its development, both inside and outside formal EU structures.

Organization and capacities of EU institutions

With the new powers attributed to it under the ToA, the Commission gradually expanded its organizational basis in JHA. One of the first moves of the new President of the Commission (1999–2004), Romano Prodi, was to transform the small Task Force which had been established within the Secretariat of the Commission under the TEU into a new Directorate-General on Justice and Home Affairs, later renamed Justice, Liberty and Security (DG JLS). It was widely recognized that the task force, with only forty-six full-time employees in 1998, had been desperately understaffed and therefore had had little impact on third-pillar developments. Since the creation of the new DG, the number of personnel has been constantly increased, to 283 employees in 2002 and 440 in 2008, a size that is comparable to that of DG Trade (456 employees) and DG Markt (423 employees). Its expenditures also saw a steep increase, from €219.4 million in 2000 to €461.7 million in 2006, with 53.5 per cent of the total flowing to border control measures (Commission 2008j).

The responsible unit in the Council Secretariat, DG H, was more generously staffed than the Commission Task Force on JHA during the 1990s, with additional staff recruited in 1998–9. The ToA furthermore provided for the separate Schengen Secretariat to be integrated into DG H. Permanent representations of the member states in Brussels were also drawn in, adding legal advisors and officials seconded from interior ministries to their staffs.

The JHA Council inherited from Trevi and from the TEU's third pillar a heavily hierarchical structure of policy-making. It is one of the few areas in the Council that has four decision-making layers. Agendas for JHA Councils are prepared by Coreper II, which meets weekly at ambassadorial level. Between Coreper and the working groups, the JHA structure has an additional intermediary level composed of special coordinating committees, which bring together in Brussels senior officials from national ministries, normally meeting once a month. The lowest level is composed of working groups of specialists from national ministries and operational bodies (see Figure 19.1).

The former 'Coordinating Committee' (the K4 Committee) was renamed the Article 36 Committee, and then the Coordinating Committee for Police and Judicial Cooperation in Criminal Matters (CATS). At the same time, its mandate was narrowed to cover only the remaining third-pillar issues. Two new committees were created for those issues falling under the Community pillar: the Strategic Committee on Immigration, Frontiers and Asylum (SCIFA) and the Committee on Civil Law Matters. Set up initially for a five-year transitional period, these new committees of senior national officials were another sign of the intergovernmental legacy of JHA cooperation, and an anomaly under first-pillar procedures. Rather than phasing out this additional layer of consultation, in summer 2002 a new 'external borders practitioners' common unit', the 'SCIFA+', regrouped the members of the SCIFA with the heads of national border control authorities.

Although not foreseen by the treaties, the European Council's growing importance has been particularly salient in JHA where it has developed a lead function through multi-annual strategic programming. The ground was laid with the first European Council focused specifically on JHA held under the Finnish Council Presidency in Tampere in 1999, which set out far-reaching objectives and fixed deadlines for their adoption. The 2004 European Council in The Hague followed with a new, ambitious JHA multi-annual programme; it is expected that the new JHA multi-annual programme will be adopted by the European Council under the Swedish Council Presidency in autumn 2009. These strategic planning documents were devised to counter the incrementalism of cooperation under the Maastricht Treaty and to assure a greater efficiency in implementing agreed commitments. However, the flow of policies shows that under the current institutional procedures and given the domestic sensitivity of the field, a certain gap between ambitions and implementation persists (see below).

The most remarkable change in the formal decision-making structure has been the strengthening of the role of the European Parliament (EP) with the realization of the co-decision procedure for most aspects of JHA that fall under

FIGURE 19.1   Decision-making in justice and home affairs after Maastricht

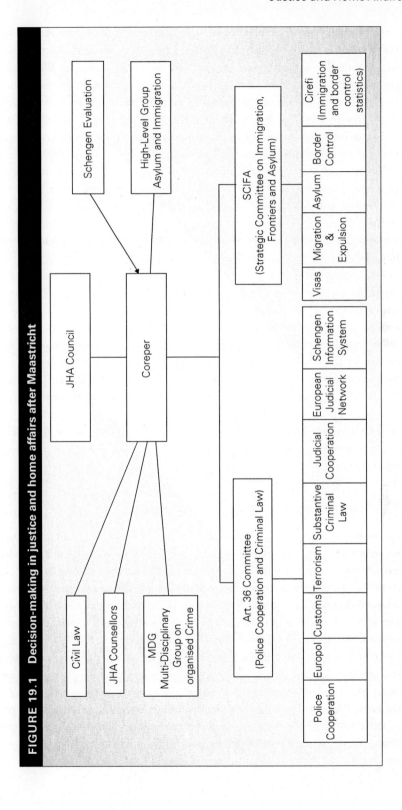

the first pillar: visas, border control, irregular migration, asylum policy, and judicial cooperation in civil law. Until 2005, when the transitional period of the ToA expired, the EP had not been granted any powers to amend or block legislation by the Council and the Council had only to consult the EP prior to adopting a measure—a requirement that was repeatedly violated (Lavenex 2006a). In its June 2006 Resolution on the AFSJ, the EP explicitly complained that it often did not get all of the preparatory documents necessary to participate in the decision-making process from the outset. The Council's failure to comply with the consultation requirements had been a topic of contention during several legislative procedures and had led the EP to file legal complaints before the ECJ, including concerning the 2003 Family Reunification Directive and the 2005 Asylum Procedures Directive.

As co-decision has not been extended to the third pillar, the EP's involvement in matters under the third pillar has been even less satisfactory. In order to allow it a real opportunity to examine and, where necessary, to suggest amendments to proposed measures, the EP must be given at least three months. Despite a much improved inter-institutional dialogue, relations between the EP and the Council continue to be contentious, and the EP has tried to enhance its grip also on third-pillar legislation. Given that third-pillar legislation often has elements that could fall under the first pillar, such as with regard to the access by law-enforcement authorities to the Visa Information System (VIS; see below), the EP has sought to link its assent to the issues under co-decision to the Council's consideration of its positions on the third-pillar issues negotiated under the consultation procedure, thus de facto widening its right to co-decision to police and judicial cooperation in criminal matters. Associated quarrels have repeatedly led to delays in the legislative process.

The reinvention of intergovernmentalism

Faced with the increasingly assertive role of the EP, but also with the expansion of member states participating in JHA Council meetings 'in a large, windowless conference hall of the Council building in Brussels' accommodating 'some 150 representatives of the Presidency, the European Commission, the Council Secretariat and national delegations' and speaking in twenty-three different official languages (Oel and Rapp-Lücke 2008: 23), several member states, under German lead, have made recourse to intergovernmental forms of cooperation outside EU structures. The Prüm Treaty mentioned above is but one manifestation of this trend. In May 2003 the interior ministers of the five biggest member states—France, Germany, Italy, Spain, and the UK—created the so-called G5 in order to try to speed up the move towards operational goals and to circumvent the lengthy decision-making processes of the Council of Ministers. In 2006 Poland joined the group, making it the G6. The G6 meet twice a year at the ministerial level and have a rotating presidency.

Over time, they have developed extensive substructures and expert working groups charged with the implementation of projects. In 2009, eighteen projects in the fields of counter-terrorism, organized crime, and migration were being conducted based on the conclusions of the ministerial meetings in Heiligendamm and Stratford-upon-Avon in 2006.

A second intergovernmental forum in JHA is the Salzburg Forum founded in 2000 on the initiative of Austria and involving Austria, the Czech Republic, Hungary, Poland, Slovakia, and Slovenia. In 2006 Romania and Bulgaria joined the group and Croatia has been participating as an observer since 2006. Like the G6, this group meets twice a year at ministerial level and has a rotating presidency. It has created substructures for operational cooperation including working groups on witness protection, country of origin information, traffic police, Schengen evaluation, exchange of DNA data, and major events.

Both groups see their role in the elaboration and testing, in a smaller context of like-minded states or contiguous neighbours, of measures that can subsequently be exported to all member states. Whereas both face criticism for circumventing the official institutions of the EU and for their lack of transparency and accountability, the composition of the G6 based on country size has faced particular contention. This notwithstanding, the 2007 German Council Presidency expanded this model of enhanced intergovernmental cooperation by creating, with the support of DG JLS, the so-called Future Group, which is charged with elaborating priorities for JHA cooperation after expiry of the Hague Programme, i.e. from 2010 to 2014. Like the G6 and the Salzburg Forum, the Future Group gathers only the ministries of the interior, and not their partners from the justice ministries. In order to avoid an arbitrary selection of member states, the Group is composed of the 'troika', including the outgoing and incoming Presidencies with the acting Council Presidency and the Commission serving as co-chairs.

These intergovernmental structures are reminiscent of the 'Schengen laboratory' that drove JHA cooperation from 1995 to 1999. With the Future Group, the Commission has accepted the perpetuation of variable geometries in JHA, even if limited to strategic planning, justified on the basis of efficiency.

The proliferation of semi-autonomous agencies and bodies

Another special characteristic of the governance of the JHA is the proliferation of semi-autonomous special agencies and bodies. The multiplication of actors and the widening of their competences over the past eight years have been impressive and illustrate the dynamism of this field of cooperation. Yet, given that the member states have so far not transferred any operational powers to these agencies, their capabilities have repeatedly failed to meet the expectations. As it stands, the JHA agencies and bodies are mainly concerned with information exchange and co-ordination between national law-enforcement authorities, often supported by the establishment of databases. The model of governance by this type of agency illustrates the choice for promoting European integration through the better coordination of national law-enforcement systems rather than by replacing them with new supranational structures.

The earliest agencies were established on the basis of first-pillar secondary legislation; the European Monitoring Centre for Drugs and Drug Addiction (EMCDDA) set up in 1993 in Lisbon, and the European Monitoring Centre on Racism and Xenophobia (EUMC) established in 1997 in Vienna, which in 2007 was replaced by the European Fundamental Rights Agency (FRA). Most subsequent developments, however, have taken place in the framework of the third pillar. Here the earliest agency was UCLAF (*Unité de coordination de la lutte anti-fraude*), the predecessor of OLAF, the now communitarized European Anti-Fraud Office (see Chapter 4). The Europol Convention had been adopted in 1995, but it was not until 1998 that it entered into force, after lengthy national ratification procedures, and Europol became operational a year later. In 1998 the European Judicial Network was launched, as a predecessor to Eurojust, the 'college' of senior magistrates, prosecutors, and judges which became operational in 2002, to coordinate cross-border prosecutions. The European Council in Tampere in 1999 proposed the creation of two new bodies: the European Police College (CEPOL), based in the UK, to develop cooperation between the national training institutes for senior police officers in the member states; and the European Police Chiefs' Task Force (PCTF) to develop personal and informal links among the heads of the various law-enforcement agencies across the EU and to promote information exchange. In 2009 an Asylum Support Office was created to gather and exchange information on countries of origin and asylum proceedings in the member states. The hope is to thereby not only assist countries in implementing EU asylum directives but also to promote the approximation of recognition practices through closer coordination.

The most dynamic agency is the Agency for the Management of Operational Cooperation at the External Borders (Frontex), which was established in Warsaw in 2005. While Frontex is primarily for coordination and risk analysis, its mandate was extended considerably in 2007 through the creation of Rapid Border Intervention Teams (RABITs) as a means of providing rapid operational assistance for a limited period to a requesting member state facing a situation of 'urgent and exceptional pressure' at external borders. The creation of RABITs was a reaction to the difficulties encountered in mobilizing the necessary personnel and equipment from the member states for joint operations such as the HERA I–III operations (2006–7) to tackle irregular migration from West Africa to the Canary Islands. Frontex's operational burden-sharing dimension has been further enhanced through the European Patrol Network (EPN) for Mediterranean and Atlantic coastal waters. This organizational expansion has been backed by a steep rise of the agency's budget from €19 million in 2006 to €70 million in

2008, thus indicating the enduring political salience of border management in Europe. This political priority which is attributed to securing the EU's external borders has again been stressed in the European Pact on Immigration and Asylum adopted under the French Council Presidency in October 2008, which calls for strengthening Frontex's own operational resources. Together with the suggestion of examining the creation of a European border-guard system, this declaratory document hints at the possibility of developing more collective capabilities in this area.

With these new common bodies, the number of common databases has also proliferated. These common databases constitute the core coordination instrument between domestic law-enforcement and immigration authorities and are meant to boost their surveillance capacities over mobile undesired individuals in the common territory. The data of EU and third-country nationals are stored and scrutinized partly under Commission supervision (Eurodac, Customs Information System), but mostly monitored by a special joint supervisory authority within the Council Secretariat (Europol and Eurojust databases). The most recent development is the establishment of a Visa Information System (VIS), a database with personal information (including biometrics) on every visa application. Due to unexpected technical problems and poor strategic planning, the idea of a revamped SIS II has not yet materialized, and interior and justice ministers have extended the deadline for establishing the system to June 2009; failing that, they will opt for a revision of the current SIS. The last step in this technological surveillance race has been the decision, in the Pact for Asylum and Immigration adopted in autumn 2008, to establish an electronic recording of entry and exit into the EU, covering both EU and non-EU citizens, and inspired by similar developments in the United States.

As in most other areas of JHA cooperation, security prerogatives in developing the databases have been granted more attention than the concurrent civil liberties or human rights aspects. Member states have taken more than three years to agree on the Framework Decision 2008/977/JHA on the protection of personal data processed in the framework of police and judicial cooperation in criminal matters adopted on 27 November 2008. This instrument is widely seen as crucial for ensuring adequate personal data protection under these information systems. Yet, in its Decision, the Council has neither taken account of the three very critical reports issued by the EP, nor the criticism of the European Data Protection Supervisor.

The proliferation of actors indicates the strong impetus for more intensive cooperation in internal security, but it also reflects the tension between, on the one hand, the case for tighter collective policy management and legislative harmonization by the EU institutions and, on the other, the persistence of integration by looser transgovernmental coordination with low levels of transparency and accountability.

BOX 19.2   **JHA agencies and bodies**

- European Monitoring Centre for Drugs and Drug Addiction (EMCDDA), set up in 1993 in Lisbon to provide factual information on the European drug problems, *http:// www.emcdda.europa.eu.*
- European Police Office (Europol), set up in 1999 in The Hague to share and pool intelligence to prevent and combat serious international organized crime, *http://www. europol.europa.eu.*
- European Police College (CEPOL), set up in 2000 in Bramshill UK to approximate national police training systems, *http://www.cepol.net.*
- European Police Chiefs' Task Force (PCTF), set up in 2000 to promote exchange, in cooperation with Europol, of best practices and information on cross-border crime and to contribute to the planning of operative actions, without headquarters and web page.
- Eurojust, set up in 2002 in The Hague to coordinate cross-border prosecutions, *http://www.eurojust.europa.eu.*
- Frontex, set up in 2005 in Warsaw to coordinate operational cooperation at the external border, *http://www.frontex.europa.eu.*
- European Fundamental Rights Agency (FRA), set up in 2007 in Vienna as the successor to the European Monitoring Centre on Racism and Xenophobia (EUMC) to provide the Community and its member states when implementing Community law with assistance and expertise relating to fundamental rights, *http://fra.europa.eu/.*
- European Asylum Support Office, proposed in 2009 to promote the approximation of national asylum recognition practices.

The flow of policy

The flow of policy has evolved in the context of the multi-annual work programmes on the AFSJ adopted since 1999. Actual policy developments have, however, remained responsive to the changing conjunctures of external events and national priorities. Moreover, Commission monitoring and evaluation reports have repeatedly highlighted delays in and deviations from the realization of agreed commitments.

The extensive use of non-binding texts by the Council, the expansion of policy objectives, and the lack of infringement procedures in the third pillar motivated the Commission to introduce half-yearly 'scoreboards'—reports monitoring progress in implementing the treaty and programme provisions. The initial reports were quite general and had little impact on the Council's work. Monitoring, however, was reinvigorated on the basis of an extensive mandate of the European Council in 2005 with the so-called 'Scoreboard Plus' for the implementation of the Hague

Programme. These second-generation scoreboards, which are published openly on the Commission's website, contain detailed information on implementation deficits by individual member states, and thus try to induce compliance by 'naming and shaming'.

The scoreboards regularly give a rather mixed picture of progress in implementing the work programmes. The Commission's 2007 implementation report concluded that, 'The general overall assessment is *rather unsatisfactory*. A significant number of actions envisaged in the Action Plan ... had to be abandoned or delayed' (Commission 2007i: 2).

The shortcomings of implementing cooperation in JHA are perhaps not surprising. A constant feature of JHA cooperation is the pre-eminence of national concerns over Commission initiatives and, hence, the jostling of short-term national priorities with long-term common objectives. Generally speaking, cooperation has focused most consistently on the fight against irregular migration and cross-border crime, while measures of operational cooperation have been easier to achieve than legislative harmonization. Insofar as harmonization measures have been adopted, they have been limited to setting minimum standards, allow many exceptions, and leave large margins of discretion to the member states.

Asylum and immigration policy

In contrast to the protracted progress of internal communitarization, particularly since 2001, JHA has developed a dynamic external dimension. It now has a foreign-policy agenda of its own. One of the most advanced areas of JHA integration is asylum policy. Substantive harmonization towards a 'common European asylum system' (CEAS) by 2010, as provided in the Hague Programme, has, however, proved much more difficult than agreement on the allocation of responsibility for the examination of asylum claims (see Box 19.3; Lavenex 2006a).

Agreement on which forms of immigration to classify as legal has proved even more controversial. The main achievements were the adoption of two directives: Council Directive 2003/109/EC on the status of third-country nationals who are long-term residents in a member state of the European Union and Council Directive 2003/86/EC on the right to family reunification, both adopted on 22 September 2003. The Council's failure to consult the EP and the possibility that children over the age of 12 could be excluded from the right to family reunification led the EP to file a complaint with the ECJ, which was however rejected (Case C-540/03 of 27.6.2006). A Commission proposal on the admission of immigrants for the purpose of work and self-employment, like the two before it, has found little support in the Council. In October 2007 the Commission proposed the so-called 'Blue Card', which would introduce a fast-track procedure for the admission of highly qualified third-country workers and would allow them economic mobility within the EU after an initial stay of two years in the first country of admission. The Commission justified the proposal on the grounds of needing to offer attractive conditions in the

---

BOX 19.3   **Common European asylum system**

- The cornerstone of EU asylum policy is the system of exclusive responsibility for the examination of asylum claims based on Regulation 343/2003 of 18 February 2003, establishing the criteria and mechanisms for determining the member state responsible for examining an asylum application. This instrument replaces the Dublin Convention and its implementation is linked to the Eurodac database.

- The mutual recognition of asylum determination outcomes implied by the system of responsibility allocation necessitated minimum standards on reception conditions, the definition of the term refugee, and asylum procedures. These 'Phase I' directives were adopted only after significant delays, and are riddled with delicate compromises and open questions.

- A Commission Green Paper on the future Common European Asylum System (CEAS) of 2007 (Commission 2007*j*) gives a critical assessment of progress achieved so far and identifies the need for fuller harmonization of substantive and procedural asylum law in order to realize a CEAS by 2010. It also calls for a re-examination of the cornerstone of EU asylum cooperation, the Dublin system, when it states that this system 'may *de facto* result in additional burdens on Member States that have limited reception and absorption capacities and that find themselves under particular migratory pressures because of their geographical location'.

- The reluctance to accept supranational rules in this sensitive field of domestic policy has shifted asylum cooperation to more operational aspects, e.g. through the creation of a European Asylum Support Office.

- Burden-sharing remains a challenge, although the European Refugee Fund to support reception, integration, and voluntary return measures in the member states has more than tripled from €216 million (2000–4) to just under €700 million (2005–10). More significant sums of money have been allocated for border controls in the border fund (€1,820 million for the same period), as well as to Frontex activities.

- Particular attention is now paid to cooperation with countries of transit and origin of asylum-seekers. Mainly geared toward enhancing migration control in those countries, this cooperation has focused on the conclusion of readmission agreements as well as, more hesitantly, the promotion of asylum procedures and reception capacities (Lavenex 2006*b*; Lavenex and Kunz 2008).

---

global competition for highly skilled workers. The proposal has, however, raised objections from several member states. New member states, particularly the Czech government in the 2009 Council presidency, have claimed that a scheme favouring third-country nationals should be introduced only after the full implementation of free-movement rights for their own nationals. Several other member states have opposed the proposal because they want to prioritize their domestic programmes (the UK) or they are hostile to EU competence over economic immigration (Austria, Germany, and The Netherlands).

In the absence of a common policy, cooperation regarding the integration of third-country nationals is dealt with by a 'soft' mode of coordination between the member states. These deliberations flow into an EU Handbook on Integration for Policy-Makers, the second edition of which was published in 2007 (European Communities 2007). By the end of 2007 all member states were integrated in the network of 'National Contact Points' on integration. The 'Common Basic Principles on Integration', adopted on a Dutch initiative in 2004, have remained declaratory and have not led to any legislative action.

From the outset of cooperation in the mid-1980s, the emphasis has been on the fight against illegal immigration rather than on which legal immigrants to accept (Lavenex and Wallace 2005). Most instruments relate to entry controls. A 2007 Commission proposal for a directive providing for sanctions against employers of illegal third-country nationals (Commission 2007k) has faced the opposition of several member states, because of sovereignty concerns, particularly over European provisions for criminal sanctions in serious cases.

In the light of enduring immigration pressure and of the internal resistance to stronger legislative integration, the emphasis of cooperation has moved outwards to the attempt to engage countries of transit and origin in the management of migration flows. Initially focused on coercive measures and the conclusion of readmission agreements, the failure to ensure compliance by third countries has led to the re-emergence of a more comprehensive vision of external migration cooperation and the launch of the so-called 'Global Approach' in December 2005.

Consequently, immigration has become a main focus of the European Neighbourhood Policy (see Chapter 17), and consultations have also intensified with African countries. Yet, given internal blockages against EU competence over economic migration, the EU has little to offer to these countries in return for their cooperation in securing the EU's borders. The visa facilitation agreements offered to eastern neighbours, in exchange for their agreement to readmit their own as well as foreign nationals who stay irregularly in the EU, remain limited.

The newest device in implementing the 'global approach' has been the conclusion of 'mobility partnerships' in which opportunities for 'circular', that is temporary, labour migration into the EU and development cooperation are linked as well as cooperation on readmission and the fight against irregular migration. The first mobility partnerships were concluded with Cap Verde and Moldova in 2008. Negotiations on such a partnership with Senegal were suspended in 2009 because Senegal was dissatisfied with the EU's offer. Indeed, the existing partnerships reflect very little innovation as they largely summarize existing bilateral cooperation programmes with individual member states under a new heading (Lavenex 2006b; Lavenex and Kunz 2008).

Police and judicial cooperation in criminal matters

The dominance of non-binding instruments and the focus on operational cooperation have been even stronger in the third pillar. One of the main developments in police cooperation was the decision by the JHA Council to replace the Europol Convention with a 'third pillar' Decision by 2010 (Council Document 5055/07 EUROPOL 2 of 19 April 2008). This will facilitate adaptation of Europol's mandate by omitting (sometimes lengthy) ratification procedures by national parliaments and turn it into a regular EU agency. Apart from the facilitation of information exchange between national law-enforcement authorities through Europol and its network of European Liaison Officers (ELOs), as well as expertise and technical support activities, integration in police matters has focused on networking and the development of common operational practices such as through the Police Chiefs' Task Force and the European Police College. These networks are to address the main impediment to more effective cooperation between national police forces, which is the need for mutual understanding and trust between highly diverse domestic systems of law enforcement (Occhipinti 2003). With enlargement, both issues—the need for trust and problems associated with diversity—have clearly increased, prompting concern about how to invigorate the operational aspects of police cooperation. In the meantime, the Prüm Treaty and the proliferation of intergovernmental consultations confirm the continuity of concentric circles in this area of cooperation.

In comparison, while cooperation in the judicial sphere was initially slower to develop, it has been one of the most dynamic aspects of JHA cooperation since the Tampere European Council (de Kerchove and Weyembergh 2002). It has, however, also faced problems of a lack of trust and complex interaction. This cooperation centres on the principle of mutual recognition, which forms the basis of the main instrument adopted so far in this area, the European arrest warrant (EAW, see Box 19.4).

Terrorist attacks have also spurred cooperation. Trevi had its roots in fighting terrorism, and just ten days after the 9/11 attacks on the US in 2001, the European Council adopted the EU Action Plan on Combating Terrorism. The bombings in Madrid (March 2004) and London (July 2005) induced new initiatives, such as the establishment of a special EU Counter-Terrorism Coordinator. This new office has, however, had to contend with problems, similar to those faced by the other EU agencies. Its first representative, Gijs de Vries, stood down from the post in 2007 partly over his lack of operational powers and partly because of the overall reluctance within member states to supply information regarding anti-terror activities or to develop the legal instruments specified in the Action Plan. In 2007, Gilles de Kerchove, a senior Council official with extensive JHA experience and international contacts, was appointed to fill the post.

The external dimension of police and judicial cooperation has also expanded. Europol, Eurojust, and Frontex have all concluded cooperation agreements with a series of European and non-European countries, and at the end of 2005 the JHA Council adopted a Strategy on the external aspects of JHA (Council Document 14366/3/05 REV 3). Cooperation with the US has been particularly close and has spurred major controversies both between EU institutions and between the EU and civil-rights activists, especially in the area of data protection. The 2004 US–EU passenger name record (PNR) agreement, which requires European

BOX 19.4	European arrest warrant

- The Tampere European Council adopted four basic principles for establishing a common European judicial space: mutual recognition of judicial decisions; approximation of national substantive and procedural laws; the creation of Eurojust; and the development of the external dimension of criminal law.
- The 11 September 2001 terrorist attacks in the US spurred the adoption of the Framework Decision on the European arrest warrant in 2002.
- The European arrest warrant is a judicial decision issued by a member state with a view to the arrest and surrender by another member state of a person being sought for a criminal prosecution or a custodial sentence. It eliminates the use of extradition and is based on the principle of mutual recognition of decisions in criminal matters.
- In the absence of EU harmonization of criminal law, the implementation of the EAW has encountered difficulties (Lavenex 2007).
- In sum, as in the case of migration, restrictive measures, such as the EAW, have been easier to adopt than those harmonizing the rights of individuals, as illustrated by the protracted process of agreeing the Framework Decision on certain procedural rights in criminal proceedings that has been on the table since 2004 (Commission 2004*d*).

airlines flying to the US to provide US authorities with information on their passengers, was annulled by the ECJ in 2006 because the EP had not been adequately consulted. The successor agreement, which remains the same in substance, was adopted under treaty provisions that do not require the EP's opinion. PNR has raised grave concerns among the EP, the European Data Protection Supervisor (Peter Hustinx), and civil liberties groups for failing to comply with European data protection rules.

These developments underline the blurring of distinctions between notions of internal and external security. As with efforts to combat immigration, they move JHA cooperation closer and closer into traditional domains of the CFSP (see Chapter 18).

The agenda for reform

JHA occupied a central stage in recent European integration efforts, and the Treaty of Lisbon (ToL), having largely taken over the far-reaching changes proposed by the Constitutional Treaty, continues that trend. The justification for the Lisbon reforms draws heavily on public concerns about internal security and citizens' expectations that the EU should do something about it (e.g. Eurobarometer 2008). A second motivation is dissatisfaction with the implementation of agreed commitments, in particular in third-pillar issues.

The ToL includes far-reaching reform proposals that centre on the 'reunification' of JHA into a common general legal framework, and, herewith, the abolition of the pillar structure. The final compromise will bring the AFSJ as an area of 'shared competence' closer to the Community method and extend qualified majority voting and co-decision to legal migration and most areas of criminal law and policing. Germany's support for this shift could be won, however, only by inserting an explicit clause on the right of member states to determine the numbers of economic immigrants. It is generally expected that extending 'first pillar' decision-making rules will reduce the risks of blockages and lowest-common-denominator agreements in the Council, thereby increasing the EU's decision-making capacity and the quality of those decisions. Furthermore, the abolition of current restrictions on ECJ powers should enhance compliance with JHA legislation.

Apart from co-decision with the EP, democratic control will be enhanced by increasing scrutiny by national parliaments, both as guardians of the principles of proportionality and subsidiarity and as participants in the evaluation of the work of the JHA bodies and agencies. The possibility for national parliaments to block a legislative process when it is deemed to be in breach of the subsidiarity principle has, however, also raised concerns about the potential obstructive use of this right in deeply politicized issues such as migration and criminal law.

Most of these changes can be introduced also irrespective of the ToL through the use of the so-called 'passerelle' of the existing Article 42 TEU, which allows for the transfer of third-pillar matters to the first pillar by a unanimous vote in the Council of Ministers. In using this possibility, however, the Council is free to 'determine the relevant voting conditions', which means that this solution could go beyond or remain below the level of communitarization foreseen in the ToL.

Conclusions

Initially justified in limited terms as compensatory measures to the abolition of internal border controls, cooperation in JHA, now metaphorically framed as the creation of an 'area of freedom, security, and justice', has been elevated to a central objective of the EU. The Treaty of Lisbon lists it second after the overall commitment to peace promotion, and before the internal market, environmental, or social policies.

Beyond these symbolic steps, integration in these sensitive fields of state sovereignty remains constrained by multiple tensions and difficult compromises. Among these tensions the relationship between integration through increased harmonization and centralized EU structures on the one hand and through enhanced coordination of national structures on the other remains unsettled.

There are limitations on what can be achieved through dependence on transgovernmental networks, mutual recognition, and initiatives by member governments. In a field where concerns about civil liberties are powerful, these methods have regularly favoured 'security' over 'freedom' and 'justice', and they pose major problems for scrutiny and transparency. Cooperation among twenty-seven member governments may increase pressures for common rules and effective monitoring of their implementation, and play in favour of the exploitation of the ToL or the use of the 'passerelle' for moving towards the Community method of decision-making. In the absence of political will, however, the opposite could equally well occur. The re-emergence of intergovernmental cooperation outside the EU and the preference of operational coordination over legislative harmonization both point in this direction.

FURTHER READING

For a fairly comprehensive overview of the JHA *acquis* see Peers (2007) and Mitsilegas et al. (2003). On the development of immigration policy, see Geddes (2008), and on the effects of EU policies on the member states see Ette and Faist (2007). Mitsilegas (2009) gives an excellent introduction into EU criminal law cooperation, and Occhipinti (2003) on police cooperation.

Ette, A., and Faist, T. (2007) (eds.), *The Europeanization of National Policies and Politics of Immigration* (Basingstoke: Palgrave Macmillan).

Geddes, A. (2008), *Immigration and European Integration: Towards Fortress Europe?*, 2nd edn. (Manchester: Manchester University Press).

Mitsilegas, V. (2009), *EU Criminal Law* (London: Hart).

Mitsilegas, V., Monar, J., and Rees, W. (2003), *The European Union and Internal Security: Guardian of the People?* (Basingstoke: Palgrave Macmillan).

Occhipinti, J. D. (2003), *The Politics of EU Police Cooperation: Towards a European FBI?* (Boulder, CO: Lynne Rienner).

Peers, S. (2007), *EU Justice and Home Affairs Law* (Oxford: Oxford University Press).

PART III

Conclusions

CHAPTER 20

EU Policy-Making in Challenging Times

Adversity, Adaptability, and Resilience

Mark A. Pollack, Helen Wallace, and Alasdair R. Young

Summary

Policy-making in the European Union (EU) continues to develop against a backcloth of both functional demands and systemic pressures. Experience over recent years suggests that the trends are towards greater diversification of policy methods and modes within the EU system itself, and also at the interfaces with the national processes of the member states and *vis-à-vis* the global system. These trends in policy-making have taken place in the face of major challenges to EU policy-making. Enlargement seems to have been less dislocating than many had feared. Institutional processes have adapted to the context of working in an EU of twenty-seven. Our case studies show wide variations in the impacts of enlargement on the substance of policies, whether as regards how policy issues are framed or as regards the outcomes. In many areas policies have evolved rather straightforwardly to incorporate the larger number of members. The going is tougher on distributive, social, and environmental issues, as well as on those where the new political geography of the EU27 impinges. The institutional stalemate pending ratification of treaty reforms has had less of an impact on day-to-day policy-making than might have been expected. By and large both the formal and informal processes of EU policy-making have demonstrated significant adaptability and resilience in the face of new challenges. It is less easy to read the preliminary impacts of the financial crisis and recession, but our case studies indicate several policy areas where existing policies and policy templates are under test.

Introduction

Time never stands still for the EU. Old policies face new challenges and new policy issues come onto the agenda. The interdependence between the EU and the wider world continues to throw up questions to be addressed, both in the immediate European neighbourhood and in the global system. The EU started out as an organization with core political objectives, and with an initial emphasis on developing collective economic policies. It thus has to grapple with the events and disturbances, both political and economic, which form the context for its operations. In the past few years there have been plenty of both. The world is an unsettled place for which there is no clear map to guide policy-makers' judgements, and the financial crisis has muddied the picture as well. An underlying question is thus whether the EU system is robust enough to adapt.

In this concluding chapter we offer a broad, cross-issue analysis of how EU policy-making has developed in the five years since the previous edition of this volume—a period marked by the Union's largest-ever enlargement, a 'constitutional crisis' over the aborted Constitutional Treaty and the finally ratified Treaty of Lisbon, and the shock of a financial crisis that by 2009 had become a major economic crisis for the EU and its member states.

In the first section of this chapter we identify the main trends in EU policy-making that emerge from our policy case studies, indicating both continuing patterns and new features. Three features particularly stand out: experimentation with and adoption of new modes of policy-making, often in conjunction with more established modes, leading to hybridization; renegotiation of the role of the member states (and their domestic institutions) in the policy process; and erosion of traditional boundaries between internal and external policies. EU institutions and policy processes, we argue, have demonstrated considerable adaptability and resilience in the face of new challenges, even during a period when the overarching treaty structure of the Union was effectively frozen.

The phenomenon of EU policy-making under stress—notably the stresses of enlargement in 2004 and 2007, the institutional stalemate provoked by non-ratification of treaty reforms, and the financial and economic crises—is the focus of the second section of this chapter. Both individually and collectively, these three challenges have led commentators to brand the EU as being in a period of crisis, and indeed the challenges thrown up by these developments have been substantial. Here again, however, we, like other scholars, find that EU policy-making has demonstrated significant continuity in the face of both enlargement and the long institutional 'crisis', with member states again demonstrating significant pragmatism and adaptability in day-to-day policy-making. It is early days, at this writing, to assess the effects of the exogenous shock from the financial and economic crisis, but early signs suggest that these effects will be varied, placing some EU policies under significant strain, but having little impact on many others.

Trends in EU policy-making

The policy-making system of the EU has never been static (H. Wallace 2001*b*). As we have observed in previous editions, over time there have typically been patterns of gradual evolution and episodes of experimentation, interspersed with moments of explicit institutional change through reforms to the treaties. In recent years, as we shall see below, treaty-based institutional change has been stalled. To be sure, as we shall also see later, this stalemate has interfered with policy-making in some sectors. It has not, however, prevented a plethora of more informal changes taking place in the ways that policies are developed, decided, and implemented. Nor has it frozen the relationships among the main policy actors, whether articulated through the EU institutions or the interfaces between the EU and, on the one hand, its member states, or, on the other hand, the organs of global governance.

On the contrary, our case studies reveal a good many changes both in policy-making methods and in policy content. These have not, however, been in one direction. Instead the trends are towards greater diversification within the EU system itself, and also at the interfaces with the national processes of the member states and *vis-à-vis* the global system. Thus it has become harder rather than easier to provide a shorthand summary of the key features of EU policy-making.

Nonetheless, some overarching trends stand out. First, there is not a stable 'institutional balance' among the political institutions of the EU, i.e. the Commission, the Council and European Council, the European Parliament (EP), and the European Court of Justice (ECJ). Within this shifting institutional landscape, there appear to be two secular trends. First, the ECJ and national courts have become increasingly important in non-traditional areas. Indeed, in both social and employment policy (see Chapters 11 and 12) there seems to be a move toward extensive judicialization, as an increasingly sclerotic legislative process loses importance and the significance of EU and national court rulings becomes an increasingly important driver of policy developments. An increase in the importance of judicial politics is evident in other chapters as well, most notably in Chapter 6, where Stephen Wilks demonstrates the changes in EU competition policy wrought by increasing judicial oversight. By contrast with this greater role for the judiciary, we see a secular trend away from the centrality of the Commission as the classic agenda-setter within the EU. However, there is no obvious replacement source of initiatives on a recurrent basis, in that the traditional Franco-German couple operates erratically and the European Council has, as yet, not taken systematic command of the agenda, despite its considerable importance. Indeed, as we shall see presently, the shifts in the EU's institutional balance have corresponded with an equally striking period of diversification and experimentation in modes of policy-making within and across different issue areas.

Second, domestic politics within the member states has become increasingly 'sticky' on European issues, as sources of criticism of the EU process have become more vocal and national politicians have become more timorous and more inclined to play to their domestic audiences. The financial crisis increases the pressures in this direction. At the same time, however, the growing influence of policy coordination processes and networks of national regulators has implicated an ever-growing collection of domestic institutions and actors into the making as well as the implementation of EU policy.

Third, the interface between Europeanization and globalization has become more pertinent, yet also more difficult for European policy-makers to handle, with 'internal' EU policies both influencing, and influenced by, the broader international environment.

Experimentation and hybridization of policy modes

From the first edition of this volume (Wallace et al. 1977), the editors have resisted the temptation to identify a single EC or EU policy style, noting instead the diversity of EU policy-making across issue areas. Against that background, the policy modes identified in Chapter 4 were always intended as a series of ideal types, which laid out the main variants in the EU system, rather than as a literally accurate description of EU policy-making in any particular issue area. Nevertheless, as ideal types, our classification of policy modes provides a useful starting point for our analysis and for the identification of trends over time. We identify three such trends, all clearly visible and arguably accelerating over the past five years, on the basis of our contributors' findings.

First, the chapters in this edition demonstrate the continued presence and viability of all five policy modes, with certainly no evidence of convergence toward a single policy mode over time. Nevertheless, we do detect some trends in the frequency or prevalence of particular policy modes over time. The classic Community method, for example, has traditionally been associated with well-established and strongly 'communitarized' policies, such as competition policy, the common agricultural policy, and trade policy, yet our case studies of these areas show policies and policy processes in flux. The CAP, in particular, is taking on elements of the regulatory mode. Competition policy is incorporating inter-agency networks reminiscent of the policy-coordination mode. Hence, while it may be premature to announce the death of the traditional Community method (Dehousse 2008), it is clear that Community method has become less common, and combined with elements of other modes, over time. By contrast, the regulatory policy mode, the ascendance of which was associated in previous editions with the completion of the internal market, remains the dominant mode for many issue areas, and arguably the predominant mode for the Union as a whole. Perhaps the most striking development of the latter part of the 2000s has been the further flowering and spread of the 'policy coordination' mode, elements of which have spread beyond the European Employment Strategy (EES) and other formal open methods of coordination (OMCs) to a growing number of issue areas where networking, benchmarking, and loose coordination are increasingly commonplace—although, as Martin Rhodes makes clear in Chapter 12, the efficacy of such policy coordination remains very much in doubt. The distributive and intensive transgovernmentalist modes, finally, retain their importance in specific, core issue areas, with the former evident in the making of the EU budget, cohesion policy, and elements of the CAP, and the latter continuing to dominate in the increasingly productive fields of common foreign and security policy (CFSP) and justice and home affairs (JHA).

Beneath these overall trends in the prevalence of particular policy modes, we find an additional trend, which is the increasing use of multiple modes of governance *within individual issue areas*. In Chapter 11, for example, Stephan Leibfried points to several distinct tracks or policy modes operating within the social policy realm, with a regulatory programme of positive integration existing alongside a somewhat encapsulated social dialogue, which, in turn, exists alongside a strong negative-integration dynamic dominated by national courts and the ECJ. In Chapter 12, Martin Rhodes is at pains to point out that EU employment policy is *not* synonymous with the policy-coordination mode of the OMC and the European employment strategy, but is also characterized by extensive and ongoing EU regulation as well as a growing series of landmark court cases that are reshaping European and national employment law in an enlarged EU. David Buchan, in Chapter 15, finds an EU energy policy proceeding along three distinct tracks—energy market liberalization, energy security, and climate change—each with distinct legal bases, formal legislative processes, and dominant players. As Sandra Lavenex demonstrates in Chapter 19, certain elements of justice and home affairs have become increasingly 'communitarized' over time, with the Commission and other EU institutions becoming increasingly associated with specific aspects of policy, even as member governments maintain a firm hold over other aspects. Economic and monetary union (EMU), covered by Dermot Hodson in Chapter 7, is perhaps the most extreme example of multiple, distinct policy modes within a single issue area, characterized by a strong ECB-centred Community method for monetary policy, policy coordination for national fiscal policies, and an ongoing debate over the procedures for banking regulation.

In sum, we are seeing plural policy modes operating within what EU scholars have traditionally considered distinct issue areas. The diversity of EU policy-making has thus increased within as well as across issue areas.

A further trend we observe is related to this diversification, but goes a step further, comprising a rise in 'innovative' (Tömmel and Verdun 2008), 'experimental' (Sabel and Zeitlin 2008), or 'hybrid' policy modes that combine, adapt, and adjust new and traditional policy modes and instruments in highly flexible and innovative ways in order to adjust to the ever-changing demands of the policy environment, as well as the continuing sensitivities of EU member governments. Indeed, in a provocative article, Sabel and Zeitlin (2008: 278) argue that the EU is witnessing nothing less than a 'Cambrian explosion' of new and hybrid institutional forms.

Sabel and Zeitlin contend that legislation adopted under the Community method or regulatory policy mode increasingly incorporates not only traditional command-and-control regulations but also the full range of so-called new-governance instruments, including policy-coordination efforts such as the OMC as well as the creation of European networks of regulators that seek to coordinate national regulations in an informal, non-binding fashion (Coen and Thatcher 2008b; and see below). The recast Equal Treatment Directive (2002/73/EC), for example, includes classic elements of the regulatory mode—it was adopted under the co-decision procedure and substantially strengthened the legally binding requirements of previous directives—but also required all member states to establish gender-equality bodies and created an EU-wide network of such bodies (Pollack 2008). We see a similar mix of policy instruments in environmental policy, where 'command and control' rules are employed alongside voluntary codes, self-regulation, and co-regulation, among other 'new instruments' (Chapter 13). More generally, the Commission's 2007 initiative on 'A Single Market for 21st Century Europe' aims to make use of a '"smarter" mix' of policy instruments in the pursuit of market liberalization, including competition policy, self-regulation, and 'soft law' (see Chapter 5). These examples suggest that the nature of EU regulation may be changing substantially, with new and innovative policy modes emerging in response to functional demands and/or to the political sensitivities of EU member governments.

'Brussels' and national governance

The national governments of the member states have always been deeply implicated in EU policy-making, both as negotiators in the Council and as those responsible for the implementation of policies on the ground. The ECJ and national courts are also intertwined in the EU legal order. Nevertheless, there is increasing complexity in the interactions between 'Brussels' and national governance, and there is evidence of increasing contention and contestation around the ways that the boundaries are drawn between these two layers of governance.

One striking development, which accelerated during the mid-2000s, has been the extent to which domestic governments and/or independent regulatory authorities are increasingly drawn (or co-opted) into transgovernmental networks. The modernization of EU competition policy, discussed in Chapter 6, combines centralized EU policy-making by the Commission with policy coordination and power-sharing among an ever more cohesive network of national competition regulators. Even the single-market programme, long the exemplar of the EU regulatory policy mode, similarly relies increasingly on cooperation among national financial and utilities regulators both to devise and to implement common EU policies (Chapters 5 and 15; Coen and Thatcher 2008*b*). The development of networks of national officials has been particularly pronounced in justice and home affairs, where semi-autonomous special agencies and bodies have proliferated to facilitate information exchange and coordination between national law-enforcement authorities, often supported by the establishment of new EU-wide databases (see Chapter 19). This trend illustrates that increased cooperation can occur largely horizontally among domestic policy-makers and not just vertically between Brussels and the member states.

The development of a network of national competition regulators is in part intended to manage the increased authority of national regulators (see Chapter 6), which is part of a second recent development: the (partial) renationalization of some EU policies. The renationalization of policy is even evident in the common agricultural policy (CAP) where recent reforms have increased the scope for variation to accommodate national circumstances (see Chapter 8). This development underlines that there is not a singular trend towards greater centralization in EU policy-making.

These developments take place against a background of persistent argument about where 'Brussels' reigns and where national responsibilities prevail. Generally speaking, this boundary has not become less contested with the passage of time (Szczerbiak and Taggart 2008). Indeed developments in some policy sectors, such as those in competition policy and the CAP, suggest that the national domain has become more not less important in determining outcomes. The task of the Commission has thus also become harder as it attempts to craft policies that can be made to work across twenty-seven heterogeneous member states. This involves a range of practical problems, as has always been the case in an EU composed of countries with diverse features. However, the diversities and parochialisms of national politics are also constraining factors. It remains the case that domestic politicians prefer to claim the credit for popular EU policies and to shift the blame to 'Brussels' for decisions that may be necessary rather than popular. The prolonged arguments about treaty ratification have not helped to increase confidence in the EU policy system and the financial crisis encourages retreat into domestic political spaces. The outcome of the 2009 European Parliament elections has been shaped, as were previous elections, mainly by the contours of domestic politics in individual member states.

Over the years it has been commonplace for commentators on the EU to identify ways in which participation in the EU policy process enables national politicians and policy-makers to exploit the Brussels arena in order to take forward policies that would be more difficult to implement in a narrowly national context (see Chapters 5 and 13). Yet there is increasing evidence of national politicians and policy-makers becoming more reluctant, more risk-averse, and more prudent as regards agreement to EU policy initiatives. Cooperation thus remains limited in a number of policy areas, such as with regard to energy security (see Chapter 15) and police and judicial cooperation (see Chapter 19). The development of cooperation in employment policy remains highly contested, and member-state opposition has required advocates to deploy creative interpretations of the treaty base, transferring legislation to the 'inter-professional dialogue', and shifting emphasis to the soft-law European Employment Strategy (see Chapter 12). Member states' caution about further integration is even evident within the context of the single market, as the politics leading to the Services Directive illustrate (see Chapter 5). Moreover, member governments remain vigilant about their contributions to and receipts from the EU's budget (see Chapters 9 and 10). Indeed, this seems in part to account for the trend, noted above, towards a stronger role for the Council and the European Council in the EU institutional system and to the detriment of the Commission, now led by a college in which the national identities of individual Commissioners are more prominent.

Interacting European and global governance

EU policy-making has never taken place in a vacuum, as evidenced most clearly by the EU's policies for external trade, foreign and security policy, and enlargement, and these EU 'external policies' have continued to develop in institutional and substantive terms. EU trade policy, as Stephen Woolcock demonstrates in Chapter 16, has been institutionalized and strengthened over the years, with increasing thematic coverage (e.g. of trade in services and intellectual property) and greater centralization of power in Brussels, although the growing number of actors has made it increasingly difficult for the EU (or its traditional partner/rival, the United States) to shape the form and substance of the global trade regime. By contrast, the EU's common foreign and security policy remains largely transgovernmental (Chapter 18), with at best a secondary and supporting role for the Commission and other EU institutions. Yet here as well we find extremely rapid institutional development, with an ever-growing set of transgovernmental committees and an increasingly prominent defence component alongside the EU's traditional 'civilian power' instruments. In addition, as Ulrich Sedelmeier demonstrates in Chapter 17, EU enlargement policy has developed from a largely reactive process of accepting and negotiating membership applications from candidate countries to a distinctive regional foreign policy aiming to shape EU relations with its immediate neighbours and exert substantial influence over their internal politics and institutions. In all three areas, then, the institutional as well as the substantive policies of the Union have continued to develop impressively even in the short span of the past half-decade.

Our point here, however, is a broader one, namely that the EU's traditional distinction between external relations or 'RELEX' policies and 'internal' policies has grown increasingly artificial. More precisely, the EU's internal policies have become increasingly intermeshed with relations with other states and with a range of international and global regimes. Causation in these cases runs both ways: on the one hand, the growing number and density of EU policies has led the EU's members to act, to negotiate, and to litigate together on the broader international stage, 'externalizing' internal policies at the global level. On the other hand, increasing issue coverage of international and global regimes, and in particular the increased coverage and legalization of the multilateral trading system with the creation of the World Trade Organization (WTO) in 1995, have increasingly placed external pressures on the EU to reshape and reform its internal policies to be compatible with its international commitments. Causation, put differently, is both 'inside-out' from EU to global policies, as well as 'outside-in' from global pressure to internal reform.

The concept of 'externalization' of internal policies is not a new one. The EU has long recognized the imperative to negotiate collectively with the rest of the world in areas where the Union has adopted common or harmonized policies, and previous editions have demonstrated the empirical significance of this phenomenon (see e.g. Sbragia 2000). In many respects the externalization of EU's internal policies has been inadvertent. Single-market and European-environmental regulations have internal objectives, but can set requirements for products entering the EU, creating both the potential for international trade and regulatory conflicts, as well as a strong incentive for the EU to negotiate common or mutually recognized standards with major trading partners (see Chapters 5, 13, and 14). Externalization has also been evident in the area of competition policy, where the EU has increasingly asserted extraterritorial jurisdiction over mergers and anti-competitive practices of foreign firms that have an impact within the EU (see Chapter 6). The European Central Bank (ECB) sets its monetary policy according to domestic objectives, but those decisions have significant implications for other countries by influencing exchange rates and interest rates (see Chapter 7). The intensification of cooperation on immigration and asylum also has implications for those seeking to enter the EU to live or work (see Chapter 19). Because of the EU's economic size, all of these 'domestic' decisions can have profound ramifications for firms and people in other countries.

The explicit externalization of internal policies is greatest in the EU's pre-accession and enlargement policies (see Chapters 5 and 17; A. R. Young and Wallace 2000). Having agreed internal policies has also facilitated the EU's participation in external trade negotiations by providing common negotiating positions (see Chapters 5 and 16; A. R. Young 2002). Externalization of EU policy can also be seen in the area of agricultural biotechnology, where the common EU policy has implications for and has led EU member states to negotiate collectively within international regimes dedicated to environmental protection, food safety, and international trade, among others (Chapter 14). The EU's efforts to externalize its energy policy have been mixed: it has created an Energy Community for south-eastern Europe, but Russia has refused to ratify the Energy Charter Treaty (see Chapter 15).

By 2006, the Commission had adopted a broader and more explicit strategy to externalize its domestic regulations, 'promoting European standards internationally through international organization and bilateral agreements' (Commission 2007*n*;

see Chapter 5). The EU, therefore, has not simply negotiated collectively, but has actively sought to 'export' or to 'upload' basic principles (such as the precautionary principle) and specific regulatory standards from the EU to global regulatory regimes (Drezner 2007).

There are, however, also external pressures on internal policies. The Commission (2001: 6) has estimated that 30 per cent of all of its legislative proposals arise from the EU's international obligations. Our cases illustrate two distinct types of external impacts: a dynamic interaction between internal policies and external negotiations and the pressure to change rules that are not compatible with international obligations. The dynamic interaction is most evident among our cases with regard to agriculture and the environment. Reforms of the CAP have been facilitated by the potential cross-sectoral trade-offs made possible by multilateral trade negotiations and the desire for the EU to play a leadership role. Moreover, those reforms have made progress in trade negotiations possible, although this effect was more pronounced in the Uruguay Round than in the Doha Round (see Chapters 8 and 16; Woolcock and Hodges 1996). The EU's desire to play a leadership role in the development of the climate-change regime has created an impetus for the EU to demonstrate its capacity to meet its Kyoto commitments and to present concrete proposals to achieve ambitious targets for reducing further greenhouse gas emissions and boosting renewable energy production (see Chapters 13 and 15). The case of biotechnology illustrates both the intense pressures for reform generated by international organizations such as the WTO, as well as the path-dependence of existing policies that have changed only at the margins in response to such pressures (see Chapter 14). Most of our cases, as with most of the policy-making literature (see A. R. Young 2008), however, do not explicitly discuss how international obligations shape EU policy-making—a promising subject for future research.

EU policy-making under stress

All of these trends in policy-making have taken place against a backdrop of major challenges to the EU since the publication of the last edition of this volume in 2005. In the mid-2000s it was widely expected that the big-bang enlargement to an EU of twenty-seven by 2007 would be the major source of stress within the EU system. However, there were hopes that institutional reforms via the then-anticipated Constitutional Treaty would go some way to offset that stress and might even lead to a new dynamism in policy-making and political credibility for the EU. The jury was out on the economic outlook. On the one hand, the eurozone was settling down rather well. On the other hand, growth had slowed and commentaries such as the Sapir Report (2003) had drawn attention to the need to rethink some policies to revive the economy and to adapt EU governance in order to achieve this. The new

European Commission college which took office in late 2004 under the presidency of José Manuel Barroso was not expected to have an easy ride and committed itself to the slogan of doing 'less but better'.

None of these three sources of stress has turned out quite as had been expected. Enlargement seems to have been less dislocating than many had feared. In contrast, the quest for major treaty reforms was set back by the failure to ratify the Constitutional Treaty and the long delay over ratification of the Treaty of Lisbon. The European economy seemed to be recovering, only to be disrupted by the 2007–8 financial crisis. All three of these disturbances are still very much history-in-the-making. We draw together here some preliminary observations, helped by the insights from our case studies, but conscious that it is premature to draw hard and fast conclusions.

The impacts of enlargement

Enlargements have always been something of a shock to the EU system in the past, but were generally judged to have brought benefits as well as costs, the classic statement being that widening (of membership) and deepening (of cooperation) go hand-in-hand. Yet the scale and nature of the enlargements of 2004 and 2007 were expected by many practitioners and many commentators to be much more of a challenge. The jump from EU15 to EU27 was, after all, almost a doubling of the membership, and the new members came to the EU with very different backgrounds and concerns from those of the old 'west' European membership. Thus it was a reasonable expectation that these might both cause strains within the institutional system and complicate policy development and policy implementation. In the absence of institutional reforms (see below) there were widespread fears of gridlock and the stalling of new policies.

Of course these are still early days to be reaching definitive judgements. After all, the EU entered this enlargement phase with a good deal of policy development work in hand, and, as is explained in Chapter 17, the acceding member states had been through a gruelling and monitored schooling experience in what became the routines of the pre-accession process. Thus the twelve member states that came on board had been particularly thoroughly prepared for life inside the EU as full members. It may well also be that there is a time-lag between accession and impact, and that even the passage of five years since the 2004 enlargement wave may not reveal the medium-term trends. In particular, it is still hard to judge how much of an implementation problem there is in the new member states, and we have as yet little by way of European case law on issues of compliance. Yet, by and large, enlargement seems to have been much less dislocating than expected. Institutional adaptation has taken place on an informal basis. On the policy side the impacts of enlargement seem to vary a good deal sector by sector and, hardly surprisingly, are most marked in those policy sectors where relative economic under-development is most pertinent or where the new European geography impacts on policy options.

Institutional adaptation in the EU27

Accession treaties generally simply make arithmetic adaptations to existing institutional rules in order to cater for the arrival of acceding members, as was done in the treaties leading to the 2004 and 2007 enlargements. More far-reaching reforms had been sought through, first, the Treaty of Nice (inadequate), next the Constitutional Treaty (not ratified), and then the Treaty of Lisbon (ratified in November 2009). Hence in the period 2004–9 under review here the only plausible scenarios for institutional change were either informal adaptation or gridlock. Identifying firm evidence for what has happened is not straightforward, and what there is remains patchy. We have some quantitative data, although these do not yet cover very well the arrival of Bulgaria and Romania in 2007. We have some qualitative analysis, although not particularly thorough in its extent. Beyond lie some broader issues of how far changes that we might observe in 2004–9 result from enlargement as opposed to other factors simultaneously affecting the development of the EU.

The quantitative studies published so far (Dehousse et al. 2007; H. Wallace 2007; Best et al. 2008) are pretty much agreed that the indicators of activity and productivity inside the EU institutions since 2004 are very similar to those that could be observed previously. The Commission produces annually similar numbers of policy proposals now to those in the years that preceded 2004, and indeed it is hard to find evidence for the Barroso Commission's claim that it would be doing less. Legislative decisions that come through the bicameral processes of the Council and the EP are similar in number, with the key change being that an increasing number of new laws are resolved in the first reading of co-decision. In non-legislative fields, levels of activity in the Council have remained similar. The Council continues to reach a large proportion of its decisions by consensus, even when taking decisions under the QMV rule. Indeed, informal processes seem to have been at work inside the institutions, with the practitioners looking for—and finding—ways of mitigating the impacts of larger numbers of participants and a wider range of interests to be accommodated. The pre-accession process also served to prepare policy-makers from the new member states for the routines of the EU institutions. Within the EP the party groups have remained primary frames of reference for guiding MEPs' behaviour (Hix and Noury 2009). The ECJ has made some real progress in cutting its backlog of cases, and in reducing the time taken for judgments to be issued, although as yet few cases have been adjudicated concerning the new member states. Thus, in a nutshell, we find no evidence of post-enlargement gridlock.

Nonetheless, not all of those involved are as sanguine about enlargement as this evidence suggests that they might be. Discussions with insiders indicate some frustration at the decreasing intimacy within the club. It is common for particular criticisms to be made of Bulgaria and Romania as having arrived insufficiently prepared to take on the responsibilities of effective membership. There are worries that yet further enlargement might not be so easily handled, not least given that among the actual or potential candidates are some very small and not entirely viable states, on the one hand, or, on the other hand, Turkey, which would become the largest member state in terms of population.

Some specific concerns regarding the functioning of the EU institutions have certainly been aggravated by enlargement. The college of commissioners has become unwieldy at twenty-seven, not least with the increasingly firm identification of individual commissioners with their countries of origin. The college finds it harder to operate as an executive team and there are huge variations in the weight of commissioners' policy portfolios, which militate against 'joined-up' policy-making. The rotating Council presidency remains vulnerable to the vagaries of domestic politics, although this phenomenon long predates the 2004 enlargement. National politics impinges for new member states as well as for old on the way in which their EU negotiating positions are defined, and the severe impact of the financial crisis on some of the new member states is an additional complication. Early evidence shows a high 'success rate' for the new member states in transposing EU legislation into national law (Sedelmeier 2008), but suggests that constrained administrative and judicial capacities impede effective policy implementation (Falkner and Treib 2008).

Cross-issue variation in the policy impacts of enlargement

Our case studies show wide variations in the impacts of enlargement on the substance of policies, whether as regards how policy issues are framed or as regards the outcomes. Broadly stated, in the core areas of economic regulation that constitute the single market, as well as in trade policy (Chapters 5 and 16), the patterns of policy-making and the outcomes remain much in line with those evident before 2004, except with respect to the controversial issue of the free movement of labour within the EU (see Chapters 5 and 12). In those areas of regulation dealing with the environmental and social dimensions the new member states are more hesitant about accepting strong EU disciplines (Chapters 11 and 13). Similarly across the agenda of distributional policy issues, the arrival of a cohort of poorer countries has complicated the nature of bargaining (Chapters 9 and 10). One or two areas of policy have so far been insulated against the influence of enlargement, notably the management of the single currency given the high entry threshold for joining it (Chapter 7).

From a different angle we can observe impacts of enlargement on politics and policy debates within the old EU member states—employment and migration issues figure particularly prominently, accentuated by the financial crisis (Chapters 12 and 19). In other areas the eastwards geographical extension of the EU has radically altered the nature of the policy issues to be addressed and introduced quite different policy concerns into the discussion, as in the cases of energy security, JHA, and the CFSP (Chapters 15, 18 and 19).

As regards economic regulation, competition, and external trade, the new member states have largely taken on the obligations and accepted the implications of long-standing EU policies and legislation (Chapters 5, 6, and 15). There is little evidence of a distinctive grouping of new members with respect to the internal market: some are more liberal, and some a little less so, than older members. Evidence on voting records in the Council indicates that, since their accession, the new members have tended to align to the more market-promoting side of the discussion and not in this respect to be laggards (Mattila 2008). By and large, EU policy templates have played a key role in shaping the transformation of these countries towards becoming modern market economies, and much of this transformation took place during the pre-accession period as the EU *acquis* shaped the domestic legislation being set in place or 'downloaded' (Chapter 17). In some parts of the economy the substantial presence of foreign ownership of banks or retail has in any case meant that policy priorities have been shaped by big players from the old EU. Nonetheless and not surprisingly, there are some signs that strong pro-market disciplines are not always popular, and hence on competition and state-aid issues there has been some friction.

As regards regulation that bites into social and environmental matters, however, the picture is less straightforward (Chapters 11, 12, and 13). The long-standing debate in the old EU between the 'leaders' and the 'laggards' finds expression in the post-2004 EU. Poorer countries tend understandably to be less enthusiastic in rushing towards higher social or environmental standards than wealthier countries, even without the added constraints of the financial crisis. High process standards imply significant extra costs and could undermine what would otherwise be cost-competitiveness for central and east European countries. Moreover, physical legacies, such as the continued importance of coal (sometimes brown coal) for some new members, impinge on their policy concerns (Chapter 15). More broadly, the climate-change agenda carries less immediacy for some of these countries than it supposedly has for the old EU members (Chapters 13 and 15). In relation to the social and employment agendas the new members come to the EU without the constraints of welfare states to protect (Chapters 11 and 12), and also with less vocal non-governmental groups clamouring for higher standards of social protection. In these areas, enlargement has both changed the politics, and limited the prospects, of future regulation.

It is on the explicitly distributional issues that the new member states form the most distinct grouping and make the most explicit difference to the line-up of positions to be accommodated in the development of collective EU policies—for good and for ill. The prospect of eastwards enlargement, for example, has been one of the driving forces pressing for reform of the CAP. The budgetary and consumer costs of extending the old CAP eastwards served to increase the incentives for acceptance of a shift from product and market support towards the new forms of farm payments, buttressed by the delayed provisions for extending the CAP eastwards (Chapter 8). At least as clear is the impact of enlargement on the development of cohesion policy—and in two senses (Chapter 10). On the one hand, on objective criteria for distributing funding the new member states would be in line for pride of place as recipients, given their evident need to improve their economic infrastructures both regionally and nationally. On the other hand, old beneficiaries of the structural funds have been at pains not to let go of all their benefits of incumbency. These two factors, combined with the pressures on the net contributors to the EU budget, have made negotiations on these issues even tougher than they were before (Chapter 9).

The development of economic and monetary union (EMU) had been, since the drafting of the terms of the Maastricht Treaty on European Union, hedged to protect the 'project' from the baggage of less capable member states (Chapter 7). Thus the commitment to membership of the single currency was reserved for only those member states with economies that would meet stringent performance tests. Since 2004 only four of the new member states of the EU have been admitted into the eurozone: Cyprus, Malta, Slovakia, and Slovenia. Hence the members of the eurozone have had an autonomous capability to control the impact of enlargement, as regards both who has voice and which economies are included. Meanwhile, on the macroeconomic side of EMU the development of policy discussions is so much more open-ended that enlargement has limited implications.

Over the years enlargement has always been accompanied by a discussion of whether and when new member states would be included in the Treaty of Rome's original provisions for the free movement of labour (Chapters 11 and 12). This was a bone of contention in earlier years as the EU opened up to Greece, Portugal, and Spain as new member states, countries with then lower wage costs and populations apparently willing to move countries in search of employment. A similar debate accompanied the run-up to the 2004/2007 enlargements. Incumbent member states were able to delay the application of free-labour-movement provisions to the prospective new member states for up to seven years—and most of them chose to do so. This has turned out to be perhaps the most politically sensitive dimension of enlargement, given the coincidence of the timing of the EU's recent enlargements with wider patterns of migration towards Europe (for quite other reasons) and given the more recent impact of the financial crisis on EU labour markets and increasing levels of unemployment. Both Chapters 11 and 12 report aspects of this, including the series of controversial ECJ cases on 'posted' workers, that is workers from one (usually lower-wage-cost) member state recruited to work in another member state (usually with higher wage costs and higher ancillary obligations). Chapter 5 discusses how these concerns influenced the Services Directive. Analyses of the roots of euroscepticism also tell us that EU citizens are prone to confusion as to the difference between intra-EU mobility of labour and migration (whether legal or illegal, whether economic or political) into the EU from outside the EU. Thus these issues are scrambled up inside the EU policy debate with the questions that arise under the provisions for developing JHA, with a component that addresses migration policy (Chapter 19).

The new EU geography is a powerful factor in driving debates about EU policy developments, and especially so in a period in which forms of instability permeate the EU neighbourhood. Several of our case studies shed light on this. Self-evidently the attempt to elaborate the CFSP provokes difficult discussions about how to address the several and different groups of neighbours, most importantly Russia and the US (see Chapter 18). Efforts to improve energy security have been plagued by the differences of view among EU members as regards their degrees of dependence on Russian-sourced energy supplies, which have sent member states old and new scurrying in different directions to look after their diverse national interests (see Chapter 15). EU member states are torn also in different directions about when and whether to admit this or that neighbouring country as an actual or potential candidate for EU membership—or whether and if so how to develop alternatives to an EU membership track for some neighbours (see Chapter 17). The development of JHA has taken on many features that derive from the specificities of the new EU geography, which has altered the definition of where the relevant boundaries lie for 'controlling' the licit and the illicit movements of people and objects (see Chapter 19). Here, in contrast to the EMU story, in practice the EU boundaries (and specifically the Schengen Area's boundaries) have come to be defined inclusively rather than exclusively. Thus all of the new member states except Bulgaria, Cyprus, and Romania have now been accepted within Schengen, and several non-EU countries have also been incorporated—Iceland, Norway, and Switzerland.

The long constitutional stalemate

The first decade of the twenty-first century has been characterized by a long constitutional debate: the negotiation of the Constitutional Treaty (CT); its rejection in referendums in France and The Netherlands in 2005; and its renegotiation as the Treaty of Lisbon (ToL). A first negative referendum in Ireland in 2008 was reversed by a second positive one in October 2009. Signatures of ratification followed in Poland and, after the completion of legal or parliamentary procedures in the Czech Republic and Germany. This messy history raises two questions in particular for us: first, has the widely perceived 'crisis' in the EU affected day-to-day policy-making in our issue areas? And, second, what difference will Lisbon make in the policy areas that we cover in this volume?

With respect to the first question, the long stalemate on treaty reform infected the political climate in which EU policy-making takes place and generally eroded the legitimacy of the EU system. Nonetheless, as we have seen above, policy-making continues and policy initiatives have continued to be rolled out. Moreover, by and large our case studies suggest that where policies have been stalled in recent years, the reasons seem to lie in substantive disagreements about what to do rather than to be a function of specific institutional rules awaiting amendment by the ToL.

With respect to the second question, the ratification of the ToL introduces some changes to the formal procedures under which EU policies are made (for good reviews see e.g. Centre for European Policy Studies 2007 and Europolitics 2007). It should be noted that changes to the policy-making process emerged more from the politics of the processes of treaty reform than from a sober assessment of what might be needed to promote the functional effectiveness of the EU as a policy-making and policy-delivery system. The Constitutional Treaty had been drafted with institutional changes in sight for political reasons rather than as a function of well-specified policy requirements. Those responsible for drafting the ToL were more concerned to retrench on the ambitions of the CT than to add new elements. As a consequence, the potential impact of the ToL varies across policy areas.

There are many areas of EU policy-making where the impact of the ToL will be trivial in the sense of altering the main procedural patterns of work. Thus, for example, the new treaty brings little by way of formal change to the economic governance of the EU as regards either EMU or the single market (Chapters 5, 6, and 7). Interestingly, in the light of the political salience of climate change and energy security issues, the ToL provides only small additional elements of leverage for those seeking to strengthen the EU capability to act collectively (Chapter 15), which reflects the desire not to go beyond the CT, despite the way in which both climate change and energy security had risen on the policy agenda in the interim. In these areas policy-makers will thus be left to work within the pre-existing framework, or now and then to devise more informal ways of adapting their working methods. This is in line with the wider phenomenon highlighted above of experimentation and evolution in the absence of treaty reform.

In a number of other policy areas specific changes to decision-making practices will follow the ratification of the ToL. Thus agricultural legislation will become subject to co-decision by the Council and the EP (Chapter 8). On the one hand, this should strengthen the accountability mechanisms, but, on the other hand, it might raise the obstacles to reform. Similarly, the EP will acquire a greater voice in trade policy, yielding again increased accountability and again perhaps a tougher ride in the quest for consensus and perhaps delays in responding to global negotiations (Chapter 16).

In two policy domains, however—CFSP and JHA—the ToL introduces important reforms, which could have far-reaching consequences. As regards CFSP and its sister, European security and defence policy (ESDP), the ToL contains substantial and detailed new rules and procedures (Chapter 18). In particular, the envisaged full-time European Council President can be expected to spend a good deal of the time in office focusing on foreign-policy issues, while the High Representative will belong to both the Council and to the Commission, and a treaty base is provided for developing a kind of EU diplomatic service. Yet, as is indicated in Chapter 18, it is by no means evident that these changes will provide clarity of institutional responsibilities, and the practical effectiveness of these innovations can by no means be taken for granted.

As regards JHA, the implementation of the ToL explicitly brings this domain of policy-making inside the core institutional framework of the EU and in this sense procedurally 'mainstreams' its ways of working. The current 'pillar' arrangements will be abolished, whereby some parts of JHA are inside the first 'Community' pillar and others are kept within a segmented third pillar. This sounds like a potentially radical change. Yet, as is argued in Chapter 19, appearances can be deceptive. The existing and famous 'passerelle' clause already allows EU policy-makers, and notably the member governments acting by consensus, to shift JHA topics from the third to the first pillar, as indeed has already been done in a number of instances. Thus the pre-Lisbon treaty framework already has procedural elasticity.

In sum, according to the evidence in this volume, the ToL as such does not appear to be set on radically transforming either the policy-making processes of the EU or the policy effectiveness of the EU. As has been the case in the past, there remains a good deal of scope for evolution and experimentation, just as there remain a good many areas where the proof of the pudding will be in the eating, which is to say that the outcomes will depend on how policy-makers interpret rule changes and on how the persisting confusions in institutional responsibilities under the ToL are handled in and shaped by practice. It cannot be denied, however, that the institutional stalemate has cast a long political shadow. Indeed it may be that the most significant impact of the ToL's final ratification in November 2009 will be the end of the ill-humour and sense of 'constitutional crisis' that had gripped Europe for nearly half a decade. It also removes a tempting alibi for failures to reach agreement on this or that policy proposal.

The financial crisis

The centrepiece of the EU is the creation of a single European market with common rules and rule-making, and, for the eurozone members, with an experiment in common monetary and coordinated fiscal policy. All of these have been put under stress by the financial crisis of 2007–8 and the subsequent economic recession. We are still too close to this crisis for it yet to be clear how far and in what ways the EU and its policies will be affected or for it to be evident what the impacts are likely to be in the medium term. This is not the first time that the EU has been tested by economic turbulence or recession. After all, in the 1970s and early 1980s the oil-price shocks initially found the then member states searching for national responses rather than a collective European approach. In that case it became fashionable for commentators to speak of 'Eurosclerosis', although this did not prevent the EU from eventually getting its act together with the series of initiatives that led to the single European market (see Chapter 5). Moreover, faced with the political upheavals in Europe after 1989, EU leaders took the very big step of agreeing to create the euro and a single monetary policy (see Chapter 7). We make these points simply to show that events can have unexpected consequences, and that the EU has been known to make bold decisions against a background of economic and/or political stress.

What then of EU responses so far to the financial and economic crises? Some of our case studies offer preliminary insights into these, while others stress that the time lags are such that the impacts of the crisis have yet to show themselves. With this caution in mind, we highlight some of the issues that have been manifest in the brief period since the start of the crisis, and that seem likely to need to be addressed in the coming years.

- *The EU economic template on test.* The single-market model based on essentially liberal regulation and a pro-competition rule-book may be increasingly vulnerable in a period when the temptations to rewrite—and to make more restrictive—the regulation of financial services will be enormous (Chapters 5 and 7). The financial crisis has already begun to call into question the state-aid provisions of EU competition policy, as EU member states undertake large, and in some cases unprecedented, rescues of troubled banks, automobile makers, and other industries, and the Commission comes under intense pressure to accept these extraordinary measures (see Chapter 6; Wilks 2009). Economic and monetary union has conveyed clear benefits to its members since the beginning of the financial crisis, most notably by avoiding exchange-rate crises that have aggravated the problems of European states outside the eurozone; yet the EMU model based on a sound monetary policy and price stability looks vulnerable for rethinking given the substantial increases in unfunded government spending (either as explicit fiscal stimulus or through 'automatic stabilizers') and the resulting threat to the Stability and Growth Pact designed to coordinate eurozone fiscal policies (see Chapter 7).

- *Liberalism versus protectionism.* Two huge achievements of the EU in the past have been the insistence on the four economic freedoms within the EU and a broadly liberal stance in trade relations with the rest of the world (see Chapters 5 and 16). Both are vulnerable in circumstances of prolonged recession and in a period in which governments are under pressure for protection from their electorates across the range of manufacturing and service sectors. For this reason, speculation has been rife that, in the words of former Trade Commissioner Peter Mandelson, 'the crisis may spark a new wave of economic nationalism' and 'an "every man for himself" approach', both within the EU and vis-à-vis the rest of the world (quoted in *The Sunday Telegraph*, 5 October 2008: 1; see also *New York Times*, 26 February 2009).

- *Our workers—or their workers?* It was evident ahead of the financial crisis that migration was becoming an increasingly contentious issue in the domestic politics of many EU member states. The combination of migratory pressures from the rest of the world together with the acceleration of intra-EU migration following enlargement had already generated considerable resentment, as several of our case studies illustrate (see Chapters 5, 11, 12, and 19). Add to this the unemployment consequences of the recession and there is an explosive cocktail. Politicians and policy-makers across the EU will not easily rally behind free movement of labour within the EU let alone behind generous policies towards would-be migrants, refugees, or asylum-seekers from elsewhere.

- *Not enough money to go round.* Public budgets across the EU are being doubly stretched by the financial crisis. On the one hand, the bail-out of the banks is expensive and its extent as yet not known. On the other hand, the welfare budgets of member states are also being stretched as tax revenues fall and claims for unemployment benefits rise as consequences of retracting economies. Hence the Maastricht criteria for EMU were immediately breached, and, equally importantly, rising levels of public expenditure are squeezing what might otherwise be available to fund collective EU policies. We already knew that budgetary bargains were among the toughest to resolve within the EU, as Chapters 8, 9, and 10 illustrate. The outlook for the forthcoming rounds of distributive bargaining thus looks stormy.

- *How green an economy in a recession?* The timing of the financial crisis has been particularly inconvenient as regards the climate-change and energy agendas of the EU. The crisis bit just as the EU reached the point of accepting that mitigating climate change was a crucial priority and one on which the EU could provide global leadership. Already, as we can see from Chapters 13 and especially 15, EU politicians are standing back from far-reaching commitments to green their economies and to meet those environmental and energy targets that might make a real difference. Here a set of long-term risks being subverted by short-term constraints.

- *Strength in numbers—or not?* Early evidence on reactions to the crisis suggests that some member states have been much more severely affected than others, and that in particular some of the new member states have been especially hard hit. The temptations will be strong in all member states, old as well as new, to adopt *sauve qui peut* national policies rather than to opt for collective EU actions. As in earlier periods of economic disruption, it is likely to take time for member governments to figure out that there may rather be merit in developing shared responses. And the extent to which they do will also depend on the robustness of the EU policy-making process in providing a forum that can adapt and deliver appropriate collective policies.

In all of these areas, the financial and economic crises of recent years threaten to set back both the core liberalizing policies of the EU (the single market, competition policy, the free movement of labour, and economic and monetary union), as well as flanking social, environmental, and energy policies, and future budgetary agreements regarding the CAP and the structural funds. The ultimate impact of the crisis in each of these areas will depend on the length and depth of the current recession and on the policy and political responses of EU institutions and member governments, which may accept or resist the temptation of beggar-thy-neighbour policies.

Conclusions

If there is a common denominator in the previous pages, it is the adaptability and resilience of the EU policy process, both in its day-to-day operations and in its response to the major challenges and crises of the day.

In terms of responding to the stresses the EU has faced, neither enlargement nor the institutional crisis (nor the combination of the two) has led to gridlock, not least because the Commission, member governments, and EP have found practical working methods. This underlines that cooperation within the EU can advance even in the absence of treaty reform and that cooperation has always been more extensive than what is formally required by the treaties. Moreover, derogations have been permitted from common rules to accommodate politically difficult and economically diverse circumstances. Thus incumbent member states were allowed to restrict immigration from the new member states in order to sustain political support for enlargement. In the face of the financial crisis, member states have been permitted to breach the deficit requirements of the Stability and Growth Pact and to violate (within limits) state-aid rules, threatening the integrity of those policies yet also providing member states with de facto pressure valves or escape clauses in tough times.

Routine policy-making occurs through a variety of different modes and combinations of modes; deploys myriad different policy instruments; and engages different constellations of member states within diverse institutional frameworks. In some policy areas centralized legislation is the dominant policy output. In others the emphasis is on coordination among national officials or promotion of best practice. In many policy areas it is common to find a mix of parallel methods and modes. Some policy areas engage all of and only the member states, while in others only subsets of member states participate, and in yet others non-member states participate.

To a significant extent, one can argue that the adaptability of the EU's policy processes and the multiplication and variation of policy modes reflect the *limits* to the member states' willingness to engage in close cooperation. Indeed, many experiments and innovations in policy-making—including the open method of coordination, the Stability and Growth Pact in EMU, intensive transgovernmentalism in CFSP, and partial communitarization in JHA, among others—can be seen as the result of member-state reluctance to embrace the traditional Community method or to empower supranational actors such as the Commission, Parliament, and Court of Justice. Confronted by these limits to European integration, and by the persistent difficulty of reforming the Union's constitutional structure, EU member governments and institutions have pioneered new policy processes to respond to shocks and manage stresses. Paradoxically, then, the limits to European integration also help to explain the adaptability of the EU policy processes and the resilience, so far, of the European project in hard times.

APPENDIX: Caseloads of EU Courts

TABLE A.1 New caseload of the European Court of Justice by subject matter, 1953–1991

Subject matter	1953–1971	1972	1973	1974–1975	1976	1977	1978	1979	1980	1981	1972–1981 Σcol. 2–10	1982	1983	1984	1985	1986	1987	1988	1989	1990°	1991	1982–1991 Σcol. 12–21	1972–1991 Σcol. 11+22	1953–1991 Σcol. 1+23
	1	2	3	4	5	6	7	8	9	10	11	12	13	14	15	16	17	18	19	20	21	22	23	24
1 Accession of new member states	n.a.										n.a.											n.a.	n.a.	n.a.
2 Agriculture and fisheries	135	36	36	84	47	61	94	48	48	55	509	83	47	47	70	70	81	88	63	155	97	801	1310	1445
3 Approximation of laws	n.a.										n.a.											n.a.	n.a.	n.a.
4 Brussels convention	n.a.										n.a.											n.a.	n.a.	n.a.
5 Commercial policy	n.a.										n.a.											n.a.	n.a.	n.a.
6 Competition (incl. line 19 before 1992)	44	6	26	16	6	10	64	14	13	7	162	42	18	21	34	27	34	16	69	20	30	311	473	517
7 Energy	n.a.										n.a.											n.a.	n.a.	n.a.
8 Environment & consumers	n.a.										n.a.											n.a.	n.a.	n.a.
9 External Relations	n.a.										n.a.											n.a.	n.a.	n.a.

10 Free movement for persons (incl. line 18 before 1992)	48	11	12	27	17	19	20	25	17	26	174	17	31	26	37	24	35	39	40	37	77	363	537	585
11 Freedom of establishment & to provide services, company law	1	0	0	8	3	2	7	2	2	12	36	4	15	10	17	12	12	7	19	27	10	133	169	170
12 Free movement of capital	n.a.										n.a.											n.a.	n.a.	n.a.
13 Free movement of goods & customs	56	3	11	18	16	25	24	41	55	53	246	56	38	68	62	33	45	70	72	39	36	519	765	821
14 Industrial policy	n.a.										n.a.												n.a.	n.a.
15 Intellectual property	n.a.										n.a.												n.a.	n.a.
16 Law governing the institutions	n.a.										n.a.												n.a.	n.a.
17 Principles of Community law	n.a.										n.a.												n.a.	n.a.

TABLE A.1 (Continued)

Subject matter	1953–1971	1972	1973	1974–1975	1976	1977	1978	1979	1980	1981	1972–1981 Σcol. 2–10	1982	1983	1984	1985	1986	1987	1988	1989	1990c	1991	1982–1991 Σcol. 12–21	1972–1991 Σcol. 11+22	1953–1991 Σcol. 1+23
	1	2	3	4	5	6	7	8	9	10	11	12	13	14	15	16	17	18	19	20	21	22	23	24
18 Social policy (see line 10 before 1992)	n.a.										n.a.											n.a.	n.a.	n.a.
19 State aid (see line 6 before 1992)	n.a.										n.a.											n.a.	n.a.	n.a.
20 Taxation	27	1	0	4	3	2	9	7	7	20	53	9	13	17	39	18	35	30	19	26	24	230	283	310
21 Transport	3	0	1	1	1	2	6	2	0		13	4	5	5	6	6	5	5	4	16	7	63	76	79
22 Rest (EC)	8	2	2	4[a]	11	16	10	12	12	23	92	21	22	35	68	53	44	48	56	37	44	428	557	565
23 Other (ECSC, EAEC)	282	0	4	3	2	0	12	7	3	33	64	25	40	42	35	28	27	10	3	1	1	212	276	558
24 Staff of EU institutions	291	23	100	67	19	25	22	1163	117	94	1630	85	68	41	65	57	77	59	40	0	0	492	2122	2413

25 All (officially reported sums)	895	82	192	238	120	162	268	1322	280	323	2987	348	297	312	433	328	395[b]	372	385	358[c]	326[d]	3196	6183	7078
26 All[e] (mathematical sums)	895	82	192	232	125	162	268	1321	274	323	2979	346	297	312	433	328	395	372	385	358	326	3552	6531	7426

Sources: fifth to twenty-fifth *General Report of the European Commission*, 1972–1992. For 1974 and 1975 (8th and 9th Report) values were not reported but could be calculated as follows: per each category from the total number of cases at the end of 1976 the new 1976 caseload (both 10th Report) and also the total caseload at the end of 1973 (7th Report) could be subtracted to arrive at the added caseload for that two-year period. Compiled by Josef Falke, Centre for European Law and Policy (ZERP) and Research Centre Tran State (Transformations of the State), and by Stephan Leibfried, Research Centre Tran State and Centre for Social Policy Research (CeS), and tabulated by Monika Sniegs of Trans State, all University of Bremen.

Legend: n.a. = not applicable.

[a] Under 'Rest (EC)' 1974–75 (line 22) the new 1976-category 'treaties' in the 10th Report could be ignored as no case dated to an earlier year.

[b] Own calculation; no total number reported in the 21st Report.

[c] In 1990 the Court of First Instance was founded which reduced the original 36 competition cases (line 6) by 16 appeals, left only one EAEC case remaining under 'Other' (line 23), and moved all staff cases (line 24) to the new court. The statistics were adjusted accordingly, leading to a different 1990 total of ECJ cases.

[d] Without 14 appeal cases.

[e] Sums different from line 25 are underlined.

TABLE A.2   New caseload of the European Court of Justice by subject matter, 1953–2007

Subject matter[a]	Until 1971	Distribution (Icol. 1 in %)	1972–1981	Distribution (col. 3 in %)	1982–91	Distributions (col. 5 in %)	1992	1993	1994	1995	1996	1997	1998	1999	2000	2001	2002	2003	2004	2005	2006	2007	1992–2007 Σ7–22	Distribution (col. 23 in %)
	1	2	3	4	5	6	7	8	9	10	11	12	13	14	15	16	17	18	19	20	21	22	23	24
1 Accession of new member states	n.a.		n.a.		n.a.			1	0	13	9	6	1	0	2	1	2	1	4	0	0	0	40	0.52
2 Agriculture & fisheries	135	15.08	509	17.08	801	22.55	197	207	63	64	55	64	38	80	88	55	58	60	58	41	62	37	1227	15.98
3 Approximation of laws	n.a.		n.a.		n.a.		4	7	27	11	32	38	43	42	26	63	38	50	41	27	18	60	527	6.87
4 Brussels convention	n.a.		n.a.		n.a.		8	9	2	9	3	6	0	2	9	6	10	6	3	2	2	3	80	1.04
5 Commercial policy	n.a.		n.a.		n.a.		6	13	8	4	3	2	7	11	9	5	2	1	1	2	1	0	75	0.98
6 Competition (included line 19 before 1992)	44	4.92	162	5.43	311	8.76	34	17	13	24	20	24	28	29	22	30	13	21	33	10	32	31	381	4.96
7 Energy	n.a.		n.a.		n.a.						3	2	0	2	0	1	2	4	2	9	6	2	33	0.43
8 Environment & consumers	n.a.		n.a.		n.a.		18	16	15	44	36	42	30	41	57	55	71	69	48	51	60	60	713	9.29
9 External Relations	n.a.		n.a.		n.a.		6	14	8	13	10	8	11	12	7	8	10	13	8	10	11	10	159	2.07

10 Free movement for persons (included line 18 before 1992)	48	5.36	174	5.84	363	10.22	35	45	71	42	69	50	36	69	32	13	21	23	23	25	14	28	596	7.76
11 Freedom of establishment & to provide services, company law	1	0.11	36	1.21	133	3.74	6	6	10	14	15	17	53	33	43	62	55	57	69	45	79	44	608	7.92
12 Free movement of capital	n.a.	n.a.	n.a.	n.a.	n.a.	n.a.		1	4	1	2	2	6	3	6	6	3	5	9	10	7	7	72	0.94
13 Free movement of goods & customs	56	6.26	246	8.26	519	14.61	33	54	55	62	31	28	32	23	28	20	31	29	25	27	29	33	540	7.03
14 Industrial policy	n.a.	n.a.	n.a.	n.a.	n.a.	n.a.								5	16	4	10	16	12	8	16	25	112	1.46
15 Intellectual property	n.a.	n.a.	n.a.	n.a.	n.a.	n.a.								2	6	15	8	9	8	24	23	28	123	1.60
16 Law governing the institutions	n.a.	n.a.	n.a.	n.a.	n.a.	n.a.		5	8	14	10	13	11	13	9	13	15	27	14	10	10	22	205	2.67
17 Principles of Community law	n.a.	n.a.	n.a.	n.a.	n.a.	n.a.	4	4	1	4	16	25	4	4	7	4	1	2	2	2	5	3	88	1.15
18 Social policy (before 1992 see line 10)	n.a.	n.a.	n.a.	n.a.	n.a.	n.a.	20	26	15	25	42	26	33	33	45	35	33	39	40	48	47	44	551	7.18
19 State aid (before 1992 see line 6)	n.a.	n.a.	n.a.	n.a.	n.a.	n.a.	13	12	6	12	7	18	13	15	22	15	18	30	24	9	20	18	252	3.28
20 Taxation	27	3.02	53	1.78	230	6.48	19	20	22	31	29	36	73	61	30	36	36	33	40	49	34	48	607	7.91

TABLE A.2   (Continued)

Subject matter[*]	Until 1971	Distribution (col. 1 in %)	1972–1981	Distribution (col. 3 in %)	1982–91	Distributions (col. 5 in %)	1992	1993	1994	1995	1996	1997	1998	1999	2000	2001	2002	2003	2004	2005	2006	2007	1992–2007 Σ7–22	Distribution (col. 23 in %)
	1	2	3	4	5	6	7	8	9	10	11	12	13	14	15	16	17	18	19	20	21	22	23	24
21 Transport	3	0.34	13	0.44	63	1.77	12	9	7	4	3	9	27	22	22	22	9	23	21	14	9	15	228	2.97
22 Rest (EC) including	8	0.89	92	3.09	428	12.05	2	9	5	4	0	1	5	2	3	1	2	6	6	8	4	5	63	0.82
22a Justice & home affairs	n.a.		n.a.		n.a.		n.a.									3	0	5	12	8	15	31	74	0.96
22b Common foreign & security policy	n.a.		n.a.		n.a.		n.a.												2	3	3	0	8	0.10
22c Economic & monetary policy	n.a.		n.a.		n.a.		n.a.											1	1	2	0	1	5	0.07
22d European citizenship									1	0	0	1	0	2	0	0	4	1	4	2	5	2	22	0.29
22e Regional policy									1	2	2	2	0	2	1	3	0	7	3	2	3	3	31	0.40
23 Other (ECSC, EAEC)	282	31.51	64	2.15	212	5.97	7	0	2	5	4	10	4	18	5	14	8	3	6	7	3	3	99	1.29
24 Staff of EU institutions	291	32.51	1630	54.72	492	13.85	12	9	5	11	13	13	19	16	8	16	10	10	5	11	14	10	182	2.37
25 All (officially reported sums, including appeals)	895	100.0	2987	100.0	3196	100.0	442	469	354	408	416	443	481	541	500	503	470	555	526	467	535	573	7677	100.0

25a Appeals	n.a.		n.a.		n.a.		25	16	13	48	28	35	70	72	79	72	46	63	52	66	80	80	945	n.c.
26 Allb (mathematical sums)	895	100.0	2979	100.0	3552	100.0	441	487	354	408	416	442	475	541	504	503	470	535	524	466	535	573	7674	

Sources: For columns 1, 3, and 5 see Table A.1. For columns 7–22 see the *Annual Reports of the Court of Justice and the Court of First Instance of the European Communities*, 1992–2007. Compiled by Josef Falke, Centre for European Law and Policy (ZERP) and Research Centre TranState (Transformations of the State), and by Stephan Leibfried, Research Centre TranState and Center for Social Policy Research (CeS) and tabulated by Monika Sniegs of TranState and Gitta Klein of CeS, University of Bremen.

Legend: n.a. = not applicable; n.c. = not comparable.

a Over time, in particular since 1992, the court statistics have had to become more differentiated because increasing caseload required some categories to be subdivided, e.g. 'approximation of laws' which was included in line 22 ('Rest EC') is now reported separately (line 3); and because new competencies were created or old ones decisively extended, like 'industrial policy' (line 14) in Art. 157 ToA (1997), such that separate reporting was deemed necessary.

b Sums different from line 25 are underlined.

TABLE A.3 Number of new cases at the Court of First Instance, 1992–2007

Subject matter	1992	1993	1994	1995	1996	1997	1998	1999	2000	2001	2002	2003	2004	2005	2006	2007	1992–2007 Σ1–16	Distribution (col. 17 in %)
	1	2	3	4	5	6	7	8	9	10	11	12	13	14	15	16	17	18
1 Agriculture		420	216	46	33	73	19	42	23	17	9	11	25	21	18	34	1007	16.16
2 Commercial policy			20	11	6	15	12	5	8	4	5	6	12	5	18	9	136	2.18
3 Competition	36	28	59	74	28	22	23	34	36	39	61	43	36	40	81	62	702	11.27
4 Customs		1	2	2	3	17	0	0	0	2	5	5	11	2	0	4	54	0.87
5 Environment & consumer policy		3	2	3	0	0	4	5	14	2	8	13	30	18	21	41	164	2.63
6 External Relations							10	5	14	26	11	13	3	2	2	1	87	1.40
7 Fisheries		5	7	3	2	2	0	2	1	3	6	25	3	2	0	5	66	1.06
8 Free movement for persons & social policy		14	2	3	9	4	17	14	15	4	5	9	6	11	7	9	129	2.07
9 Free movement of goods		1	0	0	2	1	7	10	17	1	0	0	1	0	0	1	41	0.66

Subject															Total	%
10 Freedom of establishment & to provide services, company law	1	0	3	1	3	3	3	4	7	3	3	7	12	12	10	72	1.16
11 Intellectual property						1	18	34	37	83	101	110	98	145	168	795	12.76
12 Law governing the institutions			8	13		10	19	29	12	18	26	33	28	15	28	218	3.50
13 State aid	13	12	13	25	28	16	100	80	42	51	25	46	25	28	37	541	8.68
14 Taxation		3	0	0	0	0	0	0	0	1	5	0	0	1	2	12	0.19
15 Transport	1	1	0	0	1	3	0	0	2	1	1	3	0	1	4	20	0.32
16 Justice & home affairs									1	1	0	0	1	0	3	6	0.10
17 Common foreign & security policy								1	3	6	2	4	0	5	12	33	0.53
18 Economic & monetary policy												1	1	2	0	3	0.05
19 Regional policy	1	1	2	2	1	2	2	0	1	6	7	10	12	16	18	76	1.22

TABLE A.3 (Continued)

Subject matter	1992	1993	1994	1995	1996	1997	1998	1999	2000	2001	2002	2003	2004	2005	2006	2007	1992–2007 Σ1–16	Distribution (col. 17 in %)
	1	2	3	4	5	6	7	8	9	10	11	12	13	14	15	16	17	18
20 Rest (EC)		16	18	1	2	2	2	1	4	7	3	8	8	13	12	15	467	7.49
21 Other (ECSC, EAEC)		2	23	6	5	6	12	8	1	4	3	11	1	0	1	0	83	1.33
22 Staff of EU institutions	79	84	85	79	107	155	79	86	106	111	112	124	146	151	11	29	1544	24.78
23 All (officially reported sums)	115	589	460	249	237	636	215	356	387	327	393	438	496	442	398	493	6231	100.00
24 All [a] (mathematical sums)	115	589	450	252	237	636	220	356	387	325	392	438	496	442	398	493	6226	—

Sources: *Annual Reports of the Court of Justice and the Court of First Instance of the European Communities*, 1992–2007. Compiled by Josef Falke, Centre for European Law and Policy (ZERP) and Research Centre TranState (Transformations of the State), and by Stephan Leibfried, Research Centre TranState and Center for Social Policy Research (CeS) and tabulated by Monika Sniegs of TranState and Gitta Klein of CeS, University of Bremen.

[a] Sums different from line 23 are underlined.

▌ REFERENCES

In addition to the substantial body of scholarly research cited below, students of the European Union can find extensive and up-to-date information about the EU's institutions and policies on-line. The EU's 'gateway' website provides profiles (in all of the Union's official languages) of the EU's various policies or 'activities' at: *http:// europa.eu*. In addition, each of the individual institutions maintains a dedicated website, including those for the Commission (*http://ec.europa.eu*), the Council of Ministers (*http://www.consilium.europa.eu*), the Court of Justice (*http://curia. europa.eu/jcms/jcms/j_6/home*), and the European Parliament (*http://www.europarl. europa.eu*). The EU also maintains several useful databases related to EU policies and policy-making, including most notably EUR-Lex (*http://eur-lex.europa.eu*), a keyword-searchable directory of EU treaties and legislation, and Pre-Lex (*http:// ec.europa.eu/prelex/apcnet.cfm?CL=en*), which provides access to documents from all stages and from the various institutions of the EU legislative process for thousands of individual pieces of legislation. In addition to these official websites, there are a growing number of publications (such as *Agence Europe, European Report*, and *European Voice*) and websites (such as *EUobserver.com*) that provide dedicated press coverage of EU institutions and policies.

Ackrill, R. (2000), *The Common Agricultural Policy* (Sheffield: Sheffield Academic Press).

Ackrill, R., and Kay, A. (2004), 'CAP Reform, Path Dependence and the EU Budget', paper presented at the 78th Annual Conference of the Agricultural Economics Society, Imperial College, London, 2–4 April.

Ackrill, R., and Kay, A. (2006), 'Historical-Institutionalist Perspectives on the Development of the EU Budget System', *Journal of European Public Policy*, 13/1: 113–33.

Agence Europe, various issues.

Aggarwal, V. K., and Foggerty, E. A. (2005), 'The Limits of Interregionalism: The EU and North America,' *European Integration*, 27/3: 327–46.

Allen, D. (2000), 'Cohesion and the Structural Funds: Transfers and Trade Offs', in H. Wallace and W. Wallace (eds.), *Policy-Making in the European Union*, 4th edn. (Oxford: Oxford University Press), 243–66.

Allen, D. (2005), 'Cohesion and the Structural Funds: Competing Pressures for Reform', in H. Wallace, W. Wallace, and M. A. Pollack (eds.), *Policy-Making in the European Union*, 5th edn. (Oxford: Oxford University Press), 213–41.

Allison, G. (1969), 'Conceptual Models and the Cuban Missile Crisis', *American Political Science Review*, 63/3: 689–718.

Allison, G. (1971), *Essence of Decision: Explaining the Cuban Missile Crisis* (Boston, MA: Little Brown).

Allison, G., and Zelikow, P. (1999), *Essence of Decision: Explaining the Cuban Missile Crisis*, 2nd edn. (New York, NY: Longman).

Alter, K. J. (2001), *Establishing the Supremacy of European Law: The Making of an International Rule of Law in Europe* (Oxford: Oxford University Press).

Alter, K. J., and Meunier-Aitsahalia, S. (1994), 'Judicial Politics in the European Community: European Integration and the Pathbreaking *Cassis de Dijon* Decision', *Comparative Political Studies*, 26/4: 535–61.

Amato, G. (1997), *Antitrust and the Bounds of Power* (Oxford: Hart).

Andersen, M. S., and Liefferink, D. (1997) (eds.), *European Environmental Policy: The Pioneers* (Manchester: Manchester University Press).

Angenendt, S. (1997) (ed.), *Migration und Flucht: Aufgaben und Strategien für Deutschland, Europa und die internationale Gemeinschaft* (Bonn/Munich: Bundeszentrale für politische Bildung/R. Oldenbourg).

Ansell, C., and Vogel, D. (2006) (eds.), *Why the Beef? The Contested Governance of European Food Safety* (Cambridge, MA: The MIT Press).

Apeldoorn, B. van (2001), 'The Struggle over European Order: Transnational Class Agency in the Making of "Embedded Neo-Liberalism"', in A. Bieler and A. D. Morton (eds.), *Social Forces in the Making of the New Europe: The Restructuring of European Social Relations in the Global Political Economy* (Basingstoke: Palgrave Macmillan), 70–89.

Apeldoorn, B. van (2002), *Transnational Capitalism and the Struggle over European Integration* (London: Routledge).

Armstrong, K., and Bulmer, S. (1998), *The Governance of the Single European Market* (Manchester: Manchester University Press).

Arnold, C. U. (2002), 'How Two-Level Entrepreneurship Works: The Influence of the Commission on the Europe-Wide Employment Strategy', paper presented at the conference of the American Political Science Association, Boston, 29 August–1 September.

Arnold, C. U., Hosli, M. O., and Pennings, P. (2004), 'Social Policy-Making in the European Union: A New Mode of Governance?', paper presented at the Conference of Europeanists, Chicago, 11–13 March.

Artis, M., and Buti, M. (2000), 'Close-to-Balance or in Surplus: A Policy-Maker's Guide to the Implementation of the Stability and Growth Pact', *Journal of Common Market Studies*, 38/4: 563–92.

Aspinwall, M. D., and Schneider, G. (1999), 'Same Menu, Separate Tables: The Institutionalist Turn in Political Science and the Study of European Integration', *European Journal of Political Research*, 38: 1–36.

Atkinson, M. M., and Coleman, W. D. (1989), *State, Business and Industrial Change in Canada* (Toronto: Toronto University Press).

Avery, G. (2004), 'The Enlargement Negotiations', in F. Cameron (ed.), *The Future of Europe: Integration and Enlargement* (London: Routledge), 35–62.

Averyt, W. (1977), *Agropolitics in the European Community* (New York, NY: Praeger Publishers).

Axelrod, R. (1970), *Conflict of Interest* (Chicago, IL: Markham).

Axelrod, R. (1984), *The Evolution of Cooperation* (New York, NY: Basic Books).

Bache, I. (1998), *The Politics of European Union Regional Policy: Multi-Level Governance or Flexible Gatekeeping?* (Sheffield: Sheffield Academic Press).

Bache, I. (1999), 'The Extended Gatekeeper: Central Government and the Implementation of the EC Regional Policy in the UK', *Journal of European Public Policy*, 6/1: 28–45.

Bache, I. (2004), 'Multi-Level Governance and EU Regional Policy', in I. Bache and M. Flinders (eds.), *Multi-Level Governance* (Oxford: Oxford University Press), 165–78.

Bache, I. (2008), *Europeanization and Multi-Level Governance: Cohesion Policy in the European Union and Britain* (Lanham, MD: Rowman & Littlefield).

Bache, I., and Bristow G. (2003), 'Devolution and the Gate-Keeping Role of the Core Executive: The Struggle for European Funds', *British Journal of Politics and International Relations*, 5/3: 405–27.

Bache, I., and Flinders, M. (2004), 'Themes and Issues in Multi-Level Governance', in I. Bache and M. Flinders (eds.), *Multi-Level Governance* (Oxford: Oxford University Press), 1–11.

Bachtler, J., and Mendez, C. (2007), 'Who Governs EU Cohesion Policy? Deconstructing the Reforms of the Structural Funds', *Journal of Common Market Studies*, 45/3: 535–64.

Bachtler, J., Mendez, C., and Wishlade, F. (2008), *Ideas for Budget and Policy Reform: Reviewing the Debate on Cohesion Policy 2014+*, European Policy Research Paper 08/04 (Glasgow: University of Strathclyde; European Policies Research Centre).

Bailey, D., and De Propris, L. (2004), 'A Bridge too Phare? EU Pre-Accession Aid and Capacity Building in the Candidate Countries', *Journal of Common Market Studies*, 42/1: 77–98.

Baker, S. (2003), 'The Dynamics of European Union Biodiversity Policy: Interactive, Functional and Institutional Logics', *Environmental Politics*, 12/3: 23–41.

Balassa, B. (1975), *European Economic Integration* (Amsterdam: North-Holland).

Baldwin, M. (2006), 'EU Trade Politics Heaven or Hell?', *Journal of European Public Policy*, 13/6: 926–42.

Barbé, E. (1998), 'Balancing Europe's Eastern and Southern Dimensions', in J. Zielonka (ed.), *Paradoxes of European Foreign Policy* (The Hague: Kluwer Law International), 117–30.

Barnard, C. (2007), *The Substantive Law of the EU: The Four Freedoms*, 2nd edn. (Oxford: Oxford University Press).

Barnard, C. (2008a), 'Unravelling the Services Directive', *Common Market Law Review*, 45/2: 323–94.

Barnard, C. (2008b), 'Employment Rights, Free Movement under the EC Treaty and the Services Directive', Mitchell Working Paper Series, Edinburgh Europa Institute, No. 5/2008.

Barnard, C., and Deakin, S. (2002), '"Negative" and "Positive" Harmonization of Labor Law in the European Union', *Columbia Journal of European Law*, 8: 389–413.

Barysch, K. (2008) (ed.), *Pipelines, Politics and Power: The Future of EU–Russia Relations* (London: Centre for European Reform).

Baumgartner, F. R., and Jones, B. D. (1993), *Agendas and Instability in American Politics* (Chicago, IL: University of Chicago Press).

Baumgartner, F. R., and Leech, B. L. (1998), *Basic Interests: The Importance of Groups in Politics and Political Science* (Princeton, NJ: Princeton University Press).

Baun, M. (2000), *A Wider Europe: The Process and Politics of EU Enlargement* (Lanham, MD: Rowman & Littlefield).

Baun, M., and Marek, D. (2008), *EU Cohesion Policy after Enlargement* (Basingstoke: Palgrave Macmillan).

Beach, D. (2005), *The Dynamics of European Integration: Why and When EU Institutions Matter* (Basingstoke: Palgrave Macmillan).

Becker, U. (1998), 'Brillen aus Luxemburg und Zahnbehandlung in Brüssel: die Gesetzliche Krankenversicherung im Europäischen Binnenmarkt', *Neue Zeitschrift für Sozialrecht*, 7/8: 359–64.

Becker, U. (2004a) 'Die soziale Dimension des Binnenmarktes', in J. Schwarze (ed.), *Der Verfassungsentwurf des Europäischen Konvents: Verfassungsrechtliche Grundstrukturen und wirtschaftsverfassungsrechtliches Konzept* (Baden-Baden: Nomos), 201–19.

Becker, U. (2004b) 'Grenzüberschreitende Versicherungsleistungen in der (gesetzlichen) Krankenversicherung—Die juristische Persektive', in J. Basedow et al. (eds.), *Versicherungswissenschaftliche Studien*, 26 (Baden-Baden: Nomos), 171–88.

Becker, U. (2005a), 'Stationäre und ambulante Krankenhausleistungen im grenzüberschreitenden Dienstleistungsverkehr—von Entgrenzungen und neuen Grenzen in der EU', *Neue Zeitschrift für Sozialrecht*, 14/9: 449–56.

Becker, U. (2005b), 'Das Gemeinschaftsrecht, die deutschen Sozialleistungssysteme und die Debatte um deren Reform', in U. Becker (ed.), *Reformen des deutschen Sozial- und Arbeitsrechts im Lichte supra- und internationaler Vorgaben: wissenschaftliches Kolloquium zum 70. Geburtstag von Bernd Baron von Maydell* (Baden-Baden: Nomos), 15–32.

Becker, U. (2007a), 'Sozialrecht in der europäischen Integration—eine Zwischenbilanz', *ZFSH/SGB*, 46/3: 134–43.

Becker, U. (2007b), 'EU-Beihilfenrecht und soziale Dienstleistungen', *Neue Zeitschrift für Sozialrecht*, 16/4: 169–76.

Beer, S. (1982), *Modern British Politics: Parties and Pressure Groups in the Collectivist Age* (London: Faber & Faber).

Begg, I. (2008a), 'Economic Governance in an Enlarged Euro Area', *European Economy*, Economic Papers, No. 311.

Begg, I. (2008b), 'Subsidiarity in Regional Policy', in G. Gelauff, I. Grilo, and A. Lejour (eds.), *Subsidiarity in Economic Reform in Europe* (Berlin/Heidelberg: Springer), 291–310.

Begg, I., and Grimwade, N. (1998), *Paying for Europe* (Sheffield: Sheffield Academic Press).

BEPA (Bureau of Economic Policy Advisors) (2008), *Public Finances in the EU* (Luxembourg: Office for Official Publications of the European Communities).

Bercusson, B. (2007), *European Labour Law*, 2nd edn. (London: Butterworths).

Bernauer, T. (2003), *Genes, Trade and Regulation: The Seeds of Conflict in Food Biotechnology* (Princeton, NJ: Princeton University Press).

Besson, S. (2007) (ed.), 'EU Citizenship', *European Law Journal*, 13/5: 573–694 (special issue).

Besson, S., and Utzinger, A. (2007), 'Introduction: Future Challenges of European Citizenship—Facing a Wide-Open Pandora's Box', *European Law Journal*, 13/5: 573–690.

Best, E., Christiansen, C., and Settembri, P. (2008) (eds.), *The Institutions of the Enlarged European Union* (Cheltenham: Edward Elgar).

Bieback, K.-J. (1993), 'Marktfreiheit in der EG und nationale Sozialpolitik vor und nach Maastricht', *Europarecht*, 28/2: 150–72.

Bieback, K.-J. (2003) 'Die Bedeutung der sozialen Grundrechte für die Entwicklung der EU', *Zeitschrift für Sozialhilfe und Sozialgesetzbuch (ZFSH/SGB)*, 42/10: 579–88.

Black, R. E. (1977), 'Plus Ça Change, Plus C'est la Même Chose: Nine Governments in Search of a Common Energy Policy', in H. Wallace, W. Wallace, and C. Webb (eds.), *Policy-Making in the European Communities* (Chichester: John Wiley), 165–96.

Blinder, A. (2007), 'Monetary Policy by Committee: Why and How?', *European Journal of Political Economy*, 23/1: 106–23.

Blom-Hansen, J. (2005), 'Principals, Agents, and the Implementation of EU Cohesion Policy', *Journal of European Public Policy*, 12/4: 624–48.

Boecken, W. (2005), 'EG-rechtlicher Zwang zu Unisex-Tarifen in der betrieblichen Altersversorgung?', in A. Söllner, W. Gitter, and R. Waltermann (eds.), *Gedächtnisschrift für Meinhard Heinze* (Munich: Beck), 57–68.

Boeri, T., and Brücker, H. (2006) (eds.), *Immigration Policy and the Welfare System: A Report for the Fondazione Rodolfo Debenedetti* (Oxford: Oxford University Press).

Bohman, J. (1998), 'Survey Article: The Coming of Age of Deliberative Democracy', *Journal of Political Philosophy*, 6/4: 400–25.

Boldrin, M., and Canova, F. (2001), 'Inequality and Convergence in Europe's Regions: Reconsidering European Regional Policies', *Economic Policy: A European Forum*, 0/32: 205–45.

Borrás, S., and Greve, B. (2004) (eds.), 'The Open Method of Coordination in the European Union', *Journal of European Public Policy*, 11/2: 181–336 (special issue).

Borrás, S., and Jacobsson, K. (2004), 'The Open Method of Coordination and the New Governance Patterns in the EU', *Journal of European Public Policy*, 11/2: 185–208.

Börzel, T. A. (2001), 'Non-Compliance in the European Union. Pathology or Statistical Artifact?', *Journal of European Public Policy*, 8/5: 803–24.

Börzel, T. A., and Hosli, M. (2003), 'Brussels between Bern and Berlin. Comparative Federalism Meets the European Union', *Governance*, 16/2: 179–202.

Börzel, T. A., and Risse, T. (2007), 'Europeanization: The Domestic Impact of EU Politics', in K. E. Jørgensen, M. A. Pollack, and B. Rosamond (eds.), *The Handbook of European Union Politics* (London: Sage), 483–504.

Bourgeois, J. (1982), 'The Tokyo Round Agreements on Technical Barriers and Government Procurement in International and EEC Perspective', *Common Market Law Review*, 19/1: 5–33.

Bradley, K. St Clair (1998), 'The GMO-Committee on Transgenic Maize: Alien Corn, or the Transgenic Procedural Maize', in M. P. C. M. van Schendelen (ed.), *EU Committees as Influential Policymakers* (Aldershot: Ashgate), 207–22.

Bretherton, C., and Vogler, J. (2006), *The EU as a Global Actor*, 2nd edn. (London: Routledge).

Buchan, D. (2009), *Energy and Climate Change: Europe at the Crossroads* (Oxford: Oxford University Press).

Budzinski, O. (2008), 'Monoculture versus Diversity in Competition Economics', *Cambridge Journal of Economics*, 32/2: 295–324.

Bueno de Mesquita, B., and Stokman, S. N. (1994), *European Community Decision Making* (New Haven, CT: Yale University Press).

Buigues, P., and Sheehy, J. (1994), 'European Integration and the Internal Market Programme', paper presented at the ESRC/COST A7 conference, University of Exeter, 8–11 Sept.

Bull, H. (1982), 'Civilian Power Europe: A Contradiction in Terms?', *Journal of Common Market Studies*, 21/1: 149–65.

Bulmer, S., and Lequesne, C. (2005) (eds.), *Member States and the European Union* (Oxford: Oxford University Press).

Burgess, M. (1989), *Federalism and European Union: Political Ideas, Influences and Strategies in the European Community, 1972–1987* (London: Routledge).

Burley, A.-M., and Mattli, W. (1993), 'Europe Before the Court: A Political Theory of Legal Integration', *International Organization*, 47/1: 41–76.

Buti, M., and Nava, M. (2008), '"Constrained Flexibility" As a Tool to Facilitate Reform of the EU Budget', *European Economy*, Economic Papers 326, DG Economic and Financial Affairs, European Commission.

Buti, M., Eijffinger, S., and Franco, D. (2003), 'Revisiting EMU's Stability Pact: A Pragmatic Way Forward', *Oxford Review of Economic Policy*, 19/1: 100–11.

Buzan, B., Wæver, O., and de Wilde, J. (1998), *Security: A New Framework for Analysis* (Boulder, CO: Lynne Rienner).

Buzogány, A. (2008), 'Confrontation or Cooperation? State-Society Relations and the Europeanization of Environmental Policy in the New Member States', paper presented at the 2008 ECPR Joint Sessions of Workshops (Rennes).

Cameron, D. (1992), 'The 1992 Initiative: Causes and Consequences', in A. M. Sbragia (ed.), *Euro-Politics: Institutions and Policymaking in the 'New' European Community* (Washington, DC: Brookings Institution), 23–74.

Cameron, P. (2007), *Competition in Energy Markets: Law and Regulation in the European Union*, 2nd edn. (Oxford: Oxford University Press).

Cantley, M. (1995), 'The Regulation of Modern Biotechnology: A Historical and European Perspective: A Case Study in How Societies Cope with New Knowledge in the Last Quarter of the Twentieth Century', in H. J. Rehm and G. Reed (eds.) in cooperation with A. Pühler and P. Stadler, *Biotechnology*, vol. xii: *Legal, Economic and Ethical Dimensions* (Weinheim: VCH), 506–681.

Capelletti, M., Seccombe, M., and Weiler, J. (1986) (eds.), *Integration through Law: Europe and the American Federal Experience* (New York, NY: De Gruyter).

Carbone, M. (2008), 'Mission Impossible: The European Union and Policy Coherence for Development', *Journal of European Integration*, 30/3: 323–42.

Carlsnaes, W., Sjursen, H., and White, B. (2004) (eds.), *Contemporary European Foreign Policy* (London: Sage).

Casey, B. (2003), 'Coordinating "Coordination": Beyond "Streamlining"', in Verband Deutscher Rentenversicherungsträger (VDR) (ed.), *Offene Koordinierung in der Alterssicherung in der Europäischen Union* (Frankfurt am Main: VDR), DRV Schriften 34, 89–97 (special issue, *Deutsche Rentenversicherung*).

Castles, F. G., Leibfried, S., Lewis, J., Obinger, H., and Pierson, C. (forthcoming), *Oxford Handbook of Comparative Welfare States* (Oxford: Oxford University Press).

Cecchini, P., with Catinat, M., and Jacquemin, A. (1988), *The European Challenge 1992: The Benefits of a Single Market* (Aldershot: Wildwood House).

Centre for European Policy Studies (CEPS) (2007), *The Treaty of Lisbon: Implementing the Institutional Innovations* (Brussels: CEPS).

Chalmers, D. (2003), 'Food for Thought: Reconciling European Risks and Traditional Ways of Life', *Modern Law Review*, 66/4: 532–64.

Chalmers, D. (2004), *The Dynamics of Judicial Authority and the Constitutional Treaty*, Jean Monnet Working Paper 5/04 (New York, NY: New York University School of Law, Jean Monnet Program/Woodrow Wilson School of Government, Princeton University).

Checkel, J. T. (2001), *Taking Deliberation Seriously*, ARENA Working Paper WP 01/14, available at *http://www.arena.uio.no/publications/*.

Checkel, J. T. (2005), 'International Institutions and Socialization in Europe: Introduction and Framework', *International Organization*, 59/4: 801–26.

Checkel, J. T., and Moravcsik, A. (2001), 'A Constructivist Research Program in EU Studies?', *European Union Politics*, 2/2: 219–49.

Christian Science Monitor, various issues.

Christiansen, T., Jørgensen, K. E., and Wiener, A. (1999), 'The Social Construction of Europe', *Journal of European Public Policy*, 6/4: 528–44.

Cini, M., and McGowan, L. (1998), *Competition Policy in the European Union* (London: Macmillan).

Cini, M., and McGowan, L. (2009), *Competition Policy in the European Union*, 2nd edn. (Basingstoke: Palgrave Macmillan).

Citi, M., and Rhodes, M. (2007), 'New Forms of Governance in the EU', in K. E. Jørgensen, M. A. Pollack, and B. Rosamond (eds.), *The Handbook of European Union Politics* (London: Sage), 463–82.

Clark, A. M., Friedman, E. J., and Hochstetler, K. (1998), 'The Sovereign Limits of Global Civil Society: A Comparison of NGO Participation in UN World Conferences on the Environment, Human Rights and Women', *World Politics*, 51/1: 1–35.

Clarke, R. (2006), 'Dominant Firms and Monopoly Policy in the UK and EU', in R. Clarke and E. Morgan (eds.), *New Developments in UK and EU Competition Policy* (Cheltenham: Edward Elgar), 22–50.

Cleveland, H. van B. (1966) (ed.), *The Atlantic Idea and its European Rivals* (New York, NY: McGraw-Hill).

Closa, C. (2004), 'The Convention Method and the Transformation of EU Constitutional Politics', in E.O. Eriksen, J. E. Fossum, and A. J. Menéndez (eds.), *Developing a Constitution for Europe* (London: Routledge), 183–206.

Cockfield, Lord (1994), *The European Union: Creating the Single Market* (London: Wiley Chancery Law).

Coen, D., (2007), 'Empirical and Theoretical Studies in EU Lobbying', *Journal of European Public Policy*, 14/3: 333–45.

Coen, D., and Richardson, J. (2009) (eds.), *Lobbying in the European Union: Institutions, Actors and Issues* (Oxford: Oxford University Press).

Coen, D., and Thatcher, M. (2005) (eds.), 'The New Governance of Markets and Non-Majoritarian Regulators', *Governance*, 18/3 (special issue).

Coen, D., and Thatcher, M. (2008a), 'Reshaping European Regulatory Space: An Evolutionary Analysis', *West European Politics*, 31/4: 806–36.

Coen, D., and Thatcher, M. (2008b). 'Network Governance and Multi-level Delegation: European Networks of Regulatory Agencies,' *Journal of Public Policy*, 28/1: 49–71.

Cohen, B. (2003), 'Global Currency Rivalry: Can the Euro Ever Challenge the Dollar?', *Journal of Common Market Studies*, 41/4: 575–95.

Cohen, J., and Sabel, C. (2003), 'Sovereignty and Solidarity in the EU', in J. Zeitlin and D. Trubek (eds.), *Governing Work and Welfare in a New Economy: European and American Experiments* (Oxford: Oxford University Press), 345–75.

Cohen, M., March, J., and Olsen, J. P. (1972), 'A Garbage Can Model of Organizational Choice', *Administrative Science Quarterly*, 17: 1–25.

Coleman, W. D., Skogstad, G. D., and Atkinson, M. M. (1997), 'Paradigm Shifts and Policy Networks: Cumulative Change in Agriculture', *Journal of Public Policy*, 16/3: 273–301.

Collins, D. (1975), *The European Communities: The Social Policy of the First Phase*, 2 vols. (London: Martin Robertson).

Collins, K., and Earnshaw, D. (1992), 'The Implementation and Enforcement of European Community Environment Legislation', *Environmental Politics*, 1/4: 213–49.

Commission (1969), Memorandum to the Council on the Co-ordination of Economic Policies and Monetary Co-operation Within the Community, *Bulletin of the EC*, Supplement 3/69.

Commission (1977–), *The Agricultural Situation in the European Union*, DG AGRI (previously *The Agricultural Situation in the Community*).

Commission (1981–), *Annual Reports on Competition Policy* (Luxembourg: Office for Official Publications of the European Communities).

Commission (1985a), *Completing the Internal Market: White Paper from the Commission to the European Council*, COM (85) 310 final.

Commission (1985b), Internal memo from DGIII to DGXI, photocopy.

Commission (1986), *A Community Framework for the Regulation of Biotechnology*, Communication from the Commission to the Council, COM (86) 573.

Commission (1988), *Proposal for a Council Directive on the Deliberate Release to the Environment of Genetically Modified Organisms*, COM (88) 160 final.

Commission (1990), *The Development of the Community's Relations with the Countries of Central and Eastern Europe*, SEC (90) 194.

Commission (1993a). *Towards Sustainability: A European Community Programme of Policy and Action in Relation to the Environment and Sustainable Development* (Luxembourg: Office for Official Publications of the European Communities).

Commission (1993b), *Growth, Competitiveness, Employment: The Challenges and Ways Forward into the 21st Century*, White Paper. Parts A and B, COM (93) 700 final/A and B.

Commission (1994), *European Social Policy: A Way Forward for the Union, A White Paper*.

Commission (1995), *Preparation of the Associated Countries of Central and Eastern Europe for Integration into the Internal Market of the Union*, White Paper, COM (95) 163 final.

Commission (1996), *Report on Directive 90/220/EEC on Genetically Modified Organisms*, IP/96/1148 (10 December 1996).

Commission (1997), Agenda 2000: For a Stronger and Wider Union, COM (1997) 2000, *Bulletin of the EU*, Supplement, 5/97.

Commission (1999–2007). *Sixteenth to Twenty-fourth Annual Report on Monitoring the Application of Community Law* (Brussels: Commission), accessible at: *http://ec.europa.eu/community_law/infringements/infringements_annual_report_en.htm*.

Commission (2000a), *Seventeenth Annual Report on Monitoring the Application of Community Law* (1999), COM (2000) 92 final.

Commission (2000b), *White Paper on Food Safety*, COM (1999) 719 final.

Commission (2000c), *Commission Communication on the Precautionary Principle*, COM (2000) 1 final.

Commission (2000d), *Social Policy Agenda*, COM (2000) 379 final.

Commission (2000e), *Reforming the Commission: White Paper*, Part 1, COM (2000) 200 final.

Commission (2001), *Improving and Simplifying the Regulatory Environment: Interim Report from the Commission to the Stockholm European Council*, COM (2001) 130 final.

Commission (2002a), *Second Biennial Report on the Application of the Principle of Mutual Recognition in the Single Market*, COM (2002) 419 final.

Commission (2002b), *The Internal Market: Ten Years without Frontiers*, available at: *http://ec.europa.eu/internal_market/10years/docs/workingdoc/workingdoc_en.pdf*.

Commission (2002c), *The State of the Internal Market for Services*, COM (2002) 441 final.

Commission (2002d) *Proposed Draft Directive on Security of Gas Supply*, COM (2002) 488 final.

Commission (2003a), *Commission Recommendation on the Broad Guidelines of the Economic Policies of the Member States and the Community [2003–2005]*, COM (2003) 170 final.

Commission (2003b), *Communication from the Commission to the Council, Strengthening the Social Dimension of the Lisbon Strategy: Streamlining Open Coordination in the Field of Social Protection [2003–2009]*, COM (2003) 261 final.

Commission (2003c), *Communication from the European Commission: Modernising Social Protection for More and Better Jobs—A Comprehensive Approach Contributing to Making Work Pay*, COM (2003) 842 final.

Commission (2003d), *Green Paper on Services of General Interest*, COM (2003) 270 final.

Commission (2003e), *Wider Europe—Neighbourhood: A New Framework for Relations with our Eastern and Southern Neighbours*, 11 March 2003, COM (2003) 104 final.

Commission (2003f), *Reviving the DDA Negotiation—The EU Perspective*, Communication, Brussels, 26 Nov.

Commission (2003g), *Financial Report 2002* (Luxembourg: Office for Official Publications of the European Communities).

Commission (2004a), *Third Report on Economic and Social Cohesion*, COM (2004) 107 final.

Commission (2004b), *Proposal for a Directive of the European Parliament and of the Council on Services in the Internal Market*, COM (2004) 2 final.

Commission (2004c), *White Paper on Services of General Interest*, COM (2004) 374 final.

Commission (2004d), *Proposal for a Council Framework Decision on Certain Procedural Rights in Criminal Proceedings throughout the European Union*, COM (2004) 328 final.

Commission (2005), *Cohesion Policy in Support of Growth and Jobs: Community Strategic Guidelines, 2007–2013*, COM (2005) 299 final.

Commission (2006a), *EU Economy Review* (Luxembourg: Office for Official Publications of the European Communities).

Commission (2006b), *An Energy Policy for Europe*, COM (2007) 1 final.

Commission (2006c), *23rd Annual Report from the Commission on Monitoring the Application of Community Law (2005)*, COM (2006) 416 final.

Commission (2006d), *Modernizing Labour Law to Meet the Challenges of the 21st Century*, Green Paper, COM (2006) 708 final.

Commission (2006e), *Infosheet on the Single Farm Payment: The Concept*, available at *http://ec.europa.eu/agriculture/capreform/infosheets/pay_en.pdf*.

Commission (2006f), *Enlargement Strategy and Main Challenges 2006–2007, ANNEX 1: Special Report on the EU's Capacity to Integrate New Members*, 8 Nov., COM (2006) 649 final.

Commission (2006g), *Global Europe: Competing in the World: A Contribution to the EU's Growth and Jobs Strategy*, COM (2006) 567 final, 4 Oct.

Commission (2006h), *Report from the Commission on the Working of Committees During 2005*, COM (2006) 446 final.

Commission (2007a), *A Single Market for 21st Century Europe*, COM (2007) 724 final, 20 Nov.

Commission (2007b), *Instruments for a Modernised Single Market Policy*, SEC (2007) 1518, 20 Nov.

Commission (2007c), *The Single Market: Review of Achievements*, SEC (2007) 1521, 20 Nov.

Commission (2007d), *Keeping up the Pace of Change: Strategic Report on the Renewed Lisbon Strategy for Growth and Jobs: Launching the New Cycle (2008–2010)*, Communication from the Commission to the Spring European Council, COM (2007) 803 final.

Commission (2007e), *Translating for a Multilingual Community*, DG Translation (Brussels).

Commission (2007f), 'Together for Health: A Strategic Approach for the EU 2008–2013', White Paper, COM (2007) 630 final, 23 Nov.

Commission (2007g), *Towards Common Principles of Flexicurity: More and Better Jobs through Flexibility and Security*, COM (2007) 359 final.

Commission (2007h), *Strategic Report on the Renewed Lisbon Strategy for Growth and Jobs: Launching the New Cycle 2008–2010*, COM (2007) 803 final.

Commission (2007i), *Report on the Implementation of the Hague Programme 2007*, COM (2008) 373 final.

Commission (2007j), *Green Paper on the Future Common European Asylum System of 2007*, COM (2007) 301 final.

Commission (2007k), *Proposal for a Directive of the European Parliament and of the Council Providing for Sanctions Against Employers of Illegally Staying Third-country Nationals*, COM (2007) 249 final.

Commission (2007l), *Fourth Report on Economic and Social Cohesion*, COM (2007) 273 final.

Commission (2007m), *Member States and Regions Delivering the Lisbon Strategy for Growth and Jobs through the EU Cohesion Policy, 2007–2013*, COM (2007) 798 final.

Commission (2007n), *A Single Market for Citizens: Interim Report to the 2007 Spring European Council*, COM (2007) 60 final.

Commission (2008a), *Second Strategic Review of Better Regulation in the European Union*, COM (2008) 32 final, 30 Jan.

Commission (2008b), *Internal Market Scoreboard*, 17.

Commission (2008c), *From Financial Crisis to Recovery: A European Framework for Action*, COM (2008) 706 final, 29 Oct.

Commission (2008d), *One Currency for One Europe: The Road to the Euro* (Luxembourg: Office for Official Publications of the European Communities).

Commission (2008e), *EMU@10: Successes and Challenges After 10 Years of Economic and Monetary Union* (Luxembourg: Office for Official Publications of the European Communities).

Commission (2008f), *Renewed Social Agenda: Opportunities, Access and Solidarity in 21st Century Europe*, COM (2008) 412 final.

Commission (2008g), *Proposal for a Directive of the European Parliament and the Council on the Application of Patients' Rights in Cross-Border Healthcare*, COM (2008) 414 final.

Commission (2008h), *Overview of the Implementation of Direct Payments under the CAP in Member States*, Version 1.1 Jan. (DG AGRI).

Commission (2008i), *European Union Public Finance* (Luxembourg: Office for Official Publications of the European Communities).

Commission (2008j), *Financial Report 2007* (Luxembourg: Office for Official Publications of the European Communities).

Commission (2008k), *Communication Concerning Measures to Safeguard Security of Natural Gas Supply*, COM (2008) 769 final.

Commission (2008l), *Second Strategic Energy Review: An EU Energy Security and Solidarity Action Plan*, COM (2008) 781 final.

Commission (2008m), *The Environment Directorate General's Legal Enforcement Activities in 2007*, available at: *http://ec.europa.eu/environment/legal/law/pdf/report_activities2007.pdf*.

Commission (2008n), *Implementing European Community Environmental Law*, COM (2008) 773/4.

Commission (2008o), *Report on Competition Policy 2007: Report and Commission Staff Working Paper*, Brussels.

Commission (2008p), *Growing Regions, Growing Europe: Fifth Progress Report on Economic and Social Cohesion*, COM (2008) 371 final.

Commission (2008q), *General Report on the Activities of the European Union 2007*.

Commission (2009a), *Internal Market Scoreboard*, 18.

Commission (2009b), *Financial Markets: Commission Adopts Measures to Strengthen Supervisory Committees and Standard-Setting Bodies for Accounting and Auditing*, IP/09/125, 26 Jan.

Commission (2009c), *Third Progress Report on the Strategy for Simplifying the Regulatory Environment, Commission Working Document*, COM (2009) 17/3.

Committee of Independent Experts (1999), *First Report on Allegations regarding Fraud, Mismanagement and Nepotism in the European Commission*, 15 March, available at: *http://www.europarl.eu.int/experts/*.

Conant, L. (2002), *Justice Contained: Law and Politics in the European Union* (Ithaca, NY: Cornell University Press).

Conant, L. (2007a), 'Review Article: The Politics of Legal Integration', *Journal of Common Market Studies*, 45/s1: 45–66.

Conant, L. (2007b), 'Judicial Politics', in K. E. Jørgensen, M. A. Pollack, and B. Rosamond (eds.), *The Handbook of European Union Politics* (London: Sage), 213–29.

Cooper, R. (2003), *The Breaking of Nations: Order and Chaos in the Twenty-First Century* (London: Atlantic Books).

Costello, C., and Davies, G. (2006), 'The Case Law of the Court of Justice in the Field of Sex Equality since 2000', *Common Market Law Review*, 43/6: 1567–616.

Council of the European Union (1988), *Presidency Conclusions*, European Council in Rhodes, 2–3 Dec., SN 4443/1/88.

Council of the European Union (1989), *Presidency Conclusions*, European Council in Strasbourg, 8–9 Dec., SN 441/2/89.

Council of the European Union (1994), *Presidency Conclusions*, European Council in Corfu, 24–25 June, SN 150/94.

Council of the European Union (1995), *Presidency Conclusions*, Madrid European Council, 15–16 Dec., SN 400/95.

Council of the European Union (1999*a*), *Presidency Conclusions*, European Council in Berlin, 24–25 Mar, SN 100/1/99 rev.

Council of the European Union (1999*b*), '2194th Council Meeting—Environment—Luxembourg, June 24–25, 1999', Press 203—Nr 9406/99.

Council of the European Union (1999*c*), *Presidency Conclusions*, Helsinki European Council 10–11 Dec., SN 300/1/99 available at: *http://www.europarl.europa.eu/summits/hel1_en.htm*.

Council of the European Union (2000), *Presidency Conclusions*, Santa Maria da Feira European Council, 19–20 June 2000, SN 200/00.

Council of the European Union (2001), *Presidency Conclusions*, Laeken European Council, 14–15 Dec. 2001; SN 300/1/01 REV 1.

Council of the European Union (2002), *Presidency Conclusions*, Copenhagen European Council, 12–13 Dec. 2002; SN 400/02.

Council of the European Union (2003*a*), *Council Regulation No. 1/2003 of 16 December 2002 on the Implementation of the Rules on Competition laid down in Articles 81 and 82 of the Treaty* (OJ L 1/1, 4.1.2003).

Council of the European Union (2003*b*), 'A Secure Europe in a Better World: European Security Strategy', *Presidency Conclusions*, Brussels, 12 Dec., available at: *http://www.consilium.europa.eu/uedocs/cmsUpload/78367.pdf*.

Council of the European Union (EU) (2004), 'Headline Goal 2010, approved by General Affairs and External Relations Council on 17 May 2004 and endorsed by the European Council of 17 and 18 June 2004', available at: *http://www.consilium.eu.int/uedocs/cmsUpload/2010%20Headline%20Goal.pdf*.

Council of the European Union (2008), *Presidency Conclusions*, Brussels European Council, 15 and 16 Oct., 14368/08.

Council of the European Union (2009), *Presidency Conclusions*, Brussels European Council, 19/20 March, 7880/1/09, REV1, CONCL1.

Court of Auditors (2008), *Annual Report on the Implementation of the Budget*, Official Journal of the European Union (2008/C 286/01), Chapter 6, section 27.

Cowles, M. G. (1994), 'The Politics of Big Business in the European Community: Setting the Agenda for a New Europe', Ph.D. dissertation, The American University, Washington, DC.

Cowles, M. G. (1997), 'Organizing Industrial Coalitions: A Challenge for the Future?', in H. Wallace and A. R. Young (eds.), *Participation and Policy-Making in the European Union* (Oxford: Clarendon), 116–40.

Cowles, M. G., Caporaso, J. A., and Risse, T. (2001) (eds.), *Transforming Europe: Europeanization and Domestic Change* (Ithaca, NY: Cornell University Press).

Craig, P., and de Búrca, G. (2008), *EU Law*, 4th edn. (Oxford: Oxford University Press).

Culpepper, P. D. (1993), 'Organisational Competition and the Neo-Corporatist Fallacy in French Agriculture', *West European Politics*, 16/3: 295–315.

Dahl, R. (1961), *Who Governs? Democracy and Power in an American City* (New Haven, CT: Yale University Press).

Daly, M. (2008), 'Whither EU Social Policy? An Account and Assessment of Developments in the Lisbon Social Inclusion Process', *Journal of Social Policy*, 37/1: 1–19.

Dashwood, A. (1977), 'Hastening Slowly: The Communities' Path Towards Harmonization', in H. Wallace, W. Wallace, and C. Webb (eds.), *Policy-Making in the European Communities* (Chichester: Wiley), 273–99.

Dashwood, A. (1983), 'Hastening Slowly: The Communities' Path towards Harmonization', in H. Wallace, W. Wallace, and C. Webb (eds.), *Policy-Making in the European Communities*, 2nd edn. (Chichester: Wiley), 177–208.

Daugbjerg, C. (1999), 'Reforming the CAP: Policy Networks and Broader Institutional Structures', *Journal of Common Market Studies*, 37/3: 407–28.

Daugbjerg, C., and Swinbank, A. (2009), *Ideas, Institutions and Trade: The WTO and the Curious Role of EU Farm Policy in Trade Liberalization* (Oxford: Oxford University Press).

Daviter, F. (2007), 'Policy Framing in the European Union', *Journal of European Public Policy*, 14/4: 654–66.

Deakin, S. (2007), 'Reflexive Governance and European Company Law', Working Paper No. 346, Centre for Business Research, University of Cambridge, available at: *http://www.cbr.cam.ac.uk/pdf/wp346.pdf*.

De Grauwe, P. (2006), 'What Have We Learnt about Monetary Integration since the Maastricht Treaty?', *Journal of Common Market Studies*, 44/4: 711–30.

De Grauwe, P. (2007), *The Economics of Monetary Union*, 7th edn. (Oxford: Oxford University Press).

Dehousse, R. (1998), *The European Court of Justice* (Basingstoke: Palgrave Macmillan).

Dehousse, R. (2008), 'The "Community Method": Chronicle of a Death Too Early Foretold', in B. Kohler-Koch and F. Larat (eds.), *Efficient and Democratic Governance in the European Union*, CONNEX Report, vol. ix (Mannheim: Connex), 79–107.

Dehousse, R., Deloche-Gaudez, F., and Duhamel, O. (2007), *Élargissement: Comment l'Europe s'adapte* (Paris: Les Presses Sciences Po).

De Kerchove, G., and Weyembergh, A. (2002) (eds.), *L'espace penal européen: enjeux et perspectives* (Brussels: Éditions de l'Université de Bruxelles).

De La Porte, C., and Nanz, P. (2004), 'OMC—A Deliberative-Democratic Mode of Governance? The Cases of Employment and Pensions', *Journal of European Public Policy*, 11/2: 267–88.

della Sala, V. (2004) 'Maastricht to Modernization: EMU and the Italian Social State', in A. Martin and G. Ross (eds.), *Euros and Europeans: Monetary Integration and the European Model of Society* (Cambridge: Cambridge University Press), 126–41.

Deroose, S., Hodson, D., and Kuhlmann, J. (2008), 'The Broad Economic Policy Guidelines: Before and After the Re-launch of the Lisbon Strategy', *Journal of Common Market Studies*, 46/4: 827–48.

Derthick, M., and Quirk, P. J. (1986), *The Politics of Deregulation* (Washington, DC: Brookings Institution).

Devuyst, Y. (1995), 'The EC and the Conclusion of the Uruguay Round', in C. Rhodes and S. Mazey (eds.), *The State of the European Union, vol. iii: Building a European Polity?* (Boulder, CO/Harlow: Lynne Rienner and Longman), 449–68.

Dinan, D. (2004), *Europe Recast: A History of European Union* (Basingstoke: Palgrave Macmillan).

Dølvik, J. E. (2006), 'Industrial Relations Responses to Migration and Posting of Workers after EU Enlargement: Nordic Trends and Differences', *Transfer: European Review of Labour and Research*, 12/2: 213–30.

Donahue, J. D., and Pollack, M. A. (2001), 'Centralization and Its Discontents: The Rhythms of Federalism in the United States and the European Union', in K. Nicolaïdis and R. Howse (eds.), *The Federal Vision: Legitimacy and Levels of Governance in the United States and the European Union* (Oxford: Oxford University Press), 73–117.

Dowding, K. (1995), 'Model or Metaphor? A Critical Review of the Policy Network Approach', *Political Studies*, 43/1: 136–58.

Downs, A. (1972), 'Up and Down with Ecology—The Issue-Attention Cycle', *Public Interest*, 28/3: 38–50.

Drahos, M. (2001), *Convergence of Competition Laws and Policies in the European Community* (Duventer: Kluwer).

Drezner, D. W. (2007), *All Politics is Global: Explaining International Regulatory Regimes* (Princeton, NJ: Princeton University Press).

Duina, F., and Raunio, T. (2007), 'The Open Method of Co-Ordination and National Parliaments: Further Marginalization or New Opportunities?', *Journal of European Public Policy*, 14/4: 489–506.

Dunleavy, P. (1997), 'Explaining Centralization of the European Union: A Public Choice Analysis', *Aussenwirtschaft*, 55/1–2: 183–212.

Dür, A., and Zimmermann, H. (2007) (eds.), 'The EU in International Trade Negotiations', *Journal of Common Market Studies*, 45/4 (special issue).

Dyson, K. (2000), *The Politics of the Euro-Zone: Stability or Breakdown?* (Oxford: Oxford University Press).

Dyson, K. (2006) (ed.), *Enlarging the Euro Area: External Empowerment and Domestic Transformation in East Central Europe* (Oxford: Oxford University Press).

Dyson, K., and Featherstone, K. (1999), *The Road to Maastricht: Negotiating Economic and Monetary Union* (Oxford: Oxford University Press).

Eberlein, B., and Grande, E. (2005), 'Beyond Delegation: Transnational Regulatory Regimes and the EU Regulatory State', *Journal of European Public Policy*, 12/1: 89–112.

ECB (European Central Bank) (2003), *Monthly Bulletin*, 05/03 (Frankfurt am Main: ECB).

ECB (European Central Bank) (2008a), *Monthly Bulletin (10th Anniversary of the ECB)*, 05/08 (Frankfurt am Main: ECB).

ECB (European Central Bank) (2008b), *The International Role of the Euro* (Frankfurt am Main: ECB).

Economist, various issues.

ECOTECH (2003), *Evaluation of the Added Value and Costs of the European Structural Funds in the UK, Final Report to Department of Trade and Industry (DTI) and Office of the Deputy Prime Minister (ODPM)* (London: DTI/ODPM).

EEA (European Environment Agency) (1999), *Environment in the European Union at the Turn of the Century*, Environmental Assessment Report No. 2 (Copenhagen: EEA), available on-line at: *http://reports.eea.eu.int*.

Eeckhout, P. (2004), *External Relations of the European Union: Legal and Constitutional Foundations* (Oxford: Oxford University Press).

Egeberg, M. (2008), 'European Government(s): Executive Politics in Transition?', *West European Politics*, 31/1–2: 235–57.

Eichener, V. (1997), 'Effective European Problem Solving: Lessons from the Regulation of Occupational Safety and Environmental Protection', *Journal of European Public Policy*, 4/4: 591–608.

Eichener, V. (2000), *Das Entscheidungssystem der Europäischen Union: institutionelle Analyse und demokratietheoretische Bewertung* (Opladen: Leske & Budrich).

Eichengreen, B. (1992), *Should the Maastricht Treaty be Saved?*, Princeton Studies in International Finance, No. 74 (Princeton, NJ: Princeton University Economics Department).

Eichengreen, B. (2007), *The European Economy Since 1945: Coordinated Capitalism and Beyond* (Princeton, NJ: Princeton University Press).

Eichenhofer, E. (2003), 'Unionsbürgerschaft—Sozialbürgerschaft?', *Zeitschrift für ausländisches und internationales Arbeits- und Sozialrecht*, 17/3–4: 404–17.

Eichenhofer, E. (2004), 'Diskriminierungsschutz und Privatautonomie', *Deutsches Verwaltungsblatt*, 119/17 (1 Sept.): 1078–86.

Eichenhofer, E. (2006), *Sozialrecht der Europäischen Union*, 3rd edn. (Berlin: Erich Schmidt).

Eichhorst, W. (1998), *European Social Policy between National and Supranational Regulation: Posted Workers in the Framework of Liberalized Services Provisions*, MPIfG Discussion Paper 98/6. (Cologne: Max Planck Institute for the Study of Societies).

Eichorst, W. (2000), *Europäische Sozialpolitik zwischen nationaler Autonomie und Marktfreiheit: die Entsendung von Arbeitnehmern in der EU* (Frankfurt am Main: Campus).

Eliasoph, I. H. (2007–8), 'A "Switch in Time" for the European Community? Lochner Discourse and the Recalibration of Economic and Social Rights in Europe', *Columbia Journal of European Law*, 14/3: 467–508.

Elsig, M. (2002), *The EU's Common Commercial Policy: Institutions, Interests and Ideas* (Farnham: Ashgate).

Elsig, M. (2008), 'EU Trade Policy After Enlargement: Does the Expanded Trade Power Have New Clothes?', paper for the APSA Annual Conference, Boston, 28-31 Aug.

Elster, J. (1998) (ed.), *Deliberative Democracy* (Cambridge: Cambridge University Press).

Emmert, F. (1996), *Europarecht* (Munich: C. H. Beck).

Epiney, A. (2007), 'The Scope of Article 12EC: Some Remarks on the Influence of European Citizenship', *European Law Journal*, 13/5: 611–22.

Epstein, D., and O'Halloran, S. (1999), *Delegating Powers: A Transaction Cost Politics Approach to Policy Making under Separate Powers* (Cambridge: Cambridge University Press).

ERGEG (2007), 'EU Energy Regulators Back the European Commission's 3rd Energy Package of Measures, available at: *http://www.energy-regulators.eu/portal/page/portal/ EER_HOME/EER_PUBLICATIONS/PRESS_RELEASES/2007/PR-07-09_ERGEG_ Support_3rdPackage 19-09-2007Final.doc.*

Eriksen, E. O., and Fossum, J. E. (2000), 'Post-national Integration', in E. O. Eriksen and J. E. Fossum (eds.), *Democracy in the European Union* (London: Routledge), 1–28.

Eriksen, E. O., and Fossum, J. E. (2003), 'Closing the Legitimacy Gap?', available at *http:// www.arena.uio.no/ecsa/papers/FossumEriksen.pdf.*

Ette, A., and Faist, T. (2007) (eds.), *The Europeanization of National Policies and Politics of Immigration* (Basingstoke: Palgrave Macmillan).

EUobserver.com, various issues.

EurActiv (2008), 'Enlargement Split in EU Climate Feud?', 26 November 2008, available at: *http://www.euractiv.com/en/climate-change/enlargement-split-eu-climate-feud/article-177513.*

Eureport, various issues.

Eureport social, various issues.

Eurobarometer (2006*a*), 'Internal Market: Opinion and Experiences of Businesses in EU-15', *Flash Eurobarometer* 180, June.

Eurobarometer (2006*b*), 'Internal Market: Opinion and Experiences of Businesses in the 10 New Member States', *Flash Eurobarometer* 190, Sept.

Eurobarometer (2008) 'The Role of the EU in Justice, Freedom and Security Policy Areas', *Special Eurobarometer* 290, Brussels.

European Communities (1969), 'Communiqué of the Meeting of Heads of State or Government of the Member States at The Hague, 1–2 December 1969', available at: *http://www.ena.lu/.*

European Communities (2007), *Handbook on Integration for Policy-Makers and Practitioners*, 2nd edn. (Brussels: European Communities).

European G8 members (2008), *Joint Statement on the International Financial Situation*, Press Release, 4 Oct.

European Parliament (1964), *Towards Political Union: A Selection of Documents*, General Directorate of Parliamentary Documentation and Information, January 1964, available at: *http://aei.pitt.edu/944/01/towards_political_union_1.pdf.*

European Parliament (1984), *Draft Treaty Establishing the European Union* (Luxembourg: European Parliament).

European Parliament (1996), *Working Document on Implementation of Community Environmental Law*, Committee on the Environment, Public Health and Consumer Protection, PE 219. 240.

European Parliament (2003), *Report on the Proposal for a Directive to Safeguard Security of Natural Gas Supply*, Ref no. A5-0295/2003.

European Parliament (2007*a*), *Report on the Future of the European Union's Own Resources*, 2006/2205(INI), Committee on Budgets.

European Parliament (2007*b*), *Report on a Common Foreign Energy Policy*, Ref no. A6-0312/2007.

European Parliament (2008*a*), *Draft report on a Regulation Establishing an Agency for the Cooperation of Energy Regulators*, 11 Feb.

European Parliament (2008*b*), *Interim Report on the Scientific Facts of Climate Change: Findings and Recommendations for Decision-making*, A6-0136/2008.

European Report, various issues.

Europolitics (2007), 'Treaty of Lisbon: Here is What Changes!', special edition, 7 November, No. 3407.

European Voice, various issues.

Evans, P. B. (1993), 'Building an Integrative Approach to International and Domestic Politics: Reflections and Projections', in P. B. Evans, H. K. Jacobson, and R. D. Putnam (eds.), *Double-Edged Diplomacy: International Bargaining and Domestic Politics* (Berkeley, CA: University of California Press), 397–430.

Evenett, S., and Meier, M. (2007), 'An Interim Assessment of US Trade Policy of "Competitive Liberalization"', University of St Gallen, Economic Discussion Paper No. 18, February.

Falkner, G. (1998), *EU Social Policy in the 1990s: Towards a Corporatist Policy Community* (London: Routledge).

Falkner, G., and Treib, O. (2008), 'Three Worlds of Compliance or Four? The EU-15 Compared to New Member States', *Journal of Common Market Studies*, 46/2: 293–313.

Falkner, G., Hartlapp, M., and Treib, O. (2007), 'Worlds of Compliance: Why Leading Approaches to European Union Implementation Are Only "Sometimes-True Theories"', *European Journal of Political Research*, 46/3, 395–416.

Falkner, G., Treib, O., Hartlapp, M., and Leiber, S. (2005), *Complying with Europe: EU Harmonisation and Soft Law in the Member States* (Cambridge: Cambridge University Press).

Falkner, G., Treib, O., and Holzleithner, E., in cooperation with Causse, E., Furtlehner, P., Schulze, M., and Wiedermann, C. (2008), *Compliance in the Enlarged European Union: Living Rights or Dead Letters?* (Aldershot: Ashgate).

FCO (Foreign and Commonwealth Office) (2008), *Consolidated Text of the EU Treaties as Amended by the Treaty of Lisbon*, Command 7310, January (London: TSO).

Feldstein, M. (2005), 'The Euro and the Stability Pact', NBER Working Paper, No. W11249.

Felsenthal, D. S., and Machover, M. (1997), 'The Weighted Voting Rule in the Council of Ministers, 1958–95: Intentions and Outcomes', *Electoral Studies*, 16/1, 34–47.

Felsenthal, D. S., and Machover, M. (2004), 'A Priori Voting Power: What is it All About?' *Political Studies Review*, 2/1: 1–24.

Fennell, R. (1997), *The Common Agricultural Policy: Continuity and Change* (Oxford: Clarendon Press).

Ferrera, M., and Gualmini, E. (2004), *Rescued by Europe? Social and Labour Market Reforms in Italy from Maastricht to Berlusconi* (Amsterdam: Amsterdam University Press).

Financial Times, various issues.

Fisher, R., and Ury, W. (1982), *Getting to Yes: How to Reach Agreement without Giving In* (London: Hutchinson).

Flora, P. (1999) (ed.), *State Formation, Nation-Building and Mass Politics in Europe: The Theory of Stein Rokkan* (Oxford: Oxford University Press).

Foden, D., and Magnusson, L. (2003) (eds.), *Five Years' Experience of the Luxembourg Employment Strategy* (Brussels: European Trade Union Institute).

Forwood, N. (2008), 'The Court of First Instance, Its Development, and Future Role in the Legal Architecture of the European Union', in A. Arnull, P. Eeckhout, and T. Tridimas (eds.), *Continuity and Change in EU Law: Essays in Honour of Sir Francis Jacobs* (Oxford: Oxford University Press), 34–47.

Fouilleux, E. (2003), *La Politique Agricole Commune et ses Réformes* (Paris: L'Harmattan).

Franchino, F. (2004), 'Delegating Powers in the European Community', *British Journal of Political Science*, 34/2: 449–76.

Franchino, F. (2007), *The Powers of the Union: Delegation in the EU* (Cambridge: Cambridge University Press).

Franklin, M., Marsh, M., and McLaren, L. (1994), 'Uncorking the Bottle: Popular Opposition to European Unification in the Wake of Maastricht', *Journal of Common Market Studies*, 32/4: 455–73.

Franzius, C. (2003), 'Der "Gewährleistungsstaat": ein neues Leitbild für den sich wandelnden Staat', *Der Staat*, 42/4: 493–517.

Freyer, T. (2006), *Antitrust and Global Capitalism, 1930–2004* (Cambridge: Cambridge University Press).

Friedrich, A., Tappe, M., and Wurzel, R. (2002), 'A New Approach to EU Environmental Policy-making? The Auto-Oil I Programme', *Journal of European Public Policy*, 7/4: 593–612.

Friedrich, C. J. (1969), *Europe: An Emergent Nation* (New York, NY: Harper & Row).

Friis, L. (1998), 'The End of the Beginning of Eastern Enlargement: Luxembourg Summit and Agenda-Setting', *European Integration online Papers*, 2/7; available at: *http://eiop.or.at/eiop*.

Friis, L., and Murphy, A. (2000), 'Turbo-Charged Negotiations: The EU and the Stability Pact for South Eastern Europe', *Journal of European Public Policy*, 7/5: 767–86.

Fuchs, M. (2003), 'Koordinierung oder Harmonisierung des europäischen Sozialrechts?', *Zeitschrift für ausländisches und internationales Arbeits- und Sozialrecht*, 17/3–4: 379–90.

Fuchs, M. (2005) (ed.), *Nomos Kommentar zum europäischen Sozialrecht*, 4th edn. (Baden-Baden: Nomos).

Fukuda-Parr, S. (2007) (ed.), *The Gene Revolution: GM Crops and Unequal Development* (London: Earthscan Publications).

Gabel, M., Hix, S., and Schneider, G. (2002), 'Who is Afraid of Cumulative Research? The Scarcity of EU Decision-Making Data and What Can Be Done about This', *European Union Politics*, 3/4: 481–500.

Garrett, G. (1992), 'International Cooperation and Institutional Choice: The European Community's Internal Market', *International Organization*, 46/2: 533–60.

Garrett, G., and Tsebelis, G. (1996), 'An Institutional Critique of Intergovernmentalism', *International Organization*, 50/2: 269–99.

Garrett, G., and Weingast, B. (1993), 'Ideas, Interests, and Institutions: Constructing the European Community's Internal Market', in J. Goldstein and R. O. Keohane (eds.), *Ideas and Foreign Policy* (Ithaca, NY: Cornell University Press), 173–206.

Garzon, I. (2006), *Reforming the Common Agricultural Policy: History of a Paradigm Change* (Basingstoke: Palgrave Macmillan).

Gaskell, G., Allum, N., and Stares, S. (2003), *Eurobarometer 58.0: A Report to the EC Directorate General for Research from the project 'Life Sciences in European Society'*, QLG7-CT-1999-00286.

Geddes, A. (2008), *Immigration and European Integration: Towards Fortress Europe?*, 2nd edn. (Manchester: Manchester University Press).

Genieys, W., Guglielmi, M., and Le Pape, Y. (2000), 'Les traductions régionales du partenariat: la mise en œuvre des programmes 5 B', in D. Perraud (ed.), *L'Europe Verte: les acteurs régionaux des politiques communautaires agricoles et rurales* (Paris: INRA), 17–32.

George, S. (1991), *Politics in the European Union* (Oxford: Oxford University Press).

Gheciu, A. (2005), 'Security Institutions as Agents of Socialization? NATO and the "New Europe"', *International Organization*, 59/4: 973–1012.

Giegerich, B. (2008), *European Military Crisis Management: Connecting Ambition and Reality*, Adelphi Paper No. 397 (Abingdon: Routledge for the International Institute for Strategic Studies).

Giegerich, B., and Wallace, W. (2004), 'Not Such a Soft Power: The External Deployment of European Forces', *Survival*, 46/2: 63–82.

Giesen, R. (2005), 'Nationales Sozialrecht und europäisches Wettbewerbsrecht—das Wettbewerbsziel in der Rationalitätenfalle', in U. Becker and W. Schön (eds.), *Steuer- und Sozialstaat im europäischen Systemwettbewerb* (Tübingen: Mohr-Siebeck), 141–70.

Glière, C. (2008), *EU Security and Defence: Core Documents 2007, Vol. VIII*, Chaillot Paper No. 112 (Paris: EU Institute for Security Studies).

Global Competition Review (2007), 'Rating Enforcement: The Annual Ranking of the World's Top Antitrust Authorities', June.

Gnesotto, N. (1990), 'Défence européenne: pourquoi pas les douze?', *Politique Étrangère*, 55/4: 881–3.

Goebel, R. (2006), 'Court of Justice Oversight Over the European Central Bank: Delimiting the ECB's Constitutional Autonomy and Independence in the Olaf Judgment', *Fordham International Law Journal*, 29/4: 600–54.

Goetschy, J. (2003), 'The European Employment Strategy, Multi-level Governance and Policy Coordination: Past, Present and Future', in J. Zeitlin and D. Trubek (eds.) *Governing Work and Welfare in a New Economy: European and American Experiments* (Oxford: Oxford University Press), 61–88.

Goetz, K. H. (2008), 'Governance as a Path to Government', *West European Politics*, 31/1–2: 258–79.

Goldstein, J., and Keohane, R. O. (1993), 'Ideas and Foreign Policy: An Analytical Framework', in J. Goldstein and R. O. Keohane (eds.), *Ideas and Foreign Policy: Beliefs, Institutions and Political Change* (Ithaca, NY: Cornell University Press), 11–26.

Goodin, R. E., Rein, M., and Moran, M. (2006), 'The Public and its Policies', in M. Moran et al. (eds.), *The Oxford Handbook of Public Policy* (Oxford: Oxford University Press), 3–35.

Gordon, C. (2008), 'The Stabilisation and Association Process in the Western Balkans: An Effective Instrument of Post-Conflict Management?', paper presented at the workshop 'The Role of the EU in Conflict Management', London School of Economics and Political Science, 4 Oct.

Gowan, R. (2007) *EUFOR RD Congo, UNIFIL and Future European Support to the UN*, SDA Discussion Paper (Brussels: Security and Defence Agenda).

Goyder, D. (2003), *EC Competition Law*, 4th edn. (Oxford: Oxford University Press).

Grabbe, H. (2006), *The EU's Transformative Power: Europeanization through Conditionality in Central and Eastern Europe* (Basingstoke: Palgrave Macmillan).

Grant, W. (1997), *The Common Agricultural Policy* (Basingstoke: Palgrave Macmillan).

Grant, W. (2005), 'An Insider Group under Pressure: The NFU in Britain', in D. Halpin (ed.), *Surviving Global Change?* (Aldershot: Ashgate), 31–50.

Grant, W., Matthews, D., and Newell, P. (2000), *The Effectiveness of European Union Environmental Policy* (Basingstoke: Palgrave Macmillan).

Graser, A. (2004), 'Sozialrecht ohne Staat? Politik und Recht unter Bedingungen der Globalisierung und Dezentralisierung', in A. Windhoff-Héritier, M. Stolleis, and F. W. Scharpf (eds.), *European and International Regulation after the Nation State* (Baden-Baden: Nomos), 163–84.

Greenwood, J., and Young, A. R. (2005), 'EU Interest Representation or US-Style Lobbying?', in N. Jabko and C. Parsons (eds.), *The State of the European Union*, vol. vii: *With US or Against US? European Trends in American Perspective* (Oxford: Oxford University Press), 275–95.

Greer, A. (2005), *Agricultural Policy in Europe* (Manchester: Manchester University Press).

Greven, M. T. (2000), 'Can the European Union Finally Become a Democracy?', in M. T. Greven and L. Pauly (eds.), *Democracy Beyond the State? The European Dilemma and the Emerging World Order* (Lanham, MD: Rowman & Littlefield), 35–61.

Gros, D. (2003), 'Reforming the Composition of the ECB Governing Council in View of Enlargement: An Opportunity Missed', CEPS Policy Brief No. 32 (Brussels: Centre for European Policy Studies).

Gros, D. (2008), 'How to Achieve a Better Budget for the European Union?', *CEPS Working Document* No. 289 (Brussels: Centre for European Policy Studies).

Grosser, A. (1980), *The Western Alliance: European–American Relations since 1945* (London: Macmillan).

Grossman, G. M., and Helpman, E. (2001), *Special Interest Politics* (Cambridge, MA: MIT Press).

Gualina, E. (2003), 'Challenges to Multi-level Governance: Contradictions and Conflicts in the Europeanization of Italian Regional Policy', *Journal of European Public Policy*, 10/4: 618–36.

Guersent, O. (2003), 'The Fight Against Secret Horizontal Agreement in the EC Competition Policy', paper presented to the Fordham Corporate Law Institute.

Guillén, A. M., and Palier, B. (2004) (eds.), 'EU Enlargement and Social Policy', *Journal of European Public Policy*, 14/3: 203–349 (special issue).

Haas, E. B. (1961), 'International Integration: The European and Universal Process', *International Organization*, 15/3 : 366–92.

Haas, E. B. (1975), *The Obsolescence of European Integration Theory* (Berkeley, CA: University of California Press).

Haas, E. B. (2004) [1958], *The Uniting of Europe* (Stanford, CA: Stanford University Press; reprinted in 2004 by Notre Dame University Press, South Bend, IN.

Haas, P. M. (1992), 'Introduction: Epistemic Communities and International Policy Coordination', *International Organization*, 46/1, 1–35.

Habermas, J. (1985), *The Theory of Communicative Action*, vol. ii (Boston, MA: Beacon Press).

Habermas, J. (1998), *Between Facts and Norms: Contributions to a Discourse Theory of Law and Democracy* (Cambridge, MA: The MIT Press).

Häge, F. (2008), 'Who Decides in the Council of the European Union?', *Journal of Common Market Studies*, 46/3: 533–58.

Hagen, K. P. (1998), 'Towards a Europeanisation of Social Policies? A Scandinavian Perspective', in MIRE, *Comparing Social Welfare Systems in Nordic Countries and France* (Paris: MIRE), 405–22.

Hagen, K. P., Norrman, E., and Sørensen, P. B. (1998), 'Financing the Nordic Welfare States in an Integrating Europe', in P. B. Sørensen (ed.), *Tax Policy in the Nordic Countries* (Basingstoke: Palgrave Macmillan), 138–203.

Hague, R., and Harrop, M. (2007), *Comparative Government and Politics: An Introduction*, 7th edn. (Basingstoke: Palgrave Macmillan).

Haigh, N. (2004) (ed.), *Manual of Environmental Policy: The EU and Britain*, Institute of European Environmental Policy (IEEP) (Leeds: Maney Publishing).

Hailbronner, K. (2004*a*), 'Die Unionsbürgerschaft und das Ende rationaler Jurisprudenz', *Neue Juristische Wochenschrift*, 57/31: 2185–9.

Hailbronner, K. (2004*b*), 'Diskriminierungsverbot, Unionsbürgerschaft und gleicher Zugang zu Sozialleistungen', *Zeitschrift für ausländisches öffentliches Recht und Völkerrecht*, 64/3: 603–19.

Hall, P. A. (1986), *Governing the Economy: The Politics of State Intervention in Britain and France* (Oxford: Oxford University Press).

Hall, P. A. (1999), 'The Political Economy of Europe in an Era of Interdependence', in H. Kitschelt, P. Lange, G. Marks, and J. Stephens (eds.), *Continuity and Change in Contemporary Capitalism* (Cambridge: Cambridge University Press), 135–63.

Hall, P. A., and Taylor, R. C. R. (1996), 'Political Science and the Three New Institutionalisms', *Political Studies*, 44/5: 936–57.

Hall, P. A., and Thelen, K. (2009), 'Institutional Change in Varieties of Capitalism', *Socio-Economic Review*, 7/1: 7–34.

Halliday, F. (2001), 'The Romance of Non-State Actors', in D. Josselin and W. Wallace (eds.), *Non-State Actors in World Politics* (Basingstoke: Palgrave Macmillan), 21–37.

Hancher, L., and Moran, M. (1989), 'Introduction: Regulation and Deregulation', *European Journal of Political Research*, 17/2: 129–36.

Hanson, B. T. (1998), 'What Happened to Fortress Europe? External Trade Policy Liberalization in the European Union', *International Organization*, 52/1: 55–85.

Hantrais, L. (2007), *Social Policy in the European Union*, 3rd edn. (Basingstoke: Palgrave Macmillan).

Harding, C., and Joshua, J. (2003), *Regulating Cartels in Europe* (Oxford: Oxford University Press).

Hartlapp, M. (2007), 'On Enforcement, Management and Persuasion: Different Logics of Implementation Policy in the EU and the ILO', *Journal of Common Market Studies*, 45/3: 653–74.

Hartlapp, M., and Falkner, G. (2008),. 'Problems of Operationalization and Data in EU Compliance Research', WZB Discussion Paper, Social Science Research Centre Berlin, ISSN Nr. 1011-9523, March.

Hawkins, D. (2004), 'Explaining Costly International Institutions: Persuasion and Enforceable Human Rights Norms', *International Studies Quarterly*, 48/4: 779–804.

Hay, C. (2007), 'What Doesn't Kill You Can Only Make You Stronger: The Doha Development Round, the Services Directive and the EU's Conception of Competitiveness', *Journal of Common Market Studies*, 45/s1: 25–43.

Hayes-Renshaw, F., and Wallace, H. (2006), *The Council of Ministers*, 2nd edn. (Basingstoke: Palgrave Macmillan).

Hayes-Renshaw, F., van Aken, W., and Wallace, H. (2006), 'When and Why the EU Council of Ministers Votes Explicitly', *Journal of Common Market Studies*, 44/1: 161–94.

Heidenheimer, A. J. (1985), 'Comparative Public Policy at the Crossroads', *Journal of Public Policy*, 5/4: 441–65.

Heidenreich, M. (2003), 'Regional Inequalities in the Enlarged Europe', *Journal of European Social Policy*, 13/4: 313–33.

Heidenreich, M., and Bischoff, G. (2008), 'The Open Method of Coordination: A Way to the Europeanization of Social and Employment Policies?', *Journal of Common Market Studies*, 46/3: 497–532.

Heidenreich, M., and Zeitlin, J. (2009) (eds.), *Changing European Employment and Welfare Regimes: The Influence of the Open Method of Coordination on National Reforms* (London: Routledge).

Helm, D. (2007), 'European Energy Policy: Securing Supplies and Meeting the Challenge of Climate Change', in D. Helm (ed.), *The New Energy Paradigm* (Oxford: Oxford University Press), 440–51.

Hemerijck, A., Keune, M., and Rhodes, M. (2006), 'European Welfare States: Diversity, Challenges and Reforms', in E. Jones, P. Heywood, M. Rhodes, and U. Sedelmeier (eds.), *Development in European Politics* (Basingstoke: Palgrave Macmillan), 259–79.

Hendrickx, F. (2008), 'The Services Directive and the Alleged Issue of Social Dumping', in J. W. van de Gronden (ed.), *The EU and WTO Law on Services: Limits to the Realisation of General Interest Policies Within the Services Markets?* (Austin: Wolters Kluwer), 97–118.

Héritier, A. (2002), 'New Modes of Governance in Europe: Policy-making without Legislating?', in A. Héritier (ed.), *The Provision of Common Goods: Governance Across Multiple Arenas* (Boulder, CO: Rowman & Littlefield), 185–206.

Héritier, A., Kerwer, D., Knill, C., Lehmkuhl, D., Teutsch, M., and Douillet, A.-C. (2001), *Differential Europe: The European Union Impact on National Policymaking* (Lanham, MD: Rowman & Littlefield).

Hey, C., Jacob K., and Volkery, A. (2008), 'REACH als Beispiel für hybride Formen von Steuerung und Governance', in G. Folke Schuppert and M. Zürn (eds.), 'Governance in einer sich wandelnden Welt', *Politische Vierteljahresschrift*, Sonderheft 41, 430–51.

Heydon, K., and Woolcock, S. (2009), *The Rise of Bilateralism: Comparing American, European and Asian Approaches to Preferential Trade Agreements* (Tokyo/New York: United Nations University Press).

Hibbs, D. A., and Madsen, H. J. (1981), 'Public Reactions in the Growth of Taxation and Government Expenditure', *World Politics*, 33/3: 413–35.

Hildebrand, P. M. (1993), 'The European Community's Environmental Policy, 1957 to 1992: From Incidental Measures to an International Regime?', in D. Judge (ed.), *A Green Dimension for the European Community: Political Issues and Processes* (London: Frank Cass), 13–44.

Hill, C. (2003), *The Changing Politics of Foreign Policy* (Basingstoke: Palgrave Macmillan).

Hill, C., and Smith, M. (2005) (eds.), *International Relations and the European Union* (Oxford: Oxford University Press).

Hix, S. (1994), 'The Study of the European Community: The Challenge to Comparative Politics', *West European Politics*, 17/1: 1–30.

Hix, S. (1998), 'The Study of the European Union II: The "New Governance" Agenda and its Rival', *Journal of European Public Policy*, 5/1: 38–65.

Hix, S. (1999), *The Political System of the European Union* (Basingstoke: Palgrave Macmillan).

Hix, S. (2001), 'Legislative Behaviour and Party Competition in European Parliament: An Application of Nominate to the EU', *Journal of Common Market Studies*, 39/4: 663–88.

Hix, S. (2005), *The Political System of the European Union*, 2nd edn. (Basingstoke: Palgrave Macmillan).

Hix, S. (2008a), 'The EU as a Political System', in D. Caramani (ed.), *Comparative Politics* (Oxford: Oxford University Press), 573–601.

Hix, S. (2008b), *What's Wrong with the European Union and How to Fix It* (Cambridge: Polity).

Hix, S., and Noury, A. G. (2009), 'After Enlargement: Voting Patterns in the Sixth European Parliament', *Legislative Studies Quarterly*, 34/2: 159–74.

Hix, S., Noury, A., and Roland, G. (2007), *Democratic Politics in the European Parliament* (Cambridge: Cambridge University Press).

HM Treasury (2003), *UK Membership of the Single Currency: An Assessment of the Five Economic Tests* (London: HM Treasury).

Hocking, B. (2004), 'Diplomacy', in W. Carlsnaes, H. Sjursen, and B. White (eds.), *Contemporary European Foreign Policy* (London: Sage), 91–109.

Hodson, D. (2009), 'EMU and Political Union: What, If Anything, Have We Learned From the Euro's First Decade?', *Journal of European Public Policy*, 16/4: 508–26.

Hodson, D., and Maher, I. (2001), 'The Open Method of Coordination as a New Mode of Governance: The Case of Soft Economic Policy Co-ordination', *Journal of Common Market Studies*, 39/4: 719–46.

Hodson, D., and Maher, I. (2004), 'Soft Sanctions and the Reform of the Stability and Growth Pact', *Journal of European Public Policy*, 11/5: 798–813.

Hodson, D., and Quaglia, L. (2009) (eds.) 'European Perspectives on the Global Financial Crisis', *Journal of Common Market Studies* 47/4: 939–1128 (special issue).

Hoffmann, S. (1966), 'Obstinate or Obsolete? The Fate of the Nation-State and the Case of Western Europe', *Daedalus*, 95/3: 862–915.

Holmes, P., and McGowan, F. (1997), 'The Changing Dynamics of EU–Industry Relations: Lessons from the Liberalization of the European Car and Airline Markets', in H. Wallace and A. R. Young (eds.), *Participation and Policy-Making in the European Union* (Oxford: Clarendon Press), 159–84.

Holzinger, K. (1994), *Politik des kleinsten gemeinsamen Nenners? Umweltpolitische Entscheidungsprozesse in der EG am Beispiel des Katalysatorautos* (Berlin: Edition Sigma).

Holzinger, K., Knill, C., and Lenschow, A. (2008), 'Governance in EU Environmental Policy', in I. Tömmel and A. Verdun (eds.), *Innovative Governance in the European Union: The Politics of Multilevel Policymaking* (Boulder, CO: Lynne Rienner), 45–62.

Hooghe, L. (1996) (ed.), *Cohesion Policy and European Integration: Building Multi-level Governance* (Oxford: Oxford University Press).

Hooghe, L. (2002), *The European Commission and the Integration of Europe* (Cambridge: Cambridge University Press).

Hooghe, L. (2005), 'Several Roads Lead to International Norms, but Few Via International Socialization: A Case Study of the European Commission', *International Organization* 59/4: 861–98.

Hooghe, L., and Keating, M. (1994), 'The Politics of European Union Regional Policy', *Journal of European Public Policy*, 1/3: 367–93.

Hooghe, L., and Marks, G. (2001), *Multi-Level Governance and European Integration* (Lanham, MD: Rowman & Littlefield).

Hoskyns, C. (1996), *Integrating Gender: Women, Law and Politics in the European Union* (London: Verso).

Hosli, M. O. (1994), *Coalitions and Power: Effects on Qualified Majority Voting in the European Union's Council of Ministers* (Maastricht: European Institute of Public Administration).

House of Commons (2004), *The EU's Financial Perspective for 2007–13 and Reform of the Structural and Cohesion Funds*, European Scrutiny Committee, Fifteenth Report of Session 2003–04, HC 42-xv (London: TSO).

House of Lords (2000), *Report on EU Proposals to Combat Discrimination*, European Union Committee, 9th Report, HL Paper 68 (London: TSO).

House of Lords (2004), *Equality in Access to Goods and Services Report*, Sub-Committee G (Social and Consumer Affairs), HL Paper 165–I (London: TSO).

House of Lords (2008), *The Future of EU Regional Policy*, European Union Committee, 19th Report, HL paper 141 (London: TSO).

Howarth, D. (2007a), 'Internal Policies: Reinforcing the New Lisbon Message of Competitiveness and Innovation', *Journal of Common Market Studies*, 45/s1: 89–106.

Howarth, D. (2007b), 'Making and Breaking the Rules: French Policy on EU Economic Governance', *Journal of European Public Policy*, 14/7: 1–18.

Howorth, J. (2007), *Security and Defence Policy in the European Union* (Basingstoke: Palgrave Macmillan).

Huber, J. D., and Shipan, C. R. (2002), *Deliberate Discretion? The Institutional Foundations of Bureaucratic Autonomy* (Cambridge: Cambridge University Press).

Hughes, J., Sasse, G., and Gordon, C. (2004*a*), 'Conditionality and Compliance in the EU's Eastern Enlargement: Regional Policy and the Reform of Sub-National Government', *Journal of Common Market Studies*, 42/3: 523–51.

Hughes, J., Sasse, G., and Gordon, C. (2004*b*), *Europeanization and Regionalization in the EU's Enlargement to Central and Eastern Europe: The Myth of Conditionality* (Basingstoke: Palgrave Macmillan).

Hurrell, A., and Menon, A. (1996), 'Politics Like Any Other? Comparative Politics, International Relations and the Study of the EU', *West European Politics*, 19/2: 386–402.

Hurrelmann, A., Leibfried, S., Martens, K., and Mayer, P. (2008) (eds.), *Transforming the Golden Age Nation State* (Basingstoke: Palgrave Macmillan).

Husmann, M. (1998), 'Koordinierung der Leistungen bei Arbeitslosigkeit durch EG-Recht', *Die Sozialgerichtsbarkeit*, 45/6: 245–52 (pt. 1); 7: 291–8 (pt. 2).

Husmann, M. (2005), 'Die EG-Gleichbehandlungs-Richtlinien 2000/2002 und ihre Umsetzung in das deutsche, englische und französische Recht', *Zeitschrift für europäisches Sozial- und Arbeitsrecht* (ZESAR), 4/3: 107–14 (pt. I); 4/4: 167–75 (pt. II).

Ieraci, G. (1998), 'European Integration and the Relationship between State and Regions in Italy: The Interplay between National and Common Agricultural Policies', *Regional and Federal Studies*, 8/2: 21–33.

Ilzkovitz, F., Dierx, A., Kovacs, V., and Sousa, N. (2007), 'Steps Towards a Deeper Economic Integration: The Internal Market in the 21st Century', *European Economy, Economic Papers 271* (Brussels: European Commission).

IISS (International Institute for Strategic Studies) (2008), *European Military Capabilities* (London: International Institute for Strategic Studies).

Inside US Trade, various issues.

Institute for Security Studies (2004), *EU Security and Defence: Core Documents 2004*, Chaillot Paper No. 75 (Paris: EU Institute for Security Studies).

International Herald Tribune, various issues.

International Monetary Fund (2008), *Global Financial Stability Report* (Washington, DC: International Monetary Fund).

Iversen, T., and Soskice, D. (2006), 'New Macroeconomics and Political Science', *Annual Review of Political Science*, 9: 425–53.

Jabko, N. (2006), *Playing the Market: A Political Strategy for Uniting Europe, 1985–2005* (Ithaca, NY: Cornell University Press).

Jachtenfuchs, M. (1995), 'Theoretical Perspectives on European Governance', *European Law Journal*, 1/2: 115–33.

Jachtenfuchs, M. (2001), 'The Governance Approach to European Integration', *Journal of Common Market Studies*, 39/2: 245–64.

Jachtenfuchs, M. (2007), 'The European Union as a Polity (II)', in K. E. Jørgensen, M. A. Pollack, and B. Rosamond (eds.), *The Handbook of European Union Politics* (London: Sage), 159–73.

Jachtenfuchs, M., and Kohler-Koch, B. (2004), 'Governance and Institutional Development', in A. Wiener, and T. Diez (eds.), *European Integration Theory*, 1st edn. (Oxford: Oxford University Press), 97–115.

Jacobs, F., Corbett, R., and Shackleton, M. (2007), *The European Parliament*, 7th edn. (London: John Harper).

Jacobsson, K. (2004), 'The Methodology of the European Employment Strategy: Achievement and Problems', mimeo (SCORE, Stockholm University).

Jacobsson, K., and Vifell, Å. (2003), 'Integration by Deliberation: On the Role of Committees in the Open Method of Coordination', in E.O. Eriksen, C. Joerges, and J. Neyer (eds.), *European Governance, Deliberation and the Quest for Democratisation*, Arena Report 2/03 (Oslo/Florence: ARENA/EUI), 417–58.

Jacobsson, K., and Vifell, Å. (2007), 'New Governance Structures in Employment Policy Making: Loose Co-ordination in Action', in I. Linsenmann, C. Meyer, and W. Wessels (eds.), *Economic Government of the EU: A Balance Sheet of New Modes of Policy Coordination* (Basingstoke: Palgrave Macmillan), 53–71.

Jacoby, W. (2004), *The Enlargement of the European Union and NATO: Ordering from the Menu in Central Europe* (Cambridge: Cambridge University Press).

Jasanoff, S. (2005), *Designs on Nature: Science and Democracy in Europe and the United States* (Princeton, NJ: Princeton University Press).

Jobelius, S. (2003), 'Who Formulates the European Employment Guidelines? The OMC between Deliberation and Power Games', paper presented to the ESPAnet conference, 'Changing European Societies: The Role for Social Policy', Copenhagen, 13–15 Nov.

Joerges, C. (2001a), '"Deliberative Supranationalism": A Defence', European Integration online Papers, 5/8; available at *http://eiop.or.at/eiop*.

Joerges, C. (2001b), 'Law, Science and the Management of Risks to Health at the National, European and International Level: Stories on Baby Dummies, Mad Cows and Hormones in Beef', *Columbia Journal of European Law*, 7: 1–19.

Joerges, C., and Neyer, J. (1997a), 'From Intergovernmental Bargaining to Deliberative Political Process: The Constitutionalization of Comitology', *European Law Journal*, 3/3: 273–99.

Joerges, C., and Neyer, J. (1997b), 'Transforming Strategic Interaction into Deliberative Political Process: The Constitutionalization of Comitology in the Foodstuffs Sector', *Journal of European Public Policy*, 4/4: 609–25.

Johansson, K. M. (1999), 'Tracing the Employment Title in the Amsterdam Treaty: Uncovering Transnational Coalitions', *Journal of European Public Policy*, 6/1: 85–101.

John, P. (1998), *Analysing Public Policy* (London: Continuum).

Johnson, M. (1998), *European Community Trade Policy and the Article 113 Committee* (London: Royal Institute of International Affairs).

Johnson, S. P., and Corcelle, G. (1989), *The Environmental Policy of the European Communities* (London: Graham and Trotman).

Jones, E. (2002), *The Politics of Economic and Monetary Union: Integration and Idiosyncrasy* (Boulder, CO: Rowman & Littlefield).

Jones, S. G. (2007), *The Rise of European Security Cooperation* (Cambridge: Cambridge University Press).

Jordan, A. (2002a) (ed.), *Environmental Policy in the European Union: Actors, Institutions and Processes* (London: Earthscan).

Jordan, A. (2002b), *The Europeanization of British Environmental Policy: A Departmental Perspective* (Basingstoke: Palgrave Macmillan).

Jordan, A. (2003), 'The Europeanization of National Government and Policy: A Departmental Perspective', *British Journal of Political Science*, 33/2: 261–82.

Jordan, A. (2005) (ed.), *Environmental Policy in the European Union: Actors, Institutions and Processes*, 2nd edn. (London: Earthscan).

Jordan, A., and Lenschow, A. (2008), *Innovation in Environmental Policy? Integrating the Environment for Sustainability* (Cheltenham: Edward Elgar).

Jordan, A., and Schout, A. (2006), *The Coordination of the European Union: Exploring the Capacities of Networked Governance* (Oxford: Oxford University Press).

Jordan, A., Schout, A., and Unfried, M. (2008), 'The European Union', in A. Jordan and A. Lenschow (eds.), *Innovation in Environmental Policy? Integrating the Environment for Sustainability* (Cheltenham: Edward Elgar), 159–79.

Jordan, A., Wurzel, R. K. W., and Zito, A. R. (2003), *'New' Instruments of Environmental Governance: National Experiences and Prospects* (London: Frank Cass).

Jordan, A., Wurzel, R. K. W., and Zito, A. R. (2005), 'The Rise of "New" Policy Instruments in Comparative Perspective: Has Governance Eclipsed Government?', *Political Studies*, 53: 477–96.

Jordan, G., (1998), 'What Drives Associability at the European Level? The Limits of the Utilitarian Explanation', in J. Greenwood and M. Aspinwall (eds.), *Collective Action in the European Union: Interests and the New Politics of Associability* (London: Routledge), 31–62.

Jordan, G., and Maloney, W. A. (1996), 'How Bumble-bees Fly: Accounting for Public Interest Participation', *Political Studies*, 44/4: 668–85.

Jorens, Y., and Schulte, B. (1998) (eds.), *European Social Security Law and Third Country Nationals* (Bruges: die Keure).

Jørgensen, K. E. (2007), 'Overview: The European Union and the World', in K. E. Jørgensen, M. A. Pollack, and B. Rosamond (eds.), *The Handbook of European Union Politics* (London: Sage), 507–25.

Jørgensen, K. E., Pollack, M. A., and Rosamond, B. (2007) (eds.), *The Handbook of European Union Politics* (London: Sage).

Jupille, J. (2005), 'Knowing Europe: Metatheory and Methodology in EU Studies', in M. Cini and A. Bourne (eds.), *Palgrave Advances in European Union Studies* (Basingstoke: Palgrave Macmillan), 209–32.

Jupille, J., Caporaso, J. A., and Checkel, J. (2003), 'Integrating Institutions: Rationalism, Constructivism, and the Study of the European Union', *Comparative Political Studies*, 36/1–2: 7–40.

Kahan, D., Slovic, P., Braman, D., and Gastil, J. (2006), 'Fear of Democracy: A Cultural Evaluation of Sunstein on Risk', *Harvard Law Review*, 119/4: 1071–109.

Kahler, M. (2002), 'The State of the State in World Politics', in I. Katznelson and H. V. Milner (eds.), *Political Science: State of the Discipline* (New York, NY: W. W. Norton), 56–83.

Kapteyn, P. (1996), *The Stateless Market: The European Dilemma of Integration and Civilization* (London: Routledge).

Kassim, H. (1994), 'Policy Networks, Networks and European Union Policy Making: A Sceptical View', *West European Politics*, 17/4: 15–27.

Kassim, H., Peters, B. G., and Wright, V. (2000) (eds.), *The National Co-ordination of EU Policy: The Domestic Level* (Oxford: Oxford University Press).

Keck, M., and Sikkink, K. (1998), *Activists Beyond Borders: Advocacy Networks in International Politics* (Ithaca, NY: Cornell University Press).

Keeler, J. T. S. (1987), *The Politics of Neocorporatism in France* (New York, NY: Oxford University Press).

Keeler, J. T. S. (2005), 'Mapping EU Studies: The Evolution from Boutique to Boom Field 1960–2001', *Journal of Common Market Studies*, 43/3: 551–82.

Kelemen, R. D. (2002), 'The Politics of "Eurocratic" Structures and the New European Agencies', *West European Politics*, 25/4: 93–118.

Kelemen, R. D. (2003), 'The Structure and Dynamics of EU Federalism', *Comparative Political Studies*, 36/1–2: 184–208.

Kelemen, R. D. (2004), *The Rules of Federalism: Institutions and Regulatory Politics in the EU and Beyond* (Cambridge, MA: Harvard University Press).

Keller, B. (2008), 'Social Dialogue—The Specific Case of the European Union', *The International Journal of Comparative Labour Law and Industrial Relations*, 24/2: 201–26.

Kelley, J. G. (2004), *Ethnic Politics in Europe: The Power of Norms and Incentives* (Princeton, NJ: Princeton University Press).

Kelley, J. G. (2006), 'New Wine in Old Wineskins: Promoting Political Reforms through the New European Neighbourhood Policy', *Journal of Common Market Studies*, 44/1: 29–55.

Kenner, J. (2003), *EU Employment Law: From Rome to Amsterdam and Beyond* (Oxford: Hart).

Keohane, R. O. (1986), 'Reciprocity in International Relations', *International Organization*, 40/1: 1–27.

Keohane, R. O., and Nye, J. S. (2001), *Power and Interdependence*, 3rd edn. (New York, NY: Longman).

Kerremans, B. (2004), 'What Went Wrong in Cancun? A Principal–Agent View on the EU's Rationale Towards the Doha Development Round', *European Foreign Affairs Review*, 9/3: 363–93.

Kiewiet, R. D., and McCubbins, M. (1991), *The Logic of Delegation: Congressional Parties and the Appropriations Process* (Chicago, IL: University of Chicago Press).

Kingdon, J. W. (2003), *Agendas, Alternatives and Public Policies*, 2nd edn. (New York, NY: Longman).

Kingreen, T. (2007), 'The Fundamental Rights of the European Union: Basic Rights of Equality and Social Rights', in D. Ehlers (ed.), *European Fundamental Rights and Freedoms* (Berlin: De Gruyter), 466–89.

Kleinman, M. (2001), *A European Welfare State? European Union Social Policy in Context* (Basingstoke: Palgrave Macmillan).

Kleinman, M., and Piachaud, D. (1992), 'European Social Policy: Conceptions and Choices', *Journal of European Social Policy*, 3/1: 1–19.

Klumpes, P., Fenn, P., Diacon, S., O'Brien, C., and Yildirim, C. (2007), 'European Insurance Markets: Recent Trends and Future Regulatory Developments', in J. D. Cummins and B. Venard (eds.), *Handbook of International Insurance: Between Global Dynamics and Local Contingencies* (New York, NY: Springer), 789–848.

Knill, C. (2001), *The Europeanisation of National Administration: Patterns of Institutional Change and Persistence* (Cambridge: Cambridge University Press).

Knill, C., and Lenschow, A. (2000) (eds.), *Implementing EU Environmental Policy: New Directions and Old Problems* (Manchester: Manchester University Press).

Knill, C., and Liefferink, D. (2007) (eds.), *Environmental Politics in the European Union: Policy-making, Implementation and Patterns of Multi-level Governance* (Manchester: Manchester University Press).

Knudsen, A.-C. Lauring (2009), *Farmers on Welfare: The Making of Europe's Common Agricultural Policy* (Ithaca, NY: Cornell University Press).

Kochan, T., Locke, R., Osterman, P., and Piore, M. (2001), *Working in America: Blueprint for a New Labor Market* (Cambridge, MA: The MIT Press).

Koeck, H. F. and Karollus, M. M. (2008) (eds.), *Die neue Dienstleistungsrichtlinie der Europäischen Union: Hoffnungen und Erwartungen angesichts einer (weiteren) Vervollständigung des Binnenmarktes* (Baden-Baden: Nomos; Vienna: Facultas-WUV).

Kohler-Koch, B. (2003) (ed.), *Linking EU and National Governance* (Oxford: Oxford University Press).

Kok, W. (2004), *Facing the Challenge, Report of Wim Kok to the European Commission* (The Kok Report) (Brussels).

Kooiman, J. (1993), 'Social-Political Governance: Introduction', in J. Kooiman (ed.), *Modern Governance* (London: Sage), 1–6.

Kotzian, P. (2002), *Stuck in the Middle: Welfare Effects of the European Pharmaceutical Markets' Incomplete Integration and a Possible Remedy*, MZES Working Paper 59 (Mannheim: Mannheimer Zentrum für Europäische Sozialforschung).

Kotzian, P. (2003), *Verhandlungen im europäischen Arzneimittelsektor: Initiierung–Institutionalisierung–Ergebnisse* (Baden-Baden: Nomos).

Kramer, H. (1993), 'The European Community's Response to the "New Eastern Europe"', *Journal of Common Market Studies*, 31/2: 231–44.

Krämer, L. (2008), 'Environmental Judgements by the Court of Justice and their Duration', *Research Papers in Law*, 4/2008, (Bruges: College of Europe).

Krapohl, S. (2004), 'Credible Commitments in Non-Independent Regulatory Agencies: A Comparative Analysis of the European Agencies for Pharmaceuticals and Foodstuffs', *European Law Journal*, 10/5: 518–38.

Kreppel, A. (2001), *The European Parliament and Supranational Party System: A Study in Institutional Development* (Cambridge: Cambridge University Press).

Kreppel, A. (2002), 'The Environmental Determinants of Legislative Structure: A Comparison of the US House of Representatives and the European Parliament', paper presented at the conference, 'Exporting Congress? The Influence of the US Congress on World Legislatures', Jack D. Gordon Institute for Public Policy and Citizenship Studies, Florida International University, 6–7 Dec.

Kreppel, A., and Hix, S. (2003), 'From "Grand Coalition" to Left-Right Confrontation: Explaining the Shifting Structure of Party Competition in the European Parliament', *Comparative Political Studies*, 36/1–2: 75–96.

Kroes, N. (2007), Press Conference, Brussels, 19 Sep.

Kubicek, P. (2003) (ed.) *The European Union and Democratization* (London: Routledge).

Kuijper, P. J. (2000), 'Some Legal Problems Associated with the Communitarisation of Policy on Visas, Asylum and Immigration Under the Amsterdam Treaty and Incorporation of the Schengen Acquis', *Common Market Law Review*, 37/2: 345–66.

Kvist, J. (2004), 'Does EU Enlargement Start a Race to the Bottom? Strategic Interaction among EU Member States in Social Policy', *Journal of European Social Policy*, 14/3: 301–18.

Laatikainen, K. V., and Smith, K. E. (2006), 'Introduction—The European Union at the United Nations: Leader, Partner or Failure?', in K. V. Laatikainen and K. E. Smith (eds.), *The European Union at the United Nations: Intersecting Multilateralisms* (Basingstoke: Palgrave MacMillan).

Laffan, B. (1996), 'The Politics of Identity and Political Order in Europe', *Journal of Common Market Studies*, 34/1: 81–102.

Laffan, B. (1997), *The Finances of the European Union* (Basingstoke: Palgrave Macmillan).

Laffan, B., O'Donnell, R., and Smith, M. (1999), *Europe's Experimental Union: Rethinking Integration* (London: Routledge).

Lamy, P. (2004), *Trade Policy in the Prodi Commission, 1999–2004*, available at: www.acp-eu-trade.org/library/library_detail.php?library_detail_id=1827&doc_language.

Lange, P. (1992), 'The Politics of the Social Dimension', in A. M. Sbragia (ed.), *Euro-Politics: Institutions and Policy-Making in the 'New' European Community* (Washington, DC: Brookings Institution), 225–56.

Langhammer, R. L. (2005), 'The EU Offer of Services Trade Liberalization in the Doha Round: Evidence of a Not-Yet-Perfect Customs Union', *Journal of Common Market Studies*, 43/2: 311–25.

Larsen, T. P., and Andersen, S. K. (2007), 'A New Mode of European Regulation? The Implementation of the Autonomous Framework Agreement on Telework in Five Countries', *European Journal of Industrial Relations*, 13/2: 181–98.

Laudati, L. (1996), 'The European Commission as Regulator: The Uncertain Pursuit of the Competitive Market', in G. Majone (ed.), *Regulating Europe* (London: Routledge), 229–61.

Lavenex, S., (2006a), 'Towards a Constitutionalization of Aliens' Rights in the European Union?', *Journal of European Public Policy*, 13/8: 1284–301.

Lavenex, S., (2006b), 'Shifting Up and Out: The Foreign Policy of European Immigration Control', *West European Politics*, 29/2: 329–50.

Lavenex, S. (2007), 'Mutual Recognition and the Monopoly of Force: Limits of the Single Market Analogy', *Journal of European Public Policy*, 14/5: 762–79.

Lavenex, S., and Kunz, R. (2008), 'The Migration-Development Nexus in EU External Relations', *Journal of European Integration*, 30/3: 439–57.

Lavenex, S., and Wallace, W. (2005), 'Justice and Home Affairs: Towards a "European Public Order?"', in H. Wallace, W. Wallace, and M. A. Pollack (eds.), *Policy-Making in the European Union*, 5th edn. (Oxford: Oxford University Press), 457–80.

Le Cacheux, J. (2007), *Funding the EU Budget with a Genuine Own Resource: The Case for a European Tax*, Studies 57 (Paris: Notre Europe).

Leibfried, S. (1994), 'The Social Dimension of the European Union: En Route to a Positive Joint Sovereignty?', *Journal of European Social Policy*, 4/4: 239–62.

Leibfried, S. (2001), 'Über die Hinfälligkeit des Staates der Daseinsvorsorge: Thesen zur Zerstörung des äußeren Verteidigungsringes des Sozialstaats', in Schader-Stiftung (ed.),

Die Zukunft der Daseinsvorsorge: öffentliche Unternehmen im Wettbewerb (Darmstadt: Schader-Stiftung), 158–66.

Leibfried, S. (2005), 'Social Policy: Left to the Judges and the Markets?', in H. Wallace, W. Wallace, and M. A. Pollack (eds.), *Policy-Making in the European Union*, 5th edn. (Oxford: Oxford University Press), 243–78.

Leibfried, S., and Mau, S. (2008) (ed.), *Welfare States: Construction, Deconstruction, Reconstructions*, 3 vols. (Cheltenham: Edward Elgar).

Leibfried, S., and Obinger, H. (2008), 'Nationale Sozialstaaten in der Europäischen Union', in M. Höpner and A. Schäfer (eds.), *Die politische Ökonomie der europäischen Integration* (Frankfurt am Main: Campus), 335–65.

Leibfried, S., and Pierson, P. (1995) (eds.), *European Social Policy: Between Fragmentation and Integration* (Washington, DC: Brookings Institution).

Leibfried, S., and Pierson, P. (2000), 'Social Policy: Left to the Courts and Markets?', in H. Wallace and W. Wallace (eds.), *Policy-Making in the European Union*, 4th edn. (Oxford: Oxford University Press), 267–92.

Leibfried, S., and Starke, P. (2008), 'Transforming the "Cordon Sanitaire": The Liberalization of Public Services and the Restructuring of European Welfare States', *Socio-Economic Review*, 6/1: 175–82.

Leibfried, S., and Zürn, M. (2005), 'Reconfiguring the National Constellation', in S. Leibfried and M. Zürn (eds.), *Transformations of the State?* (Cambridge: Cambridge University Press), 1–36.

Lenschow, A. (2003), 'New Regulatory Approaches in Greening EU Policies', *European Law Journal*, 8/1: 19–37.

Lenschow, A. (2005), 'Environmental Policy: Contending Dynamics of Policy Change', in H. Wallace, W. Wallace, and M. A. Pollack (eds.), *Policy-Making in the European Union*, 5th edn. (Oxford: Oxford University Press), 304–27.

Lenschow, A. (2007), 'Environmental Policy in the European Union: Bridging Policy, Politics and Polity Dimensions', in K. E. Jørgensen, M. A. Pollack, and B. Rosamond (eds.), *The Handbook of European Union Politics* (London: Sage), 413–32.

Lequesne, C. (2005), 'Fisheries Policy: Letting the Little Ones Go', in H. Wallace, W. Wallace, and M. A. Pollack (eds.), *Policy-Making in the European Union*, 5th edn. (Oxford: Oxford University Press), 353–76.

Lewis, J. (2005), 'The Janus Face of Brussels: Socialization and Everyday Decision Making in the European Union', *International Organization*, 59/4: 937–71.

Liefferink, D., and Jordan, A. (2004) (eds.), *Environmental Policy in Europe: The Europeanisation of National Environmental Policy* (London: Routledge).

Lindberg, L. N. (1963), *The Political Dynamics of European Economic Integration* (Stanford, CA: Stanford University Press).

Lindberg, L. N., and Scheingold, S. A. (1970), *Europe's Would-Be Polity* (Englewood Cliffs, NJ: Prentice-Hall).

Lindblom, C. (1977), *Politics and Markets* (New York, NY: Basic Books).

Lindner, J. (2006), *Conflict and Change in EU Budgetary Politics* (London: Routledge).

Linklater, A. (2005), 'A European Civilising Process?', in C. Hill and M. Smith (eds.), *International Relations and the European Union* (Oxford: Oxford University Press), 367–87.

Linsenmann, I., Meyer, C., and Wessels, W. (2007) (eds.), *Economic Government of the EU: A Balance Sheet of New Modes of Policy Coordination* (Basingstoke: Palgrave Macmillan).

Lowe, P. (2006), 'Preserving and Promoting Competition: A European Response', *Competition Policy Newsletter*, 2, Summer.

Lowe, P., Buller, H., and Ward, N. (2002), 'Setting the Next Agenda? British and French Approaches to the Second Pillar of the Common Agricultural Policy', *Journal of Rural Studies*, 18/1: 1–17.

Lowi, T. J. (1964), 'American Business, Public Policy, Case-Studies, and Political Theory', *World Politics*, 16/4: 677–715.

Lowi, T. J. (1972), 'Four Systems of Policy, Politics and Choice', *Public Administration Review*, 32/4: 298–310.

McCormick, J. (2006), 'Policymaking in the European Union', in E. E. Zeff and E. B. Pirro (eds.), *The European Union and the Member States*, 2nd edn. (Boulder, CO: Lynne Rienner), 11–31.

McDonagh, B. (1998), *Original Sin in a Brave New World: The Paradox of Europe: An Account of the Negotiation of the Treaty of Amsterdam* (Dublin: Institute of European Affairs).

McElroy, G. (2007), 'Legislative Politics', in K. E. Jørgensen, M. A. Pollack, and B. Rosamond (eds.), *The Handbook of European Union Politics* (London: Sage), 175–94.

McGowan, L. (2005), 'Europeanization Unleashed and Rebounding: The Modernization of EU Cartel Policy', *Journal of European Public Policy*, 12/6: 986–1004.

McNamara, K. (1998), *The Currency of Ideas: Monetary Politics in the European Union* (Ithaca, NY: Cornell University Press).

McNamara, K. (2005), 'Economic and Monetary Union: Innovation and Challenges for the Euro', in H. Wallace, W. Wallace, and M. A. Pollack (eds.), *Policy-Making in the European Union*, 5th edn. (Oxford: Oxford University Press), 141–60.

Maes, I. (2004), 'On the Origins of the Franco-German EMU Controversies', *European Journal of Law and Economics*, 17/1: 21–39.

Magnette, P. (2004), 'Deliberation or Bargaining? Coping with Constitutional Conflicts in the Convention on the Future of Europe', in E. O. Eriksen, J. E. Fossum, and A. J. Menéndez (eds.), *Developing a Constitution for Europe* (London: Routledge), 207–25.

Maher, I. (2004), 'Economic Policy Co-ordination and the European Court: Excessive Deficits and Ecofin Discretion', *European Law Review*, 29/6: 831–41.

Majone, G. (1991), 'Cross-National Sources of Regulatory Policymaking in Europe and the United States', *Journal of Public Policy*, 2/1: 79–106.

Majone, G. (1993), 'The European Community between Social Policy and Social Regulation', *Journal of Common Market Studies*, 31/2: 153–70.

Majone, G. (1994), 'The Rise of the Regulatory State in Europe', *West European Politics*, 17/3: 77–101.

Majone, G. (1995a), *La Communauté européenne: un Etat régulateur* (Paris: Montchestien).

Majone, G. (1995b), 'Quelle politique sociale pour l'Europe?', in Y. Mény, P. Muller, and J.-L. Quermonne (eds.), *Politiques Publiques en Europe* (Paris: L'Harmattan), 271–86.

Majone, G. (1996) (ed.), *Regulating Europe* (London: Routledge).

Majone, G. (2000a), 'Two Logics of Delegation: Agency and Fiduciary Relations in EU Governance', *European Union Politics*, 2/1: 103–21.

Majone, G. (2000*b*), 'The Credibility Crisis of Community Regulation', *Journal of Common Market Studies*, 38/2: 273–302.

Majone, G. (2002), 'What Price Safety? The Precautionary Principle and its Policy Implications', *Journal of Common Market Studies*, 40/1: 89–109.

Majone, G. (2003), 'Foundations of Risk Regulation: Science, Decision-Making, Policy Learning and Institutional Reform', in G. Majone (ed.), *Risk Regulation in the European Union: Between Enlargement and Internationalization* (Florence: European University Institute), 9–32.

Majone, G. (2005), *Dilemmas of European Integration: The Ambiguities and Pitfalls of Integration by Stealth* (Oxford: Oxford University Press).

Manners, I. (2007), 'Another Europe is Possible: Critical Perspectives on European Union Politics', in K. E. Jørgensen, M. A. Pollack, and B. Rosamond (eds.), *The Handbook of European Union Politics* (London: Sage), 77–96.

Manners, I. (2008), 'The Normative Ethics of the European Union', *International Affairs*, 84/1: 45–60.

Manow, P., Schäfer, A., and Zorn, H. (2004), *European Social Policy and Europe's Party-Political Center of Gravity, 1957–2003*, MPifG Discussion Paper 04/6 (Cologne: Max Planck Institute for the Study of Societies), available at: *http://www.mpifg.de/pu/mpifg_dp/dp046.pdf*).

Manzella, G., and Mendez, C. (2009), *The Turning Points of EU Cohesion Policy*, European Policies Research Centre, available at: *http://ec.europa.eu/regional_policy/policy/future/pdf/8_manzella_final-formatted.pdf*.

March, J. G., and Olsen, J. P. (1984), 'The New Institutionalism: Organizational Factors in Political Life', *European Union Politics*, 2/1: 103–21.

March, J. G., and Olsen, J. P. (1989), *Rediscovering Institutions: The Organizational Basis of Politics* (New York, NY: Free Press).

Marks, G. (1992), 'Structural Policy in the European Community', in A. M. Sbragia (ed.), *Euro-politics: Institutions and Policy-Making in the 'New' European Community* (Washington, DC: Brookings Institution), 191–224.

Marks, G. (1993), 'Structural Policy and Multilevel Governance in the EC', in A. W. Cafruny and G. G. Rosenthal (eds.), *The State of the European Community*, vol. ii: *The Maastricht Debates and Beyond* (Boulder, CO: Lynne Rienner), 390–410.

Marks, G., Hooghe, L., and Blank, K. (1996), 'European Integration from the 1980s: State-Centric v Multi-Level Governance', *Journal of Common Market Studies*, 34/3: 341–78.

Martin, A., and Ross, G. (2004), *Euros and Europeans: Monetary Integration and the European Model of Society* (Cambridge: Cambridge University Press).

Matlary, J. H. (1996), 'Energy Policy: From a National to a European Framework?', in H. Wallace and W. Wallace (eds.), *Policy-Making in the European Union*, 3rd edn. (Oxford: Oxford University Press), 257–77.

Mattila, M. (2004), 'Contested Decisions—Empirical Analysis of Voting in the EU Council of Ministers', *European Journal of Political Research*, 43/1: 29–50.

Mattila, M. (2008), 'Voting and Coalitions in the Council after the Enlargement', in D. Naurin and H. Wallace (eds.), *Unveiling the Council of the European Union: Games Governments Play in Brussels* (Basingstoke: Palgrave Macmillan), 23–35.

Mattli, W., and Slaughter, A.-M. (1995), 'Law and Politics in the European Union: A Reply to Garrett', *International Organization*, 49/1: 183–90.

Mattli, W., and Slaughter, A.-M. (1998), 'Revisiting the European Court of Justice', *International Organization*, 52/1: 177–210.

Mau, S., and Verwiebe, R. (2009), *Die Sozialstruktur Europas* (Konstanz: UVK Verlagsgesellschaft).

Maurer, A. (2003*a*), 'Less Bargaining—More Deliberation: The Convention Method for Enhancing EU Democracy', *Internationale Politik und Gesellschaft*, 1: 167–90.

Maurer, A. (2003*b*), 'The Legislative Powers and Impact of the European Parliament', *Journal of Common Market Studies*, 41/2: 227–47.

Maydell, B. Baron von (1991), 'Einführung in die Schlussdiskussion', in B. Schulte, and H. F. Zacher (eds.), *Wechselwirkungen zwischen dem europäischen Sozialrecht und dem Sozialrecht der Bundesrepublik Deutschland* (Berlin: Duncker & Humblot), 229–36.

Maydell, B. Baron von (1999), 'Auf dem Weg zu einem gemeinsamen Markt für Gesundheitsleistungen in der Europäischen Gemeinschaft', *Vierteljahresschrift für Sozialrecht*, 1: 3–19.

Maydell, B. Baron von, Borchardt, K., Henke, K.-D., Leitner, R., Muffels, R., Quante, M., Rauhala, P.-L. K., Verschraegen, G., and Zukowski, M. (2006) (eds.), *Enabling Social Europe* (Berlin: Springer).

Mayhew, A. (1998), *Recreating Europe: The European Union's Policy towards Central and Eastern Europe* (Cambridge: Cambridge University Press).

Mazey, S. (1998), 'The European Union and Women's Rights: From the Europeanization of National Agendas to the Nationalization of a European Agenda?', *Journal of European Public Policy*, 5/1: 131–52.

Mazower, M. (1999), *Dark Continent: Europe's Twentieth Century* (London: Penguin).

Meester, G. (1999), 'European Agricultural Policy in Transformation: The CAP Decision Making Process', unpublished paper.

Mendez, C., Wishlade, F., and Yuill, D. (2006), 'Conditioning and Fine Tuning Europeanization: Negotiating Regional Policy Maps under the EU's Competition and Cohesion Policies', *Journal of Common Market Studies*, 44/3: 581–605.

Menon, A. (2004), 'From Crisis to Catharsis: ESDP after Iraq', *International Affairs*, 80/4: 631–48.

Menon, A., Forster, A., and Wallace, W. (1992), 'A Common European Defence?', *Survival*, 34/3: 98–118.

Menz, G. (2003), 'Re-regulating the Single Market: National Varieties of Capitalism and Their Responses to Europeanization', *Journal of European Public Policy*, 10/4: 532–55.

Menzie, C., and Frankel, J. (2008), 'The Euro May Over the Next 15 Years Surpass the Dollar as Leading International Currency', Faculty Research Working Paper RWP08-016 (Cambridge, MA: Harvard University, John F. Kennedy School of Government).

Meunier, S. (2005), *Trading Voices: The European Union in International Commercial Negotiations* (Princeton, NJ: Princeton University Press).

Meyer, C. O., and Kunstein, T. (2007), 'Towards a "Grand Débat Européen" on Economic Governance? Publicised Discourses as Indicators for the Performance and Evolution of Policy Coordination Modes', in I. Linsenmann, C. O. Meyer, and W. Wessels (eds.), *Economic Government of the EU: A Balance Sheet of New Modes of Policy Coordination* (Basingstoke: Palgrave Macmillan), 187–210.

Milner, H. V. (1998), 'Rationalizing Politics: The Emerging Synthesis of International, American and Comparative Politics', *International Organization*, 52/4: 759–86.

Milward, A. S. (1992), *The European Rescue of the Nation-State* (London: Routledge).

Milward, A. S. (2000), *The European Rescue of the Nation-State*, 2nd edn. (London: Routledge).

Milward, A. S., and Lynch, F. M. B. (1993) (eds.), *The Frontiers of National Sovereignty: History and Theory 1945–1992* (London: Routledge).

Mirwaldt, K., McMaster, I., and Bachtler, J. (2009), *Reconsidering Cohesion Policy: The Contested Debate on Territorial Cohesion*, European Policy Research Paper, no. 66 (Glasgow: University of Strathclyde; European Policies Research Centre).

Mitsilegas, V. (2009), *EU Criminal Law* (London: Hart).

Mitsilegas, V., Monar, J., and Rees, W. (2003), *The European Union and Internal Security: Guardian of the People?* (Basingstoke: Palgrave Macmillan).

Moe, T. (1984), 'The New Economics of Organization', *American Journal of Political Science*, 28/4: 739–77.

Molyneux, C. G. (1999), 'The Trade Barriers Regulation: The European Union as a Player in the Globalization Game', *European Law Journal*, 5/4: 375–418.

Monar, J. (1997), 'European Union—Justice and Home Affairs: A Balance Sheet and an Agenda for Reform', in G. Edwards and A. Pijpers (eds.), *The Politics of European Treaty Reform: The 1996 Intergovernmental Conference and Beyond* (London: Pinter/Cassell), 326–39.

Monar, J. (2001), 'The Dynamics of Justice and Home Affairs: Laboratories, Driving Factors and Costs', *Journal of Common Market Studies*, 39/4: 747–64.

Monar, J. (forthcoming), 'Experimentalist Governance in EU Justice and Home Affairs', in C. Sabel and J. Zeitlin (eds.), *Experimentalist Governance in the European Union: Towards a New Architecture* (Oxford: Oxford University Press).

Monti, M. (2003), 'EU Competition Policy after May 2004', paper presented at the Fordham Corporate Law Institute.

Moran, M., Rein, M., and Goodin, R. E. (2006) (eds.), *The Oxford Handbook of Public Policy* (Oxford: Oxford University Press).

Moravcsik, A. (1991), 'Negotiating the Single European Act: National Interests and Conventional Statecraft in the European Community', *International Organization*, 45/1: 19–56.

Moravcsik, A. (1993a), 'Preferences and Power in the European Community: A Liberal Intergovernmentalist Approach', *Journal of Common Market Studies*, 31/4: 473–524.

Moravcsik, A. (1993b), 'Introduction: Integrating International and Domestic Theories of International Bargaining', in P. B. Evans, H. K. Jacobson, and R. D. Putnam (eds.), *Double-Edged Diplomacy: International Bargaining and Domestic Politics* (Berkeley, CA: University of California Press), 3–42.

Moravcsik, A. (1998), *The Choice for Europe: Social Purpose and State Power from Messina to Maastricht* (Ithaca, NY: Cornell University Press).

Moravcsik, A. (1999), 'Is Something Rotten in the State of Denmark? Constructivism and European Integration', *Journal of European Public Policy*, 6/4: 669–81.

Moravcsik, A. (2001), 'Federalism in the European Union: Rhetoric and Reality', in K. Nicolaïdis and R. Howse (eds.), *The Federal Vision: Legitimacy and Levels of*

Governance in the United States and the European Union (Oxford: Oxford University Press), 161–87.

Moravcsik, A. (2002), 'In Defense of the Democratic Deficit: Reassessing Legitimacy in the European Union', *Journal of Common Market Studies*, 40/4: 603–24.

Moravcsik, A., and Schimmelfennig, F. (2009), 'Liberal Intergovernmentalism', in A. Wiener and T. Diez (eds.), *European Integration Theory*, 2nd edn. (Oxford: Oxford University Press), 67–87.

Moravcsik, A., and Vachudova, M. A. (2003), 'National Interests, State Power, and EU Enlargement', *East European Politics and Societies*, 17/1: 42–57.

Morgan, E. (2006), 'Merger Policy in the EU', in R. Clarke and E. Morgan (eds.), *New Developments in UK and EU Competition Policy* (Cheltenham: Edward Elgar), 78–109.

Mortished, C. (2008), 'Frankenstein Foods Are Not Monsters', *TimesOnline*, 8 January, *http://business.timesonline.co.uk/tol/business/columnists/article3155919.ece* (accessed 14 January 2008).

Mosher, J. S., and Trubek, D. (2003), 'Alternative Approaches to Governance in the EU: EU Social Policy and the European Employment Strategy', *Journal of Common Market Studies*, 41/1: 63–88.

Mossialos, E., and McKee, M. (2002), *EU Law and the Social Character of Health Care* (Brussels: PLE-Peter Lang).

Mossialos, E., Dixon, A., Figueras, J., and Kutzin, J. (2002) (eds.), *Funding Health Care: Options for Europe* (Buckingham: Open University Press).

Motta, M. (2004), *Competition Policy: Theory and Practice* (Cambridge: Cambridge University Press).

Moyer, H., and Josling, T. (2002), *Agricultural Policy Reform: Politics and Processes in the EU and in the US in the 1990s* (Aldershot: Ashgate).

Müller, H., (2003), 'Interests or Ideas? The Regulation of Insurance Services and the European Single Market: Trade Liberalisation, Risk Regulation and Limits to Market Integration', D.Phil. thesis, University of Sussex, Falmer.

Mundell, R. A. (1961), 'A Theory of Optimum Currency Areas', *American Economic Review*, 51/4: 657–65.

Nanetti, R. (1996), 'EU Cohesion and Territorial Restructuring in the Member States', in L. Hooghe (ed.), *Cohesion Policy and European Integration: Building Multilevel Governance* (Oxford: Oxford University Press), 59–88.

Nato (1999), 'Washington Summit Communiqué Issued by the Heads of State and Government participating in the meeting of the North Atlantic Council in Washington, DC on 24th April 1999', Press Release NAC-S(99)64, available at: *http://www.nato.int/docu/pr/1999/p99-064e.htm*.

Naurin, D., and Wallace, H. (2008) (eds.), *Unveiling the Council of the European Union: Games Governments Play in Brussels* (Basingstoke: Palgrave Macmillan).

Nedergaard, P. (2006), 'Market Failures and Government Failures: A Theoretical Model of the Common Agricultural Policy', *Public Choice*, 127/3–4: 393–413.

Neergard, U., Nielsen, R., and Roseberry, L. M. (2008) (eds.), *The Services Directive: Consequences for the Welfare State and the European Social Model* (Copenhagen: DJØF Publishers).

Neven, D. (2006), 'Competition Economics and Antitrust in Europe', *Economic Policy*, 21/48: 741–91.

Neville-Jones, P. (1997), 'Dayton, IFOR and Alliance Relations', *Survival*, 38/4: 45–65.

Neville-Rolfe, E. (1984), *The Politics of Agriculture in the European Community* (London: Policy Studies Institute).

New York Times, various issues.

Neyer, J. (2000), 'The Regulation of Risks and the Power of the People: Lessons from the BSE Crisis', *European Integration online Papers*, 4/6, available at: *http://eiop.or.at/eiop* (accessed on 8 January 2008).

Niblett, R., and Wallace, W. (2001) (eds.), *Rethinking European Order: West European Responses, 1989–1997* (Basingstoke: Palgrave Macmillan).

Nicolaïdis, K., and Schmidt, S. K. (2007), 'Mutual Recognition "On Trial": The Long Road to Services Liberalization', *Journal of European Public Policy*, 14/5: 717–34.

Niskanen, W. A. (1971), *Bureaucracy and Representative Government* (Chicago, IL: Aldine-Atherton).

Nivola, P. S. (1998), 'American Social Regulation Meets the Global Economy', in P. S. Nivola (ed.), *Comparative Disadvantages: Social Regulations and the Global Economy* (Washington, DC: Brookings Institution), 16–65.

Noord, P. van den, Döhring, B., Langedijk, S., Nogueira-Martins, J., Pench, L., Temprano-Arroyo, H., and Thiel, M. (2008), 'The Evolution of Economics Governance in EMU', *European Economy*, Economic Papers, No. 328.

North, D. C. (1990), *Institutions, Institutional Change and Economic Performance* (Cambridge: Cambridge University Press).

Nugent, N. (2004*a*), 'Previous Enlargement Rounds', in N. Nugent (ed.), *European Union Enlargement* (Basingstoke: Palgrave Macmillan), 22–33.

Nugent, N. (2004*b*) (ed.), *European Union Enlargement* (Basingstoke: Palgrave Macmillan).

Nugent, N. (2006), *The Government and Politics of the European Union*, 6th edn. (Basingstoke: Palgrave Macmillan).

Obermaier, A. J. (2008), 'Fine-Tuning the Jurisprudence: The ECJ's Judicial Activism and Self-Restraint' (Vienna: Austrian Academy of Sciences, Working Paper 02/08).

Oberthür, S., and Roche Kelly, C. (2008), 'EU Leadership in International Climate Policy: Achievements and Challenges', *The International Spectator*, 43/3: 1–16.

Obinger, H., Leibfried, S., and Castles, F. G. (2005), 'Bypasses to a Social Europe? Lessons from Federal Experience', *Journal of European Public Policy*, 12/3: 545–71.

Occhipinti, J. D. (2003), *The Politics of EU Police Cooperation: Towards a European FBI?* (Boulder, CO: Lynne Rienner).

O'Donnell, P. (2008), 'Commission GMO Debate Achieves No Resolution', *BioWorld International*, 20/13: 3.

OECD (Organization for Economic Co-operation and Development) (2007), *Agriculture and Food*, 2005/4: 78–118.

Oel, M., and Rapp-Lücke, J. (2008), 'Preparing Decision-Making on the Political Level in the EU-27 Plus: The Example of European Home Affairs', Working Paper Series on EU Internal Security Governance, no. 11, Securint Collection (Strasbourg: Université Robert Schuman).

Offe, C. (2000), 'The Democratic Welfare State in an Integrating Europe', in M. T. Greven and L. Pauly (eds.), *Democracy Beyond the State? The European Dilemma and the Emerging Global Order* (Lanham, MD: Rowman & Littlefield), 63–89.

Offe, C. (2003), 'The European Model of "Social" Capitalism: Can It Survive European Integration?', *Journal of Political Philosophy*, 11/4: 437–69.

Olson, M. (1965), *The Logic of Collective Action* (Cambridge, MA: Harvard University Press).

Orden, D., Paarlberg, R., and Roe, T. (1999), *Policy Reform in American Agriculture: Analysis and Prognosis* (Chicago, IL: University of Chicago Press).

Ostner, I., and Lewis, J. (1995), 'Gender and the Evolution of European Social Policy', in S. Leibfried and P. Pierson (eds.), *European Social Policy: Between Fragmentation and Integration* (Washington, DC: Brookings Institution), 159–93.

Padoa-Schioppa, T. (2000), *The Road to Monetary Union in Europe: The Emperor, the Kings and the Genies* (Oxford: Oxford University Press).

Page, E. C. (1997), *People who Run Europe* (Oxford: Clarendon Press).

Page, E. C. (2006), 'The Origins of Policy', in M. Moran, M. Rein, and R. E. Goodin (eds.), *The Oxford Handbook of Public Policy* (Oxford: Oxford University Press), 207–27.

Pallemaerts, M. (2009, continuously updated), (ed.), *Manual of Environmental Policy: The EU and Britain*, Institute of European Environmental Policy (IEEP) (Leeds: Maney Publishing).

Parsons, C. (2008), 'The SEA Story and Globalization', paper presented to the 38th UACES Annual Conference, Edinburgh, 1–3 Sept.

Patterson, L. A. (2000), 'Biotechnology', in H. Wallace and W. Wallace (eds.), *Policy-Making in the European Union*, 4th edn. (Oxford: Oxford University Press), 317–43.

Pearce, J. (1981), *The Common Agricultural Policy: Prospects for Change* (London: Routledge and Kagan Paul).

Pearce, J., and Sutton, J. (1985), *Protection and Industrial Policy in Europe* (London: Routledge).

Pedersen, A. W. (2004), 'The Privatization of Retirement Income? Variation and Trends in the Income Package of Old Age Pensioners', *Journal of European Social Policy*, 14/1: 5–2.

Peers, S. (2007), *EU Justice and Home Affairs Law* (Oxford: Oxford University Press).

Pelkmans, J. (1984), *Market Integration in the European Community* (The Hague: Martinus Nijhoff).

Pelkmans, J., and Murphy, A. (1991), 'Catapulted into Leadership: The Community's Trade and Aid Policies vis-à-vis Eastern Europe', *Journal of European Integration*, 14/2–3: 125–51.

Pelkmans, J., and Winters, L. A. (1988), *Europe's Domestic Market* (London: Royal Institute of International Affairs).

Perraud, D. (1999), *Europe, états, régions: La gouvernance multi-niveaux et le rôle des régions dans les politiques agricoles et rurales* (Grenoble: INRA-ESR).

Pesendorfer, D. (2006), 'EU Environmental Policy under Pressure: Chemicals Policy Change between Antagonistic Goals?', *Environmental Politics*, 15/1: 95–114.

Peters, B. G. (1992), 'Bureaucratic Politics and the Institutions of the European Community', in A. M. Sbragia (ed.), *Euro-Politics: Institutions and Policy-Making in the 'New' European Community* (Washington, DC: Brookings Institution), 75–122.

Peters, B. G. (1994), 'Agenda-Setting in the European Community', *Journal of European Public Policy*, 1/1: 9–26.

Peters, B. G. (1997), 'Escaping the Joint-Decision Trap: Repetition and Sectoral Politics in the European Union', *West European Politics*, 20/2: 22–37.

Peters, B. G. (1999), *Institutional Theory in Political Science: The 'New Institutionalism'* (London: Continuum).

Peters, B. G. (2001), *The Future of Governing*, 2nd edn. (Lawrence, KS: University of Kansas Press).

Petersen, J. H. (1991), 'Harmonization of Social Security in the EC Revisited', *Journal of Common Market Studies*, 29/5: 505–26.

Petersen, J. H. (2000), 'Financing of the Welfare State: Possibilities and Limits', in B. Baron von Maydell (ed.), *Entwicklungen der Systeme sozialer Sicherheit in Japan und Europa* (Berlin: Duncker & Humblot), 289–318.

Peterson, J. (1995), 'Decision-Making in the European Union: Towards a Framework for Analysis', *Journal of European Public Policy*, 2/1: 69–93.

Peterson, J. (1997), 'States, Societies and the European Union', *West European Politics*, 20/4: 1–24.

Peterson, J. (2004), 'Policy Networks', in A. Wiener and T. Diez (eds.), *European Integration Theory*, 1st edn. (Oxford: Oxford University Press), 117–35.

Peterson, J. (2009), 'Policy Networks', in A. Wiener and T. Diez (eds.), *European Integration Theory*, 2nd edn. (Oxford: Oxford University Press), 105–24.

Peterson, J., and Bomberg, E. (1999), *Decision-Making in the European Union* (Basingstoke: Palgrave Macmillan).

Peterson, J., and Shackleton (2005) (eds.), *The Institutions of the European Union*, 2nd edn. (Oxford: Oxford University Press).

Peterson, J., and Young, A. R. (2006) (eds.), 'The European Union and the New Trade Politics', *Journal of European Public Policy*, 13/6 (special issue).

Peterson, P. E., and Rom, M. C. (1990), *Welfare Magnets: A New Case for a National Standard* (Washington, DC: Brookings Institution).

Petit, M., de Benedictis, M., Bitton, D., de Groot, M., Henrichsmeyer, H., and Lechi, F. (1987), *Agricultural Policy Formation in the European Community: The Birth of Milk Quotas and CAP Reform* (Amsterdam: Elsevier).

Phinnemore, D. (1999), *Association: Stepping-Stone or Alternative to EU Membership?* (Sheffield: Sheffield Academic Press).

Phinnemore, D. (2003), 'Stabilisation and Association Agreements: Europe Agreements for the Western Balkans?', *European Foreign Affairs Review*, 8/1: 77–103.

Pierson, P. (1993), 'When Effects Become Cause: Policy Feedback and Political Change', *World Politics*, 45/4: 595–628.

Pierson, P. (1995*a*), 'The Creeping Nationalization of Income Transfers in the United States', in S. Leibfried and P. Pierson (eds.), *European Social Policy: Between Fragmentation and Integration* (Washington, DC: Brookings Institution), 301–28.

Pierson, P. (1995*b*), 'Federal Institutions and the Development of Social Policy', *Governance*, 8/4: 449–78.

Pierson, P. (1996*a*), 'The New Politics of the Welfare State', *World Politics*, 48/2: 147–79.

Pierson, P. (1996*b*), 'The Path to European Integration: A Historical Institutionalist Analysis', *Comparative Political Studies*, 29/2: 123–63.

Pierson, P. (2000), 'Increasing Returns, Path Dependence, and the Study of Politics', *American Political Science Review*, 94/2: 251–67.

Pierson, P. (2001) (ed.), *The New Politics of the Welfare State* (Oxford: Oxford University Press).

Pierson, P., and Leibfried, S. (1995), 'The Dynamics of Social Policy Integration', in S. Leibfried and P. Pierson (eds.), *European Social Policy: Between Fragmentation and Integration* (Washington, DC: Brookings Institution), 432–65.

Pinder, J. (1968), 'Positive Integration and Negative Integration: Some Problems of Economic Union in the EEC', *World Today*, 24/3: 88–110.

Pinder, J. (1991), *The European Community and Eastern Europe* (London: Pinter).

Pippan, C. (2004), 'The Rocky Road to Europe: The EU's Stabilization and Association Process for the Western Balkans and the Principle of Conditionality', *European Foreign Affairs Review*, 9/2: 219–45.

Pisani-Ferry, J. (2006), 'Only One Bed for Two Dreams: A Critical Retrospective on the Debate over the Economic Governance of the Euro Area', *Journal of Common Market Studies*, 44/4: 823–44.

Pisani-Ferry, J., and Sapir, A. (2007), 'Last Exit to Lisbon', Bruegel Policy Brief 2006/02 (Brussels: Bruegel).

Pochet, P. (2003), 'Pensions: The European Debate', in G. L. Clark and N. C. Whiteside (eds.), *Pension Security in the 21st Century: Redrawing the Public-Private Debate* (Oxford: Oxford University Press), 44–63.

Polanyi, K. (1994) [1944], *The Great Transformation* (New York, NY: Rinehart).

Pollack, M. A. (1995), 'Regional Actors in an Intergovernmental Play: The Making and Implementation of EC Structural Policy', in C. Rhodes and S. Mazey (eds.), *The State of the European Union*, vol. iii: *Building a European Polity?* (Boulder, CO: Lynne Rienner): 361–90.

Pollack, M. A. (1997), 'Delegation, Agency and Agenda Setting in the European Community', *International Organization*, 51/1: 99–134.

Pollack, M. A. (2003), *The Engines of European Integration: Delegation, Agency and Agenda Setting in the EU* (Oxford: Oxford University Press).

Pollack, M. A. (2004), 'The New Institutionalisms and European Integration', in A. Wiener and T. Diez (eds.), *European Integration Theory*, 1st edn. (Oxford: Oxford University Press), 137–56.

Pollack, M. A. (2008), 'Discussion: The Community Method and New Modes of Governance', in B. Kohler-Koch and F. Larat (eds.), *Efficient and Democratic Governance in the European Union*, CONNEX Report Series, vol. ix (Mannheim: Connex), 151–62, available at:*http://www.connex-network.org*

Pollack, M. A. (2009), 'The New Institutionalisms and European Integration', in A. Wiener and T. Diez (eds.), *European Integration Theory*, 2nd edn. (Oxford: Oxford University Press), 125–43.

Pollack, M. A., and Shaffer, G. S., (2009), *When Cooperation Fails: The International Law and Politics of Genetically Modified Organisms* (Oxford: Oxford University Press).

Preston, C. (1997), *Enlargement and Integration in the European Union* (London: Routledge).

Price, R. (2003), 'Transnational Civil Society and Advocacy in World Politics', *World Politics*, 55/4: 579–606.

Pridham, G. (2005), *Designing Democracy: EU Enlargement and Regime Change in Post-Communist Europe* (Basingstoke: Palgrave Macmillan).

Prügl, E. (2007), 'Gender and European Union Politics', in K. E. Jørgensen , M. A. Pollack, and B. Rosamond (eds.), *The Handbook of European Union Politics* (London: Sage), 433–48.

Puchala, D. (1972), 'Of Blind Men, Elephants, and International Integration', *Journal of Common Market Studies*, 10/3: 267–84.

Puetter, U. (2006), *The Eurogroup: How a Secretive Circle of Finance Ministers Shape European Economic Governance* (Manchester: Manchester University Press).

Puetter, U. (2007), 'Intervening From Outside: The Role of EU Finance Ministers in Constitutional Politics', *Journal of European Public Policy*, 14/8: 1293–310.

Putnam, R. D. (1988), 'Diplomacy and Domestic Politics: The Logic of Two-Level Games', *International Organization*, 42/3: 427–60.

Quaglia, L. (2008), 'Committee Governance in the Financial Sector', *Journal of European Integration*, 30/3: 565–80.

Rabinowicz, E. (1999), 'EU Enlargement and the Common Agricultural Policy: Finding Compromise in a Two-Level Repetitive Game', *International Politics*, 36: 397–417.

RAPID (European Commission press release service), various items.

Rasmussen, A. (2007), 'Early Conclusion in the Co-Decision Legislative Procedure', *EUI Working Papers*, MWR 2007/31 (Florence: European University Institute).

Raustiala, K., and Slaughter, A.-M. (2002), 'International Law, International Relations and Compliance', in W. Carlsnaes, T. Risse, and B. A. Simmons (eds.), *Handbook of International Relations* (New York, NY: Sage) 538–58.

Raveaud, G. (2007), 'The European Employment Strategy: Towards More and Better Jobs?', *Journal of Common Market Studies*, 45/2: 411–34.

Recchi, E., and Favell, A. (2009) (eds.), *Pioneers of European Integration: Citizenship and Mobility in the EU* (Cheltenham: Edward Elgar).

Reif, K. (1994), 'Less Legitimation through Lazy Parties? Lessons from the 1994 European Elections', paper presented at the XVIth World Congress of the International Political Science Association, Berlin, 21–25 Aug.

Rein, M., and Rainwater, L. (1986) (eds.), *Public-Private Interplay in Social Protection: A Comparative Study* (Armonk, NY: M. E. Sharpe).

Reinicke, W. H. (1999–2000), 'The Other World Wide Web: Global Public Policy Networks', *Foreign Policy*, 117: 44–57.

Rhodes, M. (1991), 'The Social Dimension of the Single European Market: National versus Transnational Regulation', *European Journal of Political Research*, 19/2–3: 245–80.

Rhodes, M. (1992), 'The Future of the "Social Dimension": Labour Market Regulation in Post-1992 Europe', *Journal of Common Market Studies*, 30/1: 23–51.

Rhodes, M. (1995), 'A Regulatory Conundrum: Industrial Relations and the Social Dimension', in S. Leibfried and P. Pierson (eds.), *European Social Policy: Between Fragmentation and Integration* (Washington, DC: Brookings Institution), 78–122.

Rhodes, M. (1999), 'An Awkward Alliance: France, Germany and Social Policy', in D. Webber (ed.), *The Franco-German Relationship in the European Union* (London: Routledge), 130–47.

Rhodes, R. A. W. (1996), 'The New Governance: Governing without Government', *Political Studies*, 44/3: 652–7.

Rhodes, R. A. W. (1997), *Understanding Governance* (Buckingham: Open University Press).

Rhodes, R. A. W. (2006), 'Policy Network Analysis', in M. Moran, M. Rein, and R. E. Goodin (eds.), *The Oxford Handbook of Public Policy* (Oxford: Oxford University Press), 425–47.

Richardson, J. J. (1982) (ed.), *Policy Styles in Western Europe* (London: George Allen & Unwin).

Richardson, J. J. (2000), 'Government, Interest Groups and Policy Change', *Political Studies*, 48/5: 1006–25.

Richardson, J. J. (2006), 'Policy-Making in the EU: Interests, Ideas and Garbage Cans of Primeval Soup', in J. Richardson (ed.), *European Union: Power and Policy-Making*, 3rd edn. (London: Routledge), 3–30.

Rieger, E. (2005), 'The Common Agricultural Policy', in H. Wallace, W. Wallace, and M. A. Pollack (eds.), *Policy-Making in the European Union*, 5th edn. (Oxford: Oxford University Press), 161–90.

Rieger, E., and Leibfried, S. (2003), *Limits to Globalization: Welfare States in the World Economy* (Cambridge: Polity).

Riel, B. van, and Meer, M. van der (2002), 'The Advocacy Coalition for European Employment Policy: The European Integration Process after EMU', in H. Hegman and B. Neumaerker (eds.), *Die Europäische Union aus Politökonomischer Perspektive* (Marburg: Metropolis Verlag), 117–37.

Riker, W. H. (1962), *The Theory of Political Coalitions* (New Haven, CT: Yale University Press).

Risse, T. (2000), '"Let's Argue!": Communicative Action in World Politics', *International Organization*, 54/1: 1–39.

Risse, T. (2002), 'Constructivism and International Institutions: Towards Conversations across Paradigms', in I. Katznelson and H. V. Milner (eds.), *Political Science: State of the Discipline* (New York, NY: W. W. Norton), 597–623.

Risse, T. (2004), 'Social Constructivism and European Integration', in A. Wiener and T. Diez (eds.), *European Integration Theory*, 1st edn. (Oxford: Oxford University Press), 159–76.

Risse, T. (2009), 'Social Constructivism and European Integration', in A. Wiener and T. Diez (eds.), *European Integration Theory*, 2nd edn. (Oxford: Oxford University Press), 144–61.

Risse-Kappen, T. (1991), 'Public Opinion, Domestic Structure and Foreign Policy in Liberal Democracies', *World Politics*, 43/4: 479–512.

Risse-Kappen, T. (1996), 'Exploring the Nature of the Beast: International Relations Theory and Comparative Policy Analysis Meet the European Union', *Journal of Common Market Studies*, 34/1: 51–80.

Robertson, D. B. (1989), 'The Bias of American Federalism: The Limits of Welfare State Development in the Progressive Era', *Journal of Polity History*, 1/3: 261–91.

Roederer-Rynning, C. (2002), 'Farm Conflict in France and the Europeanization of Agricultural Policy', *West European Politics*, 25/3: 107–26.

Roederer-Rynning, C. (2003a), 'From "Talking Shop" to "Working Parliament"? The European Parliament and Agricultural Change', *Journal of Common Market Studies*, 41/1: 113–35.

Roederer-Rynning, C. (2003b), 'Impregnable Citadel or Leaning Tower? Europe's Common Agricultural Policy at Forty', *SAIS Review*, 23/1: 133–51.

Romero, F. (1993), 'Migration as an Issue in European Interdependence and Integration: The Case of Italy', in A. S. Milward, F. M. B. Lynch, F. Romero, R. Ranieri, and V. Sørensen (eds.), *The Frontier of National Sovereignty: History and Theory, 1945–1991* (London: Routledge), 33–58, 205–8.

Rosamond, B. (2000), *Theories of European Integration* (Basingstoke: Palgrave Macmillan).

Rosati, J. A. (1981), 'Developing a Systematic Decision-Making Framework: Bureaucratic Politics in Perspective', *World Politics*, 33/2: 234–52.

Rosenau, J. N. (1992), 'Governance, Order and Change in World Politics', in J. N. Rosenau and E. O. Czempiel (eds.), *Governance without Government: Order and Change in World Politics* (Cambridge: Cambridge University Press), 1–29.

Rosenau, J. N., and Czempiel, E.-O. (1992) (eds.), *Governance Without Government: Order and Change in World Politics* (Cambridge: Cambridge University Press).

Rosenthal, G. G. (1975), *The Men Behind the Decisions: Cases in European Policy-Making* (Lanham, MD: Lexington Books).

Ross, G. (1995a), *Jacques Delors and European Integration* (Cambridge: Polity).

Ross, G. (1995b), 'Assessing the Delors Era in Social Policy', in S. Leibfried and P. Pierson (eds.), *European Social Policy: Between Fragmentation and Integration* (Washington, DC: Brookings Institution), 357–88.

Rothgang, H. (2007), *Differenzierung privater Krankenversicherungstarife nach Geschlecht* (Baden-Baden: Nomos).

Sabatier, P. A. (1998), 'The Advocacy Coalition Framework: Revisions and Relevance for Europe', *Journal of European Public Policy*, 5/1: 98–130.

Sabatier, P. A. (1999), 'The Need for Better Theories', in P. A. Sabatier (ed.), *Theories of the Policy Process* (Boulder, CO: Westview Press), 3–17.

Sabatier, P. A., and Jenkins-Smith, H. C. (1993), *Policy Change and Learning: An Advocacy Coalition Approach* (Boulder, CO: Westview Press).

Sabel, C., and Zeitlin, J. (2008), 'Learning from Difference: The New Architecture of Experimentalist Governance in the EU', *European Law Journal*, 14/3: 271–327.

Sadeh, T., and Verdun, A. (2009), 'Explaining Europe's Economic and Monetary Union: A Survey of the Literature', *International Studies Review*, 11/2: 277–301.

Sandholtz, W., and Zysman, J. (1989), '1992: Recasting the European Bargain', *World Politics*, 42/1: 95–128.

Sapir, A., Aghion, P., Bertola, G., Hellwig, M., Pisani-Ferry, J., Rosati, D., Vinals, J., and Wallace, H. (2004), *An Agenda for a Growing Europe: Making the EU Economic System Deliver, Report of an Independent High Level Study Group* (Chairman: André Sapir) (Oxford: Oxford University Press; originally published on-line by the EU Commission, 2003).

Sbragia, A. (1992a) (ed.), *Euro-Politics: Institutions and Policymaking in the 'New' European Community* (Washington, DC: Brookings Institution).

Sbragia, A. (1992b), 'Thinking about the European Future: The Uses of Comparison', in A. Sbragia (ed.), *Euro-Politics: Institutions and Policymaking in the 'New' European Community* (Washington, DC: Brookings Institution), 257–91.

Sbragia, A. (1993), 'The European Community: A Balancing Act', *Publius*, 23/3: 23–38.

Sbragia, A. (1998), 'Institution-Building from Below and Above: The European Community in Global Environmental Politics', in A. Stone Sweet and W. Sandholtz (eds.), *European Integration and Supranational Governance* (Oxford: Oxford University Press), 283–303.

Sbragia, A. (2000), 'Environmental Policy: Economic Constraints and External Pressures', in H. Wallace and W. Wallace (eds.), *Policy-Making in the European Union*, 4th edn. (Oxford: Oxford University Press): 235–55.

Sbragia, A., and Damro, C. (1999), 'The Changing Role of the European Union in International Environmental Politics: Institution Building and the Politics of Climate Change', *Environment and Planning C: Government and Policy*, 17/1: 53–8.

Schalk, J., Torenvlied, R., Weesie, J., and Stokman, F. (2007), 'The Power of the Presidency in EU Council Decision-Making', *European Union Politics*, 8/2: 229–50.

Scharpf, F. W. (1988), 'The Joint-Decision Trap: Lessons From German Federalism and European Integration', *Public Administration*, 66/3: 239–78.

Scharpf, F. W. (1994), 'Community and Autonomy: Multi-level Policy-making in the European Union', *Journal of European Public Policy*, 1/2: 219–42.

Scharpf, F. W. (1997), *Games Real Actors Play: Actor-Centered Institutionalism in Policy Research* (Boulder, CO: Westview Press).

Scharpf, F. W. (1999), *Governing in Europe: Effective and Democratic?* (Oxford: Oxford University Press).

Scharpf, F. W. (2006), 'The Joint-Decision Trap Revisited', *Journal of Common Market Studies*, 44/4: 845–64.

Schelkle, W. (2006) (ed.), 'Economic Governance in EMU Revisited', *Journal of Common Market Studies*, 44/4: 669–864.

Schimmelfennig, F. (2008), 'EU Political Accession Conditionality after the 2004 Enlargement: Consistency and Effectiveness', *Journal of European Public Policy*, 15/6: 918–37.

Schimmelfennig, F., and Sedelmeier, U. (2002), 'Theorizing EU Enlargement: Research Focus, Hypotheses, and the State of Research', *Journal of European Public Policy*, 9/4: 500–28.

Schimmelfennig, F., and Sedelmeier, U. (2005a) (eds.), *The Europeanization of Central and Eastern Europe* (Ithaca, NY: Cornell University Press).

Schimmelfennig, F., and Sedelmeier, U. (2005b) (eds.), *The Politics of EU Enlargement: Theoretical Approaches* (London: Routledge).

Schimmelfennig, F., Engert, S., and Knobel, H. (2006), *International Socialization in Europe: European Organizations, Political Conditionality and Democratic Change* (Basingstoke: Palgrave Macmillan).

Schmidt, S. K. (1998), 'Commission Activism: Subsuming Telecommunications and Electricity under European Competition Law', *Journal of European Public Policy*, 5/1: 169–84.

Schmidt, S. K. (2004a), *Die Folgen der europäischen Integration für die Bundesrepublik Deutschland: Wandel durch Verflechtung*, MPIfG Discussion Paper 02/4 (Cologne: Max Planck Institute for the Study of Societies).

Schmidt, S. K. (2004b), *Rechtsunsicherheit statt Regulierungswettbewerb: die nationalen Folgen des europäischen Binnenmarkts für Dienstleistungen*, habilitation thesis, FernUniversität Hagen, Hagen.

Schmidt, V. (2002), *The Futures of European Capitalism* (Oxford: Oxford University Press).

Schmitter, P. C. (1996), 'Examining the Present Euro-Polity with the Help of Past Theories', in G. Marks, F. W. Scharpf, P. C. Schmitter, and W. Streeck (eds.), *Governance in the European Union* (London: Sage), 1–14.

Schneider, G., Steunenberg, B., and Widgrén, M. (2006), 'Evidence with Insight: What Models Contribute to EU Research,' in R. Thomson, F. N. Stokman, C. H. Achen, and T. König (eds.), *The European Union Decides* (Cambridge: Cambridge University Press), 299–316.

Schneider, V., Fink, S., and Tenbücken, M. (2005), 'Buying out the State: A Comparative Perspective on the Privatization of Infrastructures', *Comparative Political Studies*, 38/6: 704–27.

Schreiber, K. (1991), 'The New Approach to Technical Harmonization and Standards', in L. Hurwitz and C. Lequesne (eds.), *The State of the European Community*, vol. i: *Politics, Institutions and Debates in the Transition Years* (Boulder, CO: Lynne Rienner), 97–112.

Schuler, M. (2005), 'Comments on Arts. 10a of Reg. 1408/71', in K.-J. Bieback and M. Fuchs (eds.), *Europäisches Sozialrecht: Nomos-Kommentar*, 4th edn. (Baden-Baden: Nomos), 151–3.

Schulte, B. (2008), 'Supranationales Recht', in B. Baron von Maydell and F. Ruland (eds.), *Sozialrechtshandbuch (SRH)*, 4th edn. (Baden-Baden: Nomos), 1611–76.

Schulz-Weidner, W. (1997), 'Die Konsequenzen des europäischen Binnenmarktes für die deutsche Rentenversicherung', *Deutsche Rentenversicherung*, 8: 445–73.

Schulz-Weidner, W. (2003), 'Die Öffnung der Sozialversicherung im Binnenmarkt und ihre Grenzen: zugleich eine Betrachtung zu der Entscheidung des Europäischen Gerichtshofs vom 3. Oktober 2002 in der Rechtssache "Danner" C 136/00', *Zeitschrift für europäisches Sozial- und Arbeitsrecht*, 2/2: 58–68.

Schulz-Weidner, W. (2004), 'Das europäische Beihilferecht und sein Einfluss auf die Sozialversicherung', *Deutsche Rentenversicherung*, 10: 592–613.

Schüssel, W. (2007), 'Europas Finanzen — Das alte System ist ausgereizt', *Spotlight Europe*, 2007/08 (Gütersloh: Bertelsmann Stiftung und Centrum für angewandte Politikforschung).

Schwark, P. (2003), 'Unisex-Tarife: Gebot der Gleichbehandlung oder Umverteilungsinstrument?', *Wirtschaftsdienst*, 83/10: 647–54.

Schwarze, J. (1998), 'Die Bedeutung des Territorialitätsprinzips bei mitgliedstaatlichen Preiskontrollen auf dem europäischen Arzneimittelmarkt', in J. Schwarze (ed.), *Unverfälschter Wettbewerb für Arzneimittel im europäischen Binnenmarkt* (Baden-Baden: Nomos), 59–74.

Sciarra, S. (2001) (ed.), *Labour Law in the Courts: National Judges and the European Court of Justice* (Oxford: Hart).

Sciarra, S. (2007), 'EU Commission Green Paper "Modernising Labour Law to Meet the Challenges of the 21st Century"', *Industrial Law Journal*, 36/3: 375–82.

Scott, J. (2003), 'European Regulation of GMOs and the WTO', *Columbia Journal of European Law*, 9: 213–39.

Scott, J., and Trubek, D. (2002), 'Mind the Gap: Law and New Approaches to Governance in the European Union', *European Law Journal*, 8/1: 1–18.

Sedelmeier, U. (1994), *The European Union's Association Policy Towards Central Eastern Europe: Political and Economic Rationales in Conflict*, SEI Working Paper No. 7 (Falmer: Sussex European Institute).

Sedelmeier, U. (2005*a*), 'Eastern Enlargement: Towards a European EU?', in H. Wallace, W. Wallace, and M. A. Pollack (eds.), *Policy-Making in the European Union*, 5th edn. (Oxford: Oxford University Press), 401–28.

Sedelmeier, U. (2005*b*), *Constructing the Path to Eastern Enlargement: The Uneven Policy Impact of EU Identity* (Manchester: Manchester University Press).

Sedelmeier, U. (2008), 'After Conditionality: Post-Accession Compliance with EU Law in East Central Europe', *Journal of European Public Policy*, 15/6: 806–25.

Sedelmeier, U., and Wallace, H. (1996), 'Policies Towards Central and Eastern Europe', in H. Wallace and W. Wallace (eds.), *Policy-Making in the European Union*, 3rd edn. (Oxford: Oxford University Press), 353–87.

Selin, H. (2007), 'Coalition Politics and Chemicals Management in a Regulatory Ambitious Europe', *Global Environmental Politics*, 7/3: 63–93.

Selznick, P. (1984) [1949], *TVA and the Grassroots: A Study of Politics and Organization* (Berkeley, CA: University of California Press; original edition, Berkeley, CA: University of California).

Shackleton, M. (1990), *Financing the European Community* (London: Pinter).

Shackleton, M. (1993*a*), 'The Community Budget After Maastricht', in A. W. Cafruny and G. G. Rosenthal (eds.), *The State of the European Community*, vol. II: *The Maastricht Debates and Beyond* (Boulder, CO: Lynne Rienner), 373–90.

Shackleton, M. (1993*b*), 'The Budget of the EC: Structure and Process', in J. Lodge (ed.), *The European Community and the Challenge of the Future* (London: Pinter).

Shapiro, M., and Stone, A. (1994), 'The New Constitutional Politics of Europe', *Comparative Political Studies*, 26/4: 397–420.

Shaw, J. (2000) (ed.), *Social Law and Policy in an Evolving European Union* (Oxford: Hart).

Shaw, J. (2007), 'EU-Citizenship and Political Rights in an Evolving European Union', *Fordham Law Review*, 75/5: 2549–78.

Sheingate, A. (2001), *The Welfare State for Farmers: Institutions and Interest Group Power in the United States, France, and Japan* (Princeton, NJ: Princeton University Press).

Shepsle, K. (1979), 'Institutional Arrangements and Equilibrium in Multidimensional Voting Models', *American Journal of Political Science*, 23/1: 27–60.

Shepsle, K. (1986), 'Institutional Equilibrium and Equilibrium Institutions', in H. F. Weisberg (ed.), *Political Science: The Science of Politics* (New York, NY: Agathon), 51–81.

Sissenich, B. (2005), 'The Transfer of EU Social Policy to Poland and Hungary', in F. Schimmelfennig and U. Sedelmeier (eds.), *The Europeanization of Central and Eastern Europe* (Ithaca, NY: Cornell University Press), 156–77.

Sjursen, H. (2007) (ed.), *Civilian or Military Power? European Foreign Policy in Perspective* (London: Routledge).

Skjaerseth, J. B., and Wettestad, J. (2008), *EU Emissions Trading: Initiation, Decision-making and Implementation* (Farnham: Ashgate).

Skogstad, G. (1998), 'Ideas, Paradigms and Institutions: Agricultural Exceptionalism in the European Union and the United States', *Governance*, 11/4: 463–90.

Skogstad, G. (2003), 'Legitimacy and/or Policy Effectiveness? Network Governance and GMO Regulation in the European Union', *Journal of European Public Policy*, 10/3: 321–38.

Slaughter, A.-M. (2004), *A New World Order* (Princeton, NJ: Princeton University Press).

Slaughter, A.-M., Stone Sweet, A., and Weiler, J. H. H. (1997), *The European Court and National Courts* (Oxford: Hart).

Smismans, S. (2007), 'Transnational Private Governance in the EU: When Social Partners Bargain Beyond Borders', in J.-C. Graz and A. Nolke (eds.), *Transnational Private Governance and its Limits* (London: Routledge), 185–95.

Smismans, S. (2008a), 'The European Social Dialogue in the Shadow of Hierarchy', *Journal of Public Policy*, 26/1: 161–80.

Smismans, S. (2008b), 'New Modes of Governance and the Participatory Myth', *West European Politics*, 32/5: 874–95.

Smith, E. W. (1999), 'Re-Regulation and Integration: The Nordic States and the European Economic Area', D.Phil. thesis, University of Sussex.

Smith, K. E. (1998), 'The Use of Political Conditionality in the EU's Relations with Third Countries: How Effective?', *European Foreign Affairs Review*, 3/2: 253–74.

Smith, K. E. (2003), *European Union Foreign Policy in a Changing World* (Cambridge: Polity).

Smith, M. A. M., and Wallace, H. (1994), 'The European Union: Towards a Policy for Europe', *International Affairs*, 70/3: 429–44.

Smith, M. E. (2004), *Europe's Foreign and Security Policy: The Institutionalization of Cooperation* (Cambridge: Cambridge University Press).

Smith, M. P. (2008), 'All Access Points are not Created Equal: Explaining the Fate of Diffuse Interests in the EU', *British Journal of Politics & International Relations*, 10/1: 64–83.

Snyder, F. G. (1985), *Law of the Common Agricultural Policy* (London: Sweet & Maxwell).

Spence, D. (2005) (ed.), *The European Commission*, 3rd edn. (London: John Harper).

Starke, P., Obinger, H., and Castles, F. G. (2008), 'Convergence Towards Where: In What Ways, If Any, Are Welfare States Becoming More Similar?', *Journal of European Public Policy*, 15/7: 975–1000.

Stern, N. (2006), *The Economics of Climate Change: The Stern Review* (London: HM Treasury).

Steunenberg, B. (2007), 'A Policy Solution to the European Union's Transposition Puzzle: Interaction of Interests in Different Domestic Arenas', *West European Politics*, 30/1: 23–49.

Stewart, T. P., and Johanson, D. S. (1999), 'Policy in Flux: The European Union's Laws on Agricultural Biotechnology and their Effects on International Trade', *Drake Journal of Agricultural Law*, 4: 243–95.

Stone Sweet, A., and Brunell, T. L. (1998a), 'The European courts and national courts: a statistical analysis of preliminary references 1961–95', *Journal of European Public Policy*, 5: 66–97.

Stone Sweet, A., and Brunell, T. L. (1998b), 'Constructing a Supranational Constitution: Dispute Resolution and Governance in the European Community', *American Political Science Review*, 92/1: 63–81.

Stone Sweet, A., and Caporaso, T. (1998), 'From Free Trade to Supranational Policy', in W. Sandholtz and A. Stone Sweet (eds.), *European Integration and Supranational Governance* (Oxford: Oxford University Press), 92–133.

Streeck, W. (1995), 'From Market-Making to State Building?', in S. Leibfried and P. Pierson, *European Social Policy: Between Fragmentation and Integration* (Washington, DC: Brookings Institution), 92–133.

Streeck, W. (1998), *The Internationalization of Industrial Relations in Europe: Prospects and Problems*, MPIfG Discussion Paper 98/2 (Cologne: Max Planck Institute for the Study of Societies).

Streeck, W. (2000), 'Competitive Solidarity: Rethinking the "European Social Model"', in K. Hinrichs, H. Kitschelt, and H. Wiesenthal (eds.), *Kontingenz und Krise: Institutionenpolitik in kapitalistischen und postsozialistischen Gesellschaften* (Frankfurt am Main: Campus), 245–61.

Streeck, W., and Schmitter, P. C. (1991), 'From National Corporatism to Transnational Pluralism: Organized Interests in the Single European Market', *Politics and Society*, 19/2: 133–64.

Streeck, W., and Thelen, K. (2005), 'Introduction: Institutional Change in Advanced Political Economies', in W. Streeck and K. Thelen (eds.), *Beyond Continuity: Institutional Change in Advanced Political Economies* (Oxford: Oxford University Press), 1–39.

Sunstein, C. (2005), *The Laws of Fear: Beyond the Precautionary Principle* (New York, NY: Cambridge University Press).

Sutcliffe, J. B. (2000), 'The 1999 Reform of the Structural Fund Regulations: Multi-Level Governance or Renationalization?', *Journal of European Public Policy*, 7/2: 290–309.

Swaan, A. de (1973), *Coalition Theories and Cabinet Formation* (Amsterdam: Elsevier).

Swaan, A. de (1992), 'Perspectives for a Transnational Social Policy', *Government and Opposition*, 27/1: 33–52.

Swinbank, A. (1989), 'The Common Agricultural Policy and the Politics of European Decision Making', *Journal of Common Market Studies*, 27/4: 303–22.

Swinbank, A., and Daugbjerg, C. (2006), 'The 2003 CAP Reform: Accommodating WTO Pressures', *Comparative European Politics*, 4/1: 47–64.

Syrpis, P. (2002), 'Legitimizing European Governance: Taking Subsidiarity Seriously within the Open Method of Coordination', Department of Law Working Papers 2002/10 (Florence: European University Institute).

Syrpis, P. (2007), *EU Intervention in Domestic Labour Law* (Oxford: Oxford University Press).

Syrpis, P. (2008), 'The Treaty of Lisbon: Much Ado ... But About What?', *Industrial Law Journal*, 37/3: 219–35.

Szczerbiak, A., and Taggart, P. P. (2008), *Opposing Europe?: The Comparative Politics of Euroscepticism*, 2 vols. (Oxford: Oxford University Press).

Tallberg, J. (2000), 'The Anatomy of Autonomy: An Institutional Account of Variation in Supranational Influence', *Journal of Common Market Studies*, 38/5: 843–64.

Tallberg, J. (2002), 'Paths to Compliance: Enforcement, Management and the European Union', *International Organization*, 56/3: 609–43.

Tallberg, J. (2003), *European Governance and Supranational Institutions: Making States Comply* (London: Routledge).

Tallberg, J. (2006), *Leadership and Negotiation in the European Union* (Cambridge: Cambridge University Press).

Tallberg, J. (2007), 'Executive Politics', in K. E. Jørgensen, M. A. Pollack, and B. Rosamond (eds.), *The Handbook of European Union Politics* (London: Sage), 195–212.

Tallberg, J. (2008), 'The Power of the Chair: Formal Leadership by the Council Presidency', in D. Naurin and H. Wallace (eds.), *Unveiling the Council of the European Union: Games Governments Play in Brussels* (Basingstoke: Palgrave Macmillan), 187–202.

Taylor, P. (1983), *The Limits of European Integration* (New York, NY: Columbia University Press).

Tenbücken, M. (2006), *The Regulation of Network Infrastructures in the New European Union* (Ph.D. Konstanz; *http://www.ub.uni-konstanz.de/kops/volltexte/2006/1736/index.html*).

Thatcher, M. (1984), 'Europe: The Future', paper presented to the European Council, Fontainebleau, 25–26 June.

Thatcher, M., and Stone Sweet, A. (2002) (eds.), 'The Politics of Delegation: Non-Majoritarian Institutions in Europe', *West European Politics*, 25/1 (special issue).

Thelen, K., and Steinmo, S. (1992), 'Introduction', in K. Thelen and S. Steinmo (eds.), *Structuring Politics: Historical Institutionalism in Comparative Politics* (Cambridge: Cambridge University Press), 1–32.

Thomas, D. C. (2006), 'Constitutionalization through Enlargement: The Contested Origins of the EU's Democratic Identity', *Journal of European Public Policy*, 13/8: 1190–210.

Thomson, R. (2007), 'The Impact of Enlargement on Legislative Decision Making in the European Union', paper presented at the General Conference of the European Consortium for Political Research, Pisa, Italy, 6–8 Sept.

Thomson, R. (2008), 'The Council Presidency in the European Union: Responsibility with Power', *Journal of Common Market Studies*, 46/3: 593–617.

Thomson, R., and Hosli, M. (2006), 'Who Has Power in the EU? The Commission, Council and Parliament in Legislative Decision-Making', *Journal of Common Market Studies*, 44/2: 391–417.

Thomson, R., Stokman, F. N., Achen, C. H., and Konig, T. (2006), *The European Union Decides: Testing Theories of European Decision-Making* (Cambridge: Cambridge University Press).

Thomson, S., and Mossialos, E. (2007), 'Regulating Private Health Insurance in the European Union: The Implications of Single Market Legislation and Competition Policy', *Journal of European Integration*, 29/1: 89–107.

Tiberghien, Y. (2007), 'Europe: Turning Against Agricultural Biotechnology in the Late 1990s', in S. Fukuda-Parr (ed.), *The Gene Revolution: GM Crops and Unequal Development* (London: Earthscan), 51–69.

Tidow, S. (2003), 'The Emergence of a European Employment Policy', in H. Overbeek (ed.), *The Political Economy of European Employment* (London: Routledge), 77–98.

Tömmel, I., and Verdun, A. (2008) (eds.), *Innovative Governance in the European Union* (Boulder, CO: Lynne Rienner).

Toshkov, D. (2007), 'In Search of the Worlds of Compliance: Culture and Transposition Performance in the European Union', *Journal of European Public Policy*, 14/6: 933–59.

Townsend, M. (2007), *The Euro and Economic and Monetary Union: An Historical, Institutional and Economic Description* (London: John Harper).

Tracy, M. (1989), *Government and Agriculture in Western Europe* (New York, NY: Harvester Wheatsheaf).

Tranholm-Mikkelsen, J. (1991), 'Neo-functionalism: Obstinate or Obsolete? A Reappraisal in Light of the New Dynamism of the EC', *Millennium: Journal of International Studies*, 20/1: 1–21.

Treib, O. (2008), 'Implementing and Complying with EU Governance Outputs', *Living Reviews in European Governance*, 3/5, available at: *http://www.livingreviews.org/lreg-2008-5* (accessed 3 March 2009).

Treib, O., Bähr, H., and Falkner, G. (2007), 'Modes of Governance: Towards a Conceptual Clarification', *Journal of European Public Policy*, 14/1: 1–20.

Trondal, J. (2007), 'The Public Administration Turn in Integration Research', *Journal of European Public Policy*, 14/6: 960–72.

Tsebelis, G. (1994), 'The Power of the European Parliament as a Conditional Agenda Setter', *American Political Science Review*, 88/1: 128–42.

Tsebelis, G. (1995), 'Decision Making in Political Systems: Veto Players in Presidentialism, Parliamentarism, Multicameralism and Multipartyism', *British Journal of Political Science*, 25/3: 289–325.

Tsebelis, G., and Garrett, G. (2000), 'Legislative Politics in the European Union', *European Union Politics*, 1/1: 9–36.

Tsebelis, G., and Garrett, G. (2001), 'The Institutional Foundations of Intergovernmentalism and Supranationalism in the European Union', *International Organization*, 55/2: 357–90.

Tsebelis, G., Jensen, C., Kalandrakis, A., and Kreppel, A. (2001), 'Legislative Procedures in the European Union: An Empirical Analysis', *British Journal of Political Science*, 31/4: 573–99.

Tugendhat, C. (1985), 'How to Get Europe Moving Again', *International Affairs*, 61/3: 421–9.

Uhl, S. (2008), 'Europe, the Nation State, and Taxation', in A. Hurrelmann, S. Leibfried, K. Martens, and P. Mayer (eds.), *Transforming the Golden Age Nation State* (Basingstoke: Palgrave Macmillan), 24–41.

Ujupan, A. (2009), 'Reform Perspectives for Cohesion Policy in the Budget Review Process', paper presented at the Midwest Political Science Association National Annual Conference, Chicago, IL, 2–5 April, available at: *http://www.allacademic.com//meta/p_mla_apa_research_citation/3/6/3/0/5/pages363056/p363056-1.php*.

UNICE, UEAPME, CEEP (2006), 'Implementation of the Framework Agreement on Telework. Report by the European Social Partners, adopted by the Social Dialogue Committee on 28 June 2006' (Brussels 2006), available at *http://ec.europa.eu/employment_social/news/2006/oct/telework_implementation_report_en.pdf*.

Vachudova, M. A. (2005), *Europe Undivided: Democracy, Leverage and Integration after Communism* (Oxford: Oxford University Press).

Vaubel, R. (1986), 'A Public Choice Approach to International Organization', *Public Choice*, 51/1: 39–57.

Vaughan-Whitehead, D. (2003), *EU Enlargement versus Social Europe? The Uncertain Future of the European Social Model*. (Cheltenham: Edward Elgar)

Vaughan-Whitehead, D. (2007), 'Work and Employment Conditions in New EU Member States: A Different Reality?', in P. Leisink, B. Steijn, and U. Veersma (eds.), *Industrial Relations in the New Europe: Enlargement, Integration and Reform* (Cheltenham: Edward Elgar), 41–62.

Vauhkonen, J., and Pylkkönen, P. (2004), 'Integration of European Banking and Insurance', in H. Koskenkylä (ed.), *Financial Integration*, Bank of Finland studies, A 108 (Helsinki: Suomen Pankki), 73–115.

Veljanovski, C. (2004), 'EC Merger Policy after *GE/Honeywell* and *Airtours*', *The Antitrust Bulletin*, Spring–Summer: 153–93.

Verdun, A. (1999), 'The Role of the Delors Committee in the Creation of EMU: An Epistemic Community', *Journal of European Public Policy*, 6/2: 308–28.

Versluis, E. (2007), 'Even Rules, Uneven Practices: Opening the "Black Box" of EU Law in Action', *West European Politics*, 30/1: 50–67.

Vickers, J. (2003), 'Competition Economics and Policy', *European Competition Law Review*, 24/3: 95–102.

Vogel, D. (1986), *National Styles of Regulation* (Ithaca, NY: Cornell University Press).

Vogel, D. (1989), *Fluctuating Fortunes: The Political Power of Business in America* (New York, NY: Basic Books).

Vogel, D. (1995), *Trading Up: Consumer and Environmental Regulation in a Global Economy* (Cambridge, MA: Harvard University Press).

Vogel, D. (2001), 'Ships Passing in the Night: GMOs and the Contemporary Politics of Risk Regulation in Europe', Working Paper No. 2001/16 (Florence: European University Institute), available at, *http://www.iue.it/RSCAS/WP-Texts/01_16.pdf.*

Vogel, D. (2003), 'The Hare and the Tortoise Revisited: The New Politics of Consumer and Environmental Regulation in Europe', *British Journal of Political Science*, 33/4: 557–80.

Vogt, L. (2005), 'The EU's Single Market: At Your Service?', Economics Department Working Paper No. 449, ECO/WKP(2005)36 (Paris: Organization for Economic Cooperation and Development), 7 October.

Vos, E. (2000), 'EU Food Safety Regulation in the Aftermath of the BSE Crisis', *Journal of Consumer Policy*, 23/3: 227–55.

Waarden, F. van, and Drahos, M. (2002), 'Courts and (Epistemic) Communities in the Convergence of Competition Policies', *Journal of European Public Policy*, 9/6: 913–34.

Walby, S. (2005) (ed.), 'Gender Mainstreaming', *Social Politics* 12/3: 321–450 (special issue).

Wallace, H. (1973), *National Governments and the European Communities* (London: Chatham House).

Wallace, H. (1977), 'The Establishment of the Regional Development Fund: Common Policy or Pork Barrel?', in H. Wallace, W. Wallace, and C. Webb (eds.), *Policy-Making in the European Communities* (Chichester: Wiley), 136–64.

Wallace, H. (1983), 'Distributional Politics: Dividing up the Community Cake', in H. Wallace, W. Wallace, and C. Webb (eds.), *Policy-Making in the European Communities*, 2nd edn. (Chichester: Wiley), 81–113.

Wallace, H. (1984), 'Bilateral, Trilateral and Multilateral Negotiations in the European Community', in R. Morgan, and C. Bray (eds.), *Partners and Rivals in Western Europe: Britain, France and Germany* (Aldershot: Gower), 156–74.

Wallace, H. (1999), 'Whose Europe Is It Anyway?', *European Journal of Political Research*, 35/3: 287–306.

Wallace, H. (2000), 'EU Enlargement: A Neglected Subject', in M. G. Cowles and M. Smith (eds.), *The State of the European Union, vol v: Risks, Reforms, Resistance and Revival* (Oxford: Oxford University Press), 149–63.

Wallace, H. (2001a) (ed.), *Interlocking Dimensions of European Integration* (Basingstoke: Palgrave Macmillan).

Wallace, H. (2001b), 'The Changing Politics of the European Union: An Overview', *Journal of Common Market Studies*, 39/4: 581–94.

Wallace, H. (2007), 'Adapting to Enlargement of the European Union: Institutional Practice', *TEPSA Working Paper* (Brussels: TEPSA).

Wallace, H., Wallace, W., and Webb, C. (1977) (eds.), *Policy-Making in the European Communities* (Chichester: Wiley).

Wallace, W. (1982), 'Europe as a Confederation: The Community and the Nation-State', *Journal of Common Market Studies*, 20/1–2: 57–68.

Wallace, W. (1996), *Opening the Door: The Enlargement of NATO and the European Union* (London: Centre for European Reform).

Wapner, P. (1996), *Environmental Activism and World Civic Politics* (Albany, NY: SUNY Press).

Ward, N., and Lowe, P. (2004), 'Europeanizing Rural Development? Implementing the CAP's Second Pillar in England', *International Planning Studies*, 9/2–3: 121–37.

Warntjen, A. (2008), 'Steering but not Dominating: The Impact of the Council Presidency on EU Legislation', in D. Naurin and H. Wallace (eds.), *Unveiling the Council of the European Union: Games Governments Play in Brussels* (Basingstoke: Palgrave Macmillan), 203–18.

Watt, A. (2004), 'Reform of the European Employment Strategy after Five Years: A Change of Course or Merely Presentation?', *European Journal of Industrial Relations*, 10/2: 117–37.

Weale, A. (1992), *The New Politics of Pollution* (Manchester: Manchester University Press).

Weaver, R. E. (1986), 'The Politics of Blame Avoidance', *Journal of Public Policy*, 6/4: 371–98.

Webb, C. (1977), 'Introduction: Variations on a Theoretical Theme', in H. Wallace, W. Wallace, and C. Webb (eds.), *Policy-Making in the European Communities* (Chichester: Wiley), 1–32.

Webster, R. (1998), 'Environmental Collective Action: Stable Patterns of Cooperation and Issue Alliances at the European Level', in J. Greenwood and M. Aspinwall (eds.), *Collective Action in the European Union: Interest and the New Politics of Associability* (London: Routledge), 176–95.

Weiler, J. H. H. (1994), 'A Quiet Revolution: The European Court of Justice and its Interlocutors', *Comparative Political Studies*, 24/4: 510–34.

Weiler, J. H. H. (1995), 'Does Europe Need a Constitution? Reflections on Demos, Telos, and the German Maastricht Decision', *European Law Journal*, 1/2: 219–58.

Weiler, J. H. H. (1999), *The Constitution of Europe: 'Do the New Clothes Have an Emperor?' and Other Essays on European Integration* (Cambridge: Cambridge University Press).

Wendler, F. (2004), 'The Paradoxical Effects of Institutional Change for the Legitimacy of European Governance: The Case of EU Social Policy', *European Integration online Papers*, 8/7, available at: *http://eiop.or.at/eiop*.

Westlake, M., and Galloway, D. (2005) (eds.), *The Council of the European Union*, 3rd edn. (London: John Harper).

Whish, R. (2008), *Competition Law*, 6th edn. (Oxford: Oxford University Press).

Wiener, A., and Diez, T. (2009) (eds.), *European Integration Theory*, 2nd edn. (Oxford: Oxford University Press).

Wiener, J. B., and Rogers, M. D. (2002), 'Comparing Precaution in the United States and Europe', *Journal of Risk Research*, 5/4: 317–49.

Wigger, A. (2007), 'Towards a Market-Based Approach: The Privatization and Micro-economization of EU Antitrust Law Enforcement', in H. Overbeek et al. (eds.), *The Transnational Politics of Corporate Governance Regulation* (London: Routledge), 98–118.

Wigger, A., and Nölke, A. (2007), 'Enhanced Roles of Private Actors in EU Business Regulation and the Erosion of Rhenish Capitalism: The Case of Antitrust Enforcement', *Journal of Common Market Studies*, 45/2: 487–513.

Williams, S. (1991), 'Sovereignty and Accountability in the European Community', in R. O. Keohane and S. Hoffmann (eds.), *The New European Community* (Boulder, CO: Westview), 155–76.

Wilks, S. (2005*a*), 'Agency Escape: Decentralization or Dominance of the European Commission in the Modernization of Competition Policy?', *Governance*, 18/3: 431–52.

Wilks, S. (2005*b*), 'Competition Policy', in H. Wallace, W. Wallace, and M. A. Pollack (eds.), *Policy-Making in the European Union*, 5th edn. (Oxford: Oxford University Press), 113–40.

Wilks, S. (2007), 'Agencies, Networks, Discourses and the Trajectory of European Competition Enforcement', *European Competition Journal*, 3/2: 437–64.

Wilks, S. (2009), 'Competition Policy in the Recession: Industrial Crisis and Implications for the Economic Constitution', paper presented at the Biennial Conference of the European Union Studies Association, Los Angeles, 22–25 April.

Wilks, S. (2010), 'Competition Policy', in D. Coen, W. Grant, and G. Wilson (eds.), *The Oxford Handbook of Business and Government* (Oxford: Oxford University Press), 730-56.

Wilks, S., with Bartle, I. (2002), 'The Unanticipated Consequences of Creating Independent Competition Agencies', *West European Politics*, 25/1: 148–72.

Wilks, S., with McGowan, L. (1996), 'Competition Policy in the European Union: Creating a Federal Agency?', in G. B. Doern and S. Wilks (eds.), *Comparative Competition Policy: National Institutions in a Global Market* (Oxford: Clarendon Press), 225–67.

Wilson, J. Q. (1980), *The Politics of Regulation* (New York, NY: Basic Books).

Witney, N. (2008), *Re-Energising Europe's Security and Defence Policy* (Brussels: European Council on Foreign Relations).

Woll, C. (2009), 'Trade Policy Lobbying in the European Union: Who Captures Whom', in D. Coen and J. Richardson (eds.), *Lobbying in the European Union: Institutions, Actors and Issues* (Oxford: Oxford University Press), 268–89.

Woolcock, S. (1996), 'Competition among Rules in the Single European Market', in J. McCahery, W. W. Bratton, S. Picciotto, and C. Scott (eds.), *International Regulatory Competition and Coordination: Perspectives on Economic Regulation in Europe and the United States* (Oxford: Clarendon Press), 289–321.

Woolcock, S. (2005), 'Trade Policy', in H. Wallace, W. Wallace and M. A. Pollack (eds.), *Policy-Making in the European Union*, 5th edn. (Oxford: Oxford University Press), 377–400.

Woolcock, S. (2008), 'The Potential Impact of the Lisbon Treaty on European Union External Trade Policy', Policy Papers (Stockholm: Swedish Institute for European Policy Studies).

Woolcock, S., and Hodges, M. (1996), 'EU Policy in the Uruguay Round: The Story Behind the Headlines', in H. Wallace and W. Wallace (eds.), *Policy-Making in the European Union*, 3rd edn. (Oxford: Oxford University Press), 301–24.

Wright, G. (1953), 'Agrarian Syndicalism in Postwar France', *The American Political Science Review*, 47/2: 402–16.

WTO (2008), 'Thirteenth Annual Review of the Implementation and Operation of the TBT Agreement', G/TBT/23 (Geneva: World Trade Organization Committee on Technical Barriers to Trade), 20 Feb.

Young, A. R. (1995), 'Ideas, Interests and Institutions: The Politics of Liberalisation in the EC's Road Haulage Industry', in D. Mayes (ed.), *The Evolution of Rules for a Single European Market, Part i: Industry and Finance* (Brussels: Office for Official Publications of the European Communities).

Young, A. R. (1997), 'Consumption without Representation? Consumers in the Single Market', in H. Wallace and A. R. Young (eds.), *Participation and Policy-Making in the European Union* (Oxford: Clarendon Press), 206–34.

Young, A. R. (1998), 'European Consumer Groups: Multiple Levels of Governance and Multiple Logics of Collective Action', in J. Greenwood and M. Aspinwall (eds.), *Collective Action in the European Union: Interests and the New Politics of Associability* (London: Routledge), 149–75.

Young, A. R. (2002), *Extending European Cooperation: The European Union and the 'New' International Trade Agenda* (Manchester: Manchester University Press).

Young, A. R. (2003), 'Political Transfer and "Trading Up"? Transatlantic Trade in Genetically Modified Food and US Politics', *World Politics*, 55/4: 457–84.

Young, A. R. (2004), 'The Incidental Fortress: The Single European Market and World Trade', *Journal of Common Market Studies*, 42/2: 393–414.

Young, A. R. (2007a), 'The Politics of Regulation and the Internal Market', in K. E. Jørgensen, M. A. Pollack, and B. Rosamond (eds.), *The Handbook of European Union Politics* (London: Sage), 373–94.

Young, A. R. (2007b), 'Trade Politics Ain't What it Used To Be: The European Union in the Doha Round', *Journal of Common Market Studies*, 45/4: 789–811.

Young, A. R. (2008), 'Explaining EU Compliance with WTO Rules: A Research Project', paper to the UACES Conference, Edinburgh, 1–3 Sept.

Young, A. R. (2009), 'Analysing Compliance: The EU and the WTO', paper presented to the International Studies Association Conference, New York, 15–18 Feb.

Young, A. R., and Peterson, J. (2006), 'The EU and the New Trade Politics', *Journal of European Public Policy*, 13/6: 795–814.

Young, A. R., and Wallace, H. (2000), *Regulatory Politics in the Enlarging European Union: Weighing Civic and Producer Interests* (Manchester: Manchester University Press).

Young, O. R. (1999), *Governance in World Affairs* (Ithaca, NY: Cornell University Press).

Zeitlin, J. (2008), 'The Open Method of Co-ordination and the Governance of the Lisbon Strategy', *Journal of Common Market Studies*, 46/2: 436–50.

Zeitlin, J., and Pochet, P., with Magnusson L. (2005) (eds.), *The Open Method of Coordination in Action: The European Employment and Social Inclusion Strategies* (Brussels: PLE-Peter Lang).

Zito, A.R. (1999), 'Task Expansion: A Theoretical Overview', *Environment and Planning C: Government and Policy*, 17/1: 19–35.

Zito, A. R. (2001), 'Epistemic Communities, Collective Entrepreneurship and European Integration', *Journal of European Public Policy*, 8/4: 585–603.

Zürn, M. (2000), 'Democratic Governance Beyond the Nation-State', in M. T. Greven and L. Pauly (eds.), *Democracy Beyond the State? The European Dilemma and the Emerging Global Order* (Lanham, MD: Rowman & Littlefield), 91–114.

Zürn, M., and Checkel, J. T. (2005), 'Getting Socialized to Build Bridges: Constructivism and Rationalism, Europe and the Nation-State', *International Organization*, 59/4: 1045–79.

Zwanenberg, P. van, and Millstone, E. (2005), *BSE: Risk, Science, and Governance* (Oxford: Oxford University Press).

▌ INDEX

Note page references for all legislation – decisions, directives, and regulations – and European court judgements are provided in the lists in the preliminary matter, pp. xxxiii–xl

1992 programme 113, 116, 131
  see also single European market

A

abuse of dominance *see* antitrust
accession 5–7, 19, 109, 130n, 150, 182, 196, 200, 204n, 215, 217, 219–20, 227, 235, 237, 238, 244, 302, 314, 326, 349, 391, 401–28, 433, 437, 462, 489, 491–2, 494, 504, 508
  see also pre-accession strategy; enlargement
accession partnership (AP) 402, 408, 416–17
accountability 71, 79, 148, 166, 199, 244, 299, 316, 387–8, 427, 432, 434, 460, 467, 469, 497
  democratic 39, 461
  government 314
  financial 209
  parliamentary 316
  political 100
acquis communautaire 23, 38, 128, 137, 150, 226, 263, 382, 385–6, 388, 406–7, 410–11, 415–17, 419, 422, 424, 461, 494
  environmental *acquis* 314, 328
  JHA *acquis* 462, 477
acts of accession (accession treaties) 6–7, 407–9, 420, 425, 428, 492
Ad Hoc Committee on Institutional Reform (Dooge Committee) 113
adaptability/adaptation 37, 63, 100, 128, 136, 142, 173, 236, 240, 243, 255–6, 276, 295–8, 307, 328, 376, 482–3, 491–2, 500–1
additionality, *see* structural funds
Aer Lingus 136
Afghanistan xvii, 434, 441, 444, 446, 447–8, 452
African, Caribbean and Pacific (ACP)
  countries 382, 393, 398
  see also Cotonou Agreement; economic partnership agreements; Lomé Convention
Agency for the Cooperation of Energy Regulators (ACER) 367
Agency for the Management of Operational Cooperation at the External Borders, *see* Frontex

Agenda 2000 182, 192, 196, 201–2, 207, 215, 218–19, 234, 235, 386
  see also budget; common agricultural policy; enlargement; European Council (Berlin1999); structural funds
agenda-setting 22, 30, 45–7, 50, 52–6, 59, 60, 92, 121, 188, 196, 296, 364, 418
agriculture, *see* common agricultural policy
air transport 114–15, 122, 146, 276, 448
Albania 373, 405, 410, 413, 427
Algeria 267, 370–1
Americanization 134, 151
Andreasen, Marta 224
animal health and welfare 192, 203, 345
animal rights groups 315
anti-discrimination 253, 259, 263–4, 304
anti-dumping 225, 384–5, 394–5, 413
antitrust 133–5, 138, 139–42, 144, 148, 150–1, 154, 358, 360, 362, 365–7
  abuse of dominance 140
  restrictive practices 133, 135, 139–40, 146, 148
  see also competition policy
approximation 109, 114–15, 117, 126, 288, 321, 458, 468, 470, 475, 504, 508, 511
Arab–Israeli war 434
area of freedom, security and justice (AFSJ) 458, 462–3, 466, 470, 476
  see also justice and home affairs
Argentina 347
argumentative rationality 40, 60
  see also communicative action; logic of arguing; governance approach
Armenia 426
Article 36 (ex K4) Committee *see* Coordinating Committee for Police and Judicial Cooperation in Criminal Matters (CATS)
Article 133 (ex 113) Committee 76, 388–90, 392, 396–8
association agreements 383–4, 393, 298, 402, 407–10, 412–15, 422, 426–7
  see also Europe agreements
Association of South East Asian Nations (ASEAN) 397
asylum 425, 457–8, 460–1, 465, 466, 469, 489, 499
  Asylum Support Office 468, 470–2